RAND McNALLY

TODAY'S WORLD

A NEW WORLD ATLAS

FROM

THE CARTOGRAPHERS

OF

RAND McNALLY

TODAY'S WORLD

A NEW WORLD ATLAS FROM
THE CARTOGRAPHERS OF RAND McNALLY

RAND McNALLY

CHICAGO • NEW YORK • SAN FRANCISCO

CONTENTS

TODAY'S WORLD

Copyright ©1992 by Rand McNally & Company

1995 Edition

All rights reserved. No part of this publication may be reproduced, stored in a retrieval system, or transmitted, in any form or by any means - electronic, mechanical, photocopied, recorded, or other - without the prior written permission of Rand McNally & Company.

Printed in the United States of America

Library of Congress Cataloging-in-Publication Data
Rand McNally and Company.
    Today's world: A new world atlas from the cartograhers of
    Rand McNally. – 1993 rev. ed.
        p.   cm.
        Shows changes for Europe, Russia, and Eritrea.
        Includes index.
        ISBN 0-528-83778-8
        1. Atlases. 1. Title.
G1021.R4867   1993 <G&M : fol.>
912—dc20   93-7143
                                            CIP
                                            MAP

Title page photo, Mount Cook, New Zealand, J. Amos/SUPERSTOCK

USING THE ATLAS

MAPS AND ATLASES

Satellite images of the world (figure 1) constantly give us views of the shape and size of the earth. It is hard, therefore, to imagine how difficult it once was to ascertain the look of our planet. Yet from early history we have evidence of humans trying to work out what the world actually looked like.

Twenty-five hundred years ago, on a tiny clay tablet the size of a hand, the Babylonians inscribed the earth as a flat disk (figure 2) with Babylon at the center. The section of the Cantino map of 1502 (figure 3) is an example of a *portolan* chart used by mariners to chart the newly discovered Americas. Handsome and useful maps have been produced by many cultures. The Mexican map drawn in 1583 marks hills with wavy lines and roads with footprints between parallel lines (figure 4). The methods and materials used to create these maps were dependent upon the technology available, and their accuracy suffered considerably. A modern topographic map (figure 5), as well as those in this atlas, shows the detail and accuracy that cartographers are now able to achieve. They benefit from our ever-increasing technology, including satellite imagery and computer assisted cartography.

In 1589 Gerardus Mercator used the word *atlas* to describe a collection of maps. Atlases now bring together not only a variety of maps but an assortment of tables and other reference material as well. They have become a unique and indispensable reference for graphically defining the world and answering the question *where*. Only on a map can the countries, cities, roads, rivers, and lakes covering a vast area be simultaneously viewed in their relative locations. Routes between places can be traced, trips planned, boundaries of neighboring states and countries examined, distances between places measured, the meandering of rivers and streams and the sizes of lakes visualized— and remote places imagined.

FIGURE 1

FIGURE 4

FIGURE 2

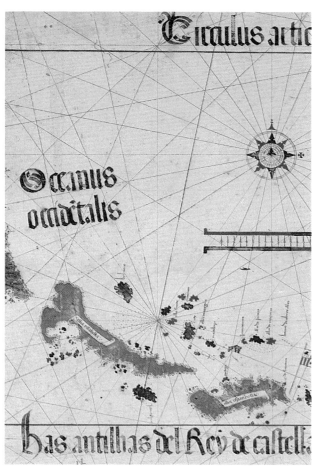

FIGURE 3

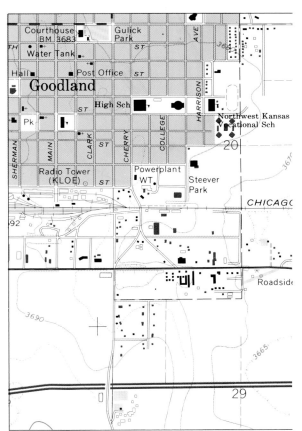

FIGURE 5

SEQUENCE OF THE MAPS

The world is made up of seven major landmasses: the continents of Europe, Asia, Africa, Antarctica, Australia, South America, and North America (figure 6). The maps in this atlas follow this continental sequence. To allow for the inclusion of detail, each continent is broken down into a series of maps, and this grouping is arranged so that as consecutive pages are turned, a continuous successive part of the continent is shown. Larger-scale maps are used for regions of greater detail (having many cities, for example) or for areas of global significance.

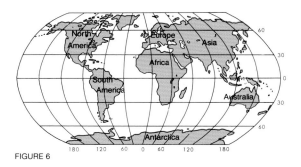

FIGURE 6

GETTING THE INFORMATION

An atlas can be used for many purposes, from planning a trip to finding hot spots in the news and supplementing world knowledge. To realize the potential of an atlas the user must be able to:

1. Find places on the maps
2. Measure distances
3. Determine directions
4. Understand map symbols

FINDING PLACES

One of the most common and important tasks facilitated by an atlas is finding the location of a place in the world. A river's name in a book, a city mentioned in the news, or a vacation spot may prompt your need to know where the place is located. The illustrations and text below explain how to find Yangon (Rangoon), Myanmar.

1. Look up the place-name in the index at the back of the atlas. Yangon, Myanmar can be found on the map on page 38, and it can be located on the map by the letter-number key *B2* (figure 7).

Yangguanpu, China	**C4**	34
Yangjia, China	**I7**	32
Yangjiang, China	**G9**	30
Yangkoushi, China	**G7**	34
Yangliuqing, China	**D5**	32
Yanglousi, China	**F2**	34
Yangon (Rangoon), Mya. . .	**B2**	38
Yangp'yŏng, S. Kor.	**F15**	32
Yangquan, China	**F1**	32
Yangsan, S. Kor.	**H17**	32
Yangshuling, China	**B6**	32
Yangtze see Chang, stm., China	**E10**	30
Yangxiaodian, China	**D5**	34
Yangyang, S. Kor.	**E16**	32
Yangzhou, China	**C8**	34
Yanheying, China	**C7**	32
Yanji, China	**A17**	32
Yankdŏk, N. Kor.	**D14**	32

FIGURE 7

2. Turn to the map of Southeastern Asia found on page 38. Note that the letters *A* through *H* and the numbers *1* through *11* appear in the margins of the map.

3. To find Yangon, on the map, place your left index finger on *B* and your right index finger on *2*. Move your left finger across the map and your right finger down the map. Your fingers will meet in the area in which Yangon is located (figure 8).

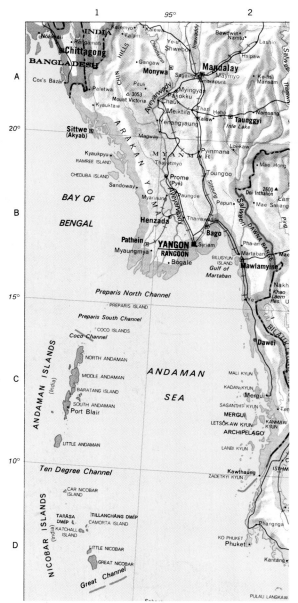

FIGURE 8

MEASURING DISTANCES

In planning trips, determining the distance between two places is essential, and an atlas can help in travel preparation. For instance, to determine the approximate distance between Paris and Rouen, France, follow these three steps:

1. Lay a slip of paper on the map on page 14 so that its edge touches the two cities. Adjust the paper so one corner touches Rouen. Mark the paper directly at the spot where Paris is located (figure 9).

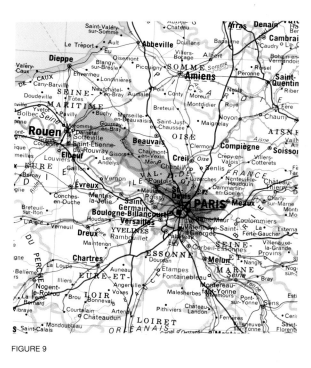

FIGURE 9

2. Place the paper along the scale of miles beneath the map. Position the corner at 0 and line up the edge of the paper along the scale. The pencil mark on the paper indicates Rouen is between 50 and 100 miles from Paris (figure 10).

3. To find the exact distance, move the paper to the left so that the pencil mark is at 100 on the scale. The corner of the paper stands on the fourth 5-mile unit on the scale. This means that the two towns are 50 plus 20, or 70 miles apart (figure 11).

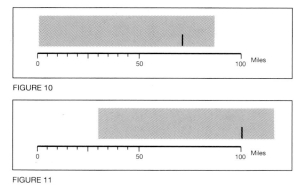

FIGURE 10

FIGURE 11

DETERMINING DIRECTION

Most of the maps in the atlas are drawn so that when oriented for normal reading, north is at the top of the map, south is at the bottom, west is at the left, and east is at the right. Most maps have a series of lines drawn across them—the lines of *latitude* and *longitude*. Lines of latitude, or *parallels* of latitude, are drawn east and west. Lines of longitude, or *meridians* of longitude, are drawn north and south (figure 12).

Parallels and meridians appear as either curved or straight lines. For example, in the section of the map of Europe (figure 13) the parallels of latitude appear as curved lines. The meridians of longitude are straight lines that come together toward the top of the map. Latitude and longitude lines help locate places on maps. Parallels of latitude are numbered in degrees north and south of the *Equator*. Meridians of longitude are numbered in degrees east and west of a line called the *Prime Meridian*, running through Greenwich, England, near London. Any place on earth can be located by the latitude and longitude lines running through it.

To determine directions or locations on the map, you must use the parallels and meridians. For example, suppose you want to know which is farther north, Bergen, Norway, or Stockholm, Sweden. The map in figure 13 shows that Stockholm is south of the 60° parallel of latitude and Bergen is north of it. Bergen is farther north than Stockholm. By looking at the meridians of longitude, you can determine which city is farther east. Bergen is approximately 5° east of the 0° meridian (Prime Meridian), and Stockholm is almost 20° east of it. Stockholm is farther east than Bergen.

UNDERSTANDING MAP SYMBOLS

In a very real sense, the whole map is a symbol, representing the world or a part of it. It is a reduced representation of the earth; each of the world's features—cities, rivers, etc.—is represented on the map by a symbol. Map symbols may take the form of points, such as dots or squares (often used for cities, capital cities, or points of interest), or lines (roads, railroads, rivers). Symbols may also occupy an area, showing extent of coverage (terrain, forests, deserts). They seldom look like the feature they represent and therefore must be identified and interpreted. For instance, the maps in this atlas define political units by a colored line depicting their boundaries. Neither the colors nor the boundary lines are actually found on the surface of the earth, but because countries and states are such important political components of the world, strong symbols are used to represent them. The Map Symbols page in this atlas identifies the symbols used on the maps.

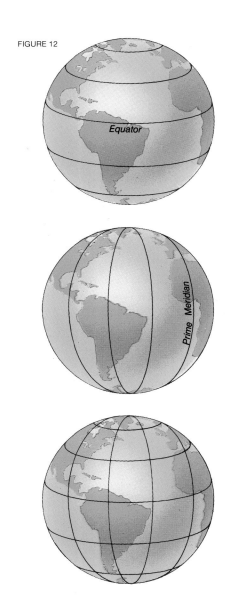

FIGURE 12

FIGURE 13

World Time Zones

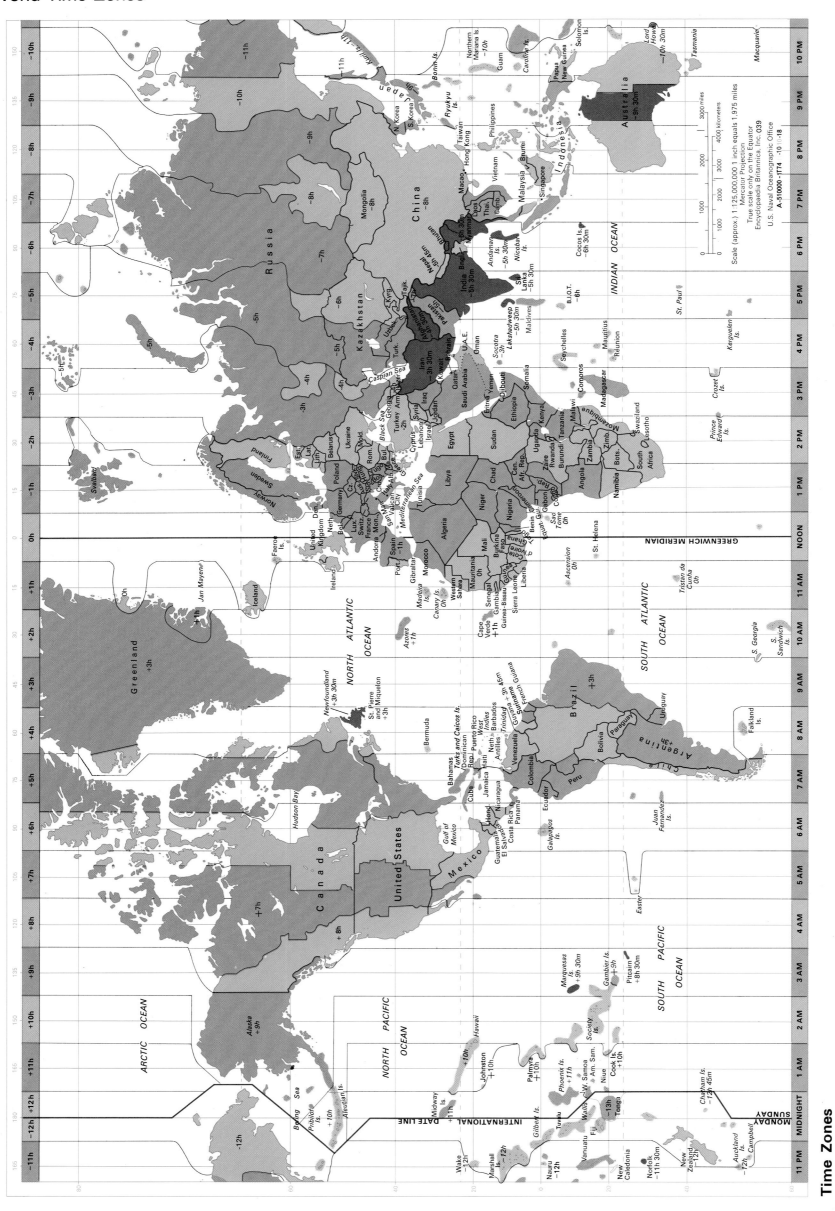

The standard time zone system, fixed by international agreement and by law in each country, is based on a theoretical division of the globe into 24 zones of 15° longitude each. The mid-meridian of each zone fixes the hour for the entire zone. The zero time zone extends 7½° east and 7½° west of the Greenwich meridian, 0° longitude. Since the earth rotates toward the east, time zones to the west of Greenwich are earlier, to the east, later.

Plus and minus hours at the top of the map are added to or subtracted from local time to find Greenwich time. Local standard time can be determined for any area in the world by adding one hour for each time zone counted in an easterly direction from one's own, or by subtracting one hour for each zone counted in a westerly direction. To separate one day from the next, the 180th meridian has been designated as the international date line. On both sides of the line the time of day is the same, but west of the line it is one day later than it is to the east. Countries that adhere to the international zone system adopt the zone applicable to their location. Some countries, however, establish time zones based on political boundaries, or adopt the time zone of a neighboring unit. For all or part of the year some countries also advance their time by one hour, thereby utilizing more daylight hours each day.

Scale (approx.) 1:125,000,000 1 inch equals 1,975 miles
Mercator Projection
True scale only on the Equator
Encyclopædia Britannica, Inc. Q39
U.S. Naval Oceanographic Office
A-510000-1T74 -10 -18

h m hours, minutes

Time Zones

- Standard time zone of even-numbered hours from Greenwich time
- Standard time zone of odd-numbered hours from Greenwich time
- Time varies from the standard time zone by half an hour
- Time varies from the standard time zone by other than half an hour

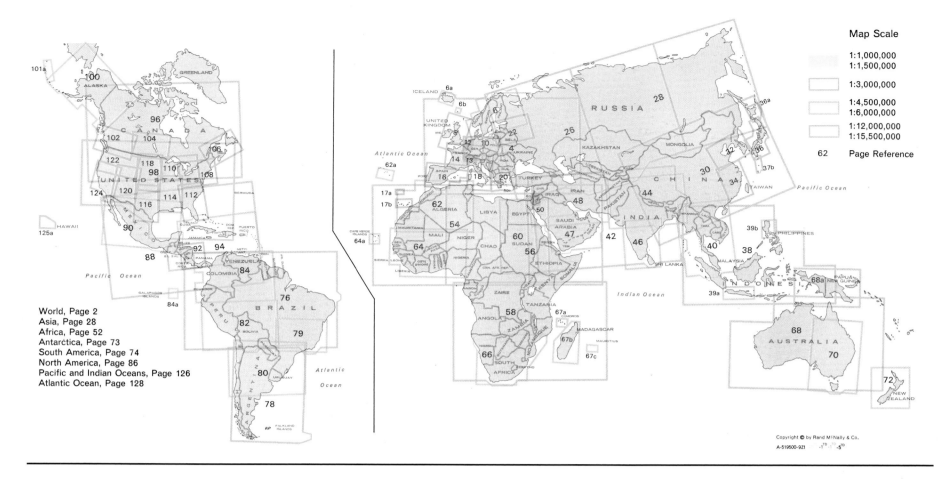

World, Page 2
Asia, Page 28
Africa, Page 52
Antarctica, Page 73
South America, Page 74
North America, Page 86
Pacific and Indian Oceans, Page 126
Atlantic Ocean, Page 128

Map Scale

1:1,000,000
1:1,500,000
1:3,000,000
1:4,500,000
1:6,000,000
1:12,000,000
1:15,500,000

62   Page Reference

World Maps Symbols

Inhabited Localities

The size of type indicates the relative economic
and political importance of the locality

Écommoy   Lisieux   **Rouen**

Trouville   **Orléans**   **PARIS**

Bi'r Safâjah ° Oasis

Alternate Names

MOSKVA
MOSCOW
        English or second official language
        names are shown in reduced size
Basel   lettering
Bâle

Volgograd   Historical or other alternates in
(Stalingrad)   the local language are shown in
              parentheses

Urban Area (Area of continuous industrial,
commercial, and residential development)

Capitals of Political Units

BUDAPEST   Independent Nation

Cayenne   Dependency
           (Colony, protectorate, etc.)

Recife   State, Province, County, Oblast, etc.

Political Boundaries

International (First-order political unit)

Demarcated and Undemarcated

Disputed de jure

Indefinite or Undefined

Demarcation Line

Internal

State, Province, etc.
(Second-order political unit)

MURCIA   Historical Region
          (No boundaries indicated)

GALAPAGOS
(Ecuador)   Administering Country

Transportation

Primary Road

Secondary Road

Minor Road, Trail

Railway

Canal du Midi   Navigable Canal

Bridge

Tunnel

TO MALMÖ   Ferry

Hydrographic Features

Shoreline

Undefined or Fluctuating Shoreline

Amur   River, Stream

Intermittent Stream

Rapids, Falls

Irrigation or Drainage Canal

Reef

The Everglades   Swamp

RIMO GLACIER   Glacier

L. Victoria   Lake, Reservoir

Tuz Gölü   Salt Lake

Intermittent Lake, Reservoir

Dry Lake Bed

(395)   Lake Surface Elevation

Topographic Features

Matterhorn △
4478   Elevation Above Sea Level

76 ▽   Elevation Below Sea Level

Mount Cook ▲
3764   Highest Elevation in Country

133 ▼   Lowest Elevation in Country

Khyber Pass =
1067   Mountain Pass

Elevations are given in meters.
The highest and lowest elevations in a
continent are underlined

Sand Area

Lava

Salt Flat

1

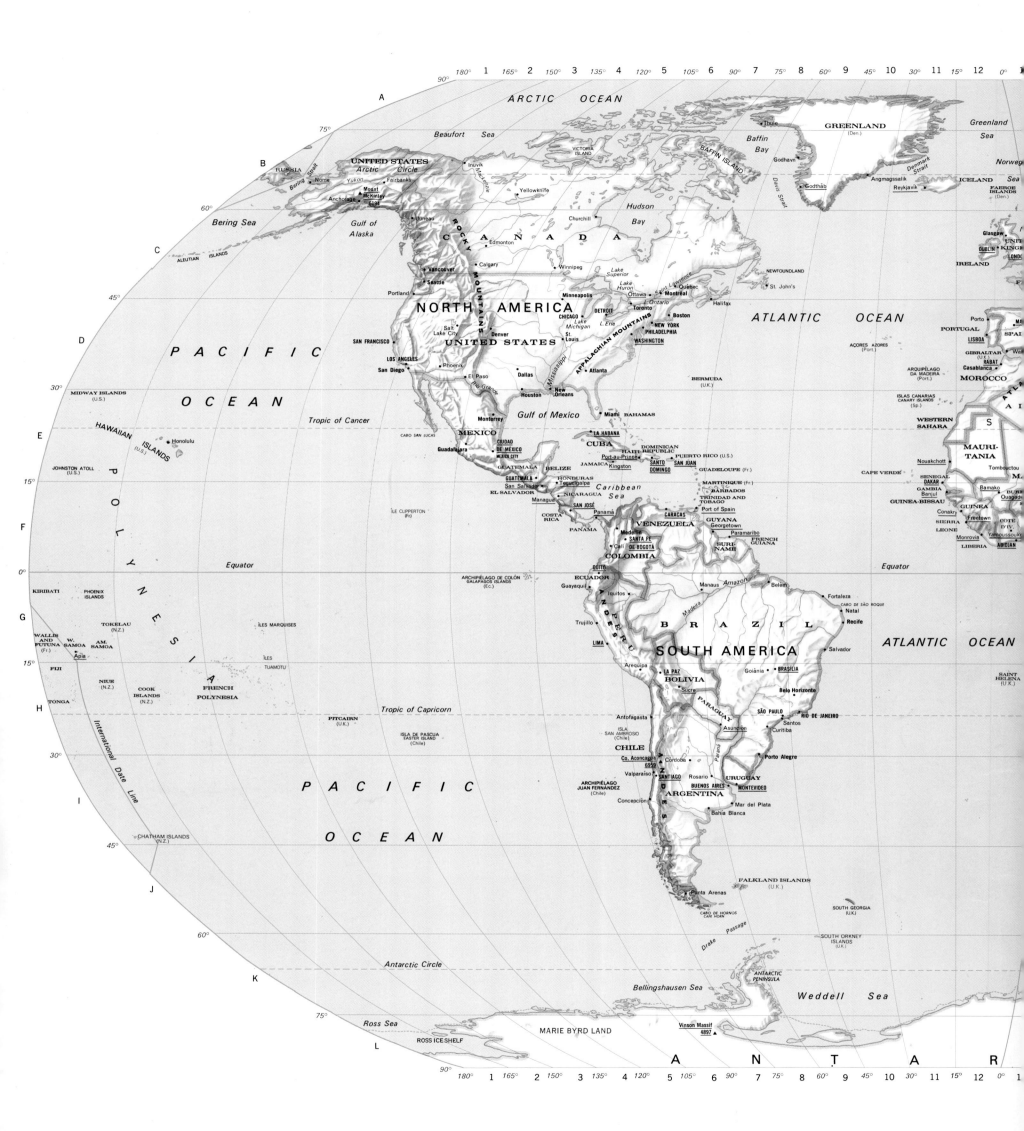

One centimeter represents 750 kilometers.
One inch represents approximately 1200 miles.
Robinson Projection
Scale 1:75,000,000

Kilometers

Statute Miles

Scale 1:12,000,000

One centimeter represents 120 kilometers.
One inch represents approximately 190 miles.

Miller Oblated Stereographic Projection

Map labels (Iceland inset — a):

GREENLAND SEA

Denmark Strait

Arctic Circle

ICELAND
ÍSLAND

ATLANTIC OCEAN

Reykjavík

Keflavík

Kópavogur

Hafnarfjörður

VATNAJÖKULL

MÝRDALSJÖKULL

SKAFTAFELL NATIONAL PARK

HOFSJÖKULL

Akureyri

Húnaflói

Faxaflói

SNÆFELLSNESS

Faeroe Islands inset (b):

FAEROE ISLANDS
FØROYAR
(Denmark)

NORWEGIAN SEA

ATLANTIC OCEAN

Tórshavn

Slættaratindur

Klaksvík

Main map:

NORWEGIAN SEA

Arctic Circle

LOFOTEN

Bodø

NORDLAND

Trondheim

MØRE OG ROMSDAL

SØR TRØNDELAG

NORD TRØNDELAG

JÄMTLANDS LÄN

Östersund

SOGN OG FJORDANE

OPPLAND

HEDMARK

KOPPARBERGS LÄN

GÄVLEBORGS LÄN

Ålesund

Bergen

HORDALAND

BUSKERUD

Falun

Sandviken

Gävle

Borlänge

Haugesund

TELEMARK

Oslo

AKERSHUS

VÄRMLANDS LÄN

VÄSTMANLANDS LÄN

Uppsala

Örebro

Västerås

Stavanger

ROGALAND

AUST AGDER

VEST AGDER

ØSTFOLD

Skien

Drammen

Fredrikstad

Karlstad

SÖDERMANLANDS LÄN

STOCKHOLM

Eskilstuna

Kristiansand

NORTH SEA

Skagerrak

Göteborg
Gothenburg

ÄLVSBORGS LÄN

Norrköping

ÖSTERGÖTLANDS LÄN

Linköping

Uddevalla

GÖTEBORGS OCH BOHUS LÄN

Vänern

Vättern

Kattegat

JÄLLANDS

Ålborg

Randers

JYLLAND

Viborg

Århus

Esbjerg

HALLANDS LÄN

Halmstad

Jönköping

KRONOBERGS LÄN

Växjö

GOTLANDS LÄN

GOTLAND

BALTIC SEA

ÖLAND

Kalmar

BLEKINGE LÄN

Karlskrona

Kristianstad

KØBENHAVN
COPENHAGEN

Odense

FYN

Svendborg

Helsingborg

Lund

Malmö

Trelleborg

SJÆLLAND

DENMARK
DANMARK

GERMANY
DEUTSCHLAND

SCHLESWIG
HOLSTEIN

Flensburg

Kiel

Rendsburg

Neumünster

BORNHOLM

Rønne

TO LERWICK

TO NEWCASTLE

TO HARWICH

Copyright © by Rand McNally & Co.
A-554490-264

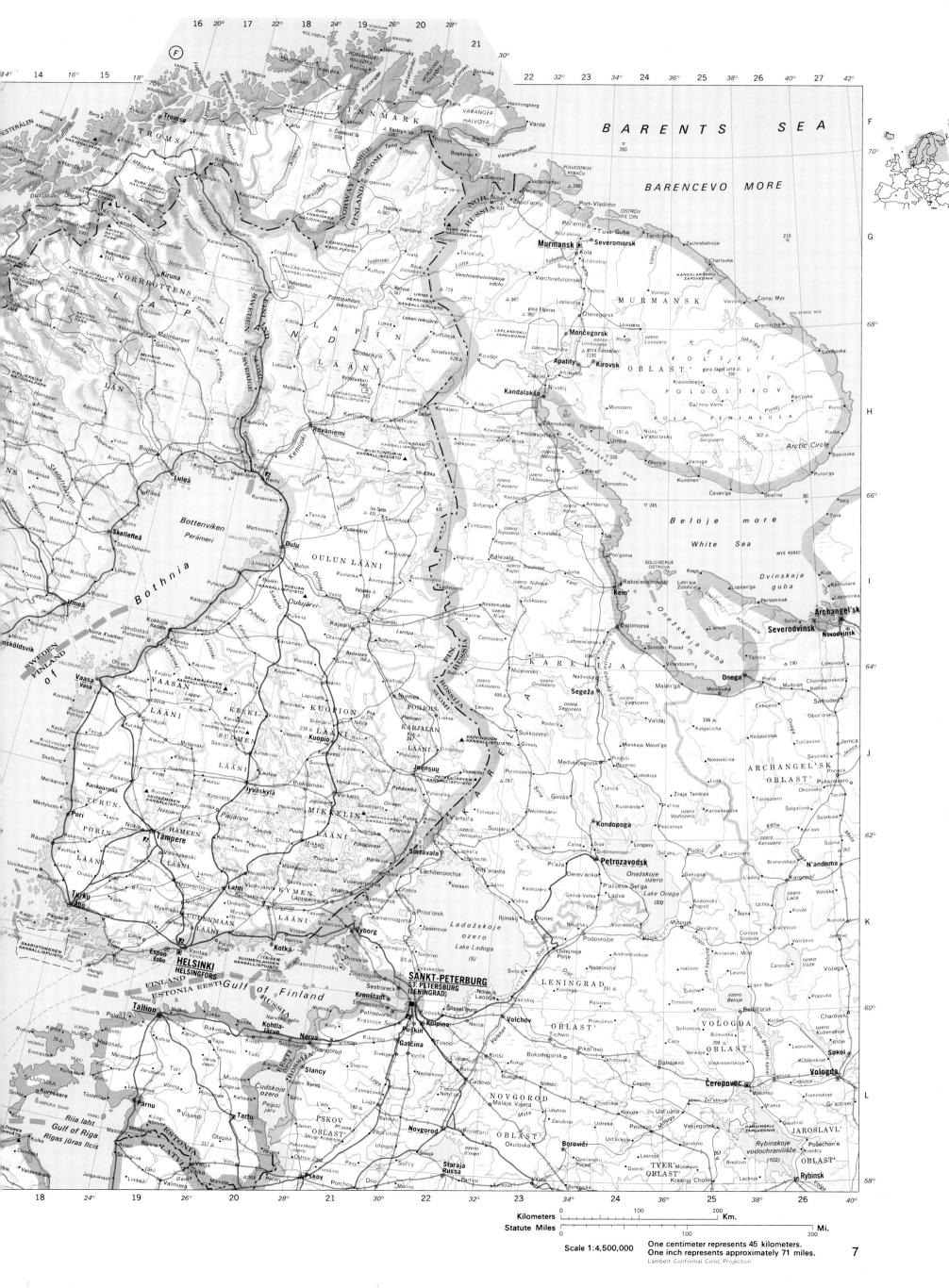

Kilometers 0 100 200 Km.

Statute Miles 0 100 200 Mi.

Scale 1:4,500,000
One centimeter represents 45 kilometers.
One inch represents approximately 71 miles.
Lambert Conformal Conic Projection

British Isles

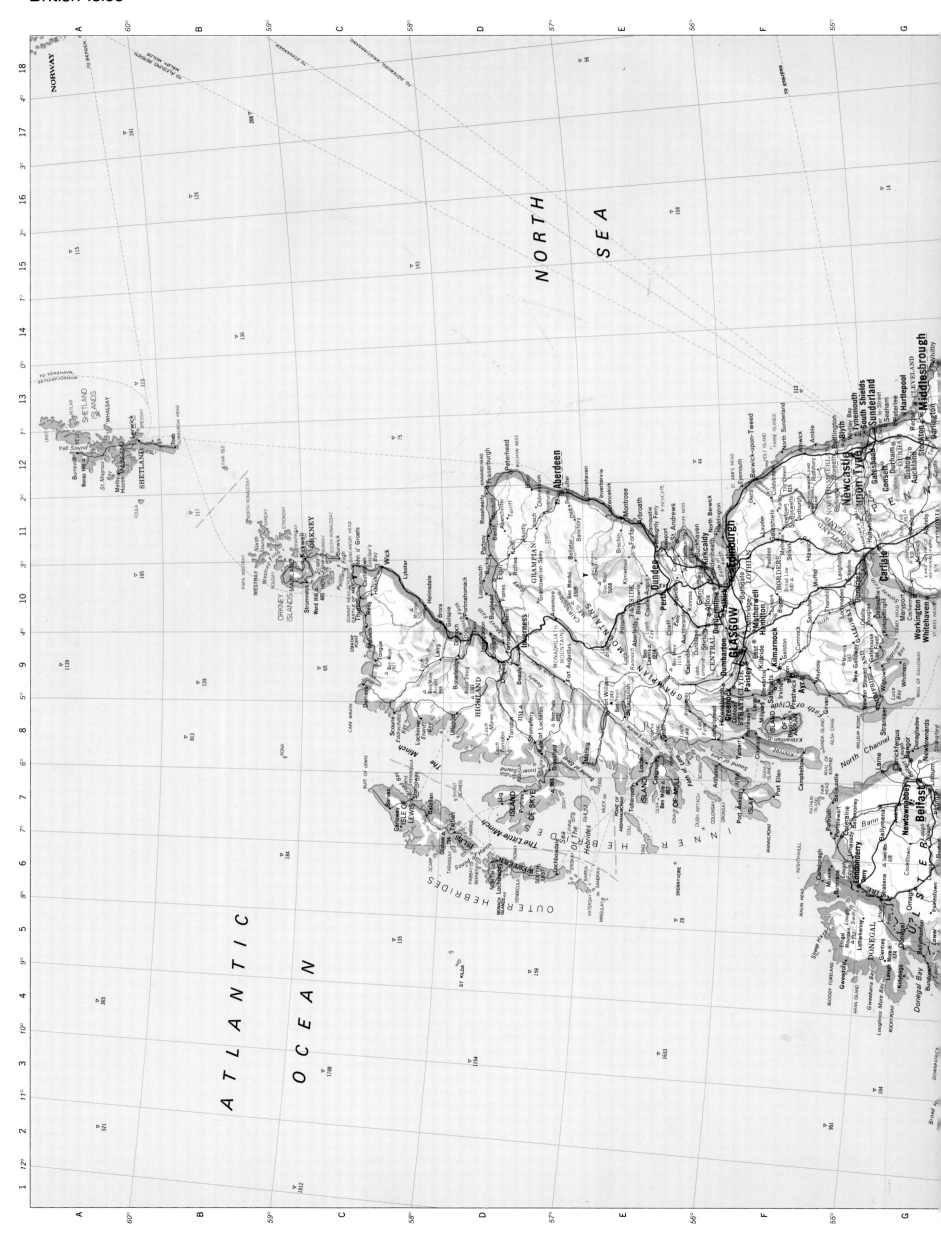

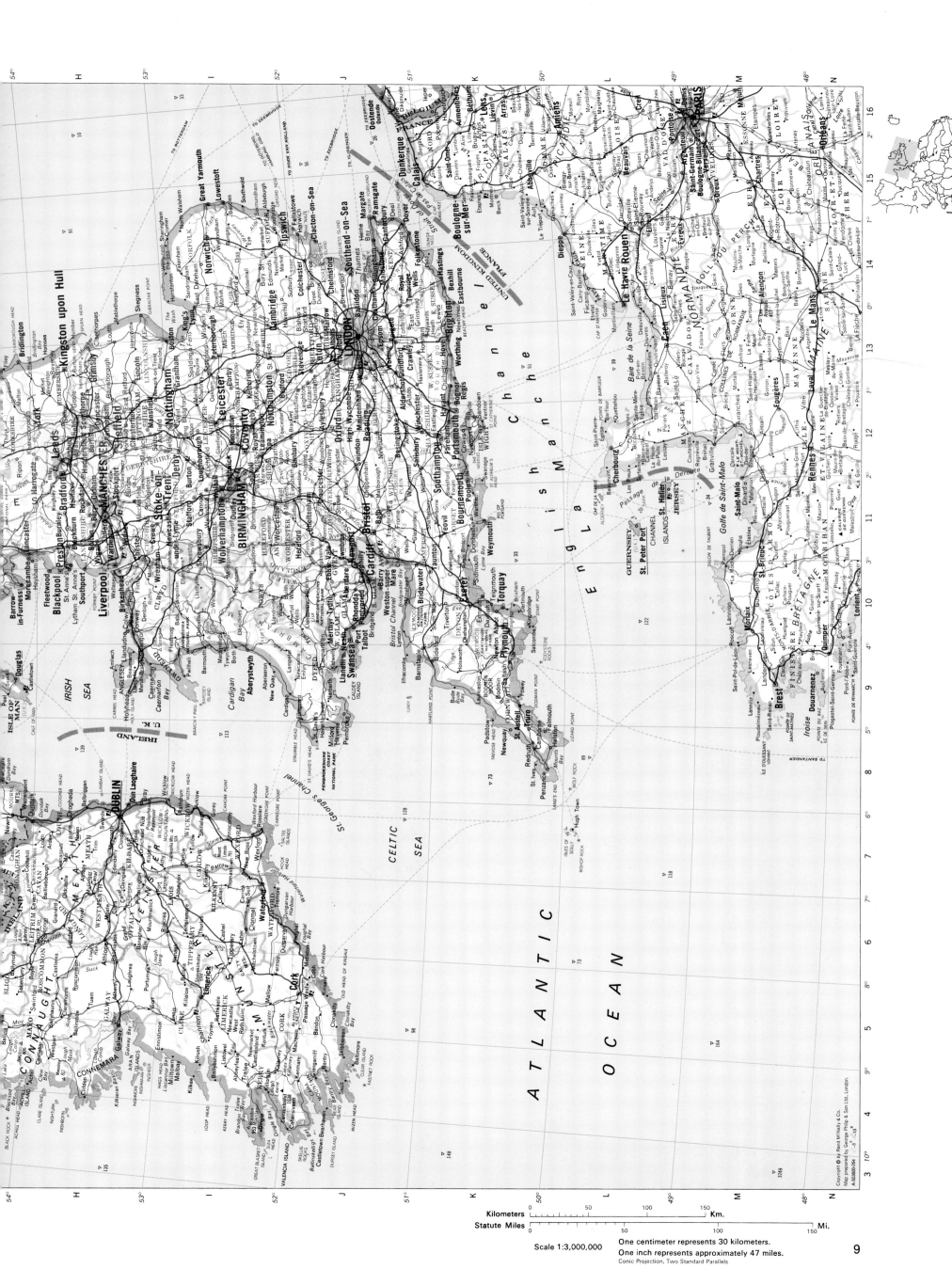

Kilometers

Statute Miles

One centimeter represents 30 kilometers.
One inch represents approximately 47 miles.

Scale 1:3,000,000

Conic Projection, Two Standard Parallels

Km.

Mi.

Kilometers
Statute Miles

Scale 1:3,000,000 One centimeter represents 30 kilometers.
One inch represents approximately 47 miles.
Conic Projection, Two Standard Parallels.

Scale 1:1,500,000

One centimeter represents 15 kilometers.
One inch represents approximately 24 miles.

Lambert Conformal Conic Projection

Kilometers |0 10 20 30 40 50 Km.

Statute Miles |0 10 20 30 40 50 Mi.

Copyright © by Rand McNally & Co.
A-553101364

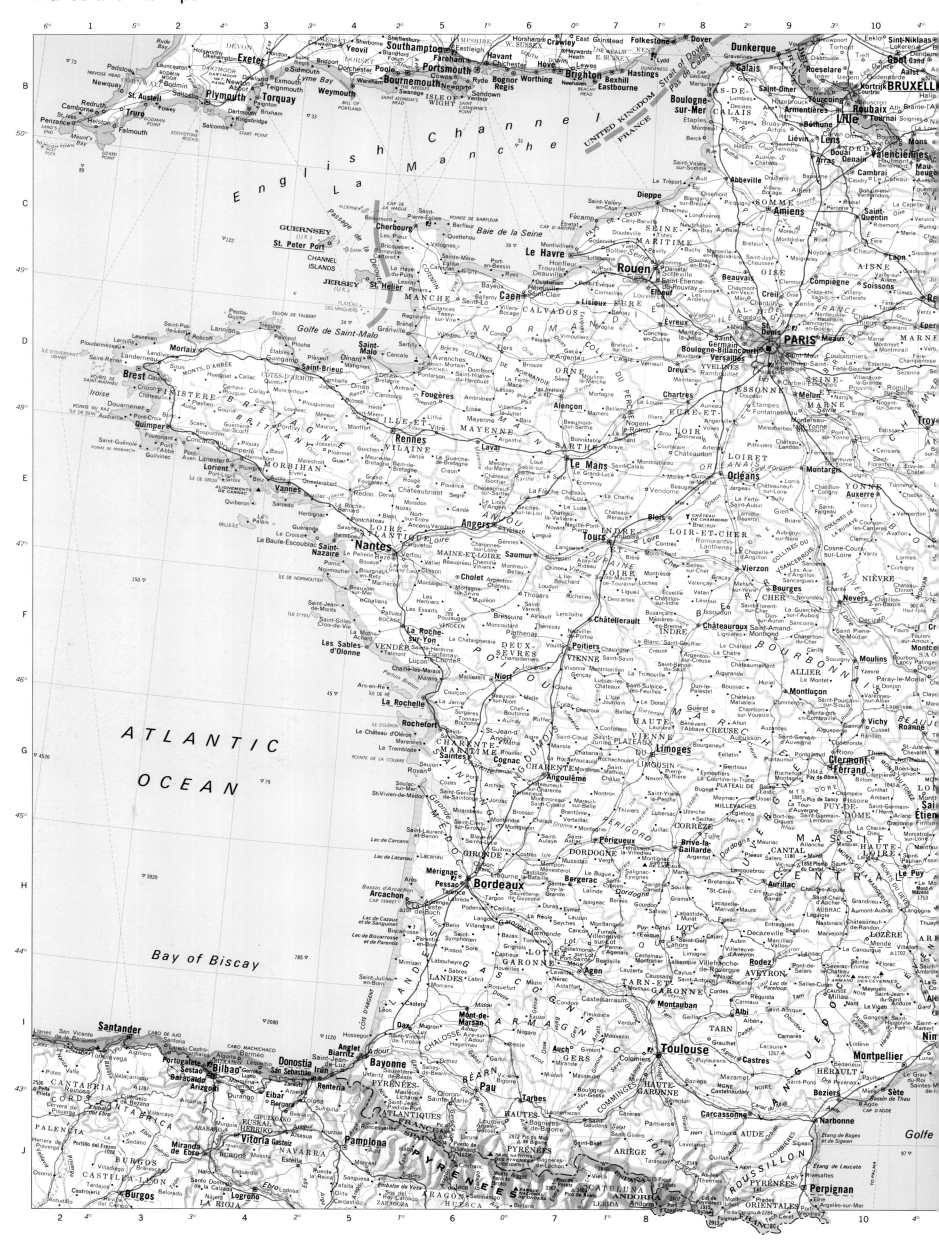

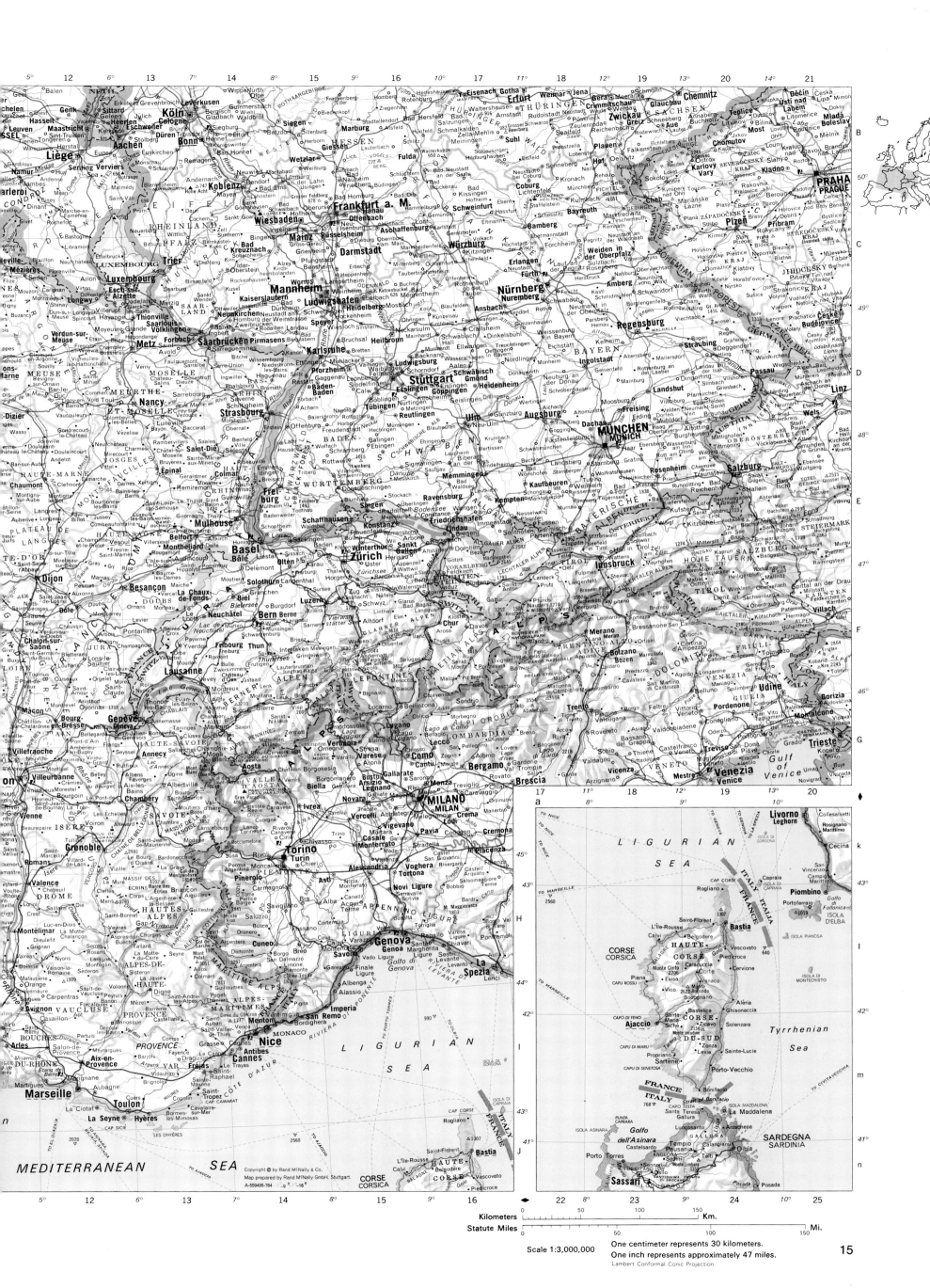

One centimeter represents 30 kilometers.
One inch represents approximately 47 miles.

Scale 1:3,000,000

Lambert Conformal Conic Projection

Kilometers
Statute Miles

15

Kilometers
Statute Miles

Scale 1:3,000,000

One centimeter represents 30 kilometers.
One inch represents approximately 47 miles.

Conic Projection, Two Standard Parallels

17

ADRIATIC SEA
LIGURIAN SEA
Gulf of Venice
MILANO
Torino Turin
Genova Genoa
Venezia Venice
Bologna
Firenze Florence
Trieste
Ljubljana
Zagreb
WIEN VIENNA
BUDAPEST
Bratislava
MÜNCHEN MUNICH
Zürich
Innsbruck
Salzburg
Graz
Verona
Padova
Parma
Ancona
Pescara
Split
Sarajevo
Bastia
Nice
Monaco
CORSE CORSICA
ITALY ITALIA
FRANCE

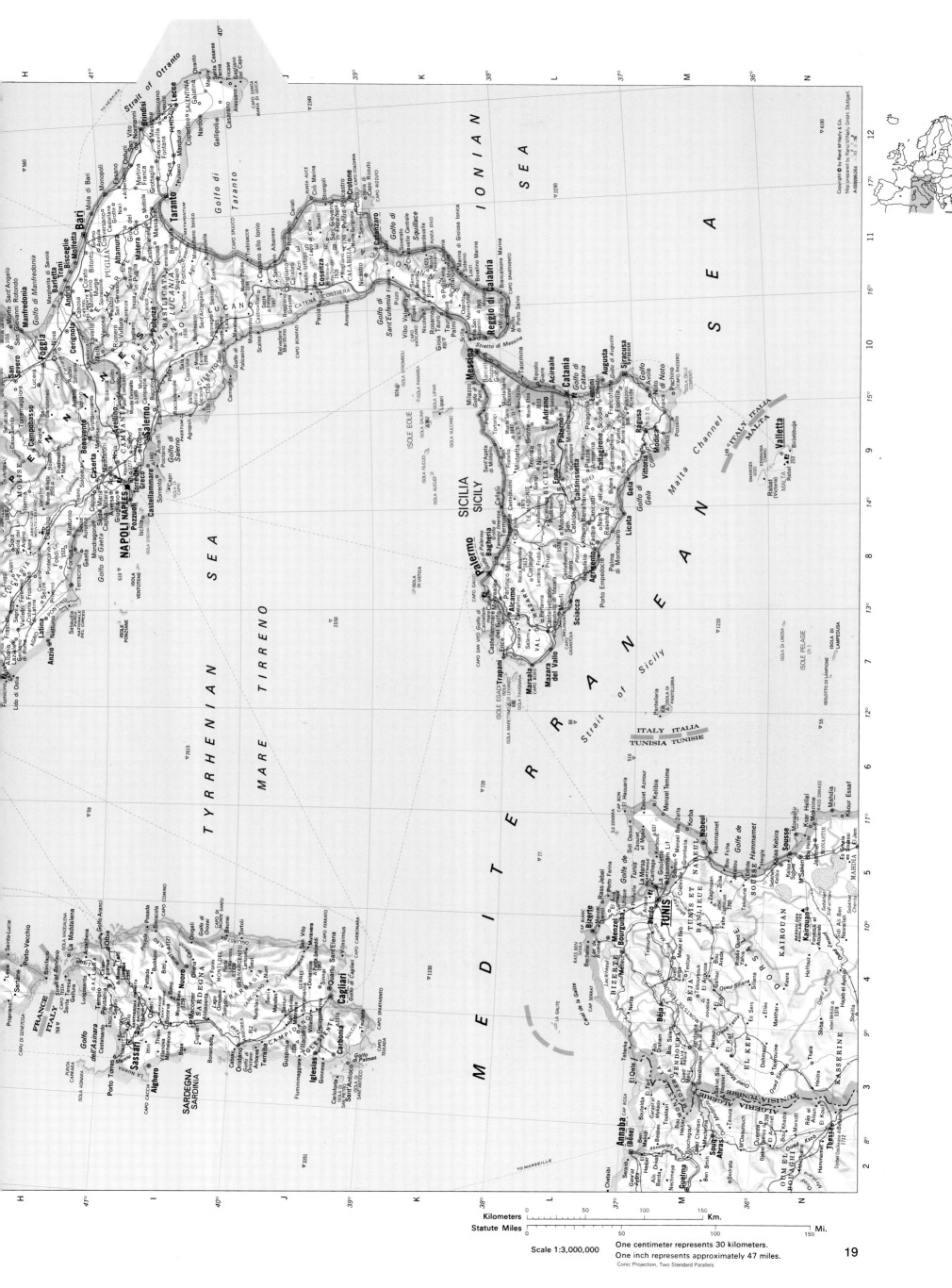

Kilometers

Statute Miles

Scale 1:3,000,000

One centimeter represents 30 kilometers.
One inch represents approximately 47 miles.

Conic Projection, Two Standard Parallels

19

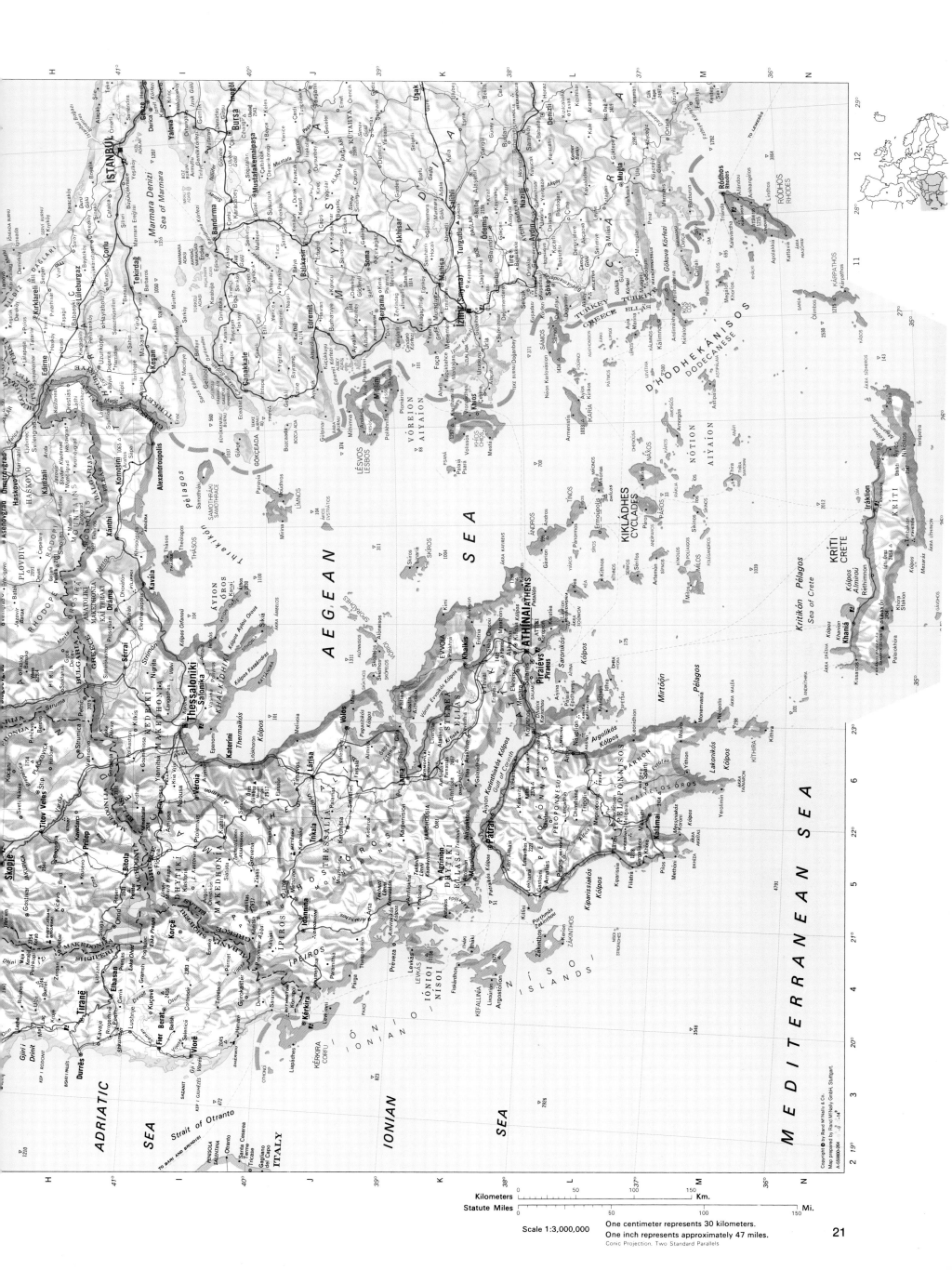

Scale 1:3,000,000

Kilometers
Statute Miles

One centimeter represents 30 kilometers.
One inch represents approximately 47 miles.
Conic Projection, Two Standard Parallels

21

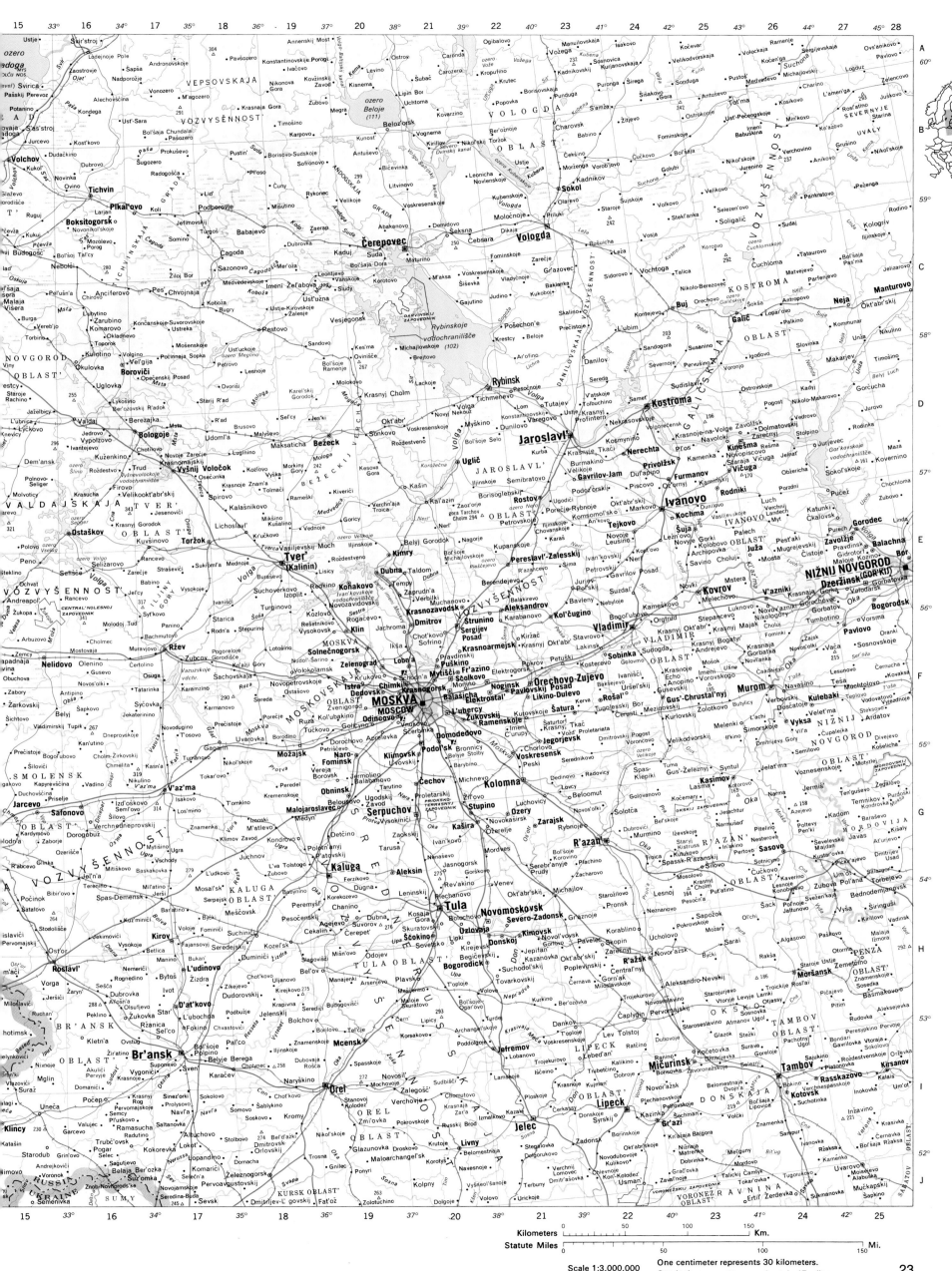

Scale 1:3,000,000

One centimeter represents 30 kilometers.
One inch represents approximately 47 miles.
Lambert Conformal Conic Projection

Kilometers
Statute Miles

Km.
Mi.

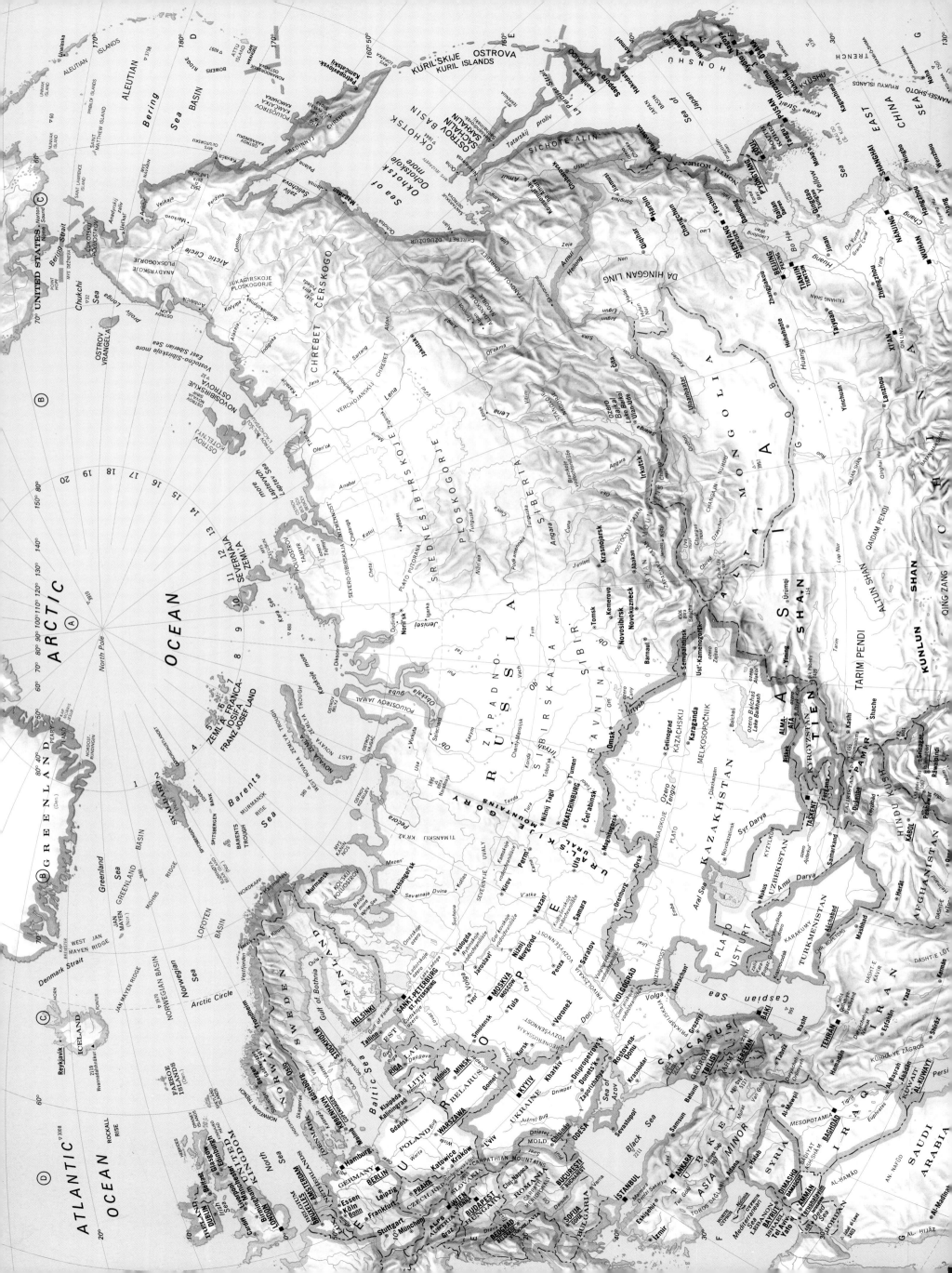

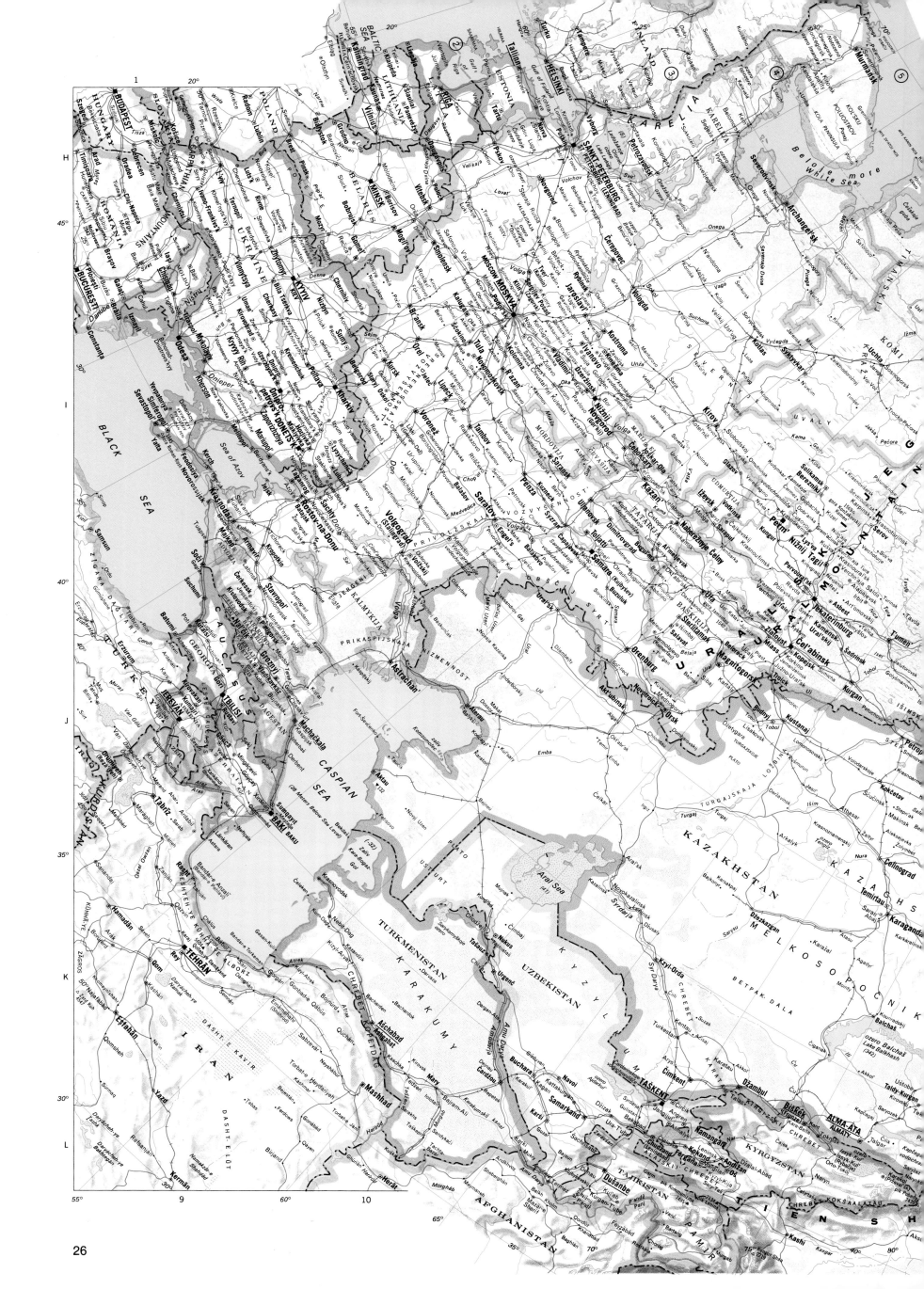

Scale 1:12,000,000

One centimeter represents 120 kilometers.
One inch represents approximately 190 miles.

Lambert Conformal Conic Projection

Kilometers

Statute Miles

Copyright © by Rand McNally & Co.
Map prepared by Esselte Map Service AB, Stockholm.
A-579594-264

Scale 1:12,000,000

One centimeter represents 120 kilometers.
One inch represents approximately 190 miles.

Lambert Conformal Conic Projection

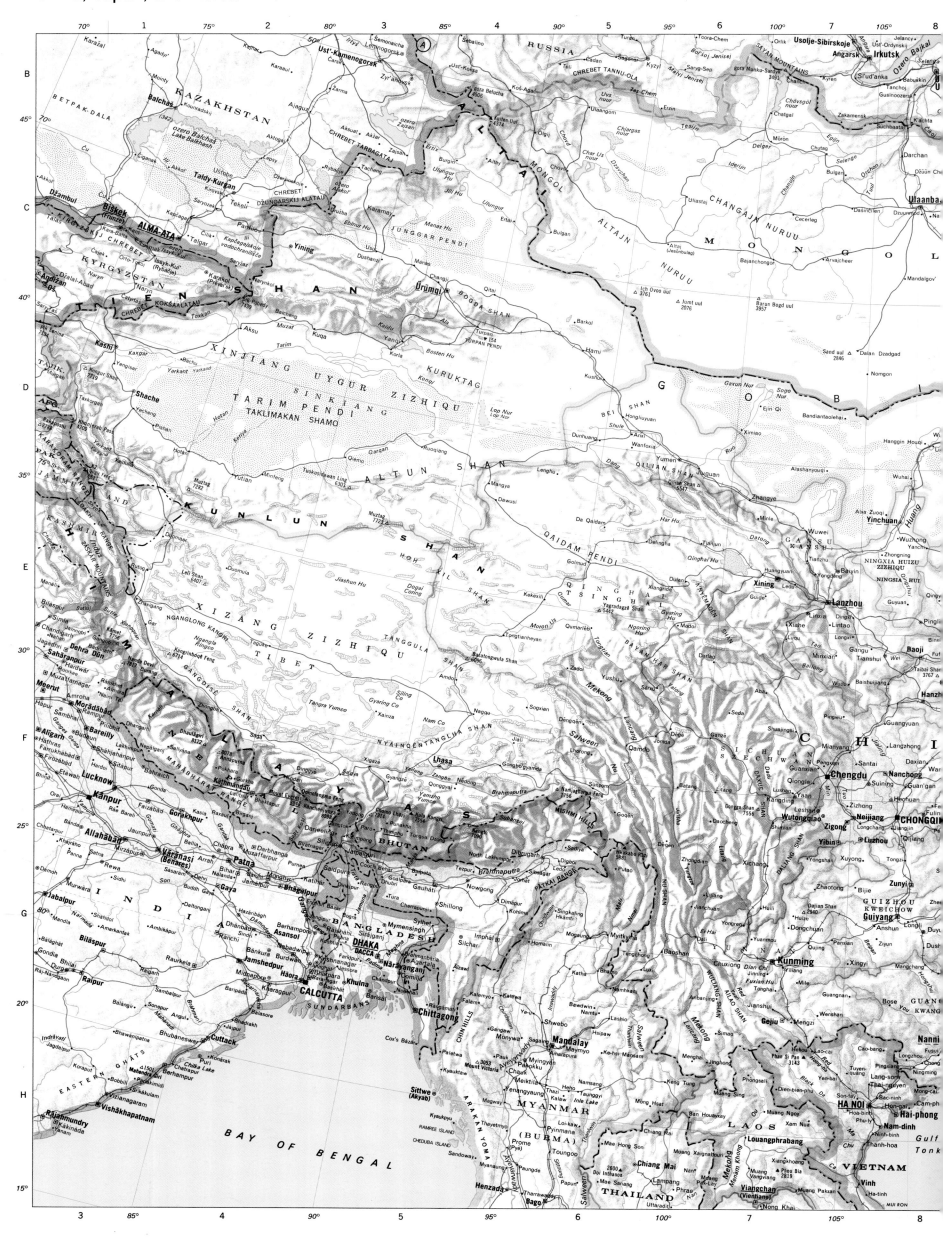

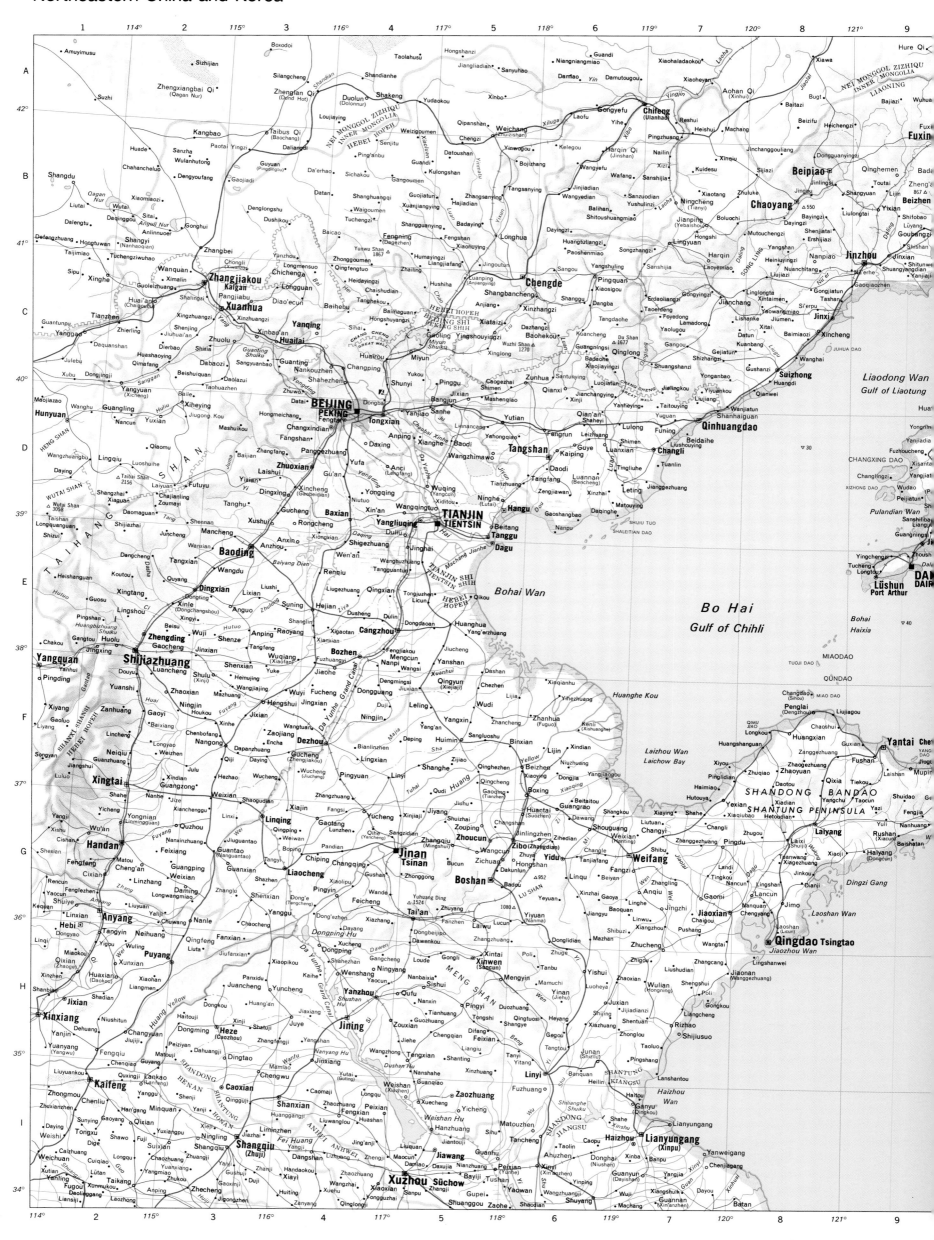

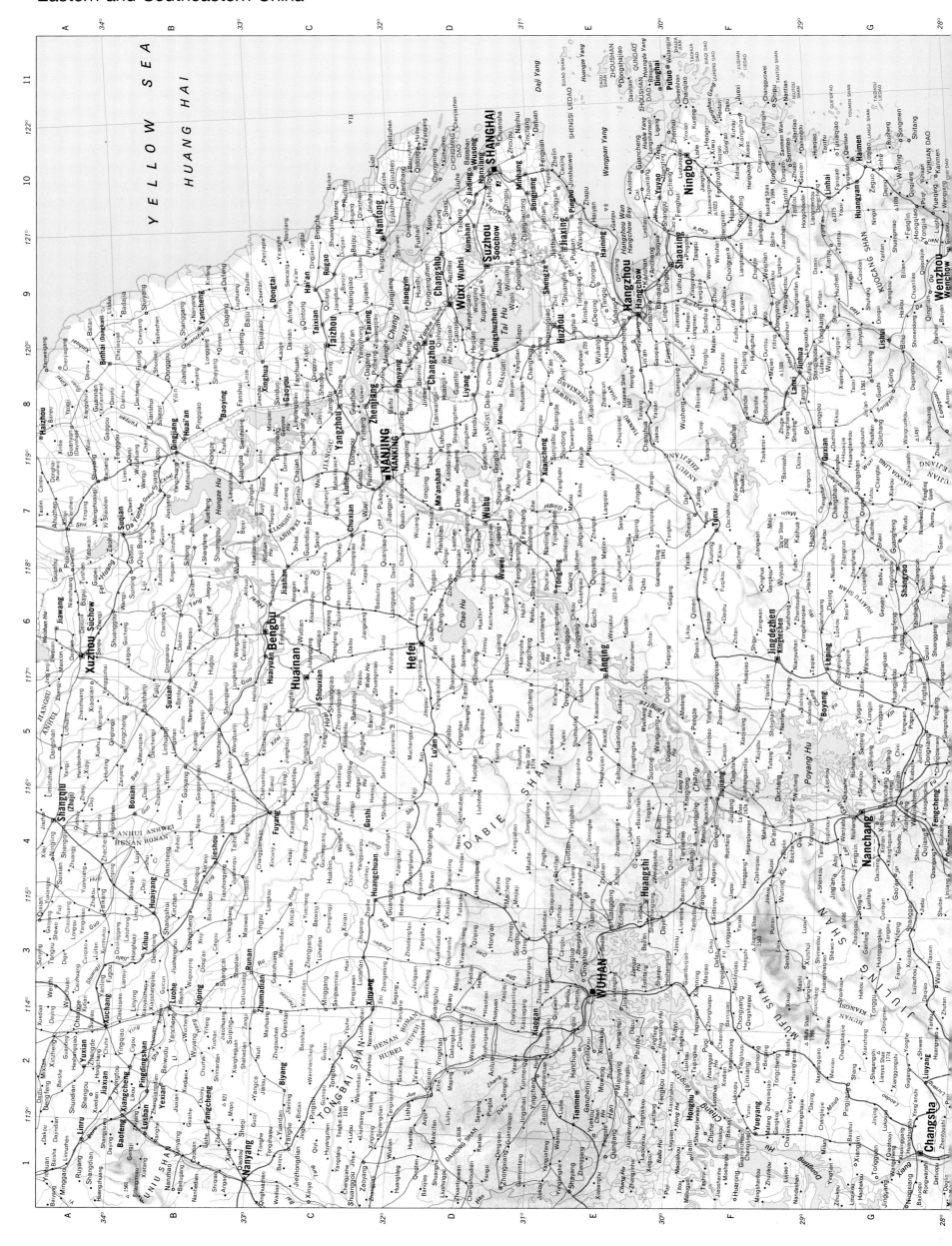

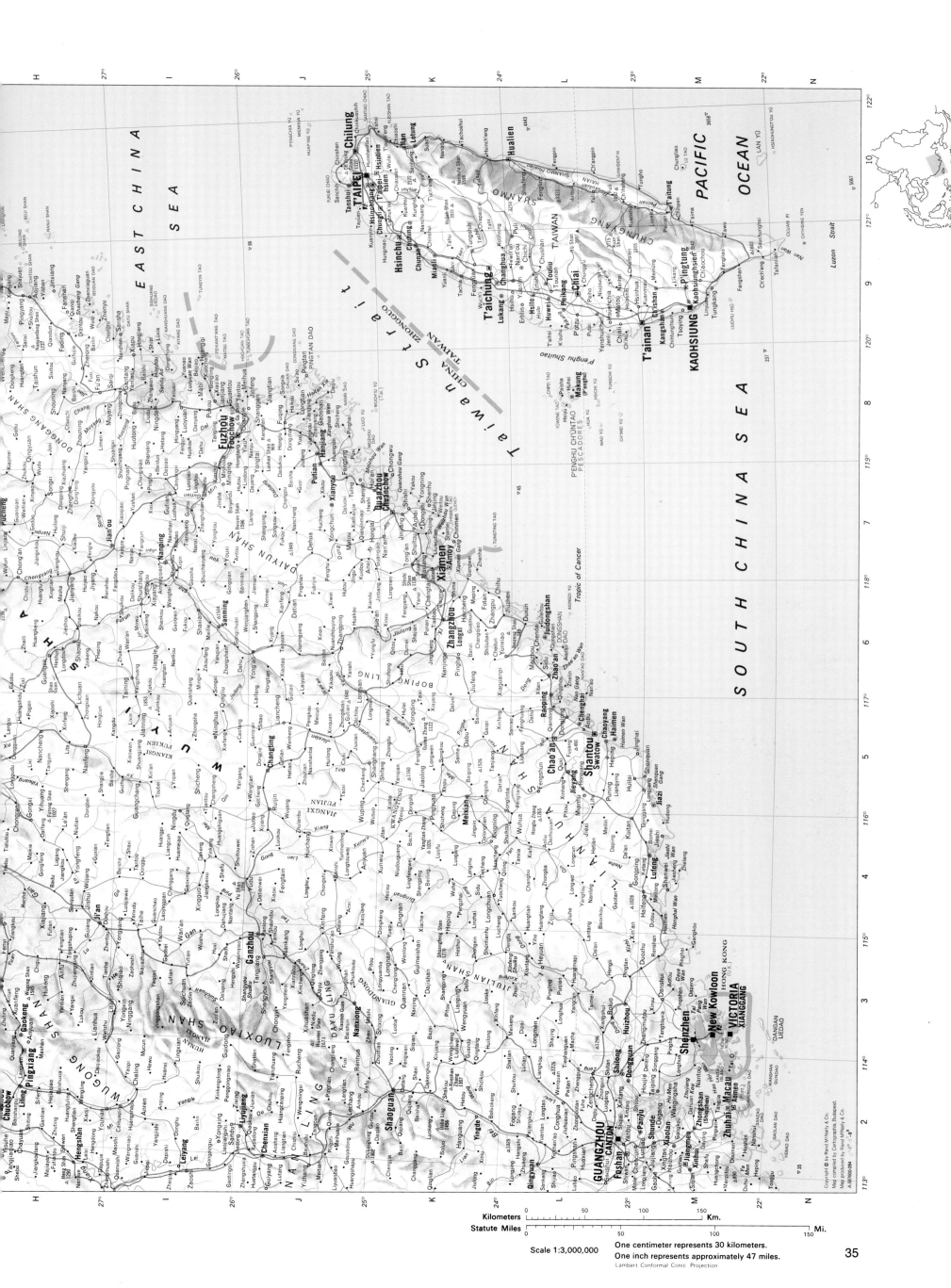

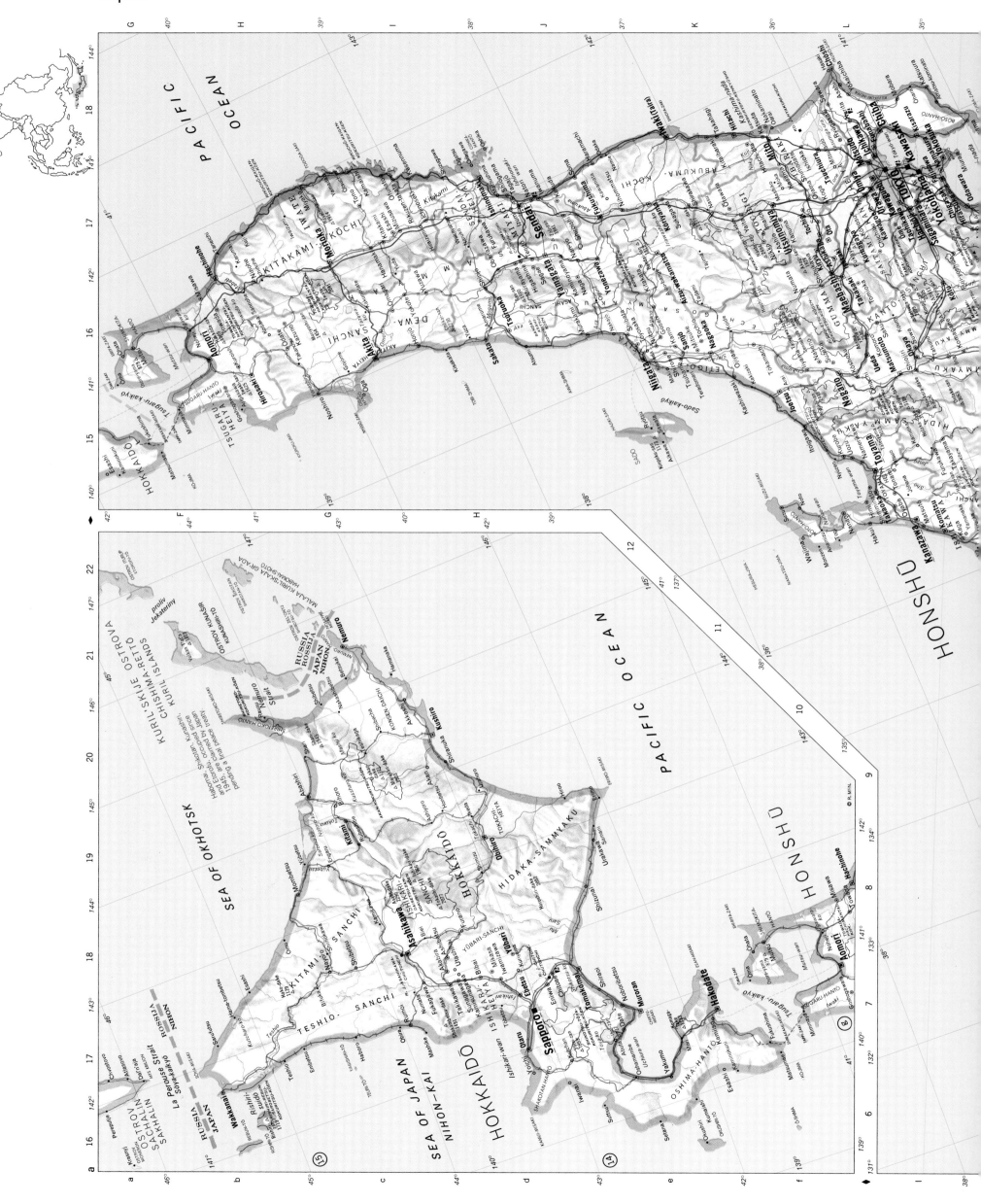

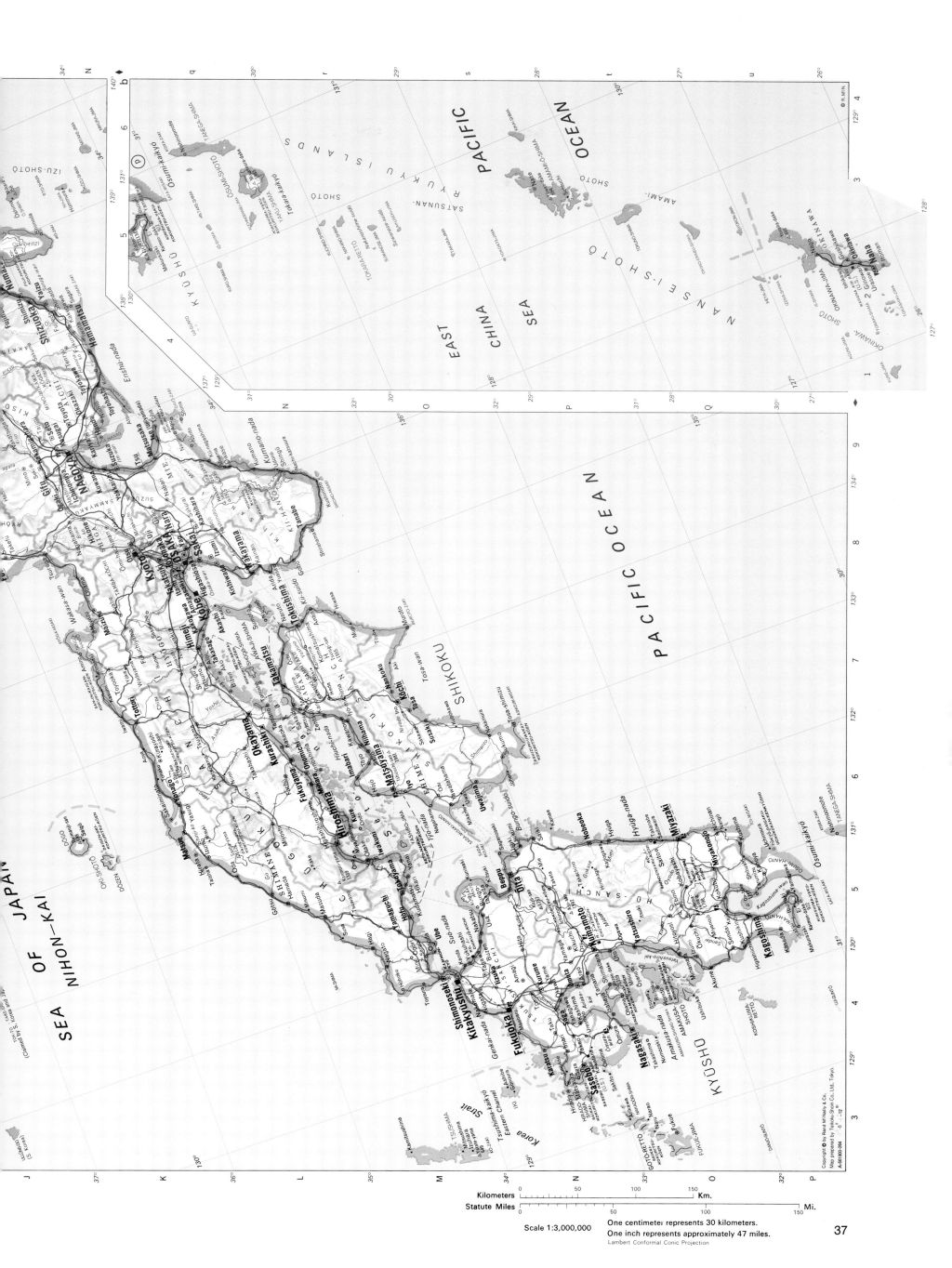

SEA OF JAPAN
NIHON-KAI

PACIFIC OCEAN

EAST CHINA SEA

PACIFIC OCEAN

RYUKYU ISLANDS

NANSEI-SHOTO

KYUSHU

SHIKOKU

NAGOYA
KYOTO
OSAKA
Kobe
Hiroshima
Okayama
Matsuyama
Kōchi
Takamatsu
Tokushima
Matsue
Tottori
Yamaguchi
Shimonoseki
Kitakyūshū
Fukuoka
Nagasaki
Sasebo
Kumamoto
Miyazaki
Kagoshima
Ōita
Beppu
Nobeoka

Kilometers
Statute Miles

Km.
Mi.

Scale 1:3,000,000
One centimeter represents 30 kilometers.
One inch represents approximately 47 miles.
Lambert Conformal Conic Projection

Copyright © by Rand McNally & Co.
Map prepared by Teikoku-Shoin Co., Ltd., Tokyo.

37

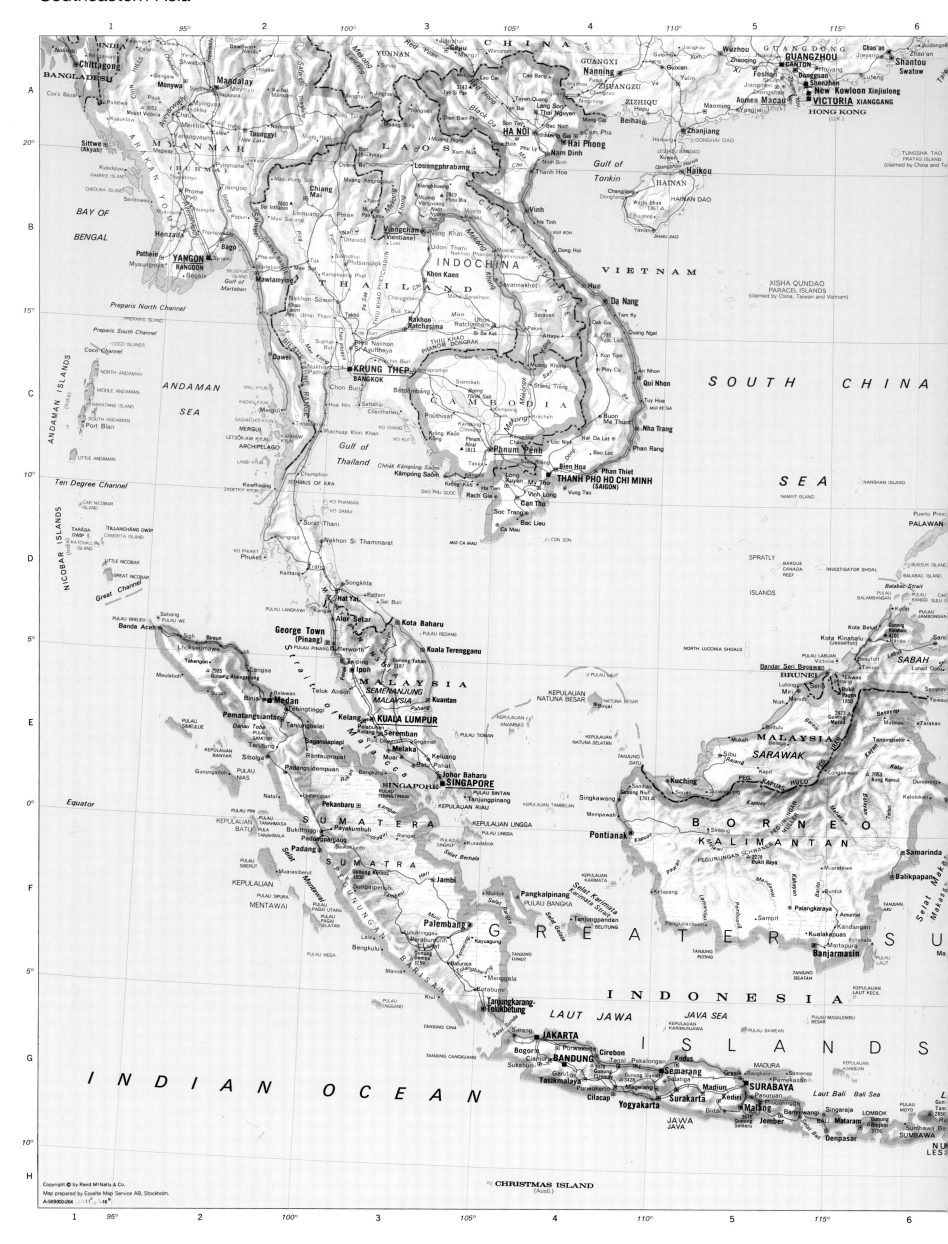

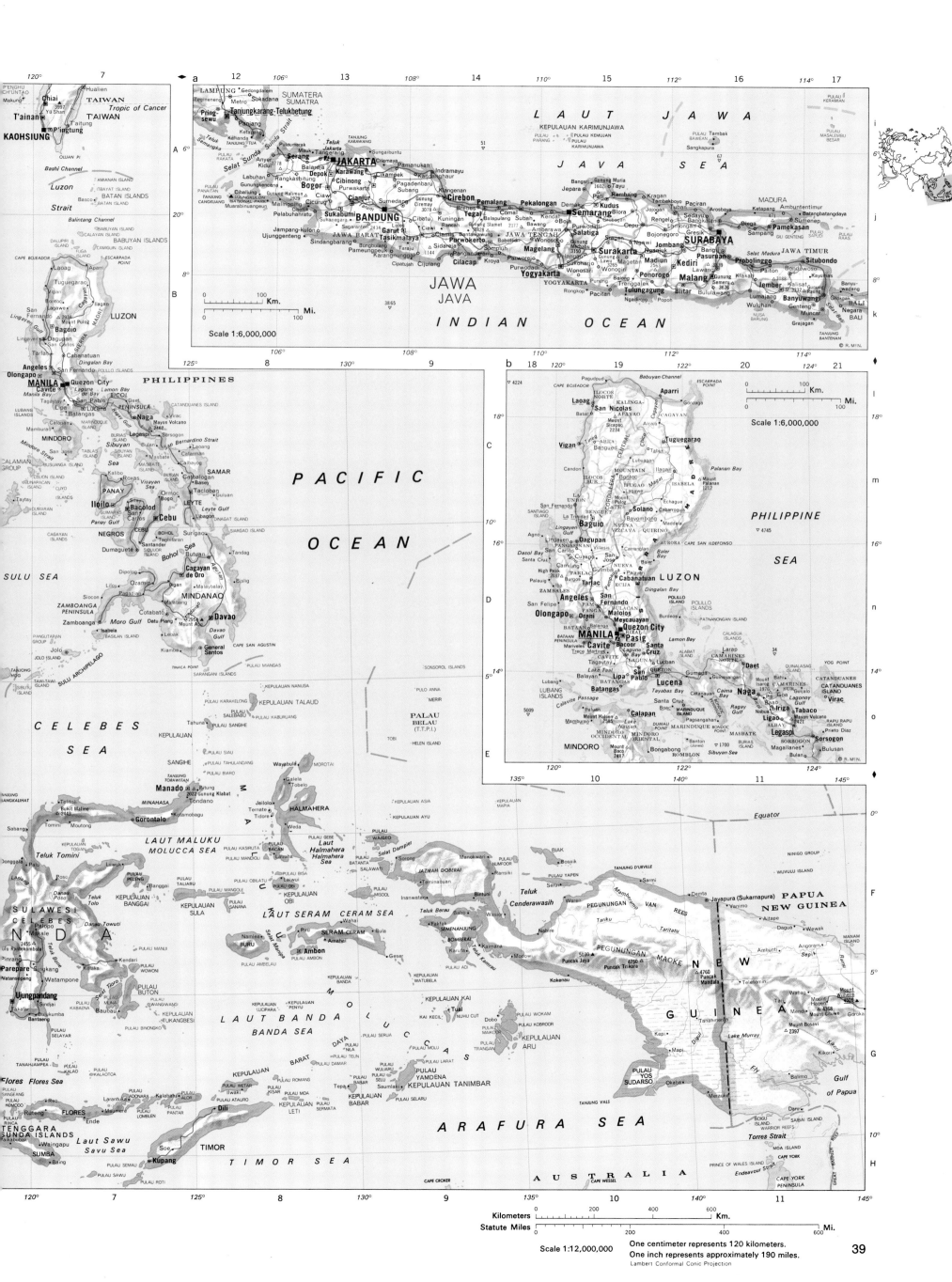

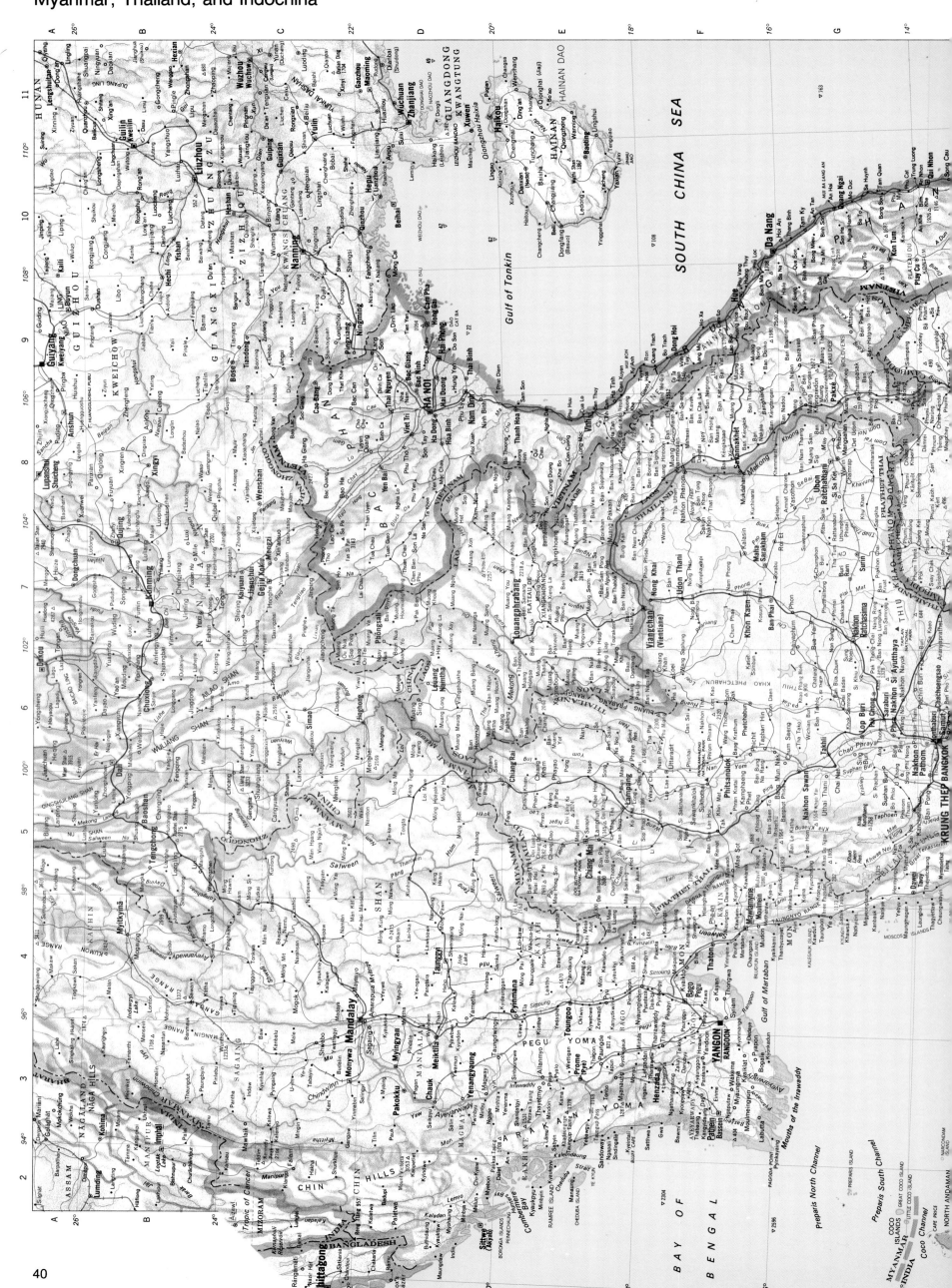

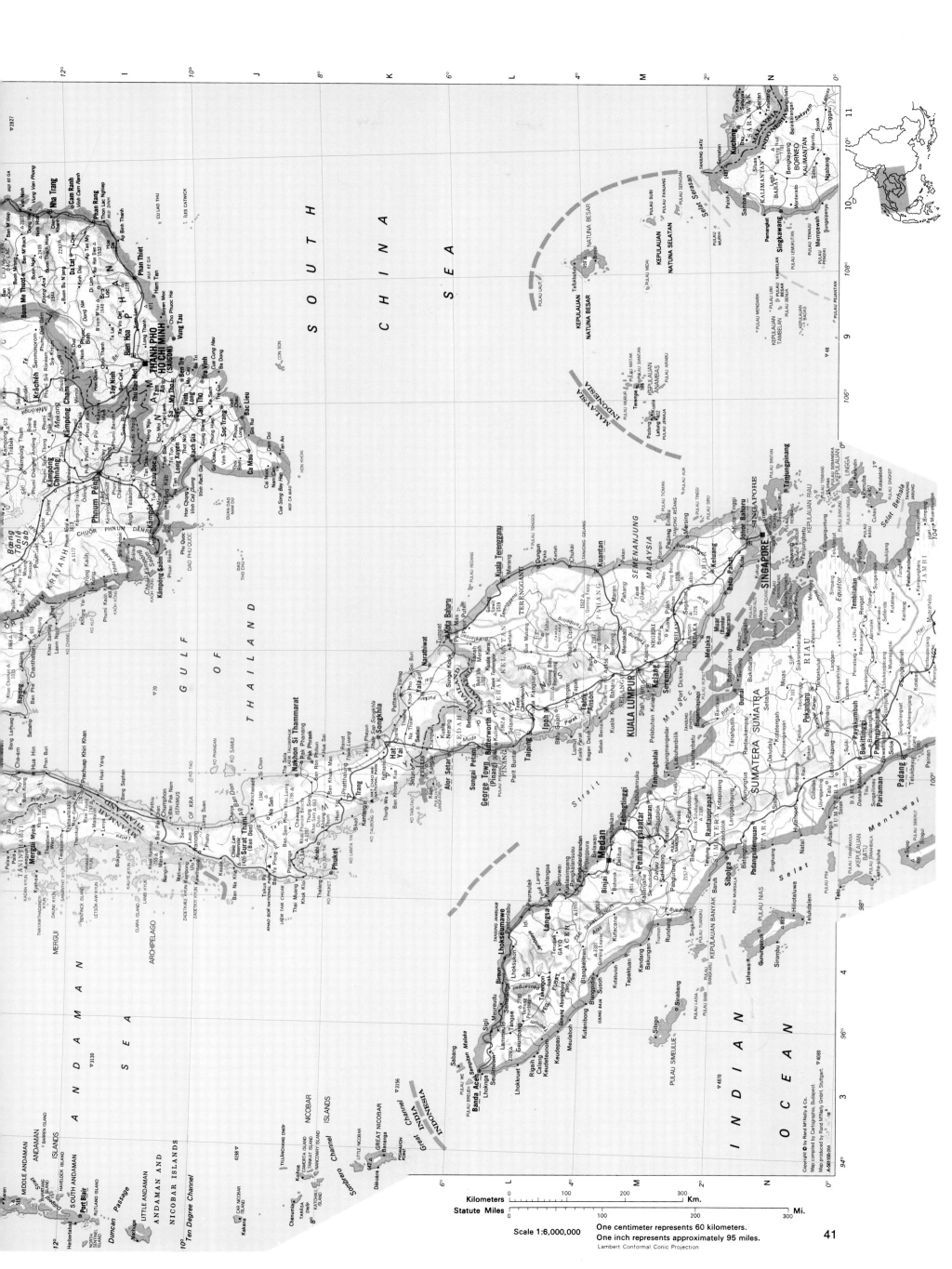

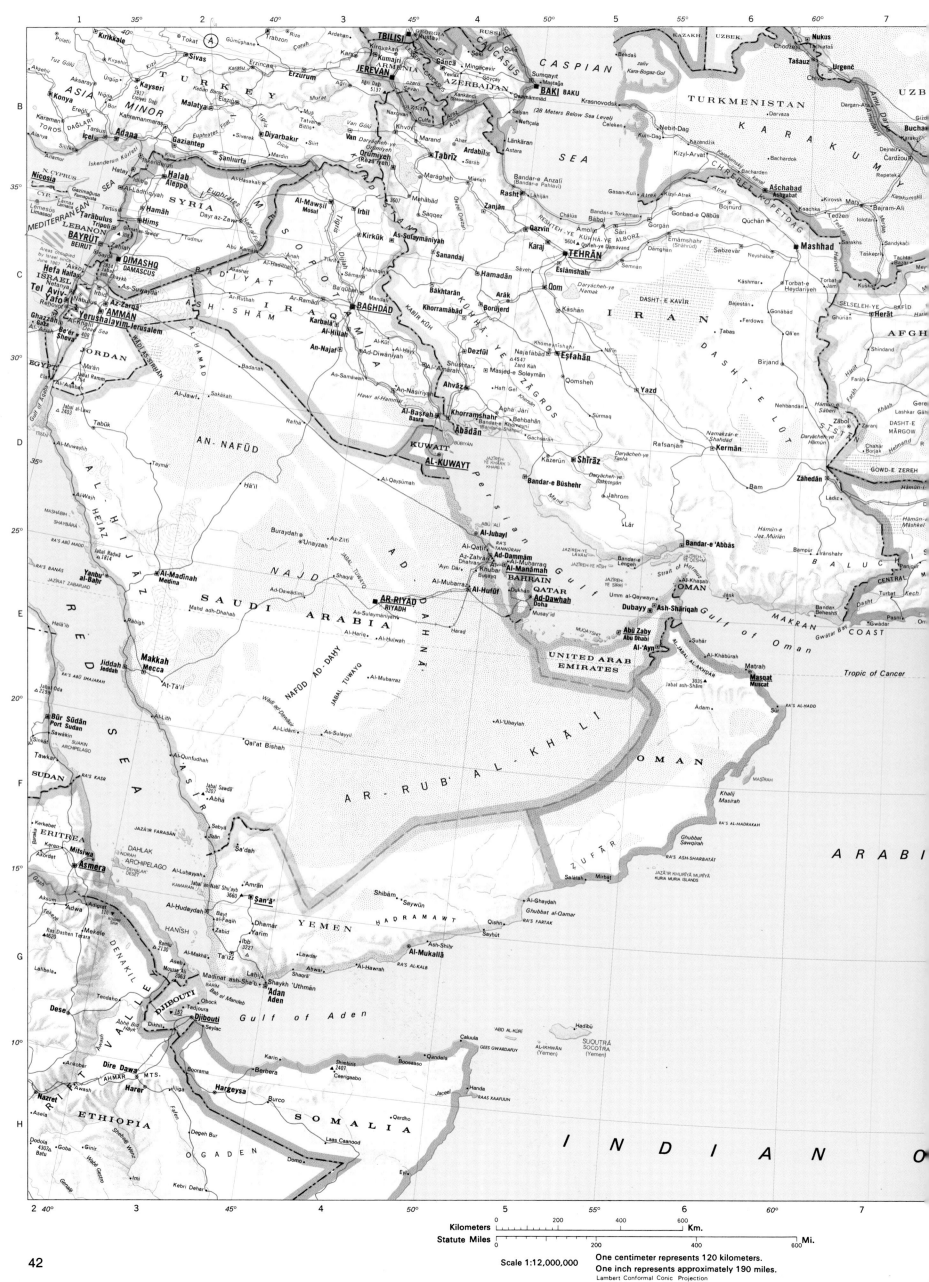

Kilometers
Statute Miles

Scale 1:12,000,000
One centimeter represents 120 kilometers.
One inch represents approximately 190 miles.
Lambert Conformal Conic Projection

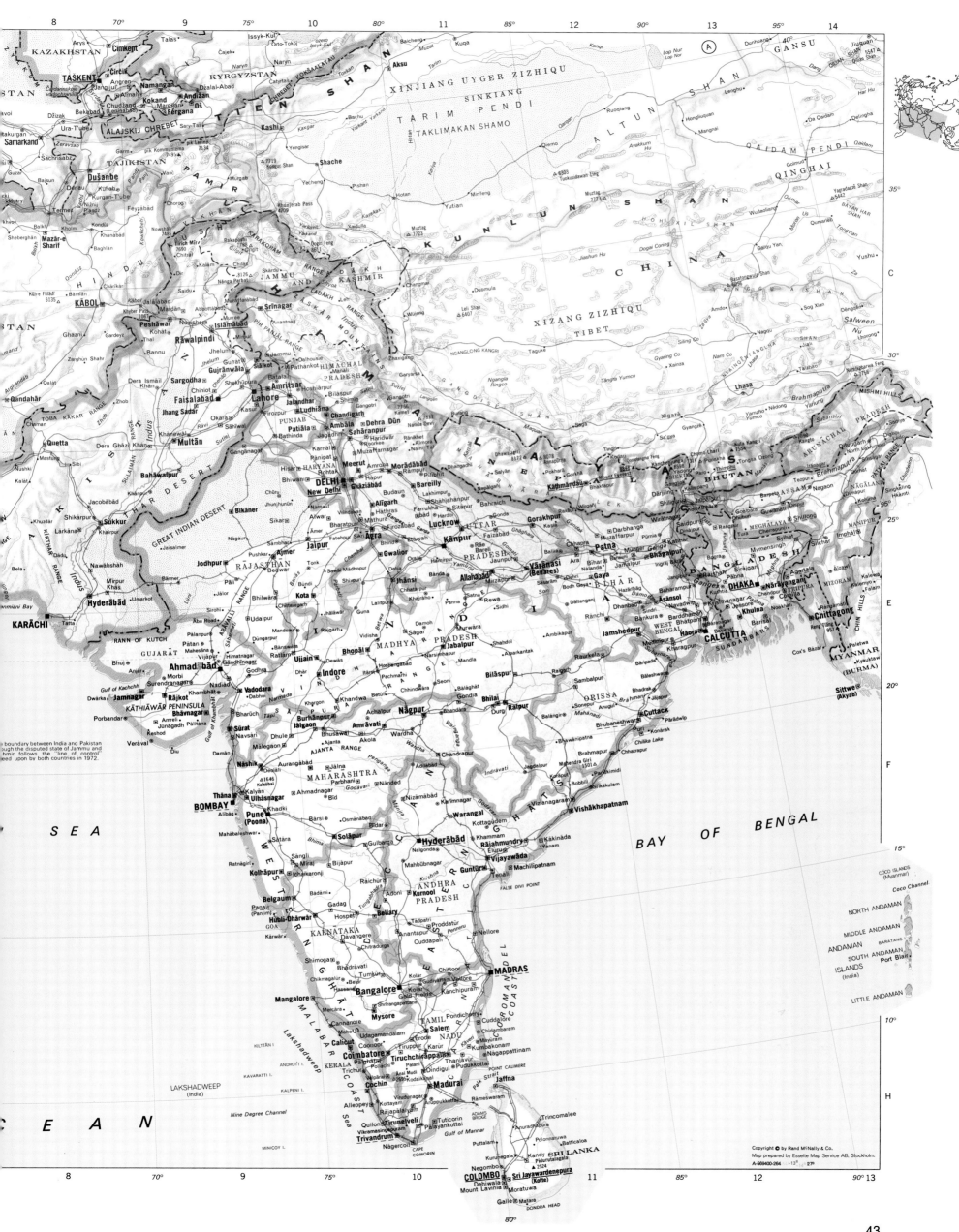

43

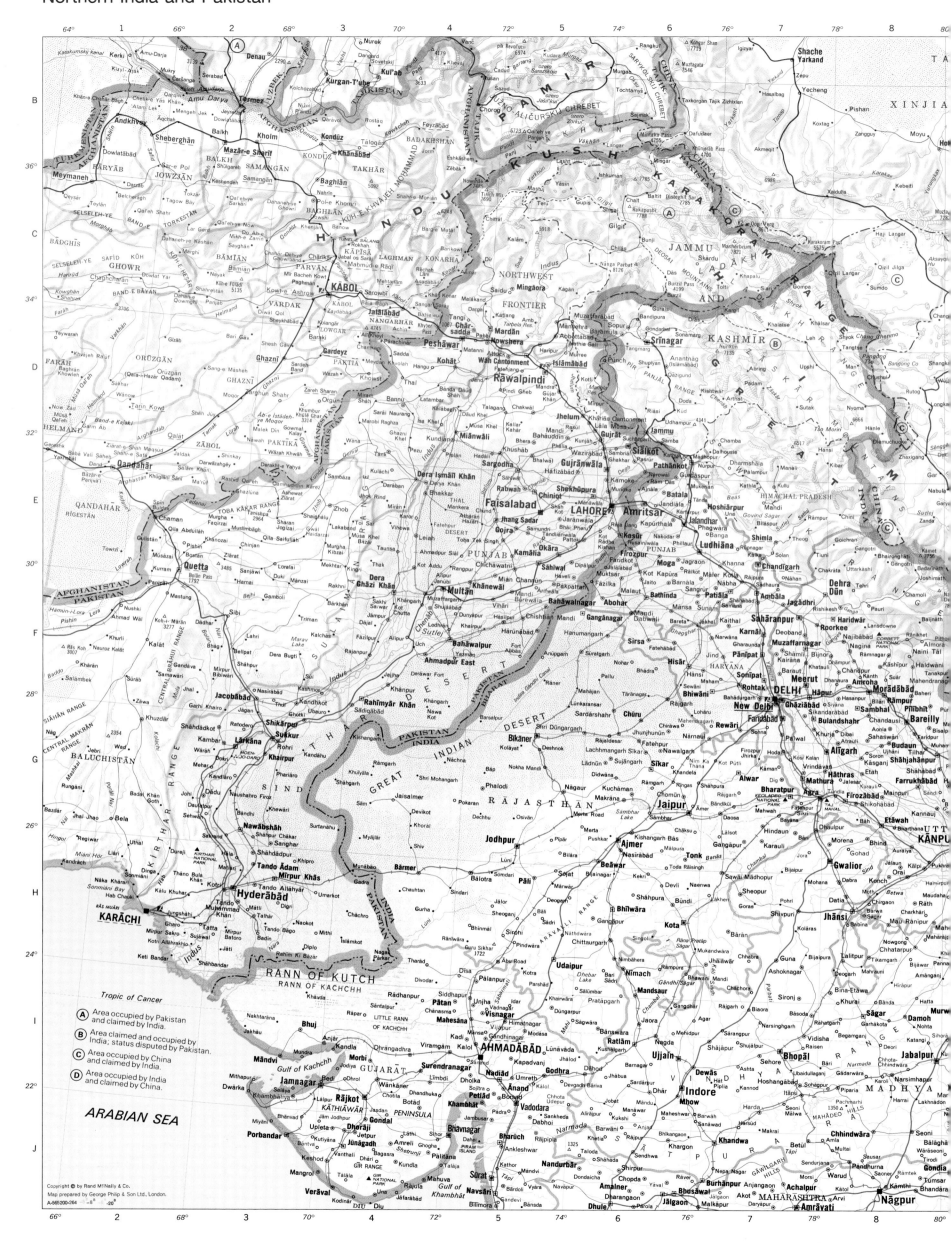

Kilometers
Statute Miles

Scale 1:6,000,000
One centimeter represents 60 kilometers.
One inch represents approximately 95 miles.
Lambert Conformal Conic Projection

Copyright © by Rand McNally & Co.
Map prepared by George Philip & Son Ltd., London.
A-565300-264

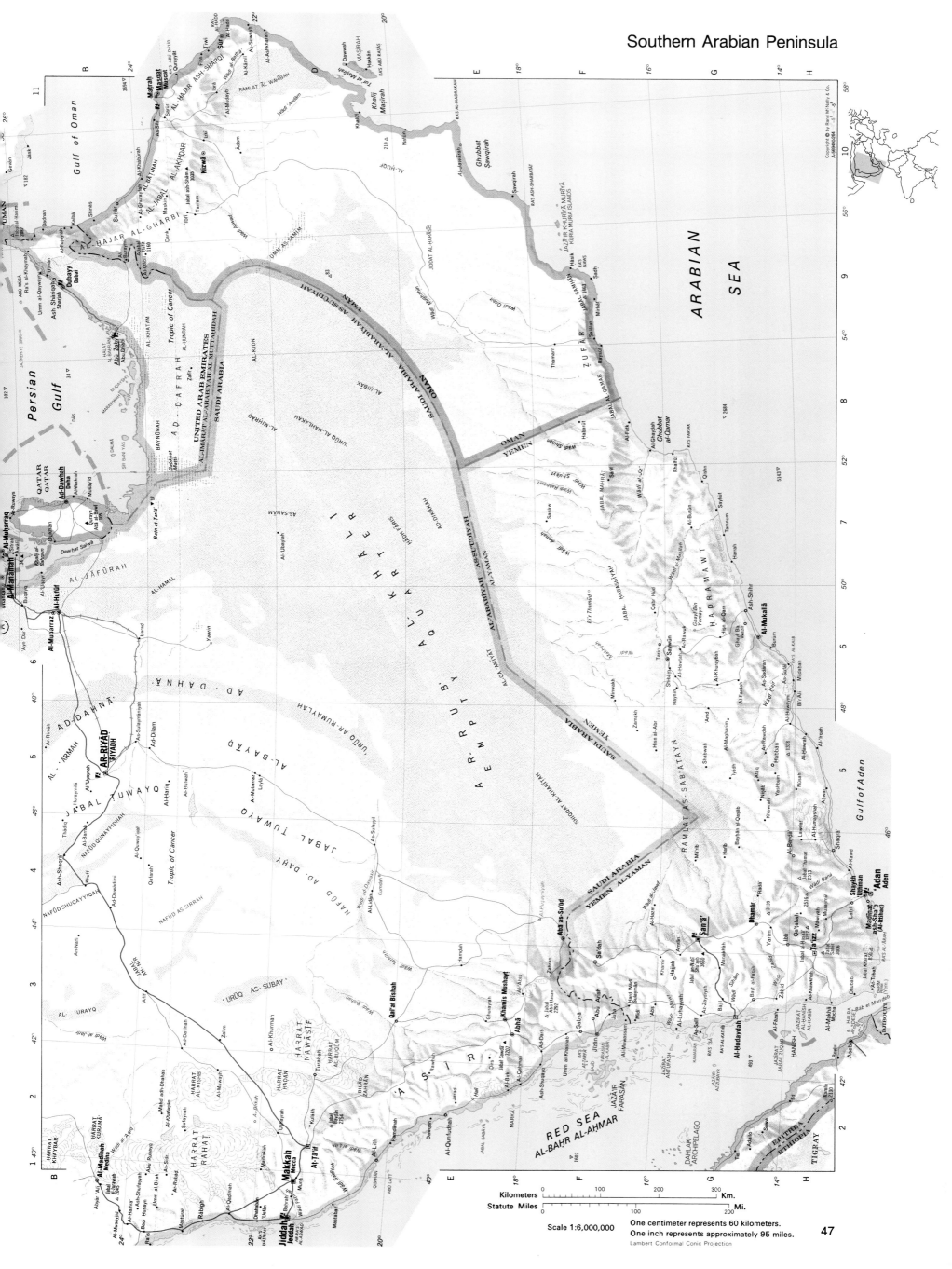

Southern Arabian Peninsula

Gulf of Oman

Persian Gulf

ARABIAN SEA

RED SEA
AL-BAHR AL-AHMAR

Gulf of Aden

AR-RUB' AL-KHALI

AD-DAHNA

JABAL TUWAYQ

SAUDI ARABIA

OMAN

YEMEN

UNITED ARAB EMIRATES
AL-IMARAT AL-'ARABIYAH AL-MUTTAHIDAH

QATAR

ZUFAR

HADRAMAWT

'ASIR

Scale 1:6,000,000
One centimeter represents 60 kilometers.
One inch represents approximately 95 miles.
Lambert Conformal Conic Projection

Kilometers
Statute Miles

47

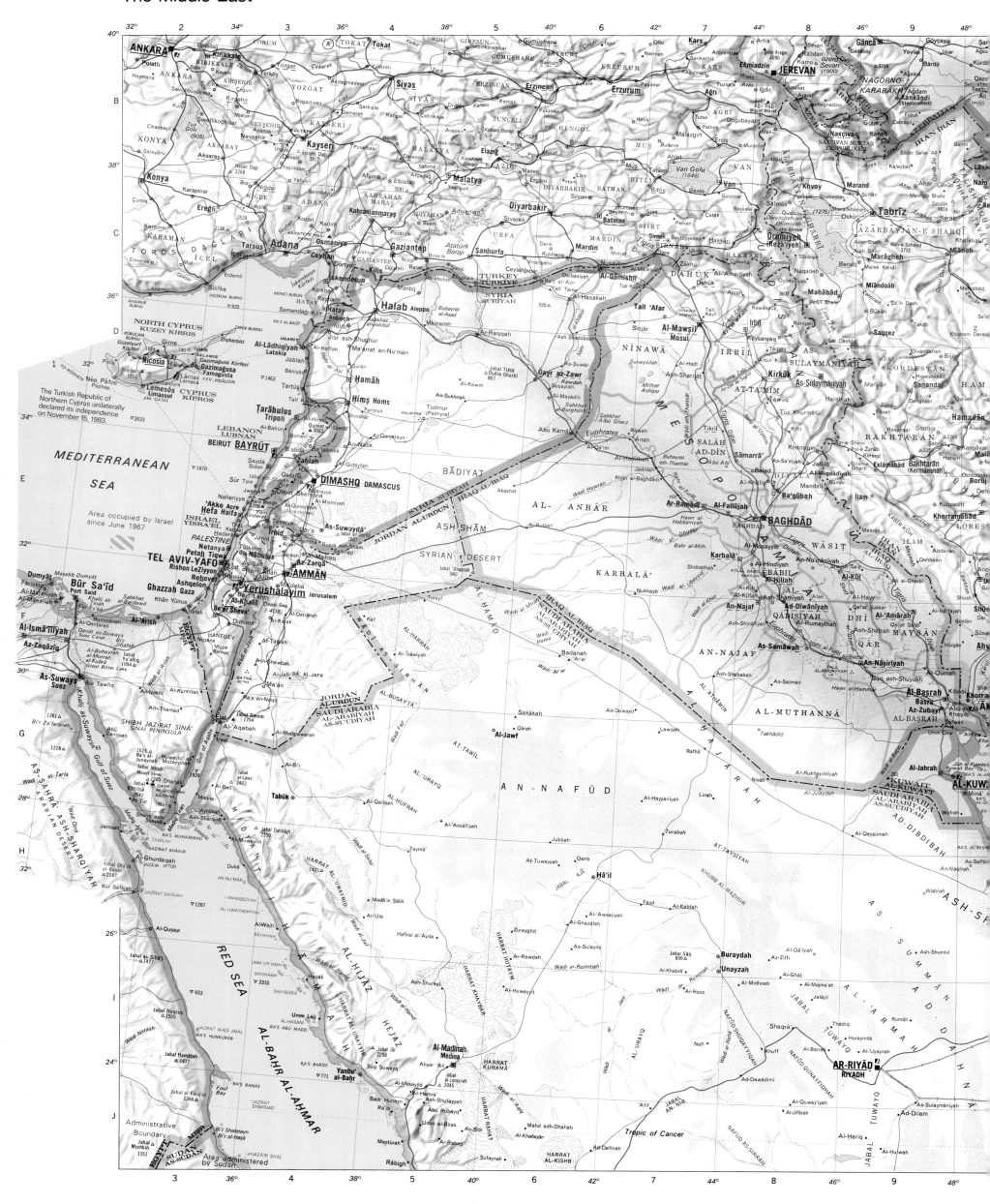

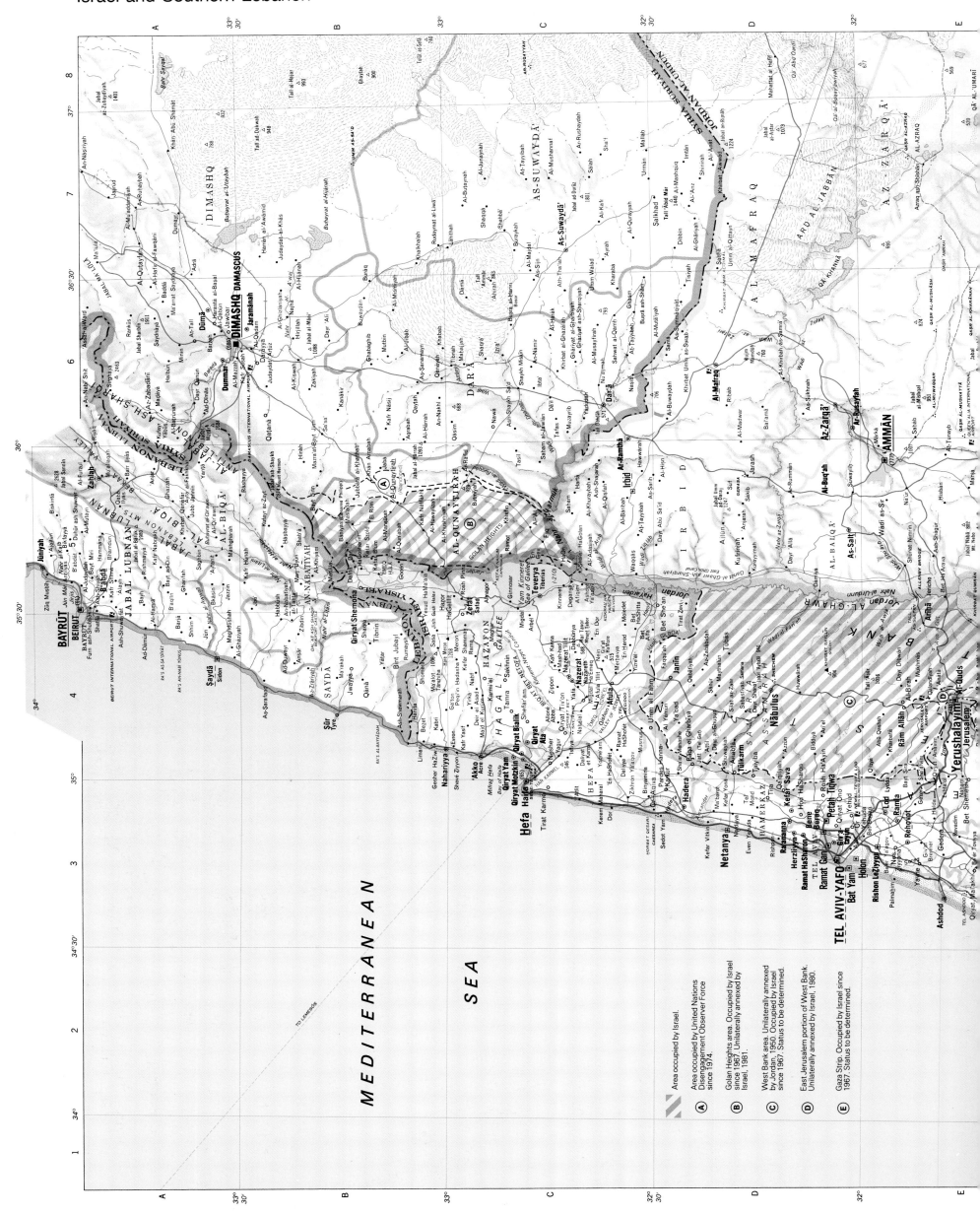

MEDITERRANEAN

SEA

Ⓐ Area occupied by United Nations
Disengagement Observer Force
since 1974.

Ⓑ Golan Heights area. Occupied by Israel
since 1967. Unilaterally annexed by
Israel, 1981.

Ⓒ West Bank area. Unilaterally annexed
by Jordan, 1950. Occupied by Israel
since 1967. Status to be determined.

Ⓓ East Jerusalem portion of West Bank.
Unilaterally annexed by Israel, 1980.

Ⓔ Gaza Strip. Occupied by Israel since
1967. Status to be determined.

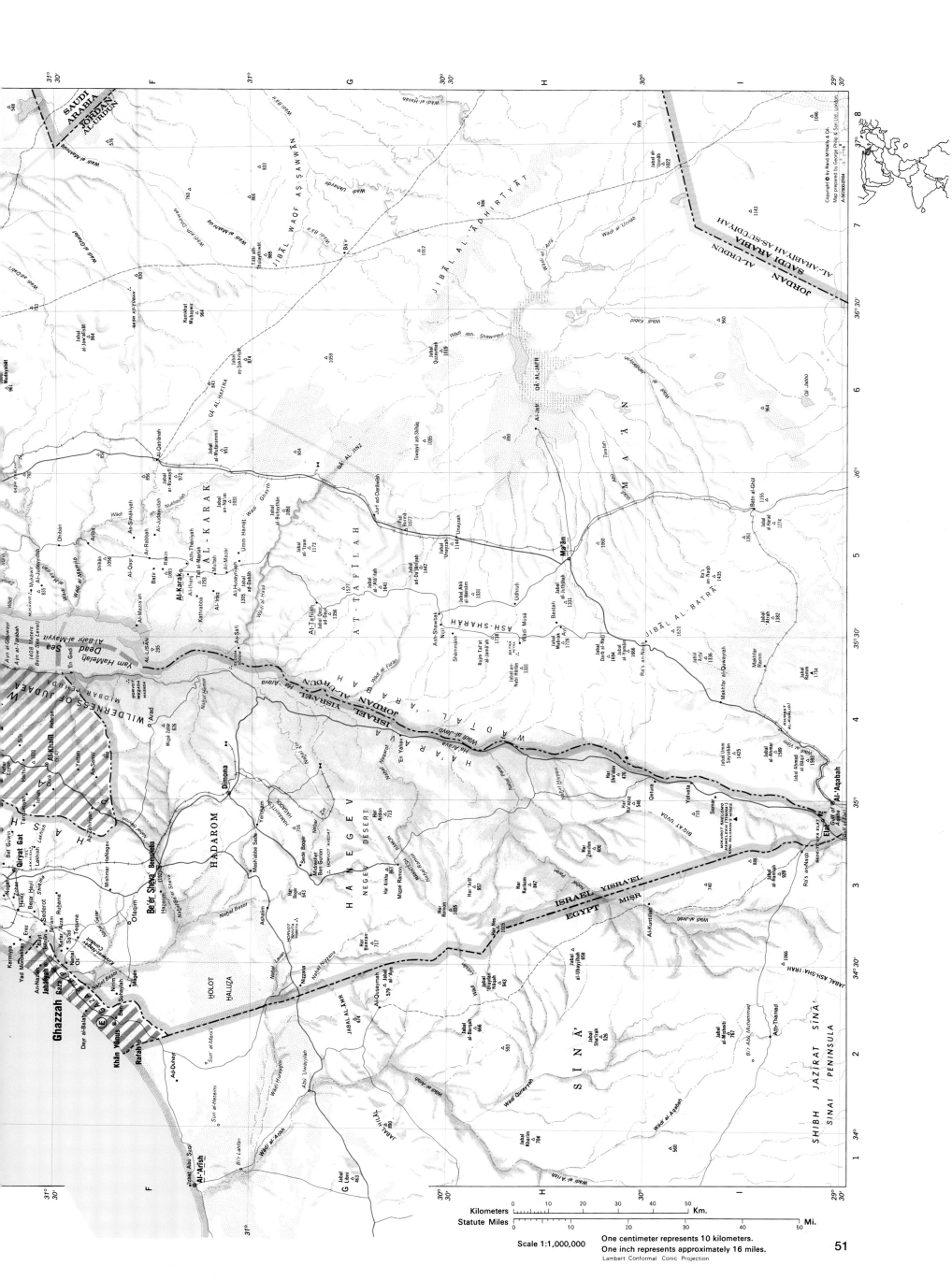

Kilometers

Statute Miles

Scale 1:1,000,000

One centimeter represents 10 kilometers.
One inch represents approximately 16 miles.

Lambert Conformal Conic Projection

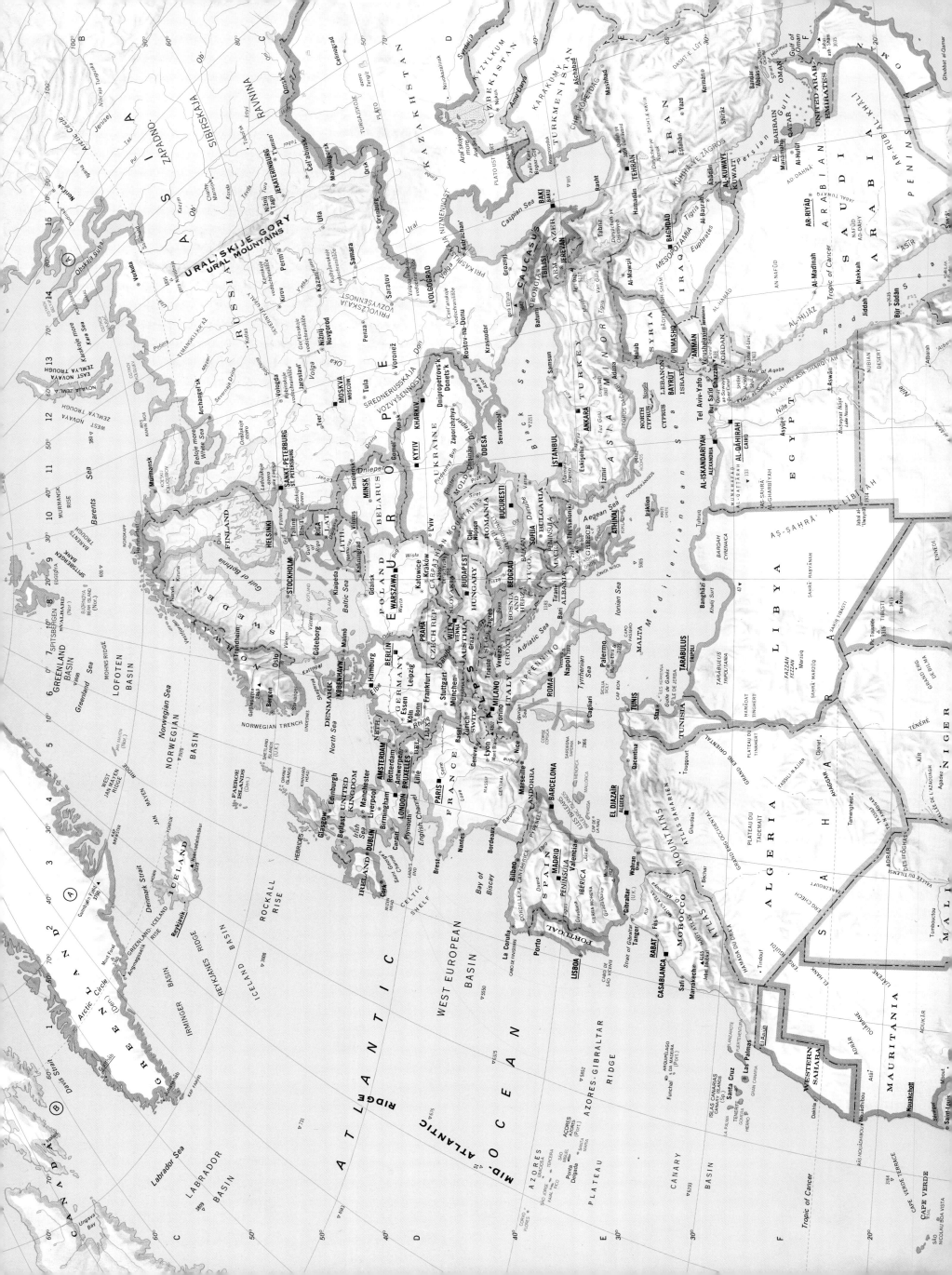

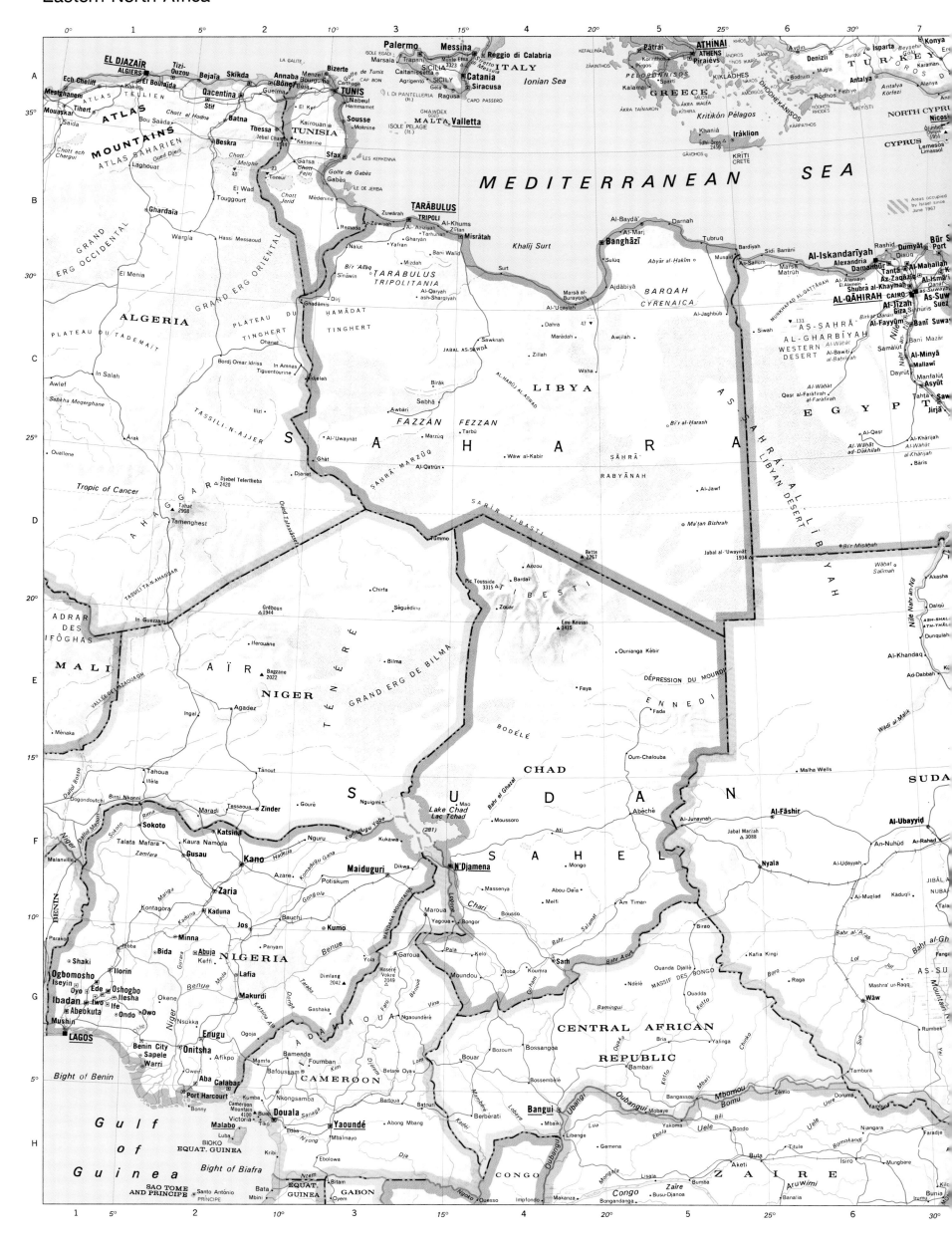

Kilometers

Statute Miles

Copyright © by Rand McNally & Co.
Map prepared by Esselte Map Service AB, Stockholm.
A-589391 -264   -11°   -24°

Scale 1:12,000,000
One centimeter represents 120 kilometers.
One inch represents approximately 190 miles.
Miller Oblated Stereographic Projection

INDIAN OCEAN

SOMALIA

KENYA

NAIROBI

Mombasa

TANZANIA

Dodoma

DAR ES SALAAM

MALAWI

MOZAMBIQUE

Beira

COMOROS

MADAGASCAR

ANTANANARIVO

Antsirabe

Fianarantsoa

Toliara

Faradofay

SEYCHELLES

Victoria

Port Louis
MAURITIUS

Saint-Denis
REUNION

MASCARENE
ISLANDS

Tropic of Capricorn

INDIAN OCEAN

Copyright © by Rand McNally & Co.
Map prepared by Esselte Map Service AB, Stockholm.
A-589200-264

Kilometers
Statute Miles

Scale 1:12,000,000
One centimeter represents 120 kilometers.
One inch represents approximately 190 miles.
Miller Oblated Stereographic Projection

59

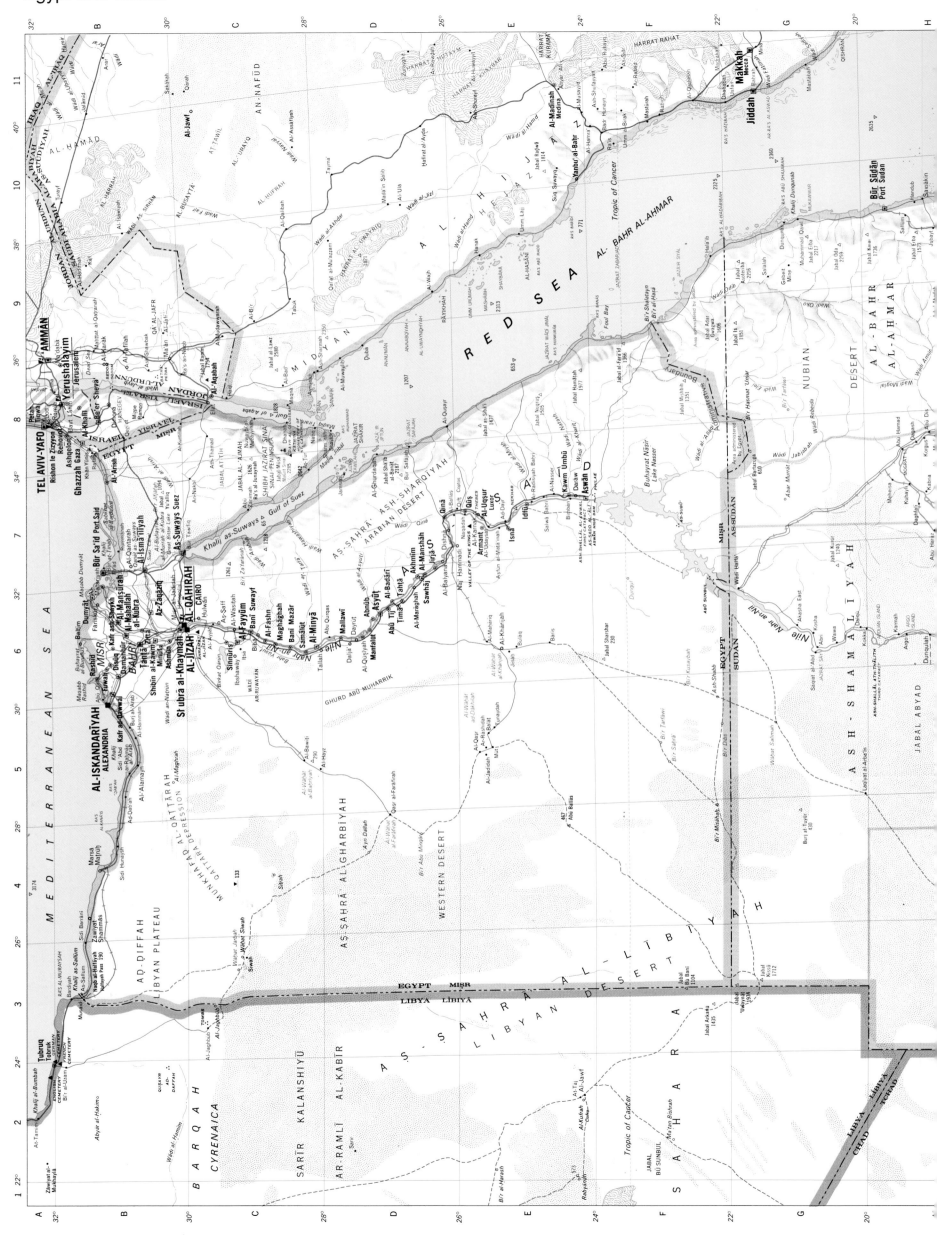

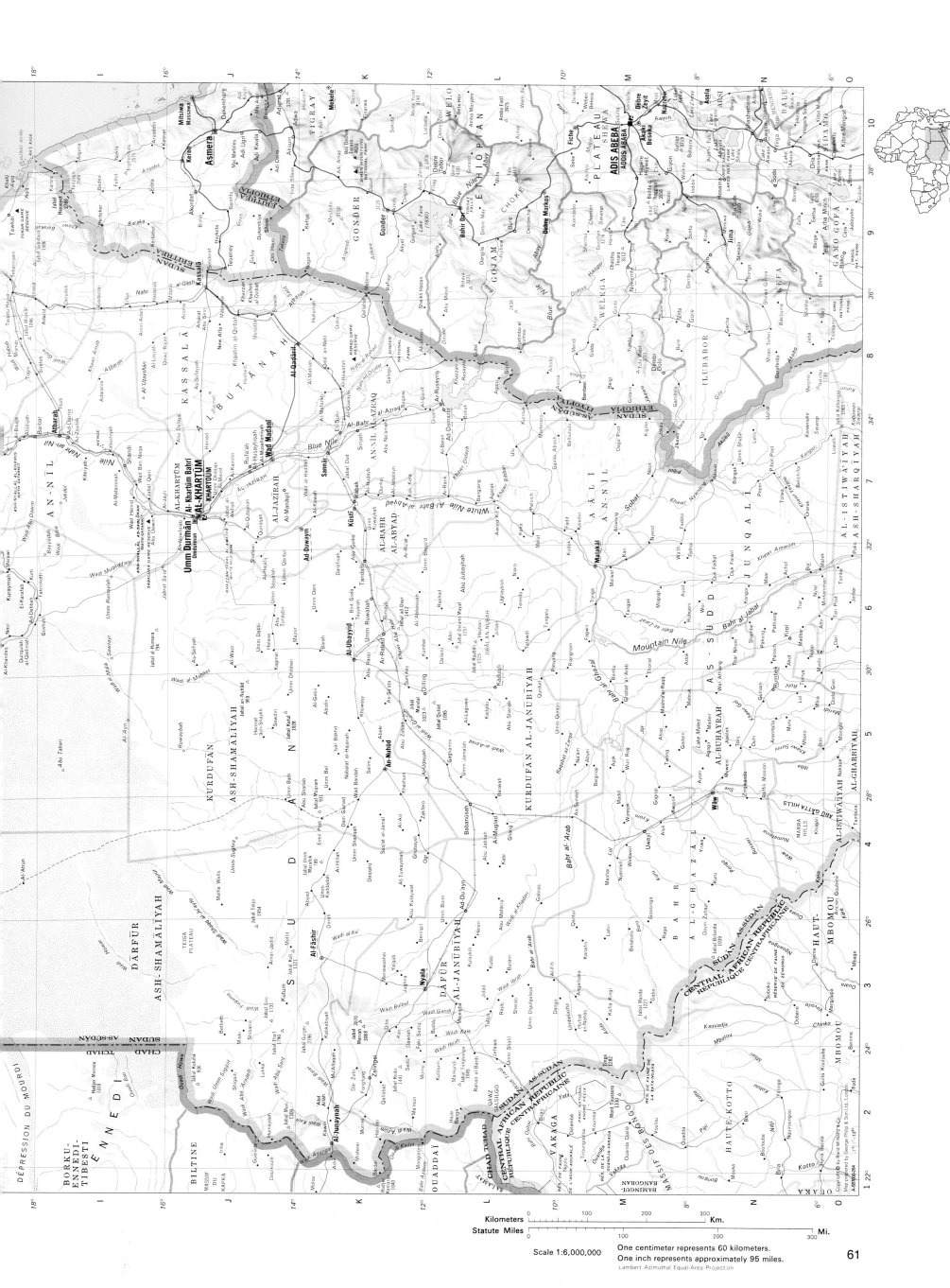

Kilometers 0 100 200 300 Km.

Statute Miles 0 100 200 300 Mi.

Scale 1:6,000,000

One centimeter represents 60 kilometers.
One inch represents approximately 95 miles.

Lambert Azimuthal Equal-Area Projection

61

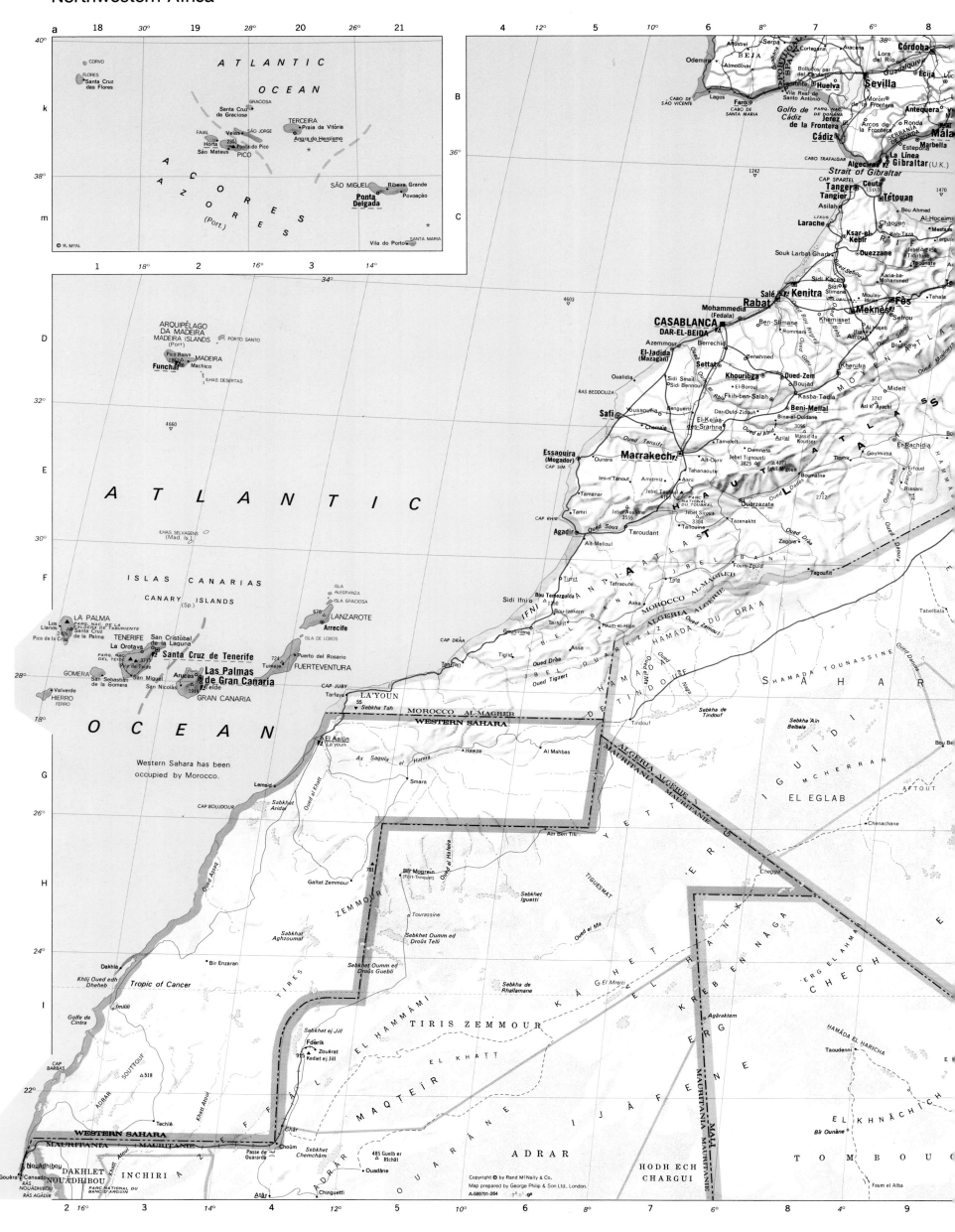

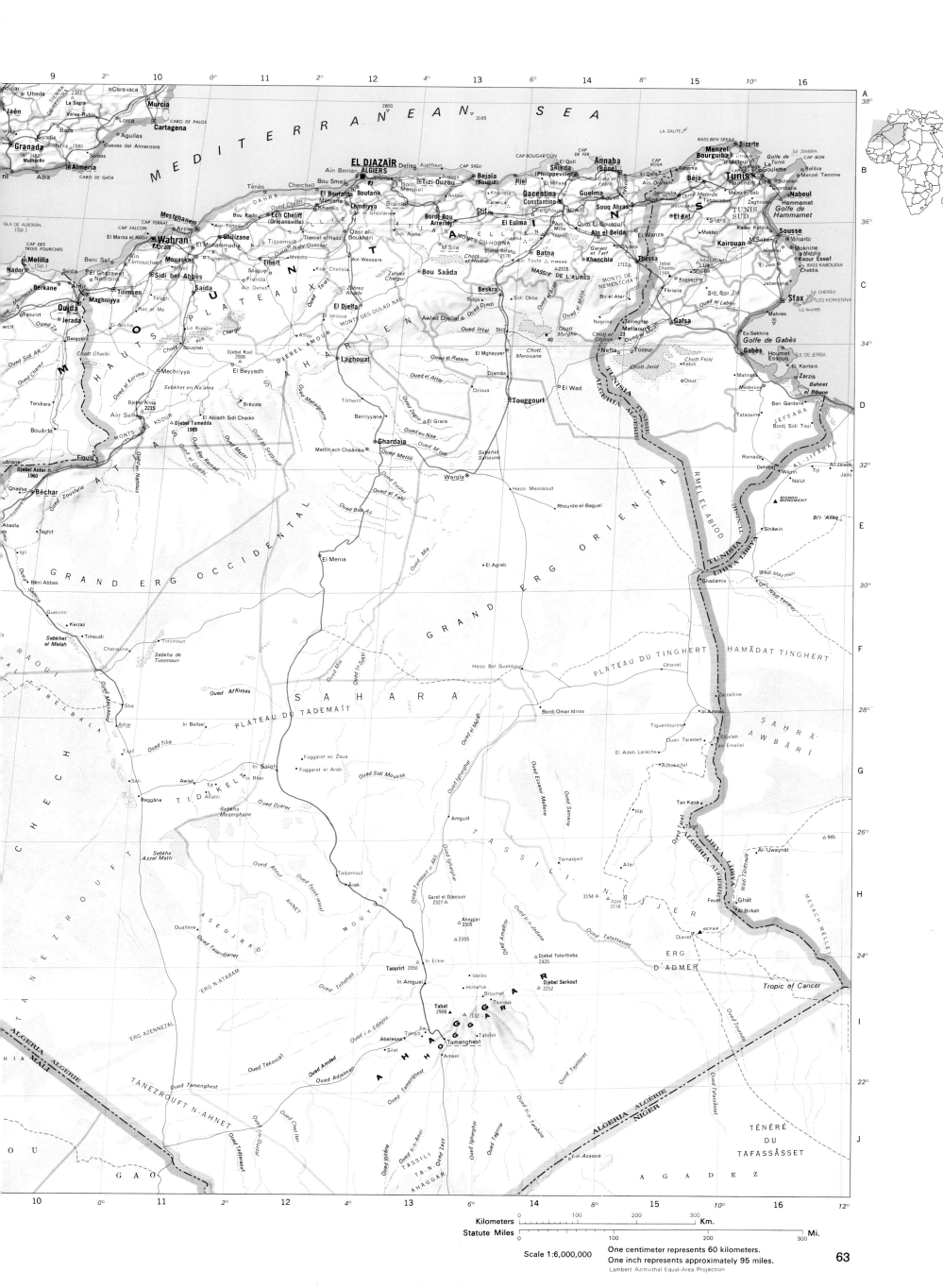

West Africa

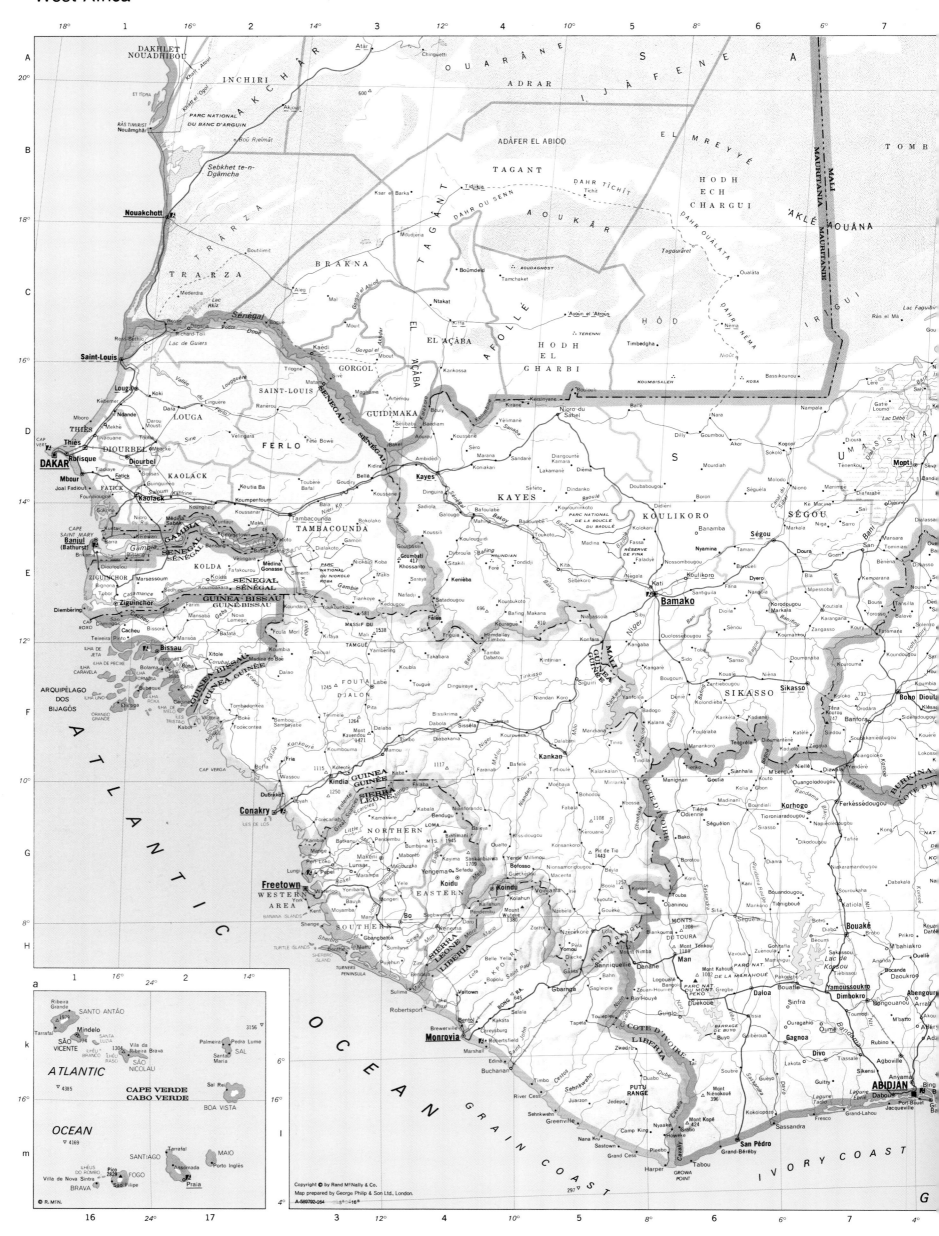

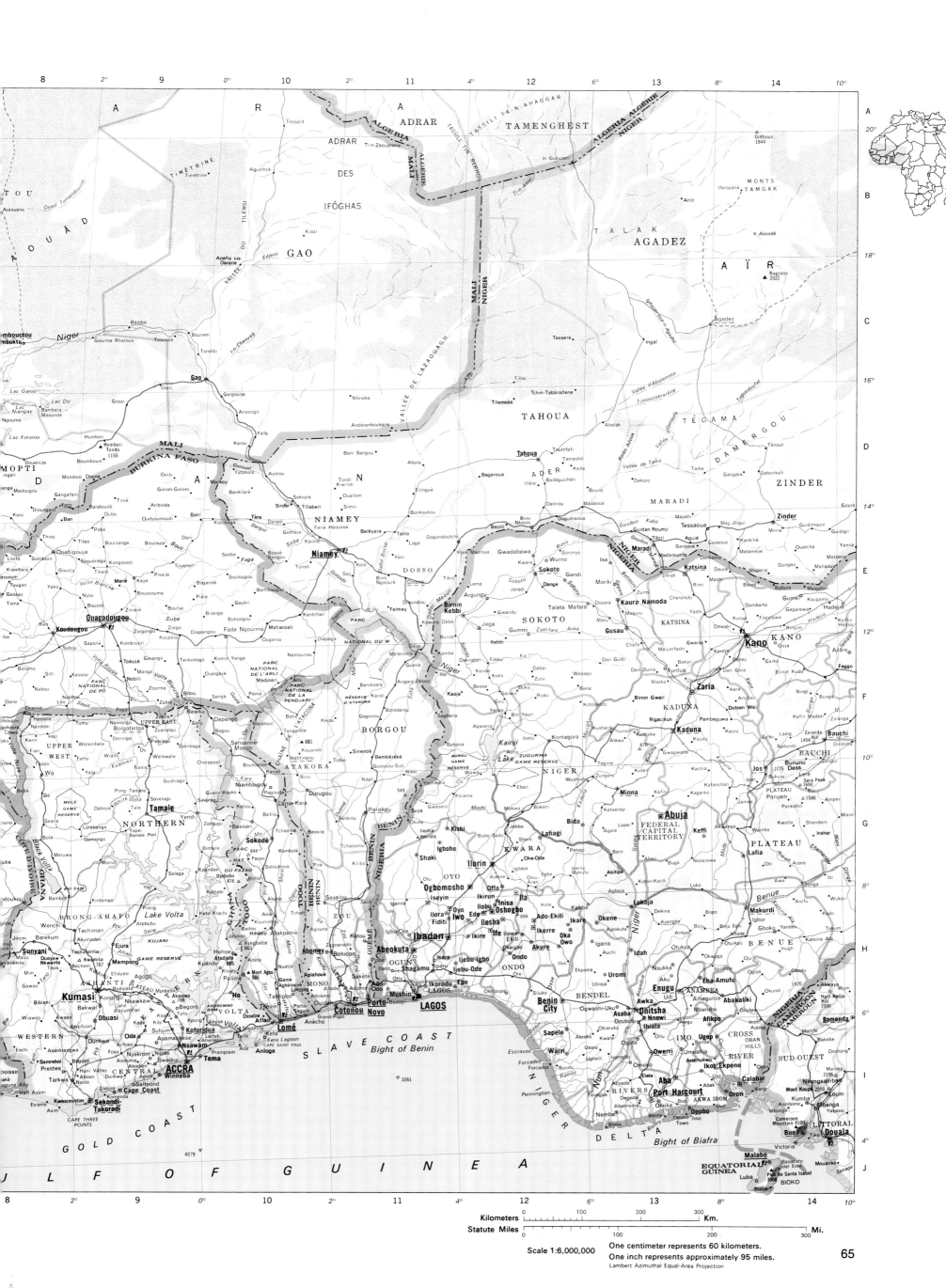

Kilometers
Statute Miles

Scale 1:6,000,000

One centimeter represents 60 kilometers.
One inch represents approximately 95 miles.
Lambert Azimuthal Equal-Area Projection

Copyright © by Rand McNally & Co.
Map prepared by George Philip & Son Ltd., London.
A-589292-264

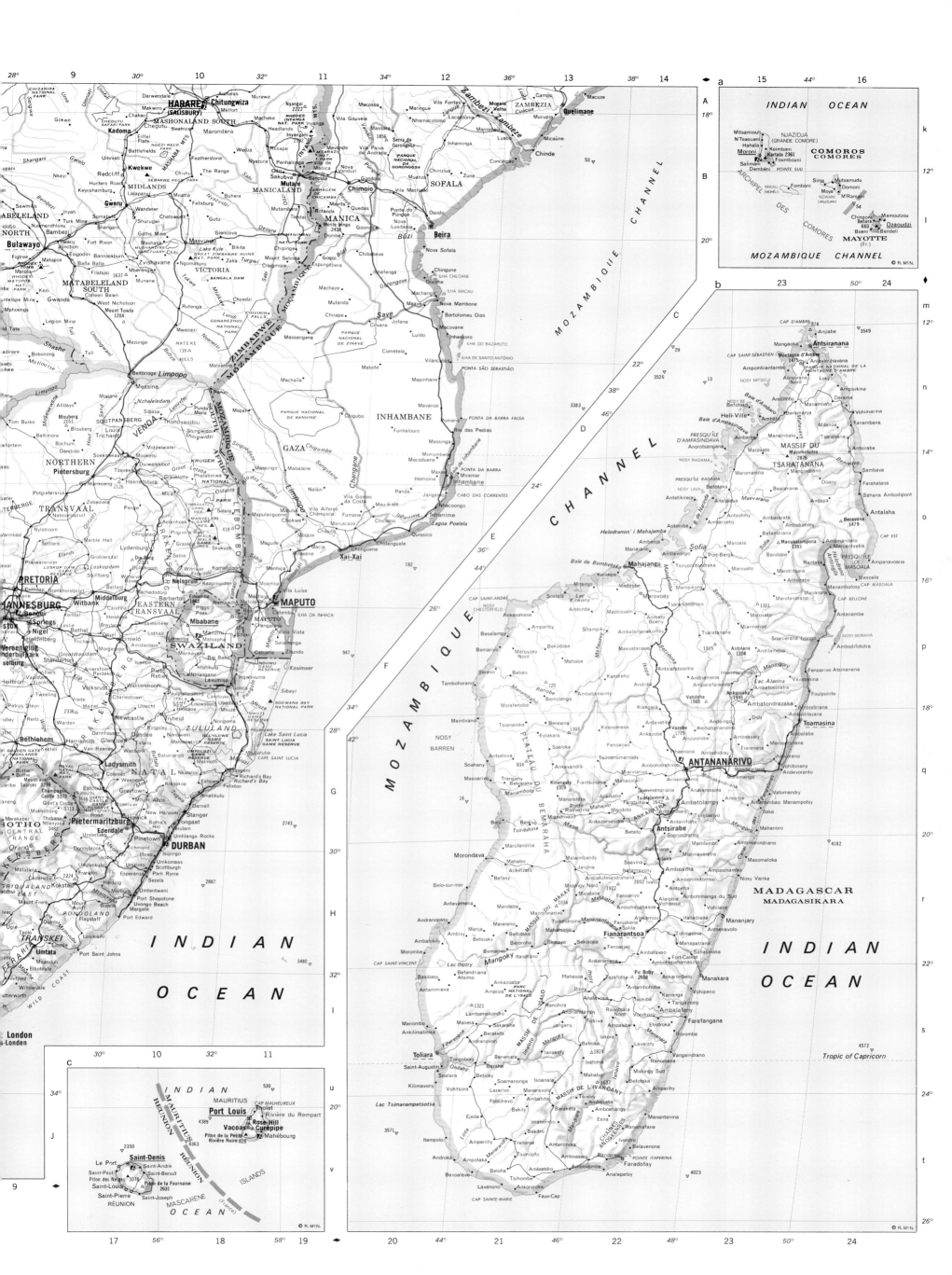

Australia

Scale 1:12,000,000
One centimeter represents 120 kilometers.
One inch represents approximately 190 miles.
Lambert Conformal Conic Projection

Kilometers

Statute Miles

Km.

Mi.

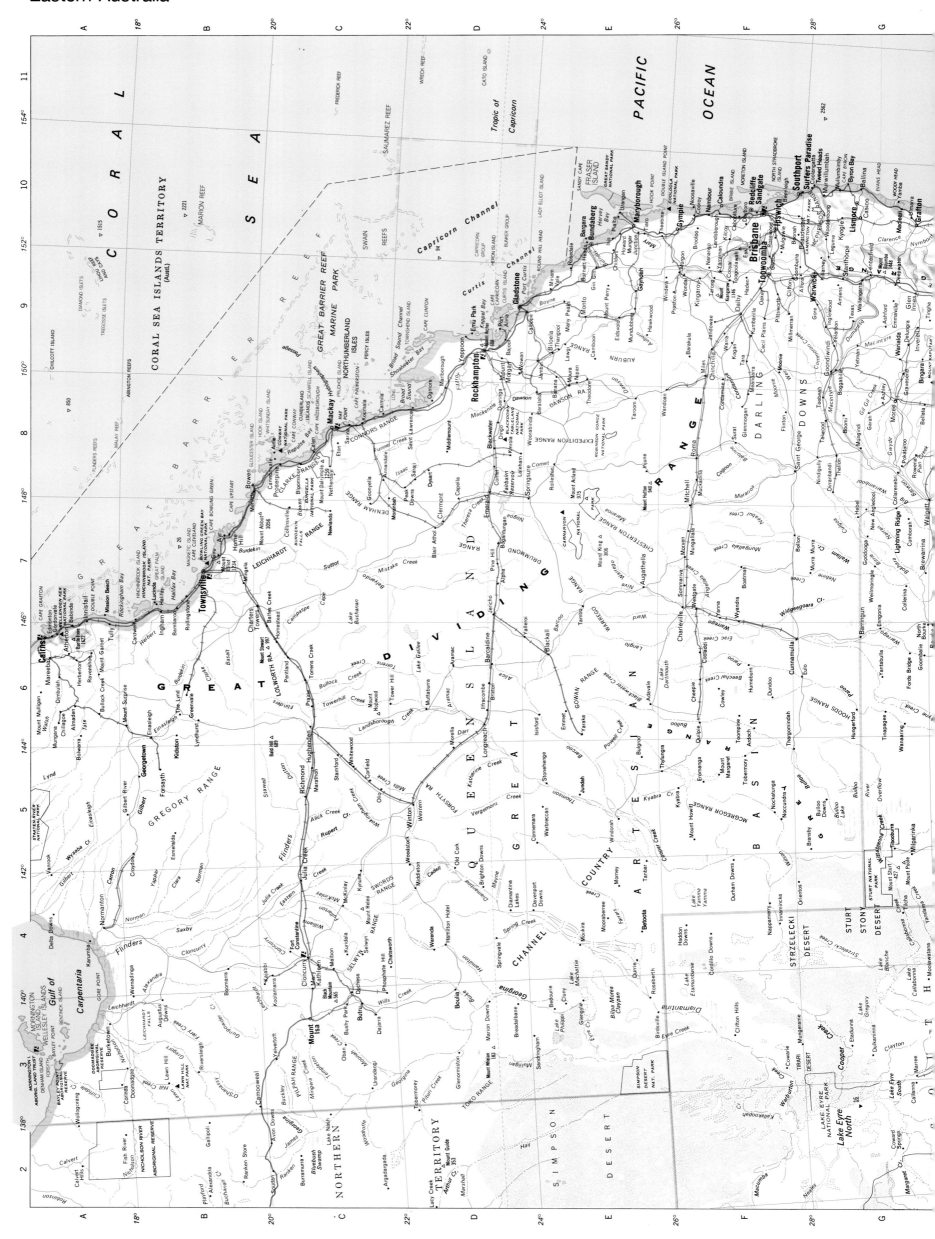

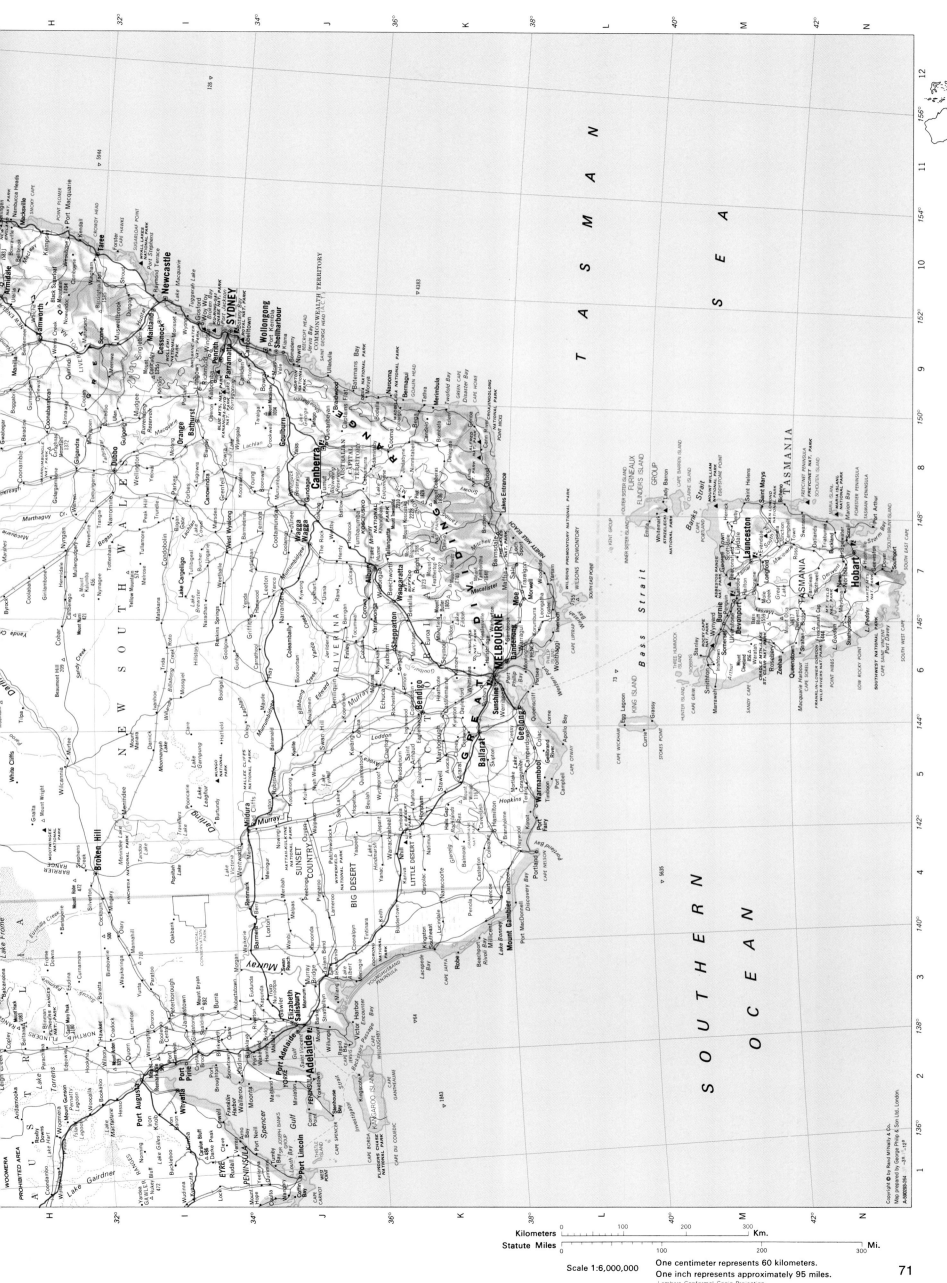

Kilometers

Statute Miles

Km.

Mi.

Scale 1:6,000,000

One centimeter represents 60 kilometers.
One inch represents approximately 95 miles.

Lambert Conformal Conic Projection

New Zealand

PACIFIC OCEAN

CAPE REINGA
NORTH CAPE
Rangaunu Bay
Ahipara Bay
Doubtless Bay
TAUROA POINT
CAPE BRETT
Okaihau
Opua

Whangarei

Dargaville
Bream Bay

GREAT BARRIER ISLAND

Wellsford
Kaipara Harbour
Hauraki Gulf

COROMANDEL PENINSULA

Takapuna
Devonport
Auckland
Manukau Harbour
Pukekohe
Thames
Waiuku
Waihi

NORTH

Hamilton
Morrinsville
Tauranga
Huntly
Te Awamutu
Cambridge
Kawhia Harbour
Whakatane
Opotiki

ISLAND

Bay of Plenty
CAPE RUNAWAY
EAST CAPE

Te Kuiti
Tokoroa
Rotorua
Murupara

RAUKUMARA RANGE

TASMAN

SEA

North Taranaki Bight
Taumarunui
Taupo
Lake Taupo

New Plymouth
Waitara
Mt. Egmont 2518

Gisborne

Stratford
Opunake
Hawera
Raetihi
Wairoa

South Taranaki Bight
Patea
Taihape

KAIMANAWA MTS

MAHIA PENINSULA

Hawke Bay
CAPE KIDNAPPERS
Napier
Hastings

Wanganui

Waipukurau

Palmerston North
Woodville
Dannevirke

CAPE FAREWELL
Golden Bay
Takaka
D'URVILLE ISLAND
Levin
Otaki

Masterton

TARARUA

Tasman Bay
Motueka
Lower Hutt
Wellington

Karamea Bight
1875
Mount Owen
Nelson
Picton
Richmond
Blenheim
Cook Strait
Lake Wairarapa
CAPE PALLISER

Seddonville
CAPE FOULWIND
Mt. Uriah 1501
Westport
Wairau
CAPE CAMPBELL

Reefton
2337
Mount Travers 2885
Tapuaenuku 2885

SPENSER MTS

SOUTH

Runanga
Greymouth
Manakau 2610
Kaikoura

Hokitika
Hurunui
Waiau

Ross

ISLAND
Mount Murchison 2400
Waipara
Oxford
Pegasus Bay
Whataroa
Sheffield
Kaiapoi
Christchurch

SOUTHERN ALPS

Mount Cook 3764
Lake Tekapo
Mount Somers
Methven
Little River

CASCADE POINT
Haast
Fairlie
Southbridge
BANKS PENINSULA

Ashburton

Canterbury Bight

Mount Aspiring 3035
Lake Wanaka
Omarama
Timaru

PACIFIC

2756 Mount Tutoko
Wanaka
Mount Saint Bathans 2086
Kurow
Waitaki
Waimate

Queenstown
Cromwell
Ranfurly
Oamaru

OCEAN

Doubtful Sound
Lake Te Anau
LIVINGSTONE MTS
Lake Wakatipu
Kingston
Alexandra
Roxburgh
Palmerston

RESOLUTION ISLAND
Te Anau
Mossburn
Beaumont
Port Chalmers

CAPE PROVIDENCE
Nightcaps
Edievale
Dunedin

Otautau
Winton
Gore
Milton

Riverton
Tokanui
Kaitangata

Invercargill
Bluff
Tahakopa

Foveaux Strait
Mt Raglan 1978

STEWART ISLAND

Scale 1:6,000,000

One centimeter represents 60 kilometers.
One inch represents approximately 95 miles.

Lambert Conformal Conic Projection

Kilometers   0   100   200   300   Km.

Statute Miles   0   100   200   300   Mi.

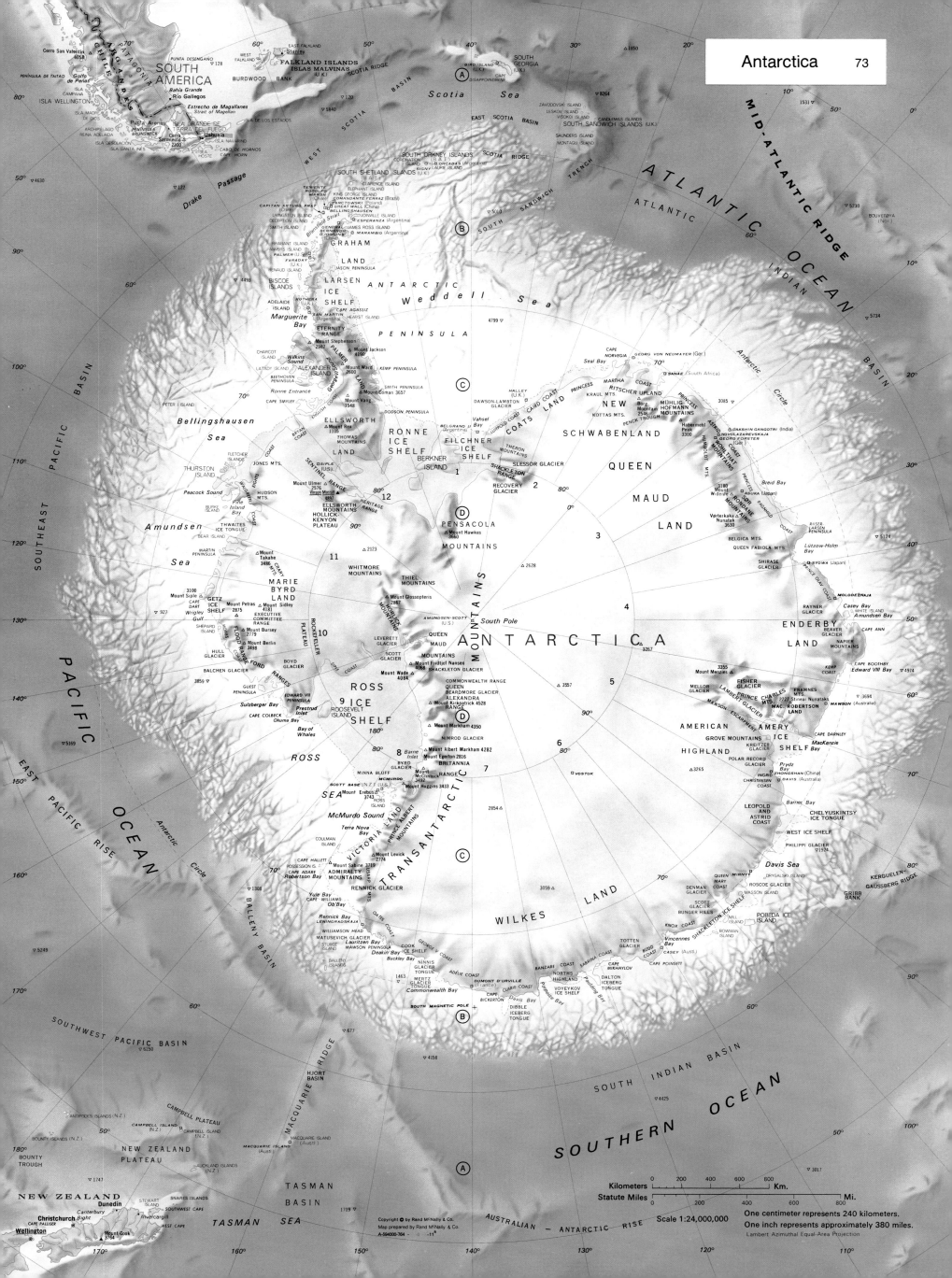

Kilometers
Statute Miles

One centimeter represents 240 kilometers.
One inch represents approximately 380 miles.
Scale 1:24,000,000

Lambert Azimuthal Equal-Area Projection

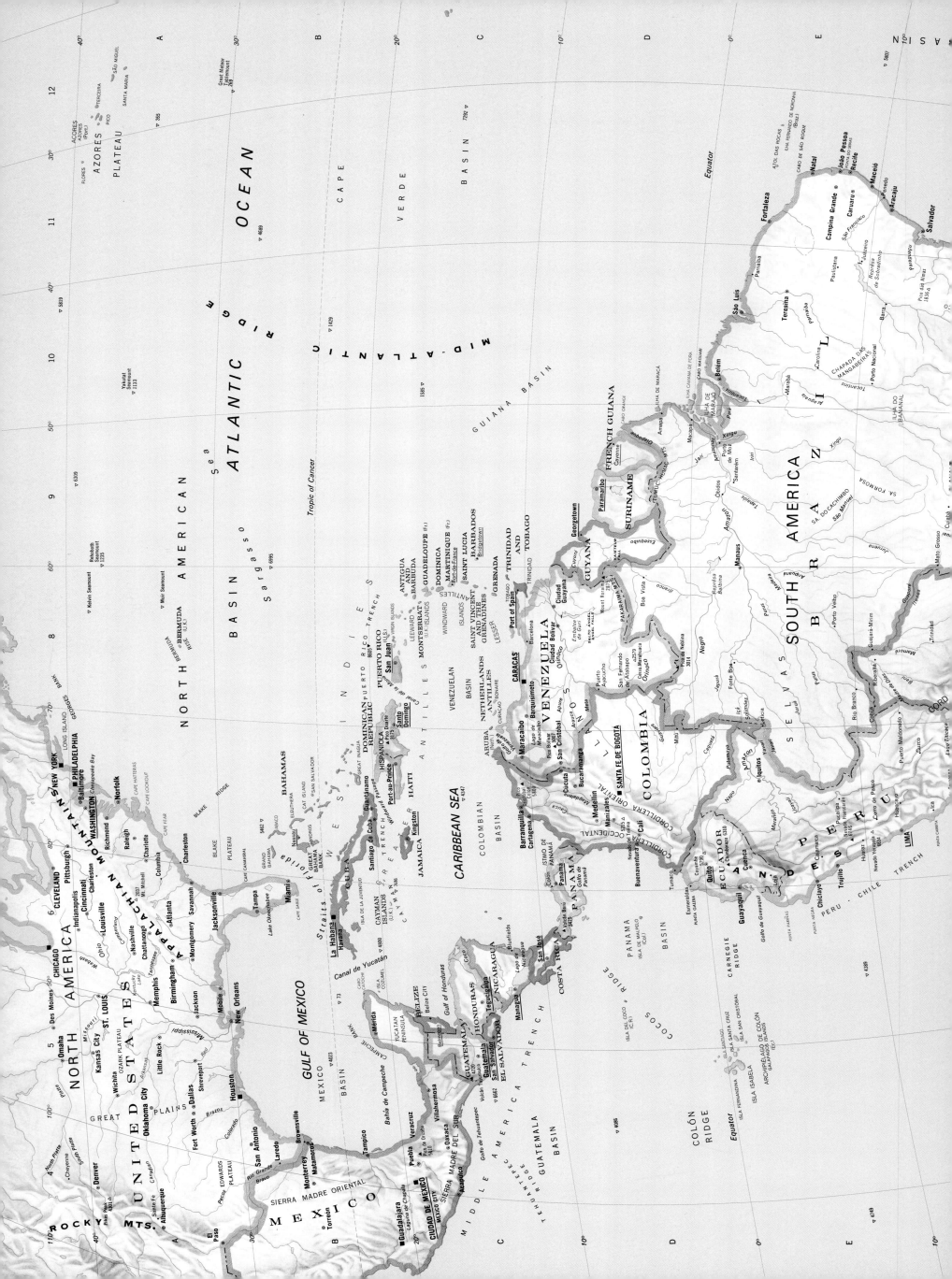

PACIFIC OCEAN

CARIBBEAN SEA

Kilometers
Statute Miles

Scale 1:12,000,000   One centimeter represents 120 kilometers.
One inch represents approximately 190 miles.
Oblique Conic Conformal Projection

Copyright © by Rand McNally & Co.
Map prepared by Esselte Map Service AB, Stockholm.
A-549100-264

BARBADOS
Bridgetown

A

TOBAGO

10°

ATLANTIC   OCEAN

B

GUYANA

Charity
Georgetown
Parika
Hyde Park
Bartica
Rosignol
Linden   New Amsterdam
Corriverton   Totness
Wismar

Paramaribo
Nieuw Amsterdam
Moengo   Saint-Laurent-du-Maroni
Onverwacht   Paranam   Albina
Kwakoegron   São Sinnamary   ÎLE DU DIABLE
Brokopondo   Cayenne
Stuwmeer   Saint-Élie   Matoury
Regina
SURINAME   Saint-Georges
▲ Juliana Top   Oiapoque
1230   Saül   ▲ 830   CABO ORANGE
Oiapoque

5°

**FRENCH
GUIANA**

Calçoene

C

AMAPÁ   Cunani
Serra do Navio   Amapá
ILHA DE MARACÁ

TUMUC-HUMAC MTS.

ACARAI MTS.

Macapá   CABO MAGUARI
Mazagão   ILHA BAILIQUE
Canal do Norte   ILHA DO CURUÁ
ILHA JANAUCU
Equator   0°

ILHA CAVIANA DE FORA
ILHA MEXIANA

Amazon   ILHA DE MARAJÓ   CABO MAGUARI
Amazonas   Baía de Marajó
Óbidos   Breves   **Belém**
Faro   Oriximiná   Almeirim   Gurupá   Abaetetuba   Bragança
Alenquer   Porto de   Carutapera
Parintins   Moz   ILHA DA   Carupi
Itacoatiara   Monte Alegre   LAGUNA   Cametá   Camiranga
Maués   **Santarém**   Portel   Pinheiro   Alcântara
Viana   São Luís
Rosário   Tutóia
Itaitúba   Altamira   São Bento   Parnaíba
Tucuruí   Monção   Itapecuru-Mirim   Camocim   Acaraú
Represa   Brejo   Sobral   D
de Tucuruí   Pindaré   Maranguape   **Fortaleza**
PARÁ   Barras   Ipu   Baturité   ILHA FERNANDO
Pedro II   Quixadá   Russas   DE NORONHA
Marabá   São João   Imperatriz   Codó   União   Campo Maior   Aracati   ATOL DAS ROCAS   (Brazil)
do Araguaia   MARANHÃO   **Teresina**   Crateús   Senador   Areia Branca
Araguatins   Grajaú   Colinas   Caxias   Pompeu   CEARÁ   Macau   5°
SERRA DOS CARAJÁS   Bacabal   Anga   Iguatu   Angicos   CABO DE SÃO ROQUE
Carajás   Amarante   Senador   Lajes   Ceará-Mirim
Tocantinópolis   Pedreiras   Floriano   PIAUÍ   Pompeu   RIO GRANDE DO NORTE   **Natal**
Carolina   Mirador   Picos   Icó   Currais Novos
SERRA DO CACHIMBO   Loreto   Benedito Leite   Oeiras   Crato   Sousa   Caicó
Riachão   Represa Boa   Juazeiro   Cajazeiras   Patos   Guarabira
Gradaús   Esperança   Balsas   do Norte   Sertânia   **Campina Grande**   Sape
Conceição do Araguaia   Santa Filomena   PARAÍBA   Itabaiana   **João Pessoa**
Alto Parnaíba   PERNAMBUCO   Gravatá   Goiana   PONTA DO SEIXAS
Miracema do Tocantins   Tocantínia   Arcoverde   Jaboatão   **Olinda**   E
Recife
Gilbués   São Raimundo Nonato   Remanso   Caruaru
TOCANTINS   Represa de Petrolina   Garanhuns   Palmares
Cristalândia   Palmas   Sobradinho   União dos Palmares   Barreiros
Porto Nacional   Paulistana   **Juazeiro**   Paulo   ALAGOAS   Rio Largo
Natividade   Parnaguá   Afonso   São   Arapiraca   **Maceió**
Dianópolis   Senhor   Jeremoabo   Propriá   Cabo de Pedras
BRAZIL   do Bonfim   Francisco   SERGIPE   Coruripe
Xique-Xique   Tucano   Itabaiana   **Aracaju**
ILHA   Taguatinga   Jacobina   Itapicuru   São Cristóvão   10°
DO   Arraias   Barra   Morro do Chapéu   Estância
BANANAL   Corrente   Serrinha   F
Posse   Bom Jesus   **BAHIA**   Santo Amaro   Feira de Santana   Inhambupe
da Lapa   Santo Antônio de Jesus   Candeias   **Salvador**
Cavalcante   Paramirim   Caetité   Valença   ILHA DE TINHARÉ
Pilar de Goiás   ▲ Pico das   Nazaré
Almas   Jequié   ILHA DE ITAPARICA
1836

Alto Araguaia   SERRA DO CAIAPÓ   Araçá   SERRA DO ESPINHAÇO

MATO GROSSO

PLANALTO   DO

MATO   GROSSO   Cuiabá

Rondonópolis   Poxoréo   Barra
de Melgaço

Cáceres

Barão
de Melgaço

Corumbá   MATO GROSSO
DO SUL

Campo Grande

UAY

Presidente Prudente

G

15°

20°

77

Kilometers
Km.
Statute Miles
Mi.

Scale 1:12,000,000
One centimeter represents 120 kilometers.
One inch represents approximately 190 miles.
Oblique Conic Conformal Projection

Copyright © by Rand McNally & Co.
Map prepared by Esselte Map Service AB, Stockholm.
A-549200-264

ATLANTIC OCEAN

Scale 1:6,000,000
One centimeter represents 60 kilometers.
One inch represents approximately 95 miles.
Oblique Conic Conformal Projection

Kilometers
Statute Miles

Km.
Mi.

Scale 1:6,000,000

Kilometers

Statute Miles

One centimeter represents 60 kilometers.
One inch represents approximately 95 miles.
Oblique Conic Conformal Projection

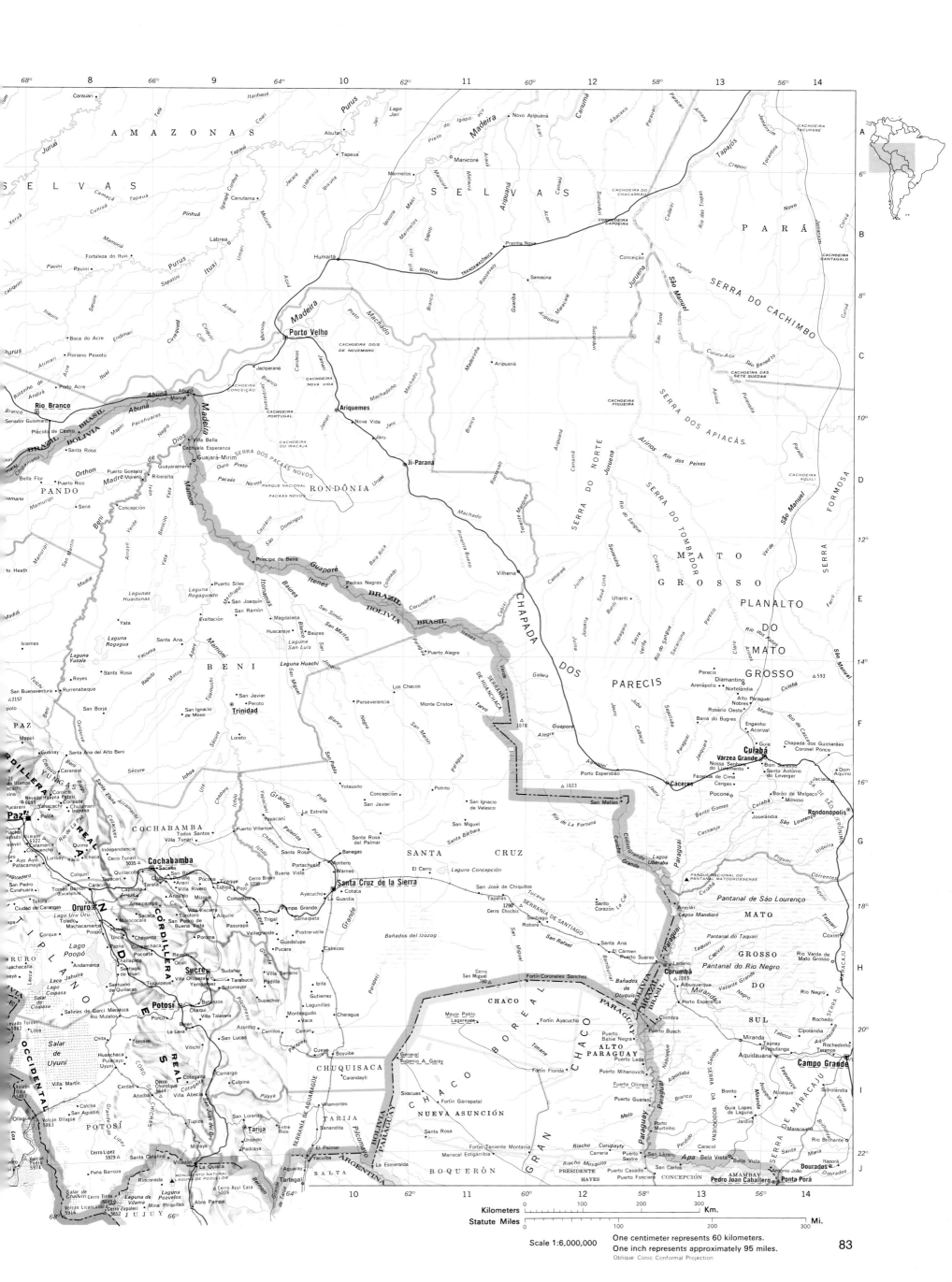

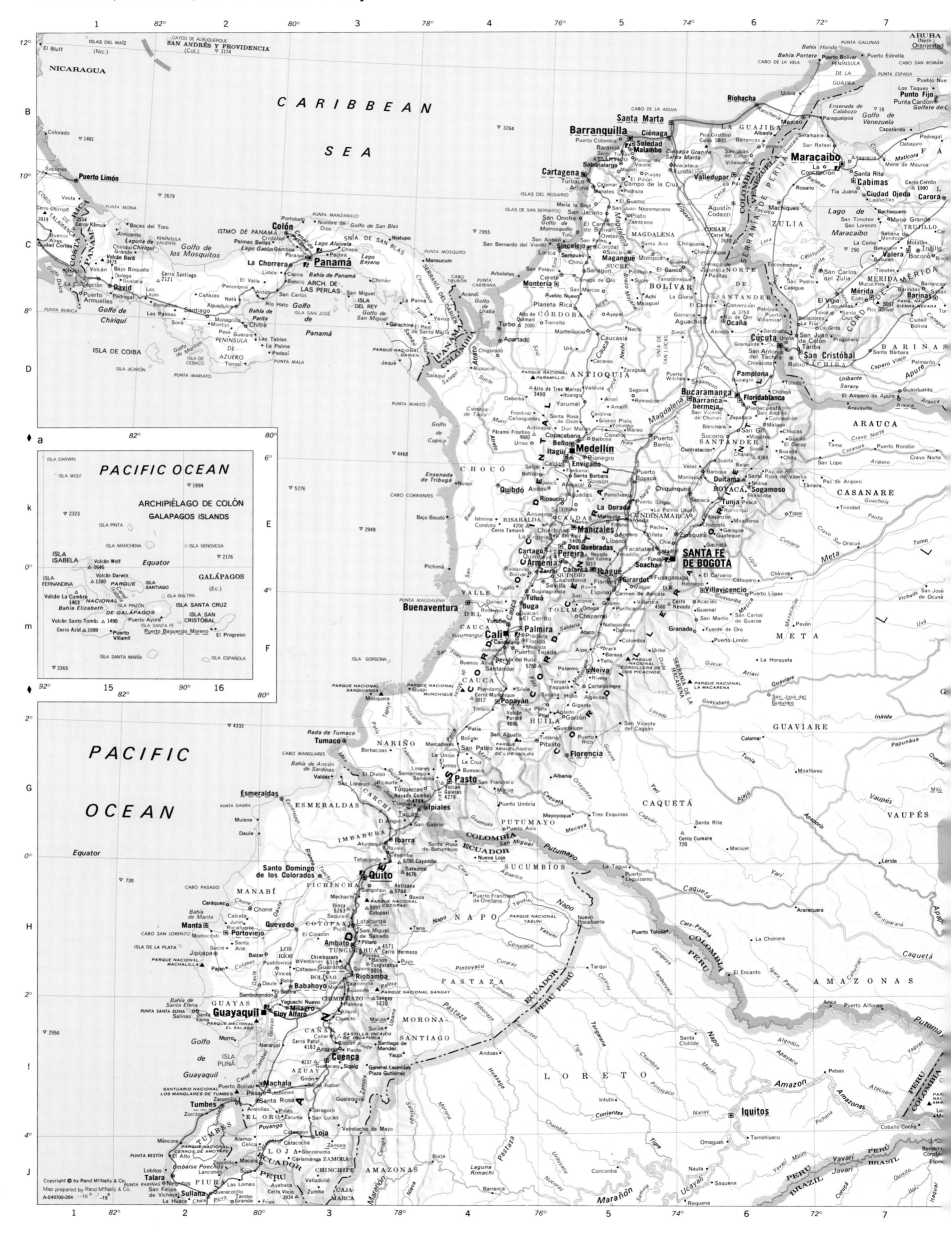

Kilometers

Statute Miles

One centimeter represents 60 kilometers.
One inch represents approximately 95 miles.

Scale 1:6,000,000
Oblique Conic Conformal Projection

Mexico

Kilometers
Statute Miles

Scale 1:6,000,000
One centimeter represents 60 kilometers.
One inch represents approximately 95 miles.
Lambert Conformal Conic Projection

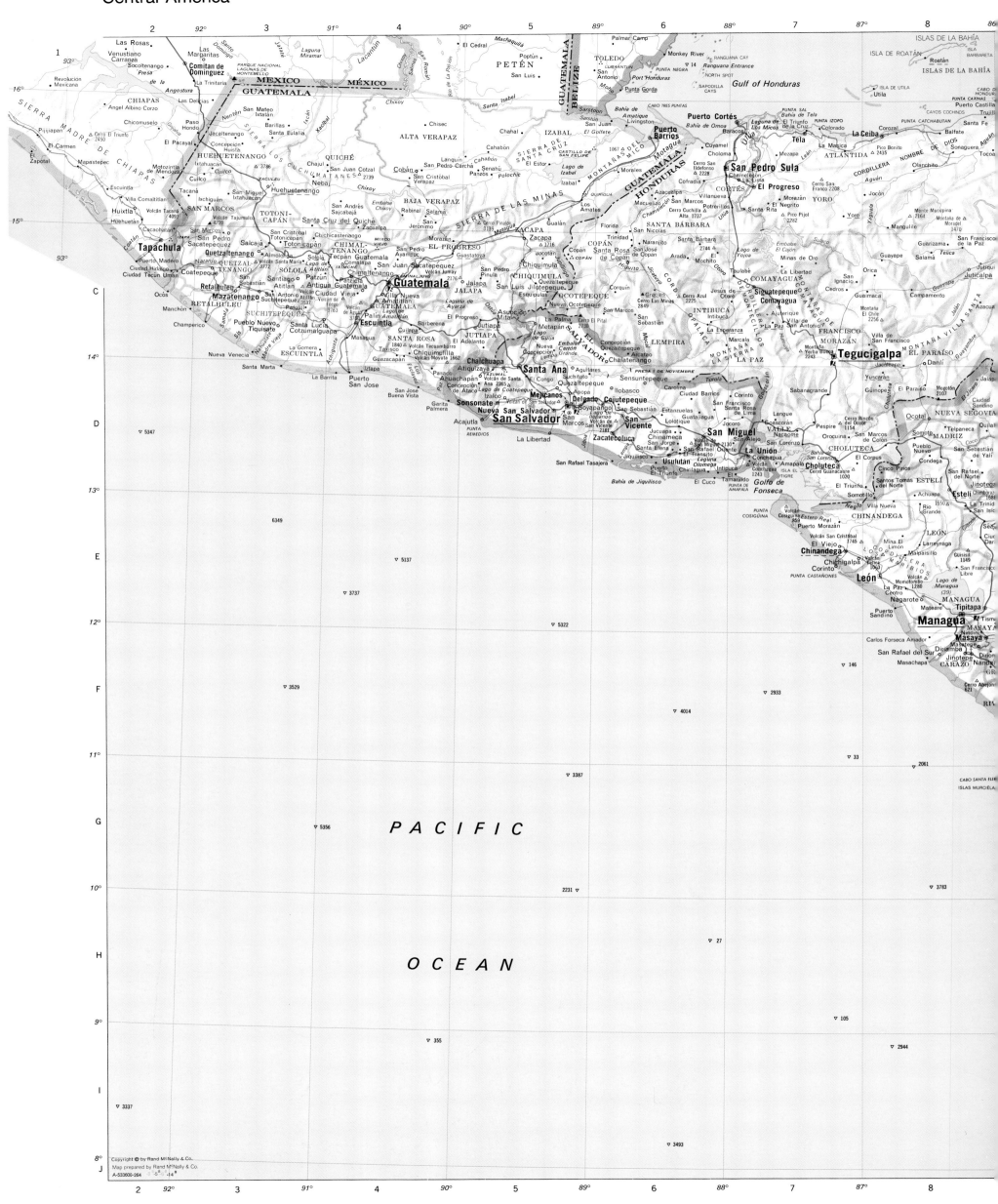

GULF OF MEXICO

88°   1   86°   2   84°

26°   3

A

7

UNITED STATES
FLORIDA
The Everglades

West Palm Beach
Fort Myers
Belle Glade
Lake Worth
Palm Beach
Delray Beach
Boca Raton
Pompano Beach
Fort Lauderdale
Hollywood
Hialeah
MIAMI
Miami Beach
Coral Gables
Homestead
Naples
Everglades
Everglades City
TEN THOUSAND ISLANDS
CAPE SABLE
EVERGLADES NATIONAL PARK
BISCAYNE NATIONAL PARK
Key Largo

West End
GRAND BAHAMA
Freeport
Marsh Harbour
ABACO
LITTLE ABACO

Northwest Providence Channel

4919

BAHAMA

B

Florida Bay
DRY TORTUGAS
MARQUESAS KEYS
Key West
FLORIDA KEYS
868

Straits of Florida

Nicholl's Town
ANDROS
Andros Town
Adelaide
Nassau
NEW PROVIDENCE
Rock Sound
Governor's Harbour
ELEUTHERA

GREAT BAHAMA BANK

Berry Islands
SOUTHWEST POINT
NORTHEAST PROVIDENCE CHANNEL

BIMINI ISLANDS
Alice Town
5

5

Mangrove Cay
Kemps Bay
37

TONGUE OF THE OCEAN

ELEUTHERA POINT
New Bight
CAT ISLAND
Mount Alvernia
Port Howe
COLUMBUS POINT

4292

24°

841
34
3401
3584

GULF OF MEXICO

HAWKS NEST POINT
GREAT GUANA CAY
CISTERN POINT
1382

EXUMA
Georgetown

JUMENTOS CAYS
GREAT EXUMA
LONG ISLAND

EXUMA SOUND

GREAT SANTA MARIA

RAGGED ISLAND
Clarence Town
Deadman's Cay
Island

C

CAY SAL
CAY SAL BANK
7
ANGUILLA CAYS

Nicholas Channel

ARCHIPIÉLAGO DE SABANA

Old Bahama Channel

CAY LOBOS

10

W E S T

RUM CAY

1827
LA HABANA
HAVANA
San Antonio de los Baños
San José de las Lajas
Artemisa
Matanzas
Cárdenas
Bahía de Cárdenas
Jovellanos
Quemado de Güines
Sagua la Grande
Calbarién
Yaguajay
Bahía de Perros

RAGGED ISLAND RANGE
2542
2596
SALINA POINT

22°

1188
La Esperanza
Los Palacios
Candelaria
Güira de Melena
Güines
Unión de Reyes
Colón
Cruces
Lajas
Palmira
Aguada de Pasajeros
Yaguaramas
Sancti Spíritus
Morón
Esmeralda
CAYO COCO
Bahía de Jiguey

CAYO GUAJABA

Crooked Island

Minas de Matahambre
Mantua
La Fe
Guane
PUNTA GORDA
Ensenada de la Broa
PENÍNSULA DE ZAPATA
Jagüey Grande
Cienfuegos
Santa Clara
Placetas
Cabaiguán
Presa Zaza
Pico San Juan 1145
Ciego de Ávila
Florida
Minas
Nuevitas
Puerto Manatí
CAYO SABINAL

Pinar del Río
Consolación del Sur
Golfo de Batabanó
CAYOS DE SAN FELIPE
Nueva Gerona
Cárdenas
Trinidad
Tunas de Zaza
Júcaro
Golfo de Ana María
Vertientes
Najasa
Martí
Jesús Menéndez
Gibara

2688

Golfo de Guanahacabibes
CABO CORRIENTES
Ensenada de la Siguanea
ISLA DE LA JUVENTUD
(ISLA DE PINOS)
ARCHIPIÉLAGO DE LOS CANARREOS
CAYO LARGO
65
CUBA
Golfo de Zaza
Camagüey
Santa Cruz del Sur
Guayabal
Puerto Padre
Holguín
Banes
Bahía de Nipe
Mayarí
Sagua de Tánamo

D

20°

4352
4307
CABO DE SAN ANTONIO
Bahía de Cortés

ARCH. DE LOS JARDINES DE LA REINA
Golfo de Guacanayabo
Manzanillo
Campechuela
Niquero
Marea de Portillo
CABO CRUZ

Las Tunas
Bayamo
Salado
San Germán
Cueto
Alto Cedro
Tiguabos
San Luis
Guantánamo
Caimanera
Baracoa

SIERRA MAESTRA
Pico Turquino 1972
Palma Soriano
Santiago de Cuba

Antilla
PUNTA DE MULAS
Baracoa

1176

YUCATÁN
CABO CATOCHE
Laguna Yalahau
Kantunilkin
Puerto Juárez
Isla Mujeres
MÉXICO
X-Can
Cancún
PUNTA CANCÚN
Chemax
coná
Puerto Morelos
Playa del Carmen
ISLA COZUMEL
Cozumel
1005

LITTLE CAYMAN
CAYMAN BRAC
Pedro Turquino

GREATER

E

18°

QUINTANA ROO
Tulum
TULUM
YUCATÁN PENINSULA
PENÍNSULA DE YUCATÁN

Bahía Emiliano Zapata

3017

Bahía Venustiano Carranza

BANCO CHINCHORRO

1097

MISTERIOSA BANK
16

ROSARIO BANK

5464

CAYMAN ISLANDS
(U.K.)
George Town
GRAND CAYMAN

7119

4702

4627

7238

5215

Montego Bay
Falmouth
Ocho Rios
Port Maria
Saint Ann's Bay
Port Antonio
Savanna-la-Mar
Mandeville
Mount Denham 986
Spanish Town
Kingston
Blue Mountain Peak 2256
Morant Point
PORTLAND POINT
Morant Bay
Portland Bight

JÉRÉ
d'Hainault
POINTE FANCHON

SOUTH NEGRIL POINT
JAMAICA
May Pen
PORTLAND POINT

NAVASSA ISLAND (U.S.)

Windward

F

16°

ISLAS SANTANILLA
(Hond.)

1519

1982

3090

PEDRO CAYS (Jam.)

MORANT CAYS (Jam.)

Gulf of Honduras
GLOVERS REEF (Belize)
3001
LIGHTHOUSE REEF (Belize)
ISLAS DE LA BAHÍA
Guanaja
ISLA DE GUANAJA
Roatán
ISLA DE ROATÁN
Utila
ISLA DE UTILA
CABO DE HONDURAS

5193
804

Colorado
Trujillo
Limón
Aguán
Tocoa
Sico Tinto
Brus Laguna
Laguna Caratasca
40
27

105

BAJO NUEVO (Col.)

ROSALIND BANK

G

Tela
La Ceiba
Pico Bonito 2435
Olanchito
Yoro
Salamá
MONTAÑAS DE COMAYAGUA
Juticalpa
Catacamas
Paya
Patuca
Wampú
LA MOSQUITIA
CABO CAMARÓN
CABO GRACIAS A DIOS
Waspam

CAYO DE SERRANILLA (Col.)

145
ARRECIFES DE LA MEDIA LUNA

1975

CARIBBEA

14°

Minas de Oro
Montaña El Chile 2256
San Ignacio
Guaimaca
Guayape
Salamá
Bilwaskarma
Coco
Wewa
Yablis
Waspam
HONDURAS
NICARAGUA
CORD. ISABELIA
Cerro Kilambé 1750
Cerro Saslaya 1650
Bonanza
Siuna
Prinzapolka
Puerto Cabezas
COSTA DE MOSQUITOS

530

87

Cayo de Serrana
QUITASUEÑO

4263

Tegucigalpa
Yuscarán
Danlí
Ocotal
Somoto
Condega
Estelí
San Rafael del Norte
Jinotega
Matagalpa
Sébaco
Ciudad Darío
Boaco
CORDILLERA DARIENSE
Tuma
Grande de Matagalpa
Río Grande
La Cruz de Río Grande
Kurinwás
Tungla
Prinzapolka
Wounta

1755
105

CAYOS DE RONCADOR

H

El Corpus
Choluteca
El Triunfo
San Marcos de Colón
Río Grande
San Cristóbal 1745
Volcán Momotombo 1280
Matagalpa
Boaco
Santo Domingo
Rama
Siquia
Bluefields
El Bluff

3292

ISLA DE PROVIDENCIA
SAN ANDRÉS Y PROVIDENCIA (Col.)

3174

CAYOS DE ALBUQUERQUE

12°

El Viejo
Chinandega
León
La Paz Centro
Nagarote
Managua
Masaya
Granada
Diriamba
Jinotepe
Nandaime
Masatepe
Juigalpa
La Libertad
Santo Tomás
Muelle de los Bueyes
Acoyapa
Volcán Concepción 1610
Volcán Madera

Lago de Managua
Lago de Nicaragua (31)
ISLA DE OMETEPE

ISLA DE SAN ANDRÉS
San Andrés
CAYOS DEL ESTE SUDESTE

4157

ISLAS DEL MAÍZ (Nic.)

I

10°

PACIFIC

33
2061
SANTA ELENA
CABO VELAS
PENÍNSULA DE NICOYA
Liberia
Cañas
Santa Cruz
Nicoya
Bagaces
Golfo de Papagayo
GOLFO DE NICOYA
Golfo de Nicoya
NICARAGUA
COSTA RICA
CORD. DE GUANACASTE
Volcán Miravalles 2028
San Carlos
Fortuna
San Juan
Colorado
San Juan del Norte
San Juan del Sur
Rivas
San Carlos
El Castillo de La Concepción
Bahía de Punta Gorda
Punta Gorda
3264

Santa Marta
Barranquilla
Soledad
Ciénaga
ATLÁNTICO
Puerto Colombia
Puerto de Varela
Baranoa
Sabanagrande
Malambo

J

417
1481
2679
3224
2944

OCEAN

San José
Cartago
Heredia
Alajuela
Volcán Irazú
Volcán Turrialba
Puntarenas
Cerro Azul 1063
PENÍNSULA DE NICOYA
CABO BLANCO
Golfo de Nicoya
Cerro Chirripó 3819
Cerro de la Muerte 3491
Cerro Kámuk 3549
Buenos Aires
Ciudad Cortés
Bahía de Coronado
San Isidro
Volcán Barú 3475
Bajo Boquete
CORD. DE TALAMANCA
PANAMÁ
Puerto Limón
PUNTA MONA
Bocas del Toro
Chiriquí Grande
Almirante
Laguna de Chiriquí
PENÍNSULA VALIENTE
Golfo de los Mosquitos
ISTMO DE PANAMÁ
Portobelo
Nombre de Dios
Colón
Cristóbal
Lago Alajuela
Lago Gatún
Gamboa
Paraíso
Panamá
2955
SERRANÍA DE SAN BLAS
Golfo de San Blas
Nlatupo

Cartagena
Turbaco
Calamar
Malagana
BOLÍVAR
ISLAS DEL ROSARIO
San Bernardo
San Jacinto
El Carmen de Bolívar
Zambrano
CÓRDOBA
Sincé
SUCRE
Corozal
Sincelejo
Magangué
MAGDALENA

Copyright © by Rand M?Nally & Co.
Map prepared by Rand M?Nally & Co.
A-530100-264   -8° - -18°

1   86°   2   84°   3   82°   4   80°   5   78°   6   76°   7

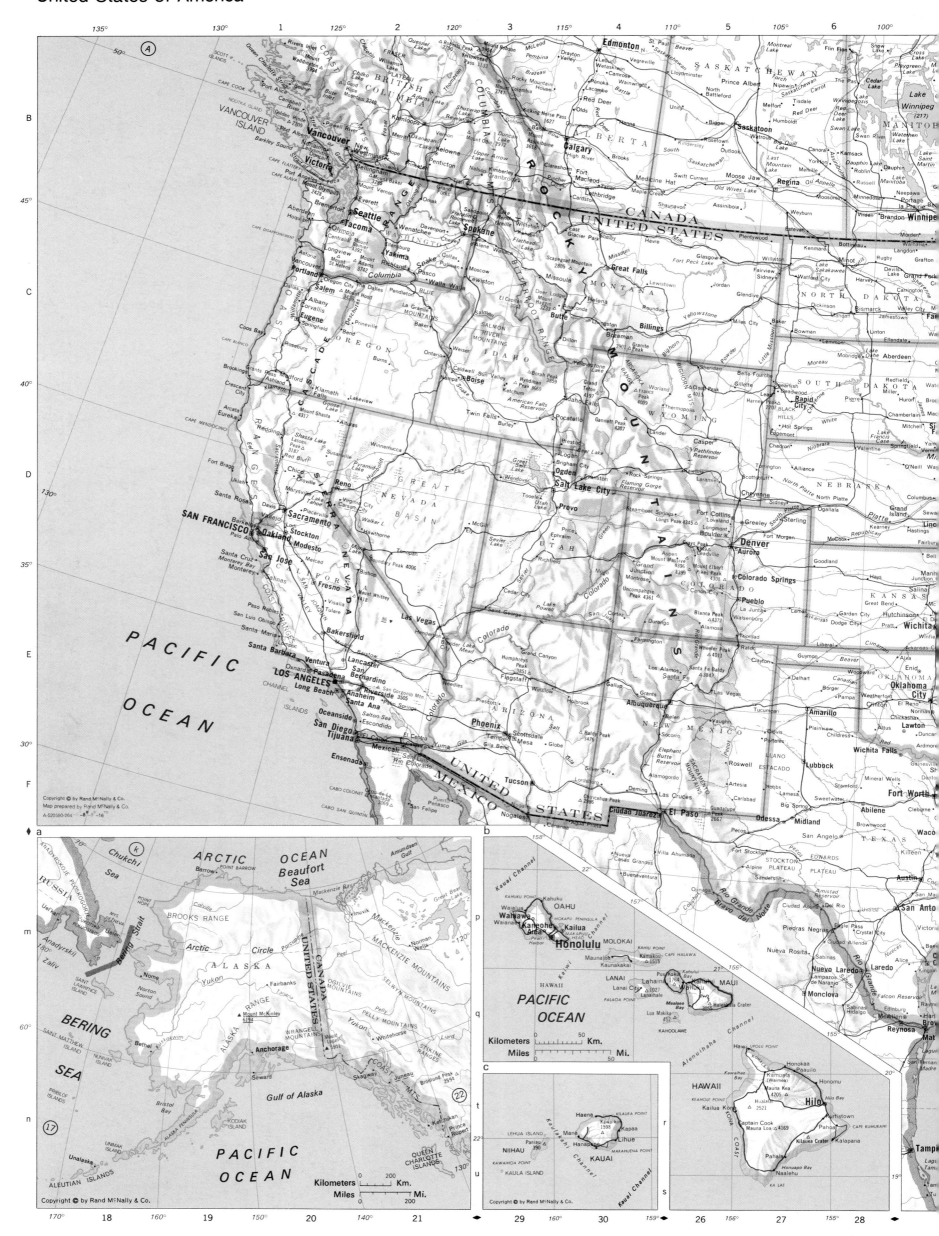

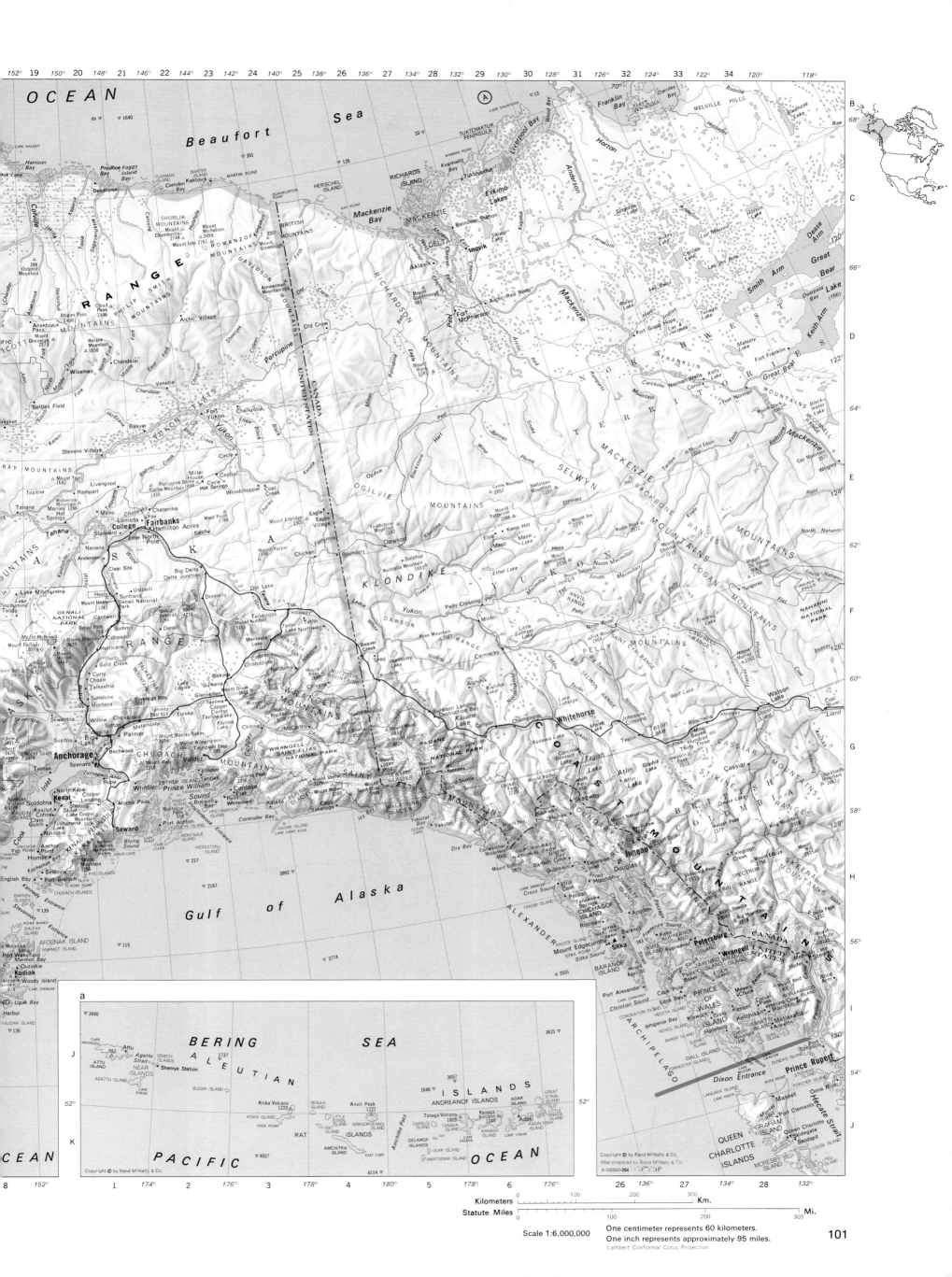

Kilometers

Statute Miles

One centimeter represents 30 kilometers.
One inch represents approximately 47 miles.

Scale 1:3,000,000
Lambert Conformal Conic Projection

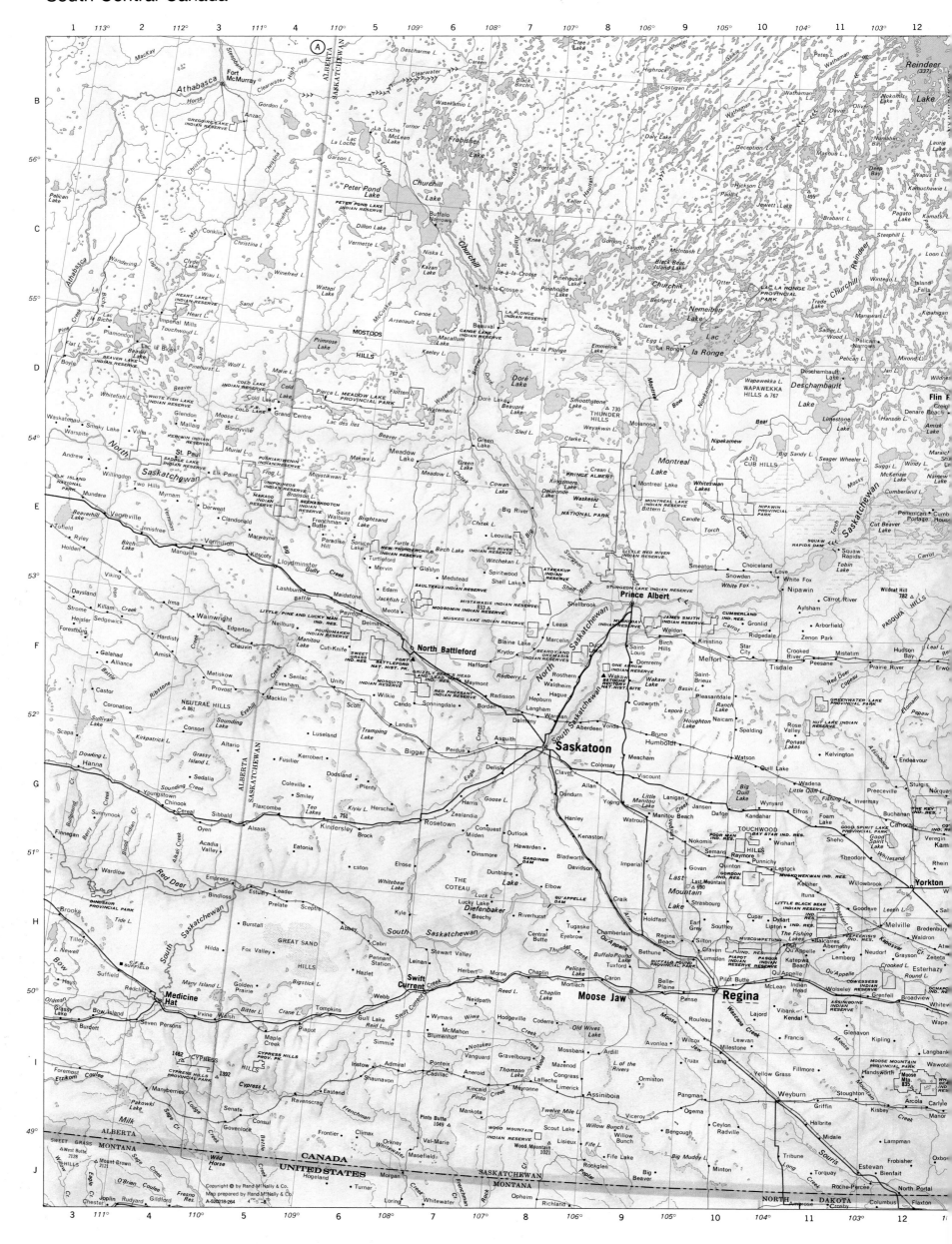

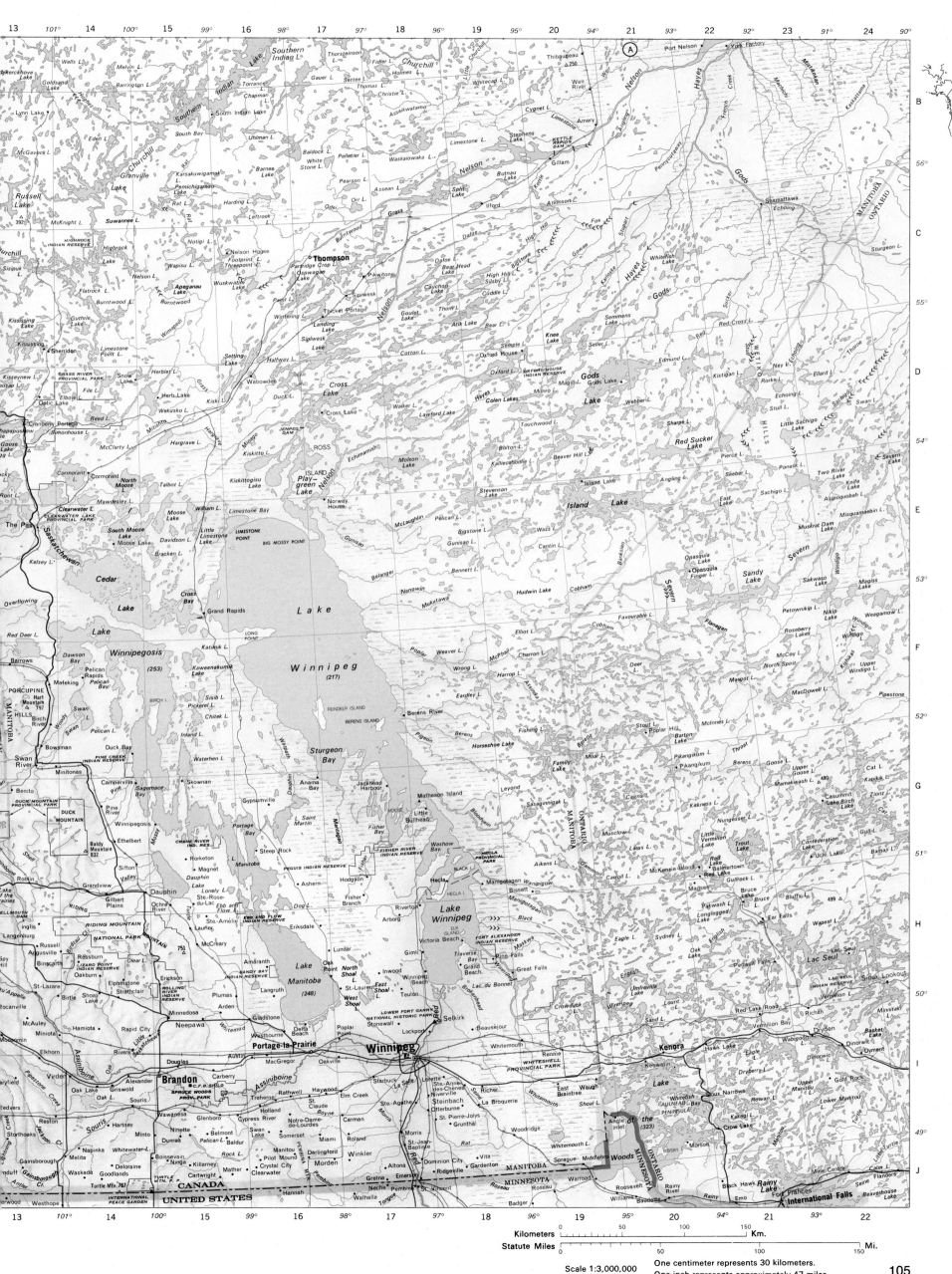

Kilometers 0   50   100   150   Km.
Statute Miles 0   50   100   150   Mi.

Scale 1:3,000,000

One centimeter represents 30 kilometers.
One inch represents approximately 47 miles.

Lambert Conformal Conic Projection

105

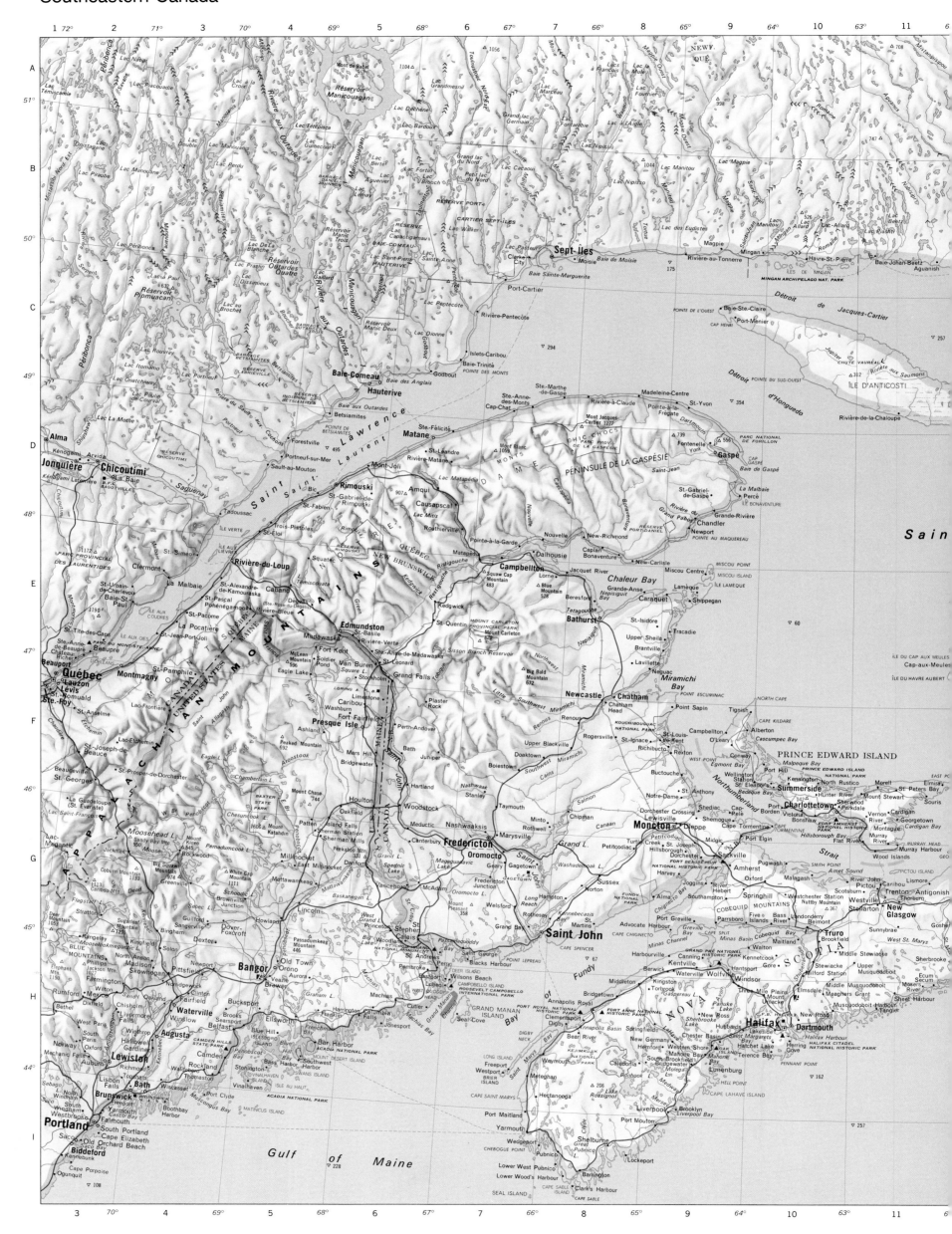

LABRADOR SEA

NEWFOUNDLAND

Gulf of Lawrence

ATLANTIC OCEAN

CAPE BRETON ISLAND

SAINT PIERRE AND MIQUELON (France)
SAINT-PIERRE-ET-MIQUELON

CANADA

St. John's

Corner Brook

Sydney

Glace Bay

SABLE ISLAND (N.S.)

Kilometers

Statute Miles

Scale 1:3,000,000
One centimeter represents 30 kilometers.
One inch represents approximately 47 miles.
Lambert Conformal Conic Projection

109

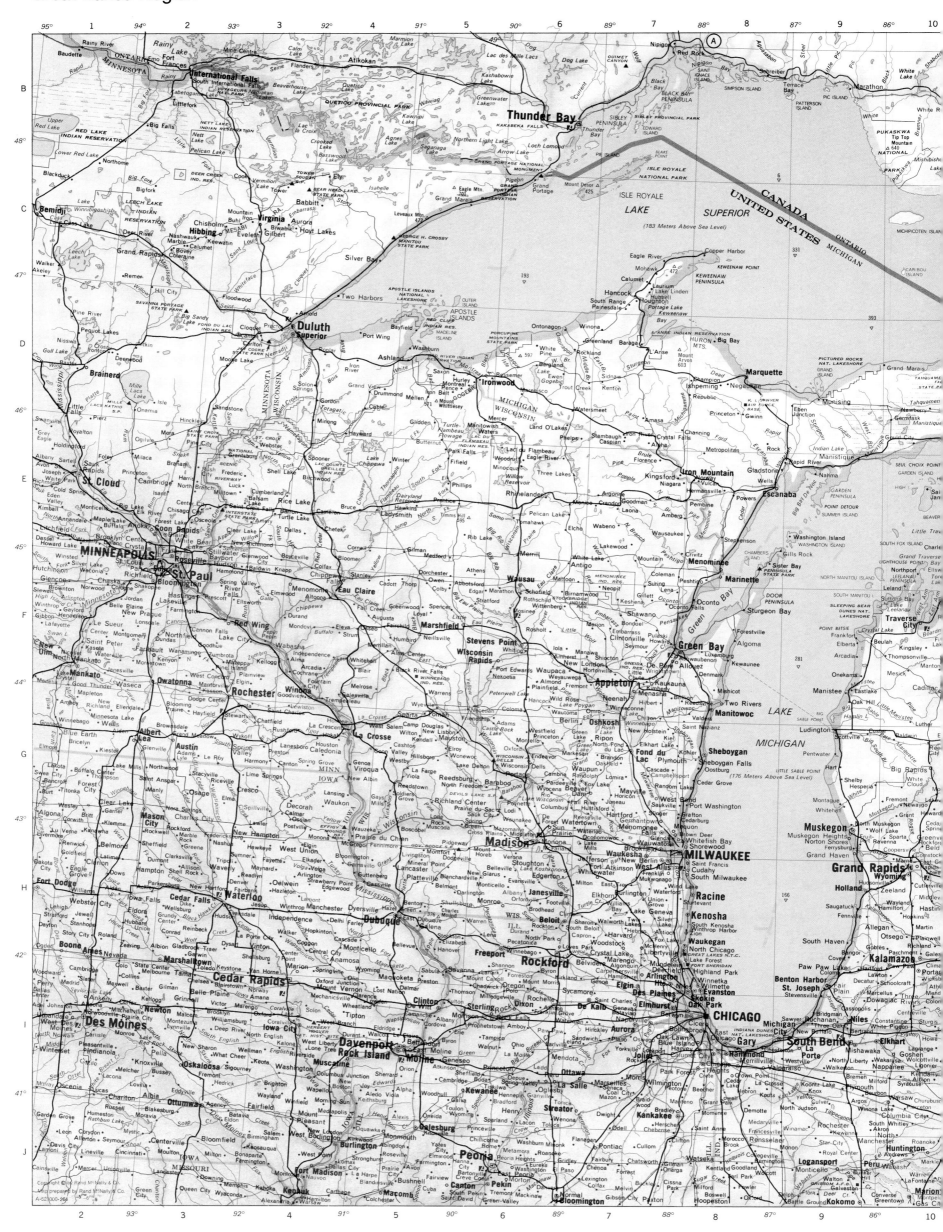

Kilometers

Statute Miles

Scale 1:3,000,000

One centimeter represents 30 kilometers.
One inch represents approximately 47 miles.

Albers Conical Equal-Area Projection

111

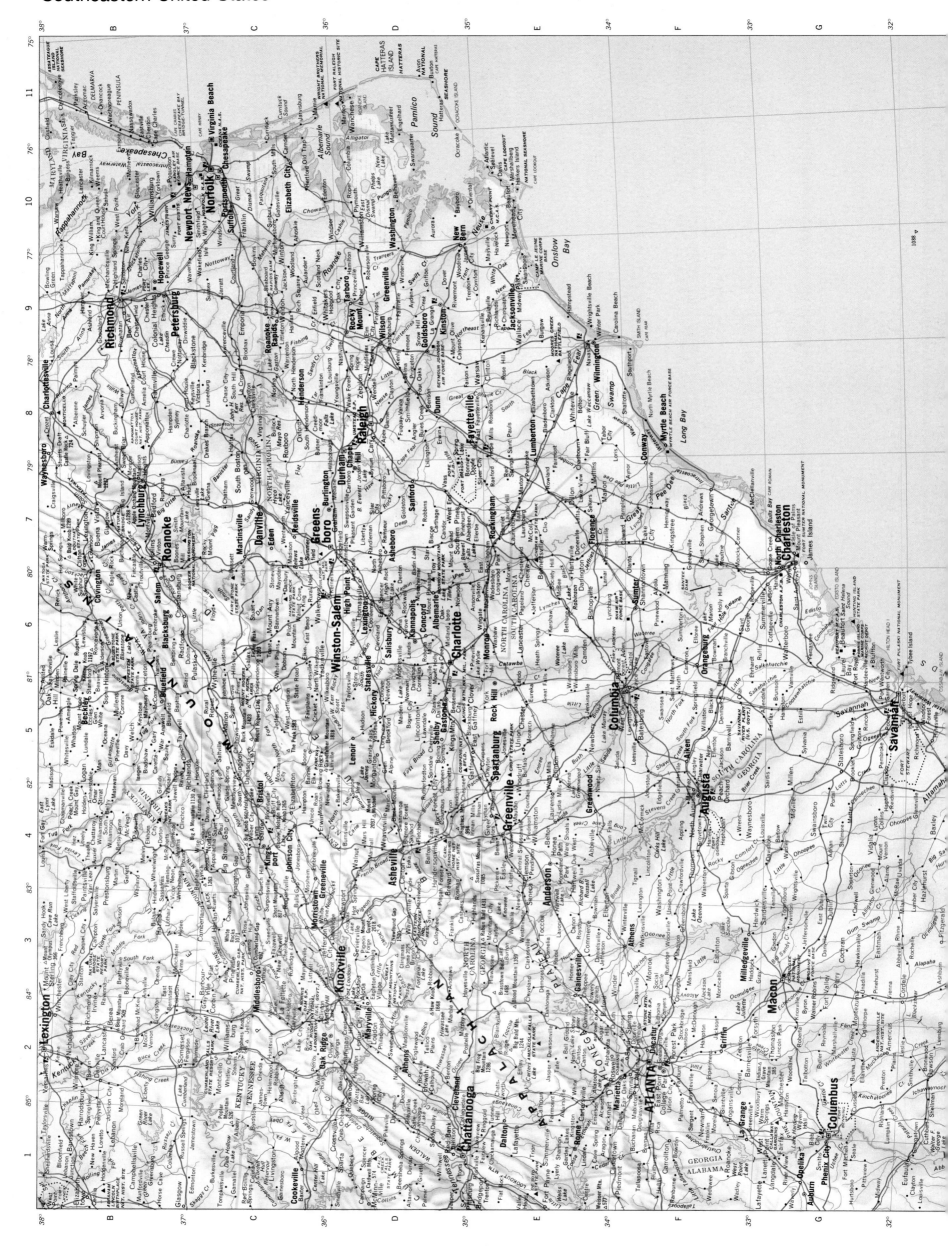

ATLANTIC

OCEAN

GULF OF MEXICO

Channel

Northwest Providence Channel

BAHAMAS

UNITED STATES

Nassau
NEW PROVIDENCE

Freeport
GRAND BAHAMA

LITTLE ABACO ISLAND
GREAT ABACO

ANDROS ISLAND

ELEUTHERA

BERRY ISLANDS

BIMINI ISLANDS

West Palm Beach
Riviera Beach
Boynton Beach
Delray Beach
Boca Raton
Pompano Beach
Fort Lauderdale
Hollywood
Hialeah
North Miami
MIAMI
Coral Gables
South Miami

Lake Okeechobee

Fort Pierce

Vero Beach

Melbourne

Cocoa Beach
Merritt Island
Cocoa
Rockledge

Titusville
JOHN F. KENNEDY SPACE CENTER
CAPE CANAVERAL

Daytona Beach

Ormond Beach
New Smyrna Beach

St. Augustine

Jacksonville

Brunswick

Waycross

Orlando
Winter Park
Sanford

Lakeland
Winter Haven

Ocala

Gainesville

Tampa
Plant City
St. Petersburg
Clearwater
Pinellas Park
Largo
Bradenton
Sarasota

Fort Myers
Cape Coral

Naples

Key West

FLORIDA KEYS

Key Largo

EVERGLADES NATIONAL PARK

BIG CYPRESS

The Everglades

Tallahassee

Thomasville
Moultrie
Valdosta

Dothan

GEORGIA

FLORIDA

ALABAMA

Okefenokee Swamp

Suwannee

DRY TORTUGAS NAT. MON.
FORT JEFFERSON NAT. MON.

Kilometers

Statute Miles

0   50   100   150   Km.

0   50   100   150 Mi.

Scale 1:3,000,000
One centimeter represents 30 kilometers.
One inch represents approximately 47 miles.

Albers Conical Equal-Area Projection

113

Scale 1:3,000,000

One centimeter represents 30 kilometers.
One inch represents approximately 47 miles.

Kilometers

Statute Miles

Albers Conical Equal-Area Projection

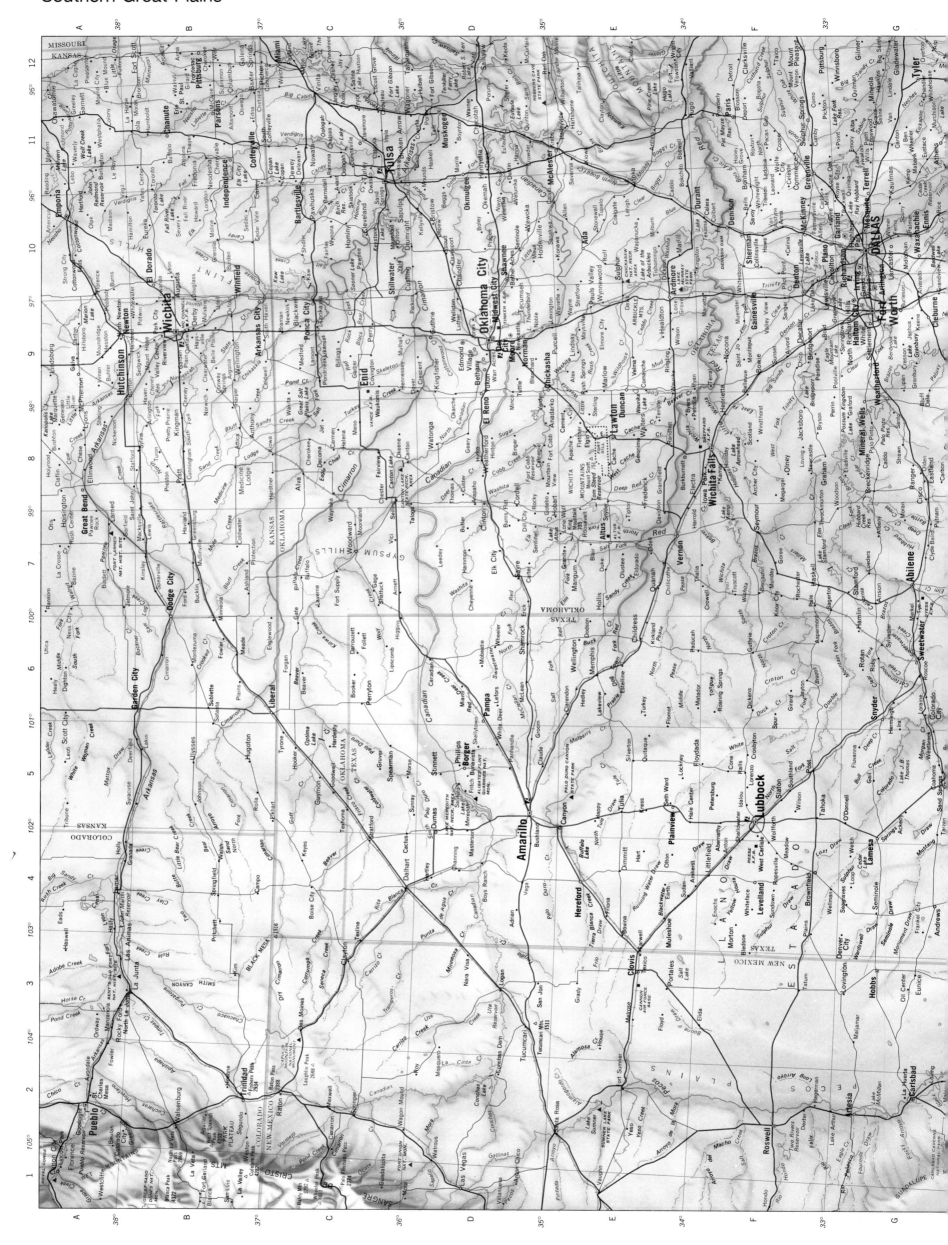

Kilometers
Statute Miles

Scale 1:3,000,000

One centimeter represents 30 kilometers.
One inch represents approximately 47 miles.

Albers Conical Equal-Area Projection

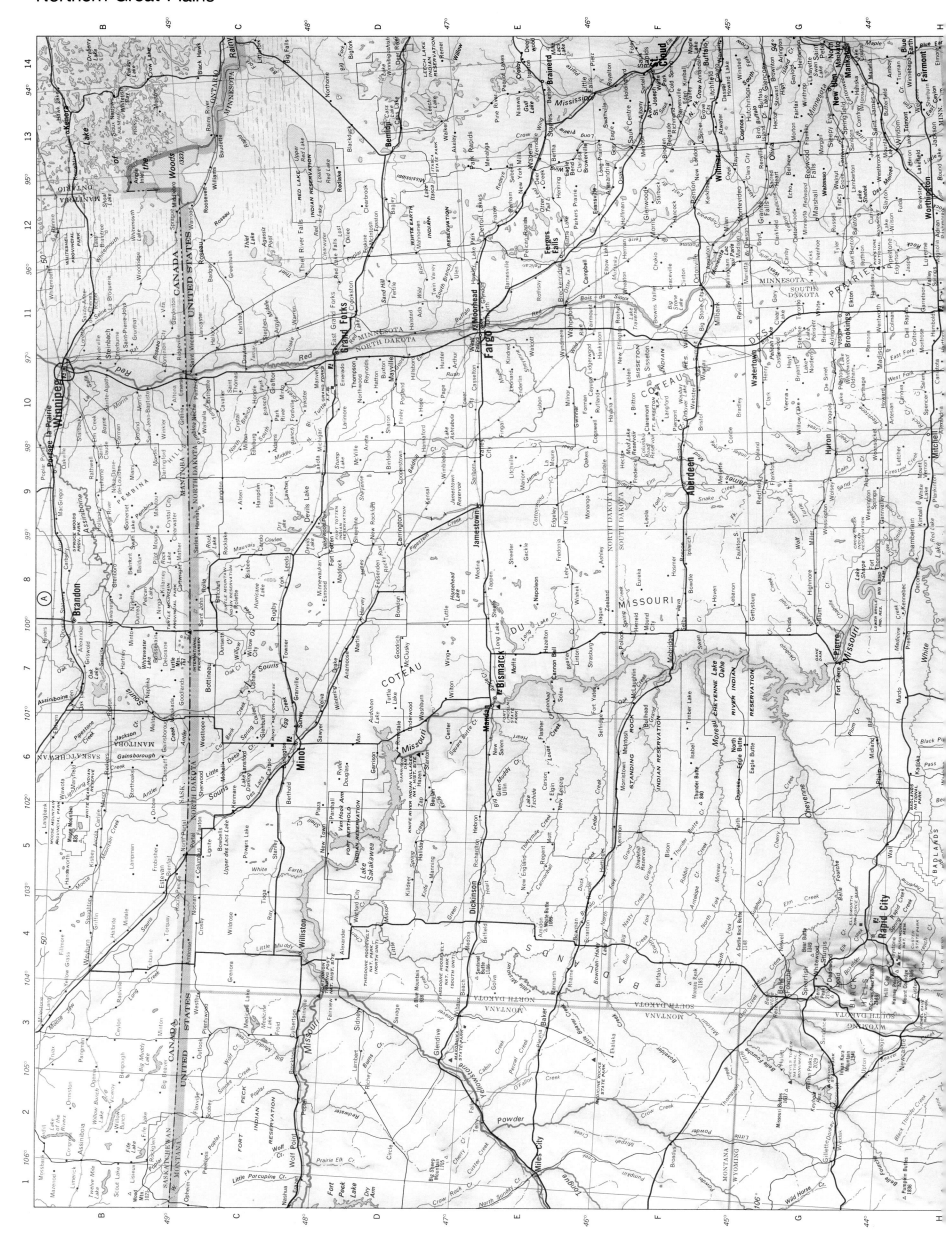

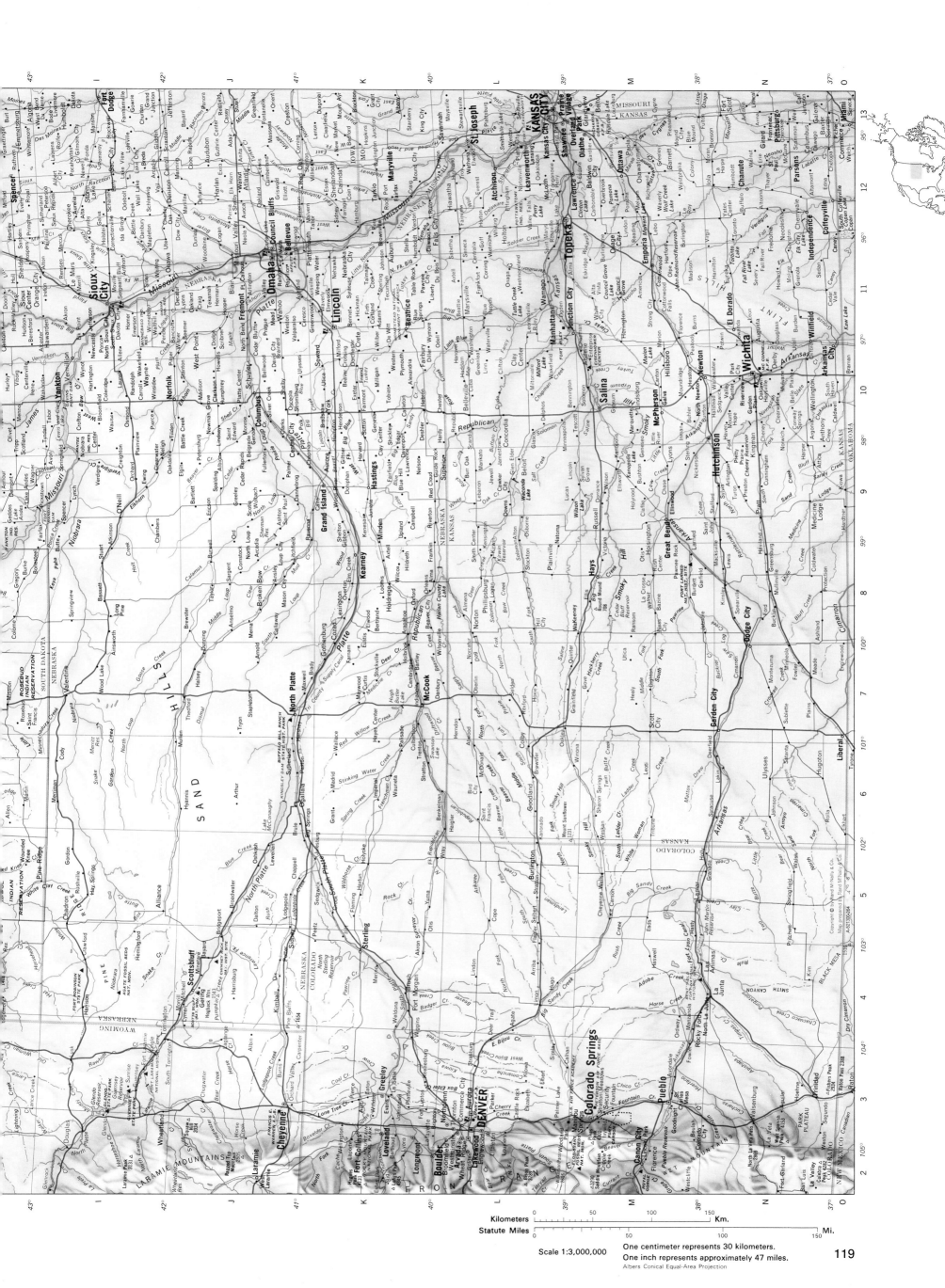

Scale 1:3,000,000
One centimeter represents 30 kilometers.
One inch represents approximately 47 miles.
Albers Conical Equal-Area Projection

Kilometers
Statute Miles

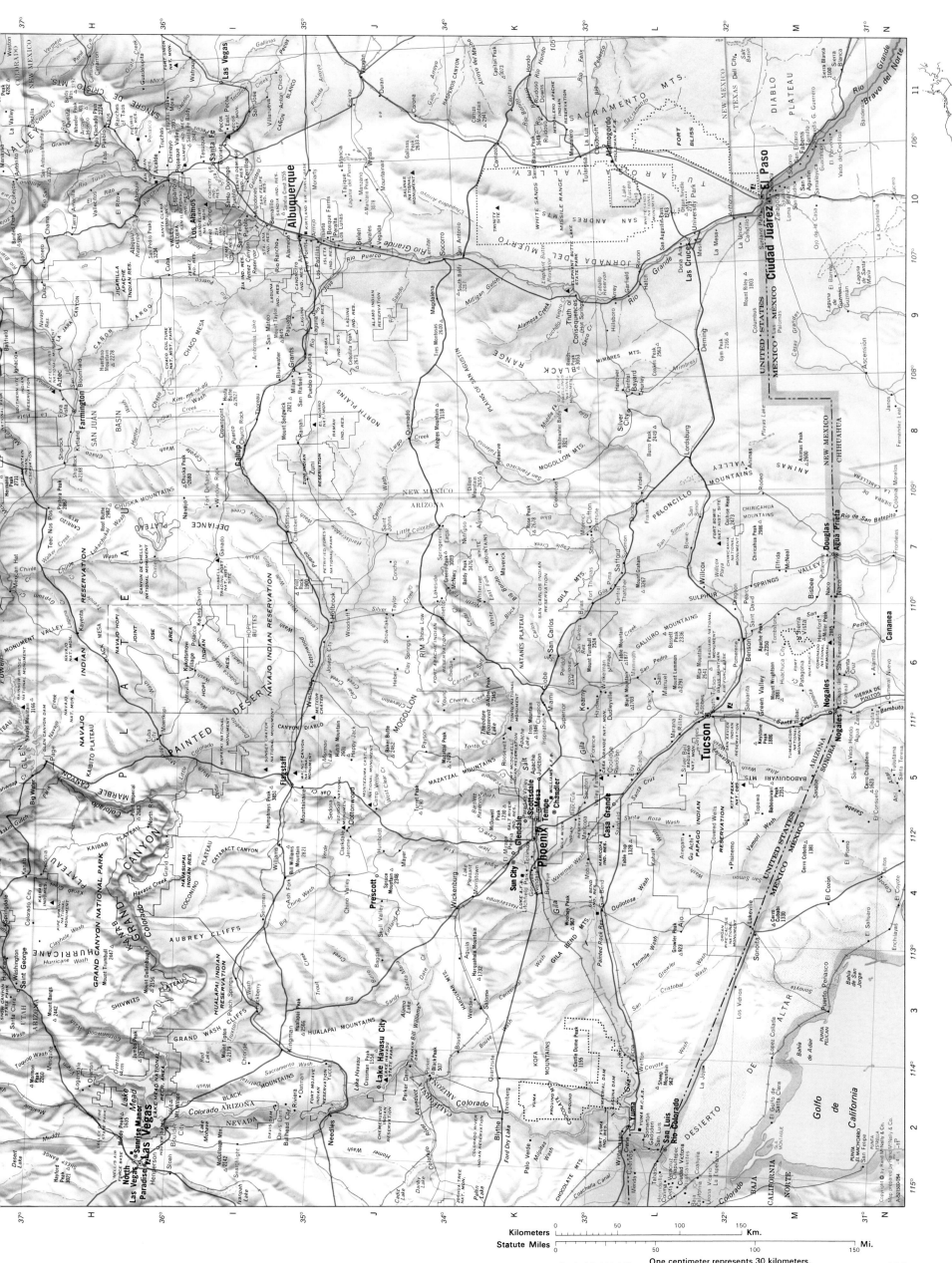

Kilometers

Statute Miles

Scale 1:3,000,000

One centimeter represents 30 kilometers.
One inch represents approximately 47 miles.

Albers Conical Equal-Area Projection

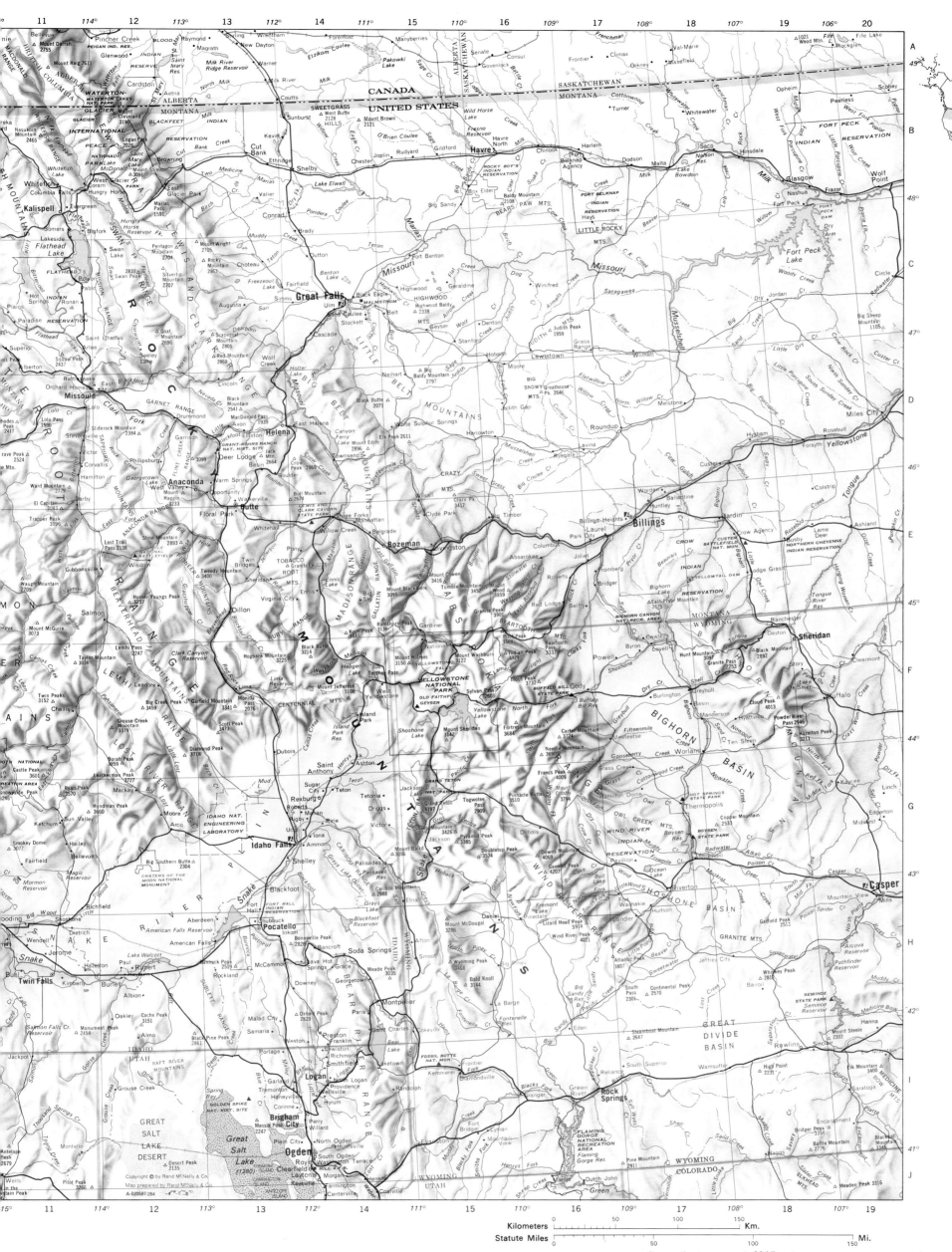

Kilometers

Statute Miles

Scale 1:3,000,000

One centimeter represents 30 kilometers.
One inch represents approximately 47 miles.
Albers Conical Equal-Area Projection

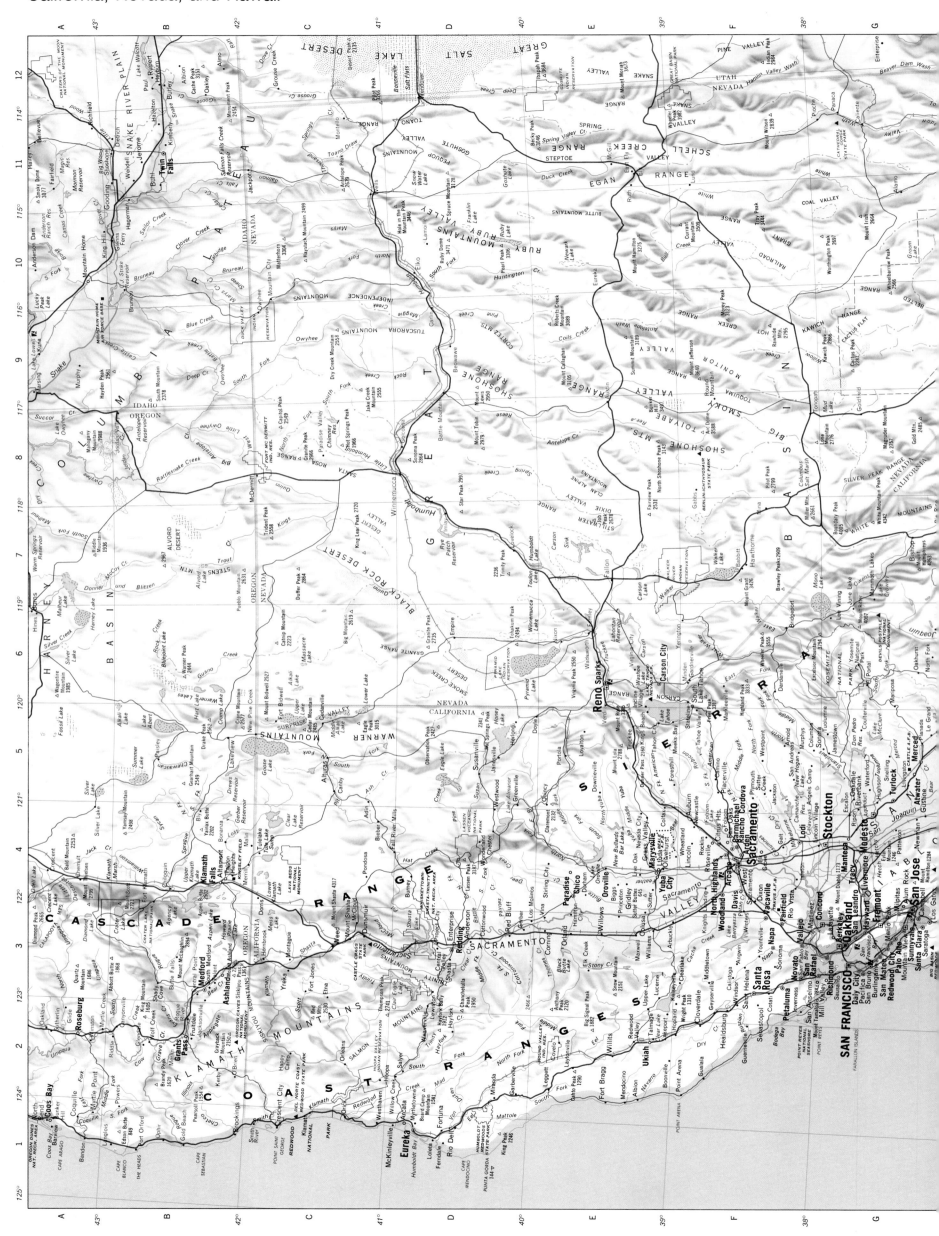

Kilometers

Statute Miles

Scale 1:3,000,000

One centimeter represents 30 kilometers.
One inch represents approximately 47 miles.

Albers Conical Equal-Area Projection

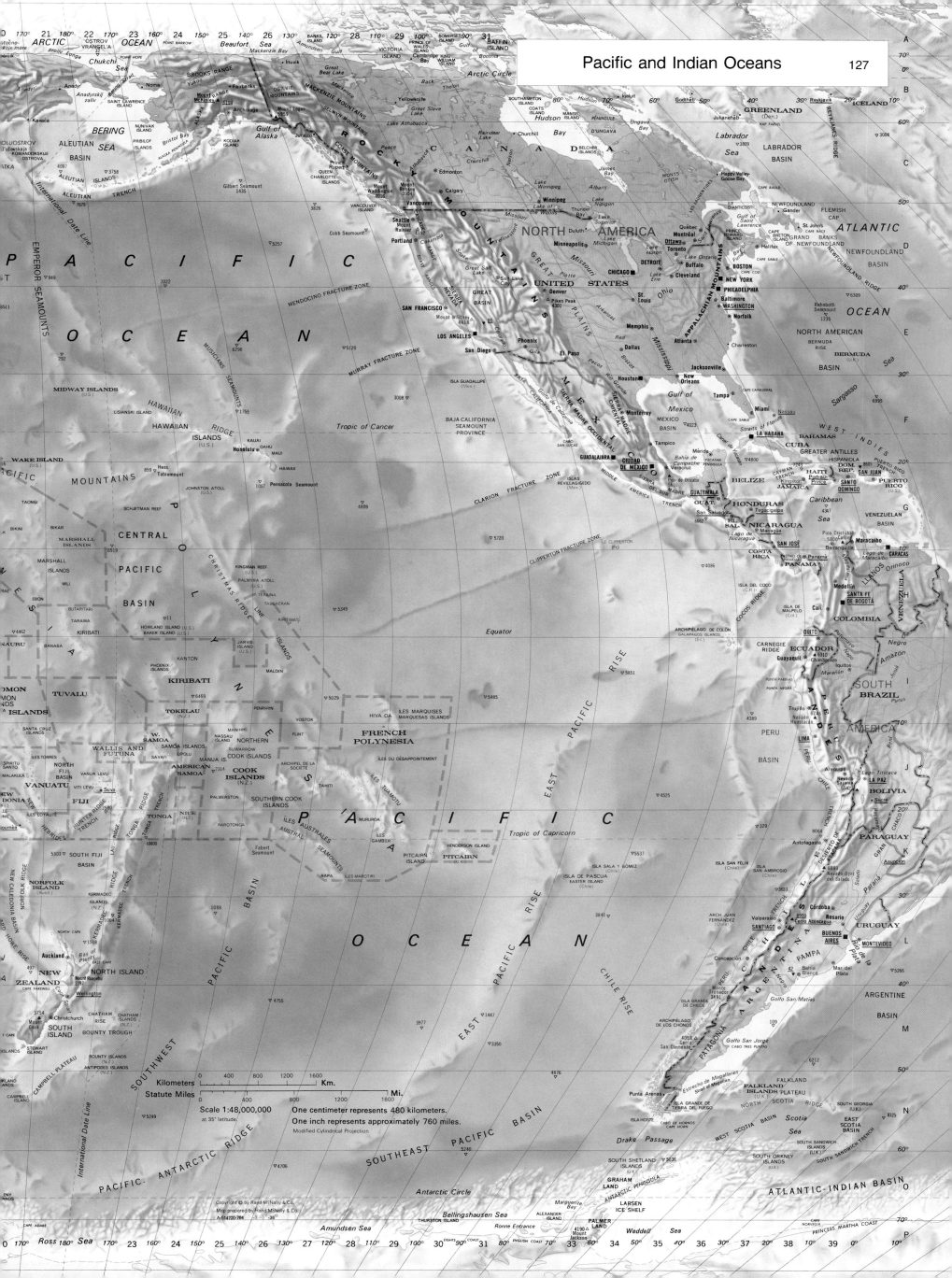

Kilometers
Statute Miles

Scale 1:48,000,000
at 35° latitude.
One centimeter represents 480 kilometers.
One inch represents approximately 760 miles.
Modified Cylindrical Projection

Copyright © by Rand McNally & Co.
Map prepared by Rand McNally & Co.
A-514700-764

Scale 1:48,000,000
at 35° latitude

One centimeter represents 480 kilometers.
One inch represents approximately 760 miles.

Modified Cylindrical Projection

Copyright © by Rand McNally & Co.
Map prepared by Rand McNally & Co.
A-513700-764

Index to World Reference Maps

Introduction to the Index

This universal index includes in a single alphabetical list over 52,000 names of features that appear on the reference maps. Each name is followed by the name of the country or continent in which it is located, a map-reference key and a page reference.

Names The names of cities appear in the index in regular type. The names of all other features appear in *italics*, followed by descriptive terms (hill, mtn., state) to indicate their nature.

Names that appear in shortened versions on the maps due to space limitations are spelled out in full in the index. The portions of these names omitted from the maps are enclosed in brackets — for example, Acapulco [de Juárez].

Abbreviations of names on the maps have been standardized as much as possible. Names that are abbreviated on the maps are generally spelled out in full in the index.

Country names and names of features that extend beyond the boundaries of one country are followed by the name of the continent in which each is located. Country designations follow the names of all other places in the index. The locations of places in the United States, Canada, and the United Kingdom are further defined by abbreviations that indicate the state, province, or political division in which each is located.

All abbreviations used in the index are defined in the List of Abbreviations below.

Alphabetization Names are alphabetized in the order of the letters of the English alphabet. Spanish *ll* and *ch*, for example, are not treated as distinct letters. Furthermore, diacritical marks are disregarded in alphabetization — German or Scandinavian *ä* or *ö* are treated as *a* or *o*.

The names of physical features may appear inverted, since they are always alphabetized under the proper, not the generic, part of the name, thus: 'Gibraltar, Strait of'. Otherwise every entry, whether consisting of one word or more, is alphabetized as a single continuous entity. 'Lakeland', for example, appears after 'La Crosse' and before 'La Salle'. Names beginning with articles (Le Havre, Den Helder, Al Manşūrah) are not inverted. Names beginning 'St.', 'Ste.' and 'Sainte' are alphabetized as though spelled 'Saint'.

In the case of identical names, towns are listed first, then political divisions, then physical features. Entries that are completely identical are listed alphabetically by country name.

Map-Reference Keys and Page References The map-reference keys and page references are found in the last two columns of each entry.

Each map-reference key consists of a letter and number. The letters appear along the sides of the maps. Lowercase letters indicate reference to inset maps. Numbers appear across the tops and bottoms of the maps.

Map reference keys for point features, such as cities and mountain peaks, indicate the locations of the symbols. For extensive areal features, such as countries or mountain ranges, locations are given for the approximate centers of the features. Those for linear features, such as canals and rivers, are given for the locations of the names.

The page number generally refers to the main map for the country in which the feature is located. Page references to two-page maps always refer to the left-hand page.

List of Abbreviations

Afg.	Afghanistan	C.V.	Cape Verde	Jord.	Jordan	N. Ire., U.K.	Northern Ireland, U.K.	Sri L.	Sri Lanka
Afr.	Africa	Cyp.	Cyprus	Kaz.	Kazakhstan			*state*	state, republic, canton
Ak., U.S.	Alaska, U.S.	Czech.	Czech Republic	Kir.	Kiribati	N.J., U.S.	New Jersey, U.S.		
Al., U.S.	Alabama, U.S.	D.C., U.S.	District of Columbia, U.S.	Ks., U.S.	Kansas, U.S.	N. Kor.	North Korea	St. Hel.	St. Helena
Alb.	Albania			Kuw.	Kuwait	N.M., U.S.	New Mexico, U.S.	St. K./N	St. Kitts and Nevis
Alg.	Algeria	De., U.S.	Delaware, U.S.	Ky., U.S.	Kentucky, U.S.	N. Mar. Is.	Northern Mariana Islands	St. Luc.	St. Lucia
Alta., Can.	Alberta, Can.	Den.	Denmark	Kyrg.	Kyrgyzstan			*stm.*	stream (river, creek)
Am. Sam.	American Samoa	*dep.*	dependency, colony	*l.*	lake, pond	Nmb.	Namibia	S. Tom./P.	Sao Tome and Principe
anch.	anchorage	*depr.*	depression	La., U.S.	Louisiana, U.S.	Nor.	Norway		
And.	Andorra	*dept.*	department, district	Lat.	Latvia	Norf. I.	Norfolk Island	St. P./M.	St. Pierre and Miquelon
Ang.	Angola	*des.*	desert	Leb.	Lebanon	N.S., Can.	Nova Scotia, Can.		
Ant.	Antarctica	Dji.	Djibouti	Leso.	Lesotho	Nv., U.S.	Nevada, U.S.	*strt.*	strait, channel, sound
Antig.	Antigua and Barbuda	Dom.	Dominica	Lib.	Liberia	N.W. Ter., Can.	Northwest Territories, Can.		
		Dom. Rep.	Dominican Republic	Liech.	Liechtenstein			St. Vin.	St. Vincent and the Grenadines
Ar., U.S.	Arkansas, U.S.	Ec.	Ecuador	Lith.	Lithuania	N.Y., U.S.	New York, U.S.		
Arg.	Argentina	El Sal.	El Salvador	Lux.	Luxembourg	N.Z.	New Zealand	Sud.	Sudan
Arm.	Armenia	Eng., U.K.	England, U.K.	Ma., U.S.	Massachusetts, U.S.	Oc.	Oceania	Sur.	Suriname
Aus.	Austria	Eq. Gui.	Equatorial Guinea			Oh., U.S.	Ohio, U.S.	*sw.*	swamp, marsh
Austl.	Australia	Erit.	Eritrea	Mac.	Macedonia	Ok., U.S.	Oklahoma, U.S.	Swaz.	Swaziland
Az., U.S.	Arizona, U.S.	*est.*	estuary	Madag.	Madagascar	Ont., Can.	Ontario, Can.	Swe.	Sweden
Azer.	Azerbaijan	Est.	Estonia	Malay.	Malaysia	Or., U.S.	Oregon, U.S.	Switz.	Switzerland
b.	bay, gulf, inlet, lagoon	Eth.	Ethiopia	Mald.	Maldives	Pa., U.S.	Pennsylvania, U.S.	Tai.	Taiwan
		Eur.	Europe	Man., Can.	Manitoba, Can.	Pak.	Pakistan	Taj.	Tajikistan
Bah.	Bahamas	Faer. Is.	Faeroe Islands	Marsh. Is.	Marshall Islands	Pan.	Panama	Tan.	Tanzania
Bahr.	Bahrain	Falk. Is.	Falkland Islands	Mart.	Martinique	Pap. N. Gui.	Papua New Guinea	T./C. Is.	Turks and Caicos Islands
Barb.	Barbados	Fin.	Finland	Maur.	Mauritania	Para.	Paraguay		
B.A.T.	British Antarctic Territory	Fl., U.S.	Florida, U.S.	May.	Mayotte	P.E.I., Can.	Prince Edward Island, Can.	*ter.*	territory
		for.	forest, moor	Md., U.S.	Maryland, U.S.			Thai.	Thailand
B.C., Can.	British Columbia, Can.	Fr.	France	Me., U.S.	Maine, U.S.	*pen.*	peninsula	Tn., U.S.	Tennessee, U.S.
Bdi.	Burundi	Fr. Gu.	French Guiana	Mex.	Mexico	Phil.	Philippines	Tok.	Tokelau
Bel.	Belgium	Fr. Poly.	French Polynesia	Mi., U.S.	Michigan, U.S.	Pit.	Pitcairn	Trin.	Trinidad and Tobago
Bela.	Belarus	F.S.A.T.	French Southern and Antarctic Territory	Micron.	Federated States of Micronesia	*pl.*	plain, flat		
Ber.	Bermuda					*plat.*	plateau, highland	Tun.	Tunisia
Bhu.	Bhutan	Ga., U.S.	Georgia, U.S.	Mid. Is.	Midway Islands	Pol.	Poland	Tur.	Turkey
B.I.O.T.	British Indian Ocean Territory	Gam.	Gambia	*mil.*	military installation	Port.	Portugal	Turk.	Turkmenistan
		Geor.	Georgia	Mn., U.S.	Minnesota, U.S.	P.R.	Puerto Rico	Tx., U.S.	Texas, U.S.
Bngl.	Bangladesh	Ger.	Germany	Mo., U.S.	Missouri, U.S.	*prov.*	province, region	U.A.E.	United Arab Emirates
Bol.	Bolivia	Gib.	Gibraltar	Mol.	Moldova	Que., Can.	Quebec, Can.		
Bos.	Bosnia and Herzegovina	Grc.	Greece	Mon.	Monaco	*reg.*	physical region	Ug.	Uganda
		Gren.	Grenada	Mong.	Mongolia	*res.*	reservoir	U.K.	United Kingdom
Bots.	Botswana	Grnld.	Greenland	Monts.	Montserrat	Reu.	Reunion	Ukr.	Ukraine
Braz.	Brazil	Guad.	Guadeloupe	Mor.	Morocco	*rf.*	reef, shoal	Ur.	Uruguay
Bru.	Brunei	Guat.	Guatemala	Moz.	Mozambique	R.I., U.S.	Rhode Island, U.S.	U.S.	United States
Br. Vir. Is.	British Virgin Islands	Gui.	Guinea	Mrts.	Mauritius	Rom.	Romania	Ut., U.S.	Utah, U.S.
Bul.	Bulgaria	Gui.-B.	Guinea-Bissau	Ms., U.S.	Mississippi, U.S.	Rw.	Rwanda	Uzb.	Uzbekistan
Burkina	Burkina Faso	Guy.	Guyana	Mt., U.S.	Montana, U.S.	S.A.	South America	Va., U.S.	Virginia, U.S.
c.	cape, point	Hi., U.S.	Hawaii, U.S.	*mth.*	river mouth or channel	S. Afr.	South Africa	*val.*	valley, watercourse
Ca., U.S.	California, U.S.	*hist.*	historic site, ruins			Sask., Can.	Saskatchewan, Can.	Vat.	Vatican City
Cam.	Cameroon	*hist. reg.*	historic region	*mtn.*	mountain			Ven.	Venezuela
Camb.	Cambodia	H.K.	Hong Kong	*mts.*	mountains	Sau. Ar.	Saudi Arabia	Viet.	Vietnam
Can.	Canada	Hond.	Honduras	Mwi.	Malawi	S.C., U.S.	South Carolina, U.S.	V.I.U.S.	Virgin Islands (U.S.)
Cay. Is.	Cayman Islands	Hung.	Hungary	Mya.	Myanmar	*sci.*	scientific station	*vol.*	volcano
Cen. Afr. Rep.	Central African Republic	*i.*	island	N.A.	North America	Scot., U.K.	Scotland, U.K.	Vt., U.S.	Vermont, U.S.
		Ia., U.S.	Iowa, U.S.	N.B., Can.	New Brunswick, Can.	S.D., U.S.	South Dakota, U.S.	Wa., U.S.	Washington, U.S.
Christ. I.	Christmas Island	Ice.	Iceland			Sen.	Senegal	Wal./F.	Wallis and Futuna
C. Iv.	Cote d'Ivoire	*ice*	ice feature, glacier	N.C., U.S.	North Carolina, U.S.	Sey.	Seychelles	Wi., U.S.	Wisconsin, U.S.
clf.	cliff, escarpment	Id., U.S.	Idaho, U.S.	N. Cal.	New Caledonia	Sing.	Singapore	W. Sah.	Western Sahara
co.	county, parish	Il., U.S.	Illinois, U.S.	N. Cyp.	North Cyprus	S. Geor.	South Georgia	W. Sam.	Western Samoa
Co., U.S.	Colorado, U.S.	In., U.S.	Indiana, U.S.	N.D., U.S.	North Dakota, U.S.	S. Kor.	South Korea	*wtfl.*	waterfall
Col.	Colombia	Indon.	Indonesia	Ne., U.S.	Nebraska, U.S.	S.L.	Sierra Leone	W.V., U.S.	West Virginia, U.S.
Com.	Comoros	I. of Man	Isle of Man	Neth.	Netherlands	Slo.	Slovenia	Wy., U.S.	Wyoming, U.S.
cont.	continent	Ire.	Ireland	Neth. Ant.	Netherlands Antilles	Slov.	Slovakia	Yugo.	Yugoslavia
C.R.	Costa Rica	*is.*	islands	Newf., Can.	Newfoundland, Can.	S. Mar.	San Marino	Yukon, Can.	Yukon Territory, Can.
Cro.	Croatia	Isr.	Israel	N.H., U.S.	New Hampshire, U.S.	Sol. Is.	Solomon Islands		
Ct., U.S.	Connecticut, U.S.	Isr. Occ.	Israeli Occupied Territories			Som.	Somalia	Zam.	Zambia
ctry.	country			Nic.	Nicaragua	Sp. N. Afr.	Spanish North Africa	Zimb.	Zimbabwe
		Jam.	Jamaica	Nig.	Nigeria				

Index

A

Name	Map Ref.	Page
Alcorn, Ms., U.S.	K5	114
Alcorta, Arg.	G8	80
Alcoutim, Port.	H4	16
Alcovy, stm., Ga., U.S.	F3	112
Aldabra Island, i., Sey.	C9	58
Aldama, Mex.	C7	90
Aldama, Mex.	F10	90
Aldan, Russia	F17	28
Aldan, stm., Russia	F18	28
Aldanskoje nagorje, plat., Russia	F17	28
Aldeburgh, Eng., U.K.	I15	8
Alden, Ia., U.S.	H2	110
Alden, Mn., U.S.	G2	110
Alderney, i., Guernsey	L11	8
Aldershot, Eng., U.K.	J13	8
Alderson, W.V., U.S.	B6	112
Aledo, Il., U.S.	I5	110
Alefa, Eth.	L9	60
Aleg, Maur.	C3	64
Alegre, Braz.	F8	79
Alegre, stm., Braz.	F12	82
Alegres Mountain, mtn., N.M., U.S.	J8	120
Alegrete, Braz.	E11	80
Alejandro Roca, Arg.	G7	80
Alejandro Selkirk, Isla, i., Chile	H6	74
Alejo Ledesma, Arg.	G7	80
Alejsk, Russia	G8	28
Aleknagik, Ak., U.S.	G15	100
Aleksandro-Nevskij, Russia	H23	22
Aleksandrov, Russia	E21	22
Aleksandrov Gaj, Russia	G7	26
Aleksandrovskoje, Russia	E13	26
Aleksandrovsk-Sachalinskij, Russia	G20	28
Aleksejevka, Kaz.	G12	26
Aleksejevka, Russia	G5	26
Aleksejevsk, Russia	F13	28
Aleksin, Russia	G20	22
Aleksinac, Yugo.	F5	20
Alemania, Arg.	C6	80
Além Paraíba, Braz.	F7	79
Alençon, Fr.	D7	14
Alenquer, Braz.	D8	76
Alentejo, hist. reg., Port.	G3	16
Alenuihaha Channel, strt., Hi., U.S.	q17	125a
Aleppo see Ḥalab, Syria	C4	48
Aléria, Fr.	G4	18
Alert, N.W. Ter., Can.	A13	86
Alert Bay, B.C., Can.	G8	102
Alès, Fr.	H11	14
Alessandria, Italy	E3	18
Ålesund, Nor.	J10	6
Aletschhorn, mtn., Switz.	F9	13
Aleutian Islands, is., Ak., U.S.	J6	100
Aleutian Range, mts., Ak., U.S.	G17	100
Aleutian Trench	D3	86
Alevina, mys, c., Russia	F22	28
Alex, Ok., U.S.	E9	116
Alexander, Man., Can.	I14	104
Alexander, N.D., U.S.	D4	118
Alexander Archipelago, is., Ak., U.S.	H27	100
Alexander Bay, S. Afr.	G3	66
Alexander City, Al., U.S.	J11	114
Alexander Indian Reserve, Alta., Can.	D21	102
Alexander Island, i., Ant.	C12	73
Alexandra, N.Z.	F2	72
Alexandra, stm., Austl.	B4	70
Alexandra Falls, wtfl, N.W. Ter., Can.	D9	96
Alexandretta see İskenderun, Tur.	C4	48
Alexandretta, Gulf of see İskenderun Körfezi, b., Tur.	H15	4
Alexandria, B.C., Can.	E12	102
Alexandria, Ont., Can.	B12	108
Alexandria see Al-Iskandarīyah, Egypt	B5	60
Alexandria, Rom.	F9	20
Alexandria, In., U.S.	B11	114
Alexandria, Ky., U.S.	I2	108
Alexandria, La., U.S.	K4	114
Alexandria, Mn., U.S.	F12	118
Alexandria, Mo., U.S.	B5	114
Alexandria, Ne., U.S.	K10	118
Alexandria, S.D., U.S.	H10	118
Alexandria, Tn., U.S.	F10	114
Alexandria, Va., U.S.	I9	108
Alexandria Bay, N.Y., U.S.	C11	108
Alexandrina, Lake, l., Austl.	J3	70
Alexandroúpolis, Grc.	I9	20
Alexis, Il., U.S.	I5	110
Alexis Creek, B.C., Can.	E11	102
Alexis Indian Reserve, Alta., Can.	D20	102
Alfaro, Spain	C10	16
Al-Fāshir, Sud.	K3	60
Al-Fashn, Egypt	C6	60
Al-Fāw, Iraq	G10	48
Al-Fayyūm, Egypt	C6	60
Alfeld, Ger.	D9	10
Alfenas, Braz.	F6	79
Al-Fifi, Sud.	L3	60
Alfiós, stm., Grc.	L5	20
Alföld, pl., Hung.	H20	10
Alfred, Ont., Can.	B12	108
Alfred, Me., U.S.	D16	108
Alfred, N.Y., U.S.	E9	108
Alga, Kaz.	H9	26
Ålgård, Nor.	L9	6
Al-Garef, Sud.	K8	60
Algarrobal, Chile	E3	80
Algarrobo, Arg.	J7	80
Algarrobo, Arg.	F4	80
Algarrobo, Chile	G3	80
Algarrobo del Águila, Arg.	I5	80
Algarve, hist. reg., Port.	H3	16
Algasovo, Russia	H24	22
Al-Gebir, Sud.	K5	60
Algeciras, Col.	F5	84
Algeciras, Spain	I6	16
Algemesí, Spain	F11	16
Algena, Erit.	I10	60
Alger, Oh., U.S.	G3	108
Algeria (Algérie), ctry., Afr.	C7	54
Al-Ghāṭ, Sau. Ar.	H8	48
Al-Ghawr, val., Asia	D5	50
Al-Ghayḍah, Yemen	F8	47
Al-Ghazālah, Sau. Ar.	H6	48
Alghero, Italy	I3	18
Al-Ghurayfah, Oman	B10	47
Al-Ghurdaqah, Egypt	D7	60
Algiers see El Djazaïr, Alg.	B12	62
Alginet, Spain	F11	16
Algodón, stm., Peru	I6	84
Algodones, N.M., U.S.	I10	120
Algoma, Wi., U.S.	F8	110
Algoma Mills, Ont., Can.	D13	110
Algona, Ia., U.S.	G1	110
Algona, Wa., U.S.	C3	122
Algonac, Mi., U.S.	H13	110
Algonquin, Il., U.S.	H7	110
Algood, Tn., U.S.	F11	114
Algorta, Spain	B8	16
Algorta, Ur.	G10	80
Al-Ḥadīthah, Iraq	D7	48
Al-Ḥadīthah, Sau. Ar.	E8	50
Al-Ḥajarah, reg., Asia	F8	48
Al Hajeb, Mor.	D8	62
Al-Ḥamād, pl., Sau. Ar.	E5	48
Alhama de Murcia, Spain	H10	16
Al-Ḥammām, Egypt	B5	60
Al-Ḥamrā', Sau. Ar.	C1	47
Al-Ḥarīq, Sau. Ar.	C5	47
Al-Harūj al-Aswad, hills, Libya	C4	56
Al-Ḥasakah, Syria	C6	48
Alhaurín el Grande, Spain	I7	16
Al-Hawātah, Sud.	K8	60
Al-Ḥawrah, Yemen	H5	47
Al-Ḥawṭah, Yemen	G6	47
Al-Ḥayy, Iraq	E9	48
Al-Ḥayyānīyah, Sau. Ar.	G7	48
Al-Ḥayz, Egypt	C5	60
Al-Ḥijāz, reg., Sau. Ar.	I5	48
Al-Ḥillah, Iraq	E8	48
Al-Ḥillah, Sud.	K4	60
Al-Hirmil, Leb.	D4	48
Al-Ḥiṣn, Jord.	D5	50
Al-Hoceïma, Mor.	A6	54
Al Hoceïma, Baie d', b., Afr.	J8	16
Alhucemas, Peñón de, i., Sp. N. Afr.	J8	16
Al-Ḥudaydah, Yemen	G3	47
Al-Hufūf, Sau. Ar.	B6	47
Al-Ḥulwah, Sau. Ar.	J9	48
Al-Ḥumayshah, Yemen	H4	47
Al-Ḥuṣayḥiṣah, Sud.	J7	60
Al-Ḥuwaylizah, Isr. Occ.	B5	50
Al-Ḥuwayyiṭ, Sau. Ar.	I6	48
ʻAlīābād, Iran	C13	48
Aliaga, Spain	E11	16
Aliákmon, stm., Grc.	I6	20
Aliákmonos, Tekhnití Límni, res., Grc.	I5	20
ʻAlī al-Gharbī, Iraq	E9	48
Alībāg, India	C2	46
Äli Bayramlı, Azer.	B10	48
Alibey, ozero, l., Ukr.	D14	20
Alibunar, Yugo.	D4	20
Alice, S. Afr.	I8	66
Alice, Tx., U.S.	L8	116
Alice Arm, B.C., Can.	B5	102
Alicedale, S. Afr.	I8	66
Alice Springs, Austl.	D6	68
Alice Town, Bah.	B5	94
Aliceville, Al., U.S.	I8	114
Alīgarh, India	G8	44
Alīgūdarz, Iran	E10	48
Alijos, Islas, is., Mex.	E2	90
Al-Ikhwān, is., Yemen	G5	42
Aliquippa, Pa., U.S.	G6	108
Al-ʻIrāq, Jord.	F5	50
Al-ʻĪsāwīyah, Sau. Ar.	F4	48
Al-Iskandarīyah (Alexandria), Egypt	B5	60
Al-Ismāʻīlīyah, Egypt	B7	60
Aliwal North, S. Afr.	H8	66
Alix, Alta., Can.	E21	102
Al-Jabalayn, Sud.	K7	60
Al-Jadīdah, Egypt	E5	60
Al-Jafr, Jord.	H6	50
Al-Jaghbūb, Libya	C3	60
Al-Jawf, Libya	E2	60
Al-Jawf, Sau. Ar.	G5	48
Al-Jaylī, Sud.	I7	60
Al-Jazīrah, reg., Sud.	J7	60
Aljezur, Port.	H3	16
Al-Jifārah, Sau. Ar.	J8	48
Al-Jifārah (Jeffara), pl., Afr.	D16	62
Al-Jīzah, Egypt	B6	60
Al-Jubayl, Sau. Ar.	H10	48
Al-Jubayn, Sud.	K8	60
Al-Judayyidah, Jord.	E5	50
Al-Julaydah, well, Asia	G8	48
Al-Junaynah, Sud.	K2	60
Aljustrel, Port.	H3	16
Al-Kafr, Syria	C7	50
Alkali Creek, stm., Alta., Can.	G4	104
Alkali Lake, B.C., Can.	F12	102
Al-Kāmil, Oman	C11	47
Al-Karabah, Sud.	H7	60
Al-Karak, Jord.	F5	50
Al-Karnak, Egypt	E7	60
Al-Kawah, Sud.	K7	60
Al-Khabrā', Sau. Ar.	H7	48
Al-Khābūrah, Oman	C10	47
Al-Khalīl (Hebron), Isr. Occ.	E4	50
Al-Khāliṣ, Iraq	E8	48
Al-Khandaq, Sud.	H6	60
Al-Khārijah, Egypt	E6	60
Al-Kharṭūm (Khartoum), Sud.	J7	60
Al-Kharṭūm Baḥrī, Sud.	J7	60
Al-Khaṣab, Oman	A10	47
Al-Khubar, Sau. Ar.	A7	47
Al-Khums, Libya	B3	56
Al-Khuraybah, Jord.	C5	50
Al-Khuraybah, Yemen	G6	47
Al-Khurmah, Sau. Ar.	D3	47
Al-Kidn, reg., Asia	C9	47
Alkmaar, Neth.	C6	12
Al-Kuntillah, Egypt	B8	60
Al-Kūt, Iraq	E8	48
Al-Kuwayt, Kuw.	G9	48
Allada, Benin	H11	64
Al-Lādhiqīyah (Latakia), Syria	D3	48
Al-Lagowa, Sud.	L5	60
Allahābād, India	H9	44
Allan, Sask., Can.	G8	104
Allanche, Fr.	G9	14
Allanmyo, Mya.	E3	40
ʻAllāq, Bi'r, well, Libya	E16	62
Allard, Lac, l., Que., Can.	B10	106
Allardt, Tn., U.S.	F12	114
Al-Layyah, Sud.	I8	60
Alldays, S. Afr.	D9	66
Allegan, Mi., U.S.	H10	110
Allegany, N.Y., U.S.	E8	108
Allegheny, stm., U.S.	G7	108
Allegheny Mountains, mts., U.S.	I6	108
Allegheny Plateau, plat., U.S.	G8	108
Allegheny Reservoir, res., U.S.	F8	108
Allemands, Lac Des, l., La., U.S.	M6	114
Allen, Arg.	J5	80
Allen, Ne., U.S.	I11	118
Allen, Ok., U.S.	E10	116
Allen, S.D., U.S.	H6	118
Allen, Tx., U.S.	F10	116
Allen, Mount, mtn., Ak., U.S.	E23	100
Allendale, Il., U.S.	D9	114
Allendale, S.C., U.S.	F5	112
Allende, Mex.	C9	90
Allenstein see Olsztyn, Pol.	B20	10
Allentown, Pa., U.S.	G11	108
Allentsteig, Aus.	G15	10
Alleppey, India	H4	46
Aller, stm., Ger.	C9	10
Allerton, Ia., U.S.	J2	110
Allgäu, reg., Ger.	H10	10
Allgäuer Alpen, mts., Eur.	E17	14
Alliance, Alta., Can.	E23	102
Alliance, Ne., U.S.	I5	118
Alliance, Oh., U.S.	G5	108
Al-Lidām, Sau. Ar.	D4	47
Allier, dept., Fr.	F9	14
Allier, stm., Fr.	F10	14
Alligator, stm., N.C., U.S.	D10	112
Allison, Ia., U.S.	H3	110
Alliston, Ont., Can.	F16	110
Al-Līth, Sau. Ar.	D2	47
Alloa, Scot., U.K.	E10	8
Allora, Austl.	G9	70
Allouez, Wi., U.S.	F7	110
Al-Luḥayyah, Yemen	G3	47
Allyn, Wa., U.S.	C3	122
Alma, N.B., Can.	G9	106
Alma, Que., Can.	D2	106
Alma, Ar., U.S.	G2	114
Alma, Ga., U.S.	H4	112
Alma, Ks., U.S.	L11	118
Alma, Mi., U.S.	G11	110
Alma, Ne., U.S.	K8	118
Alma, Wi., U.S.	F4	110
Alma-Ata (Almaty), Kaz.	I13	26
Alma Center, Wi., U.S.	F5	110
Almada, Port.	G2	16
Almadén, Spain	G7	16
Al-Madīnah (Medina), Sau. Ar.	B1	47
Al-Mafāzah, Sud.	K8	60
Al-Mafraq, Jord.	D6	50
Almafuerte, Arg.	G6	80
Almagro, Spain	G8	16
Al-Maḥallah al-Kubrā, Egypt	B6	60
Al-Maḥārīq, Egypt	E6	60
Al Mahbas, W. Sah.	G6	62
Al-Majmaʻah, Sau. Ar.	I8	48
Al-Makhā' (Mocha), Yemen	H3	47
Almalyk, Uzb.	I11	26
Al-Manāmah, Bahr.	H11	48
Almansa, Spain	G10	16
Al-Manshāh, Egypt	D6	60
Al-Manṣūrah, Egypt	B6	60
Al-Manzilah, Egypt	F1	48
Almanzor, mtn., Spain	E6	16
Al-Marāghah, Egypt	D6	60
Al-Marj, Libya	B5	56
Almas, Pico das, mtn., Braz.	B8	79
Al-Masīd, Sud.	J7	60
Almassora, Spain	F11	16
Al-Matammah, Sud.	I7	60
Al-Maṭarīyah, Egypt	B7	60
Al-Matnah, Sud.	K8	60
Al-Mawṣil (Mosul), Iraq	C7	48
Al-Mayādīn, Syria	D6	48
Al-Mazār, Jord.	F5	50
Al-Mazraʻah, Jord.	F5	50
Almeida, Port.	E5	16
Almeirim, Port.	F3	16
Almelo, Neth.	D10	12
Almena, Ks., U.S.	L8	118
Almenara, Braz.	D8	79
Almendralejo, Spain	G5	16
Almería, Spain	I9	16
Almería, Golfo de, b., Spain	I9	16
Al'metjevsk, Russia	G8	26
Al-Midhnab, Sau. Ar.	I8	48
Al-Minyā, Egypt	C6	60
Almira, Wa., U.S.	C7	122
Almirante, Pan.	C1	84
Almirante, Bahía de, b., Pan.	H12	92
Almirante Latorre, Chile	E3	80
Al-Mismīyah, Syria	B6	50
Almo, Id., U.S.	H12	122
Almodôvar, Port.	H3	16
Almolonga, Guat.	C3	92
Almond, Wi., U.S.	F6	110
Almont, Mi., U.S.	H12	110
Almonte, Ont., Can.	E19	110
Almonte, Spain	H5	16
Almora, India	F8	44
Al-Mubarraz, Sau. Ar.	C5	47
Al-Mubarraz, Sau. Ar.	B6	47
Al-Mudawwarah, Jord.	G3	48
Al-Muglad, Sud.	L4	60
Al-Muḥarraq, Bahr.	H11	48
Al-Mukallā, Yemen	G6	47
Almuñécar, Spain	I8	16
Al-Musallamīyah, Sud.	J7	60
Al-Musayfirah, Syria	C6	50
Al-Musayjid, Sau. Ar.	B1	47
Al-Mutayn, Leb.	A5	50
Al-Muwayh, Sau. Ar.	C2	47
Al-Muwayliḥ, Sau. Ar.	H3	48
Alnwick, Eng., U.K.	F12	8
Aloândia, Braz.	D4	79
Aloja, Lat.	D7	22
Alor, Pulau, i., Indon.	G7	38
Alor Setar, Malay.	K6	40
Alosno, Spain	H4	16
Alost (Aalst), Bel.	G5	12
Alpachiri, Arg.	I7	80
Alpaugh, Ca., U.S.	I6	124
Alpena, Ar., U.S.	F3	114
Alpena, Mi., U.S.	E12	110
Alpena, S.D., U.S.	G9	118
Alpes-de-Haute-Provence, dept., Fr.	H13	14
Alpes-Maritimes, dept., Fr.	I14	14
Alpha, Austl.	D7	70
Alpha, Il., U.S.	I5	110
Alpha, Mi., U.S.	D7	110
Alpharetta, Ga., U.S.	E2	112
Alpine, Az., U.S.	K7	120
Alpine, Ca., U.S.	L9	124
Alpine, Tx., U.S.	I3	116
Alpine National Park, Austl.	K7	70
Alpinópolis, Braz.	F5	79
Alps, mts., Eur.	F10	4
Al-Qābil, Oman	C9	47
Al-Qaḍārif, Sud.	J8	60
Al-Qaḍīmah, Sau. Ar.	C1	47
Al-Qāhirah (Cairo), Egypt	B6	60
Al-Qaḥmah, Sau. Ar.	E2	47
Al-Qalībah, Sau. Ar.	G4	48
Al-Qāmishlī, Syria	C6	48
Al-Qanṭarah, Egypt	B7	60
Al-Qaryah ash-Sharqīyah, Libya	B3	56
Al-Qaṣr, Egypt	E5	60
Al-Qaṣr, Jord.	F5	50
Al-Qaṭīf, Sau. Ar.	A7	47
Al-Qaṭrānah, Jord.	F6	50
Al-Qaṭrūn, Libya	D3	56
Al-Qayṣūmah, Sau. Ar.	G9	48
Al-Qiṣfah, Jord.	C5	50
Al-Quds see Yerushalayim, Isr.	E4	50
Al-Qunayṭirah, Syria	B5	50
Al-Qunfudhah, Sau. Ar.	E2	47
Al-Qurnah, Iraq	F9	48
Al-Quṣaymah, Egypt	G2	50
Al-Quṣayr, Egypt	D8	60
Al-Qūṣīyah, Egypt	D6	60
Al-Quṭayfah, Syria	A7	50
Al-Quṭaynah, Sud.	J7	60
Al-Quwayʻīyah, Sau. Ar.	B4	47
Al-Quwaysī, Sud.	K8	60
Alsace, hist. reg., Fr.	D14	14
Alsask, Sask., Can.	G5	104
Alsea, Or., U.S.	F2	122
Alsea, stm., Or., U.S.	F2	122
Alsek, stm., N.A.	G25	100
Alsen, N.D., U.S.	C9	118
Alsfeld, Ger.	E9	10
Alsina, Arg.	G9	80
Alstead, stm., Sask., Can.	C7	104
Alsunga, Lat.	E4	22
Alta, Ia., U.S.	I12	118
Alta Gracia, Arg.	F6	80
Altagracia, Nic.	F9	92
Altagracia, Ven.	B7	84
Altagracia de Orituco, Ven.	C9	84
Altai, mts., Asia	H16	26
Altaj (Jesönbulag), Mong.	B6	30
Altaj, state, Russia	G15	26
Altamaha, stm., Ga., U.S.	H5	112
Altamira, Braz.	D8	76
Altamira, Chile	C4	80
Altamira, C.R.	G10	92
Altamont, Il., U.S.	C8	114
Altamont, Ks., U.S.	N12	118
Altamont, Or., U.S.	H4	122
Altamont, Tn., U.S.	G11	114
Altamura, Italy	I11	18
Altamura, Isla, i., Mex.	E5	90
Altar, Mex.	B4	90
Altar, stm., Mex.	B4	90
Altar, Desierto de, des., Mex.	B3	90
Altar de Los Sacrificios, hist., Guat.	I14	90
Altario, Alta., Can.	G4	104
Altata, Mex.	E6	90
Alta Verapaz, dept., Guat.	B4	92
Alta Vista, Ks., U.S.	M11	118
Altavista, Va., U.S.	B7	112
Altay, China	B4	30
Altay see Altaj, state, Russia	G15	26
Altdorf, Switz.	E10	13
Altenburg, Ger.	E12	10
Altha, Fl., U.S.	I1	112
Altheimer, Ar., U.S.	H5	114
Althofen, Aus.	I14	10
Altinópolis, Braz.	F5	79
Altiplano, plat., S.A.	H7	82
Altkirch, Fr.	E14	14
Altmark, reg., Ger.	C11	10
Altmühl, stm., Ger.	F10	10
Alto, Tx., U.S.	H11	116
Alto Araguaia, Braz.	D2	79
Alto Cedro, Cuba	D7	94
Alto Coité, Braz.	C1	79
Alto del Carmen, Chile	E3	80
Alto do Rio Doce, Braz.	F7	79
Alto Garças, Braz.	D2	79
Altomünster, Ger.	G11	10
Alton, Il., U.S.	D6	114
Alton, Ia., U.S.	I11	118
Alton, Ks., U.S.	L9	118
Alton, Mo., U.S.	F5	114
Alton, N.H., U.S.	D15	108
Altona, Man., Can.	I17	104
Altoona, Al., U.S.	H10	114
Altoona, Ia., U.S.	I2	110
Altoona, Ks., U.S.	N12	118
Altoona, Pa., U.S.	G8	108
Altoona, Wi., U.S.	F4	110
Alto Paraguai, Braz.	F13	82
Alto Paraguay, dept., Para.	I12	82
Alto Paraíso de Goiás, Braz.	C5	79
Alto Paraná, dept., Para.	C11	80
Alto Parnaíba, Braz.	E9	76
Alto Purús, stm., Peru	D6	82
Alto Río Senguer, Arg.	F2	78
Alto Sucuriú, Braz.	E2	79
Altötting, Ger.	G12	10
Alto Yurua, stm., Peru	C5	82
Altstätten, Switz.	D12	13
Altuchovo, Russia	I17	22
Altunoluk, Tur.	J10	20
Altun Shan, mts., China	D4	30
Alturas, Ca., U.S.	C5	124
Altus, Ar., U.S.	G3	114
Altus, Ok., U.S.	E7	116
Al-ʻUbaylah, Sau. Ar.	D7	47
Al-Ubayyiḍ, Sud.	K6	60
Al-ʻUdaysāt, Egypt	E7	60
Al-Uḍayyah, Sud.	K5	60
Aluk, Sud.	M4	60
Alūksne, Lat.	D10	22
Al-ʻUlā, Sau. Ar.	H4	48
Aluminé, Lago, l., Arg.	J3	80
Alum Rock, Ca., U.S.	G4	124
Al-ʻUqaylah, Libya	B4	56
Al-ʻUqayr, Sau. Ar.	B7	47
Al-Uqṣur (Luxor), Egypt	E7	60
Al-ʻUwaynāt, Libya	C3	56
Al-ʻUyaynah, Sau. Ar.	B5	47
Alva, Ok., U.S.	C8	116
Alvarado, Mex.	H12	90
Alvarado, Tx., U.S.	G9	116
Alvarães, Braz.	I10	84
Álvaro Obregón, Presa, res., Mex.	D5	90
Alvdal, Nor.	J12	6
Alvear, Arg.	E10	80
Alvernia, Mount, hill, Bah.	B7	94
Alvesta, Swe.	M14	6
Alvin, Tx., U.S.	J11	116
Alvinópolis, Braz.	F7	79
Alvito, Port.	G4	16
Älvkarleby, Swe.	K15	6
Alvord, Tx., U.S.	F9	116
Älvros, Swe.	J14	6
Älvsborgs Län, co., Swe.	L13	6
Al-Wajh, Sau. Ar.	H4	48
Al-Wakrah, Qatar	I11	48
Alwar, India	G7	44
Al-Wāsiṭah, Egypt	C6	60
Al-Wazz, Sud.	J6	60
Alxa Zuoqi, China	D8	30
Alytus, Lith.	G7	22
Alzamaj, Russia	F11	28
Alzira (Alcira), Spain	F11	16
Amacuro, stm., S.A.	C12	84
Amadeus, Lake, l., Austl.	D6	68
Amadjuak Lake, l., N.W. Ter., Can.	C18	96
Amagansett, N.Y., U.S.	G14	108
Amagasaki, Japan	M10	36
Amagi, Japan	N5	36
Amagunze, Nig.	H13	64
Amahai, Indon.	F8	38
Amaichá del Valle, Arg.	D6	80
Amajac, stm., Mex.	G10	90
Amaka, stm., Nic.	C9	92
Amakusa-shotō, is., Japan	O5	36
Amakuso-Shimo-shima, i., Japan	O5	36
Åmål, Swe.	L13	6
Amalfi, Col.	D5	84
Amalfi, Italy	I9	18
Amaliás, Grc.	L5	20
Amambaí, Braz.	G1	79
Amambaí, stm., Braz.	G1	79
Amambay, dept., Para.	B10	80
Amami-Ō-shima, i., Japan	s4	37b
Amami-shotō, is., Japan	t3	37b
Amana, Ia., U.S.	I4	110
Amanã, stm., Braz.	J14	84
Amana, stm., Ven.	J13	94
Amanã, Lago, l., Braz.	I10	84
Amanda, Oh., U.S.	H4	108
Amapá, Braz.	C8	76
Amapala, Hond.	D7	92
Amapala, Punta de, c., El Sal.	D7	92
Amarante, Braz.	E10	76
Amaranth, Man., Can.	H16	104
Amarapura, Mya.	D4	40
ʻAmārat Abū Sinn, Sud.	J8	60
Amares, Port.	D3	16
Amargosa, Braz.	B9	79
Amargosa, stm., U.S.	H9	124
Amargosa Range, mts., Ca., U.S.	H9	124
Amarillo, Tx., U.S.	D5	116
ʻAmar Jadīd, Sud.	J3	60
Amarkantak, India	G3	30
Amarnāth, India	C2	46
Amasa, Mi., U.S.	D7	110
Amasya, Tur.	G15	4
Amataurá, Braz.	I8	84
Amatikulu, S. Afr.	G10	66
Amatique, Bahía de, b., N.A.	B6	92
Amatitlán, Guat.	C4	92
Amatitlán, Lago de, l., Guat.	C4	92
Amazon (Solimões) (Amazonas), stm., S.A.	D7	76
Amazonas, state, Braz.	H10	84
Amazonas, dept., Col.	H7	84
Amazonas, dept., Peru	A2	82
Amazonas, ter., Ven.	F9	84
Ambakaka, Madag.	t22	67b
Ambāla, India	E7	44
Ambalanjanakomby, Madag.	p22	67b
Ambalavao, Madag.	r22	67b
Amba Maryam, Eth.	L10	60
Ambanja, Madag.	n23	67b
Ambar, Peru	D3	82
Ambararata, Madag.	o23	67b
Ambarčik, Russia	D24	28
Ambargasta, Salinas de, pl., Arg.	E6	80
Ambarnyj, Russia	I23	6
Ambato, Ec.	H3	84
Ambatofinandrahana, Madag.	r22	67b
Ambatolampy, Madag.	q22	67b
Ambatondrazaka, Madag.	p23	67b
Ámbelos, Ákra, c., Grc.	J7	20
Ambenja, Madag.	o22	67b
Amberg, Ger.	F11	10
Amberg, Wi., U.S.	E8	110
Ambergris Cay, i., Belize	H16	90
Ambérieu-en-Bugey, Fr.	G12	14
Ambert, Fr.	G10	14
Ambevongo, Madag.	o22	67b
Ambikāpur, India	I10	44
Ambilobe, Madag.	n23	67b
Ambinanindrano, Madag.	r23	67b
Ambivy, Madag.	r21	67b
Ambo, Peru	D3	82
Amboahangy, Madag.	t22	67b
Ambodifototra, Madag.	p23	67b
Ambodiriana, Madag.	p23	67b
Ambohidray, Madag.	q23	67b
Ambohimahamasina, Madag.	r22	67b
Amboise, Fr.	E7	14
Ambon, Indon.	F8	38
Ambondro, Madag.	t21	67b
Ambositra, Madag.	r22	67b
Ambovombe, Madag.	t22	67b
Amboy, Il., U.S.	I6	110
Amboy, Mn., U.S.	G1	110
Ambre, Cap d', c., Madag.	m23	67b
Ambridge, Pa., U.S.	G6	108
Ambrières, Fr.	D6	14
Ambriz, Ang.	C2	58
Ambrose, N.D., U.S.	C4	118
Ambrosia Lake, N.M., U.S.	I9	120
Ambunti, Pap. N. Gui.	F11	38
Amchitka Island, i., Ak., U.S.	k4	101a
ʻAmd, Yemen	G6	47
Amderma, Russia	D10	26
Amdo, China	E5	30
Ameagle, W.V., U.S.	B5	112
Ameca, Mex.	G7	90
Ameca, stm., Mex.	G7	90
Amecameca [de Juárez], Mex.	H10	90
Ameghino, Arg.	H7	80
Ameland, i., Neth.	B8	12
Amelia, Italy	G7	18
Amelia Court House, Va., U.S.	B9	112
Amelia Island, i., Fl., U.S.	I5	112
Āmer, India	G6	44
Americana, Braz.	G5	79
American Falls, Id., U.S.	H13	122
American Falls Reservoir, res., Id., U.S.	H13	122
American Fork, Ut., U.S.	D5	120
American Highland, plat., Ant.	C5	73
American Samoa, dep., Oc.	J22	126
Americus, Ga., U.S.	G2	112
Americus, Ks., U.S.	M11	118
Amersfoort, Neth.	D7	12
Amersfoort, S. Afr.	F9	66
Amery, Man., Can.	B20	104
Amery, Wi., U.S.	E3	110
Amery Ice Shelf, Ant.	B5	73
Ames, Ia., U.S.	H2	110
Amesbury, Ma., U.S.	E16	108
Amet Sound, strt., N.S., Can.	G10	106
Ámfissa, Grc.	K6	20
Amga, Russia	E18	28
Amga, stm., Russia	E18	28
Amguema, stm., Russia	D27	28
Amguid, Alg.	G13	62
Amgun', stm., Russia	G19	28
Amherst, N.S., Can.	G9	106
Amherst, Ma., U.S.	E14	108
Amherst, N.Y., U.S.	E8	108
Amherst, Oh., U.S.	F4	108
Amherst, Tx., U.S.	E4	116
Amherst, Va., U.S.	B7	112
Amherst, Wi., U.S.	F6	110
Amherstburg, Ont., Can.	H12	110
Amherstdale, W.V., U.S.	J5	108
Amherstview, Ont., Can.	F19	110
Amidon, N.D., U.S.	E4	118
Amiens, Fr.	C9	14
Amili, China	F16	44
Amīndīvi Islands, is., India	G2	46
Aminga, Arg.	E5	80
Aminuis, Nmb.	D4	66
Amirante Islands, is., Sey.	C10	58
Amisk, Alta., Can.	E23	102
Amisk Lake, l., Sask., Can.	D12	104
Amistad, Parque Internacional de la, C.R.	H11	92
Amistad Reservoir (Presa de la Amistad), res., N.A.	J5	116
Amite, La., U.S.	L6	114
Amite, stm., La., U.S.	L6	114
Amity, Ar., U.S.	H3	114
Amity, Or., U.S.	E2	122
Amizmiz, Mor.	E6	62
ʻAmm-Adām, Sud.	I9	60
ʻAmmān, Jord.	E5	50
Ammarnäs, Swe.	I15	6
Ammon, Id., U.S.	G14	122
Ammonoosuc, stm., N.H., U.S.	C15	108
Amne Machin Shan see A'nyêmaqên Shan, mts., China	D6	30
Amnicon, stm., Wi., U.S.	D4	110
Amnok-kang (Yalu), stm., Asia	C13	32
Amo, stm., Asia	G13	44
Āmol, Iran	C12	48
Amolar, Braz.	H13	82
Amorgós, i., Grc.	M9	20
Amorinópolis, Braz.	D3	79
Amory, Ms., U.S.	I8	114
Amoy see Xiamen, China	K7	34
Ampanihy, Madag.	t21	67b
Amparihy, Madag.	s22	67b
Amparo, Braz.	G5	79
Ampato, Nevado, mtn., Peru	F6	82
Amper, Nig.	G14	64
Ampombiantambo, Madag.	n23	67b
Amposta, Spain	E12	16
Ampotaka, Madag.	t21	67b
Amqui, Que., Can.	D6	106
ʻAmrān, Yemen	G3	47
Amrāvati, India	J7	44
Amreli, India	J4	44
Amritsar, India	E6	44
Amroha, India	F8	44
Amsel, Alg.	I13	62
Åmsele, Swe.	I16	6
Amsteg, Switz.	E10	13
Amsterdam, Neth.	D6	12
Amsterdam, S. Afr.	F10	66
Amsterdam, N.Y., U.S.	E12	108
Amsterdam, Île, i., F.S.A.T.	L11	126
Amsterdam-Rijnkanaal, Neth.	E7	12
Amstetten, Aus.	G14	10
Am Timan, Chad	F5	56
Amubri, C.R.	H12	92
Amu-Darja, Turk.	C18	48
Amu Darya (Amudarja), stm., Asia	B2	44
Amundsen Gulf, b., N.W. Ter., Can.	B8	96
Amundsen-Scott, sci., Ant.	D10	73
Amundsen Sea, Ant.	C11	73
Amuntai, Indon.	F6	38
Amur (Heilong), stm., Asia	B14	30
Amurrio, Spain	I3	14
Amuzhong, China	E11	44
Amvrakikós Kólpos, b., Grc.	K4	20
Anabar, stm., Russia	C14	28
Anaco, Ven.	C10	84
Anacoco, La., U.S.	K3	114
Anaconda, Mt., U.S.	D13	122
Anacortes, Wa., U.S.	B3	122
Anadarko, Ok., U.S.	D8	116
Anadyr', Russia	E27	28
Anadyr', stm., Russia	E26	28
Anadyrskij zaliv, b., Russia	E28	28
Anadyrskoje ploskogorje, plat., Russia	D26	28
Anagni, Italy	H8	18
ʻĀnah, Iraq	D6	48
Anaheim, Ca., U.S.	K8	124
Anahim Lake, B.C., Can.	E9	102
Anáhuac, Mex.	D9	90
Anáhuac, Mex.	C6	90
Anahuac, Tx., U.S.	J12	116
Ānai Mudi, mtn., India	G4	46
Analalava, Madag.	o22	67b
Analapatsy, Madag.	t22	67b
Anamã, Braz.	I12	84
Anamã, Lago, l., Braz.	I12	84
Anama Bay, Man., Can.	G16	104
Ana María, Golfo de, b., Cuba	D5	94
Anambas, Kepulauan, is., Indon.	M9	40
Anamoose, N.D., U.S.	D7	118
Anamosa, Ia., U.S.	H4	110
Anamu, stm., Braz.	G14	84
Anamur, Tur.	C2	48
Ānand, India	I5	44
Ananea, Peru	F7	82
Anantapur, India	E4	46
Anantnāg (Islāmābād), India	D6	44
Anan'yiv, Ukr.	B13	20
Anápolis, Braz.	D4	79
Anār, Iran	F13	48
Anārak, Iran	E12	48
Anār Darreh, Afg.	E16	48
Anastácio, Braz.	F1	79
Anastasia Island, i., Fl., U.S.	J5	112
ʻAnātā, Isr. Occ.	E4	50
Anatolikí Makedhonía kaí Thráki, prov, Grc.	H8	20
Añatuya, Arg.	E7	80
Anauá, stm., Braz.	G12	84
Anaurilândia, Braz.	G2	79
Anavilhanas, Arquipélago das, is., Braz.	I12	84
Anawalt, W.V., U.S.	B5	112
Anbanjing, China	C6	40
Anbu, China	L5	34
Anbyŏn, N. Kor.	D15	32
Ancash, dept., Peru	C3	82
Ancaster, Ont., Can.	G15	110
Ancasti, Arg.	E6	80
Ancasti, Sierra de, mts., Arg.	E6	80
Anchang, China	E9	34
Anchorage, Ak., U.S.	F20	100
Anchorena, Arg.	H6	80
Anchor Point, Ak., U.S.	G19	100
Anci (Langfang), China	D4	32
Ancien Goubéré, Cen. Afr. Rep.	O4	60
Anciferovo, Russia	C17	22
Ancón, Peru	D3	82
Ancona, Italy	F8	18
Ancón de Sardinas, Bahía de, b., S.A.	G3	84
Ancoraimes, Bol.	F7	82
Ancud, Chile	E2	78
Ancud, Golfo de, b., Chile	E2	78
Anda, China	B12	30
Andacollo, Arg.	I3	80
Andacollo, Chile	F3	80
Andahuaylas, Peru	E5	82
Andalgalá, Arg.	D5	80
Åndalsnes, Nor.	J10	6
Andalucía, prov., Spain	H7	16
Andalucía, hist. reg., Spain	H7	16
Andalusia, Al., U.S.	K10	114
Andaman Islands, is., India	H2	40
Andaman Sea, Asia	I3	40
Andamarca, Bol.	H8	82
Andamarca, Peru	D4	82
Andamooka, Austl.	H2	70
Andapa, Madag.	o23	67b
Andaraí, Braz.	B8	79
Andaray, Peru	F5	82
Andeer, Switz.	E11	13
Andelot, Fr.	D12	14
Andenes, Nor.	G15	6
Andéranboukane, Mali	D11	64
Andermatt, Switz.	E10	13
Andernach, Ger.	E7	10
Anderson, Al., U.S.	H9	114
Anderson, Ca., U.S.	D3	124
Anderson, In., U.S.	B11	114
Anderson, Mo., U.S.	F2	114
Anderson, S.C., U.S.	E4	112
Anderson, Tx., U.S.	I11	116
Anderson, stm., N.W. Ter., Can.	B30	100
Anderson Dam, Id., U.S.	G10	122
Anderson Lake, l., B.C., Can.	G12	102
Andes, Col.	E5	84
Andes, mts., S.A.	G8	74
Andevoranto, Madag.	q23	67b
Andhra Pradesh, state, India	D5	46
Andikíthira, i., Grc.	N7	20
Andimákhia, Grc.	M11	20
Andīmeshk, Iran	E10	48
Andirá, stm., Braz.	I14	84

Andi-Arys

Name	Map Ref.	Page
Andirá, Riozinho do, stm., Braz.	C8	82
Andirlang, China	B10	44
Ándissa, Grc.	J9	20
Andižan, Uzb.	I12	26
Andkhvoy, Afg.	B1	44
Andoas, Peru	I4	84
Andong, S. Kor.	G16	32
Andorra, And.	C13	16
Andorra, ctry., Eur.	G8	4
Andover, Me., U.S.	C16	108
Andover, Ma., U.S.	E15	108
Andover, N.Y., U.S.	E9	108
Andover, Oh., U.S.	F6	108
Andover, S.D., U.S.	F10	118
Andøya, i., Nor.	G14	6
Andradina, Braz.	F3	79
Andranopasy, Madag.	r20	67b
Andranovory, Madag.	s21	67b
Andreanof Islands, is., Ak., U.S.	J6	100
Andreapol', Russia	E15	22
Andrejevo, Russia	F24	22
Andrew, Alta., Can.	D22	102
Andrews, In., U.S.	B11	114
Andrews, N.C., U.S.	D3	112
Andrews, S.C., U.S.	F7	112
Andrews, Tx., U.S.	G4	116
Andria, Italy	H11	18
Andriamena, Madag.	p22	67b
Andriandampy, Madag.	s21	67b
Andrijevica, Yugo.	G3	20
Androka, Madag.	t21	67b
Ándros, Grc.	L8	20
Andros, i., Bah.	B6	94
Ándros, i., Grc.	L8	20
Androscoggin, stm., Me., U.S.	C16	108
Andros Town, Bah.	B6	94
Āndrott Island, i., India	G2	46
Andrychów, Pol.	F19	10
Andújar, Spain	G7	16
Anécho, Togo	H10	64
Anegada, i., Br. Vir. Is.	E12	94
Anegada Passage, strt., N.A.	E13	94
Anegam, Az., U.S.	L4	120
Añelo, Arg.	J4	80
Aneroid, Sask., Can.	I7	104
Aneta, N.D., U.S.	D10	118
Aneto, Pico de, mtn., Spain	C12	16
Anfeng, China	B9	34
Anfeng, China	C9	34
Anfengqiao, China	I7	34
Anfu, China	H3	34
Angamos, Punta, c., Chile	B3	80
Ang'angxi, China	B11	30
Angao, China	B1	34
Angara, stm., Russia	F17	26
Angara-Débou, Benin	F11	64
Angarbaka, Sud.	M3	60
Angarsk, Russia	G12	28
Angastaco, Arg.	C5	80
Angatuba, Braz.	G4	79
Ángel, Salto (Angel Falls), wtfl, Ven.	E11	84
Ángel de la Guarda, Isla, i., Mex.	C3	90
Angeles, Phil.	n19	39b
Angel Falls see Ángel, Salto, wtfl, Ven.	E11	84
Angelina, stm., Tx., U.S.	K2	114
Angels Camp, Ca., U.S.	F5	124
Angereb, stm., Afr.	K9	60
Angermünde, Ger.	B14	10
Angers, Fr.	E6	14
Angerville, Fr.	D9	14
Angical, Braz.	B6	79
Angicos, Braz.	E11	76
Angier, N.C., U.S.	D8	112
Angijak Island, i., N.W. Ter., Can.	C20	96
Angikuni Lake, l., N.W. Ter., Can.	D13	96
Angkor Wat, hist., Camb.	H7	40
Ângk Tasaôm, Camb.	I8	40
Anglais, Baie des, b., Que., Can.	C5	106
Angle Inlet, Mn., U.S.	B12	118
Anglesey, i., Wales, U.K.	H9	8
Angleton, Tx., U.S.	J11	116
Angling, stm., Man., Can.	B21	104
Angling Lake, l., Man., Can.	E21	104
Angmagssalik, Grnld.	C16	86
Angoche, Moz.	E7	58
Angoche, Ilha, i., Moz.	E7	58
Angol, Chile	I2	80
Angola, In., U.S.	A12	114
Angola, N.Y., U.S.	E7	108
Angola, ctry., Afr.	D3	58
Angoon, Ak., U.S.	H27	100
Angora see Ankara, Tur.	B2	48
Angoram, Pap. N. Gui.	F11	38
Angostura, Mex.	E5	90
Angostura, Presa de la, res., Mex.	I13	90
Angoulême, Fr.	G7	14
Angoumois, hist. reg., Fr.	G6	14
Angra dos Reis, Braz.	G6	79
Angren, Uzb.	I12	26
Angualasto, Arg.	F4	80
Anguciana, Cerro, mtn., C.R.	I11	92
Anguilla, Ms., U.S.	J6	114
Anguilla, dep., N.A.	E13	94
Anguilla Cays, is., Bah.	C5	94
Anguille, Cape, c., Newf., Can.	E14	106
Anguo, China	E3	32
Angus, Ont., Can.	F16	110
Angusville, Man., Can.	H13	104
Angwin, Ca., U.S.	F3	124
Anhai, China	K7	34
Anhui (Anhwei), prov., China	E10	30
Aniak, Ak., U.S.	F15	100
Aniche, Fr.	H3	12
Anicuns, Braz.	D4	79
Anié, Togo	H10	64
Animas, N.M., U.S.	M8	120
Animas, stm., U.S.	H9	120
Animas Peak, mtn., N.M., U.S.	M8	120
Anina, Rom.	D5	20
Anita, Ia., U.S.	J13	118
Aniva, zaliv, b., Russia	H20	28
Anivorano, Madag.	q23	67b
Anjangaon, India	B4	46
Anjār, India	I4	44
'Anjar, Leb.	A5	50
Anji, China	E8	34
Anjiabe, Madag.	n23	67b
Anjiang, China	C5	32
Anjou, hist. reg., Fr.	E6	14
Anju, N. Kor.	D13	32
Ankang, China	E8	30
Ankara, Tur.	B2	48
Ankaratra, mts., Madag.	q22	67b
Ankarimbelo, Madag.	s22	67b
Ankasakasa, Madag.	p21	67b
Ankavandra, Madag.	q21	67b
Ankazoabo, Madag.	s21	67b
Ankazobe, Madag.	q22	67b
Ankazomiriotra, Madag.	q22	67b
Ankeny, Ia., U.S.	I2	110
Ankilimalinika, Madag.	s20	67b
Ankisabe, Madag.	q22	67b
Ankleshwar, India	B2	46
Ankober, Eth.	G8	56
Ankou, China	J2	34
An'kovo, Russia	E22	22
Ankpa, Nig.	H13	64
Anliu, China	L4	34
Anlu, China	D2	34
Ann, Cape, c., Ant.	B4	73
Anna, Il., U.S.	E7	114
Anna, Tx., U.S.	F10	116
Anna, Lake, res., Va., U.S.	A9	112
Annaba (Bône), Alg.	B14	62
Annaberg-Buchholz, Ger.	E13	10
An-Nabk, Syria	D4	48
An-Nafī, Sau. Ar.	B3	47
An-Nafūd, des., Sau. Ar.	G6	48
An-Najaf, Iraq	F8	48
An-Nakhl, Egypt	C7	60
Annamitique, Chaîne, mts., Asia	F9	40
Annandale, Austl.	C8	70
Annandale, Mn., U.S.	E1	110
Annapolis, Md., U.S.	I10	108
Annapolis Basin, b., N.S., Can.	H8	106
Annapolis Royal, N.S., Can.	H8	106
Annapūrṇa, mtn., Nepal	F10	44
Ann Arbor, Mi., U.S.	H12	110
Anna Regina, Guy.	D13	84
An-Nāṣirīyah, Iraq	F9	48
An-Nāṣirīyah, Syria	A7	50
An-Nawfalāb, Sud.	J7	60
Annecy, Fr.	G13	14
Annemasse, Fr.	F13	14
Annenskij Most, Russia	A20	22
Annette, Ak., U.S.	I29	100
An Nhon, Viet.	H10	40
Anniston, Al., U.S.	I11	114
Annobón, i., Eq. Gui.	B1	58
Annonay, Fr.	G11	14
An-Nuhūd, Sud.	K5	60
An-Nu'mānīyah, Iraq	E8	48
Annville, Ky., U.S.	B3	112
Annville, Pa., U.S.	G10	108
Anoka, Mn., U.S.	E2	110
Anopino, Russia	F23	22
Anori, Braz.	I12	84
Anorí, Col.	D5	84
Anping, China	D4	32
Anpu, China	D11	40
Anqing, China	E6	34
Anqiu, China	G7	32
Ansbach, Ger.	F10	10
Anse-d'Hainault, Haiti	E7	94
Anselmo, Ne., U.S.	J8	118
Anserma, Col.	E5	84
Anshan, China	B10	32
Anshun, China	A8	40
Ansina, Ur.	F11	80
Ansley, Ne., U.S.	J8	118
Anson, Tx., U.S.	G7	116
Ansŏng, S. Kor.	F15	32
Ansongo, Mali	D10	64
Ansonville, N.C., U.S.	D6	112
Ansted, W.V., U.S.	I5	108
Anta, Peru	E5	82
Antabamba, Peru	F5	82
Antalaha, Madag.	o24	67b
Antalivtsi, Ukr.	G22	10
Antalya, Tur.	H14	4
Antalya Körfezi, b., Tur.	H14	4
Antambohobe, Madag.	s22	67b
Antanambao Manampotsy, Madag.	q23	67b
Antananarivo, Madag.	q22	67b
Antanetibe, Madag.	q22	67b
Antanifotsy, Madag.	q22	67b
Antarctica	D5	73
Antarctic Peninsula, pen., Ant.	B12	73
Antas, Rio das, stm., Braz.	E13	80
Antelope Island, i., Ut., U.S.	D4	120
Antelope Mine, Zimb.	C9	66
Antelope Peak, mtn., Nv., U.S.	C11	124
Antequera, Para.	C10	80
Antequera, Spain	H7	16
Antevamena, Madag.	r21	67b
Anthon, Ia., U.S.	I12	118
Anthony, Fl., U.S.	J4	112
Anthony, Ks., U.S.	N9	118
Anthony, N.M., U.S.	L10	120
Anthony, Tx., U.S.	M10	120
Anti-Atlas, mts., Mor.	E6	62
Antibes, Fr.	I14	14
Anticosti, Île d', i., Que., Can.	C10	106
Antigo, Wi., U.S.	E6	110
Antigonish, N.S., Can.	G12	106
Antigua, i., Antig.	F14	94
Antigua and Barbuda, ctry., N.A.	F14	94
Antigua Guatemala, Guat.	C4	92
Antiguo Morelos, Mex.	F10	90
Anti-Lebanon see Sharqī, Al-Jabal ash-, mts., Asia	A6	50
Antilla, Arg.	D6	80
Antilla, Cuba	D7	94
Antimony, Ut., U.S.	F5	120
Antioch see Hatay, Tur.	C4	48
Antioch, Il., U.S.	H7	110
Antioquia, Col.	D5	84
Antioquia, dept., Col.	D5	84
Antipodes Islands, is., N.Z.	M21	126
Antizana, vol., Ec.	H3	84
Antler, stm., N.A.	I13	104
Antlers, Ok., U.S.	E11	116
Antofagasta, Chile	B3	80
Antofagasta, prov., Chile	B4	80
Antofagasta de la Sierra, Arg.	D5	80
Antofalla, Salar de, pl., Arg.	C5	80
Antofalla, Volcán, vol., Arg.	C5	80
Antón, Pan.	C2	84
Anton, Tx., U.S.	F4	116
Anton Chico, N.M., U.S.	I11	120
Antongila, Helodrano, b., Madag.	o23	67b
Antonina, Braz.	C14	80
Antonio Amaro, Mex.	E7	90
Antônio Prado, Braz.	E13	80
Antonito, Co., U.S.	G10	120
Antón Lizardo, Punta, c., Mex.	H12	90
Antopol', Bela.	I7	22
Antou, China	I7	34
Antrain, Fr.	D5	14
Antrim, N. Ire., U.K.	G7	8
Antrodoco, Italy	G8	18
Antropovo, Russia	C26	22
Antsalova, Madag.	q21	67b
Antsenavolo, Madag.	r23	67b
Antsiafabositra, Madag.	p22	67b
Antsirabe, Madag.	o23	67b
Antsirabe, Madag.	q22	67b
Antsiranana, Madag.	n23	67b
Antsla, Est.	D9	22
Antsohihy, Madag.	o22	67b
Antuševo, Russia	B20	22
Antwerp see Antwerpen, Bel.	F5	12
Antwerp, Oh., U.S.	F2	108
Antwerpen (Anvers), Bel.	F5	12
Antwerpen, prov., Bel.	F6	12
Anugul, India	B8	46
Anuradhapura, Sri L.	H6	46
Anvers (Antwerpen), Bel.	F5	12
Anvers Island, i., Ant.	B12	73
Anvik, Ak., U.S.	E14	100
Anvil Range, mts., Yukon, Can.	E28	100
Anxi, China	C6	30
Anxi, China	J7	34
Anxin, China	E3	32
Anyama, C. Iv.	I7	64
Anyang, China	G2	32
A'nyêmaqên Shan, mts., China	D6	30
Anyi, China	G4	34
Anykščiai, Lith.	F8	22
Anyox, B.C., Can.	B5	102
Anyuan, China	H2	34
Anzac, Alta., Can.	B3	104
Anzaldo, Bol.	G9	82
Anžero-Sudžensk, Russia	F15	26
Anzhen, China	D9	34
Anzhou, China	E3	32
Anzin, Fr.	B10	14
Anzio, Italy	H7	18
Anzoátegui, state, Ven.	C10	84
Anžu, ostrova, is., Russia	B20	28
Aoga-shima, i., Japan	E14	30
Aohan Qi (Xinhui), China	A7	32
Aoji, N. Kor.	A18	32
Aojiang, China	H9	34
Aojiao, China	L6	34
Aomori, Japan	G15	36
Aóös (Vijosë), stm., Eur.	J4	20
Aôral, Phnum, mtn., Camb.	H8	40
Aosta, Italy	D2	18
Aotou, China	M3	34
Aouderas, Niger	C14	64
Aouk, Bahr, stm., Afr.	G5	56
Aoukâr, reg., Maur.	B5	64
Aourou, Mali	D4	64
Aozou, Chad	D4	56
Apa, stm., S.A.	B10	80
Apache, Ok., U.S.	E8	116
Apache Junction, Az., U.S.	K5	120
Apache Peak, mtn., Az., U.S.	M6	120
Apalachicola, Fl., U.S.	J2	112
Apalachicola, stm., Fl., U.S.	I1	112
Apalachicola Bay, b., Fl., U.S.	J1	112
Apanas, Laguna de, res., Nic.	D9	92
Apaporis, stm., S.A.	H7	84
Aparados da Serra, Parque Nacional de, Braz.	E13	80
Aparri, Phil.	I19	39b
Apaseo El Grande, Mex.	G9	90
Apatin, Yugo.	D2	20
Apatity, Russia	D4	26
Apatzingán de la Constitución, Mex.	H8	90
Apaxtla de Castrejón, Mex.	H10	90
Apayacu, stm., Peru	I6	84
Ape, Lat.	D9	22
Apeganau Lake, l., Man., Can.	C15	104
Apeldoorn, Neth.	D8	12
Apennines see Appennino, mts., Italy	F7	18
Apex, N.C., U.S.	D8	112
Apex Mountain, mtn., Yukon, Can.	E25	100
Api, mtn., Nepal	F9	44
Apía, Col.	E5	84
Apia, W. Sam.	G1	2
Apiacá, stm., Braz.	C13	82
Apiacás, Serra dos, plat., Braz.	D13	82
Apiaí, Braz.	C14	80
Apiaú, stm., Braz.	F12	84
Apizaco, Mex.	H10	90
Apizolaya, Mex.	E8	90
Aplahoué, Benin	H10	64
Aplao, Peru	G5	82
Apo, Mount, mtn., Phil.	D8	38
Apolakkiá, Grc.	M11	20
Apolda, Ger.	D11	10
Apolinario Saravia, Arg.	C6	80
Apollo, Pa., U.S.	G7	108
Apolo, Bol.	F7	82
Apón, stm., Ven.	B6	84
Aponguao, stm., Ven.	E12	84
Apopa, El Sal.	D5	92
Aporé, Braz.	E2	79
Aporé, stm., Braz.	E3	79
Apostle Islands, is., Wi., U.S.	D5	110
Apóstoles, Arg.	D11	80
Apostolove, Ukr.	H4	26
Appalachia, Va., U.S.	C4	112
Appalachian Mountains, mts., N.A.	C11	98
Appennino (Apennines), mts., Italy	F7	18
Appenzell, Switz.	D11	13
Appenzell-Ausserrhoden, state, Switz.	D11	13
Apple, stm., U.S.	H5	110
Apple, stm., Wi., U.S.	E3	110
Applegate, stm., Or., U.S.	B2	124
Appleton, Mn., U.S.	F11	118
Appleton, Wi., U.S.	F7	110
Appleton City, Mo., U.S.	D2	114
Apple Valley, Ca., U.S.	J8	124
Appling, Ga., U.S.	F4	112
Appomattox, Va., U.S.	B8	112
Appomattox, stm., Va., U.S.	B8	112
Aprelevka, Russia	F20	22
Apt, Fr.	I12	14
Apuaú, stm., Braz.	I12	84
Apucarana, Braz.	G3	79
Apure, state, Ven.	D8	84
Apure, stm., Ven.	D9	84
Apurímac, dept., Peru	E5	82
Apurímac, stm., Peru	E5	82
Apurito, Ven.	D8	84
Aqaba, Gulf of, b.	C8	60
'Aqīq, Sud.	H10	60
Aquidabã, stm., Braz.	I13	82
Aquidabán, stm., Para.	B10	80
Aquidauana, Braz.	I14	82
Aquidauana, stm., Braz.	I14	82
Aquila, Mex.	H8	90
Aquila, Switz.	E10	13
Aquiles Serdán, Mex.	C7	90
Aquiles Serdán, Mex.	E11	90
Aquilla, Tx., U.S.	H9	116
Aquin, Haiti	E8	94
Aquio, stm., Col.	F9	84
Ara, India	H11	44
Arab, Al., U.S.	H10	114
'Arab, Baḥr al-, stm., Sud.	M4	60
Arab, Shatt al-, stm., Asia	G10	48
'Arab, Wādī al-, val., Jord.	C5	50
'Arabah, Wādī al- (Ha'Arava), val., Asia	G4	50
Arabako, prov., Spain	C9	16
Arabelo, Ven.	E10	84
Arabi, La., U.S.	M6	114
Arabian Desert see Sharqīyah, Aṣ-Ṣaḥrā' ash-, des., Egypt	D7	60
Arabian Gulf see Persian Gulf, b., Asia	H11	48
Arabian Peninsula, pen., Asia	G5	24
Arabian Sea	H7	24
Araçá, stm., Braz.	G11	84
Aracaju, Braz.	F11	76
Aracataca, Col.	B5	84
Aracati, Braz.	D11	76
Araçatuba, Braz.	F3	79
Aracena, Spain	H5	16
Aracruz, Braz.	E8	79
Araçuaí, Braz.	D7	79
Araçuaí, stm., Braz.	D7	79
Arad, Rom.	C5	20
Arad, co., Rom.	C5	20
Arada, Hond.	C6	92
Arafura Sea	I17	126
Aragarças, Braz.	C2	79
Aragon, Ga., U.S.	E1	112
Aragón, prov., Spain	D10	16
Aragón, stm., Spain	C10	16
Aragua, state, Ven.	B9	84
Araguacema, Braz.	E9	76
Araguaçu, Braz.	B4	79
Aragua de Barcelona, Ven.	C10	84
Aragua de Maturín, Ven.	C11	84
Araguaia, stm., Braz.	E9	76
Araguaia, Braço Menor, stm., Braz.	B3	79
Araguainha, Braz.	D2	79
Araguao, Caño, mth., Ven.	C12	84
Araguari, Braz.	E4	79
Araguari, stm., Braz.	C8	76
Araguari, stm., Braz.	E4	79
Araguatins, Braz.	E9	76
Ârak, Alg.	H12	62
Arāk, Iran	D10	48
Arakan Yoma, mts., Mya.	E3	40
Árakhthos, stm., Grc.	J4	20
Aral Sea, Asia	H10	26
Aral'sk, Kaz.	H10	26
Aramac, Austl.	D6	70
Aramac, stm., Austl.	D6	70
Aramari, Braz.	B9	79
Aramberri, Mex.	E10	90
Arampampa, Bol.	G8	82
Aramtalla, Sud.	N5	60
Ārān, Iran	D11	48
Aranda de Duero, Spain	D8	16
Arandas, Mex.	G8	90
Aranđelovac, Yugo.	E4	20
Arandis, Nmb.	D2	66
Arani, Bol.	G9	82
Aran Islands, is., Ire.	H4	8
Aranjuez, Spain	E8	16
Aransas, stm., Tx., U.S.	K9	116
Aransas Pass, Tx., U.S.	L9	116
Aranyaprathet, Thai.	H7	40
Arao, Japan	O5	36
Araouane, Mali	E6	54
Arapa, Laguna, l., Peru	F6	82
Arapaho, Ok., U.S.	D8	116
Arapahoe, Ne., U.S.	K8	118
Arapey, Ur.	F10	80
Arapey Chico, stm., Ur.	F10	80
Arapey Grande, stm., Ur.	F10	80
Arapiraca, Braz.	E11	76
Arapkir, Tur.	B5	48
Arapongas, Braz.	G3	79
Arapoti, Braz.	H4	79
'Ar'ar, Sau. Ar.	F6	48
'Ar'ar, Wādī, val., Asia	B11	60
Araranguá, Braz.	E14	80
Araraquara, Braz.	F4	79
Araras, Braz.	G5	79
Ararat, Arm.	B8	48
Ararat, Austl.	K5	70
Ararat, Mount see Ağrı Dağı, mtn., Tur.	B8	48
Ararirá, stm., Braz.	H10	84
Araruama, Lagoa de, b., Braz.	G7	79
Aras (Araz), stm., Asia	B10	48
Áratos, Grc.	H9	20
Aratuípe, Braz.	B9	79
Arauã, stm., Braz.	C9	82
Arauá, stm., Braz.	A11	82
Arauá, stm., Braz.	J10	84
Arauca, Col.	D7	84
Arauca, dept., Col.	D7	84
Arauca, stm., S.A.	D9	84
Araucária, Braz.	C14	80
Arauco, Chile	I2	80
Arauco, Golfo de, b., Chile	I2	80
Araújos, Braz.	E6	79
Arauquita, Col.	D7	84
Araure, Ven.	C8	84
Arāvalli Range, mts., India	H5	44
Araxá, Braz.	E5	79
Araya, Ven.	B10	84
Araya, Punta de, c., Ven.	B10	84
Araz (Aras), stm., Asia	B10	48
Arba Minch, Eth.	N9	60
Arboga, Swe.	L14	6
Arbois, Fr.	F12	14
Arboledas, Arg.	I8	80
Arboletes, Col.	C4	84
Arbon, Switz.	C11	13
Arborfield, Sask., Can.	E11	104
Arborg, Man., Can.	H17	104
Arbroath, Scot., U.K.	E11	8
Arbuckle, Ca., U.S.	E3	124
Arc, Bayou des, stm., Ar., U.S.	G5	114
Arcachon, Fr.	H5	14
Arcade, Ca., U.S.	J7	124
Arcade, N.Y., U.S.	E8	108
Arcadia, Ca., U.S.	J7	124
Arcadia, Fl., U.S.	L5	112
Arcadia, In., U.S.	B10	114
Arcadia, Ia., U.S.	I12	118
Arcadia, Ks., U.S.	N13	118
Arcadia, La., U.S.	J4	114
Arcadia, Mi., U.S.	F9	110
Arcadia, Mo., U.S.	E6	114
Arcadia, Ne., U.S.	J8	118
Arcadia, Pa., U.S.	G8	108
Arcadia, S.C., U.S.	E5	112
Arcadia, Wi., U.S.	F4	110
Arcanum, Oh., U.S.	H2	108
Arcas, Cayos, is., Mex.	G14	90
Arcata, Ca., U.S.	D1	124
Arcatao, El Sal.	C6	92
Arc Dome, mtn., Nv., U.S.	F8	124
Arcelia, Mex.	H9	90
Archangel'sk, Russia	E6	26
Archbold, Oh., U.S.	F2	108
Archdale, N.C., U.S.	D7	112
Archer, Fl., U.S.	J4	112
Archer City, Tx., U.S.	F8	116
Archidona, Spain	H7	16
Archipovka, Russia	E24	22
Arco, Id., U.S.	G12	122
Arcola, Sask., Can.	I12	104
Arcola, Il., U.S.	C8	114
Arcola, Ms., U.S.	I6	114
Arcos, Braz.	F6	79
Arcos de la Frontera, Spain	I6	16
Arcot, India	F5	46
Arcoverde, Braz.	E11	76
Arctic Bay, N.W. Ter., Can.	B15	96
Arctic Ocean	A1	86
Arctic Red, stm., N.W. Ter., Can.	C28	100
Arctic Red River, N.W. Ter., Can.	C28	100
Arctic Village, Ak., U.S.	B22	100
Arctowski, sci., Ant.	B1	73
Arcturus, Zimb.	A10	66
Arda, stm., Eur.	H9	20
Ardabīl, Iran	B10	48
Ardahan, Tur.	G16	4
Ardakān, Iran	F12	48
Ardakān, Iran	E12	48
Årdalstangen, Nor.	K10	6
Ardatov, Russia	F26	22
Ardèche, dept., Fr.	H11	14
Arden, Man., Can.	H15	104
Arden, Ca., U.S.	F4	124
Arden, Mount, mtn., Austl.	I2	70
Ardennes, dept., Fr.	C11	14
Ardennes, reg., Eur.	E5	10
Ardestān, Iran	E12	48
Ardila, stm., Eur.	G4	16
Ardill, Sask., Can.	I9	104
Ardino, Bul.	H9	20
Ardlethan, Austl.	J7	70
Ardmore, Al., U.S.	H10	114
Ardmore, Ok., U.S.	E9	116
Ardmore, Pa., U.S.	G11	108
Ardoch, Austl.	F6	70
Åre, Swe.	J13	6
Areado, Braz.	F5	79
Arecibo, P.R.	E11	94
Areguá, Para.	C10	80
Areia, Ribeirão da, stm., Braz.	C6	79
Areia Branca, Braz.	D11	76
Arena, Punta, c., Mex.	F5	90
Arena de la Ventana, Punta, c., Mex.	E5	90
Arenal, C.R.	G10	92
Arenal, Laguna de, l., C.R.	G10	92
Arenal, Volcán, vol., C.R.	G10	92
Arenápolis, Braz.	F13	82
Arenas, Cayo, i., Mex.	F14	90
Arendal, Nor.	L11	6
Arenillas, Ec.	I2	84
Arenys de Mar, Spain	D14	16
Arequipa, Peru	G6	82
Arequipa, dept., Peru	F5	82
Arequito, Arg.	G8	80
Arès, Fr.	H5	14
Arezzo, Italy	F6	18
Argadargada, Austl.	C2	70
Arganda, Spain	E8	16
Arga-Sala, stm., Russia	D13	28
Argelès-Gazost, Fr.	I7	14
Argelès-sur-Mer, Fr.	J10	14
Argenta, Italy	E6	18
Argenta, Il., U.S.	C8	114
Argentan, Fr.	D6	14
Argentat, Fr.	G8	14
Argentera, mtn., Italy	E2	18
Argentia, Newf., Can.	E20	106
Argentina, ctry., S.A.	C4	78
Argentino, Lago, l., Arg.	G2	78
Argenton-Château, Fr.	F6	14
Argenton-sur-Creuse, Fr.	F8	14
Argeș, co., Rom.	E8	20
Argeș, stm., Rom.	E9	20
Arghandāb, stm., Afg.	D2	44
Argo, Sud.	H6	60
Argolikós Kólpos, b., Grc.	L6	20
Argonia, Ks., U.S.	N10	118
Argonne, Wi., U.S.	E7	110
Argonne, reg., Fr.	C12	14
Árgos, Grc.	L6	20
Argos, In., U.S.	A10	114
Argostólion, Grc.	K4	20
Argun' (Ergun), stm., Asia	G16	28
Argyle, Mn., U.S.	C11	118
Argyle, Lake, res., Austl.	C5	68
Århus, Den.	M12	6
Ariana, Tun.	M5	18
Ariano Irpino, Italy	H10	18
Ariari, stm., Col.	F6	84
Arias, Arg.	G7	80
Ariaú, Braz.	I14	84
Aribinda, Burkina	D9	64
Arica, Chile	H6	82
Arica, Col.	I7	84
Arichat, N.S., Can.	G12	106
Arichuna, Ven.	D9	84
Arid, Cape, c., Austl.	F4	68
Ariège, dept., Fr.	J8	14
Ariguaní, stm., Col.	C6	84
Arīḥā (Jericho), Isr. Occ.	E4	50
Arīḥā, Jord.	F5	50
Arikaree, stm., U.S.	L5	118
Arima, Trin.	I14	94
Arinos, stm., Braz.	D12	82
Ario de Rosales, Mex.	H9	90
Ariogala, Lith.	F6	22
Ariporo, stm., Col.	D7	84
Aripuanã, Braz.	C11	82
Aripuanã, stm., Braz.	B11	82
Ariquemes, Braz.	C10	82
Arisa, stm., Ven.	D10	84
'Arīsh, Wādī al-, val., Egypt	B7	60
Arismendi, Ven.	C8	84
Aristazabal Island, i., B.C., Can.	E5	102
Ariton, Al., U.S.	K11	114
Arivonimamo, Madag.	q22	67b
Arizaro, Salar de, pl., Arg.	C5	80
Arizgoiti, Spain	B9	16
Arizona, Arg.	H6	80
Arizona, state, U.S.	E4	98
Arizpe, Mex.	B4	90
Arjay, Ky., U.S.	C3	112
Arjeplog, Swe.	H15	6
Arjona, Col.	B5	84
Arkadelphia, Ar., U.S.	H3	114
Arkalyk, Kaz.	G11	26
Arkansas, state, U.S.	D8	98
Arkansas, stm., U.S.	D8	98
Arkansas City, Ar., U.S.	I5	114
Arkansas City, Ks., U.S.	N10	118
Arkhangelsk see Archangel'sk, Russia	E6	26
Arklow, Ire.	I7	8
Arkoma, Ok., U.S.	G2	114
Arkona, Kap, c., Ger.	A13	10
Arkport, N.Y., U.S.	E9	108
Arktičeskij, mys, c., Russia	A11	28
Arktičeskogo Instituta, ostrova, is., Russia	B14	26
Arlbergpass, Aus.	D13	13
Arlberg-Tunnel, Aus.	D13	13
Arlee, Mt., U.S.	C11	122
Arles, Fr.	I11	14
Arli, Burkina	F10	64
Arlington, Ga., U.S.	H2	112
Arlington, Ia., U.S.	H4	110
Arlington, Ks., U.S.	N9	118
Arlington, Ky., U.S.	F7	114
Arlington, Mn., U.S.	F1	110
Arlington, Ne., U.S.	J11	118
Arlington, Oh., U.S.	G3	108
Arlington, Or., U.S.	E5	122
Arlington, S.D., U.S.	G10	118
Arlington, Tn., U.S.	G7	114
Arlington, Tx., U.S.	G9	116
Arlington, Vt., U.S.	D13	108
Arlington, Va., U.S.	I9	108
Arlington, Wa., U.S.	B3	122
Arlington Heights, Il., U.S.	H8	110
Arlit, Niger	B13	64
Arm, stm., Sask., Can.	H9	104
Arma, Ks., U.S.	N13	118
Armada, Mi., U.S.	H13	110
Armageddon see Tel Megiddo, hist., Isr.	C4	50
Armagh, N. Ire., U.K.	G7	8
Armagnac, hist. reg., Fr.	I7	14
Armant, Egypt	E7	60
Armavir, Russia	H6	26
Armazém, Braz.	E14	80
Armenia, Col.	E5	84
Armenia, ctry., Asia	I6	26
Armeniya see Armenia, ctry., Asia	I6	26
Armentières, Fr.	B9	14
Armería, Mex.	H8	90
Armero, Col.	E5	84
Armidale, Austl.	H9	70
Armijo, N.M., U.S.	I10	120
Armit Lake, l., N.W. Ter., Can.	D14	96
Armona, Ca., U.S.	H6	124
Armour, S.D., U.S.	H9	118
Armstrong, Arg.	G8	80
Armstrong, B.C., Can.	G15	102
Armstrong, Ia., U.S.	H13	118
Armstrong, Mo., U.S.	C4	114
Armstrong, Mount, mtn., Yukon, Can.	E28	100
Armstrong Station, Ont., Can.	F15	96
Arnaud, stm., Que., Can.	E18	96
Arnaudville, La., U.S.	L5	114
Arnay-le-Duc, Fr.	E11	14
Arnedo, Spain	C9	16
Årnes, Nor.	K12	6
Arnett, Ok., U.S.	C7	116
Arnhem, Neth.	E8	12
Arnhem, Cape, c., Austl.	B7	68
Arnhem Land, reg., Austl.	B6	68
Árnissa, Grc.	I5	20
Arno, stm., Italy	F5	18
Arno Bay, Austl.	I2	70
Arnold, Ca., U.S.	F5	124
Arnold, Mn., U.S.	D3	110
Arnold, Mo., U.S.	D6	114
Arnold, Ne., U.S.	J7	118
Arnolds Park, Ia., U.S.	H12	118
Arnprior, Ont., Can.	E19	110
Arnsberg, Ger.	D8	10
Arnstadt, Ger.	E10	10
Aro, stm., Ven.	D10	84
Aroa, Ven.	B8	84
Aroa, stm., Ven.	B8	84
Aroab, Nmb.	F4	66
Aroma, Sud.	J9	60
Arona, Italy	D3	18
Aroostook, stm., N.A.	F5	106
Aros, stm., Mex.	C5	90
Arosa, Switz.	E12	13
Arp, Tx., U.S.	G11	116
Arque, Bol.	G8	82
Ar-Rabad, Sau. Ar.	K8	47
Ar-Radīsīyah Baḥrī, Egypt	E7	60
Arraga, Arg.	E6	80
Ar-Rahad, Sud.	K6	60
Arraial do Cabo, Braz.	G7	79
Arraias, Braz.	B5	79
Arraias, stm., Braz.	B5	79
Arraias, stm., Braz.	A1	79
Ar-Ramādī, Iraq	E7	48
Ar-Ramthā, Jord.	C6	50
Arran, Island of, i., Scot., U.K.	F8	8
Ar-Rank, Sud.	L7	60
Ar-Raqqah, Syria	D5	48
Arras, Fr.	B9	14
Ar-Rāshidah, Egypt	E5	60
Ar-Rass, Sau. Ar.	I7	48
Ar-Rawḍah, Sau. Ar.	H6	48
Ar-Rāwuk, Yemen	G6	47
Ar-Rayyān, Qatar	I11	48
Arrecife, Spain	o27	17b
Arrecifes, Arg.	H8	80
Arrey, N.M., U.S.	L9	120
Arriaga, Mex.	I13	90
Arriba, Co., U.S.	L4	118
Ar-Rimāh, Sau. Ar.	B5	47
Ar-Riyāḍ (Riyadh), Sau. Ar.	B5	47
Arroio Grande, Braz.	G12	80
Arrojado, stm., Braz.	B6	79
Arronches, Port.	F4	16
Arrowrock Reservoir, res., Id., U.S.	G10	122
Arrowsmith, Mount, mtn., Austl.	H4	70
Arrowwood, Alta., Can.	G21	102
Arroyito, Arg.	F7	80
Arroyo de la Luz, Spain	F5	16
Arroyo Grande, Ca., U.S.	I5	124
Arroyo Hondo, N.M., U.S.	H11	120
Arroyo Seco, Arg.	G8	80
Arroyos y Esteros, Para.	C10	80
Ar-Ru'at, Sud.	K7	60
Ar-Rub' al-Khālī (Empty Quarter), des., Asia	D7	47
Ar-Rukhaymīyah, well, Asia	G8	48
Ar-Rumaythah, Iraq	F8	48
Ar-Rummān, Jord.	D5	50
Ar-Ruṣayfah, Jord.	D6	50
Ar-Ruṣayriṣ, Sud.	L8	60
Ar-Ruṭbah, Iraq	E6	48
Ar-Ruways, Qatar	H11	48
Arsenault Lake, l., Sask., Can.	C6	104
Arsenjev, Russia	I18	28
Arsenjevo, Russia	H19	22
Árta, Grc.	J4	20
Artašat, Arm.	B8	48
Arteaga, Mex.	H8	90
Artemisa, Cuba	C3	94
Artémou, Maur.	D3	64
Artenay, Fr.	D8	14
Artesia, Ms., U.S.	I8	114
Artesia, N.M., U.S.	G2	116
Artesian, S.D., U.S.	G10	118
Arth, Switz.	D10	13
Arthabaska, Que., Can.	A15	108
Arthur, Ont., Can.	G15	110
Arthur, Il., U.S.	C8	114
Arthur, Ne., U.S.	J6	118
Arthur, N.D., U.S.	D10	118
Arthur, Tn., U.S.	C3	112
Arthur's Town, Bah.	B7	94
Artibonite, stm., Haiti	E8	94
Artigas, Ur.	F10	80
Artik, Arm.	A7	48
Artillery Lake, l., N.W. Ter., Can.	D11	96
Artois, hist. reg., Fr.	B9	14
Art'om, Russia	I18	28
Art'omovsk, Russia	G10	28
Art'omovskij, Russia	F10	26
Artsyz, Ukr.	C13	20
Artvin, Tur.	G16	4
Artyk, Russia	E21	28
Artyom, Azer.	A11	48
Aru, Kepulauan, is., Indon.	G9	38
Aruaddin, Erit.	I10	60
Aruanã, Braz.	C3	79
Aruba, dep., N.A.	H9	94
Arunāchal Pradesh, state, India	F16	44
Aruppukkottai, India	H5	46
Arusha, Tan.	B7	58
Aruwimi, stm., Zaire	H6	56
Arvada, Co., U.S.	E11	120
Arvajcheer, Mong.	B7	30
Arvi, India	B5	46
Arvida, Que., Can.	D2	106
Arvidsjaur, Swe.	I16	6
Arvika, Swe.	L13	6
Arvin, Ca., U.S.	I7	124
Arvon, Mount, mtn., Mi., U.S.	D7	110
Arvonia, Va., U.S.	B8	112
Arvorezinha, Braz.	E12	80
Arxan, China	H15	28
Arys', Kaz.	I11	26

Name — Map Ref. — Page

Arzachena, Italy H4 18
Arzamas, Russia F6 26
Arziw, Alg. C10 62
Aš, Czech. E12 10
Aša, Russia F9 26
Asa, stm., Ven. D11 84
Asab, Nmb. E3 66
Asad, Buḩayrat al-, res., Syria C5 48
Asahikawa, Japan d17 36a
Asamankese, Ghana I9 64
Asansol, India I12 44
Asbest, Russia F10 26
Asbestos, Que., Can. B15 108
Asbury Park, N.J., U.S. G12 108
Ascensión, Mex. B6 90
Ascension, i., St. Hel. I5 52
Aŝchabad (Ashgabat), Turk. J9 26
Aschach an der Donau, Aus. A9 18
Aschaffenburg, Ger. F9 10
Aschersleben, Ger. D11 10
Ascoli Piceno, Italy G8 18
Ascona, Switz. F10 13
Ascope, Peru B2 82
Ascotán, Chile A4 80
Āseb, Erit. H3 47
Åseda, Swe. M14 6
Āsela, Eth. N10 60
Åsele, Swe. I15 6
Asendabo, Eth. M9 60
Asenovgrad, Bul. G8 20
Aşfūn al-Maţā'inah, Egypt E7 60
Ashburn, Ga., U.S. H3 112
Ashburton, N.Z. E3 72
Ashburton, stm., Austl. D3 68
Ashcroft, B.C., Can. G13 102
Ashdod, Isr. E3 50
Ashdot Ya'aqov, Isr. C5 50
Ashdown, Ar., U.S. I2 114
Asheboro, N.C., U.S. D7 112
Ashern, Man., Can. G16 104
Asherton, Tx., U.S. K7 116
Asheville, N.C., U.S. D4 112
Asheweig, stm., Ont., Can. F15 96
Ash Flat, Ar., U.S. F5 114
Ashford, Austl. G9 70
Ashford, Al., U.S. K11 114
Ash Fork, Az., U.S. I4 120
Ash Grove, Mo., U.S. E3 114
Ashibetsu, Japan d17 36a
Ashikaga, Japan K14 36
Ashkhabad see Aŝchabad, Turk. J9 26
Ashland, Al., U.S. I11 114
Ashland, Il., U.S. C6 114
Ashland, Ks., U.S. N8 118
Ashland, Ky., U.S. I4 108
Ashland, Ms., U.S. H7 114
Ashland, Mo., U.S. D4 114
Ashland, Mt., U.S. E19 122
Ashland, Ne., U.S. J11 118
Ashland, N.H., U.S. D15 108
Ashland, Oh., U.S. G4 108
Ashland, Or., U.S. H3 122
Ashland, Pa., U.S. G10 108
Ashland, Va., U.S. B9 112
Ashland, Wi., U.S. D5 110
Ashland, Mount, mtn., Or., U.S. H3 122
Ashland City, Tn., U.S. F9 114
Ashley, Il., U.S. D7 114
Ashley, Mi., U.S. G11 110
Ashley, N.D., U.S. E8 118
Ashley, Oh., U.S. G4 108
Ashmore, Il., U.S. C8 114
Ashmore Islands, is., Austl. B4 68
Ashmūn, Egypt B6 60
Ashqelon, Isr. E3 50
Ash-Shajarah, Jord. C5 50
Ash-Shaqrā', Sau. Ar. B4 47
Ash-Shāriqah (Sharjah), U.A.E. B9 47
Ash-Sharmah, Sau. Ar. G3 48
Ash-Shaṭrah, Iraq F9 48
Ash-Shawbak, Jord. G5 50
Ash-Shawmarah, Leb. B4 50
Ash-Shihr, Yemen G6 47
Ash-Shufayyah, Sau. Ar. C1 47
Ash-Shumlul, Sau. Ar. H9 48
Ash-Shuqayq, Sau. Ar. F3 47
Ash-Shurayf, Sau. Ar. I5 48
Ash-Shurayk, Sud. H7 60
Ashtabula, Oh., U.S. F6 108
Ashtabula, Lake, res., N.D., U.S. D10 118
Ashton, S. Afr. I5 66
Ashton, Id., U.S. F14 122
Ashton, Il., U.S. I6 110
Ashton, Ia., U.S. H12 118
Ashton, Ne., U.S. J9 118
Ashuanipi Lake, l., Newf., Can. F19 96
Ashuelot, stm., N.H., U.S. E14 108
Ashville, Al., U.S. I10 114
Ashville, Oh., U.S. H4 108
Ashwaubenon, Wi., U.S. F7 110
Asi (Nahr al-'Āṣī), stm., Asia C3 48
Asia D11 24
Asia, Kepulauan, is., Indon. E9 38
Asia Minor, hist. reg., Tur. H14 4
Asilah, Mor. C7 62
Asino, Russia F9 28
Asipoquobah Lake, l., Ont., Can. E23 104
'Asīr, reg., Sau. Ar. E2 47
Aşkale, Tur. B6 48
Askham, S. Afr. F5 66
Asmār, Afg. C4 44
Asmara see Asmera, Erit. E8 56
Asmera, Erit. E8 56
Asola, Italy D5 18
Asosa, Eth. F7 56
Asotin, Wa., U.S. D8 122
Asp, Spain G11 16
Aspang Markt, Aus. H16 10
Aspen, Co., U.S. E10 120
Aspen Butte, mtn., Or., U.S. H3 122
Aspermont, Tx., U.S. F6 116
Aspres-sur-Buëch, Fr. H12 14
Aspy Bay, b., N.S., Can. F13 106
Asquith, Sask., Can. F7 104
As-Sa'ata, Sud. K5 60
Aş-Şaff, Egypt C6 60
As-Saffānīyah, Sau. Ar. H10 48
Aş-Şāfī, Jord. F4 50
Aş-Şāfiyah, Sud. H4 60
Assaí, Braz. G3 79
Assaikwatamo, stm., Man., Can. B18 104
'Assāl al-Ward, Syria A6 50
As-Sallūm, Egypt B3 60
As-Salt, Jord. D5 50
Assam, state, India G15 44
As-Samāwah, Iraq F8 48
Aş-Şarīḩ, Jord. C5 50
Assateague Island, i., U.S. I11 108
Assean Lake, l., Man., Can. B18 104
Assekaifaf, Alg. G15 62
Assenede, Bel. F4 12
As-Sidr, Sau. Ar. C1 47
Assiniboia, Sask., Can. I9 104
Assiniboine, stm., Can. I16 104
Assiniboine, Mount, mtn., Can. G19 102
Assiniboine Indian Reserve, Sask., Can. H11 104
Assinika, stm., Man., Can. F19 104
Assis, Braz. G3 79
Assisi, Italy F7 18
Assomada, C.V. m17 64a
As-Sudd, reg., Sud. N6 60
Aş-Şufayyah, Sud. J8 60
As-Sulaymānīyah, Iraq D8 48
As-Sulaymānīyah, Sau. Ar. B5 47
As-Sulaymī, Sau. Ar. H6 48
As-Sulayyil, Sau. Ar. D4 47
As-Sumayh, Sud. M4 60
Assumption, Il., U.S. C7 114
Assumption Island, i., Sey. C9 58
As-Suwaydā', Syria C7 50
As-Suways (Suez), Egypt C7 60
Astaffort, Fr. H7 14
Āstāneh, Iran C10 48
Āstāneh, Iran E10 48
Astara, Azer. J7 26
Āstārā, Iran B10 48
Asti, Italy E3 18
Astica, Arg. F5 80
Astillero, Spain B8 16
Astipálaia, Grc. M10 20
Astipálaia, i., Grc. M10 20
Astorga, Braz. G3 79
Astorga, Spain C5 16
Astoria, Il., U.S. B6 114
Astoria, Or., U.S. D2 122
Astrachan', Russia H7 26
Asturias, prov., Spain B5 16
Asuka, sci., Ant. C3 73
Asunción, Para. C10 80
Asunción, Bahía, b., Mex. D2 90
Asunción Mita, Guat. C5 92
Asunción Nochixtlán, Mex. I11 90
Asunga, Wādī, val., Afr. K2 60
Aswān, Egypt E7 60
Aswān High Dam see 'Āli, As-Sadd al-, Egypt D7 60
Asyūţ, Egypt D6 60
Aszód, Hung. H19 10
Atabapo, stm., S.A. F9 84
Atacama, prov., Chile D3 80
Atacama, Desierto de (Atacama Desert), des., Chile A3 78
Atacama, Puna de, plat., S.A. C5 80
Atacama, Salar de, pl., Chile B4 80
Ataco, Col. F5 84
Atacuari, stm., Peru I7 84
Atakakup Indian Reserve, Sask., Can. E8 104
Atakpamé, Togo H10 64
Atalándi, Grc. K7 20
Atalaya, Pan. I14 92
Atalaya, Peru D5 82
Atalaya, Cerro, mtn., Peru E6 82
Atami, Japan L14 36
Atār, Maur. A3 64
Atascadero, Ca., U.S. I5 124
Atascosa, stm., Tx., U.S. K8 116
Atasu, Kaz. H12 26
Atauro, Pulau, i., Indon. G8 38
Atbara ('Aṭbarah), stm., Afr. I8 60
'Aṭbarah, Sud. I7 60
'Aṭbarah (Atbara), stm., Afr. E7 56
Atbasar, Kaz. G11 26
Atchafalaya, stm., La., U.S. L5 114
Atchafalaya Bay, b., La., U.S. M5 114
Atchison, Ks., U.S. L12 118
Atebubu, Ghana H9 64
Ateca, Spain D10 16
Atelchu, stm., Braz. B1 79
Atenguillo, Mex. G7 90
Aterau, Kaz. H8 26
Ath (Aat), Bel. G4 12
Athabasca, Alta., Can. C21 102
Athabasca, stm., Alta., Can. E10 96
Athabasca, Lake, l., Can. E10 96
Athalmer, B.C., Can. G18 102
Athapapuskow Lake, l., Man., Can. D13 104
Athārān Hazārī, Pak. E5 44
Athena, Or., U.S. E7 122
Athens, Ont., Can. C11 108
Athens see Athínai, Grc. L7 20
Athens, Al., U.S. H10 114
Athens, Ga., U.S. F3 112
Athens, Il., U.S. C7 114
Athens, La., U.S. J3 114
Athens, Mi., U.S. H10 110
Athens, N.Y., U.S. E13 108
Athens, Oh., U.S. H4 108
Athens, Pa., U.S. F10 108
Athens, Tn., U.S. D2 112
Athens, Tx., U.S. G11 116
Athens, W.V., U.S. B5 112
Athens, Wi., U.S. E5 110
Atherton, Austl. A6 70
Athiémé, Benin H10 64
Athínai (Athens), Grc. L7 20
Athlone, Ire. H6 8
Athok, Mya. F3 40
Athol, Ma., U.S. E14 108
Áthos, mtn., Grc. I8 20
Ath-Thamad, Egypt C8 60
Ati, Chad F4 56
Atico, Peru G5 82
Aticonipi, Lac, l., Que., Can. A14 106
Atigun Pass, Ak., U.S. B20 100
Atik Lake, l., Man., Can. C18 104
Atikokan, Ont., Can. B4 110
Atikonak Lake, l., Newf., Can. F20 96
Atimari, stm., Braz. C8 82
Atiparaná, mth., Braz. I9 84
Atiquizaya, El Sal. D5 92
Atitlán, Lago de, l., Guat. C3 92
Atitlán, Volcán, vol., Guat. C3 92
Atka, Russia E22 28
Atka, Ak., U.S. J7 100
Atkarsk, Russia G7 26
Atkins, Ar., U.S. G4 114
Atkinson, Il., U.S. I5 110
Atkinson, Ne., U.S. I9 118
Atkinson, N.C., U.S. E8 112
Atkinson Lake, l., Man., Can. C20 104
Atlanta, Ga., U.S. F2 112
Atlanta, Il., U.S. B7 114
Atlanta, Mi., U.S. E11 110
Atlanta, Mo., U.S. C4 114
Atlanta, Tx., U.S. I2 114
Atlantic, Ia., U.S. J12 118
Atlantic, N.C., U.S. E10 112
Atlantic Beach, Fl., U.S. I5 112
Atlantic City, N.J., U.S. H12 108
Atlantic-Indian Ridge N5 126
Atlántico, dept., Col. B5 84
Atlantic Ocean I11 128
Atlantic Peak, mtn., Wy., U.S. H16 122
Atlántida, Ur. H11 80
Atlántida, dept., Hond. B7 92
Atlas Mountains, mts., Afr. B6 54
Atlas Saharien, mts., Alg. D11 62
Atlas Tellien, mts., Alg. C11 62
Atlin, B.C., Can. G28 100
Atlin Lake, l., Can. G28 100
'Atlit, Isr. C3 50
Atmore, Al., U.S. K9 114
Atna Peak, mtn., B.C., Can. D6 102
Atnarko, stm., B.C., Can. E9 102
Atocha, Bol. I8 82
Atoka, Ok., U.S. E10 116
Atotonilco, Mex. E8 90
Atoui, Khatt (Khaṭṭ Atoui), val., Afr. J3 62
Atoyac, stm., Mex. H10 90
Atoyac de Álvarez, Mex. I9 90
Atoyaquillo, stm., Mex. I11 90
Atrak (Atrek), l., Asia C12 48
Atrato, stm., Col. D4 84
Atrek (Atrak), stm., Asia C12 48
Atri, Italy G8 18
Atrisco, N.M., U.S. J10 120
Aṭ-Ṭafīlah, Jord. G5 50
Aṭ-Ṭā'if, Sau. Ar. D2 47
At-Tāj, Libya E2 60
At-Tall, Syria A6 50
Attalla, Al., U.S. H10 114
Attapu, Laos G9 40
Attawapiskat, Ont., Can. F16 96
Attawapiskat, stm., Ont., Can. F16 96
Attawapiskat Lake, l., Ont., Can. F15 96
Attica, In., U.S. B9 114
Attica, Ks., U.S. N9 118
Attica, N.Y., U.S. E8 108
Attica, Oh., U.S. F4 108
Attigny, Fr. C11 14
Attikí, hist. reg., Grc. K7 20
Attikí, prov., Grc. K7 20
Attir, Sud. N6 60
Attleboro, Ma., U.S. F15 108
Attock, Pak. D5 44
Attoyac, stm., Tx., U.S. K2 114
Attu Island, i., Ak., U.S. j1 101a
Aṭ-Ṭunayb, Jord. E5 50
Aṭ-Ṭūr, Egypt C7 60
Āttūr, India G5 46
Aṭ-Ṭuwayshah, Sud. K4 60
Aṭ-Ṭuwayyah, Sau. Ar. H6 48
Atucatiquini, stm., Braz. B7 82
Atucha, Arg. G9 80
Atuel, stm., Arg. H5 80
Atuel, Bañados del, sw., Arg. I5 80
Atuntaqui, Ec. G3 84
Atwater, Sask., Can. H12 104
Atwater, Ca., U.S. G5 124
Atwater, Mn., U.S. F13 118
Atwood, Il., U.S. C8 114
Atwood, Ks., U.S. L6 118
Atwood, Tn., U.S. G8 114
Auari, stm., Braz. F11 84
Aubagne, Fr. I12 14
Aube, dept., Fr. D11 14
Aube, stm., Fr. D11 14
Aubigny-sur-Nère, Fr. E9 14
Aubin, Fr. H9 14
Aubrey Cliffs, clf, Az., U.S. I3 120
Aubry Lake, l., N.W. Ter., Can. C31 100
Auburn, Al., U.S. J11 114
Auburn, Ca., U.S. F4 124
Auburn, Il., U.S. C7 114
Auburn, In., U.S. A11 114
Auburn, Ky., U.S. E10 114
Auburn, Me., U.S. C16 108
Auburn, Ma., U.S. E15 108
Auburn, Mi., U.S. G11 110
Auburn, Ne., U.S. K12 118
Auburn, N.Y., U.S. E10 108
Auburn, Wa., U.S. C3 122
Auburn, stm., Austl. E9 70
Auburn Range, mts., Austl. E9 70
Aubusson, Fr. G9 14
Auca Mahuida, Arg. I4 80
Auca Mahuida, Cerro, mtn., Arg. I4 80
Aucará, Peru F4 82
Auce, Lat. E5 22
Auch, Fr. I7 14
Aucilla, stm., U.S. I3 112
Auckland, N.Z. B5 72
Auckland Islands, is., N.Z. N20 126
Aude, dept., Fr. I9 14
Aude, stm., Fr. I10 14
Audierne, Fr. D2 14
Audincourt, Fr. E13 14
Audubon, Ia., U.S. J13 118
Aue, Ger. E12 10
Augathella, Austl. E7 70
Auglaize, stm., Oh., U.S. F2 108
Au Gres, Mi., U.S. F12 110
Au Gres, stm., Mi., U.S. F12 110
Augsburg, Ger. G10 10
Augšligatne, Lat. D8 22
Augusta, Austl. F3 68
Augusta, Italy L10 18
Augusta, Ar., U.S. G5 114
Augusta, Ga., U.S. F4 112
Augusta, Il., U.S. B6 114
Augusta, Ks., U.S. N10 118
Augusta, Ky., U.S. I2 108
Augusta, Me., U.S. C17 108
Augusta, Mt., U.S. C13 122
Augusta, Wi., U.S. F4 110
Augustów, Pol. B22 10
Auila, Ribeirão, stm., Braz. B2 79
Aulander, N.C., U.S. C9 112
Aulnay, Fr. F6 14
Aulneau Peninsula, pen., Ont., Can. I20 104
Ault, Fr. B8 14
Ault, Co., U.S. D12 120
Aumale, Fr. C8 14
Auna, Nig. F12 64
Auneau, Fr. D8 14
Auob, stm., Afr. F5 66
Aurangābād, India C3 46
Auray, Fr. E4 14
Aurelia, Ia., U.S. I12 118
Aurès, Massif de l', mts., Alg. C14 62
Aurich, Ger. B7 10
Auriflama, Braz. F3 79
Aurilândia, Braz. D3 79
Aurillac, Fr. H9 14
Aurora, Ont., Can. F16 110
Aurora, Co., U.S. E12 120
Aurora, Il., U.S. I7 110
Aurora, In., U.S. C12 114
Aurora, Mn., U.S. C3 110
Aurora, Mo., U.S. F3 114
Aurora, Ne., U.S. K9 118
Aurora, N.Y., U.S. E10 108
Aurora, N.C., U.S. D10 112
Aurora, Oh., U.S. F5 108
Aurora, Ut., U.S. F5 120
Aurora, W.V., U.S. H7 108
Aurora do Norte, Braz. B5 79
Aurukun, Austl. B8 68
Aus, Nmb. F3 66
Au Sable, stm., Mi., U.S. F12 110
Au Sable Forks, N.Y., U.S. C13 108
Auschwitz see Oświęcim, Pol. E19 10
Aust-Agder, co., Nor. L10 6
Austin, Man., Can. I16 104
Austin, In., U.S. D11 114
Austin, Mn., U.S. G3 110
Austin, Nv., U.S. E8 124
Austin, Pa., U.S. F8 108
Austin, Tx., U.S. I9 116
Austin Channel, strt., N.W. Ter., Can. A12 96
Austinville, Va., U.S. C6 112
Australes, Îles, is., Fr. Poly. K24 126
Australia, ctry., Oc. D7 68
Australia Mountain, mtn., Yukon, Can. E25 100
Australian Capital Territory, ter., Austl. G9 68
Austria (Österreich), ctry., Eur. F10 4
Autazes, Braz. I13 84
Autlán de Navarro, Mex. H7 90
Autun, Fr. F11 14
Auvergne, hist. reg., Fr. G9 14
Auxerre, Fr. E10 14
Auxier, Ky., U.S. B4 112
Auxi-le-Château, Fr. B9 14
Auxonne, Fr. E12 14
Auxvasse, Mo., U.S. C5 114
Auyán Tepuy, mtn., Ven. E11 84
Auzances, Fr. F9 14
Auzangate, Nevado, mtn., Peru E6 82
Ava, Il., U.S. E7 114
Ava, Mo., U.S. F4 114
Avai, Braz. G4 79
Avallon, Fr. E10 14
Avalon, Ca., U.S. K7 124
Avalon Peninsula, pen., Newf., Can. E20 106
Ávalos, Mex. C6 90
Avanos, Tur. B3 48
Avant, Ok., U.S. C10 116
Avaré, Braz. G4 79
Avegbadje, mtn., Afr. H10 64
Aveiro, Port. E3 16
Avelgem, Bel. G3 12
Avellaneda, Arg. H9 80
Avellaneda, Arg. E9 80
Avellino, Italy I9 18
Avenal, Ca., U.S. H5 124
Aversa, Italy I9 18
Avery, Id., U.S. C10 122
Avery, Tx., U.S. I2 114
Avery Island, La., U.S. M5 114
Aveyron, dept., Fr. H9 14
Avezzano, Italy G8 18
Aviemore, Scot., U.K. D10 8
Avigliano, Italy I10 18
Avignon, Fr. I11 14
Ávila, Spain E7 16
Ávila, prov., Spain E7 16
Avilés, Spain B6 16
Avis, Pa., U.S. F9 108
Avispa, Cerro, mtn., Ven. G10 84
Aviz, Port. F4 16
Avoca, Ia., U.S. J12 118
Avoca, N.Y., U.S. E9 108
Avola, B.C., Can. F15 102
Avola, Italy M10 18
Avon, Il., U.S. J5 110
Avon, Mn., U.S. E1 110
Avon, Mt., U.S. D13 122
Avon, N.Y., U.S. E9 108
Avon, N.C., U.S. D11 112
Avon, S.D., U.S. H9 118
Avon, co., Eng., U.K. J11 8
Avon, stm., N.S., Can. H9 106
Avon, stm., Eng., U.K. I12 8
Avondale, Az., U.S. K4 120
Avondale, Co., U.S. M3 118
Avon Downs, Austl. C2 70
Avonlea, Sask., Can. H9 104
Avonmore, Pa., U.S. G7 108
Avon Park, Fl., U.S. L5 112
Avontuur, S. Afr. I6 66
Avranches, Fr. D5 14
A'waj, Nahr al-, stm., Syria B6 50
Awaji-shima, i., Japan M9 36
'Awālī, Bahr. H11 48
Awasa, Eth. N10 60
Awash, Eth. G9 56
Awash, stm., Eth. M10 60
Awaso, Ghana H8 64
Awbārī, Libya C3 56
Awe, Nig. G14 64
Awegyun, Mya. H5 40
Awjilah, Libya C5 56
Awled Djellal, Alg. C13 62
Awlef, Alg. G11 62
Aworo Kit, Sud. L7 60
Axel Heiberg Island, i., N.W. Ter., Can. B10 86
Axim, Ghana I8 64
Axinim, Braz. J13 84
Axiós (Vardar), stm., Eur. I6 20
Axis, Al., U.S. L8 114
Ax-les-Thermes, Fr. J8 14
Axtell, Ks., U.S. L11 118
Axtell, Ne., U.S. K8 118
Ayabaca, Peru J3 84
Ayabe, Japan L10 36
Ayacucho, Arg. I9 80
Ayacucho, Bol. G10 82
Ayacucho, Peru E4 82
Ayacucho, dept., Peru E4 82
Ayamonte, Spain H4 16
Ayangba, Nig. H13 64
Ayapel, Col. C5 84
Ayarza, Laguna de, l., Guat. C4 92
Ayaviri, Peru F6 82
Ayaviri, stm., Peru F6 82
Ayden, N.C., U.S. D9 112
Aydın, Tur. L11 20
Ayer, Ma., U.S. E15 108
Ayers Rock, mtn., Austl. E6 68
Ayeyarwady (Irrawaddy), stm., Mya. F3 40
Ayía Paraskeví, Grc. J10 20
Ayiássos, Grc. J10 20
Áyion Óros, pen., Grc. I8 20
Áyios Kírikos, Grc. L10 20
Áyios Nikólaos, Grc. N9 20
Áyiou Órous, Kólpos, b., Grc. I8 20
Ayl, Jord. H5 50
Aylmer, Que., Can. B11 108
Aylmer, Mount, mtn., Alta., Can. F19 102
Aylmer Lake, l., N.W. Ter., Can. D11 96
Aylmer West, Ont., Can. H15 110
Aylsham, Sask., Can. E11 104
'Ayn Dār, Sau. Ar. B6 47
Aynor, S.C., U.S. F7 112
'Aynūnah, Sau. Ar. G3 48
Ayo, Peru F5 82
Ayo Ayo, Bol. G7 82
Ayod, Sud. M6 60
Ayom, Sud. N4 60
Ayoûn el 'Atroûs, Maur. C5 64
Ayr, Austl. B7 70
Ayr, Ont., Can. G15 110
Ayr, Scot., U.K. F9 8
'Aytā al-Fakhkhār, Leb. A5 50
Ayu, Kepulauan, is., Indon. E9 38
Ayutla, Mex. G7 90
Ayutla de los Libres, Mex. I10 90
Ayvacık, Tur. J10 20
Ayvalık, Tur. J10 20
Azacualpa, Hond. C8 92
Azacualpa, Hond. B6 92
Azalea Park, Fl., U.S. K5 112
Azambuja, Port. F3 16
Āzamgarh, India G10 44
Azángaro, Peru F6 82
Azángaro, stm., Peru F6 82
Azaouagh, Vallée de l', val., Afr. D11 64
Azapa, Quebrada de, stm., Chile H6 82
Azar, val., Afr. C12 64
Azare, Nig. F15 64
Āzar Shahr, Iran C8 48
Azazga, Alg. B13 62
Azeffâl, dunes, Afr. J4 62
Azeffoun, Alg. B13 62
Azemmour, Mor. D6 62
Azerbaijan (Azarbaycan), ctry., Asia I7 26
Azerbaydzan see Azerbaijan, ctry., Asia I7 26
Azezo, Eth. K9 60
Azogues, Ec. I3 84
Azores see Açores, is., Port. k19 62a
Azoum, Bahr (Wādī 'Azūm), val., Afr. K2 60
Azov, Russia H5 26
Azov, Sea of, Eur. H5 26
Azpeitia, Spain B9 16
Azraq, Al-Bahr al- see Blue Nile, stm., Afr. K8 60
Azrou, Mor. D8 62
Aztec, N.M., U.S. H9 120
Aztec Peak, mtn., Az., U.S. K6 120
Azua, Dom. Rep. E9 94
Azuaga, Spain G6 16
Azuay, prov., Ec. I3 84
Azucena, Arg. I9 80
Azuero, Peninsula de, pen., Pan. D2 84
Azul, Arg. I9 80
Azul, Cerro, mtn., C.R. H9 92
Azul, Cerro, mtn., Hond. C6 92
Azur, Côte d', Fr. I14 14
Azurduy, Bol. H9 82
Azure Lake, l., B.C., Can. E14 102
Az-Zabadānī, Syria A6 50
Az-Zahrān (Dhahran), Sau. Ar. A7 47
Az-Zaqāzīq, Egypt B6 60
Az-Zarqā', Jord. D6 50
Az-Zāwiyah, Libya B3 56
Az-Zaydīyah, Yemen G3 47
Azzel Matti, Sebkha, pl., Alg. H11 62
Az-Zilfī, Sau. Ar. H8 48
Az-Zubayr, Iraq F9 48

B

Ba, stm., Viet. H10 40
Baar, Switz. D10 13
Baardheere, Som. H9 56
Baarle-Hertog (Baerle-Duc), Bel. F6 12
Baarle-Nassau, Bel. F6 12
Baba, Ec. H3 84
Babadag, Tur. L12 20
Babahoyo, Ec. H3 84
Babailiqiao, China C7 34
Babajevo, Russia B18 22
Babana, Nig. F11 64
Babanango, S. Afr. G10 66
Babanūsah, Sud. L4 60
Babar, Kepulauan, is., Indon. G8 38
Babar, Pulau, i., Indon. G8 38
Babbitt, Mn., U.S. C4 110
Babbitt, Nv., U.S. F7 124
Babel, Mont de, mtn., Que., Can. A5 106
Bab el Mandeb see Mandeb, Bab el, strt. H3 47
Babimost, Pol. C15 10
Babina Greda, Cro. D2 20
Babinda, Austl. A6 70
Babine, B.C., Can. B8 102
Babine, stm., B.C., Can. B8 102
Babine Lake, l., B.C., Can. C9 102
Babine Range, mts., B.C., Can. B7 102
Babino, Russia B14 22
Babino, Russia B23 22
Babo, Indon. F9 38
Bābol, Iran C12 48
Bābol Sar, Iran C12 48
Baboquivari Peak, mtn., Az., U.S. M5 120
Babuškin, Russia G13 28
Babuyan Islands, is., Phil. B7 38
Babynino, Russia G18 22
Bacabal, Braz. D10 76
Bacadéhuachi, Mex. C5 90
Bacan, Pulau, i., Indon. F8 38
Bacău, Rom. C10 20
Bacău, co., Rom. C10 20
Baccalieu Island, i., Newf., Can. D21 106
Bac Can, Viet. C8 40
Baccarat, Fr. D13 14
Bacerac, Mex. B5 90
Bac Giang, Viet. D9 40
Bachaquero, Ven. C7 84
Bacharden, Turk. J9 26
Bachi, China K4 34
Bachiniva, Mex. C6 90
Bachmutovo, Russia E17 22
Bachu, China D2 30
Bachuma, Eth. N8 60
Back, stm., N.W. Ter., Can. C13 96
Bačka Palanka, Yugo. D3 20
Bačka Topola, Yugo. D3 20
Backbone Ranges, mts., N.W. Ter., Can. E30 100
Backnang, Ger. G9 10
Backstairs Passage, strt., Austl. J2 70
Bac Lieu, Viet. J8 40
Bac Ninh, Viet. D9 40
Bacoachi, Mex. B5 90
Bacolod, Phil. C7 38
Baconton, Ga., U.S. H2 112
Bacoor, Phil. n19 39b
Bács-Kiskun, co., Hung. I19 10
Bácum, Mex. D4 90
Bad, stm., Mi., U.S. G11 110
Bad, stm., S.D., U.S. G6 118
Bad, stm., Wi., U.S. D5 110
Badagara, India G3 46
Badajia, China B9 34
Badajós, stm., Braz. I11 84
Badajós, Lago, l., Braz. I11 84
Badajoz, Spain G5 16
Badalona, Spain D14 16
Bādāmi, India E3 46
Badanah, Sau. Ar. F7 48
Badaohao, China B9 32
Badaohe, China C10 32
Bad Aussee, Aus. H13 10
Bad Axe, Mi., U.S. G13 110
Bad Brückenau, Ger. E9 10
Baddeck, N.S., Can. F13 106
Bad Doberan, Ger. A11 10
Bad Dürkheim, Ger. F8 10
Bad Dürrenberg, Ger. D12 10
Badeggi, Nig. G13 64
Badéguichéri, Niger D12 64
Bad Ems, Ger. E7 10
Baden, Erit. I9 60
Baden, Switz. D9 13
Baden-Baden, Ger. G8 10
Badenweiler, Ger. H7 10
Baden-Württemberg, state, Ger. G8 10
Badgastein, Aus. H13 10
Badger, Newf., Can. D17 106
Badger, Mn., U.S. C11 118
Bad Hall, Aus. G14 10
Bad Harzburg, Ger. D10 10
Bad Hersfeld, Ger. E9 10
Bad Homburg [vor der Höhe], Ger. E8 10
Badiraguato, Mex. E6 90
Bad Kissingen, Ger. E10 10
Bad Kreuznach, Ger. F7 10
Badlands, hills, U.S. E4 118
Badlands, hills, S.D., U.S. H5 118
Badlands National Park, S.D., U.S. H5 118
Bad Langensalza, Ger. D10 10
Bad Lauterberg, Ger. D10 10
Bad Leonfelden, Aus. G14 10
Bad Mergentheim, Ger. F9 10
Bad Muskau, Ger. D14 10
Bad Nauheim, Ger. E8 10
Bad Neustadt an der Saale, Ger. E10 10
Bad Oeynhausen, Ger. C8 10
Badogo, Mali F5 64
Bad Oldesloe, Ger. B10 10
Badou, China G5 32
Badou, Togo H10 64
Badoumbé, Mali E4 64
Bad Pyrmont, Ger. D9 10
Bad Ragaz, Switz. D12 13
Bad Reichenhall, Ger. H12 10
Badr Hunayn, Sau. Ar. C1 47
Bad Salzuflen, Ger. C8 10
Bad Salzungen, Ger. E10 10
Bad Sankt Leonhard im Lavanttal, Aus. I14 10
Bad Schwalbach, Ger. E8 10
Bad Schwartau, Ger. B10 10
Bad Segeberg, Ger. B10 10
Bad Tölz, Ger. H11 10
Badu, China I8 34
Badulla, Sri L. I6 46
Badupi, Mya. D2 40
Bad Vöslau, Aus. H16 10
Bad Waldsee, Ger. H9 10
Bad Wildungen, Ger. D9 10
Baediam, Maur. D4 64
Baena, Spain H7 16
Baependi, Braz. F6 79
Baeza, Ec. H4 84
Baezaeko, stm., B.C., Can. E10 102
Bafatá, Gui.-B. E2 64
Baffin Bay, b., N.A. B13 86
Baffin Bay, b., Tx., U.S. L9 116
Baffin Island, i., N.W. Ter., Can. C18 96
Bafing, stm., Afr. F4 54
Bafoulabé, Mali E4 64
Bafoussam, Cam. G9 54
Bāfq, Iran F13 48
Bāft, Iran G14 48
Bafwasende, Zaire A5 58
Bagaces, C.R. G9 92
Bagagem, stm., Braz. C4 79
Bāgalkot, India D3 46
Bagansiapiapi, Indon. M6 40
Bağarası, Tur. L11 20
Bagawi, Sud. K8 60
Bagdad see Baghdād, Iraq E8 48
Bagdad, Az., U.S. J3 120
Bagdad, Fl., U.S. L9 114
Bagdarin, Russia G14 28
Bagé, Braz. F11 80
Baggs, Wy., U.S. I18 122
Baghdād, Iraq E8 48
Bagheria, Italy K8 18
Baghlān, Afg. B3 44
Bagley, Mn., U.S. D12 118
Bagnères-de-Bigorre, Fr. I7 14
Bagnères-de-Luchon, Fr. J7 14
Bagnols-sur-Cèze, Fr. H11 14
Bago (Pegu), Mya. F4 40
Bagoé, stm., Afr. F6 64
Bagotville, Base des Forces canadiennes, mil., Que., Can. D3 106
Bagrationovsk, Russia G3 22
Baguio, Phil. m19 39b
Bagzane, mtn., Niger C14 64
Bahamas, ctry., N.A. D9 88
Bahār, Iran D10 48
Baharampur, India H13 44
Bahāwalnagar, Pak. F5 44
Bahāwalpur, Pak. F4 44
Bahechuan, China C12 32
Bahia, state, Braz. B7 79
Bahía, Islas de la, is., Hond. A8 92
Bahía Azul, Pan. H13 92
Bahía Blanca, Arg. J7 80
Bahía Kino, Mex. C4 90
Bahir Dar, Eth. L9 60
Baḩrah, Sau. Ar. D1 47
Bahraich, India G9 44
Bahrain (Al-Baḩrayn), ctry., Asia D5 42
Baḩrayn, Khalīj al-, b., Asia B7 47
Bāhū Kalāt, Iran I16 48
Baï, Mali E8 64
Baia Mare, Rom. B7 20
Baía Rica, stm., Braz. E10 82
Baia Sprie, Rom. B7 20
Baicao, China B4 32
Baicheng, China B11 30
Baicheng, China C3 30
Baie-Comeau, Que., Can. C5 106
Baie-Comeau-Hauterive, Réserve, Que., Can. B5 106
Baie-des-Ha] Ha], Que., Can. B15 106
Baie-des-Moutons, Que., Can. B14 106
Baie-du-Renard, Que., Can. C12 106
Baie-Johan-Beetz, Que., Can. B11 106
Baie-Sainte-Claire, Que., Can. C9 106
Baie-Saint-Paul, Que., Can. E3 106
Baie-Trinité, Que., Can. C6 106
Baie Verte, Newf., Can. C17 106
Baigong, China K5 34
Baihebu, China C4 32
Baijian, China D3 32
Baiju, China B9 34
Baikal, Lake see Bajkal, ozero, l., Russia G13 28
Bailadores, Ven. C7 84
Baile, China D2 32
Baile Átha Cliath see Dublin, Ire. H7 8
Băile Govora, Rom. D8 20
Bailén, Spain G8 16
Băilești, Rom. E7 20
Bailey, N.C., U.S. D8 112
Bailin, China H9 34
Bailique, Ilha, i., Braz. C9 76
Baillie, stm., N.W. Ter., Can. D11 96
Baillie Islands, is., N.W. Ter., Can. B7 96
Bailong, stm., China E7 30
Bailundo, Ang. D3 58
Baimaguan, China C4 32

Name	Map Ref.	Page
Baimashi, China	F7	34
Baimiaozi, China	C8	32
Bainbridge, Ga., U.S.	I2	112
Bainbridge, N.Y., U.S.	E11	108
Bainbridge, Oh., U.S.	H3	108
Bain-de-Bretagne, Fr.	E5	14
Bainiqiao, China	F3	34
Bains-les-Bains, Fr.	D13	14
Bainville, Mt., U.S.	C3	118
Baipu, China	C9	34
Baiquan, China	E11	34
Baird, Tx., U.S.	G7	116
Baird, Mount, mtn., Id., U.S.	G14	122
Bairin Zuoqi, China	C10	30
Bairnsdale, Austl.	K7	70
Bairoil, Wy., U.S.	B9	120
Bairuopu, China	G1	34
Baisha, China	E10	40
Baishanji, China	B5	34
Baishatan, China	G9	32
Baishuifan, China	E4	34
Baishuijiang, China	E8	30
Baisogala, Lith.	F6	22
Baitazi, China	A8	32
Baitu, China	D8	34
Baixa Grande, Braz.	A8	79
Baixiang, China	F2	32
Baiyin, China	D7	30
Baizhongpu, China	B3	34
Baja, Hung.	I18	10
Baja, Punta, c., Mex.	C2	90
Baja California, state, Mex.	C2	90
Baja California, pen., Mex.	C3	90
Baja California Sur, state, Mex.	E4	90
Bajada del Agrio, Arg.	J3	80
Bajanaul, Kaz.	G13	26
Bajanchongor, Mong.	B7	30
Bajánsenye, Hung.	I16	10
Baja Verapaz, dept., Guat.	B4	92
Bajdarackaja guba, b., Russia	D11	26
Bajestān, Iran	D15	48
Bajiazi, China	B11	32
Bajimba, Mount, mtn., Austl.	G10	70
Bajkal, ozero (Lake Baikal), l., Russia	G13	28
Bajkal'skoje, Russia	F13	28
Bajmak, Russia	G9	26
Bajo Baudó, Col.	E4	84
Bajo Boquete, Pan.	C1	84
Bajos de Haina, Dom. Rep.	E9	94
Bajram-Ali, Turk.	J10	26
Bakebe, Cam.	I14	64
Bakel, Sen.	D3	64
Baker, Ca., U.S.	I9	124
Baker, Fl., U.S.	L10	114
Baker, La., U.S.	L5	114
Baker, Mt., U.S.	E3	118
Baker, Or., U.S.	F8	122
Baker, Mount, mtn., Wa., U.S.	B4	122
Baker Butte, mtn., Az., U.S.	J5	120
Baker Creek, stm., B.C., Can.	E12	102
Baker Island, i., Oc.	H22	126
Baker Lake, N.W. Ter., Can.	D13	96
Baker Lake, l., N.W. Ter., Can.	D13	96
Bakersfield, Ca., U.S.	I6	124
Bakersville, N.C., U.S.	C4	112
Bākhtarān (Kermānshāh), Iran	D9	48
Bakhtegān, Daryācheh-ye, l., Iran	G13	48
Bakı (Baku), Azer.	I7	26
Bakkagerði, Ice.	B7	6a
Baklanka, Russia	C23	22
Bako, Eth.	O9	60
Bakony, mts., Hung.	H17	10
Bakoy, stm., Afr.	F5	54
Baku see Bakı, Azer.	I7	26
Bakun, China	D9	44
Bala, Sen.	D3	64
Balâ, Tur.	B2	48
Balabac Strait, strt., Asia	D6	38
Ba'labakk, Leb.	D4	48
Balabanovo, Russia	F19	22
Balachna, Russia	E26	22
Balad, Iraq	D8	48
Bālāghāt, India	J9	44
Balaguer, Spain	D12	16
Balakirevo, Russia	E21	22
Balaklava, Austl.	J3	70
Balakovo, Russia	G7	26
Balallan, Scot., U.K.	C7	8
Bālā Morghāb, Afg.	D17	48
Balāngīr, India	B7	46
Balašicha, Russia	F20	22
Balašov, Russia	G6	26
Balassagyarmat, Hung.	G19	10
Balāṭ, Egypt	E5	60
Balatina, Mol.	B11	20
Balaton, Mn., U.S.	G12	118
Balaton, l., Hung.	I17	10
Balayan, Phil.	o19	39b
Balbieriškis, Lith.	G6	22
Balbirini, Austl.	C7	68
Balboa, Pan.	I15	92
Balbriggan, Ire.	H7	8
Balcanoona, Austl.	H3	70
Balcarce, Arg.	I9	80
Balcarres, Sask., Can.	H11	104
Balchaš, Kaz.	H12	26
Balchaš, ozero (Lake Balkhash), l., Kaz.	H12	26
Balcones Escarpment, clf, Tx., U.S.	J6	116
Balde, Arg.	G5	80
Baldim, Braz.	E7	79
Bald Knob, Ar., U.S.	G5	114
Bald Mountain, mtn., Or., U.S.	G4	122
Baldock Lake, l., Man., Can.	B17	104
Baldone, Lat.	E7	22
Baldur, Man., Can.	I15	104
Baldwin, Fl., U.S.	I5	112
Baldwin, La., U.S.	M5	114
Baldwin, Mi., U.S.	G10	110
Baldwin, Wi., U.S.	F3	110
Baldwin City, Ks., U.S.	M12	118
Baldwin Peninsula, pen., Ak., U.S.	C13	100
Baldwinsville, N.Y., U.S.	D10	108
Baldwinville, Ma., U.S.	E14	108
Baldwyn, Ms., U.S.	H8	114
Baldy Mountain, mtn., B.C., Can.	F14	102
Baldy Mountain, mtn., Man., Can.	G14	104
Baldy Mountain, mtn., Mt., U.S.	B16	122
Baldy Mountain, mtn., N.M., U.S.	H11	120
Baldy Peak, mtn., Az., U.S.	K7	120
Balearic Islands see Balears, Illes, is., Spain	F15	16
Balears, prov., Spain	F15	16
Balears, Illes (Balearic Islands), is., Spain	F15	16
Baleia, Ponta da, c., Braz.	D9	79
Baleine, Grande rivière de la, stm., Que., Can.	F18	96
Baleine, Petite rivière de la, stm., Que., Can.	E18	96
Baleine, Rivière à la, stm., Que., Can.	E19	96
Balej, Russia	G15	28
Baler, Phil.	n19	39b
Bāleshwar, India	J12	44
Baléyara, Niger	E11	64
Balfate, Hond.	B8	92
Balfes Creek, Austl.	C6	70
Balfour, N.C., U.S.	D4	112
Bali, Laut (Bali Sea), Indon.	G6	38
Bali, Selat, strt., Indon.	G5	38
Balihan, China	B6	32
Balıkesir, Tur.	J11	20
Balikpapan, Indon.	F6	38
Balimo, Pap. N. Gui.	G11	38
Balin, China	B11	30
Balingen, Ger.	G8	10
Balintang Channel, strt., Phil.	B7	38
Baliza, Braz.	D2	79
Balkan Mountains see Stara Planina, mts., Eur.	G8	20
Balkan Peninsula, pen., Eur.	D9	52
Balkbrug, Neth.	C9	12
Balkh, Afg.	B2	44
Balkh, stm., Afg.	B2	44
Balkhash, Lake see Balchaš, ozero, l., Kaz.	H12	26
Ball, La., U.S.	K4	114
Ballachulish, Scot., U.K.	E8	8
Ballangen, Nor.	G15	6
Ballantine, Mt., U.S.	E17	122
Ballarat, Austl.	K5	70
Ballé, Mali	D5	64
Ballenas, Bahía de, b., Mex.	D3	90
Balleny Islands, is., Ant.	B8	73
Balleroy, Fr.	C6	14
Ballesteros, Arg.	G7	80
Balleza, Mex.	D6	90
Balleza, stm., Mex.	D6	90
Ball Ground, Ga., U.S.	E2	112
Ballia, India	H11	44
Ballina, Austl.	G10	70
Ballina, Ire.	G4	8
Ballinger, Tx., U.S.	H7	116
Ballon, Fr.	M14	8
Balls Pyramid, i., Austl.	F11	68
Ballston Spa, N.Y., U.S.	D13	108
Ballville, Oh., U.S.	F3	108
Balmaceda, Chile	F2	78
Balmertown, Ont., Can.	G21	104
Balmorhea, Tx., U.S.	I3	116
Balnearia, Arg.	F7	80
Balonne, stm., Austl.	F8	70
Bālotra, India	H5	44
Balovale, Zam.	D4	58
Baloži, Lat.	E7	22
Balrāmpur, India	G10	44
Balranald, Austl.	J5	70
Balsam Lake, Wi., U.S.	E3	110
Bálsamo, Braz.	F2	79
Balsas, Braz.	E9	76
Balsas, stm., Mex.	H8	90
Balsas, Rio das, stm., Braz.	E9	76
Balsas Sur, Mex.	I10	90
Balsthal, Switz.	D8	13
Balta, Ukr.	H3	26
Baltasar Brum, Ur.	F10	80
Bălți, Mol.	H3	26
Baltic Sea, Eur.	M16	6
Baltijsk, Russia	G2	22
Baltijskaja kosa, spit, Eur.	A19	10
Baltīm, Egypt	B6	60
Baltimore, Ire.	J4	8
Baltimore, S. Afr.	D9	66
Baltimore, Md., U.S.	H10	108
Baltimore, Oh., U.S.	H4	108
Baluarte, stm., Mex.	F7	90
Balvi, Lat.	D10	22
Balya, Tur.	J11	20
Balykši, Kaz.	H8	26
Balzac, Alta., Can.	F20	102
Balzar, Ec.	H3	84
Bam, Iran	G15	48
Bama, China	B9	40
Bamaga, Austl.	B8	68
Bamaji Lake, l., Ont., Can.	G23	104
Bamako, Mali	E5	64
Bamba, Mali	C9	64
Bambamarca, Peru	B2	82
Bambana, stm., Nic.	D11	92
Bambara Maoundé, Mali	D8	64
Bambari, Cen. Afr. Rep.	G5	56
Bambaroo, Austl.	B7	70
Bamberg, Ger.	F10	10
Bamberg, S.C., U.S.	F5	112
Bambesi, Eth.	M8	60
Bambezi, Zimb.	C9	66
Bambuí, Braz.	F6	79
Bamburral, stm., S.A.	H12	82
Bam Co, l., China	E14	44
Bamenda, Cam.	I15	64
Bamfield, B.C., Can.	I9	102
Bami, Turk.	B14	48
Bamingui, stm., Cen. Afr. Rep.	G4	56
Bampūr, Iran	H16	48
Bamumo, China	D15	44
Ba Na, Viet.	G9	40
Banaba, i., Kir.	I20	126
Banalia, Zaire	A5	58
Banana, Zaire	C2	58
Bananal, Ilha do, i., Braz.	F8	76
Banana River, b., Fl., U.S.	K6	112
Banarlı, Tur.	H11	20
Banās, Ra's, c., Egypt	F8	60
Banat, hist. reg., Eur.	D4	20
Banbuji, China	B5	34
Banco, Punta, c., C.R.	I11	92
Bancroft, Ont., Can.	E18	110
Bancroft, Id., U.S.	H14	122
Bancroft, Ia., U.S.	H13	118
Bancroft, Ne., U.S.	I11	118
Bānda, India	H9	44
Banda, Kepulauan, is., Indon.	F8	38
Banda, Laut (Banda Sea), Indon.	G8	38
Banda Aceh, Indon.	L3	40
Bānda Dāūd Shāh, Pak.	D4	44
Banda del Río Salí, Arg.	D6	80
Bandama, stm., C. Iv.	H7	64
Bandama Blanc, stm., C. Iv.	G7	64
Bandama Rouge, stm., C. Iv.	G6	64
Bandar see Machilīpatnam, India	D6	46
Bandar Beheshtī, Iran	I16	48
Bandar-e 'Abbās, Iran	H14	48
Bandar-e Anzalī (Bandar-e Pahlavī), Iran	C10	48
Bandar-e Būshehr, Iran	G11	48
Bandar-e Deylam, Iran	F11	48
Bandar-e Khomeynī (Bandar-e Shāhpūr), Iran	F10	48
Bandar-e Lengeh, Iran	H13	48
Bandar-e Māh Shahr, Iran	F10	48
Bandar-e Rīg, Iran	G11	48
Bandar-e Torkeman, Iran	C13	48
Bandar Seri Begawan, Bru.	E5	38
Banded Peak, mtn., Co., U.S.	G10	120
Bandeira, Pico da, mtn., Braz.	F8	79
Bandeirantes, Braz.	B3	79
Bandeirantes, Braz.	E1	79
Bandeirantes, Braz.	G3	79
Bandera, Arg.	E7	80
Bandera, Tx., U.S.	J7	116
Bandera, Alto, mtn., Dom. Rep.	E9	94
Banderas, Bahía de, b., Mex.	G7	90
Bandiagara, Mali	D8	64
Bandiantaolehai, China	C7	30
Bandırma, Tur.	I11	20
Bandon, Ire.	J5	8
Bandon, Or., U.S.	G1	122
Ban Don, Ao, b., Thai.	J5	40
Bandula, Moz.	B11	66
Bandundu, Zaire	B3	58
Bandung, Indon.	j13	39a
Bāneh, Iran	D8	48
Banes, Cuba	D7	94
Banff, Alta., Can.	F19	102
Banff, Scot., U.K.	D11	8
Banff National Park, Alta., Can.	F18	102
Banfora, Burkina	F7	64
Bangalore, India	F4	46
Bangaon, India	I13	44
Bangassou, Cen. Afr. Rep.	H5	56
Banggai, Indon.	F7	38
Banggai, Kepulauan, is., Indon.	F7	38
Banghāzī, Libya	B5	56
Bangil, Indon.	j16	39a
Bangjang, Sud.	L7	60
Bangjun, China	D5	32
Bangka, Pulau, i., Indon.	F4	38
Bangkalan, Indon.	j16	39a
Bangkok see Krung Thep, Thai.	H6	40
Bangladesh, ctry., Asia	E13	42
Bang Mun Nak, Thai.	F6	40
Bangolo, C. Iv.	H6	64
Bangor, N. Ire., U.K.	G8	8
Bangor, Wales, U.K.	H9	8
Bangor, Me., U.S.	C18	108
Bangor, Mi., U.S.	H9	110
Bangor, Pa., U.S.	G11	108
Bangs, Tx., U.S.	H7	116
Bang Saphan, Thai.	I5	40
Bangshi, China	C10	32
Bangued, Phil.	m19	39b
Bangui, Cen. Afr. Rep.	H4	56
Bangweulu, Lake, l., Zam.	D5	58
Ban Hin Heup, Laos	E7	40
Ban Houayxay, Laos	D6	40
Bani, Burkina	D9	64
Baní, Dom. Rep.	E9	94
Bani, stm., Mali	E7	64
Baniachang, Bngl.	H14	44
Banikoara, Benin	F11	64
Banī Mazār, Egypt	C6	60
Banī Suwayf, Egypt	C6	60
Banī Walīd, Libya	B3	56
Bāniyās, Syria	B5	50
Banja Luka, Bos.	E12	18
Banjarmasin, Indon.	F5	38
Banjin, China	C9	34
Banjul (Bathurst), Gam.	E1	64
Bankas, Mali	D8	64
Bankilaré, Niger	D10	64
Banks, Al., U.S.	K11	114
Banksian, stm., Can.	E20	104
Banks Island, i., B.C., Can.	D4	102
Banks Island, i., N.W. Ter., Can.	B8	96
Banks Lake, res., Wa., U.S.	C6	122
Banks Peninsula, pen., N.Z.	E4	72
Banks Strait, strt., Austl.	M8	70
Bānkura, India	I12	44
Ban Mit, Laos	E6	40
Bann, stm., N. Ire., U.K.	G7	8
Ban Nahin, Laos	E8	40
Ban Namnga, Laos	D7	40
Banner Elk, N.C., U.S.	C5	112
Bannertown, N.C., U.S.	C6	112
Ban Ngam, Laos	D8	40
Banning, Ca., U.S.	K9	124
Bannock Peak, mtn., Id., U.S.	H13	122
Bannu, Pak.	D4	44
Banon, Fr.	H12	14
Baños, Ec.	H3	84
Baños, Peru	D3	82
Ban Pakneun, Laos	E6	40
Ban Pong, Thai.	H5	40
Banpu, China	A8	34
Banqiao, China	E9	34
Banqiaoji, China	C5	34
Banquan, China	H6	32
Banshi, China	J4	34
Banská Bystrica, Slov.	G19	10
Banská Štiavnica, Slov.	G18	10
Ban Songkhon, Laos	F8	40
Bānswāra, India	I6	44
Ban Thanoun, Laos	E6	40
Bantry, Ire.	J4	8
Ban Xènkhalôk, Laos	E6	40
Banyak, Kepulauan, is., Indon.	M4	40
Banyoles, Spain	C14	16
Banzare Coast, Ant.	B7	73
Banzi, China	K6	34
Baode, China	D9	30
Baoding, China	E3	32
Baofeng, China	B2	34
Bao Ha, Viet.	C8	40
Baohekou, China	C6	32
Baoji, China	E8	30
Bao Lac, Viet.	I9	40
Baonian, China	D8	34
Baoquan, China	G7	32
Baoshan, China	D10	34
Baoshan, China	B5	40
Baoting, China	H8	30
Baotou, China	C8	30
Baowei, China	C9	40
Baoxinji, China	C4	34
Baoying, China	B8	34
Bāpatla, India	E6	46
Bapaume, Fr.	B9	14
Bapchule, Az., U.S.	K5	120
Bāqa el Gharbīya, Isr.	D4	50
Baqên, China	E16	44
B'aqlīn, Leb.	A5	50
Ba'qūbah, Iraq	E8	48
Baquedano, Chile	B4	80
Bar, Yugo.	G3	20
Baraawe, Som.	H9	56
Barabinsk, Russia	F7	28
Barabinskaja step', pl., Russia	F7	28
Baraboo, Wi., U.S.	G6	110
Baraboo, stm., Wi., U.S.	G6	110
Baraboulé, Burkina	D9	64
Baracaju, stm., Braz.	B3	79
Baracaldo, Spain	B9	16
Barachit, Erit.	J10	60
Barachois Pond Provincial Park, Newf., Can.	D15	106
Baracoa, Cuba	D7	94
Baracoa, Hond.	B7	92
Baradero, Arg.	G9	80
Baradine, Austl.	H8	70
Baraga, Mi., U.S.	D7	110
Baragarh, India	B7	46
Bārah, Sud.	K6	60
Barahona, Dom. Rep.	E9	94
Barak, Tur.	C4	48
Baraka, val., Afr.	E8	56
Baralaba, Austl.	E8	70
Baram, stm., Malay.	E5	38
Barama, stm., Guy.	D13	84
Baran', Bela.	G13	22
Baranagar, India	I13	44
Baranoa, Col.	B5	84
Baranof Island, i., Ak., U.S.	H27	100
Baranoviči, Bela.	H9	22
Baranya, co., Hung.	J18	10
Barão de Melgaço, Braz.	G14	82
Baratang Island, i., India	H2	40
Barataria, La., U.S.	M6	114
Barataria Bay, b., La., U.S.	M7	114
Barat Daya, Kepulauan, is., Indon.	G8	38
Bar'atino, Russia	G17	22
Barauana, stm., Braz.	G12	84
Barauni, India	H11	44
Baraut, India	F7	44
Baraya, Col.	F5	84
Barbacena, Braz.	F7	79
Barbacoas, Col.	G3	84
Barbados, ctry., N.A.	H15	94
Barbar, Sud.	H7	60
Barbareta, Isla, i., Hond.	A8	92
Barbas, Cap, c., W. Sah.	I2	62
Barbastro, Spain	C12	16
Barbate de Franco, Spain	I6	16
Barbeau Peak, mtn., N.W. Ter., Can.	A12	86
Barberena, Guat.	C4	92
Barberton, S. Afr.	E10	66
Barberton, Oh., U.S.	F5	108
Barbezieux, Fr.	G6	14
Barbil, India	I11	44
Barbosa, Col.	D5	84
Barbosa, Col.	E6	84
Barboursville, W.V., U.S.	I4	108
Barbourville, Ky., U.S.	C3	112
Barbuda, i., Antig.	F14	94
Barby, Ger.	D11	10
Barcaldine, Austl.	D6	70
Barcău (Berettyó), stm., Eur.	B6	20
Barce see Al-Marj, Libya	B5	56
Barcellona Pozzo di Gotto, Italy	K10	18
Barcelona, Mex.	D8	90
Barcelona, Spain	D14	16
Barcelona, Ven.	B10	84
Barcelos, Braz.	H11	84
Barcin, Pol.	C17	10
Barcoo, stm., Austl.	E5	70
Barcs, Hung.	J17	10
Barczewo, Pol.	B20	10
Bärdä, Azer.	A9	48
Barda del Medio, Arg.	J4	80
Bardaï, Chad	D4	56
Bardai, Sud.	K1	60
Bardawīl, Sabkhat al-, sw., Egypt	F2	48
Barddhamān, India	I12	44
Bardejov, Slov.	F21	10
Bardi, Italy	E4	18
Bardīyah, Libya	B3	60
Bardo, Tun.	M5	18
Bardonecchia, Italy	D1	18
Bardoux, Lac, l., Que., Can.	A6	106
Bardstown, Ky., U.S.	E11	114
Bardu, Nor.	G16	6
Bardufoss, Nor.	G16	6
Bardwell, Ky., U.S.	F7	114
Bareilly, India	F8	44
Barents Sea, Eur.	B4	24
Barentu, Erit.	J9	60
Barfleur, Fr.	C5	14
Barge, Eth.	N9	60
Bargnop, Sud.	M5	60
Barguzin, stm., Russia	G14	28
Bar Harbor, Me., U.S.	C18	108
Bari, Italy	H11	18
Baria, stm., Ven.	G9	84
Barichara, Col.	D6	84
Barillas, Guat.	B3	92
Barīm (Perim), i., Yemen	H3	47
Barima, stm., S.A.	C12	84
Barima-Waini, prov., Guy.	D13	84
Barinas, Ven.	C7	84
Barinas, state, Ven.	C8	84
Baring, Cape, c., N.W. Ter., Can.	B9	96
Barinitas, Ven.	C7	84
Bāripada, India	J12	44
Bariri, Braz.	G4	79
Bārīs, Egypt	E6	60
Barisāl, Bngl.	I14	44
Barisan, Pegunungan, mts., Indon.	F3	38
Barito, stm., Indon.	F5	38
Barjols, Fr.	I13	14
Bark, stm., Wi., U.S.	H7	110
Barkal, Bngl.	I15	44
Barkerville, B.C., Can.	D13	102
Barkerville Historic Park, B.C., Can.	D13	102
Barkley, Lake, res., U.S.	F9	114
Barkley Sound, strt., B.C., Can.	I9	102
Barkly East, S. Afr.	H8	66
Barkly Tableland, plat., Austl.	C7	68
Barkly West, S. Afr.	G7	66
Barkol, China	C5	30
Barksdale, Tx., U.S.	J6	116
Bârlad, Rom.	C11	20
Bar-le-Duc, Fr.	D12	14
Barlee, Lake, l., Austl.	E3	68
Barletta, Italy	H11	18
Barling, Ar., U.S.	G2	114
Barlow, Ky., U.S.	E7	114
Bārmer, India	H4	44
Barnard Castle, Eng., U.K.	G15	8
Barnaul, Russia	G14	26
Barn Bluff, mtn., Austl.	M6	70
Barnegat, N.J., U.S.	H12	108
Barnegat Bay, b., N.J., U.S.	H12	108
Barnesboro, Pa., U.S.	G8	108
Barnes Ice Cap, N.W. Ter., Can.	B18	96
Barnes Lake, l., Man., Can.	B16	104
Barnesville, Ga., U.S.	F2	112
Barnesville, Mn., U.S.	E11	118
Barnesville, Oh., U.S.	H5	108
Barnhart, Tx., U.S.	H5	116
Barnsdall, Ok., U.S.	C10	116
Barnstable, Ma., U.S.	F16	108
Barnstaple, Eng., U.K.	J9	8
Barnwell, Alta., Can.	H22	102
Barnwell, S.C., U.S.	F5	112
Baro, stm., Afr.	G8	56
Barons, Alta., Can.	G21	102
Barpeta, India	G14	44
Barqa, China	E9	44
Barqah (Cyrenaica), hist. reg., Libya	C2	60
Barque Canada Reef, rf., Asia	D5	38
Barques, Pointe aux, c., Mi., U.S.	F13	110
Barquisimeto, Ven.	B8	84
Barra, Braz.	F10	76
Barra, Ponta da, c., Moz.	D12	66
Barraba, Austl.	H9	70
Barrackville, W.V., U.S.	H6	108
Barra da Estiva, Braz.	B8	79
Barra do Bugres, Braz.	F13	82
Barra do Corda, Braz.	E9	76
Barra do Cuanza, Ang.	C2	58
Barra do Garças, Braz.	C2	79
Barra do Mendes, Braz.	A7	79
Barra do Piraí, Braz.	G7	79
Barra do Ribeiro, Braz.	F13	80
Barra Falsa, Ponta da, c., Moz.	D12	66
Barrafranca, Italy	L9	18
Barra Mansa, Braz.	G6	79
Barranca, Peru	D3	82
Barranca, Peru	A3	82
Barrancabermeja, Col.	D6	84
Barrancas, Col.	B6	84
Barrancas, Ven.	C7	84
Barrancas, Ven.	C11	84
Barrancas, stm., Arg.	I3	80
Barranqueras, Arg.	D9	80
Barranquilla, Col.	B5	84
Barras, Braz.	D10	76
Barre, Vt., U.S.	C14	108
Barreal, Arg.	F4	80
Barreiras, Braz.	B6	79
Barreirinha, Braz.	I14	84
Barreiro, Port.	G2	16
Barreiro, stm., Braz.	C2	79
Barreiros, Braz.	E11	76
Barren, stm., Ky., U.S.	E10	114
Barren, Nosy, is., Madag.	q20	67b
Barren Islands, is., Ak., U.S.	G18	100
Barren River Lake, res., Ky., U.S.	F10	114
Barretos, Braz.	F4	79
Barrhead, Alta., Can.	C20	102
Barrie, Ont., Can.	F16	110
Barrière, B.C., Can.	F14	102
Barrier Range, mts., Austl.	H4	70
Barrington, N.S., Can.	I8	106
Barrington Lake, l., Man., Can.	B14	104
Barringun, Austl.	G6	70
Barrita Vieja, Guat.	D4	92
Barro Alto, Braz.	C4	79
Barron, Wi., U.S.	E4	110
Barrow, Arg.	J8	80
Barrow, Ak., U.S.	A16	100
Barrow, Point, c., Ak., U.S.	A16	100
Barrow Creek, Austl.	D6	68
Barrow-in-Furness, Eng., U.K.	G10	8
Barrow Island, i., Austl.	D3	68
Barrows, Man., Can.	F13	104
Barrow Strait, strt., N.W. Ter., Can.	B13	96
Barry, Il., U.S.	C5	114
Barrys Bay, Ont., Can.	E18	110
Barryton, Mi., U.S.	G10	110
Bārsi, India	C3	46
Barsinghausen, Ger.	C9	10
Barstow, Ca., U.S.	J8	124
Barstow, Tx., U.S.	H3	116
Bar-sur-Aube, Fr.	D11	14
Bar-sur-Seine, Fr.	D11	14
Bartang, stm., Taj.	A5	44
Barthélemy, Deo, Viet.	E8	40
Bartholomew, Bayou, stm., U.S.	I5	114
Bartica, Guy.	D13	84
Bartle Frere, mtn., Austl.	A6	70
Bartlesville, Ok., U.S.	C11	116
Bartlett, Ne., U.S.	J9	118
Bartlett, N.H., U.S.	C15	108
Bartlett, Tn., U.S.	G7	114
Bartlett, Tx., U.S.	I9	116
Bartletts Harbour, Newf., Can.	B16	106
Bartley, Ne., U.S.	K7	118
Bartolomé de las Casas, Arg.	C9	80
Bartolomeu Dias, Moz.	C12	66
Barton, Vt., U.S.	C14	108
Barton Lake, l., Ont., Can.	F20	104
Barton-upon-Humber, Eng., U.K.	H13	8
Bartonville, Il., U.S.	J6	110
Bartoszyce, Pol.	A20	10
Bartow, Fl., U.S.	L5	112
Bartow, Ga., U.S.	G4	112
Barú, Volcán, vol., Pan.	I12	92
Baruun-Urt, Mong.	B9	30
Barva, Volcán, vol., C.R.	G10	92
Barview, Or., U.S.	G1	122
Barwāni, India	I6	44
Barwick, Ga., U.S.	I3	112
Barwon, stm., Austl.	G8	70
Barybino, Russia	F20	22
Baryš, Russia	G7	26
Basacato del Este, Eq. Gui.	J14	64
Basail, Arg.	D9	80
Basankusu, Zaire	A3	58
Basarabeasca, Mol.	C12	20
Basarabi, Rom.	E12	20
Basatongwula Shan, mtn., China	D14	44
Basavilbaso, Arg.	G9	80
Basco, Phil.	A7	38
Bascuñán, Cabo, c., Chile	E3	80
Basel (Bâle), Switz.	C8	13
Basey, Phil.	C8	38
Bashaw, Alta., Can.	E22	102
Bashi Channel, strt., Asia	G11	30
Bashkortostan see Baškirija, state, Russia	G9	26
Basile, La., U.S.	L4	114
Basilicata, prov., Italy	I11	18
Basin, Mt., U.S.	D13	122
Basin, Wy., U.S.	F17	122
Basin Lake, l., Sask., Can.	F9	104
Basīrhāt, India	I13	44
Baskakovka, Russia	G17	22
Basket Lake, l., Ont., Can.	I22	104
Baškirija, state, Russia	G9	26
Bašmakovo, Russia	H26	22
Basoko, Zaire	A4	58
Basque Lands see Euskal Herriko, prov., Spain	B9	16
Basra see Al-Baṣrah, Iraq	F9	48
Bas-Rhin, dept., Fr.	D14	14
Bassano, Alta., Can.	G22	102
Bassano del Grappa, Italy	D6	18
Bassari, Togo	G10	64
Bassas da India, rf., Afr.	F7	58
Bassecourt, Switz.	D7	13
Bassein see Pathein, Mya.	F3	40
Bassein, mth., Mya.	F3	40
Basse-Terre, Guad.	F14	94
Basseterre, St. K./N.	F13	94
Basse-Terre, i., Guad.	F14	94
Bassett, Ne., U.S.	I8	118
Bassett, Va., U.S.	C7	112
Bassett Peak, mtn., Az., U.S.	L6	120
Basse-Yutz, Fr.	J9	12
Bassfield, Ms., U.S.	K7	114
Bass Harbor, Me., U.S.	C18	108
Bassikounou, Maur.	D7	64
Bassila, Benin	G10	64
Bass River, N.S., Can.	G10	106
Bass Strait, strt., Austl.	L6	70
Basṭah, Jord.	H5	50
Bastak, Iran	H13	48
Bastelica, Fr.	I24	15a
Basti, India	G10	44
Bastia, Fr.	J16	14
Bastian, Va., U.S.	B5	112
Bastimentos, Pan.	H12	92
Bastimentos, Isla, i., Pan.	H12	92
Bastogne (Bastenaken), Bel.	H8	12
Bastrop, La., U.S.	J5	114
Bastrop, Tx., U.S.	I9	116
Bastuträsk, Swe.	I17	6
Basutoland see Lesotho, ctry., Afr.	G5	58
Bata, Eq. Gui.	A1	58
Bataan Peninsula, pen., Phil.	n19	39b
Batabanó, Golfo de, b., Cuba	C3	94
Bataguassu, Braz.	F2	79
Bataiporã, Braz.	G2	79
Batajsk, Russia	H5	26
Batala, India	E6	44
Batan, China	A9	34
Batang, China	E6	30
Batangas, Phil.	o19	39b
Batan Islands, is., Phil.	A7	38
Bátaszék, Hung.	I18	10
Batatais, Braz.	F5	79
Batavia, Arg.	H6	80
Batavia, Il., U.S.	I7	110
Batavia, Ia., U.S.	J3	110
Batavia, N.Y., U.S.	E8	108
Batavia, Oh., U.S.	H2	108
Bătdâmbâng, Camb.	H7	40
Bateckij, Russia	C13	22
Batemans Bay, Austl.	J9	70
Batesburg, S.C., U.S.	F5	112
Batesville, Ar., U.S.	G5	114
Batesville, In., U.S.	C11	114
Batesville, Ms., U.S.	H7	114
Batesville, Tx., U.S.	K7	116
Bath, N.B., Can.	F6	106
Bath, Eng., U.K.	J11	8
Bath, Me., U.S.	D17	108
Bath, N.Y., U.S.	E9	108
Bathgate, N.D., U.S.	C10	118
Bathinda, India	E6	44
Bathsheba, Barb.	H15	94
Bathurst, Austl.	I8	70
Bathurst, N.B., Can.	E8	106
Bathurst see Banjul, Gam.	E1	64
Bathurst, S. Afr.	I8	66
Bathurst, Cape, c., N.W. Ter., Can.	B7	96
Bathurst Inlet, N.W. Ter., Can.	C11	96
Bathurst Inlet, b., N.W. Ter., Can.	C11	96
Bathurst Island, i., Austl.	B6	68
Bathurst Island, i., N.W. Ter., Can.	A12	96
Batia, Benin	F10	64
Batié, Burkina	G8	64
Bāṭin, Wādī al-, val., Asia	G9	48
Batkanu, S.L.	G3	64
Batlow, Austl.	J8	70
Batman, Tur.	C6	48
Batna, Alg.	C14	62
Baṭn al-Ghūl, Jord.	I5	50
Batoche Rectory National Historic Site, hist., Sask., Can.	F8	104
Baton Rouge, La., U.S.	L5	114
Batouri, Cam.	H9	54
Batovi, Braz.	C2	79
Baṭrā (Petra), hist., Jord.	H4	50
Batson, Tx., U.S.	I12	116
Batticaloa, Sri L.	I6	46
Battle, stm., Can.	A4	98
Battle, stm., Can.	E5	104
Battle Creek, Ia., U.S.	I12	118
Battle Creek, Mi., U.S.	H10	110
Battle Creek, Ne., U.S.	J10	118
Battle Ground, In., U.S.	B10	114
Battle Ground, Wa., U.S.	E3	122
Battle Harbour, Newf., Can.	F21	96
Battle Lake, Mn., U.S.	E12	118
Battlement Mesa, mtn., Co., U.S.	E8	120
Battle Mountain, Nv., U.S.	D9	124
Battonya, Hung.	I21	10
Batu, mtn., Eth.	G8	56
Batu, Kepulauan, is., Indon.	O5	40
Batumi, Geor.	I6	26
Batu Pahat, Malay.	N7	40
Baturité, Braz.	D11	76
Bat Yam, Isr.	D3	50
Baubau, Indon.	G7	38
Bauchi, Nig.	F14	64
Baud, Fr.	E3	14
Baudette, Mn., U.S.	B1	110
Baudó, stm., Col.	E4	84
Bauld, Cape, c., Newf., Can.	A18	106
Baume-les-Dames, Fr.	E13	14
Baures, Bol.	E10	82
Baures, stm., Bol.	E10	82
Bauru, Braz.	G4	79
Baús, Braz.	E2	79
Bauska, Lat.	E7	22
Bautzen, Ger.	D14	10
Bauxite, Ar., U.S.	H4	114
Bavaria see Bayern, state, Ger.	F11	10
Bavispe, Mex.	B5	90
Bavispe, stm., Mex.	C5	90
Bavleny, Russia	E22	22
Bawdwin, Mya.	C4	40
Bawku, Ghana	F9	64
Baxian, China	D4	32
Baxley, Ga., U.S.	H4	112
Baxter, Ia., U.S.	I2	110
Baxter, Mn., U.S.	D1	110
Baxter, Tn., U.S.	F11	114
Baxter Springs, Ks., U.S.	N13	118
Baxterville, Ms., U.S.	K7	114
Bay, Ar., U.S.	G6	114
Bayamo, Cuba	D6	94
Bayamón, P.R.	E11	94
Bayan Har Shan, mts., China	E6	30
Bayano, Lago, res., Pan.	C3	84
Bayan Obo, China	C9	30
Bayard, Ia., U.S.	J13	118
Bayard, Ne., U.S.	J4	118
Bayard, N.M., U.S.	L8	120
Bayard, W.V., U.S.	H7	108
Bayboro, N.C., U.S.	D10	112
Bay Bulls, Newf., Can.	E21	106
Bayburt, Tur.	A6	48
Bay City, Mi., U.S.	G12	110
Bay City, Or., U.S.	E2	122
Bay City, Tx., U.S.	K11	116
Bay de Verde, Newf., Can.	D21	106
Baydhabo, Som.	H9	56
Bay du Nord, stm., Newf., Can.	E18	106
Bayerische Alpen, mts., Eur.	H11	10
Bayern, state, Ger.	F11	10
Bayeux, Fr.	C6	14
Bayfield, Co., U.S.	G9	120
Bayfield, Wi., U.S.	D5	110
Bayfield, Île, i., Que., Can.	A15	106
Bayiji, China	A6	34
Bayingzi, China	B8	32
Bay L'Argent, Newf., Can.	E19	106
Bay Minette, Al., U.S.	L9	114
Bayombong, Phil.	m19	39b
Bayon, Fr.	D13	14
Bayonne, Fr.	I5	14
Bayou Bodcau Reservoir, res., La., U.S.	J3	114
Bayou Cane, La., U.S.	M6	114

Name	Map Ref.	Page
Bayou D'Arbonne Lake, res., La., U.S.	J4	114
Bayou La Batre, Al., U.S.	L8	114
Bayovar, Peru	A1	82
Bay Port, Mi., U.S.	G12	110
Bayport, Mn., U.S.	E3	110
Bayreuth, Ger.	F11	10
Bayrischzell, Ger.	H12	10
Bay Roberts, Newf., Can.	E20	106
Bayrūt (Beirut), Leb.	A5	50
Bay Saint Louis, Ms., U.S.	L7	114
Bay Shore, N.Y., U.S.	G13	108
Bayside, Ont., Can.	F18	110
Bay Springs, Ms., U.S.	K7	114
Bayt al-Faqīh, Yemen	G3	47
Bayt Jinn, Syria	B5	50
Bayt Lahm (Bethlehem), Isr. Occ.	E4	50
Bayt Mirī, Leb.	A5	50
Baytown, Tx., U.S.	J12	116
Bayzo, Niger	E12	64
Baza, Spain	H9	16
Bazaruto, Ilha do, i., Moz.	C12	66
Bazas, Fr.	H6	14
Bazdār, Pak.	G1	44
Bazi, China	K2	34
Bazine, Ks., U.S.	M8	118
Be, Nosy, i., Madag.	n23	67b
Beach, N.D., U.S.	E3	118
Beach Haven, N.J., U.S.	H12	108
Beachville, Ont., Can.	G15	110
Beacon, N.Y., U.S.	F13	108
Beacon Hill, Wa., U.S.	D3	122
Beaconsfield, Austl.	M7	70
Beagle Gulf, b., Austl.	B6	68
Beagle Reef, rf., Austl.	C4	68
Bealanana, Madag.	o23	67b
Beale, Cape, c., B.C., Can.	I9	102
Bear, stm., Sask., Can.	D10	104
Bear, stm., U.S.	B5	120
Bear, stm., Ca., U.S.	E4	124
Bear Bay, b., N.W. Ter., Can.	A15	96
Bear Cove, B.C., Can.	G7	102
Bearden, Ar., U.S.	I4	114
Beardmore, Ont., Can.	G15	96
Beardstown, Il., U.S.	B6	114
Beardy and Okemasis Indian Reserves, Sask., Can.	F8	104
Bear Head Lake, l., Man., Can.	C18	104
Bear Island, i., Ant.	C11	73
Bear Island, i., Man., Can.	D16	104
Bear Island see Bjørnøya, i., Sval.	B2	24
Bear Lake, B.C., Can.	A8	102
Bear Lake, l., Alta., Can.	B15	102
Bear Lake, l., B.C., Can.	A8	102
Bear Lake, l., Man., Can.	C18	104
Bear Lake, l., U.S.	C5	120
Bear Mountain, mtn., Or., U.S.	G3	122
Béarn, hist. reg., Fr.	I6	14
Bear River, N.S., Can.	H8	106
Bear River Range, mts., U.S.	C5	120
Beartooth Pass, Wy., U.S.	F16	122
Bear Town, Ms., U.S.	K6	114
Beasain, Spain	B9	16
Beas de Segura, Spain	G9	16
Beata, Cabo, c., Dom. Rep.	F9	94
Beata, Isla, i., Dom. Rep.	F9	94
Beaton, B.C., Can.	G17	102
Beatrice, Al., U.S.	K9	114
Beatrice, Ne., U.S.	K11	118
Beatrice, Zimb.	B10	66
Beattie, Ks., U.S.	L11	118
Beatton, stm., B.C., Can.	E8	96
Beatton, stm., B.C., Can.	A14	102
Beatty, Nv., U.S.	H9	124
Beattyville, Ky., U.S.	B3	112
Beaucaire, Fr.	I11	14
Beauce, reg., Fr.	D8	14
Beauceville, Que., Can.	A16	108
Beaudesert, Austl.	F10	70
Beaufort, N.C., U.S.	E10	112
Beaufort, S.C., U.S.	G6	112
Beaufort Sea, N.A.	B5	86
Beaufort West, S. Afr.	I6	66
Beaugency, Fr.	E8	14
Beauharnois, Que., Can.	B13	108
Beaumont, Newf., Can.	C18	106
Beaumont, Fr.	C5	14
Beaumont, Ca., U.S.	K9	124
Beaumont, Ms., U.S.	K8	114
Beaumont, Tx., U.S.	L2	114
Beaumont-sur-Sarthe, Fr.	D7	14
Beaune, Fr.	E11	14
Beauport, Que., Can.	F2	106
Beaupré, Que., Can.	E3	106
Beaupréau, Fr.	E5	14
Beaupré Lake, l., Sask., Can.	D7	104
Beaurepaire, Fr.	G12	14
Beauséjour, Man., Can.	H18	104
Beauvais, Fr.	C9	14
Beauval, Sask., Can.	C7	104
Beauvoir-sur-Mer, Fr.	F4	14
Beaver, Ak., U.S.	C21	100
Beaver, Ok., U.S.	C6	116
Beaver, Pa., U.S.	G6	108
Beaver, Ut., U.S.	F4	120
Beaver, W.V., U.S.	B5	112
Beaver, stm., Can.	D7	96
Beaver, stm., Can.	D7	104
Beaver, stm., N.Y., U.S.	D11	108
Beaver, stm., Pa., U.S.	G6	108
Beaver, stm., Ut., U.S.	F4	120
Beaver City, Ne., U.S.	K8	118
Beaver Creek, Yukon, Can.	E24	100
Beaver Crossing, Ne., U.S.	K10	118
Beaver Dam, Ky., U.S.	E10	114
Beaver Dam, Wi., U.S.	G7	110
Beaverdell, B.C., Can.	H15	102
Beaver Falls, Pa., U.S.	G6	108
Beaverhead, stm., Mt., U.S.	E13	122
Beaverhead Mountains, mts., U.S.	E12	122
Beaverhill Lake, l., Alta., Can.	D22	102
Beaver Hill Lake, l., Man., Can.	D20	104
Beaver Island, i., Mi., U.S.	E10	110
Beaver Lake, l., Alta., Can.	C23	102
Beaver Lake, res., Ar., U.S.	F3	114
Beaver Lake Indian Reserve, Alta., Can.	C23	102
Beaverlodge, Alta., Can.	B15	102
Beaver Mountains, mts., Ak., U.S.	E16	100
Beaverton, Ont., Can.	F16	110
Beaverton, Mi., U.S.	G11	110
Beaverton, Or., U.S.	E3	122
Beāwar, India	G6	44
Beazley, Arg.	G5	80
Bebedouro, Braz.	F4	79
Bebeji, Nig.	F14	64
Becal, Mex.	G14	90
Bécancour, stm., Que., Can.	A15	108
Bečej, Yugo.	D4	20
Beceni, Rom.	D10	20
Becerro, Cayos, is., Hond.	B11	92
Béchar, Alg.	E9	62
Bechater, Tun.	L4	18
Bechyně, Czech.	F14	10
Beckley, W.V., U.S.	J5	108
Beckum, Ger.	D8	10
Beckville, Tx., U.S.	J2	114
Becky Peak, mtn., Nv., U.S.	E11	124
Bédarieux, Fr.	I10	14
Bedele, Eth.	M9	60
Bedeque Bay, b., P.E.I., Can.	F10	106
Bedford, Que., Can.	B14	108
Bedford, In., U.S.	D10	114
Bedford, Ia., U.S.	K13	118
Bedford, Ky., U.S.	D11	114
Bedford, Pa., U.S.	G8	108
Bedford, Va., U.S.	B7	112
Bedfordshire, co., Eng., U.K.	I13	8
Bedias, Tx., U.S.	I11	116
Bednodemjanovsk, Russia	H26	22
Beebe, Ar., U.S.	G5	114
Beech, stm., Tn., U.S.	G8	114
Beech Creek, Ky., U.S.	E9	114
Beecher, Il., U.S.	I8	110
Beech Fork, stm., Ky., U.S.	E11	114
Beech Grove, In., U.S.	C10	114
Beechworth, Austl.	K7	70
Beechy, Sask., Can.	H7	104
Beecroft Head, c., Austl.	J9	70
Beemer, Ne., U.S.	J11	118
Beenleigh, Austl.	F10	70
Bee Ridge, Fl., U.S.	L4	112
Beersheba see Be'ér Sheva', Isr.	F3	50
Beersheba Springs, Tn., U.S.	G11	114
Be'ér Sheva (Beersheba), Isr.	F3	50
Beestekraal, S. Afr.	E8	66
Beethoven Peninsula, pen., Ant.	C12	73
Beetz, Lac, l., Que., Can.	B11	106
Beeville, Tx., U.S.	K9	116
Befale, Zaire	A4	58
Befandriana, Madag.	o23	67b
Befasy, Madag.	r21	67b
Befotaka, Madag.	s22	67b
Bega, Austl.	K8	70
Bega (Begej), stm., Eur.	D5	20
Begej (Bega), stm., Eur.	D4	20
Beggs, Ok., U.S.	D10	116
Begičevskij, Russia	H21	22
Begoml', Bela.	G11	22
Begoro, Ghana	H9	64
Beguncy, Russia	B12	22
Begusarai, India	H12	44
Behbahān, Iran	F11	48
Behshahr, Iran	C12	48
Bei, stm., China	K2	34
Bei'an, China	B12	30
Beida see Al-Bayḍā', Libya	B5	56
Beidaihe, China	D7	32
Beidun, China	I7	34
Beigi, Eth.	M8	60
Beihai, China	D10	40
Beijing (Peking), China	D4	32
Beijing Shi (Peking Shih), China	C10	30
Beikan, China	C10	34
Beiling, China	K4	34
Beinwil, Switz.	D8	13
Beipan, stm., China	F8	30
Beipiao, China	B8	32
Beiqi, China	C10	32
Beira, Moz.	B12	66
Beira Baixa, hist. reg., Port.	F4	16
Beira Litoral, hist. reg., Port.	E3	16
Beirut see Bayrūt, Leb.	A5	50
Beiseker, Alta., Can.	F21	102
Beishan, China	B10	40
Bei Shan, mts., China	C6	30
Beisu, China	E2	32
Beitang, China	D5	32
Beitbridge, Zimb.	D10	66
Beixinzhen, China	D10	34
Beizhen, China	B9	32
Beja, Port.	G4	16
Béja, Tun.	M4	18
Bejaïa (Bougie), Alg.	B13	62
Béjar, Spain	E6	16
Bejuco, Pan.	C3	84
Bejuma, Ven.	B8	84
Bekabad, Uzb.	I11	26
Bekdaš, Turk.	I8	26
Békés, Hung.	I21	10
Békés, co., Hung.	I20	10
Békéscsaba, Hung.	I21	10
Bekilli, Tur.	K13	20
Bekily, Madag.	t21	67b
Bekitro, Madag.	t21	67b
Bekkaria, Alg.	N3	18
Bekkevoort, Bel.	G6	12
Bekodoka, Madag.	p21	67b
Bekoji, Eth.	N10	60
Bela, India	H9	44
Bela, Pak.	G2	44
Belabolo, Sud.	M3	60
Bela Crkva, Yugo.	E5	20
Bel Air, Md., U.S.	H10	108
Belaja, stm., Russia	G9	26
Belaja Ber'ozka, Russia	I16	22
Bélanger, stm., Man., Can.	E17	104
Bela Palanka, Yugo.	F6	20
Belarus, ctry., Eur.	E13	4
Belau see Palau, dep., Oc.	E9	38
Belavenona, Madag.	t22	67b
Bela Vista, Braz.	B10	80
Bela Vista, Moz.	F11	66
Bela Vista de Goiás, Braz.	D4	79
Bela Vista do Paraíso, Braz.	G3	79
Belawan, Indon.	M5	40
Belbubulo, Sud.	M8	60
Bełchatów, Pol.	D19	10
Belcher, La., U.S.	J3	114
Belcheragh, Afg.	C1	44
Belcher Islands, is., N.W. Ter., Can.	E17	96
Belcourt, N.D., U.S.	C8	118
Belding, Mi., U.S.	G10	110
Beled Weyne, Som.	H10	56
Belém, Braz.	D9	76
Belén, Arg.	D5	80
Belén, Chile	H7	82
Belén, Col.	D6	84
Belén, Nic.	F9	92
Belén, Para.	B10	80
Belen, N.M., U.S.	J10	120
Belén, Ur.	F10	80
Belén, stm., Arg.	D5	80
Belén de Escobar, Arg.	H9	80
Belfast, S. Afr.	E10	66
Belfast, N. Ire., U.K.	G8	8
Belfast, Me., U.S.	C17	108
Belfield, N.D., U.S.	E4	118
Belfort, Fr.	E13	14
Belfry, Ky., U.S.	B4	112
Belfry, Mt., U.S.	E16	122
Belgaum, India	E3	46
Belgium, ctry., Eur.	E8	4
Belgorod, Russia	G5	26
Belgrade, Mn., U.S.	F12	118
Belgrade, Mt., U.S.	E14	122
Belgrade, Ne., U.S.	J9	118
Belgrade see Beograd, Yugo.	E4	20
Belhaven, N.C., U.S.	D10	112
Beli Drim, stm., Eur.	G4	20
Beli Manastir, Cro.	D2	20
Belington, W.V., U.S.	H7	108
Belitung, i., Indon.	F4	38
Belize, ctry., N.A.	I15	90
Belize, stm., Belize	I15	90
Belize City, Belize	I15	90
Belize Inlet, b., B.C., Can.	F7	102
Belknap Crater, crat., Or., U.S.	F4	122
Belkofski, Ak., U.S.	I13	100
Bell, stm., Que., Can.	G17	96
Bell, stm., Yukon, Can.	C26	100
Bella Bella, B.C., Can.	E6	102
Bellac, Fr.	F8	14
Bella Coola, B.C., Can.	E8	102
Bella Coola, stm., B.C., Can.	E8	102
Bella Flor, Bol.	D8	82
Bellair, Fl., U.S.	I5	112
Bellaire, Mi., U.S.	F10	110
Bellaire, Oh., U.S.	G6	108
Bellaire, Tx., U.S.	J11	116
Bellamy, Al., U.S.	J8	114
Bellary, India	E4	46
Bella Unión, Ur.	F10	80
Bella Vista, Arg.	E9	80
Bella Vista, Arg.	D6	80
Bella Vista, Para.	B10	80
Bellavista, Peru	A1	82
Bellavista, Peru	B3	82
Bellé, Sen.	D3	64
Belle, Mo., U.S.	D5	114
Belle, W.V., U.S.	I5	108
Belle, stm., Mi., U.S.	H13	110
Belle Bay, b., Newf., Can.	E18	106
Bellefontaine, Oh., U.S.	G3	108
Bellefonte, Pa., U.S.	G9	108
Belle Fourche, S.D., U.S.	G4	118
Belle Fourche, stm., U.S.	G5	118
Bellegarde, Fr.	F12	14
Belle Glade, Fl., U.S.	M6	112
Belle-Île, i., Fr.	E3	14
Belle Isle, i., Newf., Can.	F21	96
Belle Isle, Strait of, strt., Newf., Can.	A17	106
Bellême, Fr.	D7	14
Belleoram, Newf., Can.	E18	106
Belle-Plaine, Sask., Can.	H9	104
Belle Plaine, Ia., U.S.	I3	110
Belle Plaine, Ks., U.S.	N10	118
Belle Plaine, Mn., U.S.	F2	110
Belleview, Fl., U.S.	J4	112
Belleville, Ont., Can.	C9	108
Belleville, Il., U.S.	D7	114
Belleville, Ks., U.S.	L10	118
Belleville, Pa., U.S.	G9	108
Belleville, Wi., U.S.	H6	110
Belleville-sur-Saône, Fr.	F11	14
Bellevue, Alta., Can.	H20	102
Bellevue, Id., U.S.	G11	122
Bellevue, Ia., U.S.	H5	110
Bellevue, Mi., U.S.	H10	110
Bellevue, Ne., U.S.	J12	118
Bellevue, Oh., U.S.	F4	108
Bellevue, Tx., U.S.	F8	116
Bellevue, Wa., U.S.	C3	122
Belley, Fr.	G12	14
Bellingen, Austl.	H10	70
Bellingham, Eng., U.K.	F11	8
Bellingham, Mn., U.S.	F11	118
Bellingham, Wa., U.S.	B3	122
Bellingshausen, sci., Ant.	B1	73
Bellingshausen Sea, Ant.	C11	73
Bellinzona, Switz.	F11	13
Bell Island, i., Newf., Can.	E21	106
Bell Island, i., Newf., Can.	B18	106
Bell Island Hot Springs, Ak., U.S.	B3	102
Bellmead, Tx., U.S.	H9	116
Bello, Col.	D5	84
Bellot Strait, strt., N.W. Ter., Can.	B14	96
Bellows Falls, Vt., U.S.	D14	108
Bell Peninsula, pen., N.W. Ter., Can.	D16	96
Bells, Tn., U.S.	G7	114
Bells, Tx., U.S.	F10	116
Bells Corners, Ont., Can.	B11	108
Belluno, Italy	C7	18
Bell Ville, Arg.	G7	80
Bellville, Oh., U.S.	G4	108
Bellville, Tx., U.S.	J10	116
Bellwood, Ne., U.S.	J10	118
Bellwood, Pa., U.S.	G8	108
Belly, stm., N.A.	H21	102
Belmond, Ia., U.S.	H2	110
Belmont, Man., Can.	I15	104
Belmont, N.S., Can.	G10	106
Belmont, S. Afr.	G7	66
Belmont, Ms., U.S.	H8	114
Belmont, N.H., U.S.	D15	108
Belmont, N.Y., U.S.	E8	108
Belmont, S.C., U.S.	E5	112
Belmont, Wi., U.S.	H5	110
Belmonte, Braz.	C9	79
Belmonte, Port.	E4	16
Belmopan, Belize	I15	90
Belmullet, Ire.	G3	8
Belo, Madag.	q21	67b
Belogorsk, Russia	G17	28
Belo Horizonte, Braz.	E7	79
Beloit, Ks., U.S.	L9	118
Beloit, Wi., U.S.	H6	110
Beloje, ozero, l., Russia	A20	22
Beloje more (White Sea), Russia	D5	26
Belomorsk, Russia	E4	26
Belomorsko-Baltijskij kanal, Russia	I24	6
Belomut, Russia	G22	22
Belonia, India	I14	44
Beloozersk, Bela.	I8	22
Belorečensk, Russia	I5	26
Beloreck, Russia	G9	26
Belorussia see Belarus, ctry., Eur.	E13	4
Belot, Lac, l., N.W. Ter., Can.	C31	100
Belousovo, Russia	F19	22
Bel'ov, Russia	H19	22
Belo Vale, Braz.	F6	79
Belovo, Russia	G9	28
Beloz'orsk, Russia	A20	22
Belpre, Oh., U.S.	H5	108
Belspring, Va., U.S.	B6	112
Belt, Mt., U.S.	C15	122
Belton, Mo., U.S.	D2	114
Belton, S.C., U.S.	E4	112
Belton, Tx., U.S.	H9	116
Beltrán, Arg.	D6	80
Belucha, gora, mtn., Asia	H15	26
Belūr, India	G10	42
Belvès, Fr.	H8	14
Belvidere, Il., U.S.	H7	110
Belvidere, N.J., U.S.	G11	108
Belview, Mn., U.S.	G12	118
Belvís de la Jara, Spain	F7	16
Belyando, stm., Austl.	C7	70
Belyj, Russia	F15	22
Belyj, ostrov, i., Russia	C12	26
Belyje Berega, Russia	H17	22
Belyje Stolby, Russia	F20	22
Belyj Gorodok, Russia	E20	22
Belyj Luch, stm., Russia	D27	22
Belyniči, Bela.	H12	22
Belynkoviči, Bela.	H15	22
Belzoni, Ms., U.S.	I6	114
Bemarivo, Madag.	r21	67b
Bemavo, Madag.	r21	67b
Bembèrèkè, Benin	F11	64
Bement, Il., U.S.	C8	114
Bemidji, Mn., U.S.	C1	110
Bemis, Tn., U.S.	G8	114
Benāb, Iran	C9	48
Bena-Dibele, Zaire	B4	58
Benagerie, Austl.	H4	70
Benahmed, Mor.	D7	62
Ben'akoni, Bela.	G8	22
Benalla, Austl.	K6	70
Benares see Vārānasi, India	H10	44
Ben Arous, Tun.	B16	62
Benavente, Spain	C6	16
Benavides, Tx., U.S.	L8	116
Ben Badis, Alg.	K11	16
Ben Bolt, Tx., U.S.	L8	116
Bencubbin, Austl.	F3	68
Bend, Or., U.S.	F4	122
Bendaja, Lib.	H4	64
Bende, Nig.	I13	64
Bendemeer, Austl.	H9	70
Bendigo, Austl.	K6	70
Bendugu, S.L.	G4	64
Bēne, Lat.	E6	22
Bene Beraq, Isr.	D3	50
Benedito Leite, Braz.	E10	76
Benenitra, Madag.	s21	67b
Benešov, Czech.	F14	10
Benevento, Italy	H9	18
Benfeld, Fr.	D14	14
Bengal, Bay of, b., Asia	J14	44
Ben Gardane, Tun.	D16	62
Bengbu, China	C6	34
Benghazi see Banghāzī, Libya	B5	56
Ben Giang, Viet.	G9	40
Bengkalis, Indon.	N7	40
Bengkulu, Indon.	F3	38
Bengough, Sask., Can.	I9	104
Benguela, Ang.	D2	58
Benguerir, Mor.	D7	62
Benham, Ky., U.S.	C4	112
Beni, Zaire	A5	58
Beni, dept., Bol.	E9	82
Beni, stm., Bol.	D9	82
Béni Abbas, Alg.	E9	62
Benicarló, Spain	E12	16
Benicito, stm., Bol.	D9	82
Benima, Cen. Afr. Rep.	O2	60
Beni-Mellal, Mor.	D7	62
Benin (Bénin), ctry., Afr.	G7	54
Benin, Bight of, Afr.	G7	54
Benin City, Nig.	H12	64
Beni Saf, Alg.	J10	16
Benissa, Spain	G12	16
Benito, Man., Can.	G13	104
Benito Juárez, Arg.	I9	80
Benito Juárez, Presa, res., Mex.	I12	90
Benjamin, Tx., U.S.	F7	116
Benjamín Aceval, Para.	C10	80
Benjamin Constant, Braz.	J7	84
Benjamín Hill, Mex.	B4	90
Benjamín Zorrilla, Arg.	J6	80
Benkelman, Ne., U.S.	K6	118
Benld, Il., U.S.	C7	114
Ben Lomond, Ca., U.S.	G3	124
Ben Mehidi, Alg.	M2	18
Benndale, Ms., U.S.	L8	114
Bennet, Ne., U.S.	K11	118
Bennetta, ostrov, i., Russia	B21	28
Bennett Lake, l., Can.	F27	100
Bennett Lake, l., Man., Can.	E18	104
Bennettsville, S.C., U.S.	E7	112
Bennington, Ks., U.S.	L10	118
Bennington, Vt., U.S.	E13	108
Benniu, China	D8	34
Benoit, Ms., U.S.	I5	114
Benoni, S. Afr.	F9	66
Bénoué (Benue), stm., Afr.	G9	54
Benque Viejo del Carmen, Belize	I15	90
Bensheim, Ger.	F8	10
Ben-Slimane, Mor.	D7	62
Ben Smih, Alg.	M2	18
Benson, Az., U.S.	M6	120
Benson, Mn., U.S.	F12	118
Benson, N.C., U.S.	D8	112
Bentinck Island, i., Austl.	C7	68
Bentiu, Sud.	M5	60
Bentley, Alta., Can.	E20	102
Bento Gomes, stm., Braz.	G13	82
Bento Gonçalves, Braz.	E13	80
Benton, Ar., U.S.	H4	114
Benton, Il., U.S.	E8	114
Benton, Ky., U.S.	F8	114
Benton, La., U.S.	J3	114
Benton, Ms., U.S.	J6	114
Benton, Mo., U.S.	E7	114
Benton, Pa., U.S.	F10	108
Benton, Tn., U.S.	D2	112
Benton, Wi., U.S.	H5	110
Benton City, Wa., U.S.	D6	122
Bentong, Malay.	M6	40
Benton Harbor, Mi., U.S.	H9	110
Bentonia, Ms., U.S.	J6	114
Bentonville, Ar., U.S.	F2	114
Ben Tre, Viet.	I9	40
Benue (Bénoué), stm., Afr.	G8	54
Ben Wheeler, Tx., U.S.	G11	116
Benxi (Penhsi), China	B11	32
Beograd (Belgrade), Yugo.	E4	20
Beowawe, Nv., U.S.	D9	124
Beppu, Japan	N6	36
Bequia, i., St. Vin.	H14	94
Beramanja, Madag.	n23	67b
Berat, Alb.	I3	20
Berau, Teluk, b., Indon.	F9	38
Beravina, Madag.	q21	67b
Berbera, Som.	F10	56
Berbérati, Cen. Afr. Rep.	H4	56
Berbice, stm., Guy.	D14	84
Berchtesgaden, Ger.	H13	10
Berclair, Tx., U.S.	K9	116
Berdigest'ach, Russia	E17	28
Berdsk, Russia	G8	28
Berdyans'k, Ukr.	H5	26
Berdychiv, Ukr.	H3	26
Berea, Ky., U.S.	B2	112
Berea, Oh., U.S.	F5	108
Berea, S.C., U.S.	E4	112
Berehomet, Ukr.	A9	20
Berehove, Ukr.	G22	10
Berekua, Dom.	G14	94
Berendejevo, Russia	E22	22
Berens, stm., Can.	F18	104
Berens Island, i., Man., Can.	F17	104
Berens River, Man., Can.	F17	104
Beresford, N.B., Can.	E8	106
Beresford, S.D., U.S.	H11	118
Berettyó (Barcău), stm., Eur.	B5	20
Berevo, Madag.	q21	67b
Berezajka, Russia	D16	22
Berezino, Bela.	H11	22
Berezino, Bela.	G11	22
Berezniki, Russia	F9	26
Berezyne, Ukr.	C13	20
Berg, Nor.	G15	6
Berga, Spain	C13	16
Bergama, Tur.	J11	20
Bergamo, Italy	D4	18
Bergantín, Ven.	B10	84
Bergara, Spain	B9	16
Bergby, Swe.	K15	6
Bergen (Mons), Bel.	H4	12
Bergen, Neth.	C6	12
Bergen, Nor.	K9	6
Bergen, N.Y., U.S.	D9	108
Bergen aan Zee, Neth.	C6	12
Bergen [auf Rügen], Ger.	A13	10
Bergen op Zoom, Neth.	F5	12
Bergerac, Fr.	H7	14
Bergisch Gladbach, Ger.	E7	10
Bergland, Mi., U.S.	D6	110
Bergoo, W.V., U.S.	I6	108
Bergsche Maas, stm., Neth.	E6	12
Bergsjö, Swe.	K15	6
Berguent, Mor.	C9	62
Bergues, Fr.	B9	14
Berhala, Selat, strt., Indon.	O8	40
Beringa, ostrov, i., Russia	F25	28
Bering Glacier, Ak., U.S.	F23	100
Bering Sea	C2	86
Bering Strait, strt.	D10	100
Berja, Spain	I9	16
Berkane, Mor.	C9	62
Berkeley, Ca., U.S.	G3	124
Berkeley Springs, W.V., U.S.	H8	108
Berkner Island, i., Ant.	C1	73
Berkshire, co., Eng., U.K.	J12	8
Berkshire Hills, hills, Ma., U.S.	E13	108
Berlaimont, Fr.	B10	14
Berland, stm., Alta., Can.	C17	102
Berlin, Ger.	C13	10
Berlin, S. Afr.	I8	66
Berlin, Md., U.S.	I11	108
Berlin, N.H., U.S.	C15	108
Berlin, N.J., U.S.	H12	108
Berlin, Pa., U.S.	H8	108
Berlin, Wi., U.S.	G7	110
Berlin, Mount, mtn., Ant.	C10	73
Berlinguet Inlet, b., N.W. Ter., Can.	B15	96
Berlin Lake, res., Oh., U.S.	F5	108
Bermejillo, Mex.	E8	90
Bermejo, Arg.	F5	80
Bermejo, stm., Arg.	F5	80
Bermejo, stm., S.A.	C9	80
Bermejo, Paso del, S.A.	G3	80
Bermen, Lac, l., Que., Can.	F19	96
Bermeo, Spain	B9	16
Bermuda, dep., N.A.	B12	88
Bern (Berne), Switz.	E7	13
Bern (Berne), state, Switz.	E8	13
Bernalda, Italy	I11	18
Bernalillo, N.M., U.S.	I10	120
Bernasconi, Arg.	I7	80
Bernau bei Berlin, Ger.	C13	10
Bernay, Fr.	C7	14
Bernburg, Ger.	D11	10
Berne, In., U.S.	B12	114
Berner Alpen, mts., Switz.	F7	13
Bernice, La., U.S.	J4	114
Bernie, Mo., U.S.	F7	114
Bernier Bay, b., N.W. Ter., Can.	B15	96
Bernina, mts., Eur.	F12	13
Bernina, Passo del, Switz.	F13	13
Bernina, Piz, mtn., Eur.	F16	14
Beromünster, Switz.	H8	10
Berón de Astrada, Arg.	D10	80
Beroroha, Madag.	r21	67b
Ber'ostovica, Bela.	H6	22
Beroun, Czech.	F14	10
Berounka, stm., Czech.	F13	10
Berovo, Mac.	H6	20
Ber'oza, Bela.	I7	22
Ber'ozovo, Russia	E11	26
Berrechid, Mor.	D7	62
Berri, Austl.	J4	70
Berrigan, Austl.	J6	70
Berriyyane, Alg.	D12	62
Berry, Al., U.S.	I9	114
Berry, hist. reg., Fr.	E9	14
Berry Creek, stm., Alta., Can.	F23	102
Berryessa, Lake, res., Ca., U.S.	F3	124
Berry Islands, is., Bah.	B6	94
Berryville, Ar., U.S.	F3	114
Berseba, Nmb.	F3	66
Bersenbrück, Ger.	C7	10
Bershad', Ukr.	A13	20
Berté, Lac, l., Que. Can.	B5	106
Bertha, Mn., U.S.	E12	118
Berthold, N.D., U.S.	C6	118
Berthoud, Co., U.S.	D11	120
Berthoud Pass, Co., U.S.	E11	120
Bertoua, Cam.	H9	54
Bertram, Tx., U.S.	I8	116
Bertrand, Mi., U.S.	A10	114
Bertrand, Ne., U.S.	K8	118
Beruri, Braz.	I12	84
Berwick, N.S., Can.	G9	106
Berwick, La., U.S.	M5	114
Berwick, Me., U.S.	D16	108
Berwick, Pa., U.S.	F10	108
Berwick-upon-Tweed, Eng., U.K.	F11	8
Berwyn, Il., U.S.	I8	110
Besalampy, Madag.	p21	67b
Besançon, Fr.	E13	14
Besbes, Alg.	M2	18
Bešenkoviči, Bela.	F12	22
Beskid Mountains, mts., Eur.	F20	10
Beskra, Alg.	C13	62
Besnard Lake, l., Sask., Can.	C8	104
Besni, Tur.	C4	48
Besor, Naḥal, val., Asia	F2	50
Bessarabia, hist. reg., Mol.	C12	20
Besse, Nig.	F12	64
Bessemer, Al., U.S.	I10	114
Bessemer, Mi., U.S.	D5	110
Bessemer, Pa., U.S.	G6	108
Bessemer City, N.C., U.S.	D5	112
Best'ach, Russia	E17	28
Bestobe, Kaz.	G12	26
Betafo, Madag.	q22	67b
Betanzos, Bol.	H9	82
Betanzos, Spain	B3	16
Betaré Oya, Cam.	G9	54
Betbetti, Sud.	J3	60
Bete Hor, Eth.	L10	60
Bétera, Spain	F11	16
Bétérou, Benin	G11	64
Bet Guvrin, Isr.	E3	50
Bet Ha'arava, Isr. Occ.	E5	50
Bethal, S. Afr.	F9	66
Bethalto, Il., U.S.	D6	114
Bethanien, Nmb.	F3	66
Bethany, Il., U.S.	C8	114
Bethany, Mo., U.S.	B2	114
Bethany, Ok., U.S.	D9	116
Bethel, Ak., U.S.	F14	100
Bethel, Ct., U.S.	F13	108
Bethel, Me., U.S.	C16	108
Bethel, N.C., U.S.	D9	112
Bethel, Oh., U.S.	I2	108
Bethel Acres, Ok., U.S.	D9	116
Bethel Springs, Tn., U.S.	G8	114
Bethesda, Oh., U.S.	G5	108
Bethlehem see Bayt Lahm, Isr. Occ.	E4	50
Bethlehem, S. Afr.	G9	66
Bethlehem, Pa., U.S.	G11	108
Bethlehem, W.V., U.S.	G6	108
Béthune, Sask., Can.	H9	104
Béthune, Fr.	B9	14
Bethune, S.C., U.S.	E6	112
Béticos, Sistemas, mts., Spain	H8	16
Betijoque, Ven.	C7	84
Betioky, Madag.	s21	67b
Betlica, Russia	G16	22
Betong, Thai.	L6	40
Betoota, Austl.	E4	70
Betpak-Dala, des., Kaz.	H12	26
Betroka, Madag.	s22	67b
Bet She'an, Isr.	C5	50
Bet Shemesh, Isr.	E4	50
Betsiamites, Que., Can.	D5	106
Betsiamites, stm., Que., Can.	C4	106
Betsiamites, Barrage, Que., Can.	C4	106
Betsiamites, Pointe de, c., Que., Can.	D5	106
Betsiamites, Réserve indienne de, Que., Can.	C5	106
Betsiboka, stm., Madag.	p22	67b
Betsioky, Madag.	r21	67b
Betsy Layne, Ky., U.S.	B4	112
Bette, mtn., Libya	D4	56
Bettendorf, Ia., U.S.	I5	110
Bettles Field, Ak., U.S.	C19	100
Betül, India	J7	44
Betzdorf, Ger.	E7	10
Beulah, Co., U.S.	F12	120
Beulah, Mi., U.S.	F9	110
Beulah, Ms., U.S.	I6	114
Beulah, N.D., U.S.	D6	118
Beulaville, N.C., U.S.	E9	112
Bevensen, Ger.	B10	10
B. Everett Jordan Lake, res., N.C., U.S.	D7	112
Beverley, Austl.	F3	68
Beverley, Eng., U.K.	H13	8
Beverly, Ma., U.S.	E16	108
Beverly Hills, Ca., U.S.	J7	124
Beverly Lake, l., N.W. Ter., Can.	D12	96
Beverwijk, Neth.	D6	12
Bevier, Mo., U.S.	C4	114
Bexley, Oh., U.S.	H4	108
Beyçayırı, Tur.	I10	20
Beylul, Erit.	H3	47
Beypazarı, Tur.	G14	4
Beyşehir Gölü, l., Tur.	H14	4
Bezaha, Madag.	s21	67b
Bežanicy, Russia	E12	22
Bezau, Aus.	H9	10
Bežeck, Russia	D19	22
Bezerra, stm., Braz.	B5	79
Béziers, Fr.	I10	14
Bezmein, Turk.	B15	48
Bhadrak, India	J12	44
Bhadrāvati, India	F3	46
Bhāg, Pak.	F2	44
Bhāgalpur, India	H12	44
Bhakkar, Pak.	E4	44
Bhakkar, Pak.	E4	44
Bhaktapur, Nepal	G11	44
Bhamo, Mya.	B4	40
Bhandāra, India	J8	44
Bharatpur, India	G7	44
Bharatpur, Nepal	G11	44
Bharūch, India	J5	44
Bhātāpāra, India	B6	46
Bhātpāra, India	I13	44
Bhāvnagar, India	J5	44
Bhawānipatna, India	C7	46
Bhera, Pak.	D5	44
Bhilai, India	J9	44
Bhīlwāra, India	H6	44
Bhind, India	G8	44
Bhiwandi, India	C2	46
Bhiwāni, India	F7	44
Bhongīr, India	D5	46
Bhopāl, India	I7	44
Bhubaneshwar, India	J11	44
Bhuj, India	I3	44
Bhusāwal, India	J6	44
Bhutan (Druk-Yul), ctry., Asia	D13	42
Bia, stm., Afr.	H8	64
Biá, stm., Braz.	I9	84
Bia, Phou, mtn., Laos	E7	40
Biabo, stm., Peru	B3	82
Biafra, Bight of, Afr.	H8	54
Biak, i., Indon.	F10	38
Biała, Pol.	E17	10
Biała Podlaska, Pol.	C23	10
Biała Rawska, Pol.	D20	10
Białogard, Pol.	A16	10
Białystok, Pol.	B23	10
Bianco, Monte (Mont Blanc), mtn., Eur.	G13	14
Biarritz, Fr.	I5	14
Biasca, Switz.	F10	13
Bibā, Egypt	C6	60
Bibai, Japan	d16	36a
Bibala, Ang.	D2	58
Bibb City, Ga., U.S.	G2	112
Biberach an der Riss, Ger.	G9	10
Bibiani, Ghana	H8	64
Biblián, Ec.	I3	84
Bic, Que., Can.	D5	106
Bicas, Braz.	F7	79
Bicaz, Rom.	C10	20
Bičevinka, Russia	B20	22
Biche, Lac la, l., Alta., Can.	C22	102
Bichena, Eth.	L10	60
Bicknell, In., U.S.	D9	114
Bicknell, Ut., U.S.	F5	120
Bicske, Hung.	H18	10
Bicudo, stm., Braz.	E6	79
Bīd, India	C3	46
Bida, Nig.	G13	64
Bīdar, India	D4	46
Biddeford, Me., U.S.	D16	108
Bidian, China	C2	34
Bidwell, Oh., U.S.	I4	108
Bieber, Ca., U.S.	C4	124
Biecz, Pol.	F21	10
Biedenkopf, Ger.	E8	10
Biel (Bienne), Switz.	D7	13
Bielawa, Pol.	E16	10
Bielefeld, Ger.	C8	10
Bieler Lake, l., N.W. Ter., Can.	B18	96
Bielersee, l., Switz.	D7	13
Biella, Italy	D3	18
Bielsko-Biała, Pol.	F19	10
Bielsk Podlaski, Pol.	C23	10
Bienfait, Sask., Can.	I12	104
Bien Hoa, Viet.	I9	40
Bienville, La., U.S.	J4	114
Bienville, Lac, l., Que., Can.	E18	96
Big, stm., N.W. Ter., Can.	B8	96
Big, stm., Sask., Can.	E7	104
Big, stm., Mo., U.S.	D6	114
Biga, Tur.	I11	20
Big Bald Mountain, mtn., N.B., Can.	E7	106
Big Bar Creek, B.C., Can.	F12	102
Big Bay, Mi., U.S.	D8	110
Big Bay De Noc, b., Mi., U.S.	E9	110
Big Bear Lake, Ca., U.S.	J9	124
Big Bear Lake, l., Ca., U.S.	J9	124
Big Beaver, Sask., Can.	I9	104
Big Belt Mountains, mts., Mt., U.S.	D14	122
Big Bend, Swaz.	F10	66
Big Bend National Park, Tx., U.S.	J3	116

Name — Map Ref. — Page

Big Bend Reservoir, res., Alta., Can. E19 102
Big Black, stm., Ms., U.S. J6 114
Big Blue, stm., U.S. L11 118
Big Canyon, val., Tx., U.S. I4 116
Big Clifty, Ky., U.S. E10 114
Big Creek, B.C., Can. F11 102
Big Creek, Ca., U.S. G6 124
Big Creek, stm., B.C., Can. F11 102
Big Creek Peak, mtn., Id., U.S. F12 122
Big Cypress Swamp, sw., Fl., U.S. M5 112
Big Delta, Ak., U.S. D22 100
Big Desert, des., Austl. J4 70
Big Eau Pleine, stm., Wi., U.S. F5 110
Bigelow Bight, U.S. D16 108
Big Falls, Mn., U.S. B2 110
Big Flat, Ar., U.S. F4 114
Bigfork, Mn., U.S. C2 110
Bigfork, Mt., U.S. B11 122
Big Fork, stm., Mn., U.S. B2 110
Big Frog Mountain, mtn., Tn., U.S. D2 112
Biggar, Sask., Can. F6 104
Biggar, Scot., U.K. F10 8
Biggers, Ar., U.S. F6 114
Biggs, Ca., U.S. E4 124
Big Gully Creek, stm., Sask., Can. E5 104
Big Hole, stm., Mt., U.S. E12 122
Bighorn, stm., U.S. E18 122
Bighorn Basin, U.S. F17 122
Big Horn Lake, res., U.S. E17 122
Bighorn Mountains, mts., U.S. F18 122
Big Island, Va., U.S. B7 112
Big Island, i., N.W. Ter., Can. D18 96
Big Island, i., Ont., Can. I20 104
Big Lake, Mn., U.S. E2 110
Big Lake, Tx., U.S. H5 116
Big Lookout Mountain, mtn., Or., U.S. F8 122
Big Lost, stm., Id., U.S. G12 122
Big Mossy Point, c., Man., Can. E17 104
Big Mountain, mtn., B.C., Can. H29 100
Big Mountain, mtn., Nv., U.S. C6 124
Big Mountain Creek, stm., Alta., Can. C16 102
Big Muddy, stm., Il., U.S. E7 114
Big Muddy Lake, l., Sask., Can. I10 104
Bignasco, Switz. F10 13
Bignona, Sen. E1 64
Big Otter, stm., Va., U.S. B7 112
Big Pine, Ca., U.S. G7 124
Big Pine Mountain, mtn., Ca., U.S. J6 124
Big Piney, Wy., U.S. H15 122
Big Piney, stm., Mo., U.S. E4 114
Bigpoint, Ms., U.S. L8 114
Big Quill Lake, l., Sask., Can. G10 104
Big Rapids, Mi., U.S. G10 110
Big Rib, stm., Wi., U.S. E6 110
Big River, Sask., Can. E7 104
Big River Indian Reserve, Sask., Can. E7 104
Big Sable, stm., Mi., U.S. F9 110
Big Sable Point, c., Mi., U.S. F9 110
Big Salmon, stm., Yukon, Can. F28 100
Big Salmon Range, mts., Yukon, Can. F28 100
Big Sand Lake, l., Man., Can. E13 96
Big Sandy, Mt., U.S. B15 122
Big Sandy, Tn., U.S. F8 114
Big Sandy, Tx., U.S. G11 116
Big Sandy, stm., U.S. I4 108
Big Sandy, stm., Az., U.S. J3 120
Big Sandy, stm., Tn., U.S. F8 114
Big Sandy, stm., Wy., U.S. I16 122
Big Sandy Lake, l., Sask., Can. D10 104
Bigsby Island, i., Ont., Can. I20 104
Big Sioux, stm., U.S. I11 118
Big Sky, Mt., U.S. E14 122
Big Smoky Valley, val., Nv., U.S. F8 124
Big Spring, Tx., U.S. G5 116
Big Springs, Ne., U.S. J5 118
Big Spruce Knob, mtn., W.V., U.S. I6 108
Bigstick Lake, l., Sask., Can. H5 104
Bigstone, stm., Man., Can. C19 104
Big Stone City, S.D., U.S. F11 118
Big Stone Gap, Va., U.S. C4 112
Bigstone Lake, l., Man., Can. E19 104
Big Stone Lake, l., U.S. F11 118
Big Sunflower, stm., Ms., U.S. I6 114
Big Sur, reg., Ca., U.S. I4 124
Big Thompson, stm., Co., U.S. D11 120
Big Timber, Mt., U.S. E16 122
Big Trout Lake, l., Ont., Can. F14 96
Biguaçu, Braz. D14 80
Big Valley, Alta., Can. E22 102
Big Warrambool, stm., Austl. G8 70
Big Water, Ut., U.S. G5 120
Big Wells, Tx., U.S. K7 116
Big White Mountain, mtn., B.C., Can. H16 102
Big Wood, stm., Id., U.S. G11 122
Bihać, Bos. E10 18
Bihār, India H11 44
Bihār, state, India H11 44
Bihor, co., Rom. B6 20
Bija, stm., Russia G15 26
Bijagós, Arquipélago dos, is., Gui.-B. F1 64
Bījār, Iran D9 48
Bijeljina, Bos. E3 20
Bijelo Polje, Yugo. F3 20
Bijie, China F8 30
Bijsk, Russia G9 28
Bīkāner, India F5 44
Bikeqi, China C9 30
Bikin, Russia H18 28
Bikin, stm., Russia H19 28
Bikini, atoll, Marsh. Is. G20 126
Bikoro, Zaire B3 58
Bilac, Braz. F3 79
Bilāspur, India I10 44
Bila Tserkva, Ukr. H4 26
Bilauktaung Range, mts., Asia H5 40
Bilbao, Spain B9 16
Bilhorod-Dnistrovs'kyy, Ukr. H4 26
Bilian, China G9 34
Bilimora, India B2 46
Bilin, Mya. F4 40
Bilina, Czech. E13 10
Billabong Creek, stm., Austl. J6 70
Billings, Mo., U.S. E3 114
Billings, Mt., U.S. E17 122
Billings, Ok., U.S. C9 116
Billings Heights, Mt., U.S. E17 122
Billom, Fr. G10 14
Bill Williams, stm., Az., U.S. J3 120
Bill Williams Mountain, mtn., Az., U.S. I4 120
Billy Chinook, Lake, res., Or., U.S. F4 122
Bilma, Niger E9 54
Biloela, Austl. E9 70
Biloxi, Ms., U.S. L8 114
Biloxi, stm., Ms., U.S. L7 114
Biltmore Forest, N.C., U.S. D4 112
Bilugyun Island, i., Mya. F4 40
Bilwaskarma, Nic. C11 92
Bilyayivka, Ukr. C14 20
Bimbān, Egypt E7 60
Bimbila, Ghana G10 64
Bimini Islands, is., Bah. B5 94
Binche, Bel. H5 12
Bindloss, Alta., Can. H4 104
Bindura, Zimb. E6 58
Binéfar, Spain D12 16
Binford, N.D., U.S. D9 118
Binga, Monte, mtn., Afr. B11 66
Bingara, Austl. G9 70
Bingen, Ger. F7 10
Binger, Ok., U.S. D8 116
Bingham, Me., U.S. B17 108
Binghamton, N.Y., U.S. E11 108
Bingöl, Tur. B6 48
Binhai (Dongkan), China A8 34
Binjai, Indon. M5 40
Binscarth, Man., Can. H13 104
Bintan, Pulau, i., Indon. N8 40
Bintang, Gam. E1 64
Bintimani, mtn., S.L. G4 64
Bint Jubayl, Leb. B4 50
Bintulu, Malay. E5 38
Binxian, China D8 30
Binyamina, Isr. C3 50
Binyang, China C10 40
Bin Yauri, Nig. F12 64
Bíobío, prov., Chile I3 80
Biobío, stm., Chile I2 80
Bíobío, stm., Chile F3 80
Bioko, i., Eq. Gui. J14 64
Birāk, Libya C3 56
Bi'r al-Uzam, Libya B2 60
Birao, Cen. Afr. Rep. L2 60
Birātnagar, Nepal F4 30
Birch, stm., Alta., Can. E10 96
Birch, stm., W.V., U.S. I6 108
Birch Hills, Sask., Can. F9 104
Birch Island, B.C., Can. F15 102
Birch Island, i., Man., Can. F15 104
Birch Lake, l., Alta., Can. D23 102
Birch Lake, l., Ont., Can. G22 104
Birch Lake, l., Sask., Can. E6 104
Birch Mountains, hills, Alta., Can. E10 96
Birch River, Man., Can. F13 104
Birch Run, Mi., U.S. G12 110
Birch Tree, Mo., U.S. F5 114
Birchwood, Wi., U.S. E4 110
Birchy Bay, Newf., Can. C19 106
Bird City, Ks., U.S. L6 118
Bird Island, Mn., U.S. G13 118
Bird Island, sci., S. Geor. A1 73
Bird Islet, i., Austl. D11 68
Birdsville, Austl. E3 70
Birdtail Creek, stm., Man., Can. H14 104
Birdum, Austl. C6 68
Birecik, Tur. C4 48
Bir el Ater, Alg. C15 62
Bir Enzaran, W. Sah. I3 62
Birigui, Braz. F3 79
Biril'ussy, Russia F16 26
Bīrjand, Iran E15 48
Birken, B.C., Can. G12 102
Birkenhead, Eng., U.K. H10 8
Birkfeld, Aus. H15 10
Birmingham, Eng., U.K. I12 8
Birmingham, Al., U.S. I10 114
Birmingham, Ia., U.S. J4 110
Birmingham, Mi., U.S. H12 110
Birmitrapur, India I11 44
Bîr Mogreïn (Fort-Trinquet), Maur. H5 62
Birnamwood, Wi., U.S. F6 110
Birni, Benin F10 64
Birni Ngaouré, Niger E11 64
Birnin Gwari, Nig. F13 64
Birnin Nkonni, Niger E12 64
Birnin Kudu, Nig. F14 64
Birobidžan, Russia H18 28
Birobijan see Jevrej, state, Russia H18 28
Birrie, stm., Austl. G7 70
Birsk, Russia F9 26
Birtle, Man., Can. H13 104
Bir'usa, stm., Russia F17 26
Biržai, Lith. E7 22
Biržava, stm., Eur. D5 20
Bisbee, Az., U.S. M7 120
Bisbee, N.D., U.S. C8 118
Biscarrosse, Fr. H5 14
Biscay, Bay of, b., Eur. H3 14
Biscayne Bay, b., Fl., U.S. N6 112
Bisceglie, Italy H11 18
Bischofswerda, Ger. D14 10
Biscoe, Ar., U.S. H5 114
Biscoe, N.C., U.S. D7 112
Biscoe Islands, is., Ant. B12 73
Biscucuy, Ven. C8 84
Bisha, Erit. J9 60
Bishkek see Biškek, Kyrg. I12 26
Bisho, S. Afr. I8 66
Bishop, Ca., U.S. G7 124
Bishop, Tx., U.S. L9 116
Bishop Auckland, Eng., U.K. G12 8
Bishop's Falls, Newf., Can. C18 106
Bishopville, S.C., U.S. E6 112
Bishrah, Ma'tan, well, Libya F2 60
Biškek (Frunze), Kyrg. I12 26
Bislig, Phil. D8 38
Bismarck, Mo., U.S. E6 114
Bismarck, N.D., U.S. E7 118
Bismarck Archipelago, is., Pap. N. Gui. k16 68a
Bismarck Range, mts., Pap. N. Gui. m15 68a
Bismarck Sea, Pap. N. Gui. I18 126
Bismuna, Laguna, b., Nic. C12 92
Bison, S.D., U.S. F5 118
Bison Peak, mtn., Co., U.S. E11 120
Bissau, Gui.-B. F3 54
Bissett, Man., Can. G19 104
Bissikrima, Gui. F4 64
Bissorã, Gui.-B. E2 64
Bistcho Lake, l., Alta., Can. E9 96
Bistineau, Lake, res., La., U.S. J3 114
Bistrita, Rom. B8 20
Bistrita, stm., Rom. C10 20
Bistrita-Năsăud, co., Rom. B8 20
Bisztynek, Pol. A20 10
Bitam, Gabon A2 58
Bitburg, Ger. F6 10
Bitche, Fr. C14 14
Bitlis, Tur. B7 48
Bitola, Mac. H5 20
Bitonto, Italy H11 18
Bitterfeld, Ger. D12 10
Bitterfontein, S. Afr. H4 66
Bitter Lake, l., Sask., Can. H5 104
Bittern Lake, l., Sask., Can. E9 104
Bitterroot, stm., Mt., U.S. D11 122
Bitterroot Range, mts., U.S. D11 122
Bitti, Italy I4 18
Bitung, Indon. E8 38
Bituruna, Braz. D13 80
Bivins, Tx., U.S. I2 114
Biwabik, Mn., U.S. C3 110
Biwa-ko, l., Japan L11 36
Bixby, Ok., U.S. D11 116
Biyang, China C2 34
Bizana, S. Afr. H9 66
Bizerte, Tun. L4 18
Bizkaiko, prov., Spain B9 16
Bjala Slatina, Bul. F7 20
Bjelovar, Cro. D11 18
Björna, Swe. J16 6
Bjørnøya, i., Nor. B2 24
Bjørnøya (Bear Island), i., Sval. B2 24
Bla, Mali E7 64
Black (Lixian) (Da), stm., Asia D8 40
Black, stm., Man., Can. H19 104
Black, stm., U.S. G5 114
Black, stm., Ak., U.S. C23 100
Black, stm., Az., U.S. K6 120
Black, stm., La., U.S. K5 114
Black, stm., Mi., U.S. G13 110
Black, stm., N.M., U.S. G2 116
Black, stm., N.Y., U.S. C11 108
Black, stm., S.C., U.S. F7 112
Black, stm., Vt., U.S. D14 108
Black, stm., Vt., U.S. C14 108
Black, stm., Wi., U.S. F5 110
Blackall, Austl. E6 70
Black Bear Island Lake, l., Sask., Can. C9 104
Black Birch Lake, l., Sask., Can. B7 104
Black Butte, mtn., Mt., U.S. F14 122
Black Creek, B.C., Can. H9 102
Black Diamond, Alta., Can. G20 102
Black Diamond, Wa., U.S. C3 122
Blackduck, Mn., U.S. C1 110
Black Duck, stm., Can. E15 96
Black Eagle, Mt., U.S. C14 122
Blackfalds, Alta., Can. E21 102
Blackfoot, Id., U.S. G13 122
Blackfoot, stm., Id., U.S. G14 122
Blackfoot, stm., Mt., U.S. D12 122
Blackfoot Indian Reserve, Alta., Can. G21 102
Blackfoot Reservoir, res., Id., U.S. H14 122
Black Forest see Schwarzwald, mts., Ger. G8 10
Black Hawk, Ont., Can. J21 104
Black Hawk Creek, stm., Ia., U.S. H3 110
Blackhead Bay, b., Newf., Can. D20 106
Black Hills, mts., U.S. G4 118
Black Island, i., Man., Can. G18 104
Black-Lake, Que., Can. A15 108
Black Lake, l., Sask., Can. E11 96
Black Lake, l., N.Y., U.S. C11 108
Black Lake Bayou, stm., La., U.S. J3 114
Black Mesa, mtn., U.S. B3 116
Black Mesa, mtn., Az., U.S. H6 120
Blackmore, Mount, mtn., Mt., U.S. E14 122
Black Mountain, N.C., U.S. D4 112
Black Mountain, mtn., U.S. C4 112
Black Mountain, mtn., Id., U.S. D10 122
Black Mountain, mtn., Wy., U.S. F18 122
Black Mountains, mts., Az., U.S. I2 120
Blackpool, Eng., U.K. H10 8
Black Range, mts., N.M., U.S. K9 120
Black River, N.Y., U.S. C11 108
Black River Falls, Wi., U.S. F5 110
Black Rock, Ar., U.S. F5 114
Black Rock, S. Geor. G8 78
Black Rock Desert, des., Nv., U.S. C7 124
Blacksburg, S.C., U.S. D5 112
Blacksburg, Va., U.S. B6 112
Black Sea G15 4
Blacks Fork, stm., U.S. C7 120
Blacks Harbour, N.B., Can. G7 106
Blackshear, Ga., U.S. H4 112
Blackstone, Va., U.S. B9 112
Blackstone, stm., Alta., Can. E18 102
Blackstone, stm., Yukon, Can. D26 100
Blackville, S.C., U.S. F5 112
Black Volta (Volta Noire), stm., Afr. G6 54
Black Warrior, stm., Al., U.S. I9 114
Blackwater, stm., Ire. I5 8
Blackwater, stm., Mo., U.S. D3 114
Blackwater Lake, l., N.W. Ter., Can. D33 100
Blackwell, Ok., U.S. C9 116
Blackwell, Tx., U.S. G6 116
Bladel, Neth. F7 12
Bladenboro, N.C., U.S. E8 112
Bladgrond, S. Afr. G4 66
Bladworth, Sask., Can. G8 104
Blagodarnyj, Russia H6 26
Blagoevgrad, Bul. G7 20
Blagoveščensk, Russia G17 28
Blain, Fr. E5 14
Blaine, Mn., U.S. E2 110
Blaine, Wa., U.S. B3 122
Blaine Lake, Sask., Can. F8 104
Blair, Ne., U.S. J11 118
Blair, Ok., U.S. E7 116
Blair, Wi., U.S. F4 110
Blair Athol, Austl. D7 70
Blairstown, Ia., U.S. I3 110
Blairsville, Ga., U.S. E3 112
Blairsville, Pa., U.S. G7 108
Blakely, Ga., U.S. H2 112
Blakesburg, Ia., U.S. J3 110
Blanc, Mont, mtn., Que., Can. D7 106
Blanc, Mont (Monte Bianco), mtn., Eur. G13 14
Blanca, Co., U.S. G11 120
Blanca, Bahía, b., Arg. J7 80
Blanca, Isla, i., Peru C2 82
Blanca, Punta, c., Chile C3 80
Blanca Peak, mtn., Co., U.S. G11 120
Blancas, Peñas, mts., Nic. D9 92
Blanchard, Ok., U.S. D9 116
Blanchard, stm., Oh., U.S. G3 108
Blanchardville, Wi., U.S. H6 110
Blanche, Lake, l., Austl. G3 70
Blanchester, Oh., U.S. H3 108
Blanco, Tx., U.S. I8 116
Blanco, stm., Arg. E4 80
Blanco, stm., Bol. E10 82
Blanco, stm., Ec. H3 84
Blanco, stm., Tx., U.S. I8 116
Blanco, Cabo, c., C.R. H9 92
Blanco, Cañon, val., N.M., U.S. I11 120
Blanco, Cape, c., Or., U.S. H1 122
Blanco, Río, stm., Co., U.S. G10 120
Blanc-Sablon, Que., Can. A16 106
Bland, Mo., U.S. D5 114
Bland, Va., U.S. B5 112
Blanding, Ut., U.S. G7 120
Blandinsville, Il., U.S. J5 110
Blanes, Spain D14 16
Blangy-sur-Bresle, Fr. C8 14
Blankenberge, Bel. F3 12
Blankenburg, Ger. D10 10
Blanket, Tx., U.S. H8 116
Blanquilla, Isla, i., Ven. B10 84
Blantyre, Mwi. E7 58
Blarney Castle, hist., Ire. J5 8
Blasdell, N.Y., U.S. E8 108
Blatná, Czech. F13 10
Blaufelden, Ger. F9 10
Blaye-et-Sainte-Luce, Fr. G6 14
Blayney, Austl. I8 70
Bledsoe, Tx., U.S. F3 116
Bleiburg, Aus. I14 10
Blekinge Län, co., Swe. M14 6
Blenheim, Ont., Can. H13 110
Blenheim, N.Z. D4 72
Blessing, Tx., U.S. K10 116
Bletterans, Fr. F12 14
Blind River, Ont., Can. D13 110
Blissfield, Mi., U.S. I12 110
Blitar, Indon. k16 39a
Block Island, R.I., U.S. F15 108
Block Island, i., R.I., U.S. F15 108
Blockton, Ia., U.S. K13 118
Bloedel, B.C., Can. G9 102
Bloemfontein, S. Afr. G8 66
Bloemhof, S. Afr. F7 66
Blois, Fr. E8 14
Blönduós, Ice. B3 6a
Blood Indian Creek, stm., Alta., Can. G3 104
Blood Indian Reserve, Alta., Can. H21 102
Bloodvein, stm., Can. G18 104
Bloomer, Wi., U.S. E4 110
Bloomfield, Ont., Can. G18 110
Bloomfield, In., U.S. C10 114
Bloomfield, Ia., U.S. J3 110
Bloomfield, Ky., U.S. E11 114
Bloomfield, Mo., U.S. F7 114
Bloomfield, Ne., U.S. I10 118
Bloomfield, N.M., U.S. H9 120
Blooming Grove, Tx., U.S. G10 116
Blooming Prairie, Mn., U.S. G2 110
Bloomington, Il., U.S. J7 110
Bloomington, In., U.S. C10 114
Bloomington, Mn., U.S. F2 110
Bloomington, Tx., U.S. K10 116
Bloomington, Wi., U.S. H5 110
Bloomsburg, Pa., U.S. F10 108
Bloomville, Oh., U.S. F3 108
Blora, Indon. j15 39a
Blossburg, Pa., U.S. F9 108
Blossom, Tx., U.S. F11 116
Bloumet, Alg. I14 62
Blountstown, Fl., U.S. I1 112
Blountsville, Al., U.S. H10 114
Blountville, Tn., U.S. C4 112
Blovice, Czech. F13 10
Blowering Reservoir, res., Austl. J8 70
Blowing Rock, N.C., U.S. C5 112
Bludenz, Aus. H9 10
Blue, stm., Az., U.S. K7 120
Blue, stm., Co., U.S. E10 120
Blue, stm., In., U.S. D10 114
Blue, stm., Ok., U.S. E10 116
Blue Creek, Wa., U.S. B8 122
Blue Earth, Mn., U.S. G1 110
Blue Earth, stm., U.S. G1 110
Bluefield, Va., U.S. B5 112
Bluefield, W.V., U.S. B5 112
Bluefields, Nic. E11 92
Bluefields, Bahía de, b., Nic. F11 92
Blue Hill, Me., U.S. C18 108
Blue Hill, Ne., U.S. K9 118
Blue Hill Bay, b., Me., U.S. C18 108
Blue Hills of Couteau, hills, Newf., Can. E16 106
Blue Island, Il., U.S. I8 110
Blue Mound, Il., U.S. C7 114
Blue Mound, Ks., U.S. M12 118
Blue Mountain, Ms., U.S. H7 114
Blue Mountain, mtn., N.B., Can. E7 106
Blue Mountain, mtn., Newf., Can. B16 106
Blue Mountain, mtn., Pa., U.S. G9 108
Blue Mountain Peak, mtn., Jam. E6 94
Blue Mountains, mts., U.S. F7 122
Blue Nile (Al-Bahr al-Azraq) (Abay), stm., Afr. F7 56
Bluenose Lake, l., N.W. Ter., Can. B35 100
Blue Rapids, Ks., U.S. L11 118
Blue Ridge, Alta., Can. C19 102
Blue Ridge, Ga., U.S. E2 112
Blue Ridge, mts., U.S. D10 98
Blue River, B.C., Can. E15 102
Bluesky, Alta., Can. A16 102
Blue Springs, Ne., U.S. K11 118
Bluestone, stm., U.S. B5 112
Bluestone Lake, res., U.S. B6 112
Bluewater, N.M., U.S. I9 120
Bluff, N.Z. G2 72
Bluff, Ut., U.S. G7 120
Bluff City, Tn., U.S. C4 112
Bluff Dale, Tx., U.S. G8 116
Bluff Park, Al., U.S. I10 114
Bluffs, Il., U.S. C6 114
Bluffton, In., U.S. B11 114
Bluffton, Oh., U.S. G3 108
Bluffton, S.C., U.S. G6 112
Bluffy Lake, l., Ont., Can. H22 104
Blumberg, Ger. H8 10
Blumenau, Braz. D14 80
Blumenhof, Sask., Can. H7 104
Blunt, S.D., U.S. G8 118
Bly, Or., U.S. H4 122
Blyth, Ont., Can. G14 110
Blythe, Ca., U.S. K11 124
Blytheville, Ar., U.S. G7 114
Bø, Nor. G14 6
Bø, Nor. L11 6
Bo, S.L. H4 64
Boaco, Nic. E9 92
Boaco, dept., Nic. E9 92
Boa Esperança, Braz. F6 79
Boa Nova, Braz. C8 79
Boardman, Oh., U.S. F6 108
Boardman, stm., Mi., U.S. E10 110
Boat Basin, B.C., Can. H8 102
Boatman, Austl. F7 70
Boa Vista, Braz. F12 84
Boa Vista, i., C.V. m17 64a
Boavita, Col. D6 84
Boaz, Al., U.S. H10 114
Bobai, China C10 40
Bobbili, India C7 46
Bobbio, Italy E4 18
Bobcaygeon, Ont., Can. F17 110
Böblingen, Ger. G9 10
Bobo Dioulasso, Burkina F7 64
Bobolice, Pol. B16 10
Bobonaza, stm., Ec. I4 84
Bobonong, Bots. C9 66
Bobr, Bela. G12 22
Bobrujsk, Bela. H12 22
Bobtown, Pa., U.S. H7 108
Bobures, Ven. C7 84
Boby, Pic, mtn., Madag. s22 67b
Boca Brava, Isla, i., Pan. I12 92
Boca del Monte, Pan. I12 92
Boca de Pozo, Ven. B10 84
Boca de Quadra, strt., Ak., U.S. B4 102
Boca do Acre, Braz. C8 82
Boca Grande, Fl., U.S. M4 112
Bocaiúva, Braz. D7 79
Bocanda, C. Iv. H7 64
Boca Raton, Fl., U.S. M6 112
Bocas del Toro, Pan. C1 84
Bocas del Toro, prov., Pan. I12 92
Bocas del Toro, Archipiélago de, is., Pan. H12 92
Bocay, Nic. C9 92
Bocay, stm., Nic. C9 92
Bochnia, Pol. F20 10
Bocholt, Ger. D6 10
Bochum, Ger. D7 10
Bochum, S. Afr. D9 66
Bocón, Caño, stm., Col. F8 84
Boconó, Ven. C7 84
Bodajbo, Russia F14 28
Bode, Ia., U.S. I13 118
Bodegraven, Neth. D6 12
Bodélé, reg., Chad E4 56
Boden, Swe. I17 6
Bodensee (Lake Constance), l., Eur. E16 14
Bodh Gaya, India H11 44
Bodināyakkanūr, India G4 46
Bodine, Mount, mtn., B.C., Can. B9 102
Bodø, Nor. H14 6
Bodoquena, Serra da, plat., Braz. I13 82
Bodrog, stm., Eur. A5 20
Bodrum, Tur. L11 20
Boende, Zaire B4 58
Boeo, Capo, c., Italy L7 18
Boerne, Tx., U.S. J8 116
Boeuf, stm., U.S. J5 114
Bogachiel, stm., Wa., U.S. C1 122
Bogale, Mya. F3 40
Bogalusa, La., U.S. L7 114
Bogan, stm., Austl. H7 70
Bogandé, Burkina E9 64
Bogart, Mount, mtn., Alta., Can. G19 102
Bogata, Tx., U.S. F11 116
Boğazlıyan, Tur. B3 48
Bogda Shan, mts., China C4 30
Boger City, N.C., U.S. D5 112
Boggabri, Austl. H9 70
Bogo, Phil. C7 38
Bogol'ubovo, Russia E23 22
Bogong, Mount, mtn., Austl. K7 70
Bogor, Indon. j13 39a
Bogorodick, Russia H21 22
Bogorodsk, Russia E26 22
Bogotá see Santa Fe de Bogotá, Col. E5 84
Bogotol, Russia F9 28
Bogou, Togo F10 64
Bogra, Bngl. H13 44
Bogué, Maur. C2 64
Bogue Chitto, Ms., U.S. K6 114
Bogue Chitto, stm., U.S. K6 114
Bogue Phalia, stm., Ms., U.S. I6 114
Boguševsk, Bela. G13 22
Bo Hai (Gulf of Chihli), b., China E8 32
Bohai Haixia, strt., China E9 32
Bohain-en-Vermandois, Fr. C10 14
Bohan, Bel. I6 12
Bohemia see Čechy, hist. reg., Czech. F14 10
Bohemian Forest, mts., Eur. F12 10
Bohicon, Benin H11 64
Bohol, i., Phil. D7 38
Bohol Sea, Phil. D7 38
Boiaçu, Braz. H12 84
Boiestown, N.B., Can. F7 106
Boigu Island, i., Austl. A8 68
Boiling Springs, N.C., U.S. D5 112
Boipeba, Ilha de, i., Braz. B9 79
Bois, Lac des, l., N.W. Ter., Can. C32 100
Bois, Rio dos, stm., Braz. E3 79
Bois Blanc Island, i., Mi., U.S. E11 110
Bois Brule, stm., Wi., U.S. D4 110
Bois de Sioux, stm., U.S. E11 118
Boise, Id., U.S. G9 122
Boise, stm., Id., U.S. G9 122
Boise City, Ok., U.S. C4 116
Boissevain, Man., Can. I14 104
Bojayá, stm., Col. D4 84
Bojeador, Cape, c., Phil. I19 39b
Bojnūrd, Iran C14 48
Bojonegoro, Indon. j15 39a
Boju, Nig. H13 64
Bojuru, Braz. F13 80
Bokani, Nig. G12 64
Bokchito, Ok., U.S. E10 116
Boké, Gui. F2 64
Bokhara, stm., Austl. G7 70
Bokino, Russia I24 22
Bokolako, Sen. E3 64
Boksitogorsk, Russia B16 22
Bokungu, Zaire B4 58
Bol, Cro. F11 18
Bolama, Gui.-B. F2 64
Bolaños, stm., Mex. F8 90
Bolaños de Calatrava, Spain G8 16
Bolbec, Fr. C7 14
Bolchov, Russia H19 22
Boles, Ar., U.S. H2 114
Bolesławiec, Pol. D15 10
Boleszkowice, Pol. C14 10
Boley, Ok., U.S. D10 116
Bolgatanga, Ghana F9 64
Bolhrad, Ukr. D12 20
Boli, China B13 30
Boli, Sud. N5 60
Boligee, Al., U.S. J8 114
Boling, Tx., U.S. J11 116
Bolingbrook, Il., U.S. I7 110
Bolívar, Col. E4 84
Bolívar, Col. G4 84
Bolívar, Col. E4 84
Bolívar, Peru B3 82
Bolivar, Mo., U.S. E3 114
Bolivar, N.Y., U.S. E8 108
Bolivar, Tn., U.S. G8 114
Bolívar, state, Ven. D11 84
Bolívar, prov., Ec. H3 84
Bolívar, dept., Col. C5 84
Bolívar, Cerro, mtn., Ven. D11 84
Bolívar, Pico, mtn., Ven. C7 84
Bolivar Peninsula, pen., Tx., U.S. J12 116
Bolivia, ctry., S.A. G5 76
Bollène, Fr. H11 14
Bollnäs, Swe. K15 6
Bollon, Austl. G7 70
Bollullos par del Condado, Spain H5 16
Bolobo, Zaire B3 58
Bolochovo, Russia G20 22
Bologna, Italy E6 18
Bolognesi, Peru B5 82
Bologoje, Russia D17 22
Bolomba, Zaire A3 58
Bolonchén de Rejón, Mex. G15 90
Bolotnoje, Russia F14 26
Bolovens, Plateau des, plat., Laos G9 40
Bol'šaja Balachn'a, stm., Russia C12 28
Bol'šaja Čheta, stm., Russia D14 26
Bol'šaja Čuja, stm., Russia F14 28
Bol'šaja Ižora, Russia B12 22
Bol'šaja Kuonamka, stm., Russia D13 28
Bol'šaja Lipovica, Russia I24 22
Bol'šaja Murta, Russia F16 26
Bol'šaja Višera, Russia C15 22
Bol'šakovo, Russia G4 22
Bolsena, Italy G6 18
Bolsena, Lago di, l., Italy G6 18
Bol'šereck, Russia G23 28
Bol'ševik, Bela. I13 22
Bol'ševik, Russia E21 28
Bol'ševik, ostrov, i., Russia B12 28
Bol'šezemel'skaja Tundra, reg., Russia D9 26
Bol'šoj An'uj, stm., Russia D24 28
Bol'šoj Begičev, ostrov, i., Russia C14 28
Bol'šoje Michajlovskoje, Russia E21 22
Bol'šoje Polpino, Russia H17 22
Bol'šoj Jenisej, stm., Russia G11 28
Bol'šoj L'achovskij, ostrov, i., Russia C20 28
Bol'šoj Tal'cy, Russia B16 22
Bol'šoj T'uters, ostrov, i., Russia B10 22
Bol'šoj Uzen', stm., Eur. H7 26
Bolton, Ont., Can. G16 110
Bolton, Ms., U.S. J6 114
Bolton, N.C., U.S. E8 112
Bolton Lake, l., Man., Can. D19 104
Bolu, Tur. G14 4
Boluntay, China B15 44
Boluochi, China B7 32
Bóly, Hung. J18 10
Bolzano (Bozen), Italy C6 18
Boma, Zaire C2 58
Bomaderry, Austl. J9 70
Bombala, Austl. K8 70
Bombarral, Port. F2 16
Bombay, India C2 46
Bomberai, Semenanjung, pen., Indon. F9 38
Bom Despacho, Braz. E6 79
Bomei, China M4 34
Bom Jardim de Goiás, Braz. D2 79
Bom Jesus da Lapa, Braz. B7 79
Bom Jesus de Goiás, Braz. E4 79
Bom Retiro, Braz. D14 80
Bom Sucesso, Braz. G3 79
Bom Sucesso, Braz. F13 82
Bomu (Mbomou), stm., Afr. H5 56
Bon, Cap, c., Tun. L6 18
Bon Air, Va., U.S. B9 112
Bonaire, i., Neth. Ant. H10 94
Bonampak, hist., Mex. I14 90
Bonanza, Nic. C10 92
Bonanza, Or., U.S. H4 122
Bonanza, Ut., U.S. D7 120
Bonao, Dom. Rep. E9 94
Bonaparte, Ia., U.S. J4 110
Bonaparte, stm., B.C., Can. F13 102
Bonaparte Archipelago, is., Austl. B5 68
Bonaparte Lake, l., B.C., Can. F14 102
Bonarbridge, Scot., U.K. D9 8
Bonarcado, Italy I3 18
Bonaventure, Que., Can. D8 106
Bonaventure, stm., Que., Can. D8 106
Bonaventure, Île, i., Que., Can. D9 106
Bonavista, Newf., Can. D20 106
Bonavista, Cape, c., Newf., Can. D20 106
Bonavista Bay, b., Newf., Can. D20 106
Bond, Ms., U.S. L7 114
Bondeno, Italy E6 18
Bondo, Zaire H5 56
Bondoukou, C. Iv. G8 64
Bonduel, Wi., U.S. F7 110
Bone, Teluk, b., Indon. F7 38
Bonesteel, S.D., U.S. H9 118
Bonete, Cerro, mtn., Arg. D4 80
Bonete Chico, Cerro, mtn., Arg. E4 80
Bonga, Eth. N9 60
Bongak, Sud. N7 60
Bongandanga, Zaire A4 58
Bongo, Massif des, mts., Cen. Afr. Rep. M2 60
Bongor, Chad F4 56
Bongouanou, C. Iv. H7 64
Bonham, Tx., U.S. F10 116
Bonhomme, Morne, mtn., Haiti E8 94
Bonifacio, Fr. m24 15a
Bonifacio, Strait of, strt., Eur. H4 18
Bonifay, Fl., U.S. L11 114
Bonilla Island, i., B.C., Can. D4 102
Bonita, La., U.S. J5 114
Bonita Springs, Fl., U.S. M5 112
Bonito, Braz. I13 82
Bonito, stm., Braz. D3 79
Bonito, Pico, mtn., Hond. B8 92
Bonito, Rio, stm., N.M., U.S. K11 120
Bonkoukou, Niger D11 64
Bonn, Ger. E7 10
Bonne Bay (Woody Point), Newf., Can. C16 106
Bonne Bay, b., Newf., Can. C16 106
Bonneia, Eth. O9 60
Bonner, Mt., U.S. D12 122
Bonners Ferry, Id., U.S. B9 122
Bonnet, Lac du, l., Man., Can. H19 104
Bonnétable, Fr. D7 14
Bonne Terre, Mo., U.S. E6 114
Bonnet Plume, stm., Yukon, Can. D27 100
Bonneval, Fr. D8 14
Bonneville, Fr. F13 14
Bonneville Peak, mtn., Id., U.S. H13 122
Bonneville Salt Flats, pl., Ut., U.S. D3 120
Bonnie Doone, N.C., U.S. D8 112
Bonnie Rock, Austl. F3 68
Bonny, Nig. I13 64
Bonnyville, Alta., Can. C24 102
Bono, Ar., U.S. G6 114
Bonorva, Italy I3 18
Bon Secour, Al., U.S. L9 114
Bonshaw, P.E.I., Can. F10 106
Bonthe, S.L. H3 64
Bontoc, Phil. m19 39b
Bon Wier, Tx., U.S. L3 114
Bonyhád, Hung. I18 10
Booischot, Bel. F6 12
Bookaloo, Austl. H2 70
Book Cliffs, clf, U.S. E7 120

Name	Map Ref.	Page
Campo Novo, Braz.	D12	80
Campo Quijano, Arg.	C6	80
Camporredondo, Peru	B2	82
Campos, Braz.	F8	79
Campos Altos, Braz.	E5	79
Campo Santo, Arg.	C6	80
Campos Belos, Braz.	B5	79
Campos do Jordão, Braz.	G6	79
Campos Gerais, Braz.	F6	79
Campos Novos, Braz.	D13	80
Camp Point, Il., U.S.	B5	114
Campti, La., U.S.	K3	114
Campton, Ky., U.S.	B3	112
Câmpulung, Rom.	D9	20
Câmpulung Moldovenesc, Rom.	B9	20
Campuya, stm., Peru	H5	84
Camp Verde, Az., U.S.	J5	120
Camp Wood, Tx., U.S.	J6	116
Cam Ranh, Viet.	I10	40
Cam Ranh, Vinh, b., Viet.	I10	40
Camrose, Alta., Can.	D22	102
Camsell, stm., N.W. Ter., Can.	C9	96
Camu, stm., Braz.	G14	84
Canaan, Ct., U.S.	E13	108
Canaan, Vt., U.S.	C15	108
Canaan, stm., N.B., Can.	F8	106
Cana-brava, stm., Braz.	B4	79
Cana-brava, stm., Braz.	B4	79
Canaçarí, Lago, l., Braz.	I13	84
Canada, ctry., N.A.	D13	96
Canada Bay, b., Newf., Can.	B17	106
Cañada de Gómez, Arg.	G8	80
Cañada Honda, Arg.	F4	80
Canadian, Tx., U.S.	D6	116
Canadian, stm., U.S.	D10	116
Canadian, stm., Co., U.S.	D10	120
Canaguá, stm., Ven.	C7	84
Canaima, Ven.	D11	84
Canaima, Parque Nacional, Ven.	E11	84
Canajoharie, N.Y., U.S.	E12	108
Çanakkale, Tur.	I10	20
Çanakkale Boğazı (Dardanelles), strt., Tur.	I10	20
Canal Flats, B.C., Can.	G19	102
Canal Fulton, Oh., U.S.	G5	108
Canal Point, Fl., U.S.	M6	112
Canals, Arg.	G7	80
Canal Winchester, Oh., U.S.	H4	108
Canamã, stm., Braz.	D12	82
Canandaigua, N.Y., U.S.	E9	108
Cananea, Mex.	B4	90
Cananéia, Braz.	C15	80
Canápolis, Braz.	E4	79
Cañar, Ec.	I3	84
Cañar, prov., Ec.	I3	84
Canarias, Islas (Canary Islands), is., Spain	o25	17b
Canarreos, Archipiélago de los, is., Cuba	D4	94
Canary Islands see Canarias, Islas, is., Spain	C3	54
Cañas, C.R.	G9	92
Canaseraga, N.Y., U.S.	E9	108
Cañasgordas, Col.	D4	84
Canastota, N.Y., U.S.	D11	108
Canatlán, Mex.	E7	90
Canaveral, Cape, c., Fl., U.S.	K6	112
Canavieiras, Braz.	C9	79
Cañazas, Pan.	C2	84
Canberra, Austl.	J8	70
Canby, Ca., U.S.	C5	124
Canby, Mn., U.S.	G11	118
Canby, Or., U.S.	E3	122
Cancale, Fr.	D5	14
Canchaque, Peru	A2	82
Cancún, Mex.	G16	90
Cancún, Punta, c., Mex.	D1	94
Candarave, Peru	G6	82
Candás, Spain	B6	16
Candé, Fr.	E5	14
Candeias, Braz.	B9	79
Candeias, Braz.	F6	79
Candeias, stm., Braz.	C10	82
Candela, Mex.	D9	90
Candela, stm., Mex.	D9	90
Candelaria, Arg.	D11	80
Candelaria, Arg.	G6	80
Candelária, Braz.	E12	80
Candelaria, Col.	F4	84
Candelaria, Cuba	C3	94
Candelaria, stm., Mex.	H14	90
Candeleda, Spain	E6	16
Candia see Iráklion, Grc.	N9	20
Cándido Aguilar, Mex.	E10	90
Cândido de Abreu, Braz.	C13	80
Candle, Ak., U.S.	D14	100
Candle Lake, l., Sask., Can.	E9	104
Candlemas Islands, is., S. Geor.	A2	73
Candlemas Islands, is., S. Geor.	J12	74
Candlestick, Ms., U.S.	J6	114
Candlewood, Lake, l., Ct., U.S.	F13	108
Cando, Sask., Can.	F6	104
Cando, N.D., U.S.	C8	118
Candor, N.Y., U.S.	E10	108
Candor, N.C., U.S.	D7	112
Cane, stm., La., U.S.	K4	114
Canea see Khaniá, Grc.	N8	20
Canela, Braz.	E13	80
Canelas, Mex.	E6	90
Canelli, Italy	E3	18
Canelones, Ur.	H10	80
Cañete, Chile	I2	80
Cañete, Spain	E10	16
Caney, Ks., U.S.	N12	118
Caney, stm., U.S.	C11	116
Cangallo, Peru	E4	82
Cangas, Braz.	G13	82
Cangkuang, Tanjung, c., Indon.	j12	39a
Cangombe, Ang.	D3	58
Canguçu, Braz.	F12	80
Cangzhou, China	E4	32
Caniapiscau, stm., Que., Can.	E19	96
Caniapiscau, Lac, l., Que., Can.	F19	96
Canicattì, Italy	L8	18
Canim Lake, B.C., Can.	F14	102
Canim Lake, l., B.C., Can.	F14	102
Canim Lake Indian Reserve, B.C., Can.	F14	102
Canindeyú, dept., Para.	C11	80
Canisteo, N.Y., U.S.	E9	108
Canisteo, stm., N.Y., U.S.	E9	108
Canistota, S.D., U.S.	H10	118
Cañitas de Felipe Pescador, Mex.	F8	90
Canmore, Alta., Can.	F19	102
Cannanore, India	G3	46
Cannel City, Ky., U.S.	B3	112
Cannelton, In., U.S.	E10	114
Cannes, Fr.	I14	14
Canning, N.S., Can.	G9	106
Cannington, Ont., Can.	F16	110
Cannon, stm., Mn., U.S.	F2	110
Cannon Ball, N.D., U.S.	E7	118
Cannonball, stm., N.D., U.S.	E7	118
Cannon Beach, Or., U.S.	E2	122
Cannon Falls, Mn., U.S.	F3	110
Cann River, Austl.	K8	70
Caño, Isla del, i., C.R.	I11	92
Canoas, Braz.	E13	80
Canoas, stm., Braz.	D13	80
Canoe, B.C., Can.	G15	102
Canoe, stm., B.C., Can.	E16	102
Canoe Creek Indian Reserve, B.C., Can.	F12	102
Canoe Lake, l., Sask., Can.	C6	104
Canoe Lake Indian Reserve, Sask., Can.	C6	104
Canoinhas, Braz.	D13	80
Canol, N.W. Ter., Can.	D31	100
Canon, Ga., U.S.	E3	112
Canon City, Co., U.S.	F11	120
Caño Negro, C.R.	G10	92
Canonsburg, Pa., U.S.	G6	108
Canoochee, stm., Ga., U.S.	G5	112
Canora, Sask., Can.	G12	104
Canosa [di Puglia], Italy	H11	18
Canossa, hist., Italy	E5	18
Canouan, i., St. Vin.	H14	94
Canova, S.D., U.S.	H10	118
Canova Beach, Fl., U.S.	K6	112
Canowindra, Austl.	I8	70
Cansado, Maur.	J2	62
Canso, N.S., Can.	G12	106
Canso, Strait of, strt., N.S., Can.	G12	106
Canta, Peru	D3	82
Cantabria, prov., Spain	B7	16
Cantábrica, Cordillera, mts., Spain	B6	16
Cantagalo, Braz.	F7	79
Cantal, dept., Fr.	G9	14
Cantanhede, Port.	E3	16
Cantaura, Ven.	C10	84
Canterbury, N.B., Can.	G6	106
Canterbury, Eng., U.K.	J15	8
Canterbury Bight, N.Z.	F4	72
Can Tho, Viet.	I8	40
Cantin Lake, l., Man., Can.	E19	104
Canton see Guangzhou, China	L2	34
Canton, Ga., U.S.	E2	112
Canton, Il., U.S.	J5	110
Canton, Ks., U.S.	M10	118
Canton, Mn., U.S.	G4	110
Canton, Ms., U.S.	J6	114
Canton, Mo., U.S.	B5	114
Canton, N.Y., U.S.	C11	108
Canton, N.C., U.S.	D4	112
Canton, Oh., U.S.	G5	108
Canton, Ok., U.S.	C8	116
Canton, Pa., U.S.	F10	108
Canton, S.D., U.S.	H11	118
Canton, Tx., U.S.	G11	116
Canton Lake, res., Ok., U.S.	C8	116
Cantonment, Fl., U.S.	L9	114
Cantù, Italy	D4	18
Cantu, stm., Braz.	C12	80
Cantwell, Ak., U.S.	E20	100
Cañuelas, Arg.	H9	80
Canumã, Braz.	J13	84
Canumã, stm., Braz.	J13	84
Canutama, Braz.	B9	82
Canutillo, Tx., U.S.	M10	120
Čany, ozero, l., Russia	G13	26
Cany-Barville, Fr.	C7	14
Canyon, Yukon, Can.	F26	100
Canyon, Tx., U.S.	E5	116
Canyon City, Or., U.S.	F7	122
Canyon Creek, Alta., Can.	B19	102
Canyon Ferry Lake, res., Mt., U.S.	D14	122
Canyonlands National Park, Ut., U.S.	F7	120
Canyonville, Or., U.S.	H2	122
Cao Bang, Viet.	C9	40
Caojun, China	F5	34
Caomaji, China	I4	32
Caoping, China	G7	34
Caoqiao, China	D8	34
Caota, China	F9	34
Caoxian, China	I3	32
Caoyangxi, China	I7	34
Cap, Pointe du, c., St. Luc.	G14	94
Capac, Mi., U.S.	G13	110
Čapajevsk, Russia	G7	26
Capanaparo, stm., S.A.	D9	84
Capanema, Braz.	C12	80
Capão Bonito, Braz.	H4	79
Capão Doce, Morro do, mtn., Braz.	D13	80
Capaotigamau, Lac, l., Que., Can.	B5	106
Caparaó, Parque Nacional do, Braz.	F8	79
Caparo Viejo, stm., Ven.	D7	84
Capatárida, Ven.	B7	84
Cap-aux-Meules (Grindstone Island), Que., Can.	E12	106
Cap aux Meules, Île du, i., Que., Can.	E12	106
Cap-Chat, Que., Can.	C7	106
Cape, stm., Austl.	C7	70
Cape Arid National Park, Austl.	F4	68
Cape Barren Island, i., Austl.	M8	70
Cape Breton Highlands National Park, N.S., Can.	F13	106
Cape Breton Island, i., N.S., Can.	F13	106
Cape Broyle, Newf., Can.	E21	106
Cape Canaveral, Fl., U.S.	K6	112
Cape Charles, Va., U.S.	B10	112
Cape Coast, Ghana	I9	64
Cape Cod Bay, b., Ma., U.S.	F16	108
Cape Coral, Fl., U.S.	M5	112
Cape Dorset, N.W. Ter., Can.	D17	96
Cape Elizabeth, Me., U.S.	D16	108
Cape Fear, stm., N.C., U.S.	E8	112
Cape Girardeau, Mo., U.S.	E7	114
Cape LaHave Island, i., N.S., Can.	H9	106
Cape la Hune, Newf., Can.	E17	106
Capelinha, Braz.	D7	79
Cape Lisburne, Ak., U.S.	B11	100
Capel'ka, Russia	C11	22
Capelle [aan den IJssel], Neth.	E6	12
Capelongo, Ang.	D3	58
Cape May, N.J., U.S.	I12	108
Cape May Court House, N.J., U.S.	H12	108
Cape Pole, Ak., U.S.	I28	100
Cape Porpoise, Me., U.S.	D16	108
Capernaum see Kefar Naḥum, hist., Isr.	C5	50
Cape Romanzof, Ak., U.S.	F12	100
Cape Sable Island, i., N.S., Can.	I8	106
Cape Scott Provincial Park, B.C., Can.	G6	102
Cape Tormentine, N.B., Can.	F10	106
Cape Town (Kaapstad), S. Afr.	I4	66
Cape Verde (Cabo Verde), ctry., Afr.	E2	54
Cape Vincent, N.Y., U.S.	C10	108
Cape Yakataga, Ak., U.S.	F23	100
Cape York Peninsula, pen., Austl.	B8	68
Cap-Haïtien, Haiti	E8	94
Capilla de Farruco, Ur.	G11	80
Capilla del Monte, Arg.	F6	80
Capim, stm., Braz.	D9	76
Capinópolis, Braz.	E4	79
Capinota, Bol.	G8	82
Capinzal, Braz.	D13	80
Capira, Pan.	C3	84
Capitan, N.M., U.S.	K11	120
Capitán Arturo Prat, sci., Ant.	B1	73
Capitán Bado, Para.	B11	80
Capitán Bermúdez, Arg.	G8	80
Capitán Meza, Para.	D11	80
Capitan Peak, mtn., N.M., U.S.	K11	120
Capitán Sarmiento, Arg.	H9	80
Capitola, Ca., U.S.	H4	124
Capitol Peak, mtn., Nv., U.S.	C8	124
Capitol Reef National Park, Ut., U.S.	F5	120
Capitol View, S.C., U.S.	F6	112
Capivari, Braz.	G5	79
Capivari, stm., Braz.	B8	79
Capivari, stm., Braz.	H13	82
Caplan, Que., Can.	D8	106
Çaplina, stm., Peru	G6	82
Čaplygin, Russia	H22	22
Cap Mountain, mtn., N.W. Ter., Can.	E33	100
Cap-Pelé, N.B., Can.	F9	106
Capreol, Ont., Can.	D15	110
Capri, Isola di, i., Italy	I9	18
Capricorn, Cape, c., Austl.	D9	70
Capricorn Channel, strt., Austl.	D10	70
Capricorn Group, is., Austl.	D10	70
Caprivi Zipfel (Caprivi Strip), hist. reg., Nmb.	A6	66
Capron, Il., U.S.	H7	110
Captain Cook, Hi., U.S.	r18	125a
Captains Flat, Austl.	J8	70
Capua, Italy	H9	18
Capuça I, Ang.	A5	66
Capucapu, stm., Braz.	H13	84
Caquetá, ter., Col.	G5	84
Caquetá (Japurá), stm., S.A.	H7	84
Caquiaviri, Bol.	G7	82
Çara, Eth.	O9	60
Čara, stm., Russia	E16	28
Carabaya, stm., Peru	F7	82
Carabaya, Cordillera de, mts., Peru	E6	82
Carabinani, stm., Braz.	I11	84
Carabobo, state, Ven.	J10	94
Caracal, Rom.	E8	20
Caracaraí, Braz.	G12	84
Caracas, Ven.	B9	84
Carache, Ven.	C7	84
Caracol, Braz.	B10	80
Caracollo, Bol.	G8	82
Caraguatatuba, Braz.	G6	79
Caraguatay, Para.	C10	80
Caraí, Braz.	D8	79
Caraibamba, Peru	F5	82
Caraigres, Cerro, mtn., C.R.	H10	92
Caraíva, stm., Braz.	D9	79
Carajás, Serra dos, mts., Braz.	E8	76
Caranavi, Bol.	F8	82
Carandaí, Braz.	F7	79
Carandayti, Bol.	I10	82
Carangola, Braz.	F7	79
Caransebeș, Rom.	D6	20
Carapá, stm., Para.	C11	80
Cara-Paraná, stm., Col.	H6	84
Carapeguá, Para.	C10	80
Carapo, stm., Ven.	D11	84
Caraquet, N.B., Can.	E9	106
Caráquez, Ec.	H2	84
Carare, stm., Col.	D5	84
Caraș-Severin, co., Rom.	D5	20
Caratasca, Laguna de, b., Hond.	B11	92
Caratinga, Braz.	E7	79
Carauari, Braz.	J9	84
Caravaca, Spain	G10	16
Caravaggio, Italy	D4	18
Caravelas, Braz.	D9	79
Caravelí, Peru	F5	82
Caraway, Ar., U.S.	G6	114
Carayaó, Para.	C10	80
Caraz, Peru	C3	82
Carazinho, Braz.	E12	80
Carazo, dept., Nic.	F8	92
Carballiño, Spain	C3	16
Carballo, Spain	B3	16
Carberry, Man., Can.	I15	104
Carbo, Mex.	C4	90
Carbon, Alta., Can.	F21	102
Carbon, Tx., U.S.	G8	116
Carbon, stm., Wa., U.S.	C4	122
Carbondale, Co., U.S.	E9	120
Carbondale, Il., U.S.	E7	114
Carbondale, Ks., U.S.	M12	118
Carbondale, Pa., U.S.	F11	108
Carbonear, Newf., Can.	E20	106
Carbon Hill, Al., U.S.	I9	114
Carbonia, Italy	J3	18
Carcaixent, Spain	F11	16
Carcajou, stm., N.W. Ter., Can.	D30	100
Carcarañá, Arg.	G8	80
Carcarañá, stm., Arg.	G8	80
Carcassonne, Fr.	I9	14
Carchi, prov., Ec.	G3	84
Carcross, Yukon, Can.	F27	100
Čardarinskoje vodochranilišče, res., Asia	I11	26
Cárdenas, Cuba	C4	94
Cárdenas, Mex.	F10	90
Cárdenas, Mex.	I13	90
Cárdenas, Nic.	F9	92
Cárdenas, Bahía de, b., Cuba	C4	94
Çardi, Tur.	J13	20
Cardiel, Lago, l., Arg.	F2	78
Cardiff, Wales, U.K.	J10	8
Cardigan, P.E.I., Can.	F11	106
Cardigan Bay, b., P.E.I., Can.	F11	106
Cardigan Bay, b., Wales, U.K.	I9	8
Cardinal, Ont., Can.	C11	108
Cardinal Lake, l., Alta., Can.	A17	102
Cardington, Oh., U.S.	G4	108
Cardona, Ur.	G10	80
Cardonal, Punta, c., Mex.	C4	90
Cardoso, Braz.	F4	79
Cardozo, Ur.	G10	80
Cardston, Alta., Can.	H21	102
Cardwell, Austl.	B7	70
Cardwell, Mo., U.S.	F6	114
Čardžou, Turk.	J10	26
Careen Lake, l., Sask., Can.	A6	104
Carei, Rom.	B6	20
Careiro, Braz.	I13	84
Careiro, Ilha do, i., Braz.	I13	84
Carén, Chile	F3	80
Carencro, La., U.S.	L4	114
Carentan, Fr.	C5	14
Cares, stm., Spain	B7	16
Caretta, W.V., U.S.	B5	112
Carey, Oh., U.S.	G3	108
Carey, Lake, l., Austl.	E4	68
Careysburg, Lib.	H4	64
Carhaix-Plouguer, Fr.	D3	14
Carhuamayo, Peru	D3	82
Carhuanca, Peru	E5	82
Carhuaz, Peru	C3	82
Carhué, Arg.	I7	80
Cariacica, Braz.	F8	79
Cariaco, Ven.	B11	84
Cariaco, Golfo de, b., Ven.	B10	84
Cariamanga, Ec.	J3	84
Caribana, Punta, c., Col.	C4	84
Caribbean Sea	G8	94
Cariboo, stm., B.C., Can.	E13	102
Cariboo Mountains, mts., B.C., Can.	D13	102
Caribou, N.S., Can.	G11	106
Caribou, stm., Man., Can.	E13	96
Caribou Mountain, mtn., Id., U.S.	G14	122
Caribou Mountains, mts., Alta., Can.	E9	96
Carichic, Mex.	D6	90
Carignan, Fr.	C12	14
Carinhanha, Braz.	C7	79
Carinhanha, stm., Braz.	C6	79
Carini, Italy	K8	18
Caripe, Ven.	B11	84
Caripito, Ven.	B11	84
Carleton, Mi., U.S.	H12	110
Carleton, Ne., U.S.	K10	118
Carleton, Mount, mtn., N.B., Can.	E7	106
Carleton Place, Ont., Can.	E19	110
Carlin, Nv., U.S.	D9	124
Carlinville, Il., U.S.	C7	114
Carlisle, Eng., U.K.	G11	8
Carlisle, Ar., U.S.	H5	114
Carlisle, In., U.S.	D9	114
Carlisle, Ia., U.S.	I2	110
Carlisle, Ky., U.S.	I2	108
Carlisle, Pa., U.S.	G9	108
Carl Junction, Mo., U.S.	E2	114
Carlópolis, Braz.	G4	79
Carlos Barbosa, Braz.	E13	80
Carlos Casares, Arg.	H8	80
Carlos Chagas, Braz.	D8	79
Carlos Forseca Amador, Nic.	F8	92
Carlos Pellegrini, Arg.	G8	80
Carlos Reyles, Ur.	G10	80
Carlos Tejedor, Arg.	H7	80
Carlow, Ire.	I7	8
Carlow, co., Ire.	I7	8
Carlsbad see Karlovy Vary, Czech.	E12	10
Carlsbad, Ca., U.S.	K8	124
Carlsbad, N.M., U.S.	G2	116
Carlsbad, Tx., U.S.	H6	116
Carlsbad Caverns National Park, N.M., U.S.	G2	116
Carlton, Mn., U.S.	D3	110
Carlton, Or., U.S.	E2	122
Carlton, Tx., U.S.	H8	116
Carlyle, Sask., Can.	I12	104
Carlyle, Il., U.S.	D7	114
Carlyle Lake, res., Il., U.S.	D7	114
Carmacks, Yukon, Can.	E26	100
Carmagnola, Italy	E2	18
Carman, Man., Can.	I16	104
Carmangay, Alta., Can.	G21	102
Carmanville, Newf., Can.	C19	106
Carmaux, Fr.	H9	14
Carmel, Ca., U.S.	H4	124
Carmel, In., U.S.	C10	114
Carmel, N.Y., U.S.	F13	108
Carmel, Mount see Karmel, Har, mtn., Isr.	C4	50
Carmelo, Ur.	H9	80
Carmel Valley, Ca., U.S.	H4	124
Carmel Woods, Ca., U.S.	H4	124
Carmen, Ok., U.S.	C8	116
Carmen, Ur.	G10	80
Carmen, Isla, i., Mex.	E4	90
Carmen, Isla del, i., Mex.	H14	90
Carmen, Río del, stm., Chile	E3	80
Carmen Alto, Chile	B4	80
Carmen de Apicalá, Col.	E5	84
Carmen de Areco, Arg.	H9	80
Carmen de Patagones, Arg.	E4	78
Carmi, Il., U.S.	D8	114
Carmichael, Ca., U.S.	F4	124
Carmine, Tx., U.S.	I10	116
Carmo do Paranaíba, Braz.	E5	79
Carmo do Rio Verde, Braz.	C4	79
Carmona, Spain	H6	16
Carmópolis de Minas, Braz.	F6	79
Carnarvon, Austl.	D2	68
Carnarvon, S. Afr.	H6	66
Carnatic, hist. reg., India	G10	42
Carnduff, Sask., Can.	I13	104
Carnegie, Ok., U.S.	D8	116
Carnegie, Lake, l., Austl.	E4	68
Carniche, Alpi, mts., Eur.	C8	18
Car Nicobar Island, i., India	J2	40
Carnot, Cape, c., Austl.	J1	70
Carnoustie, Scot., U.K.	E11	8
Carnsore Point, c., Ire.	I7	8
Carnwath, stm., N.W. Ter., Can.	C30	100
Caro, Mi., U.S.	G12	110
Carol City, Fl., U.S.	N6	112
Caroleen, N.C., U.S.	D5	112
Carolina, Braz.	E9	76
Carolina, Col.	D5	84
Carolina, El Sal.	D6	92
Carolina Beach, N.C., U.S.	E9	112
Caroline Islands, is., Oc.	H18	126
Caron, Sask., Can.	H9	104
Caroní, stm., Ven.	C11	84
Carora, Ven.	B7	84
Carouge, Switz.	F5	13
Carp, Ont., Can.	E19	110
Carp, stm., Mi., U.S.	D11	110
Carpathian Mountains, mts., Eur.	F12	4
Carpații Meridionali, mts., Rom.	D8	20
Carpentaria, Gulf of, b., Austl.	B7	68
Carpenter, Wy., U.S.	J3	118
Carpenter Lake, l., B.C., Can.	G12	102
Carpentersville, Il., U.S.	H7	110
Carpentras, Fr.	H12	14
Carpi, Italy	E5	18
Cărpineni, Mol.	C12	20
Carpinteria, Ca., U.S.	J6	124
Carpio, N.D., U.S.	C6	118
Carp Lake, l., B.C., Can.	C11	102
Carpolac, Austl.	K4	70
Carrabelle, Fl., U.S.	J2	112
Carranza, Cabo, c., Chile	H2	80
Carrao, stm., Ven.	D11	84
Carrara, Italy	E5	18
Carrauntoohil, mtn., Ire.	J4	8
Carrboro, N.C., U.S.	D7	112
Carreria, Para.	A9	80
Carreta, Punta, c., Peru	F3	82
Carriacou, i., Gren.	H14	94
Carrick on Shannon, Ire.	H5	8
Carrick on Suir, Ire.	I6	8
Carriere, Ms., U.S.	L7	114
Carriers Mills, Il., U.S.	E8	114
Carrillo, C.R.	H9	92
Carrillo, Mex.	D8	90
Carrington, N.D., U.S.	D8	118
Carrión de los Condes, Spain	C7	16
Carrizal Bajo, Chile	E3	80
Carrizo Mountain, mtn., N.M., U.S.	K11	120
Carrizo Springs, Tx., U.S.	K7	116
Carrizozo, N.M., U.S.	K11	120
Carroll, Ia., U.S.	I13	118
Carroll, Ne., U.S.	I10	118
Carroll Lake, l., Ont., Can.	G19	104
Carrollton, Al., U.S.	I8	114
Carrollton, Ga., U.S.	F1	112
Carrollton, Il., U.S.	C6	114
Carrollton, Ky., U.S.	D11	114
Carrollton, Mi., U.S.	G12	110
Carrollton, Ms., U.S.	I7	114
Carrollton, Mo., U.S.	C3	114
Carrollton, Oh., U.S.	G5	108
Carrollton, Tx., U.S.	G10	116
Carrolltown, Pa., U.S.	G8	108
Carrot, stm., Can.	E12	104
Carrot River, Sask., Can.	E11	104
Carrville, Al., U.S.	J11	114
Čaršanga, Turk.	B1	44
Carseland, Alta., Can.	G21	102
Čarsk, Kaz.	H14	26
Carson, N.D., U.S.	E6	118
Carson, Wa., U.S.	E4	122
Carson, stm., Nv., U.S.	E6	124
Carson City, Mi., U.S.	G11	110
Carson City, Nv., U.S.	E6	124
Carson Range, mts., U.S.	E6	124
Carson Sink, l., Nv., U.S.	E7	124
Carstairs, Alta., Can.	F20	102
Cartagena, Chile	G3	80
Cartagena, Col.	B5	84
Cartagena, Spain	H11	16
Cartago, Col.	E5	84
Cartago, C.R.	H11	92
Cartago, prov., C.R.	H11	92
Cartaxo, Port.	F3	16
Cartaya, Spain	H4	16
Carter, Ok., U.S.	D7	116
Carter Lake, Ia., U.S.	J12	118
Carter Mountain, mtn., Wy., U.S.	F16	122
Cartersville, Ga., U.S.	E2	112
Carterville, Il., U.S.	E7	114
Carthage, Tun.	M5	18
Carthage, Ar., U.S.	H4	114
Carthage, Il., U.S.	J4	110
Carthage, In., U.S.	C11	114
Carthage, Ms., U.S.	J7	114
Carthage, Mo., U.S.	E2	114
Carthage, N.Y., U.S.	D11	108
Carthage, N.C., U.S.	D7	112
Carthage, S.D., U.S.	G10	118
Carthage, Tn., U.S.	F11	114
Carthage, Tx., U.S.	J2	114
Carthage, hist., Tun.	M5	18
Cartier Islands, is., Austl.	B4	68
Cartwright, Man., Can.	I15	104
Cartwright, Newf., Can.	F21	96
Caruaru, Braz.	E11	76
Carumas, Peru	G6	82
Carúpano, Ven.	B11	84
Carutapera, Braz.	D9	76
Caruthersville, Mo., U.S.	F7	114
Carutu, stm., Ven.	E11	84
Carvin, Fr.	B9	14
Carvoeiro, Braz.	H12	84
Cary, Ms., U.S.	J6	114
Cary, N.C., U.S.	D8	112
Caryville, Fl., U.S.	L11	114
Caryville, Tn., U.S.	C2	112
Casablanca (Dar-el-Beida), Mor.	D7	62
Casa Branca, Braz.	F5	79
Casa Grande, Az., U.S.	L5	120
Casale Monferrato, Italy	D3	18
Casanare, state, Col.	E6	84
Casanare, stm., Col.	D7	84
Casanay, Ven.	B11	84
Casas Adobes, Az., U.S.	L6	120
Casas Grandes, stm., Mex.	B6	90
Casas Ibáñez, Spain	F10	16
Casasimarro, Spain	F9	16
Casavieja, Spain	E7	16
Casbas, Arg.	I7	80
Casca, Braz.	E13	80
Casca, Rio da, stm., Braz.	F14	82
Cascadas Basaseachic, Parque Nacional, Mex.	C5	90
Cascade, B.C., Can.	H16	102
Cascade, Id., U.S.	F9	122
Cascade, Ia., U.S.	H4	110
Cascade, Mt., U.S.	C14	122
Cascade, Wi., U.S.	G7	110
Cascade Locks, Or., U.S.	E4	122
Cascade Range, mts., N.A.	C2	98
Cascade Reservoir, res., Id., U.S.	F9	122
Cascais, Port.	G2	16
Cascalho Rico, Braz.	E5	79
Cascapédia, stm., Que., Can.	D7	106
Cascavel, Braz.	C12	80
Cascina, Italy	F5	18
Casco Bay, b., Me., U.S.	D16	108
Cascumpec Bay, b., P.E.I., Can.	F9	106
Caserta, Italy	H9	18
Caseville, Mi., U.S.	G12	110
Casey, Il., U.S.	C9	114
Casey, Ia., U.S.	J13	118
Cashel, Ire.	I6	8
Cashiers, N.C., U.S.	D3	112
Cashmere, Wa., U.S.	C5	122
Cashton, Wi., U.S.	G5	110
Casigua, Ven.	C6	84
Casilda, Arg.	G8	80
Casillas del Angel, Spain	o27	17b
Casino, Austl.	G10	70
Çasiquiare, stm., Ven.	F9	84
Čáslav, Czech.	F15	10
Çasma, Peru	C2	82
Čašniki, Bela.	G12	22
Časnočor, gora, mtn., Russia	H23	6
Caspe, Spain	D11	16
Casper, Wy., U.S.	B10	120
Caspian, Mi., U.S.	D7	110
Caspian Sea	I8	26
Cass, stm., Mi., U.S.	G12	110
Cassai (Kasai), stm., Afr.	C4	58
Cassanje, stm., Braz.	G13	82
Cassano allo Ionio, Italy	J11	18
Cass City, Mi., U.S.	G12	110
Casselman, Ont., Can.	B11	108
Casselton, N.D., U.S.	E10	118
Cássia, Braz.	F5	79
Cassiar, B.C., Can.	G30	100
Cassiar Mountains, mts., Can.	E7	96
Cassilândia, Braz.	E3	79
Cassinga, Ang.	E3	58
Cassino, Braz.	G12	80
Cassino, Italy	H8	18
Cass Lake, Mn., U.S.	C1	110
Cassopolis, Mi., U.S.	I9	110
Cassumba, Ilha, i., Braz.	D9	79
Cassununga, Braz.	D2	79
Cassville, Mo., U.S.	F3	114
Cassville, Wi., U.S.	H5	110
Castalia, Oh., U.S.	F4	108
Castanheira de Pêra, Port.	E3	16
Castañones, Punta, c., Nic.	E7	92
Castelbuono, Italy	L9	18
Castelfiorentino, Italy	F5	18
Castelfranco Veneto, Italy	D6	18
Castellammare del Golfo, Italy	K7	18
Castellammare [di Stabia], Italy	I9	18
Castellaneta, Italy	I11	18
Castelli, Arg.	I10	80
Castelló, prov., Spain	E11	16
Castelló de la Plana, Spain	F11	16
Castelmassa, Italy	D6	18
Castelnaudary, Fr.	I8	14
Castelo, Braz.	F8	79
Castelo Branco, Port.	F4	16
Castelsarrasin, Fr.	H8	14
Castelvetrano, Italy	L7	18
Castets, Fr.	I5	14
Castile, N.Y., U.S.	E8	108
Castilho, Braz.	F3	79
Castilla, Peru	A1	82
Castilla-La Mancha, prov., Spain	F8	16
Castilla la Nueva, hist. reg., Spain	F9	16
Castilla la Vieja, hist. reg., Spain	D7	16
Castilla-León, prov., Spain	D6	16
Castillo del Romeral, Spain	p25	17b
Castillo Incaico de Ingapirca, hist., Ec.	I3	84
Castillos, Ur.	H12	80
Castillos, Laguna de, l., Ur.	H12	80
Castine, Me., U.S.	C18	108
Castlebar, Ire.	H4	8
Castleberry, Al., U.S.	K9	114
Castle Dale, Ut., U.S.	E6	120
Castle Douglas, Scot., U.K.	G10	8
Castlegar, B.C., Can.	H17	102
Castle Hills, Tx., U.S.	J8	116
Castlemaine, Austl.	K6	70
Castle Mountain, mtn., Alta., Can.	F19	102
Castle Mountain, mtn., Yukon, Can.	D27	100
Castle Peak, mtn., Co., U.S.	E10	120
Castle Peak, mtn., Id., U.S.	F11	122
Castlerea, Ire.	H5	8
Castlereagh, stm., Austl.	H8	70
Castle Rock, Co., U.S.	E12	120
Castle Rock, Wa., U.S.	D3	122
Castle Rock, mtn., Or., U.S.	F7	122
Castle Rock Lake, res., Wi., U.S.	G6	110
Castleton, Vt., U.S.	D13	108
Castletown, Scot., U.K.	C10	8
Castlewood, S.D., U.S.	G10	118
Castlewood, Va., U.S.	C4	112
Castor, Alta., Can.	E23	102
Castor, stm., Mo., U.S.	E6	114
Castres, Fr.	I9	14
Castricum, Neth.	C6	12
Castries, St. Luc.	G14	94
Castro, Braz.	C13	80
Castro, Chile	E2	78
Castro Barros, Arg.	F6	80
Castro del Río, Spain	H7	16
Castro-Urdiales, Spain	B8	16
Castro Verde, Port.	H3	16
Castroville, Ca., U.S.	H4	124
Castroville, Tx., U.S.	J8	116
Castrovirreyna, Peru	E4	82
Castuera, Spain	G6	16
Casummit Lake, Ont., Can.	G22	104
Casupá, Ur.	H11	80
Cat, stm., Ont., Can.	G23	104
Catacamas, Hond.	C9	92
Catacaos, Peru	A1	82
Catacocha, Ec.	J3	84
Cataguases, Braz.	F7	79
Catahoula Lake, l., La., U.S.	K4	114
Catalão, Braz.	E5	79
Çatalca, Tur.	H12	20
Catalina, Newf., Can.	D20	106
Catalina, Chile	C4	80
Catalonia see Catalunya, prov., Spain	D13	16
Catalunya, prov., Spain	D13	16
Catamarca, prov., Arg.	D5	80
Catamayo, Ec.	I3	84
Catamayo, stm., Ec.	J3	84
Catanduva, Braz.	F4	79
Catania, Italy	L10	18
Catania, Golfo di, b., Italy	L10	18
Catanzaro, Italy	K11	18
Catarama, Ec.	H3	84
Catarman, Phil.	C7	38
Catarroja, Spain	F11	16
Catatumbo, stm., Ven.	C7	84
Catawba, stm., U.S.	E6	112
Catawissa, Pa., U.S.	G10	108
Cat Ba, Dao, i., Viet.	D9	40
Catbalogan, Phil.	C7	38
Catchabutan, Punta, c., Hond.	B8	92
Caterino Rodriguez, Mex.	E9	90
Catete, Ang.	C2	58
Cathcart, S. Afr.	I8	66
Cathedral City, Ca., U.S.	K9	124
Cathlamet, Wa., U.S.	D2	122
Ca' Tiepolo, Italy	E7	18
Cat Island, i., Bah.	B7	94
Cat Island, i., Ms., U.S.	L7	114
Cat Lake, l., Ont., Can.	G23	104
Catlettsburg, Ky., U.S.	I4	108
Catlin, Il., U.S.	B9	114
Catnip Mountain, mtn., Nv., U.S.	C6	124
Catoche, Cabo, c., Mex.	G16	90
Cato Island, i., Austl.	D11	70
Catonsville, Md., U.S.	H10	108
Catoosa, Ok., U.S.	C11	116
Catorce, Mex.	F9	90
Catriló, Arg.	I7	80
Catrimani, stm., Braz.	G11	84
Catskill, N.Y., U.S.	E13	108
Catskill Mountains, mts., N.Y., U.S.	E12	108
Catt, Mount, mtn., B.C., Can.	C6	102
Cattaraugus, N.Y., U.S.	E8	108
Cattolica, Italy	F7	18
Catu, Braz.	B9	79
Catwick, Îles, is., Viet.	I10	40
Cauaburi, stm., Braz.	G9	84
Caubvick, Mount (Mont d'Iberville), mtn., Can.	E20	96
Cauca, dept., Col.	F4	84
Cauca, stm., Col.	D5	84
Caucasia, Col.	C5	84
Caucasus, mts.	I6	26
Caucete, Arg.	F4	80
Cauchari, Salar de, pl., Arg.	B5	80
Cauchon Lake, l., Man., Can.	C18	104
Caudry, Fr.	B10	14
Caulonia, Italy	K11	18
Çaúngula, Ang.	C3	58
Čaunskaja guba, b., Russia	D25	28
Cauquenes, Chile	H2	80
Caura, stm., Ven.	D10	84
Caurés, stm., Braz.	H11	84
Căușani, Mol.	C13	20
Causapscal, Que., Can.	D6	106
Çaussade, Fr.	H8	14
Čausy, Bela.	H13	22

Name	Map Ref.	Page
Cautário, stm., Braz.	D9	82
Caution, Cape, c., B.C., Can.	F7	102
Cauto, stm., Cuba	D6	94
Caux, Pays de, reg., Fr.	C7	14
Cavaillon, Fr.	I12	14
Cavalaire-sur-Mer, Fr.	I13	14
Cavalcante, Braz.	B5	79
Cavalheiro, Braz.	D4	79
Cavalier, N.D., U.S.	C10	118
Cavalla (Cavally), stm., Afr.	G5	54
Cavan, Ire.	G6	8
Cavan, co., Ire.	H6	8
Cavarzere, Italy	D7	18
Cave City, Ar., U.S.	G5	114
Cave City, Ky., U.S.	E11	114
Cave In Rock, Il., U.S.	E8	114
Caveiras, stm., Braz.	D13	80
Cavelo, Ang.	A4	66
Cavendish, Austl.	K5	70
Cave Run Lake, res., Ky., U.S.	I3	108
Cave Spring, Ga., U.S.	E1	112
Caviana de Fora, Ilha, i., Braz.	C8	76
Cavite, Phil.	n19	39b
Cawker City, Ks., U.S.	L9	118
Cawood, Ky., U.S.	C3	112
Cawston, B.C., Can.	H15	102
Caxambu, Braz.	F6	79
Caxias, Braz.	D10	76
Caxias do Sul, Braz.	E13	80
Caxinas, Punta, c., Hond.	A8	92
Caxito, Ang.	C2	58
Cayambe, Ec.	G3	84
Cayambe, vol., Ec.	G4	84
Cayce, S.C., U.S.	F5	112
Cayenne, Fr. Gu.	C8	76
Cayey, P.R.	E11	94
Cayman Brac, i., Cay. Is.	E5	94
Cayman Islands, dep., N.A.	E4	94
Cayman Trench	H11	86
Cayna, Peru	D3	82
Cayo Agua, Isla, i., Pan.	H12	92
Cayucos, Ca., U.S.	I5	124
Cayuga, Ont., Can.	H16	110
Cayuga, In., U.S.	C9	114
Cayuga, N.D., U.S.	E10	118
Cayuga, Tx., U.S.	H11	116
Cayuga Heights, N.Y., U.S.	E10	108
Cayuga Lake, l., N.Y., U.S.	E10	108
Cazaclia, Mol.	C12	20
Cazenovia, N.Y., U.S.	E11	108
Cazères, Fr.	I8	14
Cazin, Bos.	E10	18
Cazombo, Ang.	D4	58
Cazorla, Spain	H8	16
Cazorla, Ven.	C9	84
Ccapi, Peru	E5	82
Cchinvali, Geor.	I6	26
Ceanannus Mór, Ire.	H7	8
Ceará-Mirim, Braz.	E11	76
Cebaco, Isla De, i., Pan.	D2	84
Çeballos, Mex.	D7	90
Čeboksary, Russia	F7	26
Cebollar, Arg.	E5	80
Cebollas, Mex.	F7	90
Cebollatí, Ur.	G12	80
Cebollatí, stm., Ur.	G11	80
Cebollita Peak, mtn., N.M., U.S.	J9	120
Céboruco, Volcán, vol., Mex.	G7	90
Čebsara, Russia	B21	22
Cebu, Phil.	C7	38
Cebu, i., Phil.	C7	38
Ceccano, Italy	H8	18
Çecerleg, Mong.	B7	30
Čečersk, Bela.	I13	22
Čečeviči, Bela.	H12	22
Čechov, Russia	F20	22
Čechtice, Czech.	F15	10
Čechy, hist. reg., Czech.	F14	10
Cecil, Ga., U.S.	H3	112
Cecilia, Ky., U.S.	E11	114
Cecina, Italy	F5	18
Cedar, stm., U.S.	I4	110
Cedar, stm., Mi., U.S.	F11	110
Cedar, stm., Ne., U.S.	J9	118
Cedar, stm., N.Y., U.S.	D12	108
Cedar Bluff Reservoir, res., Ks., U.S.	M8	118
Cedar Bluffs, Ne., U.S.	J11	118
Cedarburg, Wi., U.S.	G8	110
Cedar City, Mo., U.S.	D4	114
Cedar City, Ut., U.S.	G3	120
Cedar Creek Reservoir, res., Tx., U.S.	G10	116
Cedaredge, Co., U.S.	F9	120
Cedar Falls, Ia., U.S.	H3	110
Cedar Grove, W.V., U.S.	I5	108
Cedar Grove, Wi., U.S.	G8	110
Cedar Hill, Tn., U.S.	F10	114
Cedar Key, Fl., U.S.	J3	112
Cedar Lake, In., U.S.	A9	114
Cedar Lake, res., Man., Can.	E14	104
Cedar Mountain, mtn., Ca., U.S.	C5	124
Cedar Rapids, Ia., U.S.	I4	110
Cedar Rapids, Ne., U.S.	J9	118
Cedar Springs, Mi., U.S.	G10	110
Cedartown, Ga., U.S.	E1	112
Cedarvale, B.C., Can.	B6	102
Cedar Vale, Ks., U.S.	N11	118
Cedarville, Ca., U.S.	C5	124
Cedarville, Mi., U.S.	D11	110
Cedarville, N.J., U.S.	H11	108
Cedillo, Embalse de, res., Eur.	F4	16
Cedros, Hond.	C7	92
Cedros, Mex.	E9	90
Cedros, Isla, i., Mex.	C2	90
Ceduna, Austl.	F6	68
Ceepeecee, B.C., Can.	H8	102
Ceerigaabo, Som.	F10	56
Çefalù, Italy	K9	18
Čegdomyn, Russia	G18	28
Cegléd, Hung.	H19	10
Cehegín, Spain	G10	16
Çehu Silvaniei, Rom.	B7	20
Čekalin, Russia	G19	22
Čekujevo, Russia	J26	6
Čel'abinsk, Russia	F10	26
Celano, Italy	G8	18
Celaya, Mex.	G9	90
Celebes see Sulawesi, i., Indon.	F7	38
Çelebes Sea, Asia	E7	38
Čeleken, Turk.	J8	26
Celendín, Peru	B2	82
Celeste, Tx., U.S.	F10	116
Celestún, Mex.	G14	90
Celica, Ec.	J3	84
Celina, Oh., U.S.	G2	108
Celina, Tn., U.S.	F11	114
Celina, Tx., U.S.	F10	116
Celinograd, Kaz.	G12	26
Çelje, Slo.	C10	18
Čelkar, Kaz.	H9	26
Celle, Ger.	C10	10
Celorico da Beira, Port.	E4	16
Çeltic Sea, Eur.	J7	8
Čel'uskin, mys, c., Russia	B18	26
Çement, Ok., U.S.	E8	116
Čemerno, Bos.	F13	18
Cenderawasih, Teluk, b., Indon.	F10	38
Cenepa, stm., Peru	J3	84
Centenario, Arg.	J4	80
Centenário do Sul, Braz.	G3	79
Centennial Mountains, mts., U.S.	F14	122
Center, Co., U.S.	G10	120
Center, Mo., U.S.	C5	114
Center, Ne., U.S.	I10	118
Center, N.D., U.S.	D6	118
Center, Tx., U.S.	K2	114
Centerburg, Oh., U.S.	G4	108
Center City, Mn., U.S.	E3	110
Center Hill, Fl., U.S.	K5	112
Center Hill Lake, res., Tn., U.S.	F11	114
Center Moriches, N.Y., U.S.	G14	108
Center Mountain, mtn., Id., U.S.	E10	122
Center Point, Al., U.S.	I10	114
Center Point, Ia., U.S.	H4	110
Center Point, Tx., U.S.	J7	116
Centerville, In., U.S.	C12	114
Centerville, Ia., U.S.	J3	110
Centerville, Mo., U.S.	E6	114
Centerville, Pa., U.S.	G7	108
Centerville, S.D., U.S.	H11	118
Centerville, Tn., U.S.	G9	114
Centerville, Tx., U.S.	H11	116
Centerville, Ut., U.S.	D5	120
Cento, Italy	E6	18
Central, Az., U.S.	L7	120
Central, N.M., U.S.	L8	120
Central, S.C., U.S.	E4	112
Central, prov., Scot., U.K.	E9	8
Central, dept., Bots.	C8	66
Central, dept., Para.	C10	80
Central, Cordillera, mts., Col.	E5	84
Central, Cordillera, mts., C.R.	G10	92
Central, Cordillera, mts., Pan.	I13	92
Central, Cordillera, mts., Peru	B3	82
Central, Cordillera, mts., P.R.	E11	94
Central, Massif, mts., Fr.	G10	14
Central, Planalto, plat., Braz.	G9	76
Central, Sistema, mts., Spain	E6	16
Central African Republic, ctry., Afr.	G5	56
Central Brāhui Range, mts., Pak.	F2	44
Central Butte, Sask., Can.	H8	104
Central City, Il., U.S.	D7	114
Central City, Ia., U.S.	H4	110
Central City, Ky., U.S.	E9	114
Central City, Ne., U.S.	J9	118
Central City, Pa., U.S.	G8	108
Central Heights, Az., U.S.	K6	120
Centralia, Il., U.S.	D7	114
Centralia, Ks., U.S.	L11	118
Centralia, Mo., U.S.	C4	114
Centralia, Wa., U.S.	D3	122
Centralina, Braz.	E4	79
Central Kalahari Game Reserve, Bots.	D6	66
Central Lake, Mi., U.S.	E10	110
Central Makrān Range, mts., Pak.	G1	44
Central'nyj, Russia	H22	22
Central Point, Or., U.S.	H3	122
Central Range, mts., Leso.	G9	66
Central Square, N.Y., U.S.	D10	108
Central Valley, Ca., U.S.	D3	124
Centre, Al., U.S.	H11	114
Centre, Canal du, Fr.	F11	14
Centre Peak, mtn., B.C., Can.	B8	102
Centreville, Al., U.S.	J9	114
Centreville, Md., U.S.	H10	108
Centreville, Mi., U.S.	I10	110
Centreville, Ms., U.S.	K5	114
Century, Fl., U.S.	L9	114
Century, W.V., U.S.	H6	108
Century Village, Fl., U.S.	M6	112
Cenxi, China	C11	40
Cepu, Indon.	j15	39a
Ceram see Seram, i., Indon.	F8	38
Ceram Sea see Seram, Laut, Indon.	F8	38
Čerčany, Czech.	F14	10
Cerdas, Bol.	I8	82
Cère, stm., Fr.	H9	14
Cereal, Alta., Can.	G4	104
Cereales, Arg.	I7	80
Čeremchovo, Russia	G18	26
Čerepanovo, Russia	G14	26
Čerepet', Russia	G19	22
Čerepovec, Russia	B20	22
Ceres, Arg.	E8	80
Ceres, Braz.	C4	79
Ceres, S. Afr.	I4	66
Ceresco, Ne., U.S.	J11	118
Ceresole Reale, Italy	D2	18
Céret, Fr.	J9	14
Cereté, Col.	C5	84
Cerf Island, i., Sey.	C10	58
Çerignola, Italy	H10	18
Čerikov, Bela.	H14	22
Čerkessk, Russia	I6	26
Çerknica, Slo.	D9	18
Čerlak, Russia	G12	26
Çermei, Rom.	C5	20
Čern', Russia	H19	22
Čern'achovsk (Insterburg), Russia	G4	22
Černavčicy, Bela.	I6	22
Cernavodă, Rom.	E12	20
Çernay, Fr.	E14	14
Černogorsk, Russia	G10	28
Čern'ovo, Russia	C11	22
Černyševskij, Russia	E14	28
Cerralvo, Mex.	D10	90
Cerralvo, Isla, i., Mex.	E5	90
Cerrillos, Arg.	C6	80
Cerrillos, N.M., U.S.	I10	120
Cerritos, Mex.	F9	90
Cerro Azul, Arg.	D11	80
Cerro Azul, Braz.	C14	80
Cerro Azul, Mex.	G11	90
Cerro Azul, Peru	E3	82
Cerro Chato, Ur.	G11	80
Cerro Colorado, Ur.	G11	80
Cerro de las Mesas, hist., Mex.	H11	90
Cerro de Pasco, Peru	D3	82
Cerro Gordo, Il., U.S.	C8	114
Cerro Largo, Braz.	E11	80
Cerro Moreno, Chile	B3	80
Cerrón, Cerro, mtn., Ven.	B7	84
Cerrón Grande, Embalse, res., Hond.	C5	92
Cerros Colorados, Embalse, res., Arg.	J4	80
Çerro Vera, Ur.	G10	80
Čerskogo, chrebet, mts., Russia	E21	28
Çerusti, Russia	F23	22
Červen', Bela.	H11	22
Červen Brjag, Bul.	F8	20
Cervera, Spain	D13	16
Cervia, Italy	E7	18
Cervione, Fr.	I24	15a
Cesar, dept., Col.	C6	84
Cesar, stm., Col.	B6	84
Cesena, Italy	E7	18
Cesenatico, Italy	E7	18
Çēsis, Lat.	D8	22
Česká Lípa, Czech.	E14	10
České Budějovice, Czech.	G14	10
Českomoravská vrchovina, plat., Czech.	F15	10
Český Brod, Czech.	E14	10
Český Krumlov, Czech.	G14	10
Češskaja guba, b., Russia	D7	26
Cessnock, Austl.	I9	70
Cestos, stm., Lib.	I5	64
Cesvaine, Lat.	E9	22
Cetinje, Yugo.	G2	20
Ceuta, Sp. N. Afr.	C8	62
Ceva, Italy	E3	18
Cévennes, reg., Fr.	H10	14
Ceyhan, Tur.	C3	48
Ceylon, Sask., Can.	I10	104
Ceylon, Mn., U.S.	H13	118
Chaanling, China	F2	34
Chaatl Island, i., B.C., Can.	D2	102
Chabanais, Fr.	G7	14
Chabarovsk, Russia	H19	28
Chabás, Arg.	G8	80
Chablais, reg., Fr.	F13	14
Chablis, Fr.	E10	14
Chacabuco, Arg.	H8	80
Chacayán, Peru	D3	82
Chachani, Nevado, mtn., Peru	G6	82
Chachas, Peru	F5	82
Chachoengsao, Thai.	H6	40
Chachu, China	D9	44
Chaco, prov., Arg.	D8	80
Chaco, dept., Para.	H11	82
Chaco, stm., N.M., U.S.	H8	120
Chaco Austral, reg., Arg.	D7	80
Chaco Boreal, reg., Para.	B8	80
Chaco Central, reg., Arg.	C8	80
Chacon, Cape, c., Ak., U.S.	C2	102
Chad (Tchad), ctry., Afr.	E4	56
Chad, Lake (Lac Tchad), l., Afr.	F3	56
Chadbourn, N.C., U.S.	E8	112
Chadron, Ne., U.S.	I4	118
Chadwick, Il., U.S.	H6	110
Chaeryŏng, N. Kor.	E13	32
Chafe, Nig.	F13	64
Chaffee, Mo., U.S.	E7	114
Chāgai Hills, hills, Asia	G18	48
'Chaghcharān, Afg.	C1	44
Chagny, Fr.	F11	14
Chagos Archipelago, is., B.I.O.T.	J8	24
Chaguaramas, Ven.	C9	84
Chahal, Guat.	B5	92
Chahār Borjak, Afg.	F17	48
Chahe, China	B8	34
Chāībāsa, India	I11	44
Chaigou, China	G7	32
Chai Nat, Thai.	G6	40
Chaiqiao, China	F10	34
Chaiyaphum, Thai.	G7	40
Chajarí, Arg.	F10	80
Chajian, China	C7	34
Chajiaqiao, China	A9	34
Chajul, Guat.	B3	92
Chakasija, state, Russia	G15	26
Chākdaha, India	I13	44
Chakradharpur, India	I11	44
Chakwāl, Pak.	D5	44
Chala, Peru	F4	82
Chalatenango, El Sal.	C6	92
Chalchuapa, El Sal.	D5	92
Chalcis see Khalkís, Grc.	K7	20
Chalengkou, China	B15	44
Chaleur Bay, b., Can.	E8	106
Chalhuanca, Peru	F5	82
Chaling, China	I2	34
Chālisgaon, India	B3	46
Chalk River, Ont., Can.	D18	110
Chalkyitsik, Ak., U.S.	C23	100
Challapata, Bol.	H8	82
Challenger Deep	G18	126
Challis, Id., U.S.	F11	122
Challviri, Salar de, pl., Bol.	J8	82
Chalmette, La., U.S.	M7	114
Châlons-sur-Marne, Fr.	D11	14
Chalon-sur-Saône, Fr.	F11	14
Chalosse, reg., Fr.	I6	14
Chaltel, Cerro (Monte Fitzroy), mtn., S.A.	F2	78
Chālūs, Iran	C11	48
Cham, Ger.	F12	10
Chama, N.M., U.S.	H10	120
Chama, stm., Ven.	C7	84
Chama, Rio, stm., U.S.	H10	120
Chamaicó, Arg.	H6	80
Chaman, Pak.	E2	44
Chamaya, stm., Peru	A2	82
Chambal, stm., India	G7	44
Chamberlain, Sask., Can.	H9	104
Chamberlain, S.D., U.S.	H8	118
Chambers, Az., U.S.	I7	120
Chambers, Ne., U.S.	I9	118
Chambersburg, Pa., U.S.	H9	108
Chambéry, Fr.	G12	14
Chambi, Jebel, mtn., Tun.	C15	62
Chambira, stm., Peru	I5	84
Chambira, stm., Peru	I5	84
Chamblee, Ga., U.S.	F2	112
Chame, Pan.	I15	92
Chame, Punta, c., Pan.	I15	92
Chamelecón, Hond.	B6	92
Chamelecón, stm., Hond.	B6	92
Chamical, Arg.	F5	80
Chamo, Lake, l., Eth.	O9	60
Chamois, Mo., U.S.	D5	114
Chamonix-Mont-Blanc, Fr.	G13	14
Chāmpa, India	I10	44
Champagne, Yukon, Can.	F26	100
Champagne, hist. reg., Fr.	D11	14
Champagne Castle, mtn., Afr.	G9	66
Champagnole, Fr.	F12	14
Champaign, Il., U.S.	B8	114
Champaquí, Cerro, mtn., Arg.	F6	80
Champasak, Laos	G8	40
Champdoré, Lac, l., Que., Can.	E19	96
Champeix, Fr.	G10	14
Champerico, Guat.	C3	92
Champéry, Switz.	F6	13
Champion, Alta., Can.	G21	102
Champion, Mi., U.S.	D8	110
Champion, Oh., U.S.	F6	108
Champlain, N.Y., U.S.	C13	108
Champlain, Lake, l., N.A.	C13	108
Champlitte-et-le-Prélot, Fr.	E12	14
Champotón, Mex.	H14	90
Chamusca, Port.	F3	16
Chañar, Arg.	F6	80
Chañaral, Chile	D3	80
Chañaral, Isla, i., Chile	E3	80
Chancay, Peru	D3	82
Chancay, stm., Peru	D3	82
Chanch, Mong.	A7	30
Chanco, Chile	H2	80
Chandalar, stm., Ak., U.S.	C21	100
Chandausi, India	F8	44
Chandeleur Islands, is., La., U.S.	M8	114
Chandeleur Sound, strt., La., U.S.	M7	114
Chandīgarh, India	E7	44
Chandler, Que., Can.	D9	106
Chandler, Az., U.S.	K5	120
Chandler, In., U.S.	D9	114
Chandler, Ok., U.S.	D10	116
Chandler, Tx., U.S.	G11	116
Chandler Lake, l., Ak., U.S.	B18	100
Chandlerville, Il., U.S.	B6	114
Chandless, stm., S.A.	C6	82
Chāndpur, Bngl.	I14	44
Chāndpur, India	F8	44
Chandrapur, India	C5	46
Chandyga, Russia	E19	28
Chang (Yangtze), stm., China	E10	30
Chang, Ko, i., Thai.	H7	40
Changanācheri, India	H4	46
Changane, stm., Moz.	D11	66
Changbai Shan, mts., Asia	B15	32
Chang Cheng (Great Wall), hist., China	C4	32
Chang Chenmo, stm., Asia	C8	44
Changchou see Zhangzhou, China	K6	34
Changchow see Changzhou, China	D8	34
Changchun, China	C12	30
Changdao (Sihou), China	F8	32
Changde, China	F9	30
Change Islands, Newf., Can.	C19	106
Changguandian, China	C4	34
Changhua, Tai.	K9	34
Changhŭng, S. Kor.	I14	32
Changji, China	C4	30
Changjiang, China	J2	34
Changli, China	D7	32
Changlingzi, China	D10	32
Ch'angnyŏng, S. Kor.	H16	32
Changsha, China	G2	34
Changshan, China	G7	34
Changshoujie, China	G2	34
Changshu, China	D9	34
Changsŏng, S. Kor.	H14	32
Changsu, S. Kor.	H15	32
Changting, China	J5	34
Changuinola, Pan.	H12	92
Changuinola, stm., Pan.	H12	92
Changxing, China	D8	34
Changyŏn, N. Kor.	E13	32
Changzhi, China	D9	30
Changzhou (Changchow), China	D8	34
Chanino, Russia	G19	22
Chanka, ozero (Xingkai Hu), l., Asia	B13	30
Channel Country, reg., Austl.	E4	70
Channel Islands, is., Eur.	L11	8
Channel Islands, is., Ca., U.S.	K6	124
Channel-Port-aux-Basques, Newf., Can.	E14	106
Channelview, Tx., U.S.	J11	116
Channing, Mi., U.S.	D7	110
Channing, Tx., U.S.	D4	116
Chantajskoje, ozero, l., Russia	D10	28
Chantajskoje vodochranilišče, res., Russia	D15	26
Chantang, China	B6	34
Chanthaburi, Thai.	H7	40
Chantilly, Fr.	C9	14
Chantrey Inlet, b., N.W. Ter., Can.	C13	96
Chanty-Mansijsk, Russia	E11	26
Chanute, Ks., U.S.	N12	118
Chao, Isla, i., Peru	C2	82
Chao'an, China	L5	34
Ch'aochou, Tai.	M9	34
Chao Hu, l., China	E10	30
Chao Phraya, stm., Thai.	G6	40
Chaoshui, China	F8	32
Chaouen, Mor.	C8	62
Chaoyang, China	B8	32
Chaoyang, China	L5	34
Chaoyangchuan, China	A17	32
Chapada dos Guimarães, Braz.	F14	82
Chapala, Mex.	G8	90
Chapala, Laguna de, l., Mex.	G8	90
Chapare, stm., Bol.	G9	82
Chapare, stm., Bol.	G9	82
Chaparral, Col.	F5	84
Chapčeranga, Russia	H14	28
Chapecó, Braz.	D12	80
Chapel Hill, N.C., U.S.	D7	112
Chapel Hill, Tn., U.S.	G10	114
Chapicuy, Ur.	F10	80
Chapimarca, Peru	E5	82
Chapin, Il., U.S.	C6	114
Chapleau, Ont., Can.	C12	110
Chaplin, Sask., Can.	H8	104
Chaplin, stm., Ky., U.S.	E11	114
Chaplin Lake, l., Sask., Can.	H8	104
Chapman, Ks., U.S.	M10	118
Chapman, Ne., U.S.	J9	118
Chapman, Cape, c., N.W. Ter., Can.	C15	96
Chapman, Mount, mtn., B.C., Can.	F16	102
Chapman Lake, l., Man., Can.	B16	104
Chapman's (Okwa), stm., Afr.	D4	66
Chapmanville, W.V., U.S.	J4	108
Chappell, Ne., U.S.	J5	118
Chappell Hill, Tx., U.S.	I10	116
Chaqui, Bol.	H9	82
Chaquiago, Arg.	D5	80
Charadai, Arg.	D9	80
Charagua, Bol.	H10	82
Charalá, Col.	D6	84
Charaña, Bol.	G7	82
Charata, Arg.	D8	80
Charcana, Peru	F5	82
Charcas, Mex.	F9	90
Charco Azul, Bahía de, b., Pan.	I12	92
Charcos de Figueroa, Mex.	D8	90
Charcos de Risa, Mex.	D8	90
Chardon, Oh., U.S.	F5	108
Charente, dept., Fr.	G7	14
Charente, stm., Fr.	G6	14
Charente-Maritime, dept., Fr.	G6	14
Chari, stm., Afr.	F4	56
Chārīkār, Afg.	C3	44
Chariton, Ia., U.S.	I2	110
Chariton, stm., U.S.	C4	114
Charity, Guy.	D13	84
Charleroi, Bel.	H5	12
Charles, Cape, c., Va., U.S.	B11	112
Charles City, Ia., U.S.	G3	110
Charles City, Va., U.S.	B9	112
Charles Island, i., N.W. Ter., Can.	D18	96
Charles Mound, hill, Il., U.S.	H5	110
Charleston, Ar., U.S.	G2	114
Charleston, Il., U.S.	C8	114
Charleston, Ms., U.S.	H6	114
Charleston, Mo., U.S.	F7	114
Charleston, S.C., U.S.	G7	112
Charleston, W.V., U.S.	I5	108
Charleston Peak, mtn., Nv., U.S.	H10	124
Charlestown, St. K./N.	F13	94
Charlestown, S. Afr.	F9	66
Charlestown, In., U.S.	D11	114
Charlestown, N.H., U.S.	D14	108
Charleville, Austl.	F7	70
Charleville-Mézières, Fr.	C11	14
Charlevoix, Mi., U.S.	E10	110
Charlevoix, Lake, l., Mi., U.S.	E10	110
Charlie Lake, B.C., Can.	A14	102
Charlieu, Fr.	F11	14
Charlotte, Mi., U.S.	H11	110
Charlotte, N.C., U.S.	D6	112
Charlotte, Tn., U.S.	F9	114
Charlotte, Tx., U.S.	K8	116
Charlotte Amalie, V.I.U.S.	E12	94
Charlotte Court House, Va., U.S.	B8	112
Charlotte Harbor, b., Fl., U.S.	M4	112
Charlotte Lake, l., B.C., Can.	E9	102
Charlottesville, Va., U.S.	A8	112
Charlottetown, P.E.I., Can.	F10	106
Charlton Island, i., N.W. Ter., Can.	F17	96
Charlu, Russia	K22	6
Charmes, Fr.	D13	14
Charouine, Alg.	F10	62
Charovsk, Russia	B23	22
Charron Lake, l., Man., Can.	F19	104
Chārsadda, Pak.	C4	44
Charter Oak, Ia., U.S.	I12	118
Charters Towers, Austl.	C7	70
Chartres, Fr.	D8	14
Chasav'urt, Russia	I7	26
Chascomús, Arg.	H9	80
Chase, B.C., Can.	G15	102
Chase, Ks., U.S.	M9	118
Chase City, Va., U.S.	C8	112
Chaska, Mn., U.S.	F2	110
Chasŏng, N. Kor.	B14	32
Chasuta, Peru	B3	82
Chatanbulag, Mong.	C8	30
Chatanga, stm., Russia	C12	28
Chatangskij zaliv, b., Russia	C13	28
Chatanika, stm., Ak., U.S.	D20	100
Châteaubriant, Fr.	E5	14
Château-Chinon, Fr.	E10	14
Château d'Oex, Switz.	F7	13
Château-du-Loir, Fr.	E7	14
Châteaudun, Fr.	D8	14
Chateaugay, N.Y., U.S.	C12	108
Château-Gontier, Fr.	E6	14
Châteauguay, stm., N.A.	B12	108
Châteaulin, Fr.	D2	14
Châteauneuf-sur-Charente, Fr.	G6	14
Châteauneuf-sur-Loire, Fr.	E9	14
Château-Renault, Fr.	E7	14
Château-Richer, Que., Can.	F2	106
Châteauroux, Fr.	F8	14
Château-Salins, Fr.	D13	14
Château-Thierry, Fr.	C10	14
Châtellerault, Fr.	F7	14
Châtel-sur-Moselle, Fr.	D13	14
Chatfield, Mn., U.S.	G3	110
Chatgal, Mong.	A7	30
Chatham, N.B., Can.	E8	106
Chatham, Ont., Can.	H13	110
Chatham, Il., U.S.	C7	114
Chatham, La., U.S.	J4	114
Chatham, Ma., U.S.	F17	108
Chatham, N.Y., U.S.	E13	108
Chatham, Va., U.S.	C7	112
Chatham Head, N.B., Can.	E8	106
Chatham Islands, is., N.Z.	M22	126
Chatham Sound, strt., B.C., Can.	C4	102
Chatham Strait, strt., Ak., U.S.	H27	100
Châtillon, Italy	D2	18
Châtillon-sur-Chalaronne, Fr.	F11	14
Châtillon-sur-Indre, Fr.	F8	14
Châtillon-sur-Seine, Fr.	E11	14
Chatom, Al., U.S.	K8	114
Chatsquot Mountain, mtn., B.C., Can.	D7	102
Chatsworth, Ga., U.S.	E2	112
Chatsworth, Il., U.S.	J7	110
Chatsworth, Zimb.	B10	66
Chattahoochee, Fl., U.S.	I2	112
Chattahoochee, stm., U.S.	H2	112
Chattanooga, Tn., U.S.	G11	114
Chattaroy, W.V., U.S.	B4	112
Chaudière, stm., Que., Can.	F2	106
Chau Doc, Viet.	I8	40
Chauk, Mya.	D3	40
Chaullay, Peru	E5	82
Chaumont, Fr.	D12	14
Chaumont-en-Vexin, Fr.	C8	14
Chauncey, Oh., U.S.	H4	108
Chaungwabyin, Mya.	H5	40
Chauny, Fr.	C10	14
Chaussin, Fr.	F12	14
Chautauqua Lake, l., N.Y., U.S.	E7	108
Chauvigny, Fr.	F7	14
Chauvin, Alta., Can.	F4	104
Chauvin, La., U.S.	M6	114
Chavakkad, India	G4	46
Chavarría, Arg.	E9	80
Chaviña, Peru	F5	82
Cháviva, Col.	E6	84
Chayanta, Bol.	H8	82
Chazy, N.Y., U.S.	C13	108
Cheaha Mountain, mtn., Al., U.S.	I11	114
Cheakamus Indian Reserve, B.C., Can.	H11	102
Cheat, stm., U.S.	H7	108
Cheat, Shavers Fork, stm., W.V., U.S.	I7	108
Cheb, Czech.	E12	10
Chebanse, Il., U.S.	I8	110
Chebba, Tun.	C16	62
Chebogue Point, c., N.S., Can.	I7	106
Cheboygan, Mi., U.S.	E11	110
Chech, Erg, des., Afr.	D6	54
Chech'on, S. Kor.	F16	32
Chęciny, Pol.	E20	10
Checleset Bay, b., B.C., Can.	G7	102
Checotah, Ok., U.S.	D11	116
Chedabucto Bay, b., N.S., Can.	G12	106
Cheduba Island, i., Mya.	E2	40
Cheektowaga, N.Y., U.S.	E8	108
Chefornak, Ak., U.S.	F12	100
Chegutu, Zimb.	B10	66
Chegutu Safari Park, Zimb.	A9	66
Chehalis, stm., Wa., U.S.	D2	122
Chehe, China	B9	40
Cheju, S. Kor.	E12	30
Chekiang see Zhejiang, prov., China	F11	30
Chelan, Wa., U.S.	C5	122
Chelan, Lake, l., Wa., U.S.	C5	122
Chelelektu, Eth.	N10	60
Chelforó, Arg.	J5	80
Chelghoum el Aïd, Alg.	B14	62
Chéliff, Oued, stm., Alg.	B11	62
Chełm, Pol.	D23	10
Chełmno, Pol.	B18	10
Chelmsford, Ont., Can.	D14	110
Chełmża, Pol.	B18	10
Chelsea, Ia., U.S.	I3	110
Chelsea, Mi., U.S.	H11	110
Chelsea, Ok., U.S.	C11	116
Chelsea, Vt., U.S.	D14	108
Chelyabinsk see Čel'abinsk, Russia	F10	26
Chelyan, W.V., U.S.	I5	108
Chemaïa, Mor.	D6	62
Chemainus, B.C., Can.	I11	102
Chemax, Mex.	G16	90
Chemnitz, Ger.	E12	10
Chemult, Or., U.S.	G4	122
Chenāb, stm., Asia	E5	44
Chenachane, Alg.	G8	62
Chenango, stm., N.Y., U.S.	E11	108
Chenango Bridge, N.Y., U.S.	E11	108
Chenārān, Iran	C15	48
Chénéville, Que., Can.	B11	108
Cheney, Ks., U.S.	N10	118
Cheney, Wa., U.S.	C8	122
Cheney Reservoir, res., Ks., U.S.	N10	118
Cheneyville, La., U.S.	K4	114
Chengde, China	C5	32
Chengdu, China	E7	30
Chenghai, China	L5	34
Chengjiang, China	B7	40
Chengshan Jiao, c., China	F10	32
Chengtu see Chengdu, China	E7	30
Chengzitan, China	D10	32
Chenil, Lac, l., Que., Can.	A14	106
Chenoa, Il., U.S.	J7	110
Chenxian, China	J1	34
Cheo Reo, Viet.	H10	40
Chepén, Peru	B2	82
Chepes, Arg.	F5	80
Chepo, Pan.	C3	84
Cher, dept., Fr.	E9	14
Cher, stm., Fr.	E8	14
Cheraw, S.C., U.S.	E7	112
Cherbourg, Fr.	C5	14
Cherchell, Alg.	B12	62
Chergui, Chott ech, l., Alg.	C11	62
Cheriton, Va., U.S.	B11	112
Cherkasy, Ukr.	H4	26
Chernihiv, Ukr.	G4	26
Chernivtsi, Ukr.	A9	20
Chernobyl see Chornobyl', Ukr.	G4	26
Cherokee, Al., U.S.	H9	114
Cherokee, Ia., U.S.	I12	118
Cherokee, Ks., U.S.	N13	118
Cherokee, Ok., U.S.	C8	116
Cherokee, Tx., U.S.	I8	116
Cherokee Lake, res., Tn., U.S.	C3	112
Cherokees, Lake O' The, res., Ok., U.S.	C12	116
Cherokee Village, Ar., U.S.	F5	114
Cherquenco, Chile	J2	80
Cherrapunji, India	H14	44
Cherry Hill, N.J., U.S.	H11	108
Cherryvale, Ks., U.S.	N12	118
Cherry Valley, Ar., U.S.	G6	114
Cherryville, N.C., U.S.	D5	112
Chervonoarmiys'ke, Ukr.	D12	20
Chervonohrad, Ukr.	G2	26
Chesaning, Mi., U.S.	G11	110
Chesapeake, Va., U.S.	C10	112
Chesapeake Bay, b., U.S.	D11	98
Chesapeake Beach, Md., U.S.	I10	108
Chesapeake City, Md., U.S.	H11	108
Cheseaux, Switz.	E6	13
Cheshire, Ma., U.S.	E13	108
Cheshire, co., Eng., U.K.	H11	8
Cheslatta Lake, l., B.C., Can.	D9	102
Chesley, Ont., Can.	F14	110
Chesnee, S.C., U.S.	D5	112
Chester, Eng., U.K.	H11	8
Chester, Ca., U.S.	D4	124
Chester, Il., U.S.	E7	114
Chester, Mt., U.S.	B15	122
Chester, Ne., U.S.	K10	118
Chester, Ok., U.S.	C8	116
Chester, Pa., U.S.	H11	108
Chester, S.C., U.S.	E5	112
Chester, Vt., U.S.	D14	108
Chester, Va., U.S.	B9	112
Chester Basin, N.S., Can.	H9	106
Chesterfield, S.C., U.S.	E6	112
Chesterfield, Va., U.S.	B9	112
Chesterfield, Îles, is., N. Cal.	C11	68
Chesterfield, Nosy, i., Madag.	E8	58
Chesterfield Inlet, N.W. Ter., Can.	D14	96
Chesterfield Inlet, b., N.W. Ter., Can.	D14	96
Chesterhill, Oh., U.S.	H5	108
Chester-le-Street, Eng., U.K.	G12	8
Chesterton, In., U.S.	A9	114
Chesterton Range, mts., Austl.	E7	70
Chestertown, Md., U.S.	H10	108
Chesterville, Ont., Can.	B11	108
Chesuncook Lake, l., Me., U.S.	A17	108
Cheta, stm., Russia	C11	28
Chetaibi, Alg.	L2	18
Chetco, stm., Or., U.S.	B1	124
Chetek, Wi., U.S.	E4	110
Chéticamp, N.S., Can.	F12	106
Chetopa, Ks., U.S.	N12	118
Chetumal, Mex.	H15	90
Chetumal, Bahía, b., N.A.	H15	90
Chetwynd, B.C., Can.	B13	102
Chevak, Ak., U.S.	F12	100
Cheviot, Oh., U.S.	H2	108
Chewaucan, stm., Or., U.S.	H5	122
Chew Bahir (Lake Stefanie), l., Afr.	H8	56
Chewelah, Wa., U.S.	B8	122
Cheyenne, Ok., U.S.	D7	116
Cheyenne, Wy., U.S.	C12	120
Cheyenne, stm., U.S.	G6	118
Cheyenne Wells, Co., U.S.	M5	118
Chezhen, China	F5	32
Chhapra, India	H11	44
Chhātak, Bngl.	H14	44
Chhatarpur, India	H8	44
Chhatrapur, India	C8	46
Chhêb Kândal, Camb.	H8	40
Chhindwāra, India	I8	44
Chhukha Dzong, Bhu.	G13	44
Chi, stm., Thai.	G8	40
Chía, Col.	E5	84
Chiai, Tai.	L9	34
Chiali, Tai.	L9	34
Chiang Kham, Thai.	E6	40
Chiang Khan, Thai.	F6	40
Chiang Mai, Thai.	E5	40
Chiang Rai, Thai.	E5	40
Chiapa, Chile	H7	82
Chiapa de Corzo, Mex.	I13	90
Chiapas, state, Mex.	I14	90

Name Map Ref. Page

Chiari, Italy D4 18
Chiasso, Switz. G11 13
Chiautla de Tapia, Mex. H10 90
Chiavari, Italy E4 18
Chiavenna, Italy C4 18
Chiba, Japan L15 36
Chibougamau, Que., Can. G18 96
Chibuto, Moz. E11 66
Chicago, Il., U.S. I8 110
Chicago Heights, Il., U.S. I8 110
Chicama, stm., Peru B2 82
Chicapa, stm., Afr. C4 58
Chic-Chocs, Monts, mts., Que., Can. D8 106
Chichagof Island, i., Ak., U.S. H27 100
Chichas, Cordillera de, mts., Bol. I8 82
Chicheng, China C3 32
Chichén Itzá, hist., Mex. G15 90
Chichester, Eng., U.K. K13 8
Chichi, Tai. L9 34
Chichibu, Japan L14 36
Chichica, Pan. I13 92
Chichicastenango, Guat. C3 92
Chichigalpa, Nic. E7 92
Chichimilá, Mex. G15 90
Chichiriviche, Ven. B8 84
Chickahominy, stm., Va., U.S. B9 112
Chickaloon, Ak., U.S. F20 100
Chickamauga, Ga., U.S. E1 112
Chickamauga Lake, res., Tn., U.S. D1 112
Chickasaw, Al., U.S. L8 114
Chickasaw Bogue, stm., Al., U.S. J9 114
Chickasawhay, stm., Ms., U.S. K8 114
Chickasha, Ok., U.S. D9 116
Chiclana de la Frontera, Spain I5 16
Chiclayo, Peru B2 82
Chico, Ca., U.S. E4 124
Chico, Tx., U.S. F9 116
Chico, stm., Arg. E3 78
Chico, stm., Arg. E3 78
Chico, stm., Pan. I14 92
Chicomo, Moz. E12 66
Chicomuselo, Mex. J13 90
Chicopee, Ga., U.S. E3 112
Chicopee, Ma., U.S. E14 108
Chicoutimi, Que., Can. D2 106
Chicoutimi, stm., Que., Can. D2 106
Chicoutimi, Réserve, Que., Can. D3 106
Chicú, Cerro, mtn., Pan. I14 92
Chicxulub, Mex. G15 90
Chidambaram, India G5 46
Chiefland, Fl., U.S. J4 112
Chiemsee, l., Ger. H12 10
Chieri, Italy D2 18
Chiers, stm., Eur. I7 12
Chifeng (Ulanhad), China A7 32
Chigasaki, Japan L14 36
Chignahuapan, Mex. H10 90
Chignecto, Cape, c., N.S., Can. G9 106
Chignecto Bay, b., Can. G9 106
Chignik, Ak., U.S. H15 100
Chignik Lake, Ak., U.S. H15 100
Chigorodó, Col. D4 84
Chigyŏng, N. Kor. D15 32
Chihli, Gulf of see Bo Hai, b., China E8 32
Chihsi see Jixi, China B13 30
Chihuahua, Mex. C6 90
Chihuahua, state, Mex. C6 90
Chihuahuan Desert, des., N.A. F9 86
Chikaskia, stm., U.S. B9 116
Chik Ballāpur, India F4 46
Chikindzonot, Mex. G15 90
Chikmagalūr, India F3 46
Chikou, China E6 34
Chilakalūrupet, India D6 46
Chilako, stm., B.C., Can. D11 102
Chilanko Forks, B.C., Can. E10 102
Chilapa de Álvarez, Mex. I10 90
Chilās, Pak. C6 44
Chilca, Peru E3 82
Chilca, Peru E4 82
Chilca, Punta, c., Peru E3 82
Chilcotin, stm., B.C., Can. F12 102
Chilcott Island, i., Austl. A8 70
Childers, Austl. E10 70
Childersburg, Al., U.S. I10 114
Childress, Tx., U.S. E6 116
Chile, ctry., S.A. C2 78
Chile Chico, Chile F2 78
Chilecito, Arg. E5 80
Chilecito, Arg. G4 80
Chilete, Peru B2 82
Chilhowie, Va., U.S. C5 112
Chili, stm., Peru G6 82
Chilika Lake, l., India C8 46
Chililabombwe (Bancroft), Zam. D5 58
Chilkat Pass, B.C., Can. G26 100
Chilko, stm., B.C., Can. E11 102
Chilko Lake, l., B.C., Can. F10 102
Chilko Lake Indian Reserve, B.C., Can. F10 102
Chillagoe, Austl. A6 70
Chillán, Chile I2 80
Chillar, Arg. I9 80
Chillicothe, Il., U.S. J6 110
Chillicothe, Mo., U.S. C3 114
Chillicothe, Oh., U.S. H4 108
Chillicothe, Tx., U.S. E7 116
Chilliwack, B.C., Can. H13 102
Chillón, stm., Peru D3 82
Chillon, hist., Switz. F6 13
Chiloé, Isla Grande de, i., Chile E2 78
Chilok, Russia G14 28
Chilok, stm., Russia G13 28
Chilón, Mex. I13 90
Chiloquin, Or., U.S. H4 122
Chilpancingo de los Bravo, Mex. I10 90
Chilton, Wi., U.S. F7 110
Chiluage, Ang. C4 58
Chilung, Tai. J10 34
Chilwa, Lake, l., Afr. E7 58
Chimaltenango, Guat. C4 92
Chimaltenango, dept., Guat. C4 92
Chimán, Pan. C3 84
Chimayo, N.M., U.S. H11 120
Chimbarongo, Chile H3 80
Chimbas, Arg. F4 80
Chimborazo, prov., Ec. H3 84
Chimborazo, mtn., Nic. D9 92
Chimborazo, vol., Ec. H3 84
Chimbote, Peru C2 82
Chimichagua, Col. C6 84
Chimkent see Čimkent, Kaz. I11 26
Chimki, Russia F20 22
Chimoio, Moz. B11 66
Chimpay, Arg. J5 80
China, Mex. E10 90
China (Zhongguo), ctry., Asia D8 30
Chinácota, Col. D6 84
China Grove, N.C., U.S. D6 112
Chinameca, El Sal. D6 92
Chinandega, Nic. E7 92
Chinandega, dept., Nic. E8 92
Chinati Peak, mtn., Tx., U.S. J2 116
Chincha Alta, Peru E3 82
Chinchaga, stm., Can. E9 96
Chincheros, Peru E5 82
Chinchilla, Austl. F9 70
Chinchiná, Col. E5 84
Chinch'ŏn, S. Kor. G15 32
Chinchón, Spain E8 16
Chinchorro, Banco, Mex. H16 90
Chincolco, Chile G3 80
Chincoteague, Va., U.S. B11 112
Chinde, Moz. B13 66
Chindo, S. Kor. I14 32
Chindwinn, stm., Mya. C3 40
Chingleput, India F5 46
Chingola, Zam. D5 58
Chinguetti, Maur. A3 64
Chinhae, S. Kor. H16 32
Chinhae-man, b., S. Kor. H16 32
Chin Hills, hills, Mya. C2 40
Chinhoyi, Zimb. E6 58
Chiniot, Pak. E5 44
Chinju, S. Kor. H16 32
Chinkiang see Zhenjiang, China E10 30
Chinko, stm., Cen. Afr. Rep. G5 56
Chin Lakes, l., Alta., Can. H22 102
Chinle, Az., U.S. H7 120
Chinmen, China K7 34
Chinmen Tao, i., Tai. K7 34
Chino, Ca., U.S. J8 124
Chinook, Alta., Can. G4 104
Chinook, Mt., U.S. B16 122
Chinook Cove, B.C., Can. F14 102
Chino Valley, Az., U.S. J4 120
Chinquapin, N.C., U.S. E9 112
Chinsali, Zam. D6 58
Chintāmani, India F5 46
Chinú, Col. C5 84
Chiny, Bel. I7 12
Chioggia, Italy D7 18
Chios see Khíos, Grc. K10 20
Chipao, Peru F5 82
Chipata, Zam. D6 58
Chiperceni, Mol. B12 20
Chipinge, Zimb. C11 66
Chip Lake, l., Alta., Can. D19 102
Chipley, Fl., U.S. L11 114
Chipman, N.B., Can. F8 106
Chippewa, stm., Mi., U.S. G11 110
Chippewa, stm., Mn., U.S. F12 118
Chippewa, stm., Wi., U.S. F4 110
Chippewa, Lake, l., Wi., U.S. E4 110
Chippewa Falls, Wi., U.S. F4 110
Chiquián, Peru D3 82
Chiquimula, Guat. C5 92
Chiquimula, dept., Guat. C5 92
Chiquimulilla, Guat. C4 92
Chiquinquirá, Col. E6 84
Chiquintirca, Peru E5 82
Chiquito, stm., Mex. H9 90
Chira, stm., S.A. J2 84
Chira, Isla, i., C.R. G9 92
Chireno, Tx., U.S. K2 114
Chirfa, Niger D9 54
Chiriaco, stm., Peru A2 82
Chiricahua Mountains, mts., Az., U.S. M7 120
Chiricahua Peak, mtn., Az., U.S. M7 120
Chiriguaná, Col. C6 84
Chirikof Island, i., Ak., U.S. I17 100
Chirilagua, El Sal. D6 92
Chirinos, Peru A2 82
Chiriquí, Pan. I12 92
Chiriquí, prov., Pan. I12 92
Chiriquí, Golfo de, b., Pan. I12 92
Chiriquí, Laguna de, b., Pan. H12 92
Chiriquí Grande, Pan. C1 84
Chiriquí Viejo, stm., Pan. I12 92
Chiromo, Mwi. E7 58
Chirripó, stm., C.R. G11 92
Chirripó, Cerro, mtn., C.R. H11 92
Chirripó, Parque Nacional, C.R. H11 92
Chisago City, Mn., U.S. E3 110
Chisasibi, Que., Can. F17 96
Chiscas, Col. D6 84
Chisec, Guat. B4 92
Chi'shan, Tai. M9 34
Chisholm, Al., U.S. J10 114
Chisholm, Me., U.S. C16 108
Chisholm, Mn., U.S. C3 110
Chisholm Mills, Alta., Can. C20 102
Chishtiān Mandi, Pak. F5 44
Chişinău (Kishinev), Mol. B12 20
Chislaviči, Russia G15 22
Chisos Mountains, mts., Tx., U.S. J3 116
Chist'akovo see Torez, Ukr. F15 4
Chistochina, Ak., U.S. E22 100
Chita, Col. D6 84
Chitado, Ang. A1 66
Chitagá, Col. D6 84
Chitato, Ang. C4 58
Chiţcani, Mol. C13 20
Chitek, stm., Sask., Can. D7 104
Chitek Lake, l., Man., Can. F15 104
Chitek Lake, l., Sask., Can. E7 104
Chitembo, Ang. D3 58
Chitina, Ak., U.S. F22 100
Chitina, stm., Ak., U.S. F23 100
Chitipa, Mwi. C6 58
Chitradurga, India E4 46
Chitrāl, Pak. C4 44
Chitré, Pan. D2 84
Chittagong, Bngl. I14 44
Chittaurgarh, India H6 44
Chittoor, India F5 46
Chittūr, India G4 46
Chitu, Eth. M9 60
Chiúchiu, Chile B4 80
Chiumbe, stm., Afr. C4 58
Chiusi, Italy F6 18
Chiuta, Lake, l., Afr. D7 58
Chiva, Uzb. I10 26
Chivacoa, Ven. B8 84
Chivasso, Italy D2 18
Chivato, Punta, c., Mex. D4 90
Chivay, Peru F6 82
Chivhu, Zimb. B10 66
Chivilcoy, Arg. H8 80
Chixoy (Salinas), stm., N.A. J14 90
Chixoy, Embalse, res., Guat. B4 92
Chlevnoje, Russia I22 22
Chloride, Az., U.S. I2 120
Chŏâm Khsant, Camb. G8 40
Chobe, dept., Bots. B7 66
Chobe, stm., Afr. A7 66
Chobe National Park, Bots. B7 66
Chochis, Cerro, mtn., Bol. H11 82
Choch'iwŏn, S. Kor. G15 32
Chocó, dept., Col. D4 84
Chocolate Mountains, mts., U.S. K10 124
Chocontá, Col. E6 84
Chocope, Peru B2 82
Choctawhatchee Bay, b., Fl., U.S. L10 114
Chodecz, Pol. C19 10
Chodžakala, Turk. B14 48
Chodžejli, Uzb. I9 26
Chodzież, Pol. C16 10
Choele-Choel, Arg. J6 80
Choiceland, Sask., Can. E10 104
Choiseul, i., Sol.Is. I19 126
Choix, Mex. D5 90
Chojnice, Pol. B17 10
Chojnów, Pol. D15 10
Chokio, Mn., U.S. F11 118
Cholet, Fr. E6 14
Cholm, Russia D14 22
Cholmec, Russia E16 22
Cholmsk, Russia H20 28
Choloma, Hond. B7 92
Ch'ŏlsan, N. Kor. D12 32
Choluj, Russia E24 22
Cholula [de Rivadabia], Mex. H10 90
Choluteca, Hond. D7 92
Choluteca, dept., Hond. D7 92
Choluteca, stm., Hond. D8 92
Choma, Zam. E5 58
Chomo Lhāri, mtn., Asia G13 44
Chomūm, India G6 44
Chomutov, Czech. E13 10
Chomutovo, Russia I20 22
Ch'ŏnan, S. Kor. G15 32
Chon Buri, Thai. H6 40
Chone, Ec. H2 84
Chone, stm., Ec. H2 84
Ch'ŏngdan, N. Kor. F13 32
Ch'ŏngjin, N. Kor. B17 32
Chŏngju, N. Kor. D13 32
Ch'ŏngju, S. Kor. G15 32
Chongos Bajo, Peru E4 82
Chongoyape, Peru B2 82
Chongqing, China F8 30
Chongru, China H9 34
Ch'ŏngsong, N. Kor. B17 32
Chongzuo, China G8 30
Chŏnju, S. Kor. H15 32
Chonos, Archipiélago de los, is., Chile F2 78
Chontaleña, Cordillera, mts., Nic. F10 92
Chontales, dept., Nic. E9 92
Chop, Ukr. A6 20
Chopda, India B3 46
Chopim, stm., Braz. D12 80
Chopinzinho, Braz. C12 80
Chop'or, stm., Russia G6 26
Chopu, mtn., Asia F12 44
Chor, stm., Russia H19 28
Chorlovo, Russia F21 22
Chorna, Ukr. B13 20
Chornobyl' (Chernobyl), Ukr. G4 26
Chorog, Taj. J12 26
Chorolque, Cerro, mtn., Bol. I8 82
Choros, Isla, i., Chile E3 80
Chorreras, Mex. C7 90
Ch'ŏrwŏn, S. Kor. E15 32
Chorzele, Pol. H3 22
Ch'osan, N. Kor. C13 32
Chosen, Fl., U.S. M6 112
Chōshi, Japan L15 36
Choshui, stm., Tai. L9 34
Chosica, Peru D3 82
Chos Malal, Arg. I3 80
Choszczno, Pol. B15 10
Chota, Peru B2 82
Choteau, Mt., U.S. C13 122
Chotěboř, Czech. F15 10
Chotimsk, Bela. H15 22
Chot'kovo, Russia E21 22
Chotynec, Russia H18 22
Choûm, Maur. J4 62
Chouteau, Ok., U.S. C11 116
Chovd, Mong. B5 30
Chövsgöl Nuur, l., Mong. A7 30
Chowan, stm., N.C., U.S. C10 112
Chowchilla, Ca., U.S. G5 124
Chown, Mount, mtn., Alta., Can. D15 102
Choya, Arg. E6 80
Chrisman, Il., U.S. C9 114
Christchurch, N.Z. E4 72
Christian, Cape, c., N.W. Ter., Can. B19 96
Christiana, S. Afr. F7 66
Christiansburg, Va., U.S. B6 112
Christiansted, V.I.U.S. F12 94
Christie, Mount, mtn., Yukon, Can. E30 100
Christie Bay, b., N.W. Ter., Can. D10 96
Christie Lake, l., Man., Can. B18 104
Christina, stm., Alta., Can. B3 104
Christina Lake, l., Alta., Can. B24 102
Christina Lake, l., B.C., Can. H16 102
Christmas Island, dep., Oc. H4 38
Christopher, Il., U.S. E7 114
Christoval, Tx., U.S. H6 116
Chromtau, Kaz. G9 26
Chrudim, Czech. F15 10
Chrzanów, Pol. E19 10
Chu (Xam), stm., Asia E8 40
Chuanliao, China G9 34
Chubbuck, Id., U.S. H13 122
Chubut, stm., Arg. E3 78
Chuchi Lake, l., B.C., Can. B10 102
Chu Chua, B.C., Can. F14 102
Chuchuwayha Indian Reserve, B.C., Can. H14 102
Chucuito, Peru F7 82
Chucunaque, stm., Pan. C4 84
Chudžand (Leninabad), Taj. I11 26
Chugach Islands, is., Ak., U.S. G19 100
Chugach Mountains, mts., Ak., U.S. F21 100
Chugwater, Wy., U.S. C12 120
Chugwater Creek, stm., Wy., U.S. C11 120
Chuhuichupa, Mex. C5 90
Chuí, Braz. G12 80
Chuius Mountain, mtn., B.C., Can. C10 102
Chukai, Malay. L7 40
Chukchi Sea C2 86
Chula Vista, Ca., U.S. L8 124
Chulucanas, Peru A1 82
Chulumani, Bol. G8 82
Chuma, Bol. F7 82
Chumbicha, Arg. E5 80
Chumphon, Thai. I5 40
Chumpi, Peru F5 82
Chum Saeng, Thai. G6 40
Chunan, Tai. K9 34
Chunchi, Ec. I3 84
Ch'unch'ŏn, S. Kor. F15 32
Chunchula, Al., U.S. L8 114
Chunghwa, N. Kor. E13 32
Ch'ungju, S. Kor. G15 32
Chungking see Chongqing, China F8 30
Chungli, Tai. K10 34
Ch'ungmu, S. Kor. I16 32
Chŭngsan, N. Kor. D13 32
Chungyang Shanmo, mts., Tai. L10 34
Chunhuhux, Mex. H15 90
Chuntuquí, Guat. I14 90
Chuŏr Phnum Krâvanh, mts., Asia H7 40
Chupaca, Peru E4 82
Chuquibamba, Peru F5 82
Chuquibambilla, Peru F5 82
Chuquicamata, Chile B4 80
Chuquisaca, dept., Bol. H9 82
Chur, Switz. E12 13
Churcampa, Peru E4 82
Church Hill, Tn., U.S. C4 112
Churchill, Man., Can. E14 96
Churchill, stm., Can. E13 96
Churchill, stm., Newf., Can. F20 96
Churchill, Cape, c., Man., Can. E14 96
Churchill, Mount, mtn., B.C., Can. H11 102
Churchill Falls, wtfl, Newf., Can. F20 96
Churchill Lake, l., Sask., Can. C6 104
Church Point, La., U.S. L4 114
Church Rock, N.M., U.S. I8 120
Churdan, Ia., U.S. I13 118
Churn Creek, stm., B.C., Can. F12 102
Chūru, India F6 44
Churubusco, In., U.S. A11 114
Churuguara, Ven. B8 84
Chushan, Tai. L9 34
Chuska Peak, mtn., N.M., U.S. I8 120
Chutag, Mong. B7 30
Chutung, Tai. K10 34
Chuvashia see Čuvašija, state, Russia F7 26
Chuwang, China G2 32
Chuxiong, China B6 40
Chuy, Ur. G12 80
Chvalynsk, Russia G7 26
Chvojnaja, Russia C17 22
Ch'wiya-ri, N. Kor. E13 32
Chynadiyeve, Ukr. A6 20
Ciadâr Lunga, Mol. C12 20
Cianjur, Indon. j13 39a
Cianorte, Braz. G2 79
Cibecue, Az., U.S. J6 120
Cicero, Il., U.S. A9 114
Cicero, In., U.S. B10 114
Cichačovo, Russia D12 22
Ciechanów, Pol. C20 10
Ciechocinek, Pol. C18 10
Ciego de Ávila, Cuba D5 94
Ciempozuelos, Spain E8 16
Ciénaga, Col. B5 84
Ciénaga de Oro, Col. C5 84
Cienfuegos, Cuba C4 94
Cierna [nad Tisou], Slov. G22 10
Cieszyn, Pol. F18 10
Cieza, Spain G10 16
Čiganak, Kaz. H12 26
Cigüela, stm., Spain F8 16
Cihanbeyli, Tur. B2 48
Čiili, Kaz. I11 26
Čikoj, stm., Asia G19 26
Cikou, China F3 34
Cilacap, Indon. j14 39a
Čilik, Kaz. I13 26
Čilov ada, i., Azer. A11 48
Cimarron, Ks., U.S. N7 118
Cimarron, N.M., U.S. H12 120
Cimarron, stm., U.S. D9 116
Cimarron, stm., N.M., U.S. H11 120
Čimbaj, Uzb. I9 26
Cimişlia, Mol. C12 20
Čimkent, Kaz. I11 26
Ciml'anskoje vodochranilišče, res., Russia H6 26
Cinaruco, stm., Ven. D9 84
Cincinnati, Ia., U.S. J3 110
Cincinnati, Oh., U.S. H2 108
Cinco, Canal Numero, Arg. I10 80
Cinco Pinos, Nic. D8 92
Cinco Saltos, Arg. J4 80
Çine, Tur. L12 20
Cinema, B.C., Can. D12 102
Cingoli, Italy F8 18
Cinişeuţi, Mol. B12 20
Cintalapa, Mex. I13 90
Cinto, Monte, mtn., Fr. I23 15a
Cipa, stm., Russia F15 28
Cipó, stm., Braz. E6 79
Cipolândia, Braz. F1 79
Cipolletti, Arg. J5 80
Čirčik, Uzb. I11 26
Circle, Ak., U.S. D22 100
Circle, Mt., U.S. C20 122
Circleville, Oh., U.S. H4 108
Circleville, Ut., U.S. F4 120
Circleville Mountain, mtn., Ut., U.S. F4 120
Cirebon, Indon. j14 39a
Ciremay, Gunung, mtn., Indon. j14 39a
Cirey-sur-Vezouze, Fr. D13 14
Ciriè, Italy D2 18
Çiriquiri, stm., Braz. C9 82
Čirpan, Bul. G9 20
Cisco, Tx., U.S. G8 116
Ciskei, hist. reg., S. Afr. I8 66
Cisne, Il., U.S. D8 114
Cisneros, Col. D5 84
Cissna Park, Il., U.S. J8 110
Çistern Point, c., Bah. C6 94
Čistoje, Russia E26 22
Čistopol', Russia F8 26
Čita, Russia G14 28
Citac, Nevado, mtn., Peru E4 82
Citra, Fl., U.S. J4 112
Citronelle, Al., U.S. K8 114
Citrus Heights, Ca., U.S. F4 124
Cittadella, Italy D6 18
Città di Castello, Italy F7 18
Cittanova, Italy K11 18
City of Refuge see Pu'uhonua o Honaunau National Historic Site, hist., Hi., U.S. r18 125a
City Point, Fl., U.S. K6 112
Ciuciuleni, Mol. B12 20
Ciudad Acuña, Mex. C9 90
Ciudad Altamirano, Mex. H9 90
Ciudad Barrios, El Sal. D6 92
Ciudad Bolívar, Ven. C11 84
Ciudad Bolivia, Ven. C7 84
Ciudad Camargo, Mex. D10 90
Ciudad Constitución, Mex. E4 90
Ciudad Cortés, C.R. I11 92
Ciudad Darío, Nic. E8 92
Ciudad del Carmen, Mex. H14 90
Ciudad del Este, Para. C11 80
Ciudad del Maíz, Mex. F10 90
Ciudad de México (Mexico City), Mex. H10 90
Ciudad de Nutrias, Ven. B5 76
Ciudad de Nutrias, Ven. C8 84
Ciudad Guayana, Ven. C11 84
Ciudad Guzmán, Mex. H8 90
Ciudad Hidalgo, Mex. H9 90
Ciudad Juárez, Mex. B6 90
Ciudad Lerdo, Mex. E8 90
Ciudad Madero, Mex. F11 90
Ciudad Mante, Mex. F10 90
Ciudad Manuel Doblado, Mex. G9 90
Ciudad Miguel Alemán, Mex. D10 90
Ciudad Morelos, Mex. A2 90
Ciudad Obregón, Mex. D5 90
Ciudad Ojeda (Lagunillas), Ven. B7 84
Ciudad Piar, Ven. D11 84
Ciudad Real, Spain G8 16
Ciudad Rodrigo, Spain E5 16
Ciudad Sandino, Nic. D8 92
Ciudad Tecún Umán, Guat. C2 92
Ciudad Trujillo see Santo Domingo, Dom. Rep. E10 94
Ciudad Valles, Mex. G10 90
Ciudad Victoria, Mex. F10 90
Ciudad Vieja, Guat. C4 92
Ciutadella, Spain E15 16
Civitanova Marche, Italy F8 18
Civitavecchia, Italy G6 18
Civray, Fr. F7 14
Cizre, Tur. C7 48
Čkalovsk, Russia E26 22
Clackamas, stm., Or., U.S. E3 122
Clacton-on-Sea, Eng., U.K. J15 8
Claflin, Ks., U.S. M9 118
Claiborne, Al., U.S. K9 114
Claire, Lake, l., Alta., Can. E10 96
Clair Engle Lake, res., Ca., U.S. D3 124
Clairmont, Alta., Can. B16 102
Clairton, Pa., U.S. G7 108
Clairvaux-les-Lacs, Fr. F12 14
Clam, stm., Mi., U.S. F10 110
Clam, stm., Wi., U.S. E3 110
Clam Lake, l., Sask., Can. C9 104
Clandonald, Alta., Can. D24 102
Clanton, Al., U.S. J10 114
Clanwilliam, S. Afr. I4 66
Clara, Arg. F9 80
Clara, Ms., U.S. K8 114
Clara, stm., Austl. B4 70
Clara City, Mn., U.S. G12 118
Claraz, Arg. I9 80
Clare, Austl. I3 70
Clare, Mi., U.S. G11 110
Clare, co., Ire. I4 8
Claremont, Ca., U.S. J8 124
Claremont, N.H., U.S. D14 108
Claremont, S.D., U.S. F9 118
Claremont, mtn., Ca., U.S. E5 124
Claremore, Ok., U.S. C11 116
Clarence, Ia., U.S. I4 110
Clarence, Mo., U.S. C4 114
Clarence, stm., Austl. G10 70
Clarence Island, i., Ant. B1 73
Clarence Strait, strt., Austl. B6 68
Clarence Town, Bah. C7 94
Clarendon, Ar., U.S. H5 114
Clarendon, Pa., U.S. F7 108
Clarendon, Tx., U.S. E6 116
Clarenville, Newf., Can. D20 106
Claresholm, Alta., Can. G21 102
Clarie Coast, Ant. B7 73
Clarinda, Ia., U.S. K12 118
Clarines, Ven. C10 84
Clarion, Ia., U.S. H2 110
Clarion, Pa., U.S. F7 108
Clarion, stm., Pa., U.S. F7 108
Clarión, Isla, i., Mex. H2 90
Clarissa, Mn., U.S. E13 118
Clark, S.D., U.S. G10 118
Clark, Lake, l., Ak., U.S. F17 100
Clark, Mount, mtn., N.W. Ter., Can. D32 100
Clarkdale, Az., U.S. J4 120
Clarke, stm., Austl. B6 70
Clarke City, Que., Can. B7 106
Clarke Island, i., Austl. M8 70
Clarke Lake, l., Sask., Can. D8 104
Clarke Range, mts., Austl. C8 70
Clarkesville, Ga., U.S. E3 112
Clarkfield, Mn., U.S. G12 118
Clark Fork, Id., U.S. B9 122
Clark Fork, stm., U.S. C10 122
Clarks, La., U.S. J4 114
Clarks, Ne., U.S. J10 118
Clarks, stm., Ky., U.S. F8 114
Clarksburg, W.V., U.S. H6 108
Clarksdale, Ms., U.S. H6 114
Clark's Harbour, N.S., Can. I8 106
Clarks Hill, In., U.S. B10 114
Clarks Hill Lake, res., U.S. F4 112
Clarkson, Ky., U.S. E10 114
Clarkson, Ne., U.S. J10 118
Clarks Point, Ak., U.S. G15 100
Clarks Summit, Pa., U.S. F11 108
Clarkston, Wa., U.S. D8 122
Clarksville, Ar., U.S. G3 114
Clarksville, In., U.S. D11 114
Clarksville, Ia., U.S. H3 110
Clarksville, Tn., U.S. F9 114
Clarksville, Tx., U.S. F11 116
Clarksville, Va., U.S. C8 112
Clarkton, Mo., U.S. F7 114
Clarkton, N.C., U.S. E8 112
Claro, stm., Braz. E3 79
Claro, stm., Braz. C3 79
Claro, stm., Braz. E2 79
Clatskanie, Or., U.S. D2 122
Claude, Tx., U.S. D5 116
Clavet, Sask., Can. F8 104
Claxton, Ga., U.S. G5 112
Clay, Ky., U.S. E9 114
Clay, Tx., U.S. I10 116
Clay, W.V., U.S. I5 108
Clay Center, Ks., U.S. L10 118
Clay Center, Ne., U.S. K9 118
Clay City, Il., U.S. D8 114
Clay City, In., U.S. C9 114
Clay City, Ky., U.S. B3 112
Clayhurst, B.C., Can. A14 102
Claymont, De., U.S. H11 108
Clayoquot Sound, strt., B.C., Can. H8 102
Claypool, Az., U.S. K6 120
Claysburg, Pa., U.S. G8 108
Clay Springs, Az., U.S. J6 120
Clayton, Al., U.S. K11 114
Clayton, De., U.S. H11 108
Clayton, Ga., U.S. E3 112
Clayton, Il., U.S. B6 114
Clayton, La., U.S. K5 114
Clayton, Mo., U.S. D6 114
Clayton, N.M., U.S. C3 116
Clayton, N.Y., U.S. C10 108
Clayton, N.C., U.S. D8 112
Clayton, Ok., U.S. E11 116
Clayton, stm., Austl. G3 70
Clear, stm., Alta., Can. A15 102
Clearbrook, Mn., U.S. D12 118
Clearfield, Ia., U.S. K13 118
Clearfield, Pa., U.S. F8 108
Clearfield, Ut., U.S. C4 120
Clearlake, Ca., U.S. F3 124
Clear Lake, Ia., U.S. G2 110
Clear Lake, S.D., U.S. G11 118
Clear Lake, Wi., U.S. E3 110
Clear Lake, l., Man., Can. H14 104
Clear Lake, l., Ca., U.S. E3 124
Clear Lake Reservoir, res., Ca., U.S. C4 124
Clearmont, Wy., U.S. F19 122
Clearwater, B.C., Can. F14 102
Clearwater, Man., Can. I15 104
Clearwater, Fl., U.S. L4 112
Clearwater, Ks., U.S. N10 118
Clearwater, Ne., U.S. I9 118
Clearwater, S.C., U.S. F5 112
Clearwater, stm., Can. B4 104
Clearwater, stm., Alta., Can. E19 102
Clearwater, stm., B.C., Can. E14 102
Clearwater, stm., Id., U.S. D9 122
Clearwater, stm., Mn., U.S. D12 118
Clearwater, stm., Mt., U.S. C12 122
Clearwater Lake, l., B.C., Can. E14 102
Clearwater Lake, l., Man., Can. D13 104
Clearwater Lake Provincial Park, Man., Can. D13 104
Clearwater Mountains, mts., Id., U.S. D10 122
Clebit, Ok., U.S. E12 116
Cleburne, Tx., U.S. G9 116
Cle Elum, Wa., U.S. C5 122
Cle Elum, stm., Wa., U.S. C4 122
Clefmont, Fr. D12 14
Clementsport, N.S., Can. H8 106
Clemson, S.C., U.S. E4 112
Clendenin, W.V., U.S. I5 108
Clermont, Austl. D7 70
Clermont, Que., Can. E3 106
Clermont, Fr. C9 14
Clermont, Fl., U.S. K5 112
Clermont-en-Argonne, Fr. C12 14
Clermont-Ferrand, Fr. G10 14
Cles, Italy C6 18
Cleveland, Al., U.S. I10 114
Cleveland, Ga., U.S. E3 112
Cleveland, Ms., U.S. I6 114
Cleveland, N.C., U.S. D6 112
Cleveland, Oh., U.S. F5 108
Cleveland, Ok., U.S. C10 116
Cleveland, Tn., U.S. G12 114
Cleveland, Tx., U.S. I11 116
Cleveland, Va., U.S. C4 112
Cleveland, Cape, c., Austl. B7 70
Cleveland, Mount, mtn., Mt., U.S. B12 122
Clevelândia, Braz. D12 80
Clew Bay, b., Ire. H4 8
Clewiston, Fl., U.S. M6 112
Clifton, Az., U.S. K7 120
Clifton, Il., U.S. J8 110
Clifton, Ks., U.S. L10 118
Clifton, Tn., U.S. G9 114
Clifton, Tx., U.S. H9 116
Clifton Forge, Va., U.S. B7 112
Climax, Sask., Can. I6 104
Climax, Co., U.S. E10 120
Climax, Ga., U.S. I2 112
Climax, Mi., U.S. H10 110
Clinch, stm., U.S. C3 112
Clinchco, Va., U.S. B4 112
Clingmans Dome, mtn., U.S. D3 112
Clinton, B.C., Can. F13 102
Clinton, Ont., Can. G14 110
Clinton, Al., U.S. J8 114
Clinton, Ar., U.S. G4 114
Clinton, Ct., U.S. F14 108
Clinton, Il., U.S. B8 114
Clinton, In., U.S. C9 114
Clinton, Ia., U.S. I5 110
Clinton, Ky., U.S. F8 114
Clinton, La., U.S. L5 114
Clinton, Me., U.S. C17 108
Clinton, Ma., U.S. E15 108
Clinton, Mi., U.S. H12 110
Clinton, Mn., U.S. F11 118
Clinton, Ms., U.S. J6 114
Clinton, Mo., U.S. D3 114
Clinton, N.C., U.S. E8 112
Clinton, Ok., U.S. D8 116
Clinton, S.C., U.S. E5 112
Clinton, Tn., U.S. C2 112
Clinton, Wi., U.S. H7 110
Clinton, Cape, c., Austl. D9 70
Clinton-Colden Lake, l., N.W. Ter., Can. D11 96
Clinton Lake, res., Ks., U.S. M12 118
Clintonville, Wi., U.S. F7 110
Clintwood, Va., U.S. B4 112
Clio, Al., U.S. K11 114
Clio, Mi., U.S. G12 110
Clio, S.C., U.S. E7 112
Clipperton, Île, atoll, Oc. F3 88
Clisson, Fr. E5 14
Clodomira, Arg. D6 80
Cloncurry, Austl. C4 70
Cloncurry, stm., Austl. B4 70
Clonmel, Ire. I6 8
Cloppenburg, Ger. C8 10
Cloquet, Mn., U.S. D3 110
Cloquet, stm., Mn., U.S. C3 110
Clorinda, Arg. C10 80
Cloudcroft, N.M., U.S. L11 120
Cloud Peak, mtn., Wy., U.S. F18 122
Clover, S.C., U.S. D5 112
Cloverdale, Al., U.S. H9 114
Cloverdale, Ca., U.S. F2 124
Cloverdale, In., U.S. C10 114
Clover Pass, Ak., U.S. I29 100
Cloverport, Ky., U.S. E10 114
Clovis, Ca., U.S. H6 124
Clovis, N.M., U.S. E3 116
Cluj, co., Rom. C7 20
Cluj-Napoca, Rom. C7 20
Clunes, Austl. K5 70
Cluny, Fr. F11 14
Cluses, Fr. F13 14
Clusone, Italy D4 18
Clute, Tx., U.S. J11 116
Clwyd, co., Wales, U.K. H10 8
Clyde, Alta., Can. C21 102
Clyde, Ks., U.S. L10 118
Clyde, N.Y., U.S. D10 108
Clyde, N.C., U.S. D4 112
Clyde, Oh., U.S. F4 108
Clyde, Tx., U.S. G7 116
Clyde, stm., N.S., Can. I8 106
Clyde, stm., Scot., U.K. F10 8
Clyde, stm., Vt., U.S. C14 108
Clyde, Firth of, est., Scot., U.K. F8 8
Clyde Lake, l., Alta., Can. B23 102
Clyde Park, Mt., U.S. E15 122
Clyde River, N.W. Ter., Can. B19 96
Clymer, Pa., U.S. G7 108
Cna, stm., Russia G25 22
Coachella, Ca., U.S. K9 124
Coacoyole, Mex. E6 90
Coahoma, Tx., U.S. G5 116
Coahuila, state, Mex. C8 90
Coal, stm., Can. F31 100
Coal City, Il., U.S. I7 110
Coalcomán de Matamoros, Mex. H8 90
Coaldale, Alta., Can. H22 102
Coal Fork, W.V., U.S. I5 108
Coalgate, Ok., U.S. E10 116
Coal Grove, Oh., U.S. I4 108
Coal Harbour, B.C., Can. G7 102
Coal Hill, Ar., U.S. G3 114
Coalhurst, Alta., Can. H22 102
Coalinga, Ca., U.S. H5 124
Coalmont, B.C., Can. H14 102
Coalport, Pa., U.S. G8 108
Coal River, B.C., Can. G31 100
Coalspur, Alta., Can. D17 102
Coalville, Ut., U.S. D5 120
Coamo, P.R. E11 94
Coaraci, Braz. C9 79
Coari, Braz. J11 84

Name — Map Ref. — Page

Coari, stm., Braz. J11 84
Coari, Lago de, l., Braz. J11 84
Coast Mountains, mts., N.A. E6 96
Coast Ranges, mts., U.S. C2 98
Coatán, stm., N.A. C2 92
Coatbridge, Scot., U.K. F9 8
Coatepeque, Guat. C3 92
Coatepeque, Lago de, l., El Sal. D5 92
Coatesville, Pa., U.S. H11 108
Coaticook, Que., Can. B15 108
Coats Island, i., N.W. Ter., Can. D16 96
Coats Land, reg., Ant. C2 73
Coatzacoalcos, Mex. H12 90
Coayllo, Peru E3 82
Cobá, hist., Mex. G16 90
Cobadin, Rom. E12 20
Coballo Cocha, Peru I7 84
Cobalt, Ont., Can. C16 110
Cobán, Guat. B4 92
Cobar, Austl. H6 70
Cobberas, Mount, mtn., Austl. K8 70
Cobden, Ont., Can. E19 110
Cobden, Il., U.S. E7 114
Cobequid Bay, b., N.S., Can. G10 106
Cobequid Mountains, mts., N.S., Can. G9 106
Cobh, Ire. J5 8
Cobham, stm., Can. E20 104
Cobija, Bol. D7 82
Cobija, Chile B3 80
Cobleskill, N.Y., U.S. E12 108
Cobourg, Ont., Can. G17 110
Cobourg Peninsula, pen., Austl. B6 68
Cobquecura, Chile I2 80
Cobram, Austl. J6 70
Cobre, stm., Pan. I13 92
Cobre, Barranca del, val., Mex. D6 90
Cóbuè, Moz. D6 58
Coburg, Ger. E10 10
Coburg Island, i., N.W. Ter., Can. A17 96
Coca, stm., Ec. H4 84
Cocachacra, Peru G6 82
Cocentaina, Spain G11 16
Cochabamba, Bol. G8 82
Cochabamba, dept., Bol. G9 82
Coche, Isla, i., Ven. B11 84
Cochin, India H4 46
Cochinos, Cayos, is., Hond. B8 92
Cochise Head, mtn., Az., U.S. L7 120
Cochran, Ga., U.S. G3 112
Cochrane, Alta., Can. F20 102
Cochrane, Ont., Can. G16 96
Cochrane, Wi., U.S. F4 110
Cochrane, stm., Can. E12 96
Cochrane, Lago (Lago Pueyrredón), l., S.A. F2 78
Cochranton, Pa., U.S. F6 108
Cockburn Island, i., Ont., Can. E12 110
Coclé, prov., Pan. I14 92
Coclé del Norte, stm., Pan. I14 92
Coco, stm., N.A. G3 94
Coco, Cayo, i., Cuba C5 94
Coco, Isla del, i., C.R. G7 88
Cocoa, Fl., U.S. K6 112
Cocoa Beach, Fl., U.S. K6 112
Coco Channel, strt., Asia C1 38
Coco Islands, is., Mya. G2 40
Coconino Plateau, plat., Az., U.S. I4 120
Cocorocuma, Cayos, rf., Hond. B11 92
Cocos, Braz. C6 79
Cocos (Keeling) Islands, dep., Oc. K10 24
Cocuiza, stm., Ven. B7 84
Cocula, Mex. G8 90
Cod, Cape, pen., Ma., U.S. F16 108
Codăeşti, Rom. C11 20
Codajás, Braz. I11 84
Codera, Cabo, c., Ven. B10 84
Coderre, Sask., Can. H8 104
Codesa, Alta., Can. B16 102
Cod Island, i., Newf., Can. E20 96
Codó, Braz. D10 76
Codogno, Italy D4 18
Codpa, Chile H7 82
Codroy, Newf., Can. E14 106
Codroy Pond, Newf., Can. D15 106
Cody, Ne., U.S. I6 118
Cody, Wy., U.S. F16 122
Coeburn, Va., U.S. C4 112
Coelemu, Chile I2 80
Coen, Austl. B8 68
Coën, stm., C.R. H11 92
Coeroeni (Corentyne), stm., S.A. F14 84
Coëtivy Island, i., Sey. C11 58
Coeur d'Alene, Id., U.S. C9 122
Coeur d'Alene, stm., Id., U.S. C9 122
Coeur d'Alene Lake, l., Id., U.S. C9 122
Coevorden, Neth. C10 12
Coffeen, Il., U.S. C7 114
Coffeeville, Ms., U.S. I7 114
Coffeyville, Ks., U.S. N12 118
Coffin Bay, b., Austl. F7 68
Coffs Harbour, Austl. H10 70
Cofradía, Hond. B6 92
Cofre de Perote, Cerro, mtn., Mex. H11 90
Cofre de Perote, Parque Nacional, Mex. H11 90
Coggon, Ia., U.S. H4 110
Cognac, Fr. G6 14
Cogolin, Fr. I13 14
Cogoon, stm., Austl. F8 70
Cogswell, N.D., U.S. E10 118
Cohengu, stm., Peru D5 82
Cohocton, stm., N.Y., U.S. E9 108
Cohoe, Ak., U.S. F19 100
Cohoes, N.Y., U.S. E13 108
Cohuna, Austl. J6 70
Coiba, Isla de, i., Pan. D2 84
Coig, stm., Arg. G2 78
Coihaique, Chile F2 78
Coimbatore, India G4 46
Coimbra, Braz. F7 79
Coimbra, Braz. H13 82
Coimbra, Port. E3 16
Coín, Spain I7 16
Coin, Ia., U.S. K12 118
Coipasa, Lago, l., Bol. H7 82
Coipasa, Salar de, pl., S.A. H7 82
Čojbalsan, Mong. B9 30
Cojedes, Ven. C8 84
Cojedes, state, Ven. C8 84
Cojutepeque, El Sal. D6 92
Cokato, Mn., U.S. E1 110
Cokeville, Wy., U.S. H15 122
Colac, Austl. L5 70
Colalao del Valle, Arg. D6 80
Colatina, Braz. E8 79
Colbeck, Cape, c., Ant. C9 73
Colbert, Ok., U.S. F10 116
Colborne, Ont., Can. F18 110
Colbún, Chile H3 80
Colby, Ks., U.S. L6 118
Colby, Wi., U.S. F5 110
Colca, Peru E4 82
Colca, stm., Peru F5 82
Colcamar, Peru B3 82
Colchester, Eng., U.K. J14 8
Colchester, Ct., U.S. F14 108
Colchester, Il., U.S. J5 110
Cold Bay, Ak., U.S. I13 100
Cold Lake, Alta., Can. D4 104
Cold Lake, l., Can. D4 104
Cold Lake, Canadian Forces Base, mil., Alta., Can. D4 104
Cold Lake Indian Reserve, Alta., Can. D4 104
Cold Spring, Mn., U.S. E1 110
Coldspring, Tx., U.S. I11 116
Coldstream, Scot., U.K. F11 8
Coldwater, Ks., U.S. N8 118
Coldwater, Mi., U.S. I10 110
Coldwater, Ms., U.S. H7 114
Coldwater, Oh., U.S. G2 108
Coldwater, stm., Ms., U.S. H6 114
Coldwater Indian Reserve, B.C., Can. G14 102
Colebrook, N.H., U.S. C15 108
Cole Camp, Mo., U.S. D3 114
Coleman, Alta., Can. H20 102
Coleman, Fl., U.S. K4 112
Coleman, Mi., U.S. G11 110
Coleman, Tx., U.S. H7 116
Coleman, Wi., U.S. E7 110
Coleman, stm., Austl. B8 68
Coleman, Lake, res., Tx., U.S. G7 116
Colen Lakes, l., Man., Can. D19 104
Colenso, S. Afr. G9 66
Coleraine, Austl. K4 70
Coleraine, Mn., U.S. C2 110
Coleridge, Ne., U.S. I10 118
Coles, Ms., U.S. K5 114
Coles, Punta, c., Peru G6 82
Colesberg, S. Afr. H7 66
Coleville, Sask., Can. G5 104
Colfax, Ca., U.S. E5 124
Colfax, Il., U.S. J7 110
Colfax, In., U.S. B10 114
Colfax, Ia., U.S. I2 110
Colfax, La., U.S. K4 114
Colfax, Wa., U.S. D8 122
Colfax, Wi., U.S. F4 110
Colhué Huapi, Lago, l., Arg. F3 78
Colico, Italy C4 18
Colima, Mex. H8 90
Colima, state, Mex. H8 90
Colima, Nevado de, mtn., Mex. H8 90
Colimes, stm., Ec. H2 84
Colina, Chile G3 80
Colinas, Braz. E10 76
Colinas, Braz. C4 79
Colinet, Newf., Can. E20 106
Colinton, Alta., Can. C21 102
Collarenebri, Austl. G8 70
Collbran, Co., U.S. E9 120
College, Ak., U.S. D21 100
Collegedale, Tn., U.S. G11 114
College Park, Ga., U.S. F2 112
College Place, Wa., U.S. D7 122
College Station, Ar., U.S. H4 114
College Station, Tx., U.S. I10 116
Collegeville, In., U.S. B9 114
Collerina, Austl. G7 70
Colleymount, B.C., Can. C8 102
Colleyville, Tx., U.S. G9 116
Collie, Austl. F3 68
Collier Bay, b., Austl. C4 68
Collier Range National Park, Austl. D3 68
Collierville, Tn., U.S. G7 114
Collingwood, Ont., Can. F15 110
Collins, Ga., U.S. G4 112
Collins, Ia., U.S. I2 110
Collins, Ms., U.S. K7 114
Collins, stm., Tn., U.S. G11 114
Collins Bay, Ont., Can. F19 110
Colliston, La., U.S. J5 114
Collinsville, Austl. C7 70
Collinsville, Al., U.S. H11 114
Collinsville, Ms., U.S. J8 114
Collinsville, Ok., U.S. C11 116
Collinsville, Tx., U.S. F10 116
Collinwood, Tn., U.S. G9 114
Collipulli, Chile I2 80
Collister, Id., U.S. G9 122
Colman, S.D., U.S. H11 118
Colmar, Fr. D14 14
Colmenar de Oreja, Spain E8 16
Colmenar Viejo, Spain E8 16
Colmeneros, Mex. H9 90
Colmesneil, Tx., U.S. L2 114
Colnett, Cabo, c., Mex. B1 90
Colo, Ia., U.S. H2 110
Cologne see Köln, Ger. E6 10
Cologne, Mn., U.S. F2 110
Cololo, Nevado, mtn., Bol. F7 82
Coloma, Mi., U.S. H9 110
Coloma, Wi., U.S. F6 110
Colombey-les-Belles, Fr. D12 14
Colômbia, Braz. F4 79
Colombia, Col. F5 84
Colombia, ctry., S.A. C4 76
Colombo, Braz. C14 80
Colombo, Sri L. I5 46
Colome, S.D., U.S. H8 118
Colón, Arg. G8 80
Colón, Arg. G9 80
Colón, Cuba C4 94
Colón, Pan. C3 84
Colon, Mi., U.S. I10 110
Colón, Ur. G11 80
Colón, prov., Pan. I14 92
Colón, dept., Hond. B9 92
Colón, Archipiélago de (Galapagos Islands), is., Ec. j13 84a
Colón, Isla, i., Pan. H12 92
Colón, Montañas de, mts., Hond. C10 92
Colônia, stm., Braz. C9 79
Colonia Alvear, Arg. H5 80
Colonia Caroya, Arg. F6 80
Colonia del Sacramento, Ur. H10 80
Colonia Dora, Arg. E7 80
Colonia Elisa, Arg. D9 80
Colonia José Mármol, Arg. D8 80
Colonia Lavalleja, Ur. F10 80
Colonial Heights, Va., U.S. B9 112
Colonias Unidas, Arg. D9 80
Colonia Vicente Guerrero, Mex. B1 90
Colonia Villafañe, Arg. D9 80
Colonsay, Sask., Can. G9 104
Colony, Ks., U.S. M12 118
Colorado, C.R. G11 92
Colorado, Hond. B7 92
Colorado, state, U.S. D5 98
Colorado, stm., Arg. J7 80
Colorado, stm., Braz. E10 82
Colorado, stm., N.A. M1 120
Colorado, stm., Tx., U.S. J10 116
Colorado City, Az., U.S. H4 120
Colorado City, Co., U.S. G12 120
Colorado City, Tx., U.S. G6 116
Colorado Grande, Salina, pl., Arg. J7 80
Colorado River Aqueduct, Ca., U.S. K10 124
Colorado Springs, Co., U.S. F12 120
Colotepec, stm., Mex. J11 90
Colotlán, Mex. F8 90
Colquechaca, Bol. H8 82
Colquencha, Bol. G7 82
Colquiri, Bol. G8 82
Colquitt, Ga., U.S. H2 112
Colstrip, Mt., U.S. E19 122
Colt, Ar., U.S. G6 114
Colta, Peru F5 82
Coltauco, Chile H3 80
Colton, Ca., U.S. J8 124
Colton, S.D., U.S. H11 118
Columbia, Al., U.S. H1 112
Columbia, Ca., U.S. F5 124
Columbia, Il., U.S. D6 114
Columbia, Ky., U.S. E11 114
Columbia, La., U.S. J4 114
Columbia, Md., U.S. H10 108
Columbia, Ms., U.S. K7 114
Columbia, Mo., U.S. D4 114
Columbia, N.C., U.S. D10 112
Columbia, Pa., U.S. G10 108
Columbia, S.C., U.S. E5 112
Columbia, Tn., U.S. G9 114
Columbia, stm., N.A. G8 96
Columbia, Cape, c., N.W. Ter., Can. A12 86
Columbia, Mount, mtn., Can. E17 102
Columbia City, In., U.S. A11 114
Columbia Falls, Me., U.S. C19 108
Columbia Falls, Mt., U.S. B11 122
Columbia Icefield, Can. E17 102
Columbia Lake, l., B.C., Can. G19 102
Columbia Lake Indian Reserve, B.C., Can. G19 102
Columbia Mountains, mts., N.A. D14 102
Columbiana, Al., U.S. I10 114
Columbiana, Oh., U.S. G6 108
Columbiaville, Mi., U.S. G12 110
Columbus, Ga., U.S. G2 112
Columbus, In., U.S. C11 114
Columbus, Ks., U.S. N13 118
Columbus, Ms., U.S. I8 114
Columbus, Mt., U.S. E16 122
Columbus, Ne., U.S. J10 118
Columbus, N.M., U.S. M9 120
Columbus, N.C., U.S. D4 112
Columbus, N.D., U.S. C5 118
Columbus, Oh., U.S. H4 108
Columbus, Tx., U.S. J10 116
Columbus, Wi., U.S. G6 110
Columbus Grove, Oh., U.S. G2 108
Columbus Junction, Ia., U.S. I4 110
Columbus Point, c., Bah. B7 94
Coluna, Braz. E7 79
Colusa, Ca., U.S. E3 124
Colville, Wa., U.S. B8 122
Colville, stm., Ak., U.S. B19 100
Colville, stm., Wa., U.S. B8 122
Colville Lake, l., N.W. Ter., Can. C31 100
Comacchio, Italy E7 18
Comala, Mex. H8 90
Comalapa, Guat. C4 92
Comalapa, Nic. E9 92
Comalcalco, Mex. H13 90
Coman, Mount, mtn., Ant. C12 73
Comanche, Ok., U.S. E9 116
Comanche, Tx., U.S. H8 116
Comandante Ferraz, sci., Ant. B1 73
Comandante Fontana, Arg. C9 80
Comandante Leal, Arg. F6 80
Comandante Nicanor Otamendi, Arg. J10 80
Comarapa, Bol. G9 82
Comas, Peru D4 82
Comayagua, Hond. C7 92
Comayagua, dept., Hond. C7 92
Comayagua, Montañas de, mts., Hond. C7 92
Combahee, stm., S.C., U.S. G6 112
Combarbalá, Chile F3 80
Combeaufontaine, Fr. E12 14
Combourg, Fr. D5 14
Comboyne, Austl. H10 70
Combronde, Fr. G10 14
Come by Chance, Newf., Can. E20 106
Comendador, Dom. Rep. E9 94
Comendador Gomes, Braz. E4 79
Comer, Ga., U.S. E3 112
Comercinho, Braz. D8 79
Comfort, N.C., U.S. D9 112
Comfort, Tx., U.S. J8 116
Comfort, Cape, c., N.W. Ter., Can. C16 96
Comfrey, Mn., U.S. G13 118
Comilla, Bngl. I14 44
Comiso, Italy M9 18
Comitán de Domínguez, Mex. I13 90
Commentry, Fr. F9 14
Commerce, Ga., U.S. E3 112
Commerce, Ok., U.S. C12 116
Commerce, Tx., U.S. F11 116
Commerce City, Co., U.S. E12 120
Commercy, Fr. D12 14
Comminges, reg., Fr. I7 14
Committee Bay, b., N.W. Ter., Can. C15 96
Como, Italy D4 18
Como, Ms., U.S. H7 114
Como, Tx., U.S. F11 116
Como, Lago di, l., Italy C4 18
Comodoro Rivadavia, Arg. F3 78
Comores, Archipel des, is., Afr. D8 58
Comorin, Cape, c., India H4 46
Comoros (Comores), ctry., Afr. D8 58
Comox, B.C., Can. H10 102
Comox, Canadian Forces Base, mil., B.C., Can. H10 102
Compiègne, Fr. C9 14
Compostela, Mex. G7 90
Comprida, Ilha, i., Braz. C15 80
Compton, Ca., U.S. K7 124
Comrat, Mol. C12 20
Comstock, Ne., U.S. J8 118
Comstock, Tx., U.S. J5 116
Comstock Park, Mi., U.S. G10 110
Čona, stm., Russia E13 28
Conakry, Gui. G3 64
Conambo, stm., Ec. H4 84
Conasauga, stm., U.S. E2 112
Concarán, Arg. G6 80
Concarneau, Fr. E3 14
Conceição, Braz. B12 82
Conceição, Cachoeira, wtfl, Braz. C9 82
Conceição da Barra, Braz. E9 79
Conceição das Alagoas, Braz. E4 79
Conceição de Ipanema, Braz. E8 79
Conceição do Almeida, Braz. B9 79
Conceição do Araguaia, Braz. E9 76
Conceição do Mato Dentro, Braz. E7 79
Conceição do Maú, Braz. F13 84
Conceição do Norte, Braz. B5 79
Concepción, Arg. E10 80
Concepción, Arg. D6 80
Concepción, Bol. D8 82
Concepción, Bol. G10 82
Concepción, Chile I2 80
Concepción, Col. D6 84
Concepción, Para. B10 80
Concepción, Peru D4 82
Concepción, dept., Para. B10 80
Concepción, Bahía, b., Mex. D4 90
Concepción, Laguna, l., Bol. G11 82
Concepción, Volcán, vol., Nic. F9 92
Concepción de Ataco, El Sal. D5 92
Concepción de la Sierra, Arg. D11 80
Concepcion del Oro, Mex. E9 90
Concepción del Uruguay, Arg. G9 80
Concepción Huista, Guat. B3 92
Concepción Quezaltepeque, El Sal. C6 92
Conception Bay, b., Newf., Can. E20 106
Conception Bay, b., Nmb. D2 66
Conchagua, El Sal. D7 92
Conchagua, Volcán, vol., El Sal. D7 92
Conchas, stm., N.M., U.S. D2 116
Conchas Dam, N.M., U.S. D2 116
Conche, Newf., Can. B18 106
Conches-en-Ouche, Fr. D7 14
Conchi, Chile B4 80
Concho, Az., U.S. J7 120
Concho, stm., Tx., U.S. H7 116
Conchos, stm., Mex. C7 90
Conchos, stm., Mex. E10 90
Concise, Switz. E6 13
Concón, Chile G3 80
Concord, Ca., U.S. G3 124
Concord, Ga., U.S. F2 112
Concord, Mi., U.S. H11 110
Concord, N.H., U.S. D15 108
Concord, N.C., U.S. D6 112
Concordia, Arg. F9 80
Concórdia, Braz. D12 80
Concórdia, Braz. J9 84
Concordia, Mex. F6 90
Concordia, Peru J5 84
Concordia, Ks., U.S. L10 118
Concordia, Mo., U.S. D3 114
Concrete, Wa., U.S. B4 122
Conde, Braz. A10 79
Condé, Fr. D6 14
Conde, S.D., U.S. F9 118
Condega, Nic. D8 92
Condeúba, Braz. C8 79
Condobolin, Austl. I7 70
Condom, Fr. I7 14
Condon, Or., U.S. E5 122
Condoto, Col. E4 84
Cone, Tx., U.S. F5 116
Conecuh, stm., U.S. K10 114
Conegliano, Italy D7 18
Conejos, Co., U.S. G10 120
Conejos, stm., Co., U.S. G10 120
Confederation Lake, l., Ont., Can. G22 104
Confluence, Pa., U.S. H7 108
Confolens, Fr. F7 14
Confusion Bay, b., Newf., Can. C18 106
Confuso, stm., Para. C9 80
Congaree, stm., S.C., U.S. F6 112
Congaz, Mol. C12 20
Congo, ctry., Afr. B3 58
Congo (Zaire) (Zaïre), stm., Afr. C2 58
Congo Basin, Afr. H9 52
Congress, Sask., Can. I8 104
Coniston, Ont., Can. D15 110
Conitaca, Mex. E6 90
Conjeeveram see Kānchipuram, India F5 46
Conklin, Alta., Can. B23 102
Connaught, hist. reg., Ire. H4 8
Conneaut, Oh., U.S. F6 108
Conneautville, Pa., U.S. F6 108
Connecticut, state, U.S. C12 98
Connecticut, stm., U.S. F14 108
Connell, Wa., U.S. D7 122
Connell, Mount, mtn., B.C., Can. H19 102
Connellsville, Pa., U.S. G7 108
Connemara, reg., Ire. H4 8
Connersville, In., U.S. C11 114
Conn Lake, l., N.W. Ter., Can. B18 96
Connors Range, mts., Austl. C8 70
Cononaco, stm., Ec. H4 84
Conorochite, stm., Ven. F9 84
Conover, N.C., U.S. D5 112
Conquest, Sask., Can. G7 104
Conquista, Braz. E5 79
Conrad, Ia., U.S. H3 110
Conrad, Mt., U.S. B14 122
Conroe, Tx., U.S. I11 116
Conroe, Lake, res., Tx., U.S. I11 116
Consecon, Ont., Can. F18 110
Conselheiro Lafaiete, Braz. F7 79
Conselheiro Pena, Braz. E8 79
Consolación del Sur, Cuba C3 94
Con Son, is., Viet. J9 40
Consort, Alta., Can. F4 104
Constance, Lake see Bodensee, l., Eur. E16 14
Constanţa, Rom. E12 20
Constanţa, co., Rom. E12 20
Constantina, Spain H6 16
Constantine see Qacentina, Alg. B14 62
Constantinople see İstanbul, Tur. H12 20
Constitución, Chile H2 80
Constitución, Ur. F10 80
Consuegra, Spain F8 16
Consul, Sask., Can. I5 104
Contamana, Peru B4 82
Contas, Rio de, stm., Braz. C9 79
Contendas do Sincorá, Braz. B8 79
Continental, Oh., U.S. F2 108
Contraalmirante Cordero, Arg. J4 80
Contratación, Col. D6 84
Contumazá, Peru B2 82
Contwoyto Lake, l., N.W. Ter., Can. C10 96
Conty, Fr. C9 14
Convención, Col. C6 84
Convent, La., U.S. L6 114
Convento, C.R. H11 92
Conversano, Italy I12 18
Converse, In., U.S. B11 114
Convoy, Oh., U.S. G2 108
Conway, P.E.I., Can. F10 106
Conway, Ar., U.S. G4 114
Conway, Mo., U.S. E4 114
Conway, N.H., U.S. D15 108
Conway, N.C., U.S. C9 112
Conway, S.C., U.S. F7 112
Conway Springs, Ks., U.S. N10 118
Conyers, Ga., U.S. F2 112
Cook, Mn., U.S. C3 110
Cook, Ne., U.S. K11 118
Cook, Cape, c., B.C., Can. G7 102
Cook, Mount, mtn., N.Z. E3 72
Cookes Peak, mtn., N.M., U.S. L9 120
Cookeville, Tn., U.S. F11 114
Cookhouse, S. Afr. I7 66
Cooking Lake, l., Alta., Can. D21 102
Cook Inlet, b., Ak., U.S. F18 100
Cook Islands, dep., Oc. J23 126
Cook's Harbour, Newf., Can. A18 106
Cook Strait, strt., N.Z. D5 72
Cooktown, Austl. C9 68
Coolah, Austl. H8 70
Coolamon, Austl. J7 70
Coolangatta, Austl. G10 70
Cooleemee, N.C., U.S. D6 112
Coolgardie, Austl. F4 68
Coolidge, Az., U.S. L5 120
Coolidge, Ga., U.S. H3 112
Coolidge, Tx., U.S. H10 116
Coolin, Id., U.S. B9 122
Cooma, Austl. K8 70
Coonabarabran, Austl. H8 70
Coonamble, Austl. H8 70
Coonoor, India G4 46
Coon Rapids, Ia., U.S. J13 118
Coon Rapids, Mn., U.S. E2 110
Coon Valley, Wi., U.S. G4 110
Cooper, Tx., U.S. F11 116
Cooper, Mount, mtn., B.C., Can. G17 102
Cooper Creek, stm., Austl. G3 70
Cooper Landing, Ak., U.S. F20 100
Cooper Mountain, mtn., Ak., U.S. F20 100
Cooper Road, La., U.S. J3 114
Coopers, Al., U.S. J10 114
Cooperstown, N.Y., U.S. E12 108
Cooperstown, N.D., U.S. D9 118
Coopersville, Mi., U.S. G10 110
Cooroy, Austl. F10 70
Coosa, stm., U.S. J10 114
Coosawhatchie, stm., S.C., U.S. G5 112
Coos Bay, Or., U.S. G1 122
Coos Bay, b., Or., U.S. G1 122
Cootamundra, Austl. J8 70
Copacabana, Arg. E5 80
Copacabana, Bol. G7 82
Copainalá, Mex. I13 90
Copán, Hond. C5 92
Copan, Ok., U.S. C11 116
Copán, dept., Hond. C6 92
Copán, hist., Hond. C5 92
Copatana, Braz. I9 84
Cope, Co., U.S. L5 118
Copeá, Paraná, mth., Braz. I11 84
Copeau, stm., Sask., Can. F11 104
Copeland, Fl., U.S. N5 112
Copenhagen see København, Den. N13 6
Copenhagen, N.Y., U.S. D11 108
Copertino, Italy I13 18
Copetonas, Arg. J8 80
Copiapó, Chile D3 80
Copiapó, stm., Chile D3 80
Copley, Austl. H3 70
Copparo, Italy E6 18
Copper, stm., Ak., U.S. F22 100
Copperas Cove, Tx., U.S. H9 116
Copper Butte, mtn., Wa., U.S. B7 122
Copper Canyon see Cobre, Barranca del, val., Mex. D6 90
Copper Cliff, Ont., Can. D14 110
Copper Harbor, Mi., U.S. C8 110
Coppermine, N.W. Ter., Can. C9 96
Coppermine, stm., N.W. Ter., Can. C10 96
Copper Mountain, B.C., Can. H14 102
Coppet, Switz. F5 13
Copton Creek, stm., Alta., Can. C15 102
Coquille, Or., U.S. G1 122
Coquille, stm., Or., U.S. G1 122
Coquimbo, Chile E3 80
Coquimbo, prov., Chile F3 80
Corabia, Rom. F8 20
Coração de Jesus, Braz. D6 79
Coração de Maria, Braz. B9 79
Coracora, Peru F5 82
Coral Gables, Fl., U.S. N6 112
Coral Harbour, N.W. Ter., Can. D16 96
Coralque, stm., Peru G6 82
Coral Sea, Oc. J19 126
Coral Sea Islands Territory, ter., Austl. B9 70
Coralville, Ia., U.S. I4 110
Coralville Lake, res., Ia., U.S. I4 110
Coram, Mt., U.S. B11 122
Corangamite, Lake, l., Austl. L5 70
Corato, Italy H11 18
Corbeil-Essonnes, Fr. D9 14
Corbin, Ky., U.S. C2 112
Corcoran, Ca., U.S. H6 124
Corcovado, Golfo, b., Chile E2 78
Corcovado, Parque Nacional, C.R. I11 92
Corcovado, Volcán, vol., Chile E2 78
Cordeiro, Braz. G7 79
Cordele, Ga., U.S. H3 112
Cordell, Ok., U.S. D8 116
Cordell Hull Reservoir, res., Tn., U.S. F11 114
Corder, Mo., U.S. C3 114
Cordillera, dept., Para. C10 80
Cordillo Downs, Austl. F4 70
Cordisburgo, Braz. E6 79
Córdoba, Arg. F6 80
Córdoba, Mex. H11 90
Córdoba, Spain H7 16
Córdoba, prov., Arg. F7 80
Córdoba, dept., Col. C5 84
Córdova, Peru F4 82
Cordova, Al., U.S. I9 114
Cordova, Ak., U.S. F22 100
Cordova, Il., U.S. I5 110
Corentyne (Corantijn) (Coeroeni), stm., S.A. E14 84
Corerepe, Mex. E5 90
Corfu see Kérkira, Grc. J3 20
Corfu see Kérkira, i., Grc. J3 20
Coria, Spain F5 16
Coria del Río, Spain H5 16
Coribe, Braz. B6 79
Corigliano Calabro, Italy J11 18
Corinda, Austl. A3 70
Corinne, Ut., U.S. C4 120
Corinne, W.V., U.S. B5 112
Corinth see Kórinthos, Grc. L6 20
Corinth, Ms., U.S. H8 114
Corinth, N.Y., U.S. D13 108
Corinth, Gulf of see Korinthiakós Kólpos, b., Grc. K6 20
Corinth Canal see Korinthou, Dhiórix, Grc. L6 20
Corinto, Braz. E6 79
Corinto, El Sal. D7 92
Corinto, Nic. E7 92
Coripata, Bol. G8 82
Corire, Peru G5 82
Coris, Peru C3 82
Cork, Ire. J5 8
Cork, co., Ire. I5 8
Corlay, Fr. D3 14
Corleone, Italy L8 18
Çorlu, Tur. H11 20
Cormeilles, Fr. C7 14
Cormorant, Man., Can. D14 104
Cormorant Lake, l., Man., Can. D14 104
Cornelia, Ga., U.S. E3 112
Cornélio Procópio, Braz. G3 79
Cornelius, N.C., U.S. D6 112
Cornelius Grinnell Bay, b., N.W. Ter., Can. D20 96
Cornell, Wi., U.S. E4 110
Corner Brook, Newf., Can. D16 106
Cornersville, Tn., U.S. G10 114
Corneşti, Mol. B11 20
Corneta, Punta, c., Mex. J11 90
Corning, Ar., U.S. F6 114
Corning, Ca., U.S. E3 124
Corning, Ia., U.S. K13 118
Corning, Ks., U.S. L11 118
Corning, N.Y., U.S. E9 108
Corning, Oh., U.S. H4 108
Cornish, Me., U.S. D16 108
Corno Grande, mtn., Italy G8 18
Cornwall, Ont., Can. B12 108
Cornwall, co., Eng., U.K. K9 8
Cornwallis Island, i., N.W. Ter., Can. A14 96
Coro, Ven. B8 84
Coro, Golfete de, b., Ven. I10 94
Coroaci, Braz. E7 79
Corocoro, Bol. G7 82
Corocoro Island, i., S.A. C12 84
Coroico, Bol. G8 82
Coroico, stm., Bol. F8 82
Coromandel, Braz. E5 79
Coromandel Coast, India F6 46
Coromandel Peninsula, pen., N.Z. B5 72
Corona, Ca., U.S. K8 124
Corona, N.M., U.S. J11 120
Coronado, Mex. F9 90
Coronado, Ca., U.S. L8 124
Coronado, Bahía de, b., C.R. H11 92
Coronation, Alta., Can. E23 102
Coronation Gulf, b., N.W. Ter., Can. C10 96
Coronation Island, i., Ant. B1 73
Coronda, Arg. F8 80
Coronel, Chile I2 80
Coronel Bogado, Para. D10 80
Coronel Dorrego, Arg. J8 80
Coronel Du Graty, Arg. D8 80
Coronel Eugenio del Busto, Arg. J6 80
Coronel Fabriciano, Braz. E7 79
Coronel Moldes, Arg. C6 80
Coronel Moldes, Arg. G6 80
Coronel Murta, Braz. D7 79
Coronel Oviedo, Para. C10 80
Coronel Ponce, Braz. C1 79
Coronel Pringles, Arg. I8 80
Coronel Sapucaia, Braz. G1 79
Coronel Suárez, Arg. I8 80
Coronel Vidal, Arg. I10 80
Coronel Vivida, Braz. C12 80
Corongo, Peru C3 82
Coronie, dept., Sur. E14 84
Coropuna, Nevado, mtn., Peru F5 82
Corowa, Austl. K7 70
Corozal, Belize H15 90
Corozal, Col. C5 84
Corozal, Hond. B8 92
Corps, Fr. H12 14
Corpus, Arg. D11 80
Corpus Christi, Tx., U.S. L9 116
Corpus Christi, Lake, res., Tx., U.S. K9 116
Corpus Christi Bay, b., Tx., U.S. L9 116
Corque, Bol. H8 82
Corquín, Hond. C6 92
Corral, Chile D2 78
Corral de Almaguer, Spain F8 16
Corral de Bustos, Arg. G7 80
Corralejo, Spain o27 17b
Correctionville, Ia., U.S. I12 118
Correggio, Italy E5 18
Córrego Rico, Braz. C5 79
Corrente, stm., Braz. E3 79
Corrente, stm., Braz. B6 79
Correntes, stm., Braz. D1 79
Correntina, Braz. B6 79
Corrèze, dept., Fr. G8 14
Corrib, Lough, l., Ire. H4 8
Corrientes, Arg. D9 80
Corrientes, prov., Arg. E10 80
Corrientes, stm., Arg. E9 80
Corrientes, stm., S.A. I5 84
Corrientes, Bahía de, b., Cuba D2 94
Corrientes, Cabo, c., Arg. J10 80
Corrientes, Cabo, c., Col. E4 84
Corrientes, Cabo, c., Cuba D2 94
Corrientes, Cabo, c., Mex. G7 90
Corrigan, Tx., U.S. L2 114
Corriverton, Guy. E14 84
Corry, Pa., U.S. F7 108
Corse (Corsica), i., Fr. I24 15a
Corse, Cap, c., Fr. k24 15a
Corse-du-Sud, dept., Fr. m24 15a
Corsica, S.D., U.S. H9 118
Corsica see Corse, i., Fr. I24 15a
Corsicana, Tx., U.S. G10 116
Cortazar, Mex. G9 90
Corte, Fr. G4 18
Cortegana, Spain H5 16
Cortés, dept., Hond. B6 92
Cortez, Co., U.S. G8 120
Cortez, Sea of see California, Golfo de, b., Mex. D4 90
Cortina d'Ampezzo, Italy C7 18
Cortland, Ne., U.S. K11 118
Cortland, N.Y., U.S. E10 108
Cortland, Oh., U.S. F6 108
Cortona, Italy F6 18
Corubal (Koliba), stm., Afr. F2 64
Çoruh, stm., Asia A6 48
Çorum, Tur. J12 20
Corumbá, Braz. H13 82
Corumbá, stm., Braz. E4 79
Corumbá de Goiás, Braz. C4 79
Corumbaíba, Braz. E4 79
Corumbataí, stm., Braz. C13 80
Corumbaú, Ponta do, c., Braz. D9 79
Corumbiara, stm., Braz. E11 82
Corumo, stm., Ven. D12 84
Corunna, Ont., Can. H13 110
Corunna, Mi., U.S. H11 110

Name	Map Ref.	Page

Name	Map Ref.	Page
Epsom, Eng., U.K.	J13	8
Epukiro, stm., Afr.	C5	66
Eqlīd, Iran	F12	48
Equality, Il., U.S.	E8	114
Equatorial Guinea, ctry., Afr.	H8	54
Erath, La., U.S.	M4	114
Erciş, Tur.	B7	48
Erciyes Dağı, mtn., Tur.	B3	48
Érd, Hung.	H18	10
Erdaoliangzi, China	C7	32
Erdene, Mong.	C9	30
Erding, Ger.	G11	10
Erebato, stm., Ven.	E10	84
Erebus, Mount, mtn., Ant.	C8	73
Ereğli, Tur.	C3	48
Erenhot, China	C9	30
Erepecuru, Lago do, l., Braz.	H14	84
Eressós, Grc.	J9	20
Erétria, Grc.	K7	20
Erexim, Braz.	D12	80
Erfoud, Mor.	E8	62
Erft, stm., Ger.	D6	10
Erfurt, Ger.	E11	10
Erges (Erjas), stm., Eur.	F5	16
Ergļi, Lat.	E8	22
Ergun (Argun'), stm., Asia	A11	30
Er Hai, l., China	B6	40
Erhlin, Tai.	L9	34
Eriba, Sud.	I9	60
Erice, Italy	K7	18
Erichsen Lake, l., N.W. Ter., Can.	B16	96
Erick, Ok., U.S.	D7	116
Erickson, B.C., Can.	H18	102
Erickson, Man., Can.	H15	104
Ericson, Ne., U.S.	J9	118
Erie, Co., U.S.	D11	120
Erie, Il., U.S.	I5	110
Erie, Ks., U.S.	N12	118
Erie, Pa., U.S.	E6	108
Erie, Lake, l., N.A.	H15	110
Erie Canal see New York State Barge Canal, N.Y., U.S.	D8	108
Eriksdale, Man., Can.	H16	104
Erimo-misaki, c., Japan	f18	36a
Erin, Ont., Can.	G15	110
Erin, Tn., U.S.	F9	114
Eritrea, ctry., Afr.	E8	56
Erjas (Erges), stm., Eur.	F5	16
Erjiazhen, China	C10	34
Erkelenz, Ger.	D6	10
Erkowit, Sud.	H9	60
Erlangen, Ger.	F11	10
Ermelo, Neth.	D8	12
Ermelo, S. Afr.	F9	66
Ermenek, Tur.	C2	48
Ermineskin Indian Reserve, Alta., Can.	E21	102
Ermoúpolis, Grc.	L8	20
Erne, Lower Lough, l., N. Ire., U.K.	G6	8
Erne, Upper Lough, l., Eur.	G6	8
Ernée, Fr.	D6	14
Erode, India	G4	46
Eromanga, Austl.	F5	70
Erongo, Nmb.	C2	66
Erota, Erit.	I9	60
Er-Rachidia, Mor.	E8	62
Errol Heights, Or., U.S.	E3	122
Erskine, Mn., U.S.	D11	118
Erskine Inlet, b., N.W. Ter., Can.	A12	96
Erstein, Fr.	D14	14
Ertai, China	B5	30
Ertil', Russia	J23	22
Ertix (Irtyš), stm., Asia	H9	28
Ertuğrul, Tur.	J11	20
Erudina, Austl.	H3	70
Eruwa, Nig.	H11	64
Erval, Braz.	G12	80
Erval d'Oeste, Braz.	D13	80
Erwin, N.C., U.S.	D8	112
Erwin, Tn., U.S.	C4	112
Erwood, Sask., Can.	F12	104
Eryuan, China	A5	40
Erzgebirge (Krušné hory), mts., Eur.	E13	10
Erzin, Russia	G17	26
Erzincan, Tur.	B5	48
Erzurum, Tur.	B6	48
Esa'ala, Pap. N. Gui.	A10	68
Esashi, Japan	F15	36
Esashi, Japan	H16	36
Esbjerg, Den.	N11	6
Esca, stm., Spain	J5	14
Escalante, Ut., U.S.	G5	120
Escalante, stm., Ut., U.S.	G5	120
Escalante, stm., Ven.	C7	84
Escalante Desert, des., Ut., U.S.	G3	120
Escalón, Mex.	D7	90
Escalon, Ca., U.S.	G5	124
Escambia, stm., Fl., U.S.	L9	114
Escanaba, Mi., U.S.	E8	110
Escanaba, stm., Mi., U.S.	D8	110
Escárcega, Mex.	H14	90
Escarpada Point, c., Phil.	I20	39b
Escatawpa, stm., U.S.	L8	114
Escaut (Schelde), stm., Eur.	E3	10
Esch-sur-Alzette, Lux.	I8	12
Eschwege, Ger.	D10	10
Eschweiler, Ger.	E6	10
Escobal, Pan.	H15	92
Escobedo, Mex.	C8	90
Escocesa, Bahía, b., Dom. Rep.	E10	94
Escondido, Ca., U.S.	K8	124
Escondido, stm., Nic.	E11	92
Escudo de Veraguas, Isla, i., Pan.	H13	92
Escuinapa de Hidalgo, Mex.	F7	90
Escuintla, Guat.	C4	92
Escuintla, Mex.	J13	90
Escuintla, dept., Guat.	C3	92
Escuminac, Point, c., N.B., Can.	E9	106
Eşfahān (Isfahan), Iran	E11	48
Esfarāyen, Iran	C14	48
Eshkāshem, Afg.	B4	44
Eshowe, S. Afr.	G10	66
Esigodini, Zimb.	C9	66
Esk, Austl.	F10	70
Eskdale, W.V., U.S.	I5	108
Eskifjörður, Ice.	B7	6a
Eskilstuna, Swe.	L15	6
Eskimo Lakes, l., N.W. Ter., Can.	B28	100
Eskimo Point, N.W. Ter., Can.	D14	96
Eskişehir, Tur.	H14	4
Eskridge, Ks., U.S.	M11	118
Esla, stm., Spain	C6	16
Eslāmābād, Iran	D9	48
Eslāmshahr, Iran	D11	48
Eşme, Tur.	K12	20
Esmeralda, Austl.	B5	70
Esmeralda, Cuba	D5	94
Esmeraldas, Ec.	G3	84
Esmeraldas, prov., Ec.	G3	84
Esmeraldas, stm., Ec.	G3	84
Esmond, N.D., U.S.	C8	118
Esneux, Bel.	G8	12
Espada, Punta, c., Col.	A7	84
Espalion, Fr.	H9	14
Espanola, Ont., Can.	D14	110
Espanola, N.M., U.S.	I10	120
Esparza, C.R.	H10	92
Espejo, Spain	H7	16
Espera Feliz, Braz.	F8	79
Esperança, Braz.	J8	84
Esperance, Austl.	F4	68
Esperance Bay, b., Austl.	F4	68
Esperanza, Arg.	F8	80
Esperanza, Mex.	D5	90
Esperanza Inlet, b., B.C., Can.	H8	102
Espinal, Col.	E5	84
Espinhaço, Serra do, mts., Braz.	C7	79
Espinho, Port.	D3	16
Espinillo, Arg.	C9	80
Espino, Ven.	C9	84
Espinosa, Braz.	C7	79
Espírito Santo, state, Braz.	E8	79
Espíritu Santo, Isla, i., Mex.	E4	90
Espita, Mex.	G15	90
Espoir, Bay d', b., Newf., Can.	E18	106
Espoo (Esbo), Fin.	K19	6
Espumoso, Braz.	E12	80
Espungabera, Moz.	C11	66
Esquel, Arg.	E2	78
Esquimalt, B.C., Can.	I11	102
Esquina, Arg.	F9	80
Esquina Negra, Arg.	H9	80
Esquipulas, Guat.	C5	92
Esquipulas, Nic.	E9	92
Esquiú, Arg.	E6	80
Essaouira (Mogador), Mor.	E6	62
Es-Sekhira, Tun.	C16	62
Essen, Bel.	F5	12
Essen, Ger.	D7	10
Essequibo, stm., Guy.	E13	84
Essequibo Islands-West Demerara, prov., Guy.	D13	84
Es Sers, Tun.	M4	18
Essex, Ont., Can.	H13	110
Essex, Ia., U.S.	K12	118
Essex, Md., U.S.	H10	108
Essex, Mo., U.S.	F7	114
Essex, co., Eng., U.K.	J14	8
Essex Junction, Vt., U.S.	C13	108
Essexville, Mi., U.S.	G12	110
Esslingen, Ger.	G9	10
Es Smala es Souassi, Tun.	N5	18
Essonne, dept., Fr.	D9	14
Essoyes, Fr.	D11	14
Es-Suki, Sud.	K7	60
Est, Île de l', i., Que., Can.	E12	106
Est, Pointe de l', c., Que., Can.	C12	106
Estacada, Or., U.S.	E3	122
Estacado, Llano, pl., U.S.	F4	116
Estados, Isla de los, i., Arg.	G4	78
Eşţahbān, Iran	G13	48
Estância, Braz.	F11	76
Estancia, N.M., U.S.	J10	120
Estanislao del Campo, Arg.	C8	80
Estanzuelas, El Sal.	D6	92
Estats, Pique d', mtn., Eur.	C13	16
Estcourt, S. Afr.	G9	66
Este, Italy	D6	18
Esteio, Braz.	E13	80
Estelí, Nic.	D8	92
Estelí, dept., Nic.	D8	92
Estella, Spain	C9	16
Estelline, S.D., U.S.	G11	118
Estelline, Tx., U.S.	E6	116
Estepa, Spain	H7	16
Estepona, Spain	I6	16
Esterhazy, Sask., Can.	H12	104
Esteros, Arg.	D7	80
Estes Park, Co., U.S.	D11	120
Este Sudeste, Cayos del, is., Col.	E13	92
Estevan, Sask., Can.	I12	104
Estevan Group, is., B.C., Can.	D5	102
Estevan Point, B.C., Can.	H8	102
Estherville, Ia., U.S.	H13	118
Estill, S.C., U.S.	G5	112
Estiva, Rio da, stm., Braz.	B6	79
Eston, Sask., Can.	G6	104
Estonia (Eesti), ctry., Eur.	C8	22
Estrela, Braz.	E13	80
Estrela, mtn., Port.	E4	16
Estrela do Norte, Braz.	B4	79
Estrela do Sul, Braz.	E5	79
Estremadura, hist. reg., Port.	F3	16
Estuary, Sask., Can.	H5	104
Esztergom, Hung.	H18	10
Étables, Fr.	D4	14
Etadunna, Austl.	G3	70
Etah, Grnld.	B12	86
Etah, India	G8	44
Étain, Fr.	C12	14
Étamaniou, stm., Que., Can.	B13	106
Étampes, Fr.	D9	14
Étaples, Fr.	B8	14
Etāwah, India	G8	44
Etchemin, stm., Que., Can.	F3	106
Etchojoa, Mex.	D5	90
Ethan, S.D., U.S.	H10	118
Ethel, Ms., U.S.	I7	114
Ethel, Mount, mtn., Co., U.S.	D10	120
Ethelbert, Man., Can.	G14	104
Ethel Lake, l., Yukon, Can.	E26	100
Ethiopia (Ityopiya), ctry., Afr.	G8	56
Ethridge, Mt., U.S.	B13	122
Ethridge, Tn., U.S.	G9	114
Etna, Ca., U.S.	C3	124
Etna, Wy., U.S.	A5	120
Etna, Monte, vol., Italy	L10	18
Etobicoke, Ont., Can.	G16	110
Etomami, stm., Sask., Can.	F12	104
Etosha Pan, pl., Nmb.	B3	66
Etowah, Tn., U.S.	D2	112
Etowah, stm., Ga., U.S.	E1	112
Étretat, Fr.	C7	14
Ettelbruck, Lux.	I9	12
Et Tîdra, i., Maur.	B1	64
Ettlingen, Ger.	G8	10
Ettrick, Va., U.S.	B9	112
Etzikom Coulee, stm., Alta., Can.	I3	104
Etzná, hist., Mex.	H14	90
Eu, Fr.	B8	14
Euchiniko, stm., B.C., Can.	D10	102
Eucla, Austl.	F5	68
Euclid, Oh., U.S.	F5	108
Eucumbene, Lake, res., Austl.	K8	70
Eudistes, Lac des, l., Que., Can.	B8	106
Eudora, Ar., U.S.	I5	114
Eudora, Ks., U.S.	M12	118
Eudunda, Austl.	J3	70
Eufaula, Al., U.S.	K11	114
Eufaula, Ok., U.S.	D11	116
Eufaula Lake, res., Ok., U.S.	D11	116
Eugene, Or., U.S.	F2	122
Eugenia, Punta, c., Mex.	D2	90
Eugenio Bustos, Arg.	G4	80
Eugowra, Austl.	I8	70
Eumungerie, Austl.	H8	70
Eunice, La., U.S.	L4	114
Eunice, N.M., U.S.	G3	116
Eupen, Bel.	G9	12
Euphrates (Fırat) (Nahr al-Furāt), stm., Asia	F9	48
Eupora, Ms., U.S.	I7	114
Eure, dept., Fr.	C7	14
Eure, stm., Fr.	D8	14
Eure-et-Loir, dept., Fr.	D8	14
Eureka, Ca., U.S.	D1	124
Eureka, Il., U.S.	J6	110
Eureka, Ks., U.S.	N11	118
Eureka, Mt., U.S.	B10	122
Eureka, Nv., U.S.	E10	124
Eureka, S.C., U.S.	E5	112
Eureka, S.D., U.S.	F8	118
Eureka, Ut., U.S.	E4	120
Eureka Springs, Ar., U.S.	F3	114
Euroa, Austl.	K6	70
Europa, Île, i., Afr.	F8	58
Europa, Picos de, mts., Spain	B7	16
Europa Point, c., Gib.	I6	16
Europe	C9	52
Europoort, Neth.	E5	12
Euskal Herriko, prov., Spain	B9	16
Euskirchen, Ger.	E6	10
Eustace, Tx., U.S.	G10	116
Eustis, Fl., U.S.	K5	112
Eustis, Ne., U.S.	K7	118
Eutaw, Al., U.S.	J9	114
Eutsuk Lake, l., B.C., Can.	D8	102
Eva, Al., U.S.	H10	114
Evadale, Tx., U.S.	L2	114
Evans, Co., U.S.	D12	120
Evans, Lac, l., Que., Can.	F17	96
Evans, Mount, mtn., Co., U.S.	E11	120
Evansburg, Alta., Can.	D19	102
Evans City, Pa., U.S.	G6	108
Evansdale, Ia., U.S.	H3	110
Evans Head, c., Austl.	G10	70
Evans Strait, strt., N.W. Ter., Can.	D16	96
Evanston, Il., U.S.	H8	110
Evanston, Wy., U.S.	C6	120
Evansville, Il., U.S.	D7	114
Evansville, In., U.S.	E9	114
Evansville, Mn., U.S.	E12	118
Evansville, Wi., U.S.	H6	110
Evansville, Wy., U.S.	B10	120
Evant, Tx., U.S.	H8	116
Evart, Mi., U.S.	G10	110
Evarts, Ky., U.S.	C3	112
Eveleth, Mn., U.S.	C3	110
Evening Shade, Ar., U.S.	F5	114
Everard, Lake, l., Austl.	F7	68
Everard, Mount, mtn., B.C., Can.	F9	102
Everest, Ks., U.S.	L12	118
Everest, Mount (Qomolangma Feng), mtn., Asia	G12	44
Everett, Pa., U.S.	G8	108
Everett, Wa., U.S.	C3	122
Everglades City, Fl., U.S.	N5	112
Everglades National Park, Fl., U.S.	N6	112
Evergreen, Al., U.S.	K10	114
Evergreen, Ca., U.S.	I5	124
Evergreen, Mt., U.S.	B11	122
Everly, Ia., U.S.	H12	118
Everman, Volcán, vol., Mex.	H4	90
Evesham, Sask., Can.	F5	104
Évian-les-Bains, Fr.	F13	14
Evionnaz, Switz.	F7	13
Evisa, Fr.	G3	18
Évora, Port.	G4	16
Évreux, Fr.	C8	14
Évros (Marica) (Meriç), stm., Eur.	H10	20
Évry, Fr.	D9	14
Évvoia, i., Grc.	K7	20
Ewa, Hi., U.S.	p15	125a
Ewen, Mi., U.S.	D6	110
Ewing, Ne., U.S.	I9	118
Ewing, Va., U.S.	C3	112
Ewo, Congo	B2	58
Exaltación, Bol.	E9	82
Excelsior Mountain, mtn., Ca., U.S.	F6	124
Excelsior Springs, Mo., U.S.	C2	114
Exeter, Ont., Can.	G14	110
Exeter, Eng., U.K.	K10	8
Exeter, Ca., U.S.	H6	124
Exeter, Ne., U.S.	K10	118
Exeter, N.H., U.S.	E16	108
Exeter, stm., N.H., U.S.	D15	108
Exeter Sound, strt., N.W. Ter., Can.	C20	96
Exira, Ia., U.S.	J13	118
Exmore, Va., U.S.	B11	112
Exmouth, Austl.	D2	68
Exmouth, Eng., U.K.	K10	8
Exmouth Gulf, b., Austl.	D2	68
Expedition Range, mts., Austl.	E8	70
Experiment, Ga., U.S.	F2	112
Exploits, stm., Newf., Can.	D17	106
Exploits, Bay of, b., Newf., Can.	C18	106
Exploits Dam, Newf., Can.	D17	106
Exshaw, Alta., Can.	F19	102
Extremadura, prov., Spain	F5	16
Exuma Cays, is., Bah.	B6	94
Exuma Sound, strt., Bah.	B6	94
Eyebrow, Sask., Can.	H8	104
Eyehill Creek, stm., Can.	F4	104
Eyl, Som.	G10	56
Eymoutiers, Fr.	G8	14
Eyota, Mn., U.S.	G3	110
Eyrarbakki, Ice.	C3	6a
Eyre, Austl.	F5	68
Eyre North, Lake, l., Austl.	G2	70
Eyre Peninsula, pen., Austl.	I1	70
Eyre South, Lake, l., Austl.	G2	70
Eysturoy, i., Faer. Is.	D8	6b
Ezine, Tur.	J10	20
F		
Fabens, Tx., U.S.	M10	120
Faber Lake, l., N.W. Ter., Can.	D9	96
Fábrega, Cerro, mtn., Pan.	H12	92
Fabriano, Italy	F7	18
Facatativá, Col.	E5	84
Factoryville, Pa., U.S.	F11	108
Fada, Chad	E5	56
Fada Ngourma, Burkina	E10	64
Fadd, Hung.	I18	10
Faddeja, zaliv, b., Russia	B13	28
Fadit, Sud.	M7	60
Faenza, Italy	E6	18
Faeroe Islands (Føroyar), dep., Eur.	D8	6b
Fafa, Mali	D10	64
Fafakourou, Sen.	E2	64
Fafen, stm., Eth.	G9	56
Faga, stm., Burkina	E10	64
Făgăraş, Rom.	D8	20
Fagernes, Nor.	K11	6
Făget, Rom.	D6	20
Faguibine, Lac, l., Mali	C8	64
Fagurhólsmýri, Ice.	C5	6a
Faido, Switz.	F10	13
Fairbairn Reservoir, res., Austl.	D8	70
Fairbank, Ia., U.S.	H3	110
Fairbanks, Ak., U.S.	D21	100
Fairbanks, La., U.S.	L4	114
Fair Bluff, N.C., U.S.	E7	112
Fairborn, Oh., U.S.	H2	108
Fairburn, Ga., U.S.	F2	112
Fairbury, Il., U.S.	J7	110
Fairbury, Ne., U.S.	K10	118
Fairchance, Pa., U.S.	H7	108
Fairchild, Wi., U.S.	F5	110
Fairfax, Al., U.S.	J11	114
Fairfax, Mn., U.S.	G13	118
Fairfax, Mo., U.S.	B1	114
Fairfax, Ok., U.S.	C10	116
Fairfax, S.C., U.S.	G5	112
Fairfax, S.D., U.S.	H9	118
Fairfax, Vt., U.S.	C13	108
Fairfax, Va., U.S.	I9	108
Fairfield, Al., U.S.	I10	114
Fairfield, Ca., U.S.	F3	124
Fairfield, Id., U.S.	G11	122
Fairfield, Il., U.S.	D8	114
Fairfield, Ia., U.S.	I4	110
Fairfield, Me., U.S.	C17	108
Fairfield, Mt., U.S.	C14	122
Fairfield, Ne., U.S.	K9	118
Fairfield, Oh., U.S.	H2	108
Fairfield, Tx., U.S.	H10	116
Fairgrove, Mi., U.S.	G12	110
Fairhaven, Ma., U.S.	F16	108
Fair Haven, N.Y., U.S.	D10	108
Fair Haven, Vt., U.S.	D13	108
Fairhope, Al., U.S.	L9	114
Fairland, In., U.S.	C11	114
Fairland, Ok., U.S.	C12	116
Fairlie, N.Z.	F3	72
Fairmont, Mn., U.S.	H13	118
Fairmont, Ne., U.S.	K10	118
Fairmont, N.C., U.S.	E7	112
Fairmont, W.V., U.S.	H6	108
Fairmont Hot Springs, B.C., Can.	G19	102
Fairmount, Ga., U.S.	E2	112
Fairmount, Il., U.S.	B9	114
Fairmount, In., U.S.	B11	114
Fairmount, N.D., U.S.	E11	118
Fair Ness, c., N.W. Ter., Can.	D18	96
Fair Oaks, Ca., U.S.	F4	124
Fair Oaks, Ga., U.S.	F2	112
Fair Plain, Mi., U.S.	H9	110
Fairplains, N.C., U.S.	C5	112
Fairplay, Co., U.S.	E10	120
Fairview, Alta., Can.	A16	102
Fairview, Ga., U.S.	E1	112
Fairview, Il., U.S.	J5	110
Fairview, Ks., U.S.	L12	118
Fairview, Mi., U.S.	F11	110
Fairview, Mt., U.S.	D3	118
Fairview, Ok., U.S.	C8	116
Fairview, Tn., U.S.	G9	114
Fairview, Ut., U.S.	E5	120
Fairview, W.V., U.S.	H6	108
Fairview Park, In., U.S.	C9	114
Fairview Peak, mtn., Nv., U.S.	E7	124
Fairweather Mountain, mtn., N.A.	G26	100
Faisalabad, Pak.	E5	44
Faison, N.C., U.S.	D8	112
Faith, S.D., U.S.	F5	118
Faiyum see Al-Fayyūm, Egypt	C6	60
Faizābād, India	G10	44
Fajardo, P.R.	E12	94
Fakfak, Indon.	F9	38
Fakrinkotti, Sud.	H6	60
Faku, China	A11	32
Falaise, Fr.	D6	14
Falam, Mya.	C2	40
Falāvarjān, Iran	E11	48
Fălciu, Rom.	C12	20
Falcón, state, Ven.	B8	84
Falconara Marittima, Italy	F8	18
Falconbridge, Ont., Can.	D15	110
Falcon Heights, Or., U.S.	H4	122
Falcon Reservoir (Presa Falcón), res., N.A.	M7	116
Falémé, stm., Afr.	F4	54
Făleşti, Mol.	B11	20
Falfurrias, Tx., U.S.	L8	116
Falher, Alta., Can.	B17	102
Falkensee, Ger.	C13	10
Falkenstein, Ger.	E12	10
Falkirk, Scot., U.K.	E10	8
Falkland, B.C., Can.	G15	102
Falkland Islands, dep., S.A.	G5	78
Falkland Sound, strt., Falk. Is.	G5	78
Falkville, Al., U.S.	H10	114
Fall, stm., Ks., U.S.	N12	118
Fallais, Bel.	G7	12
Fallbrook, Ca., U.S.	K8	124
Fall Creek, Wi., U.S.	F4	110
Fallentimber Creek, stm., Alta., Can.	F19	102
Falling, stm., Va., U.S.	B8	112
Fallon, Mt., U.S.	E2	118
Fallon, Nv., U.S.	E7	124
Fall River, Ks., U.S.	N11	118
Fall River, Ma., U.S.	F15	108
Fall River, Wi., U.S.	G6	110
Fall River Mills, Ca., U.S.	C4	124
Falls City, Ne., U.S.	K12	118
Falls City, Or., U.S.	F2	122
Falls Creek, Pa., U.S.	F8	108
Falmouth, Jam.	E6	94
Falmouth, Eng., U.K.	K8	8
Falmouth, Ky., U.S.	I2	108
Falmouth, Me., U.S.	D16	108
Falmouth, Ma., U.S.	F16	108
Falmouth, Va., U.S.	I9	108
False Divi Point, c., India	E6	46
Falso, Cabo, c., Dom. Rep.	F9	94
Falso, Cabo, c., Hond.	B11	92
Falster, i., Den.	N12	6
Fălticeni, Rom.	B10	20
Falun, Swe.	K14	6
Famaillá, Arg.	D6	80
Famatina, Arg.	E5	80
Famatina, Sierra de, mts., Arg.	E5	80
Family Lake, l., Man., Can.	G19	104
Fana, Mali	E6	64
Fanado, stm., Braz.	D7	79
Fanambana, Madag.	n24	67b
Fanchon, Pointe, c., Haiti	E7	94
Fanchuan, China	C8	34
Fandriana, Madag.	r22	67b
Fang, Thai.	E5	40
Fangak, Sud.	M6	60
Fangcheng, China	B1	34
Fangdao, China	H7	34
Fangxi, China	G3	34
Fanipol', Bela.	H10	22
Fanny, Mount, mtn., Or., U.S.	E8	122
Fanny Bay, B.C., Can.	H10	102
Fano, Italy	F8	18
Fan Si Pan, mtn., Viet.	C7	40
Fanxian, China	H3	32
Faraday, sci., Ant.	B12	73
Faradje, Zaire	H6	56
Faradofay, Madag.	t22	67b
Farafangana, Madag.	s22	67b
Farāh, Afg.	E17	48
Farahalana, Madag.	o24	67b
Farā'id, Jabal al-, mtn., Egypt	J3	48
Farallon Islands, is., Ca., U.S.	G2	124
Faramana, Burkina	E7	64
Faranah, Gui.	F4	64
Farasān, Jazā'ir, is., Sau. Ar.	F2	47
Faratsiho, Madag.	q22	67b
Farewell, Cape, c., N.Z.	D4	72
Fargo, N.D., U.S.	E11	118
Faribault, Mn., U.S.	F2	110
Faribault, Lac, l., Que., Can.	E18	96
Farīdkot, India	E6	44
Farīdpur, Bngl.	I13	44
Farīmān, Iran	D15	48
Farina, Il., U.S.	D8	114
Fāriskūr, Egypt	B6	60
Farley, Ia., U.S.	H4	110
Farmer City, Il., U.S.	B8	114
Farmersburg, In., U.S.	C9	114
Farmersville, Il., U.S.	C7	114
Farmersville, Tx., U.S.	F10	116
Farmerville, La., U.S.	J4	114
Farmington, Il., U.S.	J5	110
Farmington, Ia., U.S.	J4	110
Farmington, Me., U.S.	C16	108
Farmington, Mn., U.S.	F2	110
Farmington, Mo., U.S.	E6	114
Farmington, N.H., U.S.	D15	108
Farmington, N.M., U.S.	H8	120
Farmington, Ut., U.S.	D5	120
Far Mountain, mtn., B.C., Can.	E9	102
Farmville, N.C., U.S.	D9	112
Farmville, Va., U.S.	B8	112
Farnam, Ne., U.S.	K7	118
Farnham, Que., Can.	B14	108
Farnham, Mount, mtn., B.C., Can.	G18	102
Farnhamville, Ia., U.S.	I13	118
Faro, Braz.	I14	84
Faro, Port.	H4	16
Faro, stm., Afr.	G9	54
Farquhar Group, is., Sey.	D10	58
Farragut, Ia., U.S.	K12	118
Farrāshband, Iran	G12	48
Farrell, Pa., U.S.	F6	108
Farrukhābād, India	G8	44
Fārsī, Afg.	E17	48
Farsund, Nor.	L10	6
Fartak, Ra's, c., Yemen	G8	47
Farvel, Kap, c., Grnld.	E24	96
Farwell, Mi., U.S.	G11	110
Farwell, Tx., U.S.	I3	116
Fasā, Iran	G12	48
Fasano, Italy	I12	18
Fatehpur, India	G6	44
Fathai, Sud.	M6	60
Fathom Five National Marine Park, Ont., Can.	E14	110
Fatick, Sen.	D1	64
Fátima, Port.	F3	16
Fatoto, Gam.	E3	64
Fat'ož, Russia	I18	22
Faulkton, S.D., U.S.	F8	118
Faulquemont, Fr.	C13	14
Fauquier, B.C., Can.	H16	102
Fauske, Nor.	H14	6
Faust, Alta., Can.	B19	102
Fauvillers, Bel.	I8	12
Faux-Cap, Madag.	t21	67b
Favara, Italy	L8	18
Faverges, Fr.	G13	14
Favourable Lake, l., Ont., Can.	F21	104
Fawcett, Alta., Can.	C20	102
Fawcett Lake, l., Alta., Can.	B21	102
Fawn, stm., Ont., Can.	F15	96
Fawnie Nose, mtn., B.C., Can.	D9	102
Fawnie Range, mts., B.C., Can.	D10	102
Faxaflói, b., Ice.	B2	6a
Faxinal, Braz.	G3	79
Faxinal do Soturno, Braz.	E12	80
Faya, Chad	E4	56
Fayd, Sau. Ar.	H7	48
Fayette, Al., U.S.	I9	114
Fayette, Ia., U.S.	H4	110
Fayette, Ms., U.S.	K5	114
Fayette, Mo., U.S.	C4	114
Fayette, Oh., U.S.	F2	108
Fayetteville, Ar., U.S.	F2	114
Fayetteville, Ga., U.S.	F2	112
Fayetteville, N.C., U.S.	D8	112
Fayetteville, Tn., U.S.	G10	114
Fayetteville, W.V., U.S.	I5	108
Fayl-Billot, Fr.	E12	14
Fazenda de Cima, Braz.	F13	82
Fazenda Nova, Braz.	D3	79
Fāzilka, India	E6	44
Fāzilpur, Pak.	F4	44
Fazzān (Fezzan), hist. reg., Libya	C3	56
Fdérik, Maur.	I4	62
Fear, Cape, c., N.C., U.S.	F9	112
Feather, stm., Ca., U.S.	E4	124
Feathertop, Mount, mtn., Austl.	K7	70
Fécamp, Fr.	C7	14
Federación, Arg.	F10	80
Federal, Arg.	F9	80
Federalsburg, Md., U.S.	I11	108
Fehérgyarmat, Hung.	H22	10
Fehmarn, i., Ger.	A11	10
Fehmarn Belt, strt., Eur.	A11	10
Feia, Lagoa, b., Braz.	G8	79
Feijó, Braz.	C6	82
Feira, Zam.	E6	58
Feira de Santana, Braz.	B9	79
Feixiang, China	G2	32
Fejaj, Chott, sw., Tun.	D15	62
Fejér, co., Hung.	H18	10
Felanitx, Spain	F15	16
Felda, Fl., U.S.	M5	112
Feldbach, Aus.	I15	10
Feldkirch, Aus.	H9	10
Felhit, Erit.	I10	60
Feliciano, Arroyo, stm., Arg.	F9	80
Felix, Cape, c., N.W. Ter., Can.	C13	96
Felix, Rio, stm., N.M., U.S.	K11	120
Felixlândia, Braz.	E6	79
Felixstowe, Eng., U.K.	J15	8
Felixton, S. Afr.	G10	66
Félix U. Gómez, Mex.	C4	90
Fellbach, Ger.	G9	10
Felletin, Fr.	G9	14
Fellsmere, Fl., U.S.	L6	112
Feltre, Italy	C6	18
Femund, l., Nor.	J12	6
Femundsenden, Nor.	K12	6
Fen, stm., China	D9	30
Fenelon Falls, Ont., Can.	F17	110
Fengcheng, China	C12	32
Fengcheng, China	G4	34
Fengdu, China	F8	30
Fengfeng, China	G2	32
Fenghuanjing, China	D6	34
Fengjia, China	F9	32
Fenglin, Tai.	L10	34
Fengxin, China	G4	34
Fengyang, China	E10	30
Fengyüan, Tai.	K9	34
Fengzhen, China	C9	30
Feni, Bngl.	I14	44
Fennimore, Wi., U.S.	H5	110
Fennville, Mi., U.S.	H9	110
Fenoarivo Atsinanana, Madag.	p23	67b
Fenshui'ao, China	J3	34
Fenton, Mi., U.S.	H12	110
Fentress, Tx., U.S.	J9	116
Fenwick, W.V., U.S.	I6	108
Fenyang, China	D9	30
Feodosiya, Ukr.	H5	26
Ferdinand, In., U.S.	D10	114
Ferdows, Iran	D15	48
Fergana, Uzb.	I12	26
Fergus, Ont., Can.	G15	110
Fergus Falls, Mn., U.S.	E11	118
Ferguson, B.C., Can.	G17	102
Ferguson, Ky., U.S.	B2	112
Ferguson, Mo., U.S.	D6	114
Fériana, Tun.	C15	62
Ferkéssédougou, C. Iv.	G7	64
Ferlo, Vallée du, val., Sen.	D2	64
Fermo, Italy	F8	18
Fermont, Que., Can.	F19	96
Fernández, Arg.	D7	80
Fernandina, Isla, i., Ec.	j13	84a
Fernandina Beach, Fl., U.S.	I5	112
Fernando de la Mora, Para.	C10	80
Fernando de Noronha, Ilha, i., Braz.	D12	76
Fernandópolis, Braz.	F3	79
Fernando Póo see Bioko, i., Eq. Gui.	J14	64
Fernán-Núñez, Spain	H7	16
Ferndale, Ca., U.S.	D1	124
Ferndale, Wa., U.S.	B3	122
Fernie, B.C., Can.	H19	102
Fernley, Nv., U.S.	E6	124
Fern Park, Fl., U.S.	K5	112
Fernwood, Id., U.S.	C9	122
Ferolle Point, c., Newf., Can.	A16	106
Ferrara, Italy	E6	18
Ferreñafe, Peru	B2	82
Ferreyra, Arg.	F6	80
Ferriday, La., U.S.	K5	114
Ferrières, Fr.	D9	14
Ferris, Tx., U.S.	G10	116
Ferro, stm., Braz.	B1	79
Ferrol, Península de, pen., Peru	C2	82
Ferron, Ut., U.S.	E5	120
Ferros, Braz.	E7	79
Ferryland, Newf., Can.	E21	106
Ferrysburg, Mi., U.S.	G9	110
Fertile, Mn., U.S.	D11	118
Fès, Mor.	C8	62
Feshi, Zaire	C3	58
Fessenden, N.D., U.S.	D8	118
Festus, Mo., U.S.	D6	114
Fété Bowé, Sen.	D3	64
Feteşti, Rom.	E11	20
Fethiye, Tur.	M13	20
Feuchtwangen, Ger.	F10	10
Feuet, Libya	H16	62
Feuilles, Baie aux, b., Que., Can.	E19	96
Feuilles, Rivière aux, stm., Que., Can.	E18	96
Feyzābād, Afg.	B4	44
Fez see Fès, Mor.	C8	62
Fiambalá, Arg.	D5	80
Fianarantsoa, Madag.	r22	67b
Fiantsonana, Madag.	q22	67b
Fiche, Eth.	M10	60
Fichtelberg, mtn., Ger.	E12	10
Fichtelgebirge, mts., Eur.	E11	10
Ficksburg, S. Afr.	G8	66
Fidenza, Italy	E5	18
Fidler Lake, l., Man., Can.	A18	104
Field, B.C., Can.	F18	102
Fieldale, Va., U.S.	C7	112
Fier, Alb.	I3	20
Fiesch, Switz.	F9	13
Fife, prov., Scot., U.K.	E10	8
Fife Lake, Sask., Can.	I9	104
Fife Lake, Mi., U.S.	F10	110
Fife Lake, l., Sask., Can.	I9	104
Fifield, Wi., U.S.	E5	110
Figueira da Foz, Port.	E3	16
Figueres, Spain	C14	16
Figuig, Mor.	D10	62
Fiji, ctry., Oc.	J21	126
Filabusi, Zimb.	C9	66
Filadelfia, C.R.	G9	92
Filchner Ice Shelf, Ant.	C1	73
File Lake, l., Man., Can.	D14	104
Filingué, Niger	D11	64
Fillmore, Sask., Can.	I11	104
Fillmore, Ca., U.S.	J7	124
Fillmore, Ut., U.S.	F4	120
Finale Ligure, Italy	E3	18
Finarwa, Eth.	K10	60
Fincastle, Va., U.S.	B7	112
Findlay, Il., U.S.	C8	114
Findlay, Oh., U.S.	F3	108
Findlay, Mount, mtn., B.C., Can.	G18	102
Fingal, N.D., U.S.	E10	118
Finger Lake, l., Ont., Can.	E21	104
Fíngoè, Moz.	E6	58
Finistère, dept., Fr.	D2	14
Finisterre, Cabo de, c., Spain	C2	16
Finke, Austl.	E6	68
Finke, stm., Austl.	E7	68
Finland (Suomi), ctry., Eur.	C13	4
Finland, Gulf of, b., Eur.	L20	6
Finlay, stm., B.C., Can.	E7	96
Finley, Austl.	J6	70
Finley, N.D., U.S.	D10	118
Finmoore, B.C., Can.	D11	102
Finn, stm., Eur.	G6	8
Finnegan, Alta., Can.	F22	102
Finnmark, co., Nor.	F19	6
Fins, Oman	C11	47
Finsteraarhorn, mtn., Switz.	E9	13
Finsterwalde, Ger.	D13	10
Fiora, stm., Italy	G6	18
Fīq, Isr. Occ.	C5	50
Firavitoba, Col.	E6	84
Firebaugh, Ca., U.S.	H5	124
Firenze (Florence), Italy	F6	18
Firmat, Arg.	G8	80
Firminópolis, Braz.	D3	79
Firminy, Fr.	G11	14
Firovo, Russia	D16	22
Fīrozābād, India	G8	44
Fīrozpur, India	E6	44
Firth, Ne., U.S.	K11	118
Firth, stm., N.A.	C4	96
Firth, stm., N.A.	B24	100
Fīrūzābād, Iran	G12	48
Fīrūz Kūh, Iran	D12	48
Fish (Vis), stm., Nmb.	F3	66
Fish, stm., Al., U.S.	L9	114
Fisher, Ar., U.S.	G6	114
Fisher, Il., U.S.	B8	114
Fisher, La., U.S.	K3	114
Fisher, stm., Man., Can.	G17	104
Fisher, stm., Mt., U.S.	B10	122
Fisher Bay, b., Man., Can.	G17	104
Fisher Branch, Man., Can.	G17	104
Fisher Channel, strt., B.C., Can.	E7	102
Fisher River Indian Reserve, Man., Can.	G17	104
Fishers Island, i., N.Y., U.S.	F15	108

Name	Map Ref.	Page
Fuzhuang, China	I6	32
Füzuli, Azer.	B9	48
Fyn, i., Den.	N12	6

G

Name	Map Ref.	Page
Gaalkacyo, Som.	G10	56
Gabarus, N.S., Can.	G13	106
Gabarus Bay, b., N.S., Can.	G13	106
Gabas, stm., Fr.	I6	14
Gabbs, Nv., U.S.	F8	124
Gabela, Ang.	D2	58
Gabès, Tun.	D16	62
Gabès, Golfe de, b., Tun.	C16	62
Gabiarra, Braz.	D9	79
Gabir, Sud.	M3	60
Gable Mountain, mtn., B.C., Can.	C13	102
Gabon, ctry., Afr.	B2	58
Gaborone, Bots.	E7	66
Gabriel Strait, strt., N.W. Ter., Can.	D19	96
Gabrovo, Bul.	G9	20
Gacé, Fr.	D7	14
Gachetá, Col.	E6	84
Gachsārān, Iran	F11	48
Gackle, N.D., U.S.	E8	118
Gadag, India	E3	46
Gadamai, Sud.	I9	60
Gäddede, Swe.	I14	6
Gadilovič i, Bela.	H13	22
Gadsden, Al., U.S.	H10	114
Gadsden, Az., U.S.	L2	120
Gaeta, Italy	H8	18
Gaeta, Golfo di, b., Italy	H8	18
Gaffney, S.C., U.S.	D5	112
Gafour, Tun.	M4	18
Gafsa, Tun.	C15	62
Gagarin, Russia	F18	22
Gage, Ok., U.S.	C7	116
Gagetown, N.B., Can.	G7	106
Gagetown, Canadian Forces Base, mil., N.B., Can.	G7	106
Gaggenau, Ger.	G8	10
Gaghamni, Sud.	L5	60
Gagnoa, C. Iv.	H7	64
Gagnon, Que., Can.	F19	96
Gagra, Geor.	I6	26
Gaibandha, Bngl.	H13	44
Gail, Tx., U.S.	G5	116
Gaillac, Fr.	I8	14
Gaillard, Lac, l., Que., Can.	B5	106
Gaillon, Fr.	C8	14
Gainesboro, Tn., U.S.	F11	114
Gainesville, Fl., U.S.	J4	112
Gainesville, Ga., U.S.	E3	112
Gainesville, Mo., U.S.	F4	114
Gainesville, Tx., U.S.	F9	116
Gainsborough, Sask., Can.	I13	104
Gainsborough Creek, stm., Can.	I13	104
Gairdner, Lake, l., Austl.	F7	68
Gaital, Cerro, mtn., Pan.	I14	92
Gaithersburg, Md., U.S.	H9	108
Gaixian, China	C10	32
Gajny, Russia	E8	26
Gajutino, Russia	C21	22
Galaassija, Uzb.	B18	48
Galahad, Alta., Can.	E23	102
Galán, Cerro, mtn., Arg.	C5	80
Galapagos Islands see Colón, Archipiélago de, is., Ec.	j13	84a
Galashiels, Scot., U.K.	F11	8
Galați, Rom.	D12	20
Galați, co., Rom.	D11	20
Galatia, Il., U.S.	E8	114
Galatina, Italy	I13	18
Galax, Va., U.S.	C6	112
Gáldar, Spain	o25	17b
Galdhøpiggen, mtn., Nor.	K11	6
Galeana, Mex.	B6	90
Galeana, Mex.	E9	90
Galela, Indon.	E8	38
Galena, Ak., U.S.	D16	100
Galena, Il., U.S.	H5	110
Galena, Ks., U.S.	N13	118
Galena, Mo., U.S.	F3	114
Galena Park, Tx., U.S.	J11	116
Galeota Point, c., Trin.	I14	94
Galera, stm., Braz.	F12	82
Galera, Punta, c., Ec.	G2	84
Galera Point, c., Trin.	I14	94
Galesburg, Il., U.S.	J5	110
Galesburg, Mi., U.S.	H10	110
Galesville, Wi., U.S.	F4	110
Galeton, Pa., U.S.	F9	108
Galheiros, Braz.	B5	79
Galič, Russia	C25	22
Galicia, prov., Spain	C3	16
Galicia, hist. reg., Eur.	F12	4
Galilee, Lake, l., Austl.	D6	70
Galilee, Sea of see Kinneret, Yam, l., Isr.	C5	50
Galiléia, Braz.	E8	79
Galion, Oh., U.S.	G4	108
Galiuro Mountains, mts., Az., U.S.	L6	120
Gallarate, Italy	D3	18
Gallatin, Mo., U.S.	C3	114
Gallatin, Tn., U.S.	F10	114
Gallatin, stm., U.S.	E14	122
Galle, Sri L.	I6	46
Galliano, La., U.S.	M6	114
Galliate, Italy	D3	18
Gallinas, stm., N.M., U.S.	D2	116
Gallinas, Punta, c., Col.	A7	84
Gallinas Peak, mtn., N.M., U.S.	J11	120
Gallipoli, Austl.	B2	70
Gallipoli, Italy	I12	18
Gallipoli see Gelibolu, Tur.	I10	20
Gallipoli Peninsula see Gelibolu Yarımadası, pen., Tur.	I10	20
Gallipolis, Oh., U.S.	I4	108
Gällivare, Swe.	H17	6
Galloway, Mull of, c., Scot., U.K.	G9	8
Gallup, N.M., U.S.	I8	120
Galougo, Mali	E4	64
Galt, Ca., U.S.	F4	124
Galtat Zemmour, W. Sah.	H4	62
Galty Mountains, mts., Ire.	I5	8
Galva, Il., U.S.	I5	110
Galva, Ia., U.S.	I12	118
Galva, Ks., U.S.	M10	118
Galvarino, Chile	J2	80
Galveston, In., U.S.	B10	114
Galveston, Tx., U.S.	J12	116
Galveston Bay, b., Tx., U.S.	J12	116
Galveston Island, i., Tx., U.S.	J12	116
Gálvez, Arg.	G8	80
Galway, Ire.	H4	8
Galway, co., Ire.	H5	8
Galway Bay, b., Ire.	H4	8
Gamagōri, Japan	M12	36
Gamaliel, Ky., U.S.	F11	114
Gamarra, Col.	C6	84
Gambaga, Ghana	F9	64
Gambela, Eth.	M8	60
Gambell, Ak., U.S.	E9	100
Gambia, ctry., Afr.	F3	54
Gambia (Gambie), stm., Afr.	F3	54
Gambi Atrash, Sud.	L7	60
Gambier, Oh., U.S.	G4	108
Gambier, Îles, is., Fr. Poly.	K26	126
Gambo, Newf., Can.	D19	106
Gamboa, Pan.	C3	84
Gamboma, Congo	B3	58
Gammon, stm., Can.	G19	104
Gamoep, S. Afr.	G4	66
Gamon, Sen.	E3	64
Gan, stm., China	A11	30
Gan, stm., China	G4	34
Ganado, Az., U.S.	I7	120
Ganado, Tx., U.S.	J10	116
Gananoque, Ont., Can.	F19	110
Ganāveh, Iran	G11	48
Gäncä, Azer.	I7	26
Gancevič i, Bela.	I9	22
Gand (Gent), Bel.	F4	12
Ganda, Ang.	D2	58
Gandak (Nārāyani), stm., Asia	G11	44
Gander, Newf., Can.	D19	106
Gander, stm., Newf., Can.	C19	106
Gander Bay, Newf., Can.	C19	106
Gander Bay, b., Newf., Can.	C19	106
Ganderkesee, Ger.	B8	10
Gander Lake, l., Newf., Can.	D19	106
Gāndhi Sāgar, res., India	H6	44
Gandi, Nig.	E12	64
Gandia, Spain	G11	16
Gandu, Braz.	B9	79
Ganfang, China	G3	34
Gangānagar, India	F5	44
Gangāpur, India	G7	44
Gangaw, Mya.	C3	40
Gangdisê Shan, mts., China	E9	44
Ganges, B.C., Can.	I11	102
Ganges, Fr.	I10	14
Ganges (Ganga) (Padma), stm., Asia	I13	44
Ganghu, China	D12	44
Gangi, Italy	L9	18
Gangkou, China	F4	34
Gangotri, India	E8	44
Gangotri, India	E8	44
Gangou, China	C7	32
Gangoumen, China	B4	32
Gang Ranch, B.C., Can.	F12	102
Gangtok, India	G13	44
Gangu, China	E8	30
Gannett Peak, mtn., Wy., U.S.	G16	122
Gannvalley, S.D., U.S.	G9	118
Ganq, China	B15	44
Gansu (Kansu), prov., China	D7	30
Gantt, Al., U.S.	K10	114
Ganxi, China	G7	34
Ganzê, China	E7	30
Ganzhou, China	J3	34
Ganzo Azul, Peru	C4	82
Gao, Mali	C9	64
Gaobu, China	H6	34
Gaocun, China	F10	32
Gaohe, China	M1	34
Gaokeng, China	H2	34
Gaoling, China	C5	32
Gaona, Arg.	C6	80
Gaoqiaozhen, China	C9	32
Gaoshan, China	J8	34
Gaotan, China	E6	34
Gaotingsi, China	I1	34
Gaoua, Burkina	F8	64
Gaoxinji, China	A4	34
Gaoya, China	G6	32
Gaoyou, China	C8	34
Gaoyou Hu, l., China	C8	34
Gap, Fr.	H13	14
Gar, China	E3	30
Garachiné, Pan.	C3	84
Garagoa, Col.	E6	84
Garanhuns, Braz.	E11	76
Garara, Pap. N. Gui.	A9	68
Garber, Ok., U.S.	C9	116
Garberville, Ca., U.S.	D2	124
Gârbovu, Rom.	E7	20
Garça, Braz.	G4	79
Garças, Rio das, stm., Braz.	C2	79
García, Mex.	C5	90
García de Sola, Embalse de, res., Spain	F6	16
Garcias, Braz.	F2	79
Gard, dept., Fr.	I11	14
Garda, Italy	D5	18
Garda, Lago di, l., Italy	D5	18
Gardelegen, Ger.	C11	10
Garden City, Ga., U.S.	G5	112
Garden City, Ks., U.S.	N7	118
Garden City, Mo., U.S.	D2	114
Garden City, Tx., U.S.	H5	116
Gardendale, Al., U.S.	I10	114
Garden Grove, Ca., U.S.	K8	124
Garden Grove, Ia., U.S.	J2	110
Garden Lakes, Ga., U.S.	E1	112
Garden Peninsula, pen., Mi., U.S.	E9	110
Garden Plain, Ks., U.S.	N10	118
Garden Reach, India	I13	44
Gardenton, Man., Can.	I18	104
Gardey, Arg.	I9	80
Gardeyz, Afg.	D3	44
Gardiner, Me., U.S.	C17	108
Gardiner, Mt., U.S.	E15	122
Gardiner, Or., U.S.	G1	122
Gardiner Dam, Sask., Can.	G8	104
Gardiners Bay, b., N.Y., U.S.	F14	108
Gardner, Ks., U.S.	M13	118
Gardner, Ma., U.S.	E15	108
Gardner Canal, b., B.C., Can.	D6	102
Gardnerville, Nv., U.S.	F6	124
Gardone Val Trompia, Italy	D5	18
Garešnica, Cro.	D11	18
Garfield, Ks., U.S.	M8	118
Garfield, N.M., U.S.	L9	120
Garfield, Wa., U.S.	C8	122
Garfield Mountain, mtn., Mt., U.S.	F13	122
Gargouna, Mali	D10	64
Gargždai, Lith.	F4	22
Garibaldi, Braz.	E13	80
Garibaldi, B.C., Can.	H11	102
Garibaldi, Or., U.S.	E2	122
Garibaldi, Mount, mtn., B.C., Can.	H11	102
Garibaldi Provincial Park, B.C., Can.	G12	102
Garies, S. Afr.	H4	66
Garissa, Kenya	B7	58
Garita Palmera, El Sal.	D4	92
Garko, Nig.	F14	64
Garland, Al., U.S.	K10	114
Garland, Tx., U.S.	G10	116
Garland, Ut., U.S.	C4	120
Garlasco, Italy	D3	18
Garliava, Lith.	G6	22
Garlin, Fr.	I6	14
Garm, Taj.	J12	26
Garmisch-Partenkirchen, Ger.	H11	10
Garnavillo, Ia., U.S.	H4	110
Garner, Ia., U.S.	G2	110
Garner, N.C., U.S.	D8	112
Garnett, Ks., U.S.	M12	118
Garnish, Newf., Can.	E18	106
Garonne, stm., Eur.	H6	14
Garoua, Cam.	G9	54
Garretson, S.D., U.S.	H11	118
Garrett, In., U.S.	A11	114
Garrett, Ky., U.S.	B4	112
Garrison, Mt., U.S.	D13	122
Garrison, N.D., U.S.	D6	118
Garrison, Tx., U.S.	K2	114
Garrovillas, Spain	F5	16
Garry Bay, b., N.W. Ter., Can.	C15	96
Garry Lake, l., N.W. Ter., Can.	C12	96
Garson, Ont., Can.	D15	110
Garson Lake, l., Can.	B4	104
Garub, Nmb.	F3	66
Garut, Indon.	j13	39a
Garwin, Ia., U.S.	H3	110
Garwolin, Pol.	D21	10
Garwood, Tx., U.S.	J10	116
Gary, In., U.S.	A9	114
Gary, S.D., U.S.	G11	118
Gary, Tx., U.S.	J2	114
Gary, W.V., U.S.	B5	112
Garyarsa, China	E9	44
Garza, Arg.	E7	80
Garzón, Col.	F5	84
Garzón, Ur.	H11	80
Gas City, In., U.S.	B11	114
Gascogne, hist. reg., Fr.	H6	14
Gasconade, stm., Mo., U.S.	D5	114
Gascoyne, stm., Austl.	E2	68
Gash (Nahr al-Qāsh), stm., Afr.	F8	56
Gashaka, Nig.	G9	54
Gaspar, Braz.	D14	80
Gaspard Creek, stm., B.C., Can.	F12	102
Gaspé, Que., Can.	D9	106
Gaspé, Baie de, b., Que., Can.	D9	106
Gaspé, Cap, c., Que., Can.	D9	106
Gaspé Peninsula see Gaspésie, Péninsule de la, pen., Que., Can.	D8	106
Gaspereau Lake, l., N.S., Can.	H9	106
Gaspésie, Parc Provincial de la, Que., Can.	D8	106
Gaspésie, Péninsule de la, pen., Que., Can.	D8	106
Gassaway, W.V., U.S.	I6	108
Gaston, N.C., U.S.	C9	112
Gaston, Lake, res., U.S.	C8	112
Gastonia, N.C., U.S.	D5	112
Gastre, Arg.	E3	78
Gata, Cabo de, c., Spain	I9	16
Gátas, Akrotírion, c., Cyp.	D2	48
Gatčina, Russia	B13	22
Gate, Ok., U.S.	C6	116
Gate City, Va., U.S.	C4	112
Gateshead, Eng., U.K.	G12	8
Gateshead Island, i., N.W. Ter., Can.	B12	96
Gatesville, N.C., U.S.	C10	112
Gatesville, Tx., U.S.	H9	116
Gateway, Co., U.S.	F8	120
Gatineau, Que., Can.	B11	108
Gatineau, stm., Que., Can.	G17	96
Gatineau, Parc de la, Que., Can.	B10	108
Gatlinburg, Tn., U.S.	D3	112
Gattinara, Italy	D3	18
Gatton, Austl.	F10	70
Gatún, Esclusas de, Pan.	H15	92
Gatún, Lago, res., Pan.	H15	92
Gauer Lake, l., Man., Can.	A17	104
Gauley, stm., W.V., U.S.	I5	108
Gauley Bridge, W.V., U.S.	I5	108
Gaultois, Newf., Can.	E18	106
Gaurīśaṅgkar, mtn., Asia	G12	44
Gause, Tx., U.S.	I10	116
Gauting, Ger.	G11	10
Gavà, Spain	D14	16
Gávdhos, i., Grc.	O8	20
Gavião, stm., Braz.	C8	79
Gävle, Swe.	K15	6
Gävleborgs Län, co., Swe.	K15	6
Gavrilov-Jam, Russia	D22	22
Gavrilov Posad, Russia	E23	22
Gawler, Austl.	J3	70
Gawler Ranges, mts., Austl.	F7	68
Gaxun Nur, l., China	C7	30
Gaya, India	H11	44
Gaylord, Mi., U.S.	E11	110
Gaylord, Mn., U.S.	F1	110
Gayndah, Austl.	E9	70
Gays Mills, Wi., U.S.	G5	110
Gaza see Ghazzah, Isr. Occ.	F3	48
Gaza Strip, hist. reg., Isr. Occ.	F2	50
Gaziantep, Tur.	C4	48
Gazimağusa (Famagusta), N. Cyp.	D2	48
Gbangbatok, S.L.	H3	64
Gbanhala, stm., Afr.	G5	64
Gbarnga, Lib.	H5	64
Gbongan, Nig.	H12	64
Gcoverega, Bots.	B7	66
Gdańsk (Danzig), Pol.	A18	10
Gdansk, Gulf of, b., Eur.	A19	10
Gdov, Russia	C10	22
Gdyel, Alg.	J11	16
Gdynia, Pol.	A18	10
Gearhart Mountain, mtn., Or., U.S.	H5	122
Geary, N.B., Can.	G7	106
Geary, Ok., U.S.	D8	116
Geba, stm., Afr.	F4	54
Gebeit Mine, Sud.	G9	60
Gebze, Tur.	I13	20
Gecha, Eth.	N8	60
Geddes, S.D., U.S.	H9	118
Gedera, Isr.	E3	50
Gediz, Tur.	J13	20
Gedo, Eth.	M9	60
Gedun, China	H7	34
Geel, Bel.	F7	12
Geelong, Austl.	L6	70
Geesthacht, Ger.	B10	10
Geeveston, Austl.	N7	70
Gegong, China	E6	34
Geiger, Al., U.S.	J8	114
Geikie, stm., Sask., Can.	E12	96
Geilo, Nor.	K11	6
Geiranger, Nor.	J10	6
Geislingen, Ger.	G9	10
Geistown, Pa., U.S.	G8	108
Gejiatun, China	C7	32
Gejiu (Kokiu), China	C7	40
Gela, Italy	L9	18
Gelderland, prov., Neth.	D8	12
Geldermalsen, Neth.	E7	12
Geldrop, Neth.	F8	12
Gelenbe, Tur.	J11	20
Gelgaudiškis, Lith.	F6	22
Gelibolu, Tur.	I10	20
Gelibolu Yarımadası (Gallipoli Peninsula), pen., Tur.	I10	20
Gelsenkirchen, Ger.	D7	10
Geltsa, Eth.	N9	60
Gemena, Zaire	H4	56
Gemlik, Tur.	I13	20
Gemsbok National Park, Bots.	E5	66
Gemünden, Ger.	E9	10
Gen, stm., China	A11	30
Genale (Jubba), stm., Afr.	G9	56
Gençay, Fr.	F7	14
General, stm., C.R.	H11	92
General Acha, Arg.	I6	80
General Alvear, Arg.	I8	80
General Alvear, Arg.	H5	80
General Aquino, Para.	C10	80
General Arenales, Arg.	H8	80
General Belgrano, Arg.	H9	80
General Bravo, Mex.	E10	90
General Cabrera, Arg.	G7	80
General Campos, Arg.	F9	80
General Carneiro, Braz.	C2	79
General Carrera, Lago (Lago Buenos Aires), l., S.A.	F2	78
General Cepeda, Mex.	E9	90
General Conesa, Arg.	I10	80
General Daniel Cerri, Arg.	J7	80
General Elizardo Aquino, Para.	D10	80
General Enrique Martínez, Ur.	G12	80
General Enrique Mosconi, Arg.	B7	80
General Escobedo, Mex.	E7	90
General Eugenio A. Garay, Para.	C10	80
General Eugenio A. Garay, Para.	I10	82
General Galarza, Arg.	G9	80
General Güemes, Arg.	C6	80
General Guido, Arg.	I10	80
General José de San Martín, Arg.	D9	80
General Juan José Ríos, Mex.	E5	90
General Juan Madariaga, Arg.	I10	80
General La Madrid, Arg.	I8	80
General Lavalle, Arg.	I10	80
General Leonidas Plaza Gutiérrez, Ec.	I3	84
General Levalle, Arg.	H7	80
General Manuel Belgrano, Cerro, mtn., Arg.	E5	80
General O'Brien, Arg.	H8	80
General Paz, Arg.	H9	80
General Pico, Arg.	H7	80
General Pinedo, Arg.	D8	80
General Pinto, Arg.	H8	80
General Pizarro, Arg.	C6	80
General Roca, Arg.	J5	80
General San Martín, Arg.	H9	80
General San Martín, Arg.	I7	80
General Santos, Phil.	D8	38
General Terán, Mex.	E10	90
General Viamonte (Los Toldos), Arg.	H8	80
General Villegas, Arg.	H7	80
Genesee, Id., U.S.	D9	122
Genesee, stm., U.S.	H18	110
Geneseo, Il., U.S.	I5	110
Geneseo, Ks., U.S.	M9	118
Geneseo, N.Y., U.S.	E9	108
Geneva see Genève, Switz.	F13	14
Geneva, Al., U.S.	K11	114
Geneva, Il., U.S.	I7	110
Geneva, In., U.S.	B12	114
Geneva, Ne., U.S.	K10	118
Geneva, N.Y., U.S.	E9	108
Geneva, Oh., U.S.	F6	108
Geneva, Lake, l., Eur.	F13	14
Genève (Geneva), Switz.	F5	13
Genève, state, Switz.	F5	13
Genévriers, Île des, i., Que., Can.	A15	106
Gengma, China	C5	40
Genk, Bel.	G8	12
Genlis, Fr.	E12	14
Genoa see Genova, Italy	E3	18
Genoa, Il., U.S.	H7	110
Genoa, Ne., U.S.	J10	118
Genoa, Oh., U.S.	F3	108
Genoa, Wi., U.S.	G4	110
Genova (Genoa), Italy	E3	18
Genova, Golfo di, b., Italy	E3	18
Genrijetty, ostrov, i., Russia	B23	28
Gent (Gand), Bel.	F4	12
Genthin, Ger.	C12	10
Gentry, Ar., U.S.	F2	114
Geographe Bay, b., Austl.	F3	68
Geographe Channel, strt., Austl.	D2	68
Geok-Tepe, Turk.	B14	48
George, S. Afr.	I6	66
George, Ia., U.S.	H11	118
George, stm., Que., Can.	E19	96
George, Cape, c., N.S., Can.	G12	106
George, Lake, l., Austl.	J8	70
George, Lake, l., Ug.	B6	58
George, Lake, l., Fl., U.S.	J5	112
George, Lake, l., N.Y., U.S.	D13	108
Georges Bank	E13	86
George Town, Austl.	M7	70
Georgetown, P.E.I., Can.	F11	106
George Town, Cay. Is.	E4	94
Georgetown, Gam.	E2	64
Georgetown, Guy.	D13	84
George Town (Pinang), Malay.	L6	40
Georgetown, St. Vin.	H14	94
Georgetown, Co., U.S.	E11	120
Georgetown, De., U.S.	I11	108
Georgetown, Fl., U.S.	J5	112
Georgetown, Ga., U.S.	H1	112
Georgetown, Id., U.S.	H14	122
Georgetown, Il., U.S.	C9	114
Georgetown, Ky., U.S.	I2	108
Georgetown, Ms., U.S.	K6	114
Georgetown, Oh., U.S.	I3	108
Georgetown, S.C., U.S.	F7	112
Georgetown, Tx., U.S.	I9	116
George V Coast, Ant.	B7	73
George VI Sound, strt., Ant.	C12	73
George West, Tx., U.S.	K8	116
Georgia, ctry., Asia	I6	26
Georgia, state, U.S.	E10	98
Georgia, Strait of, strt., N.A.	H11	102
Georgiana, Al., U.S.	K10	114
Georgian Bay, b., Ont., Can.	E14	110
Georgian Bay Islands National Park, Ont., Can.	F16	110
Georgijevsk, Russia	I6	26
Georgina, stm., Austl.	D3	70
Gera, Ger.	E12	10
Geral, Serra, clf, Braz.	D14	80
Gerald, Mo., U.S.	D5	114
Geral de Goiás, Serra, clf, Braz.	B5	79
Geraldine, Mt., U.S.	C15	122
Geraldton, Austl.	E2	68
Geraldton, Ont., Can.	G15	96
Gérardmer, Fr.	D13	14
Gerber, Ca., U.S.	D3	124
Gerdine, Mount, mtn., Ak., U.S.	F18	100
Gereshk, Afg.	E1	44
Gering, Ne., U.S.	J4	118
Gerlachovský štít, mtn., Slov.	F20	10
Germain, Grand lac, l., Que., Can.	A7	106
Germansen, Mount, mtn., B.C., Can.	B10	102
Germansen Lake, l., B.C., Can.	B10	102
Germansen Landing, B.C., Can.	B10	102
Germantown, Il., U.S.	D7	114
Germantown, Tn., U.S.	G7	114
Germantown, Wi., U.S.	G7	110
Germany (Deutschland), ctry., Eur.	E9	4
Germfask, Mi., U.S.	D10	110
Germiston, S. Afr.	F9	66
Gernika-Lumo (Guernica y Luno), Spain	B9	16
Geronimo, Ok., U.S.	E8	116
Gers, dept., Fr.	I7	14
Gerufa, Bots.	B8	66
Gêrzê, China	D11	44
Gesher HaZiw, Isr.	B4	50
Getafe, Spain	E8	16
Gettysburg, Pa., U.S.	H9	108
Gettysburg, S.D., U.S.	F8	118
Getulina, Braz.	F4	79
Getúlio Vargas, Braz.	D12	80
Gevgelija, Mac.	H6	20
Gévora, stm., Eur.	F4	16
Gex, Fr.	F13	14
Geyikli, Tur.	J10	20
Geyser, Mt., U.S.	C15	122
Geyserville, Ca., U.S.	F3	124
Ghaapplato, plat., S. Afr.	F7	66
Ghadāmis, Libya	E15	62
Ghāghara, stm., Asia	G10	44
Ghana, ctry., Afr.	G6	54
Ghanzi, Bots.	C5	66
Ghanzi, dept., Bots.	D6	66
Gharbi, Oued el, val., Alg.	D11	62
Gharbīyah, Aṣ-Ṣaḥrā' al- (Western Desert), des., Egypt	D4	60
Ghardaïa, Alg.	D12	62
Ghardimaou, Tun.	M3	18
Gharig, Sud.	L4	60
Gharyān, Libya	B3	56
Ghaṣm, Syria	C6	50
Ghāt, Libya	H16	62
Ghātāl, India	I12	44
Għawdex (Gozo), i., Malta	M9	18
Ghawr ash-Sharqīyah, Qanāt al- (East Ghor Canal), Jord.	D5	50
Ghayth, Wādī, val., Jord.	G5	50
Ghazāl, Baḥr al-, stm., Sud.	M5	60
Ghazal, Baḥr el, val., Chad	F4	56
Ghāziābād, India	F7	44
Ghāzīpur, India	H10	44
Ghazlūna, Pak.	E2	44
Ghaznī, Afg.	D3	44
Ghazzah (Gaza), Isr. Occ.	F3	48
Ghedi, Italy	D5	18
Ghent see Gent, Bel.	F4	12
Gheorgheni, Rom.	C9	20
Gherla, Rom.	B7	20
Ghilizane, Alg.	C11	62
Ghisonaccia, Fr.	I24	15a
Ghudāf, Wādī al-, val., Iraq	E7	48
Ghūriān, Afg.	D16	48
Giant's Castle, mtn., Afr.	G9	66
Giarre, Italy	L10	18
Gibara, Cuba	D6	94
Gibbon, Mn., U.S.	F1	110
Gibbon, Ne., U.S.	K9	118
Gibbons, Alta., Can.	D21	102
Gibbonsville, Id., U.S.	E12	122
Gibeon, Nmb.	E3	66
Gibraleón, Spain	H5	16
Gibraltar, Gib.	I6	16
Gibraltar, dep., Eur.	H6	4
Gibraltar, Strait of (Estrecho de Gibraltar), strt.	J6	16
Gibsland, La., U.S.	J3	114
Gibson, Ga., U.S.	F4	112
Gibson City, Il., U.S.	J7	110
Gibson Desert, des., Austl.	D5	68
Gibsons, B.C., Can.	H11	102
Gidami, Eth.	M8	60
Gidda, Eth.	M8	60
Giddings, Tx., U.S.	I10	116
Gideon, Mo., U.S.	F7	114
Gidole, Eth.	O9	60
Gidrotorf, Russia	E26	22
Gien, Fr.	E9	14
Giessen, Ger.	E8	10
Gifford, Fl., U.S.	L6	112
Gifford, stm., N.W. Ter., Can.	B16	96
Gifhorn, Ger.	C10	10
Gifu, Japan	L11	36
Giganta, Sierra de la, mts., Mex.	E4	90
Gigante, Col.	F5	84
Gijón, Spain	B6	16
Gila, stm., U.S.	L2	120
Gila Bend, Az., U.S.	L4	120
Gila Bend Mountains, mts., Az., U.S.	K3	120
Gila Mountains, mts., Az., U.S.	K7	120
Gilbert, La., U.S.	J5	114
Gilbert, Mn., U.S.	C3	110
Gilbert, stm., Austl.	A4	70
Gilbert, Mount, mtn., B.C., Can.	G10	102
Gilbertown, Al., U.S.	K8	114
Gilbert Plains, Man., Can.	G14	104
Gilboa', Haré, hills, Asia	D4	50
Gilbués, Braz.	E9	76
Gildford, Mt., U.S.	B15	122
Gilford Island, i., B.C., Can.	G8	102
Gilgandra, Austl.	H8	70
Gilgit, Pak.	C6	44
Gilgit, stm., Pak.	B5	44
Gil Island, i., B.C., Can.	D5	102
Gillam, Man., Can.	B20	104
Gilles, Lake, l., Austl.	I2	70
Gillespie, Il., U.S.	C7	114
Gillett, Ar., U.S.	H5	114
Gillett, Wi., U.S.	F7	110
Gillette, Wy., U.S.	G2	118
Gillian, Lake, l., N.W. Ter., Can.	C17	96
Gills Rock, Wi., U.S.	E8	110
Gilman, Il., U.S.	J8	110
Gilman, Ia., U.S.	I3	110
Gilman, Wi., U.S.	E5	110
Gilmer, Tx., U.S.	G12	116
Gilmore City, Ia., U.S.	I13	118
Gilroy, Ca., U.S.	G4	124
Giltner, Ne., U.S.	K9	118
Giluwe, Mount, mtn., Pap. N. Gui.	m15	68a
Gimbi, Eth.	M8	60
Gimie, Mount, mtn., St. Luc.	H14	94
Gimli, Man., Can.	H18	104
Gimoly, Russia	J23	6
Gimont, Fr.	I7	14
Gin Gin, Austl.	E9	70
Ginir, Eth.	G9	56
Ginosa, Italy	I11	18
Gioia del Colle, Italy	I11	18
Gioia Tauro, Italy	K10	18
Gipuzkoako, prov., Spain	B9	16
Girard, Il., U.S.	C7	114
Girard, Ks., U.S.	N13	118
Girard, Oh., U.S.	F6	108
Girard, Pa., U.S.	E6	108
Girard, Tx., U.S.	F6	116
Girardot, Col.	E5	84
Girgarre, Austl.	K6	70
Girīdīh, India	H12	44
Girne, N. Cyp.	D2	48
Giromagny, Fr.	E13	14
Girón, Ec.	I3	84
Girona, Spain	D14	16
Gironde, dept., Fr.	G6	14
Gironde, est., Fr.	G6	14
Girouxville, Alta., Can.	B17	102
Giru, Austl.	B7	70
Giruá, Braz.	E11	80
Girvas, Russia	J23	6
Gisborne, N.Z.	C7	72
Gisborne Lake, l., Newf., Can.	E19	106
Giscome, B.C., Can.	C12	102
Gisenyi, Rw.	B5	58
Gisors, Fr.	C8	14
Giswil, Switz.	E9	13
Gitega, Bdi.	B5	58
Giugliano [in Campania], Italy	I9	18
Giulianova, Italy	G8	18
Giurgiu, Rom.	F9	20
Giurgiu, co., Rom.	E9	20
Giv'atayim, Isr.	D3	50
Givet, Fr.	B11	14
Givors, Fr.	G11	14
Givry, Fr.	F11	14
Giyon, Eth.	M9	60
Giza see Al-Jīzah, Egypt	B6	60
Gīzāb, Afg.	D2	44
Giždúvan, Uzb.	I10	26
Gizen, Sud.	L8	60
Gižiginskaja guba, b., Russia	E23	28
Giżycko, Pol.	A21	10
Gjirokastër, Alb.	I4	20
Gjoa Haven, N.W. Ter., Can.	C13	96
Gjøvik, Nor.	K12	6
Gjuhëzës, Kep i, c., Alb.	I3	20
Glace Bay, N.S., Can.	F14	106
Glacier, B.C., Can.	F17	102
Glacier Bay, b., Ak., U.S.	G26	100
Glacier National Park, B.C., Can.	F17	102
Glacier National Park, Mt., U.S.	B12	122
Glacier Peak, mtn., Wa., U.S.	B4	122
Gladbach see Mönchengladbach, Ger.	D6	10
Gladbrook, Ia., U.S.	H3	110
Glade Spring, Va., U.S.	C5	112
Gladewater, Tx., U.S.	G12	116
Gladstone, Austl.	D9	70
Gladstone, Austl.	I3	70
Gladstone, Man., Can.	H16	104
Gladstone, Mi., U.S.	E8	110
Gladstone, Mo., U.S.	C2	114
Gladwin, Mi., U.S.	G11	110
Gladys Lake, l., B.C., Can.	G28	100
Glåma, stm., Nor.	K12	6
Glarner Alpen, mts., Switz.	E10	13
Glarus, Switz.	D11	13
Glarus, state, Switz.	E11	13
Glasco, Ks., U.S.	L10	118
Glasgow, Scot., U.K.	F9	8
Glasgow, Ky., U.S.	F11	114
Glasgow, Mo., U.S.	C4	114
Glasgow, Mt., U.S.	B19	122
Glasgow, Va., U.S.	B7	112
Glaslyn, Sask., Can.	E6	104
Glassboro, N.J., U.S.	H11	108
Glattfelden, Switz.	C10	13
Glauchau, Ger.	E12	10
Glaževo, Russia	B15	22
Glazov, Russia	F8	26
Glazunovka, Russia	I19	22
Gleason, Tn., U.S.	F8	114
Gleichen, Alta., Can.	G21	102
Gleisdorf, Aus.	H15	10
Glen Alpine, N.C., U.S.	D5	112
Glenavon, Sask., Can.	H11	104
Glenboro, Man., Can.	I15	104
Glenburn, N.D., U.S.	C6	118
Glen Burnie, Md., U.S.	H10	108
Glen Canyon, val., U.S.	G5	120
Glencoe, Austl.	K4	70
Glencoe, Ont., Can.	H14	110
Glencoe, Al., U.S.	I11	114
Glencoe, Mn., U.S.	F1	110
Glen Cove, N.Y., U.S.	G13	108
Glendale, Az., U.S.	K4	120
Glendale, Ca., U.S.	J7	124
Glendale, Ms., U.S.	K7	114
Glendale, Or., U.S.	H2	122
Glendale, Ut., U.S.	G4	120
Glendale, Wi., U.S.	G8	110
Glendive, Mt., U.S.	D3	118
Glendo, Wy., U.S.	B11	120
Glendon, Alta., Can.	C23	102
Gleneden Beach, Or., U.S.	F1	122
Glen Elder, Ks., U.S.	L9	118
Glen Flora, Tx., U.S.	J10	116
Glen Innes, Austl.	G9	70
Glen Lyon, Pa., U.S.	F10	108
Glenmora, La., U.S.	L4	114
Glenmorgan, Austl.	F8	70
Glennallen, Ak., U.S.	E22	100
Glenns Ferry, Id., U.S.	H10	122
Glennville, Ga., U.S.	H5	112
Glenoma, Wa., U.S.	D3	122
Glenormiston, Austl.	D3	70
Glenreagh, Austl.	H10	70
Glen Robertson, Ont., Can.	B12	108
Glen Rock, Pa., U.S.	H10	108
Glenrock, Wy., U.S.	B11	120
Glen Rose, Tx., U.S.	G9	116
Glens Falls, N.Y., U.S.	D13	108
Glenties, Ire.	G5	8
Glen Ullin, N.D., U.S.	E6	118
Glenville, Mn., U.S.	G2	110
Glenville, W.V., U.S.	I6	108
Glen White, W.V., U.S.	B5	112
Glenwood, Alta., Can.	H21	102
Glenwood, Newf., Can.	D19	106
Glenwood, Al., U.S.	K10	114
Glenwood, Ar., U.S.	H3	114
Glenwood, Ga., U.S.	G4	112
Glenwood, Ia., U.S.	J12	118
Glenwood, Mn., U.S.	F12	118
Glenwood, N.M., U.S.	K8	120
Glenwood, Ut., U.S.	F5	120
Glenwood, Va., U.S.	C7	112
Glenwood City, Wi., U.S.	E3	110
Glenwood Springs, Co., U.S.	E9	120
Glidden, Ia., U.S.	I13	118
Glidden, Wi., U.S.	D5	110
Glide, Or., U.S.	G2	122
Glinka, Russia	G15	22
Gliwice (Gleiwitz), Pol.	E18	10
Globe, Az., U.S.	K6	120
Gloggnitz, Aus.	H15	10
Głogów, Pol.	D16	10
Glória de Dourados, Braz.	G1	79
Glorieta, N.M., U.S.	I11	120
Glorieuses, Îles, is., Afr.	D9	58
Gloster, Ms., U.S.	K5	114
Gloucester, Austl.	H9	70
Gloucester, Eng., U.K.	J11	8

Name	Map Ref.	Page

H

Hana-Hira

Name — Map Ref. — Page

Hanahan, S.C., U.S. G6 112
Hanamaki, Japan H16 36
Hanapepe, Hi., U.S. p14 125a
Hanau, Ger. E8 10
Hanbury, stm., N.W. Ter., Can. D11 96
Hâncești, Mol. C12 20
Hanceville, B.C., Can. F11 102
Hanceville, Al., U.S. H10 114
Hancheng, China D9 30
Hancock, Md., U.S. H8 108
Hancock, Mi., U.S. C7 110
Hancock, Mn., U.S. F12 118
Hancock, N.Y., U.S. F11 108
Hancock, Wi., U.S. F6 110
Handa, Japan M11 36
Handa, Som. F11 56
Handan, China G2 32
Handsworth, Sask., Can. I11 104
Handub, Sud. H9 60
HaNegev (Negev Desert), reg., Isr. G3 50
Haney, B.C., Can. H12 102
Hanford, Ca., U.S. H6 124
Han'gang, China I2 32
Han-gang, stm., Asia F14 32
Hangchow see Hangzhou, China E9 34
Hanggin Houqi, China C8 30
Hanggin Qi, China D8 30
Hangö (Hanko), Fin. L18 6
Hangu, China D5 32
Hangu, Pak. D4 44
Hangzhou (Hangchow), China E9 34
Hangzhou Wan (Hangchow Bay), b., China E10 34
Hani, Tur. B6 48
Hanīsh, is., Yemen H3 47
Hanita, Isr. B4 50
Hanjiang, China J8 34
Hankey, S. Afr. I7 66
Hankinson, N.D., U.S. E11 118
Hanko see Hangö, Fin. D12 4
Hankow see Wuhan, China E3 34
Hanley, Sask., Can. G8 104
Hanmer, Ont., Can. D15 110
Hanna, Alta., Can. F23 102
Hanna, Ok., U.S. D11 116
Hanna, Wy., U.S. C10 120
Hanna City, Il., U.S. J6 110
Hannaford, N.D., U.S. D9 118
Hannah, N.D., U.S. C9 118
Hannah Bay, b., Ont., Can. F17 96
Hannibal, Mo., U.S. C5 114
Hannover, Ger. C9 10
Ha Noi, Viet. D8 40
Hanover, Ont., Can. F14 110
Hanover see Hannover, Ger. C9 10
Hanover, Il., U.S. H5 110
Hanover, In., U.S. D11 114
Hanover, Ks., U.S. L11 118
Hanover, N.H., U.S. D14 108
Hanover, N.M., U.S. L8 120
Hanover, Pa., U.S. H10 108
Hanover, Va., U.S. B9 112
Hansard, B.C., Can. C13 102
Hānsi, India F6 44
Hanska, Mn., U.S. G13 118
Hanson Lake, l., Sask., Can. D12 104
Hant's Harbour, Newf., Can. D20 106
Hantsport, N.S., Can. G9 106
Hantzsch, stm., N.W. Ter., Can. C18 96
Hanumāngarh, India F6 44
Hanušovice, Czech. E16 10
Hanwood, Austl. J7 70
Hanzhong, China E8 30
Hanzhuang, China I5 32
Haohekou, China G1 34
Hāora, India I13 44
Hapeville, Ga., U.S. F2 112
Happy, Tx., U.S. E5 116
Happy Camp, Ca., U.S. C2 124
Happy Jack, Az., U.S. J5 120
Happy Valley-Goose Bay, Newf., Can. F20 96
Hāpur, India F7 44
Haquira, Peru F5 82
Harad, Sau. Ar. B6 47
Harad, Jabal al-, mtn., Jord. I5 50
Harare (Salisbury), Zimb. A10 66
Harash, Bi'r al-, well, Libya E2 60
Harbin, China B12 30
Harbor, Or., U.S. H1 122
Harbor Beach, Mi., U.S. G13 110
Harbor Springs, Mi., U.S. E11 110
Harbour Breton, Newf., Can. E18 106
Harbour Buffett, Newf., Can. E19 106
Harbour Deep, Newf., Can. B17 106
Harbour Grace, Newf., Can. E20 106
Harbourville, N.S., Can. G9 106
Harcuvar Mountains, mts., Az., U.S. K3 120
Harda, India I7 44
Hardangerfjorden, Nor. K10 6
Hardeeville, S.C., U.S. G5 112
Harderwijk, Neth. D8 12
Hardesty, Ok., U.S. C5 116
Hardin, Il., U.S. C6 114
Hardin, Mt., U.S. E18 122
Harding, S. Afr. H9 66
Harding Lake, l., Man., Can. B16 104
Hardinsburg, Ky., U.S. E10 114
Hardisty, Alta., Can. E23 102
Hardisty Lake, l., N.W. Ter., Can. D9 96
Hardoi, India G9 44
Hardtner, Ks., U.S. N9 118
Hardwick, Ga., U.S. F3 112
Hardwick, Vt., U.S. C14 108
Hardwood Lake, l., Ont., Can. L5 114
Hardy, Ar., U.S. F5 114
Hardy, Ne., U.S. K10 118
Hardy Bay, b., N.W. Ter., Can. A9 96
Hare, Mount, mtn., Yukon, Can. C26 100
Hare Bay, Newf., Can. D19 106
Hare Bay, b., Newf., Can. A18 106
Hare Indian, stm., N.W. Ter., Can. C31 100
Harer, Eth. G9 56
Hareto, Eth. M9 60
Hargeysa, Som. G9 56
Harghita, co., Rom. C9 20
Hargrave, stm., Man., Can. D15 104
Hargrave Lake, l., Man., Can. D15 104
Har Hu, l., China D6 30
Hari, stm., Indon. F3 38
Haria, Spain n27 17b
Haridwār, India F8 44
Harihar, India E3 46
Haringvliet, strt., Neth. E5 12
Harīrūd (Tedžen), stm., Asia C16 48
Harkers Island, N.C., U.S. E10 112
Harlan, Ia., U.S. J12 118
Harlan, Ky., U.S. C3 112
Harlan County Lake, res., Ne., U.S. K8 118
Harlem, Fl., U.S. M6 112
Harlem, Ga., U.S. F4 112
Harlem, Mt., U.S. B17 122
Harlingen, Neth. B7 12
Harlingen, Tx., U.S. M9 116
Harlowton, Mt., U.S. D16 122
Harman, W.V., U.S. I7 108
Harmanli, Bul. H9 20
Harmony, In., U.S. C9 114
Harmony, Mn., U.S. G3 110
Harney Peak, mtn., S.D., U.S. H4 118
Härnösand, Swe. J15 6
Haro, Spain C9 16
Haro, Cabo, c., Mex. D4 90
Harper, Lib. I6 64
Harper, Ks., U.S. N9 118
Harper, Tx., U.S. I7 116
Harqin Qi (Jinshan), China B6 32
Harrān al-'Awāmīd, Syria B7 50
Harrell, Ar., U.S. I4 114
Harricana, stm., Can. F17 96
Harriman, Tn., U.S. D2 112
Harrington, De., U.S. I11 108
Harrington, Me., U.S. C19 108
Harrington, Wa., U.S. C7 122
Harris, Sask., Can. G7 104
Harris, Mn., U.S. E3 110
Harrisburg, Ar., U.S. G6 114
Harrisburg, Il., U.S. E8 114
Harrisburg, Ne., U.S. J4 118
Harrisburg, Or., U.S. F2 122
Harrisburg, Pa., U.S. G10 108
Harrismith, S. Afr. G9 66
Harrison, Ar., U.S. F3 114
Harrison, Id., U.S. C9 122
Harrison, Mi., U.S. F11 110
Harrison, Ne., U.S. I4 118
Harrison, Cape, c., Newf., Can. F21 96
Harrisonburg, La., U.S. K5 114
Harrisonburg, Va., U.S. I8 108
Harrison Islands, is., N.W. Ter., Can. C14 96
Harrison Lake, l., B.C., Can. H13 102
Harrisonville, Mo., U.S. D2 114
Harriston, Ont., Can. G15 110
Harriston, Ms., U.S. K5 114
Harrisville, Mi., U.S. F12 110
Harrisville, N.Y., U.S. C11 108
Harrisville, W.V., U.S. H5 108
Harrodsburg, Ky., U.S. E12 114
Harrogate, Eng., U.K. G12 8
Harrold, Tx., U.S. E7 116
Harrop Lake, l., Man., Can. F19 104
Harrow, Ont., Can. H13 110
Harrowsmith, Ont., Can. F19 110
Harry S. Truman Reservoir, res., Mo., U.S. D3 114
Harsīn, Iran D9 48
Hart, Mi., U.S. G9 110
Hart, Tx., U.S. E4 116
Hart, stm., Yukon, Can. D26 100
Hart, Lake, l., Austl. H2 70
Hartberg, Aus. H15 10
Hartford, Al., U.S. K11 114
Hartford, Ar., U.S. G2 114
Hartford, Ct., U.S. F14 108
Hartford, Ks., U.S. M12 118
Hartford, Ky., U.S. E10 114
Hartford, Mi., U.S. H9 110
Hartford, S.D., U.S. H11 118
Hartford, Wi., U.S. G7 110
Hartford City, In., U.S. B11 114
Hartington, Ne., U.S. I10 118
Hartland, N.B., Can. F6 106
Hartland, Me., U.S. C17 108
Hartlepool, Eng., U.K. G12 8
Hartley, Ia., U.S. H12 118
Hartley, Tx., U.S. D4 116
Hartley Bay, B.C., Can. D5 102
Hart Mountain, mtn., Man., Can. F13 104
Hartney, Man., Can. I14 104
Harts, stm., S. Afr. G7 66
Hartselle, Al., U.S. H10 114
Hartshorne, Ok., U.S. E11 116
Hartsville, S.C., U.S. E6 112
Hartsville, Tn., U.S. F10 114
Hartville, Mo., U.S. E4 114
Hartwell, Ga., U.S. E4 112
Hartwell Lake, res., U.S. E4 112
Harvard, Il., U.S. H7 110
Harvard, Ne., U.S. K9 118
Harvey, N.B., Can. G9 106
Harvey, Il., U.S. I8 110
Harvey, N.D., U.S. D8 118
Harwich, Eng., U.K. J15 8
Haryāna, state, India F7 44
Harz, mts., Ger. D10 10
Haṣā, Bi'r al-, well, Egypt J3 48
Ḥasan Kīādeh, Iran C10 48
Ḥāṣbānī, Nahr al-, stm., Asia B5 50
Hasenkamp, Arg. F9 80
Ḥashā', Jabal al-, mtn., Yemen H4 47
Hāsilpur, Pak. F5 44
Haskell, Ok., U.S. D11 116
Haskell, Tx., U.S. F7 116
Haskovo, Bul. H9 20
Hasperos Canyon, val., N.M., U.S. K11 120
Hassan, India F4 46
Hasselt, Bel. G7 12
Hassi Bel Guebbour, Alg. F14 62
Hassi el Ghella, Alg. J11 16
Hassi Mameche, Alg. J12 16
Hassi Messaoud, Alg. E13 62
Hassi Zehana, Alg. J11 16
Hässleholm, Swe. M13 6
Hastings, Ont., Can. F18 110
Hastings, N.Z. C6 72
Hastings, Eng., U.K. K14 8
Hastings, Fl., U.S. J5 112
Hastings, Mi., U.S. H10 110
Hastings, Mn., U.S. F3 110
Hastings, Ne., U.S. K9 118
Hasty, Co., U.S. M5 118
Haswell, Co., U.S. M4 118
Hatay, Tur. C4 48
Hatch, N.M., U.S. L9 120
Hatch, Ut., U.S. G4 120
Hatchet Lake, N.S., Can. H10 106
Hatchie, stm., U.S. G7 114
Hatfield, Ar., U.S. H2 114
Hatfield, Ma., U.S. E14 108
Hāthras, India G8 44
Ha Tien, Viet. I8 40
Ha Tinh, Viet. E8 40
Hato Mayor [del Rey], Dom. Rep. E10 94
Hatteras, N.C., U.S. D11 112
Hatteras, Cape, c., N.C., U.S. D11 112
Hatteras Island, i., N.C., U.S. D11 112
Hattiesburg, Ms., U.S. K7 114
Hatton, Al., U.S. H9 114
Hatton, N.D., U.S. D10 118
Hatvan, Hung. H19 10
Hat Yai, Thai. K6 40
Hatzic, B.C., Can. H12 102
Haugesund, Nor. L9 6
Hauge, Nor. L10 6
Haugsdorf, Aus. G16 10
Haultain, stm., Sask., Can. B8 104
Hauraki Gulf, b., N.Z. B5 72
Haut Atlas, mts., Mor. E7 62
Haute-Corse, dept., Fr. I24 15a
Haute-Garonne, dept., Fr. I8 14
Haute-Loire, dept., Fr. G10 14
Haute-Marne, dept., Fr. D12 14
Hauterive, Que., Can. C5 106
Hautes-Alpes, dept., Fr. H13 14
Haute-Saône, dept., Fr. E13 14
Haute-Savoie, dept., Fr. F13 14
Hautes Fagnes, mts., Eur. E6 10
Hautes-Pyrénées, dept., Fr. I7 14
Haute-Vienne, dept., Fr. G8 14
Haut-Folin, mtn., Fr. E11 14
Hautmont, Fr. B10 14
Haut-Rhin, dept., Fr. E14 14
Hauula, Hi., U.S. p16 125a
Havana see La Habana, Cuba C3 94
Havana, Ar., U.S. G3 114
Havana, Fl., U.S. I2 112
Havana, Il., U.S. B6 114
Havana, N.D., U.S. F10 118
Havasu, Lake, res., U.S. J2 120
Havelock, Ont., Can. F18 110
Havelock, N.C., U.S. E10 112
Haven, Ks., U.S. N10 118
Haverhill, Ma., U.S. E15 108
Hāveri, India E3 46
Haviland, Ks., U.S. N8 118
Havířov, Czech. F18 10
Havlíčkův Brod, Czech. F15 10
Havre, Mt., U.S. B16 122
Havre-Aubert, Que., Can. E12 106
Havre Aubert, Île du, i., Que., Can. E12 106
Havre aux Maisons, Île du, i., Que., Can. E12 106
Havre de Grace, Md., U.S. H10 108
Havre North, Mt., U.S. B16 122
Havre-Saint-Pierre, Que., Can. B10 106
Havsa, Tur. H10 20
Haw, stm., N.C., U.S. D7 112
Hawaii, state, U.S. q16 125a
Hawaii, i., Hi., U.S. r18 125a
Hawaiian Islands, is., Hi., U.S. q16 125a
Hawaiian Ridge F22 126
Hawaii Volcanoes National Park, Hi., U.S. r18 125a
Hawarden, Sask., Can. G8 104
Hawarden, Ia., U.S. I11 118
Hawea, Lake, l., N.Z. F2 72
Hawera, N.Z. C5 72
Hawesville, Ky., U.S. E10 114
Hawi, Hi., U.S. q18 125a
Hawick, Scot., U.K. F11 8
Hawke, Cape, c., Austl. I10 70
Hawke Bay, b., N.Z. C6 72
Hawker, Austl. H3 70
Hawkes, Mount, mtn., Ant. D1 73
Hawkesbury, Ont., Can. B12 108
Hawkesbury Island, i., B.C., Can. D5 102
Hawkins, Tx., U.S. G11 116
Hawkins, Wi., U.S. E5 110
Hawkinsville, Ga., U.S. G3 112
Hawk Junction, Ont., Can. B11 110
Hawk Lake, Ont., Can. I21 104
Hawksbill, mtn., Va., U.S. I8 108
Hawks Nest Point, c., Bah. B7 94
Hawley, Mn., U.S. E11 118
Hawley, Pa., U.S. F11 108
Hawthorne, Fl., U.S. J4 112
Hawthorne, Nv., U.S. F7 124
Hawwārah, Jord. C5 50
Hawzen, Eth. K10 60
Haxtun, Co., U.S. K5 118
Hay, Austl. J6 70
Hay, stm., Austl. D2 70
Hay, stm., Can. E9 96
Hay, stm., Wi., U.S. E4 110
Hay, Cape, c., N.W. Ter., Can. B10 96
Hay, Mount, mtn., N.A. G26 100
Hayange, Fr. C13 14
Haybān, Sud. L6 60
Hayden, Az., U.S. K6 120
Hayden, Co., U.S. D9 120
Haydenville, Oh., U.S. H4 108
Hayes, La., U.S. L4 114
Hayes, stm., Man., Can. B22 104
Hayes, stm., N.W. Ter., Can. C14 96
Hayes, Mount, mtn., Ak., U.S. E21 100
Hayes Center, Ne., U.S. K6 118
Hayesville, N.C., U.S. D3 112
Hayesville, Or., U.S. F3 122
Hayfield, Mn., U.S. G3 110
Hayfork, Ca., U.S. D2 124
Haykota, Erit. J9 60
Hay Lakes, Alta., Can. D21 102
Haymana, Tur. B2 48
Haynes, Ar., U.S. H6 114
Haynesville, La., U.S. J3 114
Hayneville, Al., U.S. J10 114
Hay River, N.W. Ter., Can. D9 96
Hays, Alta., Can. G23 102
Hays, Ks., U.S. M8 118
Hays, Mt., U.S. C17 122
Hay Springs, Ne., U.S. I5 118
Haystack Mountain, mtn., Nv., U.S. C10 124
Haysville, Ks., U.S. N10 118
Hayti, Mo., U.S. F7 114
Hayti, S.D., U.S. G10 118
Hayvoron, Ukr. A13 20
Hayward, Ca., U.S. G3 124
Hayward, Wi., U.S. D4 110
Haywood, Man., Can. I16 104
Hazard, Ky., U.S. B3 112
Hazārībāg, India I11 44
Hazebrouck, Fr. B9 14
Hazel, stm., Va., U.S. I9 108
Hazel Green, Wi., U.S. H5 110
Hazelton, B.C., Can. B7 102
Hazelton, N.D., U.S. H11 122
Hazelton, Pa., U.S. E7 118
Hazelton Mountains, mts., B.C., Can. C6 102
Hazelwood, N.C., U.S. D3 112
Hazen, Ar., U.S. H5 114
Hazen, N.D., U.S. D6 118
Hazlehurst, Ga., U.S. H4 112
Hazlehurst, Ms., U.S. K6 114
Hazlet, Sask., Can. H6 104
Hazleton, Ia., U.S. H4 110
Hazleton, Pa., U.S. G11 108
Hazor HaGelilit, Isr. C5 50
Head Bay d'Espoir, Newf., Can. E18 106
Headland, Al., U.S. K11 114
Headley, Mount, mtn., Mt., U.S. C10 122
Healdsburg, Ca., U.S. F3 124
Healdton, Ok., U.S. E9 116
Healesville, Austl. K6 70
Healy, Ak., U.S. E20 100
Healy, Ks., U.S. M7 118
Heany Junction, Zimb. C9 66
Heard Island, i., Ant. N11 126
Hearne, Tx., U.S. I10 116
Hearst, Ont., Can. G16 96
Hearst Island, i., Ant. B12 73
Heart, stm., Alta., Can. A17 102
Heart, stm., N.D., U.S. E6 118
Heart Lake, l., Alta., Can. B23 102
Heart Lake Indian Reserve, Alta., Can. B23 102
Heart's Content, Newf., Can. E20 106
Heath, stm., S.A. E7 82
Heath, Pointe, c., Que., Can. C12 106
Heathcote, Austl. K6 70
Heath Springs, S.C., U.S. E6 112
Heathsville, Va., U.S. B10 112
Heavener, Ok., U.S. H2 114
Hebbronville, Tx., U.S. L8 116
Hebei (Hopeh), prov., China D10 30
Heber, Az., U.S. J6 120
Heber, Ca., U.S. L10 124
Heber City, Ut., U.S. D5 120
Heber Springs, Ar., U.S. G4 114
Hebi, China H2 32
Hebrides, is., Scot., U.K. D6 4
Hebron, Newf., Can. E20 96
Hebron see Al-Khalīl, Isr. Occ. E4 50
Hebron, Il., U.S. H7 110
Hebron, In., U.S. A9 114
Hebron, Md., U.S. I11 108
Hebron, Ne., U.S. K10 118
Hebron, N.D., U.S. E5 118
Hebu, China H4 34
Hecate Strait, strt., B.C., Can. D3 102
Hecelchakán, Mex. G14 90
Hechi, China B10 40
Hechingen, Ger. G8 10
Hechuan, China E8 30
Hecla, Man., Can. G18 104
Hecla, S.D., U.S. F9 118
Hecla Island, i., Man., Can. G18 104
Hecla Provincial Park, Man., Can. G18 104
Hectanooga, N.S., Can. H7 106
Hector, Mn., U.S. G13 118
Hédé, Fr. D5 14
He Devil, mtn., Id., U.S. E9 122
Hedian, China C3 34
Hedley, B.C., Can. H14 102
Hedley, Tx., U.S. E6 116
Hedmark, co., Nor. K12 6
Hedrick, Ia., U.S. I3 110
Heerenveen, Neth. C8 12
Heerlen, Neth. G8 12
Ḥefa (Haifa), Isr. C4 50
Hefei, China D6 34
Heflin, Al., U.S. I11 114
Hegang, China B13 30
Heho, Mya. D4 40
Heichengzi, China A9 32
Heide, Ger. A9 10
Heidelberg, Ger. F8 10
Heidelberg, S. Afr. J5 66
Heidelberg, S. Afr. F9 66
Heidelberg, Ms., U.S. K8 114
Heidenheim, Ger. F10 10
Heidenreichstein, Aus. G15 10
Heilbron, S. Afr. F8 66
Heilbronn, Ger. F9 10
Heiligenstadt, Ger. D10 10
Heilin, China H6 32
Heilong (Amur), stm., Asia A12 30
Heilongjiang (Heilungkiang), prov., China B12 30
Heimaey, i., Ice. C3 6a
Heirnkut, Mya. H16 44
Heishan, China B10 32
Heishantou, China A13 32
Heisler, Alta., Can. E22 102
Hejian, China E4 32
Hekla, vol., Ice. C4 6a
Hekou, China C7 40
Hel, Pol. A18 10
Helen, Mount, mtn., Austl. C4 70
Helena, Ar., U.S. H6 114
Helena, Mt., U.S. D13 122
Helena, Ok., U.S. C8 116
Helensburgh, Scot., U.K. E9 8
Helenwood, Tn., U.S. C2 112
Helgoland, i., Ger. A7 10
Helgoländer Bucht, b., Ger. A8 10
Heliuji, China B5 34
Hellertown, Pa., U.S. G11 108
Hellín, Spain G10 16
Hell Point, c., N.S., Can. H9 106
Hells Canyon, val., U.S. E9 122
Hells Gate, val., B.C., Can. H13 102
Hell-Ville, Madag. n23 67b
Helmand, stm., Asia D1 44
Helmcken Falls, wtfl, B.C., Can. F14 102
Helmond, Neth. F8 12
Helmstedt, Ger. C11 10
Helper, Ut., U.S. E6 120
Helsingborg, Swe. M13 6
Helsingfors see Helsinki, Fin. K19 6
Helsingør (Elsinore), Den. M13 6
Helsinki (Helsingfors), Fin. K19 6
Helska, Mierzeja, spit, Pol. A18 10
Helvecia, Arg. F8 80
Hemau, Ger. F11 10
Hemel Hempstead, Eng., U.K. J13 8
Hemet, Ca., U.S. K9 124
Hemford, N.S., Can. H9 106
Hemingford, Ne., U.S. I4 118
Hemingway, S.C., U.S. F7 112
Hemphill, Tx., U.S. K3 114
Hempstead, Tx., U.S. I10 116
Hemujing, China F3 32
Henan (Honan), prov., China E9 30
Henderson, Arg. I8 80
Henderson, Ky., U.S. E9 114
Henderson, Mn., U.S. F2 110
Henderson, Ne., U.S. K10 118
Henderson, Nv., U.S. H11 124
Henderson, N.C., U.S. C8 112
Henderson, Tn., U.S. G8 114
Henderson, Tx., U.S. J2 114
Henderson Island, i., Pit. K27 126
Hendersonville, N.C., U.S. D4 112
Hendersonville, Tn., U.S. F10 114
Hendījān, Iran F10 48
Hendricks, Mn., U.S. G11 118
Hendricks, W.V., U.S. H7 108
Henefer, Ut., U.S. C5 120
Hengdaohe, China A11 32
Hengelo, Neth. D10 12
Henggang, China F4 34
Hengshan, China D8 30
Hengshan, China H1 34
Hengshui, China F3 32
Hengxian, China C10 40
Hengyang, China F9 30
Henlopen, Cape, c., De., U.S. I11 108
Hennaya, Alg. K10 16
Hennebont, Fr. E3 14
Hennef, Ger. E7 10
Henneman, S. Afr. F8 66
Hennepin, Il., U.S. I6 110
Hennessey, Ok., U.S. C9 116
Henniker, N.H., U.S. D15 108
Henning, Mn., U.S. E12 118
Henning, Tn., U.S. G7 114
Henri, Cap, c., Que., Can. C9 106
Henri-Chapelle (Hendrik-Kapelle), Bel. G8 12
Henrietta, N.Y., U.S. D9 108
Henrietta, N.C., U.S. D5 112
Henrietta, Tx., U.S. F8 116
Henrietta Maria, Cape, c., Ont., Can. E16 96
Henri Pittier, Parque Nacional, Ven. B9 84
Henry, Il., U.S. I6 110
Henry, S.D., U.S. G10 118
Henry, Cape, c., Va., U.S. C10 112
Henry, Mount, mtn., Mt., U.S. B10 122
Henryetta, Ok., U.S. D11 116
Henry Kater, Cape, c., N.W. Ter., Can. C19 96
Henrys Fork, stm., U.S. C6 120
Hensall, Ont., Can. G14 110
Hensley, Ar., U.S. H4 114
Hentiesbaai, Nmb. D2 66
Henty, Austl. J7 70
Henzada, Mya. F3 40
Hepburn, Sask., Can. F8 104
Hephzibah, Ga., U.S. F4 112
Heping, China K3 34
Heppenheim, Ger. F8 10
Heppner, Or., U.S. E6 122
Hepu (Lianzhou), China D10 40
Heqiao, China D8 34
Herāt, Afg. D17 48
Hérault, dept., Fr. I10 14
Herbert, Sask., Can. H7 104
Herbert, stm., Austl. B6 70
Herberton, Austl. A6 70
Herbignac, Fr. E4 14
Herb Lake, Man., Can. D15 104
Herblet Lake, l., Man., Can. D15 104
Herceg-Novi, Yugo. G2 20
Herculaneum, Mo., U.S. D6 114
Hércules, Mex. C8 90
Heredia, C.R. G10 92
Heredia, prov., C.R. G10 92
Hereford, Az., U.S. M6 120
Hereford, Tx., U.S. E4 116
Hereford and Worcester, co., Eng., U.K. I11 8
Herencia, Spain F8 16
Herentals, Bel. F6 12
Hereroland Oos, dept., Nmb. C5 66
Hereroland Wes, dept., Nmb. C4 66
Herford, Ger. C8 10
Hergla, Tun. M5 18
Herington, Ks., U.S. M11 118
Herisau, Switz. D11 13
Herkimer, N.Y., U.S. D12 108
Herleshausen, Ger. D10 10
Herlong, Ca., U.S. D5 124
Herman, Mn., U.S. F11 118
Herman, Ne., U.S. J11 118
Hermann, Mo., U.S. D5 114
Hermansville, Mi., U.S. E8 110
Hermanus, S. Afr. J4 66
Hermanville, Ms., U.S. K6 114
Hermiston, Or., U.S. E6 122
Hermitage, Newf., Can. E18 106
Hermitage, Ar., U.S. I4 114
Hermitage, Mo., U.S. E3 114
Hermitage Bay, b., Newf., Can. E17 106
Hermleigh, Tx., U.S. G6 116
Hermon, Mount see Shaykh, Jabal ash-, mtn., Asia B5 50
Hermosillo, Mex. C4 90
Hermoso, Cerro, mtn., Ec. H3 84
Hernád, stm., Eur. G21 10
Hernandarias, Para. C11 80
Hernando, Arg. G7 80
Hernando, Fl., U.S. K4 112
Hernando, Ms., U.S. H7 114
Herndon, Ks., U.S. L7 118
Herndon, Pa., U.S. G10 108
Heroica Zitácuaro, Mex. H9 90
Heron Island, i., Austl. D9 70
Heron Lake, Mn., U.S. H12 118
Herradura, Arg. D9 80
Herreid, S.D., U.S. F7 118
Herrera, Arg. E7 80
Herrera, prov., Pan. I14 92
Herrick Creek, stm., B.C., Can. C13 102
Herrin, Il., U.S. E7 114
Herring Cove, N.S., Can. H10 106
Herring Cove, Ak., U.S. I29 100
Herschel, Sask., Can. G6 104
Herschel Island, i., Yukon, Can. B25 100
Herscher, Il., U.S. I7 110
Hershey, Ne., U.S. J6 118
Hershey, Pa., U.S. G10 108
Herstal, Bel. G8 12
Hertford, N.C., U.S. C10 112
Hertfordshire, co., Eng., U.K. J13 8
Hervey Bay, b., Austl. E10 70
Herzberg, Ger. D13 10
Herzberg [am Harz], Ger. D10 10
Herzliyya, Isr. D3 50
Hesdin, Fr. B9 14
Heshangqiao, China A2 34
Heshi, China J7 34
Heshuijian, China E5 34
Hesperia, Mi., U.S. G9 110
Hesperus Mountain, mtn., Co., U.S. G8 120
Hess, stm., Yukon, Can. E28 100
Hessen, state, Ger. E9 10
Hesston, Ks., U.S. M10 118
Hetang, China I8 34
Hetch Hetchy Aqueduct, Ca., U.S. G4 124
Hetou, China K2 34
Hettinger, N.D., U.S. E5 118
Hettstedt, Ger. D11 10
Hetupu, China E5 34
Heuvelton, N.Y., U.S. C11 108
Heves, Hung. H20 10
Heves, co., Hung. H20 10
Hevron, Naḥal, val., Asia F3 50
Hexi, China K6 34
Hexian, China G9 30
Heyang, China H6 32
Heyburn, Id., U.S. H12 122
Heywood, Austl. L4 70
Heyworth, Il., U.S. B8 114
Heze (Caozhou), China H3 32
Hezhen, China F9 34
Hialeah, Fl., U.S. N6 112
Hiawassee, Ga., U.S. E3 112
Hiawatha, Ks., U.S. L12 118
Hiawatha, Ut., U.S. E5 120
Hibbing, Mn., U.S. C3 110
Hibbs, Point, c., Austl. N6 70
Hibernia Reef, rf., Austl. B4 68
Hickman, Ky., U.S. F7 114
Hickman, Ne., U.S. K11 118
Hickman's Harbour, Newf., Can. D20 106
Hickory, Ms., U.S. J7 114
Hickory, N.C., U.S. D5 112
Hickory Flat, Ms., U.S. H7 114
Hicks, Point, c., Austl. K8 70
Hickson Lake, l., Sask., Can. B10 104
Hicksville, Oh., U.S. F2 108
Hico, Tx., U.S. H8 116
Hidalgo, Mex. E10 90
Hidalgo, Mex. F8 90
Hidalgo, Mex. D10 90
Hidalgo, Mex. E9 90
Hidalgo, state, Mex. G10 90
Hidalgo del Parral, Mex. D7 90
Hida-sammyaku, mts., Japan K12 36
Hidrolândia, Braz. D4 79
Hidrolina, Braz. C4 79
Hieflau, Aus. H14 10
Hierro (Ferro), i., Spain p22 17b
Higashine, Japan I15 36
Higashiōsaka, Japan M10 36
Higbee, Mo., U.S. C4 114
Higgins, Tx., U.S. C6 116
Higginsville, Mo., U.S. C3 114
High Bar Indian Reserve, B.C., Can. F13 102
High Hill, stm., Can. B4 104
High Hill, stm., Man., Can. C20 104
High Hill Lake, l., Man., Can. C19 104
Highland, Ca., U.S. J8 124
Highland, Il., U.S. D7 114
Highland, In., U.S. A9 114
Highland, Ks., U.S. L12 118
Highland, prov., Scot., U.K. D8 8
Highland Home, Al., U.S. K10 114
Highland Park, Il., U.S. H8 110
Highland Park, Tx., U.S. G10 116
Highlands, N.J., U.S. G13 108
Highlands, N.C., U.S. D3 112
Highlands, Tx., U.S. J11 116
Highland Springs, Va., U.S. B9 112
Highmore, S.D., U.S. G8 118
High Point, N.C., U.S. D6 112
High Point, mtn., N.J., U.S. F12 108
High Prairie, Alta., Can. B18 102
High River, Alta., Can. G21 102
Highrock Indian Reserve, Man., Can. C14 104
Highrock Lake, l., Man., Can. C14 104
Highrock Lake, l., Sask., Can. A9 104
High Rock Lake, res., N.C., U.S. D6 112
High Springs, Fl., U.S. J4 112
Hightstown, N.J., U.S. G12 108
Highwood, Mt., U.S. C15 122
Highwood, stm., Alta., Can. G20 102
High Wycombe, Eng., U.K. J13 8
Higuera de Abuya, Mex. E6 90
Higuera de Zaragoza, Mex. E5 90
Higüero, Punta, c., P.R. E11 94
Higüey, Dom. Rep. E10 94
Higuito, stm., Hond. C6 92
Hiiumaa, i., Est. C5 22
Hikone, Japan L11 36
Hilbert, Wi., U.S. F7 110
Hilda, Alta., Can. H4 104
Hildburghausen, Ger. E10 10
Hildesheim, Ger. C9 10
Hildreth, Ne., U.S. K8 118
Hillaby, Mount, mtn., Barb. H15 94
Hill Bank, Belize I15 90
Hill City, Ks., U.S. L8 118
Hill City, Mn., U.S. D2 110
Hill City, S.D., U.S. H4 118
Hillcrest Center, Ca., U.S. I7 124
Hillcrest Mines, Alta., Can. H20 102
Hilli, Bngl. H13 44
Hilliard, Fl., U.S. I5 112
Hill Island Lake, l., N.W. Ter., Can. D11 96
Hillister, Tx., U.S. L2 114
Hillman, Mi., U.S. E12 110
Hills, Mn., U.S. H11 118
Hillsboro, Il., U.S. C7 114
Hillsboro, Ks., U.S. M10 118
Hillsboro, Mo., U.S. D6 114
Hillsboro, N.H., U.S. D15 108
Hillsboro, N.M., U.S. L9 120
Hillsboro, N.D., U.S. D10 118
Hillsboro, Oh., U.S. H3 108
Hillsboro, Or., U.S. E3 122
Hillsboro, Tx., U.S. G9 116
Hillsboro, Wi., U.S. G5 110
Hillsboro Canal, Fl., U.S. M6 112
Hillsborough, N.B., Can. G9 106
Hillsborough, N.C., U.S. C7 112
Hillsborough, stm., Fl., U.S. K4 112
Hillsborough, Cape, c., Austl. C8 70
Hillsborough Bay, b., P.E.I., Can. F10 106
Hillsdale, Mi., U.S. I11 110
Hillsdale Lake, res., Ks., U.S. M13 118
Hillston, Austl. I6 70
Hillsville, Va., U.S. C6 112
Hilo, Hi., U.S. r18 125a
Hilo Bay, b., Hi., U.S. r18 125a
Hilton, N.Y., U.S. D9 108
Hilton Head Island, i., S.C., U.S. G6 112
Hilversum, Neth. D7 12
Hima, Ky., U.S. B3 112
Himāchal Pradesh, state, India E7 44
Himalayas, mts., Asia F11 44
Himeji, Japan M9 36
Himi, Japan K11 36
Ḥimṣ (Homs), Syria D4 48
Hinche, Haiti E8 94
Hinchinbrook Entrance, strt., Ak., U.S. F21 100
Hinchinbrook Island, i., Austl. B7 70
Hinchinbrook Island, i., Ak., U.S. F21 100
Hinckley, Il., U.S. I7 110
Hinckley, Mn., U.S. D3 110
Hinckley, Ut., U.S. E4 120
Hindaun, India G7 44
Hindman, Ky., U.S. B4 112
Hindmarsh, Lake, l., Austl. K4 70
Hinds Lake, l., Newf., Can. D17 106
Hindu Kush, mts., Asia B4 44
Hindupur, India F4 46
Hines, Or., U.S. G6 122
Hines Creek, Alta., Can. A16 102
Hines Creek, stm., Alta., Can. A16 102
Hinesville, Ga., U.S. H5 112
Hinganghāt, India B5 46
Hingham, Ma., U.S. E16 108
Hingol, stm., Pak. H1 44
Hingoli, India C4 46
Hınıs, Tur. B6 48
Hinnøya, i., Nor. G14 6
Hinojosa del Duque, Spain G6 16
Hinsdale, Mt., U.S. B18 122
Hinsdale, N.H., U.S. E14 108
Hinterrhein, stm., Switz. E11 13
Hinton, Alta., Can. D17 102
Hinton, Ok., U.S. D8 116
Hinton, W.V., U.S. B6 112
Hipólito, Mex. E9 90
Hipólito Yrigoyen, Arg. G5 80
Hirado, Japan N4 36
Hīrākud Reservoir, res., India B7 46
Hiram, Me., U.S. D16 108
Hiratsuka, Japan L14 36

Name — Map Ref. — Page

Izbica, Pol. A17 10
Izd'oškovo, Russia F16 22
Izegem, Bel. G3 12
Īzeh, Iran F10 48
Iževsk, Russia F8 26
Izkī, Oman C10 47
Ižma, stm., Russia E8 26
Izmalkovo, Russia I20 22
Izmayil, Ukr. H3 26
İzmir (Smyrna), Tur. K11 20
İzmit, Tur. G13 4
Iznajar, Embalse de, res., Spain H7 16
Izoplit, Russia E19 22
Izopo, Punta, c., Hond. B7 92
Izozog, Bañados del, sw., Bol. H10 82
Izra', Syria C6 50
Izsák, Hung. I19 10
Iztaccíhuatl, Volcán, vol., Mex. H10 90
Iztaccíhuatl y Popocatéptl, Parques Nacionales, Mex. H10 90
Iztapa, Guat. D4 92
Izucar de Matamoros, Mex. H10 90
Izuhara, Japan M4 36
Izumi, Japan O5 36
Izumi, Japan M10 36
Izumi, Japan I15 36
Izumo, Japan L7 36
Izu-shotō, is., Japan E15 30
Izvestij CIK, ostrova, is., Russia B14 26
Izyum, Ukr. H5 26

J

Jaba, Eth. N8 60
Jabal al-Awliyā', Sud. J7 60
Jabalpur, India I8 44
Jabālyah, Isr. Occ. E2 50
Jabiru, Austl. B6 68
Jabjabah, Wādī, val., Afr. G7 60
Jablah, Syria D3 48
Jablonec nad Nisou, Czech. E15 10
Jabłonka, Pol. F19 10
Jablonovyj chrebet, mts., Russia G14 28
Jaboatão, Braz. E11 76
Jaborandi, Braz. F4 79
Jaboticabal, Braz. F4 79
Jabung, Tanjung, c., Indon. O8 40
Jaca, Spain C11 16
Jacala, Mex. G10 90
Jacaleapa, Hond. C8 92
Jacaltenango, Guat. B3 92
Jacaraci, Braz. C7 79
Jacaré, stm., Braz. B8 79
Jacaré, stm., Braz. B10 82
Jacareí, Braz. G6 79
Jacarezinho, Braz. G4 79
Jaceel, val., Som. F11 56
Jáchal, stm., Arg. F4 80
Jachroma, Russia E20 22
Jaciara, Braz. C1 79
Jacinto, Braz. D8 79
Jacinto Aráuz, Arg. J7 80
Jacinto City, Tx., U.S. J11 116
Jacinto Machado, Braz. E14 80
Jaciparaná, Braz. C9 82
Jaciparaná, stm., Braz. D9 82
Jackfish Lake, l., Sask., Can. E6 104
Jackhead Harbour, Man., Can. G17 104
Jackman, Me., U.S. B16 108
Jack Mountain, mtn., Wa., U.S. B5 122
Jackpot, Nv., U.S. C11 124
Jacksboro, Tn., U.S. C2 112
Jacksboro, Tx., U.S. F8 116
Jacks Fork, stm., Mo., U.S. E5 114
Jackson, Al., U.S. K9 114
Jackson, Ca., U.S. F5 124
Jackson, Ga., U.S. F3 112
Jackson, Ky., U.S. B3 112
Jackson, La., U.S. L5 114
Jackson, Mi., U.S. H11 110
Jackson, Mn., U.S. H13 118
Jackson, Ms., U.S. J6 114
Jackson, Mo., U.S. E7 114
Jackson, N.C., U.S. C9 112
Jackson, Oh., U.S. H4 108
Jackson, S.C., U.S. F5 112
Jackson, Tn., U.S. G8 114
Jackson, Wy., U.S. A6 120
Jackson, Mount, mtn., Ant. C12 73
Jackson Center, Oh., U.S. G2 108
Jackson Creek, stm., Can. I13 104
Jackson Lake, l., Wy., U.S. G15 122
Jackson's Arm, Newf., Can. C17 106
Jacksonville, Al., U.S. I11 114
Jacksonville, Ar., U.S. H4 114
Jacksonville, Fl., U.S. I5 112
Jacksonville, Il., U.S. C6 114
Jacksonville, N.C., U.S. E9 112
Jacksonville, Or., U.S. H3 122
Jacksonville, Tx., U.S. H11 116
Jacksonville Beach, Fl., U.S. I5 112
Jacmel, Haiti E8 94
Jaco, Mex. D7 90
Jacobābād, Pak. F3 44
Jacobina, Braz. F10 76
Jacobsdal, S. Afr. G7 66
Jacques, Lac à, l., N.W. Ter., Can. C31 100
Jacques-Cartier, Détroit de, strt., Que., Can. C10 106
Jacques-Cartier, Mont, mtn., Que., Can. D8 106
Jacquet River, N.B., Can. E7 106
Jacqueville, C. Iv. I7 64
Jacuba, stm., Braz. E2 79
Jacuí, stm., Braz. F12 80
Jacuípe, stm., Braz. B9 79
Jacumba, Ca., U.S. L9 124
Jacupiranga, Braz. C14 80
Jaén, Peru A2 82
Jaén, Spain H8 16
Jāfarābād, India B1 46
Jaffa, Cape, c., Austl. K3 70
Jaffa, Tel Aviv- see Tel Aviv-Yafo, Isr. D3 50
Jaffna, Sri L. H6 46
Jaffrey, N.H., U.S. E14 108
Jafr, Qā' al-, depr., Jord. H6 50
Jagādhri, India E7 44
Jagdalpur, India C7 46
Jagersfontein, S. Afr. G7 66
Jagodnoje, Russia E21 28
Jagraon, India E6 44
Jagtiāl, India C5 46
Jaguaquara, Braz. B9 79
Jaguarão, Braz. G12 80
Jaguarão (Yaguarón), stm., S.A. G12 80
Jaguari, Braz. E11 80
Jaguariaíva, Braz. C14 80
Jaguaribe, stm., Braz. E11 76
Jaguaripe, Braz. B9 79
Jaguaruna, Braz. E14 80
Jagüé, Arg. E4 80
Jagüey Grande, Cuba C4 94
Jahānābād, India H11 44
Jahrom, Iran G12 48
Jailolo, Indon. E8 38
Jaipur, India G6 44
Jaisalmer, India G4 44
Jaja, Russia F15 26
Jājapur, India J12 44
Jajce, Bos. E12 18
Jakarta, Indon. j13 39a
Jake Creek Mountain, mtn., Nv., U.S. C9 124
Jakobstad (Pietarsaari), Fin. J18 6
Jakša, Russia E9 26
Jakutija, state, Russia D18 28
Jakutsk, Russia E17 28
Jal, N.M., U.S. G3 116
Jalālābād, Afg. C4 44
Jalāmīd, Sau. Ar. B10 60
Jalán, stm., Hond. C8 92
Jalandhar, India E6 44
Jalapa, Guat. C5 92
Jalapa, Nic. D8 92
Jalapa, dept., Guat. C5 92
Jālgaon, India J6 44
Jalisco, state, Mex. G7 90
Jālna, India C3 46
Jālor, India H5 44
Jalostotitlán, Mex. G8 90
Jalpa, Mex. G8 90
Jalpāiguri, India G13 44
Jalpan, Mex. G10 90
Jaltepec, stm., Mex. I12 90
Jalūlā', Iraq D8 48
Jalutorovsk, Russia F11 26
Jamaame, Som. A8 58
Jamaica, ctry., N.A. E6 94
Jamaica Channel, strt., N.A. E7 94
Jamal, poluostrov, pen., Russia C12 26
Jamalo-Neneckij, state, Russia D12 26
Jamālpur, Bngl. H13 44
Jamālpur, India H12 44
Jamantau, gora, mtn., Russia G9 26
Jamanxim, stm., Braz. A13 82
Jamari, stm., Braz. C10 82
Jamarovka, Russia G14 28
Jambelí, Canal de, strt., Ec. I2 84
Jambi, Indon. F3 38
Jambol, Bul. G10 20
James, stm., Alta., Can. F20 102
James, stm., U.S. H10 118
James, stm., Mo., U.S. E3 114
James, stm., Va., U.S. B9 112
James Bay, b., Can. F16 96
James City, N.C., U.S. D9 112
James Craik, Arg. G7 80
James Island, S.C., U.S. G7 112
Jamesport, Mo., U.S. C3 114
James Ross, Cape, c., N.W. Ter., Can. B10 96
James Ross Strait, strt., N.W. Ter., Can. C13 96
James Smith Indian Reserve, Sask., Can. E10 104
Jamestown, Austl. I3 70
Jamestown, S. Afr. H8 66
Jamestown, Ca., U.S. G5 124
Jamestown, Ks., U.S. L10 118
Jamestown, Ky., U.S. F11 114
Jamestown, N.Y., U.S. E7 108
Jamestown, N.C., U.S. D7 112
Jamestown, N.D., U.S. E9 118
Jamestown, Oh., U.S. H3 108
Jamestown, Tn., U.S. F12 114
Jamestown Reservoir, res., N.D., U.S. D9 118
Jaminauá, stm., Braz. C6 82
Jamkhandi, India D3 46
Jamm, Russia C11 22
Jammu, India D6 44
Jammu and Kashmīr, dep., Asia C10 42
Jamnagar, India I4 44
Jamsah, Egypt D7 60
Jamshedpur, India I12 44
Jamsk, Russia F22 28
Jämtlands Län, co., Swe. J13 6
Jamūi, India H12 44
Jamuna, stm., Bngl. H13 44
Jamundí, Col. F4 84
Jana, stm., Russia C19 28
Janauacá, Lago, l., Braz. I12 84
Janaúba, Braz. C7 79
Janaucu, Ilha, i., Braz. C8 76
Jand, Pak. D5 44
Jandaia, Braz. D3 79
Jandaia do Sul, Braz. G3 79
Jandaq, Iran D13 48
Jandiāla, India E6 44
Jandiatuba, stm., Braz. J8 84
Janeiro, Rio de, stm., Braz. A6 79
Janesville, Ca., U.S. D5 124
Janesville, Mn., U.S. F2 110
Janesville, Wi., U.S. H6 110
Jangijul', Uzb. I11 26
Jangīpur, India H13 44
Janīn, Isr. Occ. D4 50
Janjina, Madag. r21 67b
Jan Kempdorp (Andalusia), S. Afr. F7 66
Jan Lake, l., Sask., Can. D12 104
Jan Mayen, i., Sval. B19 86
Janos, Mex. B5 90
Jánoshalma, Hung. I19 10
Jánosháza, Hung. H17 10
Janoviči, Bela. F13 22
Jansen, Sask., Can. G10 104
Janskij zaliv, b., Russia C19 28
Jantarnyj, Russia G2 22
Januária, Braz. C6 79
Janzé, Fr. E5 14
Jaora, India I6 44
Japan (Nihon), ctry., Asia D14 30
Japan, Sea of (Nihon-kai), Asia K7 36
Japim, Braz. B5 82
Japurá, Braz. H9 84
Japurá (Caquetá), stm., S.A. H8 84
Jaqué, Pan. D3 84
Jaquí, Peru F4 82
Jarābulus, Syria C5 48
Jarad, Sau. Ar. E2 47
Jaraguá, Braz. C4 79
Jaraguá do Sul, Braz. D14 80
Jaraiz de la Vera, Spain E6 16
Jarales, N.M., U.S. J10 120
Jarama, stm., Spain E8 16
Jaramānah, Syria B6 50
Jaransk, Russia F7 26
Jarash, Jord. D5 50
Jarbidge, stm., U.S. H10 122
Jarcevo, Russia F15 22
Jardim, Braz. I13 82
Jardín América, Arg. D11 80
Jardine River National Park, Austl. B8 68
Jardines de la Reina, Archipiélago de los, is., Cuba D5 94
Jardinópolis, Braz. F5 79
Jaredi, Nig. E12 64
Jarensk, Russia E7 26
Jargeau, Fr. E9 14
Jari, stm., Braz. A10 82
Jari, Lago, l., Braz. J11 84
Jaridih, India I12 44
Jarnac, Fr. G6 14
Jarocin, Pol. D17 10
Jaroměř, Czech. E15 10
Jaroslavl', Russia D22 22
Jarosław, Pol. E22 10
Jarratt, Va., U.S. C9 112
Jarreau, La., U.S. L5 114
Jaru, Braz. D10 82
Jaru, stm., Braz. D10 82
Järva-Jaani, Est. B8 22
Järvenpää, Fin. K19 6
Jarvie, Alta., Can. C21 102
Jarvis, Ont., Can. H15 110
Jarvisburg, N.C., U.S. C11 112
Jarvis Island, i., Oc. I23 126
Jaša Tomić, Yugo. D4 20
Jasikan, Ghana H10 64
Jāsk, Iran I14 48
Jasło, Pol. F21 10
Jasnogorsk, Russia G20 22
Jason Islands, is., Falk. Is. G4 78
Jasonville, In., U.S. C9 114
Jasper, Alta., Can. E16 102
Jasper, Al., U.S. I9 114
Jasper, Ar., U.S. F3 114
Jasper, Fl., U.S. I4 112
Jasper, Ga., U.S. E2 112
Jasper, In., U.S. D10 114
Jasper, Mn., U.S. H11 118
Jasper, Mo., U.S. E2 114
Jasper, Tn., U.S. G11 114
Jasper, Tx., U.S. L3 114
Jasper Lake, l., Alta., Can. D16 102
Jasper National Park, Alta., Can. E17 102
Jászapáti, Hung. H20 10
Jászberény, Hung. H19 10
Jász-Nagykun-Szolnok, co., Hung. H20 10
Jataí, Braz. D3 79
Jatapu, stm., Braz. H13 84
Jataté, stm., Mex. I14 90
Jatni, India J11 44
Jatobá, stm., Braz. B1 79
Jaú, Braz. G4 79
Jaú, stm., Braz. H12 84
Jauaperi, stm., Braz. H12 84
Jauja, Peru D4 82
Jaungulbene, Lat. D9 22
Jaunjelgava, Lat. E8 22
Jaunpiebalga, Lat. D9 22
Jaunpur, India H10 44
Jaupaci, Braz. D3 79
Jauquara, stm., Braz. F13 82
Jauru, stm., Braz. E1 79
Jauru, stm., Braz. G13 82
Java, S.D., U.S. F8 118
Java see Jawa, i., Indon. j15 39a
Javari (Yavarí), stm., S.A. D4 76
Javas, Russia G25 22
Java Sea see Jawa, Laut, Indon. G5 38
Java Trench J11 24
Jawa (Java), i., Indon. j15 39a
Jawa, Laut (Java Sea), Indon. G5 38
Jawbar, Syria A6 50
Jawor, Pol. D16 10
Jaworzno, Pol. E19 10
Jay, Fl., U.S. L9 114
Jay, Ok., U.S. C12 116
Jaya, Puncak, mtn., Indon. F10 38
Jayanca, Peru B2 82
Jayapura (Sukarnapura), Indon. F11 38
Jayb, Wādī al- (Ha'Arava), val., Asia H4 50
Jaynes, Az., U.S. L5 120
Jaypur, India C7 46
Jayton, Tx., U.S. F6 116
Jaželbicy, Russia C15 22
Jeanerette, La., U.S. M5 114
Jebba, Nig. G12 64
Jebeniana, Tun. C16 62
Jeberos, Peru A3 82
Jechegnadzor, Arm. B8 48
Jeddore Lake, res., Newf., Can. D18 106
Jędrzejów, Pol. E20 10
Jefawa, Sud. L2 60
Jeffara (Al-Jifārah), pl., Afr. D16 62
Jeffers, Mn., U.S. G12 118
Jefferson, Ga., U.S. E3 112
Jefferson, Ia., U.S. I13 118
Jefferson, N.C., U.S. C5 112
Jefferson, Oh., U.S. F6 108
Jefferson, Or., U.S. F2 122
Jefferson, S.C., U.S. E6 112
Jefferson, S.D., U.S. I11 118
Jefferson, Tx., U.S. J2 114
Jefferson, Wi., U.S. G7 110
Jefferson, stm., Mt., U.S. E13 122
Jefferson, Mount, mtn., U.S. F14 122
Jefferson, Mount, mtn., Nv., U.S. F9 124
Jefferson, Mount, mtn., Or., U.S. F4 122
Jefferson City, Mo., U.S. D4 114
Jefferson City, Tn., U.S. C3 112
Jeffersonton, Va., U.S. I9 108
Jeffersontown, Ky., U.S. D11 114
Jeffersonville, Ga., U.S. G3 112
Jeffersonville, In., U.S. D11 114
Jeffersonville, Oh., U.S. H3 108
Jeffrey City, Wy., U.S. B9 120
Jefimovskij, Russia L24 6
Jefremov, Russia G5 26
Jega, Nig. E12 64
Jegenstorf, Switz. D8 13
Jegorjevsk, Russia F22 22
Jejsk, Russia H5 26
Jēkabpils, Lat. E8 22
Jekaterinburg, Russia F10 26
Jekateriny, proliv, strt., Russia I21 28
Jekimoviči, Russia G16 22
Jekyll Island, i., Ga., U.S. H5 112
Jelabuga, Russia F8 26
Jelancy, Russia G13 28
Jel'cy, Russia E16 22
Jelec, Russia I21 22
Jelenia Góra (Hirschberg), Pol. E15 10
Jelenskij, Russia H18 22
Jelgava, Lat. E6 22
Jelizarovo, Russia C27 22
Jelizavety, mys, c., Russia G20 28
Jelizovo, Bela. H12 22
Jellico, Tn., U.S. C2 112
Jelm Mountain, mtn., Wy., U.S. C11 120
Jel'n'a, Russia G16 22
Jelnat', Russia D25 22
Jeloguj, stm., Russia E15 26
Jelšava, Slov. G20 10
Jemanželinsk, Russia G10 26
Jember, Indon. G5 38
Jemca, Russia J27 6
Jemez, stm., N.M., U.S. I10 120
Jemez Springs, N.M., U.S. I10 120
Jemmal, Tun. N5 18
Jena, Ger. E11 10
Jena, La., U.S. K4 114
Jenašimskij Polkan, gora, mtn., Russia F16 26
Jenbach, Aus. H11 10
Jendouba (Souk el Arba), Tun. M3 18
Jenisej (Yenisey), stm., Russia D15 26
Jenisejsk, Russia F10 28
Jenisejskij kr'až, mts., Russia F16 26
Jenisejskij zaliv, b., Russia C8 28
Jenkins, Ky., U.S. B4 112
Jenkinsville, S.C., U.S. E5 112
Jenkintown, Pa., U.S. G11 108
Jenks, Ok., U.S. C11 116
Jennersdorf, Aus. I16 10
Jennings, Fl., U.S. I3 112
Jennings, La., U.S. L4 114
Jenpeg Dam, Man., Can. D16 104
Jensen, Ut., U.S. D7 120
Jensen Beach, Fl., U.S. L6 112
Jens Munk Island, i., N.W. Ter., Can. C17 96
Jeparit, Austl. K4 70
Jepelacio, Peru B3 82
Jepifan', Russia H21 22
Jequeri, Braz. F7 79
Jequetepeque, stm., Peru B2 82
Jequié, Braz. B8 79
Jequitaí, Braz. D6 79
Jequitinhonha, Braz. D8 79
Jequitinhonha, stm., Braz. D9 79
Jerada, Mor. C9 62
Jeradou, Tun. M5 18
Jerba, Île de, i., Tun. D16 62
Jerécuaro, Mex. G9 90
Jérémie, Haiti E7 94
Jeremoabo, Braz. F11 76
Jerevan, Arm. I6 26
Jerez de García Salinas, Mex. F8 90
Jerez de la Frontera, Spain I5 16
Jerez de los Caballeros, Spain G5 16
Jergeni, hills, Russia H6 26
Jericho see Arīḥā, Isr. Occ. E4 50
Jericó, Col. E5 84
Jerid, Chott, sw., Tun. D15 62
Jerilderie, Austl. J6 70
Jerimoth Hill, hill, R.I., U.S. F15 108
Jermiš', Russia G25 22
Jermolajevo (Kumertau), Russia G9 26
Jermolino, Russia F19 22
Jeroaquara, Braz. C3 79
Jerofej Pavlovič, Russia G16 28
Jerome, Az., U.S. J4 120
Jerome, Id., U.S. H11 122
Jersey, dep., Eur. F7 4
Jersey City, N.J., U.S. G12 108
Jersey Mountain, mtn., Id., U.S. E10 122
Jersey Shore, Pa., U.S. F9 108
Jerseyville, Il., U.S. C6 114
Jeršov, Russia G7 26
Jerusalem see Yerushalayim, Isr. E4 50
Jervis, Cape, c., Austl. J3 70
Jervis Bay, b., Austl. J9 70
Jervis Inlet, b., B.C., Can. H10 102
Jesenice, Czech. E13 10
Jesi, Italy F8 18
Jesil', Kaz. G11 26
Jessentuki, Russia I6 26
Jessore, Bngl. I13 44
Jessup, Pa., U.S. F11 108
Jesup, Ga., U.S. H5 112
Jesup, Ia., U.S. H3 110
Jesús, Para. D11 80
Jesús Carranza, Mex. I12 90
Jesús de Otoro, Hond. C7 92
Jesús María, Arg. F6 80
Jesús María, Mex. E6 90
Jesús María, stm., Mex. F7 90
Jesús Menéndez, Cuba D6 94
Jet, Ok., U.S. C8 116
Jetmore, Ks., U.S. M8 118
Jetpur, India J4 44
Jette, Bel. G5 12
Jeumont, Fr. B11 14
Jeune Landing, B.C., Can. G7 102
Jever, Ger. B7 10
Jevrej, state, Russia H18 28
Jewell, Ia., U.S. H2 110
Jewell, Ks., U.S. L9 118
Jewell Ridge, Va., U.S. B5 112
Jewett, Il., U.S. C8 114
Jewett, Tx., U.S. H10 116
Jewett City, Ct., U.S. F15 108
Jewett Lake, l., Sask., Can. B10 104
Jezerce, mtn., Alb. G3 20
Jezerišče, Bela. F12 22
Jeziorany, Pol. B20 10
Jhābua, India I6 44
Jhālāwār, India H7 44
Jhal Jhao, Pak. G1 44
Jhang Sadar, Pak. E5 44
Jhānsi, India H8 44
Jharia, India I12 44
Jhārsuguda, India B8 46
Jhelum, Pak. D5 44
Jhelum, stm., Asia E5 44
Jhok Rind, Pak. E4 44
Jhunjhunūn, India F6 44
Jiaban, China B9 40
Jiading, China D10 34
Jiāganj, India H13 44
Jiakou, China E8 34
Jiali, China E5 30
Jialing, stm., China E8 30
Jialou, China C2 34
Jiamusi, China B13 30
Ji'an, China H3 34
Jianchang, China B12 32
Jianchuan, China A5 40
Jiangbeixu, China I4 34
Jiangbianzhai, China C6 40
Jiangcun, China G6 34
Jiangdihe, China B6 40
Jiangduo, China C9 34
Jianggezhuang, China D7 32
Jiangji, China C4 34
Jiangjin, China F8 30
Jiangkou, China G9 30
Jiangkou, China H7 34
Jiangkouji, China C5 34
Jiangliadian, China A5 32
Jiangmen, China M2 34
Jiangsu (Kiangsu), prov., China E10 30
Jiangtun, China B10 32
Jiangxi (Kiangsi), prov., China F10 30
Jiangxiang, China C6 34
Jiangyin, China D9 34
Jiangzhasiji, China E13 44
Jianli, China F1 34
Jianning, China I5 34
Jian'ou, China H7 34
Jianshan, China F9 34
Jianshui, China C7 40
Jiantouji, China I5 32
Jiaohe, China C12 30
Jiaomei, China K6 34
Jiaoshanhe, China F1 34
Jiaoxian, China G7 32
Jiaozuo, China D9 30
Jiashan, China C7 34
Jiashun Hu, l., China C12 44
Jiawang, China A6 34
Jiaxian, China B2 34
Jiaxing, China E9 34
Jiayu, China F2 34
Jiazi, China M5 34
Jibiya, Nig. E13 64
Jiboa, stm., El Sal. D5 92
Jicarón, Isla, i., Pan. D2 84
Jicatuyo, stm., Hond. C6 92
Jiddah (Jeddah), Sau. Ar. D1 47
Jidingxilin, China D15 44
Jiedong, China I2 34
Jiehe, China H5 32
Jieji, China B7 34
Jiepai, China E8 34
Jiesheng, China M4 34
Jieshou, China B4 34
Jieshou, China B8 34
Jieyang, China L5 34
Jieznas, Lith. G7 22
Jigongzhen, China A4 34
Jiguaní, Cuba D6 94
Jiguanshan, China A12 32
Jigüey, Bahía de, b., Cuba C5 94
Jihlava, Czech. F15 10
Jijel, Alg. B13 62
Jijiadianzi, China H6 32
Jikawo, Eth. M7 60
Jikawo, stm., Afr. M8 60
Jilib, Som. A8 58
Jili Hu, l., China B4 30
Jilin, China C12 30
Jilin (Kirin), prov., China C12 30
Jill, Kediet ej, mtn., Maur. I4 62
Jima, Eth. N9 60
Jimbolia, Rom. D4 20
Jiménez, Mex. D7 90
Jiménez, Mex. C9 90
Jiménez del Téul, Mex. F7 90
Jimo, China G8 32
Jim Thorpe, Pa., U.S. G11 108
Jin (Gam), stm., Asia C8 40
Jināḥ, Egypt E6 60
Jinan (Tsinan), China G4 32
Jinbang, China J7 34
Jincheng, China D9 30
Jīnd, India F7 44
Jindřichův Hradec, Czech. F15 10
Jingangtou, China H2 34
Jingcheng, China K6 34
Jingdezhen (Kingtechen), China F6 34
Jinggang, China G1 34
Jinggangshan (Ciping), China I3 34
Jinghai, China E4 32
Jinghaiwei, China G10 32
Jinghong, China C6 40
Jingning, China H8 34
Jingoutun, China B5 32
Jingxi, China C9 40
Jingxian, China F4 32
Jingyu, China A14 32
Jingzhi, China G7 32
Jinhua, China F8 34
Jining, China C9 30
Jining, China H4 32
Jinja, Ug. A6 58
Jinjiang, China A6 40
Jinjing, China G2 34
Jinkeng, China H6 34
Jinkou, China G8 32
Jinlingzhen, China G6 32
Jinning, China B7 40
Jinotega, Nic. D8 92
Jinotega, dept., Nic. D9 92
Jinotepe, Nic. F8 92
Jinping, China A10 40
Jinrui, China H3 34
Jinsha, stm., China F6 30
Jinshan, China E10 34
Jinshi, China F9 30
Jintian, China H3 34
Jinxi, China C8 32
Jinxian, China D9 32
Jinyun, China G9 34
Jinzhaizhen, China D4 34
Jinzhou (Chinchou), China B9 32
Ji-Paraná, Braz. D11 82
Jipijapa, Ec. H2 84
Jiquilisco, El Sal. D6 92
Jiquilisco, Bahía de, b., El Sal. D6 92
Jiquiriçá, stm., Braz. B8 79
Jirāfī, Wādī al- (Naḥal Paran), val. I3 50
Jirbān, Sud. L6 60
Jirjā, Egypt D6 60
Jirkov, Czech. E13 10
Jīroft, Iran G14 48
Jisr ash-Shughūr, Syria D4 48
Jitan, China K4 34
Jitaúna, Braz. C9 79
Jiu, stm., Rom. F7 20
Jiubao, China J4 34
Jiucheng, China E5 32
Jiuguan, China F9 32
Jiuhu, China F5 32
Jiuhuaxian, China L2 34
Jiujiang, China F4 34
Jiukou, China E1 34
Jiulian Shan, mts., China K3 34
Jiuling Shan, mts., China G3 34
Jiulong, China K1 34
Jiumianyang, China E2 34
Jiuningyang, China J6 34
Jiuquan, China D6 30
Jiushangshui, China B3 34
Jiutai, China C12 30
Jiuxian, China B2 34
Jiuxiangcheng, China B3 34
Jixi, China B13 30
Jixian, China H2 32
Jixian, China C5 32
Jixingji, China C5 34
Jiyang, China G5 32
Jīzān, Sau. Ar. F3 47
Joaçaba, Braz. D13 80
Joaíma, Braz. D8 79
Joanna, S.C., U.S. E5 112
João Neiva, Braz. E8 79
João Pessoa, Braz. E12 76
João Pinheiro, Braz. D5 79
Joaquim Távora, Braz. G4 79
Joaquin, Tx., U.S. K2 114
Joaquín V. González, Arg. C6 80
Job Peak, mtn., Nv., U.S. E7 124
Jocolí, Arg. G4 80
Jocón, Hond. B8 92
Jocoro, El Sal. D6 92
Jocotán, Guat. C5 92
Jódar, Spain H8 16
Jodhpur, India G5 44
Joe Batt's Arm, Newf., Can. C19 106
Joensuu, Fin. J21 6
Joetsu, Japan J13 36
Joffre, Mount, mtn., Can. G19 102
Jõgeva, Est. C9 22
Jog Falls, wtfl, India E3 46
Joggins, N.S., Can. G9 106
Jogui, stm., Braz. G1 79
Johannesburg, S. Afr. F9 66
Johannesburg, Ca., U.S. I8 124
John Day, Or., U.S. F7 122
John Day, stm., Or., U.S. E5 122
John H. Kerr Reservoir, res., U.S. C8 112
John Martin Reservoir, res., Co., U.S. M4 118
John o' Groats, Scot., U.K. C10 8
John Redmond Reservoir, res., Ks., U.S. M12 118
Johnson, Ar., U.S. F2 114
Johnson, Ks., U.S. N6 118
Johnson, Ne., U.S. K12 118
Johnson, Vt., U.S. C14 108
Johnsonburg, Pa., U.S. F8 108
Johnson City, N.Y., U.S. E11 108
Johnson City, Tn., U.S. C4 112
Johnson City, Tx., U.S. I8 116
Johnsondale, Ca., U.S. I7 124
Johnsons Crossing, Yukon, Can. F28 100
Johnsonville, S.C., U.S. F7 112
Johnston, Ia., U.S. I2 110
Johnston, S.C., U.S. F5 112
Johnston Atoll, atoll, Oc. G23 126
Johnston City, Il., U.S. E8 114
Johnstone Strait, strt., B.C., Can. G8 102
Johnstown, Co., U.S. D12 120
Johnstown, N.Y., U.S. D12 108
Johnstown, Oh., U.S. G4 108
Johnstown, Pa., U.S. G8 108
Johor Baharu, Malay. N7 40
Joigny, Fr. E10 14
Joiner, Ar., U.S. G6 114
Joinvile, Braz. D14 80
Joinville, Fr. D12 14
Joinville Island, i., Ant. B1 73
Jokkmokk, Swe. H16 6
Jolārpettai, India F5 46
Jolfā, Iran B8 48
Joliet, Il., U.S. I7 110
Joliet, Mt., U.S. E17 122
Joliette, Que., Can. A13 108
Jolo, Phil. D7 38
Jomda, China E6 30
Jonava, Lith. F7 22
Jones, Ok., U.S. D9 116
Jonesboro, Ar., U.S. G6 114
Jonesboro, Ga., U.S. F2 112
Jonesboro, Il., U.S. E7 114
Jonesboro, In., U.S. B11 114
Jonesboro, La., U.S. J4 114
Jonesboro, Tn., U.S. C4 112
Jonesburg, Mo., U.S. D5 114
Jones Mill, Ar., U.S. H4 114
Jonesport, Me., U.S. C19 108
Jones Sound, strt., N.W. Ter., Can. A15 96
Jonestown, Ms., U.S. H6 114
Jonesville, La., U.S. K5 114
Jonesville, Mi., U.S. I11 110
Jonesville, N.C., U.S. C6 112
Jonesville, S.C., U.S. E5 112
Jonesville, Va., U.S. C3 112
Joniškėlis, Lith. E7 22
Joniškis, Lith. E6 22
Jönköping, Swe. M14 6
Jonquière, Que., Can. D2 106
Jonuta, Mex. H13 90
Joplin, Mo., U.S. E2 114
Joplin, Mt., U.S. B15 122
Joppa, Il., U.S. E8 114
Jordan, Mn., U.S. F2 110
Jordan, Mt., U.S. C19 122
Jordan, N.Y., U.S. D10 108
Jordan (Al-Urdun), ctry., Asia C2 42
Jordan (Nahr al-Urdunn) (HaYarden), stm., Asia E5 50
Jordan, stm., Ut., U.S. D5 120
Jordânia, Braz. C8 79
Jordanów, Pol. F19 10
Jordan Valley, Or., U.S. H8 122
Jordão, stm., Braz. C13 80
Jordet, Nor. K13 6
Jorhāt, India G16 44
Jornado del Muerto, des., N.M., U.S. K10 120
Jos, Nig. G14 64
José Batlle y Ordóñez, Ur. G11 80
José Bonifácio, Braz. F4 79
José Francisco Vergara, Chile B4 80
Joselândia, Braz. G13 82
José Pedro Varela, Ur. G11 80
Joseph, Or., U.S. E8 122
Joseph, Lac, l., Newf., Can. F19 96
Joseph Bonaparte Gulf, b., Austl. B5 68
Joseph City, Az., U.S. J6 120
Joshua, Tx., U.S. G9 116
Joshua Tree, Ca., U.S. J9 124
Joškar-Ola, Russia F7 26
Josselin, Fr. E4 14
Joubertina, S. Afr. I6 66
Jourdanton, Tx., U.S. K8 116
Jovellanos, Cuba C4 94
Joviânia, Braz. D4 79
Jowhar, Som. H10 56
Joy, Il., U.S. I5 110
Joy, Mount, mtn., Yukon, Can. E28 100
Joyce, La., U.S. K4 114
Józefów, Pol. C21 10
J. Percy Priest Lake, res., Tn., U.S. F10 114
Juami, stm., Braz. H9 84
Juan Aldama, Mex. E8 90
Juan B. Arruabarrena, Arg. F9 80
Juan Bautista Alberdi, Arg. D6 80
Juan de Fuca, Strait of, strt., N.A. I10 102
Juan de Mena, Para. C10 80
Juan de Nova, Île, i., Afr. E8 58
Juan E. Barra, Arg. I8 80
Juan Eugenio, Mex. E8 90
Juan Fernández, Archipiélago, is., Chile C1 78
Juangriego, Ven. B11 84
Juan Guerra, Peru B3 82
Juan Jorba, Arg. G6 80
Juan José Castelli, Arg. C8 80
Juán José Perez, Bol. F7 82
Juanjuí, Peru B3 82
Juan L. Lacaze, Ur. H10 80
Juan N. Fernández, Arg. J9 80
Juan Perez Sound, strt., B.C., Can. E3 102
Juan Viñas, C.R. H11 92
Juárez, Mex. D9 90
Juárez see Ciudad Juárez, Mex. B6 90
Juárez, Mex. B5 90
Juárez, Sierra de, mts., Mex. B2 90
Juatinga, Ponta de, c., Braz. G6 79
Juàzeiro, Braz. E10 76
Juazeiro do Norte, Braz. E11 76
Jūbā, Sud. H7 56
Juba, stm., Braz. F12 82
Jūbāl, Maḍīq, strt., Egypt D7 60
Jubal, Strait of see Jūbāl, Maḍīq, strt., Egypt D7 60
Jubaysho, Eth. O9 60
Jubayt, Sud. H9 60
Jubba (Genale), stm., Afr. H9 56
Jubbah, Sau. Ar. G6 48
Jubilee Lake, l., Newf., Can. D18 106
Jubones, stm., Ec. I3 84
Juby, Cap, c., Mor. G4 62

Name Map Ref. Page

Júcar (Xúquer), stm., Spain F10 16
Juçara, Braz. C3 79
Júcaro, Cuba D5 94
Juchipila, Mex. G8 90
Juchitán de Zaragoza, Mex. I12 90
Juchnov, Russia G18 22
Juchoviči, Bela. E11 22
Jucuapa, El Sal. D6 92
Jucurucu, stm., Braz. D9 79
Judaea, hist. reg., Asia E4 50
Judas, Punta, c., C.R. H10 92
Jude Island, i., Newf., Can. E19 106
Judenburg, Aus. H14 10
Judique, N.S., Can. G12 106
Judith, stm., Mt., U.S. C16 122
Judith Gap, Mt., U.S. D16 122
Judith Mountains, mts., Mt., U.S. C16 122
Judson, S.C., U.S. E4 112
Judsonia, Ar., U.S. G5 114
Juexi, China F10 34
Jufari, stm., Braz. H11 84
Jugon, Fr. D4 14
Juḥā, Sau. Ar. F3 47
Juidongshan, China L6 34
Juigalpa, Nic. E9 92
Juina, stm., Braz. E12 82
Juiz de Fora, Braz. F7 79
Jujuy, prov., Arg. B5 80
Jukagirskoje ploskogorje, plat., Russia D23 28
Julesburg, Co., U.S. K5 118
Juli, Peru G7 82
Juliaca, Peru F6 82
Julia Creek, Austl. C4 70
Julianakanaal, Neth. F8 12
Julian Alps, mts., Eur. C8 18
Juliana Top, mtn., Sur. F14 84
Julianehåb (Qaqortoq), Grnld. D23 96
Jülich, Ger. E6 10
Julimes, Mex. C7 90
Júlio de Castilhos, Braz. E12 80
Julu, China F3 32
Juma, Russia I23 6
Jumay, Volcán, vol., Guat. C5 92
Jumbilla, Peru A3 82
Jumboo, Som. B8 58
Jumentos Cays, is., Bah. C7 94
Jumet, Bel. H5 12
Jumilla, Spain G10 16
Jump, stm., Wi., U.S. E5 110
Jūnāgadh, India J4 44
Junaynah, Ra's al-, mtn., Egypt G2 48
Junction, Tx., U.S. I7 116
Junction, Ut., U.S. F4 120
Junction City, Ar., U.S. I4 114
Junction City, Ks., U.S. L11 118
Junction City, Ky., U.S. E12 114
Junction City, Or., U.S. F2 122
Jundiaí, Braz. G5 79
Jundiaí do Sul, Braz. G3 79
Juneau, Ak., U.S. G27 100
Juneau, Wi., U.S. G7 110
Junee, Austl. J7 70
June Lake, Ca., U.S. G6 124
Jungar Qi, China D9 30
Jungfrau, mtn., Switz. E8 13
Junggar Pendi, China B4 30
Jungshāhi, Pak. H2 44
Juniata, Ne., U.S. K9 118
Juniata, stm., Pa., U.S. G9 108
Junín, Arg. H8 80
Junín, Ec. H2 84
Junín, Peru D4 82
Junín, dept., Peru D4 82
Junín, Lago de, l., Peru D3 82
Junior, W.V., U.S. I7 108
Juniper, N.B., Can. F6 106
Juniville, Fr. C11 14
Junqueirópolis, Braz. F3 79
Juntas, C.R. G9 92
Junxian, China E9 30
Juparanã, Lagoa, l., Braz. E8 79
Jupilingo, stm., Guat. C5 92
Jupiter, Fl., U.S. M6 112
Jupiter, stm., Que., Can. C10 106
Juquiá, Braz. C15 80
Juquiá, Ponta do, c., Braz. C15 80
Jur, stm., Sud. M5 60
Jura, state, Switz. D7 13
Jura, dept., Fr. F12 14
Jura, mts., Eur. F13 14
Jura, i., Scot., U.K. E8 8
Juramento, Braz. D7 79
Juratiški, Bela. G8 22
Jurbarkas, Lith. F5 22
Jurf ad-Darāwīsh, Jord. G5 50
Jurga, Russia F8 28
Jurjevec, Russia D26 22
Jurjev-Pol'skij, Russia E22 22
Jūrmala, Lat. E6 22
Jurty, Russia F17 26
Juruá, Braz. I9 84
Juruá, stm., S.A. D5 76
Juruá-mirim, stm., Braz. C5 82
Juruena, stm., Braz. B12 82
Jurupari, stm., Braz. C7 82
Jur'uzan', Russia G9 26
Juscelândia, Braz. C3 79
Jusepín, Ven. C11 84
Juskatla, B.C., Can. D2 102
Jussey, Fr. E12 14
Justiniano Posse, Arg. G7 80
Justo Daract, Arg. G6 80
Jutaí, Braz. A7 82
Jutaí, stm., Braz. D5 76
Jüterbog, Ger. D13 10
Juti, Braz. G1 79
Jutiapa, Guat. C5 92
Jutiapa, dept., Guat. C5 92
Juticalpa, Hond. C8 92
Jutiquile, Hond. C8 92
Jutland see Jylland, pen., Den. M11 6
Juva, Fin. K20 6
Juventud, Isla de la (Isla de Pinos), i., Cuba D3 94
Juxi, China H8 34
Juža, Russia E25 22
Južno-Sachalinsk, Russia H20 28
Južno-Ural'sk, Russia G10 26
Južnyj, mys, c., Russia F23 28
Jwayyā, Leb. B4 50
Jylland, reg., Den. M11 6
Jyväskylä, Fin. J19 6

K

K2 (Qogir Feng), mtn., Asia C7 44
Kaachka, Turk. J9 26
Kaachka, Turk. C15 48
Kaala, mtn., Hi., U.S. p15 125a
Kaapstad see Cape Town, S. Afr. I4 66
Kabah, hist., Mex. G15 90
Kabale, Ug. B5 58
Kabalega Falls, wtfl, Ug. H7 56
Kabalo, Zaire C5 58
Kabambare, Zaire B5 58
Kabba, Nig. H13 64
Kabetogama Lake, l., Mn., U.S. B3 110
Kabinda, Zaire C4 58
Kabīr Kūh, mts., Iran E9 48
Kabkābīyah, Sud. K3 60
Kabna, Sud. H7 60
Kābol, Afg. C3 44
Kābol, stm., Asia C4 44
Kabompo, stm., Zam. D4 58
Kabongo, Zaire C5 58
Kabot, Gui. F2 64
Kabou, Togo G10 64
Kabr, Sud. L4 60
Kābul see Kābol, Afg. C3 44
Kaburuang, Pulau, i., Indon. E8 38
Kabwe (Broken Hill), Zam. D5 58
Kačanik, Yugo. G5 20
Kačerginė, Lith. G6 22
Kachchh, Gulf of, b., India I3 44
Kachemak Bay, b., Ak., U.S. G19 100
Kachisi, Eth. M9 60
K'achta, Russia G13 28
Kačug, Russia G13 28
Kadaiyanallūr, India H4 46
Kadanai (Kadaney), stm., Asia E2 44
Kadaney (Kadanai), stm., Asia E2 44
Kadan Kyun, i., Mya. H5 40
Kade, Ghana H9 64
Kadéï, stm., Afr. H4 56
Kadi, India I5 44
Kadiana, Mali F6 64
Kadina, Austl. I2 70
Kadiri, India E5 46
Kadirli, Tur. C4 48
Kadja, Ouadi (Wādī Kaja), val., Afr. L3 60
Kadnikov, Russia B23 22
Kadnikovskij, Russia A23 22
Kado, Nig. H14 64
Kadodo, Sud. L5 60
Kadoka, S.D., U.S. H6 118
Kadom, Russia G25 22
Kadoma, Zimb. B9 66
Kaduj, Russia B20 22
Kaduna, Nig. F13 64
Kaduna, stm., Nig. G12 64
Kāduqlī, Sud. L5 60
Kadyj, Russia D26 22
Kadykčan, Russia E21 28
Kadžerom, Russia E9 26
Kaech'ŏn, N. Kor. D13 32
Kaédi, Maur. C3 64
Kaegudeck Lake, l., Newf., Can. D18 106
Kaena Point, c., Hi., U.S. p15 125a
Kaesŏng, N. Kor. E14 32
Kāf, Sau. Ar. F4 48
Kafan, Arm. B9 48
Kafanchan, Nig. G14 64
Kaffraria, hist. reg., S. Afr. H9 66
Kaffrine, Sen. D2 64
Kafia Kingi, Sud. M3 60
Kafin Madaki, Nig. F14 64
Kafirévs, Ákra, c., Grc. K8 20
Kafr ad-Dawwār, Egypt B6 60
Kafr ash-Shaykh, Egypt B6 60
Kafue, stm., Zam. E5 58
Kagan, Uzb. J10 26
Kagaznagar, India C5 46
Kagelike, China B12 44
Kagera, stm., Afr. B6 58
Kağızman, Tur. A7 48
Kagmar, Sud. J6 60
Kagoshima, Japan P5 36
Kagoshima-wan, b., Japan P5 36
Kahayan, stm., Indon. F5 38
Kahemba, Zaire C3 58
Kahnūj, Iran H14 48
Kahoka, Mo., U.S. B5 114
Kahoolawe, i., Hi., U.S. q17 125a
Kahramanmaraş, Tur. C4 48
Kahuku, Hi., U.S. p16 125a
Kahuku Point, c., Hi., U.S. p16 125a
Kahului, Hi., U.S. q17 125a
Kahului Bay, b., Hi., U.S. q17 125a
Kai, Kepulauan, is., Indon. G9 38
Kaiama, Nig. G11 64
Kaiapoi, N.Z. E4 72
Kaibab Plateau, plat., Az., U.S. H4 120
Kaibito Plateau, plat., Az., U.S. H5 120
Kaidu, stm., China C4 30
Kaieteur Fall, wtfl, Guy. E13 84
Kaifeng, China I2 32
Kaikoura, N.Z. E4 72
Kailahun, S.L. G4 64
Kaili, China A9 40
Kailu, China C11 30
Kailua, Hi., U.S. p16 125a
Kailua Kona, Hi., U.S. r18 125a
Kaimanawa Mountains, mts., N.Z. C5 72
Kainan, Japan M10 36
Kaipara Harbour, b., N.Z. B5 72
Kaiping, China G9 30
Kairāna, India F7 44
Kairouan, Tun. N5 18
Kaiserslautern, Ger. F7 10
Kaishantun, China A17 32
Kaišiadorys, Lith. G7 22
Kaitangata, N.Z. G2 72
Kaithal, India F7 44
Kaituma, stm., Guy. D13 84
Kaiwi Channel, strt., Hi., U.S. p16 125a
Kaiyuan, China A12 32
Kaja, Wādī (Ouadi Kadja), val., Afr. L3 60
Kajaani, Fin. I20 6
Kajang, Malay. M6 40
Kajnar, Kaz. H13 26
Kaka, Cen. Afr. Rep. N4 60
Kākā, Sud. L7 60
Kakadu National Park, Austl. B6 68
Kakagi Lake, l., Ont., Can. I21 104
Kakamas, S. Afr. G5 66
Kake, Ak., U.S. H28 100
Kakegawa, Japan M13 36
Kakhovs'ke vodoskhovyshche, res., Ukr. H4 26
Kākināda, India D7 46
Kakisa Lake, l., N.W. Ter., Can. D9 96
Kako, stm., Guy. E12 84
Kakoaka, Bots. B7 66
Kakogawa, Japan M9 36
Kaktovik, Ak., U.S. A23 100
Kakwa, stm., Alta., Can. C15 102
Kalaa Kebira, Tun. N5 18
Kalaallit Nunaat see Greenland, dep., N.A. B15 86
Kalaa Sghira, Tun. N5 18
Kālābāgh, Pak. D4 44
Kalabo, Zam. D4 58
Kalač, Russia G6 26
Kalačinsk, Russia F12 26
Kalač-na-Donu, Russia H6 26
Kaladan, stm., Asia D2 40
Ka Lae, c., Hi., U.S. s18 125a
Kalagwe, Mya. C4 40
Kalahari Desert, des., Afr. E5 66
Kalai-Chumb, Taj. A4 44
Kalai-Mor, Turk. D17 48
Kalajoki, Fin. I18 6
Kalakamate, Bots. C8 66
Kalām, Pak. C5 44
Kalama, Wa., U.S. D3 122
Kalámai, Grc. L6 20
Kalamalka Lake, l., B.C., Can. G15 102
Kalamazoo, Mi., U.S. H10 110
Kalamazoo, stm., Mi., U.S. H9 110
Kalapana, Hi., U.S. r19 125a
Kalasin, Thai. F7 40
Kalašnikovo, Russia D18 22
Kalāt, Pak. F2 44
Kalaw, Mya. D4 40
Kal'azin, Russia D20 22
Kalb, Ra's al-, c., Yemen G6 47
Kalbā', U.A.E. B10 47
Kalbarri, Austl. E2 68
Kale, Tur. L12 20
Kaleden, B.C., Can. H15 102
Kalemie (Albertville), Zaire C5 58
Kalemyo, Mya. C3 40
Kaletwa, Mya. D2 40
Kalevala, Russia D4 26
Kalewa, Mya. C3 40
Kálfafell, Ice. C5 6a
Kalgan see Zhangjiakou, China C2 32
Kalgoorlie-Boulder, Austl. F4 68
Kali, Mali E4 64
Kaliakra, nos, c., Bul. F12 20
Kalibo, Phil. C7 38
Kalima, Zaire B5 58
Kalimantan see Borneo, i., Asia E5 38
Kálimnos, Grc. M10 20
Kālimpang, India G13 44
Kalinin see Tver', Russia E18 22
Kaliningrad (Königsberg), Russia G3 22
Kalinkoviči, Bela. I12 22
Kalinovik, Bos. F2 20
Kalispell, Mt., U.S. B11 122
Kalisz, Pol. D18 10
Kalkaska, Mi., U.S. F10 110
Kalkfontein, Bots. D5 66
Kallaste, Est. C10 22
Kallavesi, l., Fin. J20 6
Kalliecahoolie Lake, l., Man., Can. D19 104
Kallnach, Switz. D7 13
Kalmar, Swe. M15 6
Kalmykia see Kalmykija, state, Russia H7 26
Kalmykija, state, Russia H7 26
Kālna, India I13 44
Kalnciems, Lat. E6 22
Kālol, India I5 44
Kalomo, Zam. E5 58
Kalona, Ia., U.S. I4 110
Kalone Peak, mtn., B.C., Can. E8 102
Kalpeni Island, i., India G2 46
Kalskag, Ak., U.S. F14 100
Kaltag, Ak., U.S. D15 100
Kaltan, Russia G15 26
Kaluga, Russia G19 22
Kalundborg, Den. N12 6
Kałuszyn, Pol. C21 10
Kalutara, Sri L. I5 46
Kalvarija, Lith. G6 22
Kalyān, India C2 46
Kama, stm., Russia F8 26
Kamaishi, Japan H16 36
Kamakou, mtn., Hi., U.S. p17 125a
Kamakura, Japan L14 36
Kamamaung, Mya. F4 40
Kamanjab, Nmb. B2 66
Kamarān, i., Yemen G3 47
Kamarang, stm., S.A. E12 84
Kamas, Ut., U.S. D5 120
Kamatsi Lake, l., Sask., Can. B12 104
Kamay, Tx., U.S. F8 116
Kamba, Nig. F11 64
Kambam, India H4 46
Kambar, Pak. G3 44
Kambarka, Russia F8 26
Kambia, S.L. G3 64
Kamčatka, poluostrov (Kamchatka), pen., Russia F24 28
Kamčatskij zaliv, b., Russia F24 28
Kamchatka see Kamčatka, poluostrov, pen., Russia F24 28
Kâmchay Méa, Camb. I8 40
Kamčija, stm., Bul. F11 20
Kamen', Bela. F11 22
Kamen', gora, mtn., Russia D16 26
Kamenec, Bela. I6 22
Kamenjak, Rt, c., Cro. E8 18
Kamenka, Russia G6 26
Kamen'-na-Obi, Russia G8 28
Kamennogorsk, Russia K21 6
Kamensk-Ural'skij, Russia F10 26
Kameškovo, Russia E24 22
Kāmet, mtn., Asia E8 44
Kamiah, Id., U.S. D9 122
Kamienna Góra, Pol. E16 10
Kamieńsk, Pol. D19 10
Kamilukuak Lake, l., N.W. Ter., Can. D12 96
Kamina, Zaire C5 58
Kaminak Lake, l., N.W. Ter., Can. D13 96
Kaminaljuyú, hist., Guat. J14 90
Kaminaljuyú, hist., Guat. C4 92
Kaminoyama, Japan I15 36
Kaminskij, Russia D24 22
Kaminuriak Lake, l., N.W. Ter., Can. D13 96
Kamishak Bay, b., Ak., U.S. G18 100
Kamisunagawa, Japan d17 36a
Kamloops, B.C., Can. G14 102
Kamloops Indian Reserve, B.C., Can. G14 102
Kamloops Lake, l., B.C., Can. G14 102
Kamo, Arm. A8 48
Kamoa Mountains, mts., Guy. G13 84
Kampala, Ug. A6 58
Kampar, Malay. L6 40
Kampar, stm., Indon. N7 40
Kampen, Neth. C8 12
Kamphaeng Phet, Thai. F5 40
Kamp'o, S. Kor. H17 32
Kâmpóng Cham, Camb. H8 40
Kâmpóng Chhnăng, Camb. H8 40
Kâmpóng Saôm, Camb. I7 40
Kâmpóng Saôm, Chhâk, b., Camb. I7 40
Kâmpóng Thum, Camb. H8 40
Kâmpôt, Camb. I8 40
Kampsville, Il., U.S. C6 114
Kâmpŭchéa see Cambodia, ctry., Asia C4 38
Kamsack, Sask., Can. G13 104
Kamskoje vodochranilišče, res., Russia F9 26
Kamthi, India B5 46
Kamuchawie Lake, l., Can. B12 104
Kamuela (Waimea), Hi., U.S. q18 125a
Kamuk, Cerro, mtn., C.R. H11 92
Kam'yanets'-Podil's'kyy, Ukr. H3 26
Kamyšin, Russia G7 26
Kamyšlov, Russia F10 26
Kanaaupscow, stm., Que., Can. F17 96
Kanab, Ut., U.S. G4 120
Kanab Plateau, plat., U.S. H4 120
Kanafis, Sud. M3 60
Kanaga Volcano, vol., Ak., U.S. K6 100
Kanairiktok, stm., Newf., Can. F20 96
Kananaskis, stm., Alta., Can. G19 102
Kananga (Luluabourg), Zaire C4 58
Kanarraville, Ut., U.S. G3 120
Kanaš, Russia F7 26
Kanawha, Ia., U.S. H2 110
Kanawha, stm., W.V., U.S. I4 108
Kanazawa, Japan K11 36
Kanchanaburi, Thai. G5 40
Kānchenjunga, mtn., Asia G13 44
Kānchipuram, India F5 46
Kandahar, Sask., Can. G10 104
Kandalakša, Russia D4 26
Kandalakšskaja guba, b., Russia H23 6
Kandangan, Indon. F6 38
Kandava, Lat. D5 22
Kandersteg, Switz. E8 13
Kandi, Benin F11 64
Kandi, India I13 44
Kandiāro, Pak. G3 44
Kandik, stm., N.A. D24 100
Kandos, Austl. I8 70
Kandrāch, Pak. H1 44
Kandy, Sri L. I6 46
Kane, Il., U.S. C6 114
Kane, Pa., U.S. F8 108
Kaneohe, Hi., U.S. p16 125a
Kaneohe Bay, b., Hi., U.S. p16 125a
Kang, Bots. D5 66
Kangal, Tur. B4 48
Kangalassy, Russia E17 28
Kangar, Malay. K6 40
Kangaroo Island, i., Austl. J2 70
Kangāvar, Iran D9 48
Kangding, China E7 30
Kangdong, N. Kor. D14 32
Kangean, Kepulauan, is., Indon. G6 38
Kanggye, N. Kor. C14 32
Kanghwa, S. Kor. F14 32
Kanghwa-man, b., S. Kor. F14 32
Kangiqsualujjuaq, Que., Can. E19 96
Kangiqsujuaq, Que., Can. D18 96
Kangirsuk, Que., Can. D18 96
Kangjin, S. Kor. I14 32
Kangnichumike, China D9 44
Kangnŭng, S. Kor. F16 32
Kango, Gabon A2 58
Kangping, China A11 32
Kangrinboqê Feng, mtn., China E9 44
Kangshan, Tai. M9 34
Kangsŏ, N. Kor. E13 32
Kangto, mtn., Asia G16 44
Kangyidaung, Mya. F3 40
Kani, Mya. C3 40
Kaniama, Zaire C4 58
Kanin, poluostrov, pen., Russia D7 26
Kanin Nos, mys, c., Russia D6 26
Kaniva, Austl. K4 70
Kanjiža, Yugo. C4 20
Kankakee, Il., U.S. I8 110
Kankakee, stm., U.S. A8 114
Kankan, Gui. F5 64
Kankéla, Mali F6 64
Kankossa, Maur. D4 64
Kanmaw Kyun, i., Mya. I5 40
Kannapolis, N.C., U.S. D6 112
Kannauj, India G8 44
Kano, Nig. E14 64
Kanonji, Japan M8 36
Kanopolis, Ks., U.S. M9 118
Kanorado, Ks., U.S. L5 118
Kanosh, Ut., U.S. F4 120
Kanoya, Japan P5 36
Kānpur, India G9 44
Kansas, Il., U.S. C9 114
Kansas, state, U.S. D7 98
Kansas, stm., Ks., U.S. L11 118
Kansas City, Ks., U.S. L13 118
Kansas City, Mo., U.S. C2 114
Kansau, Mya. C2 40
Kanshan, China E9 34
Kansk, Russia F11 28
Kansu see Gansu, prov., China D7 30
Kant, Kyrg. I12 26
Kantang, Thai. K5 40
Kantché, Niger E14 64
Kantishna, stm., Ak., U.S. D18 100
Kantō-sanchi, mts., Japan K13 36
Kantunilkín, Mex. G16 90
Kanuku Mountains, mts., Guy. F13 84
Kanuma, Japan K14 36
Kanus, Nmb. F4 66
Kan'utino, Russia F16 22
Kanye, Bots. E7 66
Kanyu, Bots. C7 66
Kaohsiung, Tai. M9 34
Kaohsiunghsien, Tai. M9 34
Kaokoland, hist. reg., Nmb. A1 66
Kaoko Veld, plat., Nmb. B1 66
Kaolack, Sen. D1 64
Kaoma, Zam. D4 58
Kaoshanpu, China E3 34
Kapaa, Hi., U.S. o14 125a
Kapadvanj, India I5 44
Kapanga, Zaire C4 58
Kapčagaj, Kaz. I13 26
Kapčagajskoje vodochranilišče, res., Kaz. I13 26
Kapfenberg, Aus. H15 10
Kapikik Lake, l., Ont., Can. G23 104
Kapiskau, stm., Ont., Can. F16 96
Kaplan, La., U.S. M4 114
Kapoe, Thai. J5 40
Kaposvár, Hung. I17 10
Kaposvar Creek, stm., Sask., Can. H12 104
Kappeln, Ger. A9 10
Kapps, Nmb. D3 66
Kaprun, Aus. H12 10
Kapsan, N. Kor. B16 32
Kapuas, stm., Indon. F4 38
Kapuas Hulu, Pegunungan, mts., Asia E5 38
Kapunda, Austl. J3 70
Kapūrthala, India E6 44
Kapuskasing, Ont., Can. G16 96
Kapuskasing, stm., Ont., Can. G16 96
Kapuvár, Hung. H17 10
Kara, stm., Afr. G10 64
Kara-Balta, Kyrg. I12 26
Karabanovo, Russia E21 22
Karabaš, Russia F10 26
Karabekaul, Turk. B18 48
Kara-Bogaz-Gol, zaliv, b., Turk. I8 26
Karabük, Tur. G14 4
Karacabey, Tur. I12 20
Karacadağ, Tur. H11 20
Karačev, Russia H18 22
Karāchi, Pak. H2 44
Karād, India D3 46
Karaganda, Kaz. H12 26
Karaginskij, ostrov, i., Russia F24 28
Karaginskij zaliv, b., Russia F24 28
Karagoš, gora, mtn., Russia G15 26
Kāraikāl, India G5 46
Kāraikkudi, India G5 46
Karaj, Iran D11 48
Karakax, stm., China B8 44
Karakelong, Pulau, i., Indon. E8 38
Karakol (Prževal'sk), Kyrg. I13 26
Karakoram Pass, Asia C7 44
Karakoram Range, mts., Asia C7 44
Karakoro, stm., Afr. D4 64
Karakumskij kanal, Turk. C16 48
Karakumy, des., Turk. J9 26
Karaman, Tur. L13 20
Karaman, Tur. C2 48
Karamay, China B3 30
Karamea Bight, N.Z. D3 72
Karamürsel, Tur. I13 20
Karamyševo, Russia D11 22
Kāranja, India B4 46
Karapınar, Tur. C2 48
Karasburg, Nmb. G4 66
Karasburg, dept., Nmb. G4 66
Kara Sea see Karskoje more, Russia C11 26
Karasjok, Nor. G19 6
Karasu, stm., Tur. B5 48
Karasuk, Russia G7 28
Karatau, Kaz. I12 26
Karatau, chrebet, mts., Kaz. I12 26
Karaton, Kaz. H8 26
Karatsu, Japan N4 36
Karauli, India G7 44
Karawang, Indon. j13 39a
Karawang, Tanjung, c., Indon. i13 39a
Karawanken, mts., Eur. C9 18
Karaye, Nig. F14 64
Karažal, Kaz. H12 26
Karbalā', Iraq E8 48
Karcag, Hung. H20 10
Kardhítsa, Grc. J5 20
Kärdla, Est. B5 22
Kardymovo, Russia G15 22
Kărdžali, Bul. H9 20
Karelia see Karelija, state, Russia E4 26
Karelia, hist. reg., Eur. J22 6
Karelija, state, Russia E4 26
Karesuando, Swe. G18 6
Kargopol', Russia E5 26
Karia-ba-Mohammed, Mor. C8 62
Kariba, Zimb. E5 58
Kariba, Lake, res., Afr. E5 58
Karibib, Nmb. C2 66
Karigasniemi, Fin. G19 6
Karimata, Kepulauan, is., Indon. F4 38
Karimata, Selat (Karimata Strait), strt., Indon. F4 38
Karīmnagar, India C5 46
Karimunjawa, Kepulauan, is., Indon. G5 38
Karin, Som. F10 56
Karis (Karjaa), Fin. K18 6
Karisimbi, Volcan, vol., Afr. B5 58
Kariya, Japan M11 36
Karīz, Iran D16 48
Karkaralinsk, Kaz. H13 26
Karl-Marx-Stadt see Chemnitz, Ger. E12 10
Karlovac, Cro. D10 18
Karlovo, Bul. G8 20
Karlovy Vary, Czech. E12 10
Karlsborg, Swe. I18 6
Karlskoga, Swe. L14 6
Karlskrona, Swe. M14 6
Karlsruhe, Ger. F8 10
Karlstad, Mn., U.S. C11 118
Karlstadt, Ger. F9 10
Karma, Niger E10 64
Karmah, Sud. H6 60
Karmel, Har (Mount Carmel), mtn., Isr. C4 50
Karmiyya, Isr. E3 50
Karnack, Tx., U.S. J2 114
Karnak see Al-Karnak, Egypt E7 60
Karnak, Il., U.S. E8 114
Karnāl, India F7 44
Karnālī, stm., Asia F9 44
Karnātaka, state, India E3 46
Karnes City, Tx., U.S. K9 116
Karnobat, Bul. G10 20
Kärnten, state, Aus. I13 10
Karonga, Mwi. C6 58
Karora, Sud. I10 60
Kárpathos, i., Grc. N11 20
Karpenísion, Grc. K5 20
Karpinsk, Russia F10 26
Karpogory, Russia E6 26
Karratha, Austl. D3 68
Kars, Tur. A7 48
Karsakpaj, Kaz. H11 26
Karsakuwigamak Lake, l., Man., Can. B15 104
Kärsämäki, Fin. J19 6
Kārsava, Lat. E10 22
Karši, Uzb. J11 26
Karsin, Pol. B17 10
Karskije Vorota, proliv, strt., Russia C9 26
Karskoje more (Kara Sea), Russia C11 26
Kartaly, Russia G10 26
Karthaus, Pa., U.S. F8 108
Kartuzy, Pol. A18 10
Karukuwisa, Nmb. B4 66
Karur, India G5 46
Karviná, Czech. F18 10
Kārwār, India E3 46
Karymskoje, Russia G14 28
Kas, Sud. K3 60
Kasaan, Ak., U.S. I28 100
Kasai (Cassai), stm., Afr. B3 58
Kasaji, Zaire D4 58
Kasama, Zam. D6 58
Kasan, Uzb. B18 48
Kasane, Bots. A7 66
Kasanga, Tan. C6 58
Kasaoka, Japan M8 36
Kāsaragod, India F3 46
Kasba Lake, l., N.W. Ter., Can. D12 96
Kasba-Tadla, Mor. D7 62
Kaseda, Japan P5 36
Kasempa, Zam. D5 58
Kasenga, Zaire D5 58
Kasese, Zaire B5 58
Kāsganj, India G8 44
Kāshān, Iran K8 26
Kashgar see Kashi, China D2 30
Kashi, China D2 30
Kashihara, Japan M10 36
Kashima, Japan N5 36
Kāshīpur, India F8 44
Kashiwazaki, Japan J13 36
Kāshmar, Iran D15 48
Kashmir see Jammu and Kashmīr, dep., Asia C10 42
Kashmor, Pak. F3 44
Kashunuk, stm., Ak., U.S. F12 100
Kasigluk, Ak., U.S. F13 100
Kasimov, Russia G24 22
Kašin, Russia D20 22
Kasinka, Bots. B7 66
Kašira, Russia G21 22
Kasiruta, Pulau, i., Indon. F8 38
Kaskaskia, stm., Il., U.S. D7 114
Kaskattama, stm., Man., Can. E14 96
Kaskö (Kaskinen), Fin. J17 6
Kasli, Russia F10 26
Kaslo, B.C., Can. H18 102
Kasn'a, Russia F17 22
Kasongo, Zaire B5 58
Kasongo-Lunda, Zaire C3 58
Kásos, i., Grc. N10 20
Kasota, Mn., U.S. F2 110
Kaspijsk, Russia I7 26
Kaspijskij, Russia H7 26
Kasr, Ra's, c., Afr. H10 60
Kassalā, Sud. J9 60
Kassándra, pen., Grc. I7 20
Kassándras, Kólpos, b., Grc. I7 20
Kassel, Ger. D9 10
Kasserine, Tun. C15 62
Kassikaityu, stm., Guy. G13 84
Kassinger, Sud. H6 60
Kasson, Mn., U.S. F3 110
Kastamonu, Tur. G14 4
Kastoría, Grc. I5 20
Kastrávion, Tekhnití Límni, res., Grc. K5 20
Kasūr, Pak. E6 44
Kataeregi, Nig. G13 64
Katahdin, Mount, mtn., Me., U.S. B18 108
Katanga, hist. reg., Zaire D5 58
Katanga, stm., Russia F12 28
Katanning, Austl. F3 68
Katchall Island, i., India K2 40
Katélé, Mali F7 64
Katepwa Beach, Sask., Can. H11 104
Kateríni, Grc. I6 20
Kates Needle, mtn., N.A. H28 100
Katha, Mya. B4 40
Katherine, Austl. B6 68
Kāthiāwār Peninsula, pen., India I4 44
Kāthmāndau, Nepal G11 44
Kathrabbā, Jord. F5 50
Katihār, India H12 44
Katimik Lake, l., Man., Can. F15 104
Katiola, C. Iv. G7 64
Kātmāndu see Kāthmāndau, Nepal G11 44
Katoomba, Austl. I9 70
Katoúna, Grc. K5 20
Katowice, Pol. E19 10
Kātrīnā, Jabal, mtn., Egypt C7 60
Katsepe, Madag. o22 67b
Katsina, Nig. E13 64
Katsina Ala, Nig. H14 64
Katsina Ala, stm., Afr. G8 54
Katsuta, Japan K15 36
Katsuura, Japan L15 36
Katsuyama, Japan K11 36
Kattakurgan, Uzb. J11 26
Kattavía, Grc. N11 20
Kattegat, strt., Eur. M12 6
Katun', stm., Russia G9 28
Katunki, Russia E26 22
Kātwa, India I13 44
Katwijk aan Zee, Neth. D5 12
Katyn, Russia G14 22
Kauai, i., Hi., U.S. o14 125a
Kauai Channel, strt., Hi., U.S. p15 125a
Kau Desert, des., Hi., U.S. r18 125a
Kaufbeuren, Ger. H10 10
Kaufman, Tx., U.S. G10 116
Kaukauna, Wi., U.S. F7 110
Kaukau Veld, plat., Afr. B5 66
Kauliranta, Fin. H18 6
Kaumalapau, Hi., U.S. q17 125a
Kaunakakai, Hi., U.S. p16 125a
Kaunas, Lith. G6 22
Kaura Namoda, Nig. E13 64
Kauru, Nig. F14 64
Kaustinen, Fin. J18 6
Kautokeino, Nor. G18 6
Kavacık, Tur. J12 20
Kavajë, Alb. H3 20
Kavála, Grc. I8 20
Kavalerovo, Russia I19 28
Kāvali, India E5 46
Kavaratti Island, i., India G2 46
Kāveri, stm., India G5 46
Kāveri Falls, wtfl, India F4 46
Kaverino, Russia G24 22
Kavieng, Pap. N. Gui. k17 68a
Kavimba, Bots. B7 66
Kavīr, Dasht-e, des., Iran D13 48
Kaw, Ok., U.S. C10 116
Kawagoe, Japan L14 36
Kawaguchi, Japan L14 36
Kawaihae Bay, b., Hi., U.S. q18 125a
Kawaikini, mtn., Hi., U.S. o14 125a
Kawambwa, Zam. C5 58
Kawara Débé, Niger E11 64
Kawasaki, Japan L14 36
Kawdut, Mya. H4 40
Kaweenakumik Lake, l., Man., Can. F15 104
Kawich Peak, mtn., Nv., U.S. G9 124
Kaw Lake, res., Ok., U.S. C10 116
Kawludo, Mya. E4 40
Kawm Umbū, Egypt E7 60
Kawthaung, Mya. J5 40
Kaxgar, stm., China D2 30
Kaya, Burkina E9 64
Kayak Island, i., Ak., U.S. G22 100
Kayan, Mya. F4 40
Kayan, stm., Indon. E6 38
Kāyankulam, India H4 46
Kaycee, Wy., U.S. A10 120
Kayenta, Az., U.S. H6 120
Kayes, Congo B2 58
Kayes, Mali D4 64
Kay Point, c., Yukon, Can. B25 100
Kayser Gebergte, mts., Sur. F14 84
Kayseri, Tur. B3 48
Kaysville, Ut., U.S. C5 120
Kazachskij melkosopočnik, hills, Kaz. H12 26
Kazačinskoje, Russia F16 26
Kazakhstan, ctry., Asia H11 26
Kazaki, Russia I21 22
Kazakstan see Kazakhstan, ctry., Asia H11 26
Kazalinsk, Kaz. H10 26
Kazan', Russia F7 26
Kazan, stm., N.W. Ter., Can. D13 96
Kazandžik, Turk. J9 26
Kazanlăk, Bul. G9 20
Kazan Lake, l., Sask., Can. C6 104
Kazanovka, Russia H21 22
Kazbek, gora, mtn. I6 26
Kāzerūn, Iran G11 48
Kazimierza Wielka, Pol. E20 10
Kazincbarcika, Hung. G20 10
Kazinka, Russia I22 22
Kazlų Rūda, Lith. G6 22
Kazungula, Zam. A7 66
Kazym, stm., Russia E5 28

Name — Map Ref. — Page

Kazyr, stm., Russia G17 26
Kcynia, Pol. B17 10
Kdyně, Czech. F13 10
Kéa, i., Grc. L8 20
Keaau, Hi., U.S. r18 125a
Keahole Point, c., Hi., U.S. r17 125a
Kealakekua Bay, b., Hi., U.S. r18 125a
Keams Canyon, Az., U.S. I6 120
Kearney, Mo., U.S. C2 114
Kearney, Ne., U.S. K8 118
Kearns, Ut., U.S. D5 120
Kearny, Az., U.S. K6 120
Kebeiti, China B8 44
Kébémer, Sen. D1 64
Kebili, Tun. D15 62
Kebnekaise, mtn., Swe. H16 6
Kebri Dehar, Eth. G9 56
Kecel, Hung. I19 10
Kech, stm., Pak. H17 48
Kechika, stm., B.C., Can. E7 96
Kecskemét, Hung. I19 10
Kėdainiai, Lith. F7 22
Kedgwick, N.B., Can. E6 106
Kedgwick, stm., Can. E6 106
Kediri, Indon. j16 39a
Kédougou, Sen. E3 64
Kedrikí Makedhonía, prov., Grc. I6 20
Kędzierzyn Kozle, Pol. E18 10
Keefers, B.C., Can. G13 102
Keele, stm., N.W. Ter., Can. D31 100
Keele Peak, mtn., Yukon, Can. D6 96
Keele Peak, mtn., Yukon, Can. E29 100
Keeley Lake, l., Sask., Can. D6 104
Keeling Islands see Cocos Islands, dep., Oc. K10 24
Keels, Newf., Can. D20 106
Keene, Ky., U.S. B2 112
Keene, N.H., U.S. E14 108
Keene, Tx., U.S. G9 116
Keenesburg, Co., U.S. D12 120
Keerbergen, Bel. F6 12
Keeseville, N.Y., U.S. C13 108
Keetmanshoop, Nmb. F4 66
Keewatin, Ont., Can. I20 104
Keewatin, Mn., U.S. C2 110
Kefallinía, i., Grc. K4 20
Kefar Blum, Isr. B5 50
Kefar 'Ezyon, Isr. Occ. E4 50
Kefar Naḥum (Capernaum), hist., Isr. C5 50
Kefar Sava, Isr. D3 50
Keffi, Nig. G13 64
Keffin Hausa, Nig. E14 64
Keflavík, Ice. B2 6a
Keftya, Eth. K9 60
Ke Ga, Mui, c., Viet. H10 40
Kégashka, Que., Can. B12 106
Kégashka, Lac, l., Que., Can. B12 106
Keg River, Alta., Can. E9 96
Kegums, Lat. E7 22
Kehiwin Indian Reserve, Alta., Can. C24 102
Kehra, Est. B8 22
Ke-hsi Mānsām, Mya. D4 40
Keila, Est. B7 22
Keimoes, S. Afr. G5 66
Keiser, Ar., U.S. G6 114
Keith, Scot., U.K. D11 8
Keith Arm, b., N.W. Ter., Can. C8 96
Keithley Creek, B.C., Can. E13 102
Keithsburg, Il., U.S. I5 110
Keizer, Or., U.S. F2 122
Kejimkujik National Park, N.S., Can. H8 106
Kekaha, Hi., U.S. p14 125a
Kékes, mtn., Hung. H20 10
Kekexili, China D5 30
Kelafo, Eth. G9 56
Kelang, Malay. M6 40
Kelantan, stm., Malay. L7 40
Kelegou, China B6 32
Kelibia, Tun. M6 18
Kellerberrin, Austl. F3 68
Keller Lake, l., N.W. Ter., Can. D8 96
Keller Lake, l., Sask., Can. B8 104
Kellett, Cape, c., N.W. Ter., Can. B7 96
Kelleys Island, i., Oh., U.S. F4 108
Kelliher, Sask., Can. G11 104
Kellogg, Id., U.S. C9 122
Kellogg, Ia., U.S. I3 110
Kellogg, Mn., U.S. F4 110
Kelly Lake, l., N.W. Ter., Can. D31 100
Kellyville, Ok., U.S. D10 116
Kelmė, Lith. F5 22
Kel'mentsi, Ukr. A10 20
Kelmet, Erit. I10 60
Kelo, Chad G4 56
Kelolokan, Indon. E6 38
Kelowna, B.C., Can. H15 102
Kelsey Bay, B.C., Can. G9 102
Kelsey Lake, l., Man., Can. E13 104
Kelseyville, Ca., U.S. F3 124
Kelso, Wa., U.S. D3 122
Keluang, Malay. M7 40
Kelvington, Sask., Can. F11 104
Kem', Russia E4 26
Kemah, Tx., U.S. J11 116
Kemalpaşa, Tur. K11 20
Kemano, B.C., Can. D7 102
Kemer Barajı, res., Tur. L12 20
Kemerovo, Russia F9 28
Kemi, Fin. I19 6
Kemijärvi, Fin. H20 6
Kemijoki, stm., Fin. H19 6
Kemmerer, Wy., U.S. C6 120
Kemnath, Ger. F11 10
Kemp, Tx., U.S. G10 116
Kemp, Lake, res., Tx., U.S. F7 116
Kemparana, Mali E7 64
Kempele, Fin. I19 6
Kempner, Tx., U.S. H8 116
Kemps Bay, Bah. B6 94
Kempsey, Austl. H10 70
Kempt, Lac, l., Que., Can. G18 96
Kempten [Allgäu], Ger. H10 10
Kemptville, Ont., Can. B11 108
Kenai, Ak., U.S. F19 100
Kenai Peninsula, pen., Ak., U.S. G19 100
Kenansville, Fl., U.S. L6 112
Kenansville, N.C., U.S. E9 112
Kenaston, Sask., Can. G8 104
Kenbridge, Va., U.S. C8 112
Kendal, Sask., Can. H11 104
Kendal, S. Afr. F9 66
Kendall, Fl., U.S. N6 112
Kendall, Wi., U.S. G5 110
Kendall, Cape, c., N.W. Ter., Can. D15 96
Kendallville, In., U.S. A11 114
Kendari, Indon. F7 38
Kendrāparha, India J12 44
Kendrick, Fl., U.S. J4 112
Kendrick, Id., U.S. D9 122
Kenedy, Tx., U.S. K9 116
Kenema, S.L. H4 64
Kenesaw, Ne., U.S. K9 118
Kenge, Zaire B3 58
Kengtian, China J8 34
Kēng Tung, Mya. D5 40
Kenhardt, S. Afr. G5 66
Kenilworth, Ut., U.S. E6 120
Kenitra, Mor. C7 62
Kenly, N.C., U.S. D8 112
Kenmare, N.D., U.S. C5 118
Kennard, Tx., U.S. H11 116
Kennebec, S.D., U.S. H8 118
Kennebec, stm., Me., U.S. C17 108
Kennebecasis Bay, b., N.B., Can. G8 106
Kennebunk, Me., U.S. D16 108
Kennedy, Al., U.S. I9 114
Kennedy, Zimb. B8 66
Kennedy, Cape see Canaveral, Cape, c., Fl., U.S. K6 112
Kennedy, Mount, mtn., B.C., Can. G9 102
Kennedy, Mount, mtn., Yukon, Can. F25 100
Kennedy Entrance, strt., Ak., U.S. G18 100
Kennedy Lake, l., B.C., Can. H9 102
Kenner, La., U.S. M6 114
Kennetcook, N.S., Can. G10 106
Kennett, Mo., U.S. F6 114
Kennett Square, Pa., U.S. H11 108
Kennewick, Wa., U.S. D6 122
Kenney Dam, B.C., Can. D10 102
Kenn Reef, rf., Austl. D11 68
Kénogami, Que., Can. D2 106
Kenogami, stm., Ont., Can. G15 96
Kénogami, Lac, l., Que., Can. D2 106
Keno Hill, Yukon, Can. E27 100
Kenora, Ont., Can. I20 104
Kenosha, Wi., U.S. H8 110
Kenova, W.V., U.S. I4 108
Kensal, N.D., U.S. D9 118
Kensett, Ar., U.S. G5 114
Kensington, P.E.I., Can. F10 106
Kensington, Ks., U.S. L8 118
Kensington Park, Fl., U.S. L4 112
Kent, S.L. G3 64
Kent, Oh., U.S. F5 108
Kent, Wa., U.S. C3 122
Kent, co., Eng., U.K. J14 8
Kentau, Kaz. I11 26
Kent Group, is., Austl. L7 70
Kentland, In., U.S. B9 114
Kenton, Mi., U.S. D7 110
Kenton, Oh., U.S. G3 108
Kenton, Tn., U.S. F7 114
Kent Peninsula, pen., N.W. Ter., Can. C11 96
Kentucky, state, U.S. D9 98
Kentucky, stm., Ky., U.S. D11 114
Kentucky Lake, res., U.S. F8 114
Kentville, N.S., Can. G9 106
Kentwood, La., U.S. L6 114
Kenya, ctry., Afr. B7 58
Kenya, Mount see Kirinyaga, mtn., Kenya B7 58
Kenyon, Mn., U.S. F3 110
Keokea, Hi., U.S. q17 125a
Keokuk, Ia., U.S. J4 110
Keo Neua, Col de, Asia E8 40
Keosauqua, Ia., U.S. J4 110
Keota, Ia., U.S. J4 110
Keota, Ok., U.S. D12 116
Kępice, Pol. A16 10
Kępno, Pol. D17 10
Keppel Bay, b., Austl. D9 70
Kequan, China G2 32
Kerala, state, India G4 46
Kerang, Austl. J5 70
Kerby, Or., U.S. H2 122
Kerch, Ukr. H5 26
Keremeos, B.C., Can. H15 102
Keren, Erit. J10 60
Kerend, Iran D9 48
Kerens, Tx., U.S. G10 116
Keret', ozero, l., Russia I23 6
Kerewan, Gam. E1 64
Kerguélen, Îles, is., F.S.A.T. M10 126
Kericho, Kenya B7 58
Keri Kera, Sud. K7 60
Kerinci, Gunung, mtn., Indon. F3 38
Keriya, stm., China B9 44
Kerkebet, Erit. I9 60
Kerkenna, Îles, is., Tun. C16 62
Kerkhoven, Mn., U.S. F12 118
Kerki, Turk. J11 26
Kérkira (Corfu), Grc. J3 20
Kérkira (Corfu), i., Grc. J3 20
Kerkrade, Neth. G9 12
Kermadec Islands, is., N.Z. K22 126
Kermān, Iran F14 48
Kerman, Ca., U.S. H5 124
Kermit, Tx., U.S. H3 116
Kermode, Mount, mtn., B.C., Can. E3 102
Kern, stm., Ca., U.S. I7 124
Kernersville, N.C., U.S. C6 112
Kernville, Ca., U.S. I7 124
Kérou, Benin F11 64
Kerrobert, Sask., Can. G5 104
Kerrville, Tx., U.S. I7 116
Kerry, co., Ire. I4 8
Kershaw, S.C., U.S. E6 112
Kersley, B.C., Can. E12 102
Kerulen (Cherlen) (Herlen), stm., Asia B10 30
Kerzaz, Alg. F10 62
Kerzers, Switz. E7 13
Kesagami Lake, l., Ont., Can. F16 96
Keşan, Tur. I10 20
Kesennuma, Japan I16 36
Keshena, Wi., U.S. F7 110
Keshendeh, Afg. B2 44
Keshod, India J4 44
Keskin, Tur. B2 48
Keski-Suomen lääni, prov., Fin. J19 6
Keskozero, Russia K23 6
Kes'ma, Russia C20 22
Kesova Gora, Russia D20 22
Kesra, Tun. N4 18
Kesten'ga, Russia I22 6
Keszthely, Hung. I17 10
Ket', stm., Russia F8 28
Keta, Ghana I10 64
Keta, ozero, l., Russia D10 28
Ketama, Mor. K7 16
Ketang, China M4 34
Ketchikan, Ak., U.S. I29 100
Ketchum, Id., U.S. G11 122
Kete Krachi, Ghana H9 64
Kétou, Benin H11 64
Kętrzyn (Rastenburg), Pol. A21 10
Kettering, Eng., U.K. I13 8
Kettering, Oh., U.S. H2 108
Kettle, stm., Man., Can. B20 104
Kettle, stm., N.A. I16 102
Kettle, stm., Mn., U.S. D3 110
Kettle Falls, Wa., U.S. B7 122
Kettle Rapids Dam, Man., Can. B20 104
Keuka Lake, l., N.Y., U.S. E9 108
Kevin, Mt., U.S. B14 122
Kew, T./C. Is. D8 94
Kewanee, Il., U.S. I6 110
Kewanna, In., U.S. A10 114
Kewaunee, Wi., U.S. F8 110
Keweenaw Bay, b., Mi., U.S. C7 110
Keweenaw Peninsula, pen., Mi., U.S. C7 110
Keweenaw Point, c., Mi., U.S. C8 110
Keya Paha, stm., U.S. I8 118
Keyes, Ok., U.S. C4 116
Key Largo, Fl., U.S. N6 112
Key Largo, i., Fl., U.S. N6 112
Keyser, W.V., U.S. H8 108
Keystone, Ia., U.S. I3 110
Keystone, S.D., U.S. H4 118
Keystone, W.V., U.S. B5 112
Keystone Lake, res., Ok., U.S. C10 116
Keysville, Va., U.S. B8 112
Keytesville, Mo., U.S. C4 114
Key West, Fl., U.S. O5 112
Kežmarok, Slov. F20 10
Kgalagadi, dept., Bots. E5 66
Kgatleng, dept., Bots. E8 66
Khābūr, Nahr al-, stm., Asia D6 48
Khadki (Kirkee), India C2 46
Khairpur, Pak. G3 44
Khajrāho, India H8 44
Khakassia see Chakasija, state, Russia G15 26
Khakhea, Bots. E6 66
Khalkhalah, Syria B7 50
Khalkidhikí, hist. reg., Grc. I7 20
Khalkís, Grc. K7 20
Khalūf, Oman D11 47
Khambhāliya, India I3 44
Khambhāt, India I5 44
Khambhāt, Gulf of, b., India J5 44
Khāmgaon, India B4 46
Khamir, Yemen F3 47
Khamīs Mushayṭ, Sau. Ar. E3 47
Khamkeut, Laos E8 40
Khammam, India D6 46
Khānābād, Afg. B3 44
Khān al-Baghdādī, Iraq E7 48
Khānaqīn, Iraq D8 48
Khancoban, Austl. K8 70
Khandwa, India J7 44
Khānewāl, Pak. E4 44
Khāngarh, Pak. F4 44
Khaniá, Grc. N8 20
Khānpur, Pak. F4 44
Khān Yūnus, Isr. Occ. F2 50
Kharagpur, India I12 44
Kharānoq, Iran E13 48
Khārg Island see Khārk, Jazīreh-ye, i., Iran G11 48
Khargon, India J6 44
Khāriān Cantonment, Pak. D5 44
Kharkiv, Ukr. G5 26
Kharkov see Kharkiv, Ukr. G5 26
Khartoum see Al-Kharṭūm, Sud. J7 60
Khartoum North see Al-Kharṭūm Baḥrī, Sud. J7 60
Khartum see Al-Kharṭūm, Sud. J7 60
Khasebake, Bots. C7 66
Khāsh, Afg. F17 48
Khāsh, Iran G16 48
Khashm al-Qirbah, Sud. J8 60
Khatt, Oued al, val., W. Sah. G4 62
Khawsa, Mya. G4 40
Khemis, Alg. B12 62
Khemmarat, Thai. F8 40
Khenchla, Alg. C14 62
Khenifra, Mor. D8 62
Kherrata, Alg. B13 62
Kherson, Ukr. H4 26
Khíos, Grc. K10 20
Khíos (Chios), i., Grc. K10 20
Khirbat 'Awwād, Syria D7 50
Khlong Thom, Thai. K5 40
Khmel'nyts'kyy, Ukr. H3 26
Kholm, Afg. B2 44
Khomeyn, Iran E11 48
Khomeynīshahr, Iran E11 48
Khomodimo, Bots. D6 66
Khon Kaen, Thai. F7 40
Khóra, Grc. L5 20
Khorramābād, Iran E10 48
Khorramshahr, Iran F10 48
Khossanto, Sen. E4 64
Khotyn, Ukr. A10 20
Khouribga, Mor. D7 62
Khowst, Afg. D3 44
Khuff, Sau. Ar. B4 47
Khugaung, Mya. A5 40
Khuis, Bots. F5 66
Khu Khan, Thai. G8 40
Khulna, Bngl. I13 44
Khunjerāb Pass, Asia B6 44
Khurai, India H8 44
Khurīyā Murīyā, Jazā'ir, is., Oman F10 47
Khurja, India F7 44
Khust, Ukr. H2 26
Khuzdār, Pak. G2 44
Khvāf, Iran D16 48
Khvor, Iran E13 48
Khvormūj, Iran G11 48
Khvoy, Iran B8 48
Khwae Noi, stm., Thai. G5 40
Khyber Pass, Asia C4 44
Khyriv, Ukr. F22 10
Kiama, Austl. J9 70
Kiamichi, stm., Ok., U.S. E11 116
Kiana, Ak., U.S. C14 100
Kiangarow, Mount, mtn., Austl. F9 70
Kiangsi see Jiangxi, prov., China F10 30
Kiangsu see Jiangsu, prov., China E10 30
Kibangou, Congo B2 58
Kibombo, Zaire B5 58
Kibre Mengist, Eth. O10 60
Kičevo, Mac. H4 20
Kickapoo, stm., Wi., U.S. G5 110
Kicking Horse Pass, Can. F18 102
Kidal, Mali B10 64
Kidira, Sen. D3 64
Kiel, Ger. A10 10
Kiel, Wi., U.S. G7 110
Kiel Canal see Nord-Ostsee-Kanal, Ger. A9 10
Kielce, Pol. E20 10
Kieler Bucht, b., Ger. A10 10
Kiester, Mn., U.S. G2 110
Kiev see Kyyiv, Ukr. G4 26
Kiffa, Maur. C4 64
Kifisiá, Grc. K7 20
Kifrī, Iraq D8 48
Kigali, Rw. B6 58
Kigille, Sud. M8 60
Kigoma, Tan. B5 58
Kihei, Hi., U.S. q17 125a
Kihniö, Fin. J18 6
Kihnu, i., Est. C7 22
Kii-suidō, strt., Japan N9 36
Kikerino, Russia B12 22
Kikerk Lake, l., N.W. Ter., Can. C10 96
Kikinda, Yugo. D4 20
Kikládhes (Cyclades), is., Grc. L9 20
Kikori, Pap. N. Gui. G11 38
Kikwit, Zaire C3 58
Kilambé, Cerro, mtn., Nic. D9 92
Kilauea, Hi., U.S. o14 125a
Kilauea Crater, crat., Hi., U.S. r18 125a
Kilchu, N. Kor. C17 32
Kilcoy, Austl. F10 70
Kildare, Ire. H7 8
Kildare, co., Ire. H7 8
Kildare, Cape, c., P.E.I., Can. F10 106
Kil'din, ostrov, i., Russia G24 6
Kil'dinstroj, Russia G23 6
Kildonan, B.C., Can. H9 102
Kilgore, Tx., U.S. J2 114
Kilian Island, i., N.W. Ter., Can. B11 96
Kilibo, Benin G11 64
Kilikollūr, India H4 46
Kilimanjaro, mtn., Tan. B7 58
Kilimavony, Madag. s20 67b
Kilingi-Nõmme, Est. C7 22
Kilis, Tur. C4 48
Kiliya, Ukr. D13 20
Kilkenny, Ire. I6 8
Kilkenny, co., Ire. I6 8
Kilkís, Grc. H6 20
Killaloe, Ire. I5 8
Killaloe Station, Ont., Can. E18 110
Killam, Alta., Can. E23 102
Killarney, Man., Can. I15 104
Killarney, Ont., Can. E14 110
Killarney, Ire. I4 8
Killbuck, Oh., U.S. G5 108
Killdeer, N.D., U.S. D5 118
Killeen, Tx., U.S. H9 116
Killen, Al., U.S. H9 114
Killington Peak, mtn., Vt., U.S. D14 108
Killiniq Island, i., Can. D20 96
Killinkoski, Fin. J18 6
Kilmarnock, Scot., U.K. F9 8
Kilmarnock, Va., U.S. B10 112
Kilmichael, Ms., U.S. I7 114
Kilomines, Zaire A6 58
Kilosa, Tan. C7 58
Kilpisjärvi, Fin. G17 6
Kilrush, Ire. I4 8
Kiltān Island, i., India G2 46
Kilwa, Zaire C5 58
Kim, Co., U.S. N4 118
Kim, stm., Cam. G9 54
Kimba, Austl. I2 70
Kimball, Mn., U.S. E1 110
Kimball, Ne., U.S. J4 118
Kimball, S.D., U.S. H9 118
Kimberley, B.C., Can. H19 102
Kimberley, S. Afr. G7 66
Kimberley Plateau, plat., Austl. C5 68
Kimberling City, Mo., U.S. F3 114
Kimberly, Id., U.S. H11 122
Kimberly, Wi., U.S. F7 110
Kimch'aek (Sŏngjin), N. Kor. C17 32
Kimch'ŏn, S. Kor. G16 32
Kimito (Kemiö), Fin. K18 6
Kimiwan Lake, l., Alta., Can. B18 102
Kimje, S. Kor. H14 32
Kimovsk, Russia H21 22
Kimry, Russia E20 22
Kimsquit, B.C., Can. E8 102
Kinabalu, Gunong, mtn., Malay. D6 38
Kinbasket Lake, res., B.C., Can. F17 102
Kincaid, Sask., Can. I7 104
Kincaid, Il., U.S. C7 114
Kincardine, Ont., Can. F14 110
Kincolith, B.C., Can. B5 102
Kindberg, Aus. H15 10
Kinde, Mi., U.S. G13 110
Kinder, La., U.S. L4 114
Kindersley, Sask., Can. G5 104
Kindia, Gui. F3 64
Kindred, N.D., U.S. E10 118
Kindu, Zaire B5 58
Kinel', Russia G8 26
Kinešma, Russia D25 22
King, N.C., U.S. C6 112
King and Queen Court House, Va., U.S. B10 112
Kingaroy, Austl. F9 70
King City, Ont., Can. G16 110
King City, Ca., U.S. H4 124
King City, Mo., U.S. B2 114
King Cove, Ak., U.S. I13 100
Kingfield, Me., U.S. C16 108
Kingfisher, Ok., U.S. D9 116
King George, Va., U.S. I9 108
King George, Mount, mtn., B.C., Can. G19 102
King George Island, i., Ant. B1 73
King George Islands, is., N.W. Ter., Can. E17 96
King Hill, Id., U.S. G10 122
Kingisepp, Russia B11 22
King Island, i., Austl. L6 70
King Island, i., B.C., Can. E7 102
King Lear Peak, mtn., Nv., U.S. C7 124
King Leopold Ranges, mts., Austl. C5 68
Kingman, Az., U.S. I2 120
Kingman, Ks., U.S. N9 118
Kingman Reef, rf., Oc. H23 126
King Mountain, mtn., B.C., Can. G30 100
King Mountain, mtn., Or., U.S. G7 122
Kings, Ms., U.S. J6 114
Kings, stm., Ar., U.S. F3 114
Kings, stm., Ca., U.S. H6 124
Kings, stm., Nv., U.S. C7 124
King Salmon, Ak., U.S. G16 100
Kings Beach, Ca., U.S. E5 124
Kingsburg, Ca., U.S. H6 124
Kings Canyon National Park, Ca., U.S. H7 124
Kingscote, Austl. J2 70
Kingsford, Mi., U.S. E7 110
Kingsgate, B.C., Can. H18 102
Kingsland, Ar., U.S. I4 114
Kingsland, Ga., U.S. I5 112
Kingsland, Tx., U.S. I8 116
Kingsley, Ia., U.S. I12 118
Kingsley, Mi., U.S. F10 110
King's Lynn, Eng., U.K. I14 8
Kingsmere Lake, l., Sask., Can. D8 104
Kings Mountain, N.C., U.S. D5 112
King Solomon's Mines see Mikhrot Shelomo Hamelekh, hist., Isr. I3 50
King Sound, strt., Austl. C4 68
Kings Peak, mtn., Ut., U.S. D6 120
King's Point, Newf., Can. C17 106
Kingsport, Tn., U.S. C4 112
Kingston, N.S., Can. H9 106
Kingston, Ont., Can. F19 110
Kingston, Jam. E6 94
Kingston, N.Z. F2 72
Kingston, Ga., U.S. E2 112
Kingston, Ma., U.S. F16 108
Kingston, Mo., U.S. C2 114
Kingston, N.Y., U.S. F13 108
Kingston, Oh., U.S. H4 108
Kingston, Ok., U.S. F10 116
Kingston, Pa., U.S. F11 108
Kingston, Tn., U.S. D2 112
Kingston Southeast, Austl. K3 70
Kingston upon Hull, Eng., U.K. H13 8
Kingstown, St. Vin. H14 94
Kingstree, S.C., U.S. F7 112
Kingsville, Ont., Can. H13 110
Kingsville, Tx., U.S. L9 116
King William, Va., U.S. B9 112
King William Island, i., N.W. Ter., Can. C13 96
King William's Town, S. Afr. I8 66
Kingwood, W.V., U.S. H7 108
Kinistino, Sask., Can. F9 104
Kinkony, Lac, l., Madag. p21 67b
Kinmundy, Il., U.S. D8 114
Kinnaird, B.C., Can. H17 102
Kinnaird Head, c., Scot., U.K. D11 8
Kinneret, Yam (Sea of Galilee), l., Isr. C5 50
Kinsale, Old Head of, c., Ire. J5 8
Kinshasa (Léopoldville), Zaire B3 58
Kinsley, Ks., U.S. N8 118
Kinsman, Oh., U.S. F6 108
Kinston, Al., U.S. K10 114
Kinston, N.C., U.S. D9 112
Kintampo, Ghana G9 64
Kintyre, pen., Scot., U.K. F8 8
Kintyre, Mull of, c., Scot., U.K. F8 8
Kinuseo Falls, wtfl, B.C., Can. C13 102
Kinuso, Alta., Can. B19 102
Kinyeti, mtn., Sud. H7 56
Kinzua, Or., U.S. F5 122
Kiowa, Co., U.S. L3 118
Kiowa, Ks., U.S. N9 118
Kiowa, Ok., U.S. E11 116
Kipahigan Lake, l., Can. C12 104
Kipengere Range, mts., Tan. C6 58
Kipling, Sask., Can. H12 104
Kipnuk, Ak., U.S. G12 100
Kipushi, Zaire D5 58
Kirane, Mali D4 64
Kirazlı, Tur. I10 20
Kirbyville, Tx., U.S. L3 114
Kirchberg, Ger. F9 10
Kirchheimbolanden, Ger. F8 10
Kirchmöser, Ger. C12 10
Kirchschlag in der Buckligen Welt, Aus. H16 10
Kirejevsk, Russia H20 22
Kirenga, stm., Russia F13 28
Kirensk, Russia F13 28
Kirghizia see Kyrgyzstan, ctry., Asia I13 26
Kirgizskij chrebet, mts., Asia I12 26
Kiri, Zaire B3 58
Kiribati, ctry., Oc. I22 126
Kırıkhan, Tur. C4 48
Kırıkkale, Tur. B2 48
Kirillov, Russia B21 22
Kirillovskoje, Russia A12 22
Kirin see Jilin, China C12 30
Kirin see Jilin, prov., China C12 30
Kirinyaga, mtn., Kenya B7 58
Kiriši, Russia B15 22
Kiriwina Islands, is., Pap. N. Gui. A10 68
Kırkağaç, Tur. J11 20
Kirkcaldy, Scot., U.K. E10 8
Kirkcudbright, Scot., U.K. G9 8
Kirkenes, Nor. G22 6
Kirkjubæjarklaustur, Ice. C4 6a
Kirkland, Il., U.S. H7 110
Kirkland, Tx., U.S. E6 116
Kirkland, Wa., U.S. C3 122
Kirkland Lake, Ont., Can. B15 110
Kırklareli, Tur. H11 20
Kirklin, In., U.S. B10 114
Kirkness Lake, l., Ont., Can. G21 104
Kirkpatrick, Mount, mtn., Ant. D8 73
Kirkpatrick Lake, l., Alta., Can. F23 102
Kirksville, Mo., U.S. B4 114
Kirkūk, Iraq D8 48
Kirkwall, Scot., U.K. C11 8
Kirkwood, S. Afr. I7 66
Kirkwood, Il., U.S. J5 110
Kirkwood, Mo., U.S. D6 114
Kirov, Russia G17 22
Kirov, Russia F7 26
Kirovakan, Arm. I6 26
Kirovgrad, Russia F10 26
Kirovohrad, Ukr. H4 26
Kirovsk, Bela. H12 22
Kirovsk, Russia B14 22
Kirovsk, Russia D4 26
Kirovskij, Kaz. I13 26
Kirs, Russia F8 26
Kirsanov, Russia I25 22
Kırşehir, Tur. B3 48
Kīrthar Range, mts., Pak. G2 44
Kirtland, N.M., U.S. H8 120
Kiruna, Swe. H17 6
Kirwin, Ks., U.S. L8 118
Kiryū, Japan K14 36
Kiržač, Russia E21 22
Kisa, Swe. M14 6
Kisangani (Stanleyville), Zaire A5 58
Kisarazu, Japan L14 36
Kisbey, Sask., Can. I12 104
Kisel'ovsk, Russia G9 28
Kishanganj, India G12 44
Kishangarh Bās, India G6 44
Kishi, Nig. G11 64
Kishikas, stm., Ont., Can. F23 104
Kishiwada, Japan M10 36
Kishorganj, Bngl. H14 44
Kisii, Kenya B6 58
Kiska Island, i., Ak., U.S. j3 101a
Kiskatinaw, stm., B.C., Can. B14 102
Kiski Lake, l., Man., Can. D16 104
Kiskittogisu Lake, l., Man., Can. D16 104
Kiskitto Lake, l., Man., Can. D16 104
Kiskunfélegyháza, Hung. I19 10
Kiskunhalas, Hung. I19 10
Kiskunmajsa, Hung. I19 10
Kislovodsk, Russia I6 26
Kismaayo, Som. B8 58
Kiso-sammyaku, mts., Japan L12 36
Kispiox, B.C., Can. B7 102
Kispiox, stm., B.C., Can. B7 102
Kispiox Mountain, mtn., B.C., Can. B7 102
Kisseynew Lake, l., Can. D13 104
Kissidougou, Gui. G4 64
Kissimmee, Fl., U.S. K5 112
Kissimmee, stm., Fl., U.S. L6 112
Kissimmee, Lake, l., Fl., U.S. L5 112
Kississing, Man., Can. C13 104
Kississing Lake, l., Man., Can. C13 104
Kistigan Lake, l., Can. D22 104
Kisújszállás, Hung. H20 10
Kisumu, Kenya B6 58
Kisvárda, Hung. G22 10
Kita, Mali E5 64
Kita-Daitō-jima, i., Japan F13 30
Kitaibaraki, Japan K15 36
Kitakata, Japan J14 36
Kitakyūshū, Japan N5 36
Kitale, Kenya A7 58
Kitami, Japan d18 36a
Kitami-sanchi, mts., Japan c17 36a
Kit Carson, Co., U.S. M5 118
Kitchener, Ont., Can. G15 110
Kiteiyab, Sud. I7 60
Kíthira, Grc. M7 20
Kíthira, i., Grc. M6 20
Kíthnos, i., Grc. L8 20
Kitimat, B.C., Can. C6 102
Kitimat, stm., B.C., Can. C6 102
Kitimat Ranges, mts., B.C., Can. D5 102
Kitlope, stm., B.C., Can. D7 102
Kitlope Lake, l., B.C., Can. D7 102
Kitscoty, Alta., Can. E4 104
Kitsman', Ukr. A9 20
Kittanning, Pa., U.S. G7 108
Kittery, Me., U.S. D16 108
Kittilä, Fin. H19 6
Kittitas, Wa., U.S. D5 122
Kitui, Kenya B7 58
Kitwanga, B.C., Can. B6 102
Kitwangar Indian Reserve, B.C., Can. B6 102
Kitwe, Zam. D5 58
Kitwitwi, Nmb. A4 66
Kitzbühel, Aus. H12 10
Kitzingen, Ger. F10 10
Kiukiang see Jiujiang, China F4 34
Kiviõli, Est. B9 22
Kivu, Lac, l., Afr. B5 58
Kıyıköy, Tur. H12 20
Kiyiu Lake, l., Sask., Can. G6 104
Kizel, Russia F9 26
Kızıl, stm., Tur. A2 48
Kızıltepe, Tur. C6 48
Kizl'ar, Russia I7 26
Kizyl-Arvat, Turk. J9 26
Kizyl-Atrek, Turk. J8 26
Kizyl-Su, Turk. B12 48
Kjustendil, Bul. G6 20
Kladanj, Bos. E2 20
Kladno, Czech. E14 10
Klagenfurt, Aus. I14 10
Klahoose Indian Reserve, B.C., Can. G10 102
Klaipėda (Memel), Lith. F4 22
Klaksvík, Faer. Is. D8 6b
Klamath, Ca., U.S. C1 124
Klamath, stm., U.S. C1 124
Klamath Falls, Or., U.S. H4 122
Klamath Mountains, mts., U.S. B2 124
Klangpi, Mya. C2 40
Klarälven, stm., Eur. K13 6
Kl'asticy, Bela. F11 22
Klatovy, Czech. F13 10
Klawer, S. Afr. H4 66
Klawock, Ak., U.S. I28 100
Kl'az'ma, stm., Russia E25 22
Kleck, Bela. H9 22
Kleena Kleene, B.C., Can. F10 102
Klemme, Ia., U.S. G2 110
Klemtu, B.C., Can. E6 102
Klerksdorp, S. Afr. F8 66
Klet', mtn., Czech. G14 10
Kletn'a, Russia H16 22
Kleve, Ger. D6 10
Kličev, Bela. H12 22
Klickitat, Wa., U.S. E4 122
Klickitat, stm., Wa., U.S. E4 122
Klimoviči, Bela. H14 22
Klimovo, Russia I15 22
Klimovsk, Russia F20 22
Klin, Russia E19 22
Klinaklini, stm., B.C., Can. F9 102
Klincy, Russia I15 22
Klipplaat, S. Afr. I7 66
Klishkivtsi, Ukr. A10 20
Kłobuck, Pol. E18 10
Kłodzko, Pol. E16 10
Klondike, hist. reg., Yukon, Can. E25 100
Klondike, stm., Yukon, Can. D26 100
Klosterneuburg, Aus. G16 10
Klosters, Switz. E12 13
Kloten, Switz. D10 13
Klotz, Lac, l., Que., Can. D18 96
Klötze, Ger. C11 10
Klouto, Togo H10 64
Kluane, stm., Yukon, Can. F25 100
Kluane Lake, l., Yukon, Can. F25 100
Kluane National Park, Yukon, Can. F25 100
Kl'učevskaja Sopka, vulkan, vol., Russia F24 28
Kl'uči, Russia F24 28
Kluczbork, Pol. E18 10
Klukwan, Ak., U.S. G27 100
Knapp, Wi., U.S. F3 110
Knäred, Swe. M13 6
Kn'ažji Gory, Russia E18 22
Kneehills Creek, stm., Alta., Can. F21 102
Knee Lake, l., Man., Can. C20 104
Knee Lake, l., Sask., Can. C7 104
Knevicy, Russia D15 22
Kneža, Bul. F8 20
Knić, Yugo. F4 20
Knickerbocker, Tx., U.S. H6 116
Knife, stm., N.D., U.S. D6 118
Knife Lake, l., Ont., Can. E23 104
Knight Inlet, b., B.C., Can. G9 102
Knights Landing, Ca., U.S. F4 124
Knightstown, In., U.S. C11 114
Knik Arm, b., Ak., U.S. F20 100
Knin, Cro. E11 18
Knippa, Tx., U.S. J7 116
Knittelfeld, Aus. H14 10
Knob Noster, Mo., U.S. D3 114
Knokke-Heist, Bel. F3 12
Knox, In., U.S. A10 114
Knox, Pa., U.S. F7 108
Knox, Cape, c., B.C., Can. C1 102
Knox City, Tx., U.S. F7 116
Knox Coast, Ant. B6 73
Knoxville, Ga., U.S. G3 112
Knoxville, Il., U.S. J5 110
Knoxville, Ia., U.S. I2 110
Knoxville, Tn., U.S. D3 112
Knysna, S. Afr. J6 66
Knyszyn, Pol. B22 10
Kobar Sink, depr., Eth. F9 56
Kobayashi, Japan P5 36
Kōbe, Japan M10 36
København (Copenhagen), Den. N13 6
Koblenz, Ger. E7 10
Koboža, Russia C18 22
Kobrin, Bela. I7 22
Kobrinskoje, Russia B13 22
Kobuk, Ak., U.S. C16 100
Kobylin, Pol. D17 10
Kočani, Mac. H6 20
Kočečum, stm., Russia D12 28
Kočetovka, Russia I23 22
Kočevje, Slo. D9 18
Kŏch'ang, S. Kor. H14 32
Kochanovo, Bela. G13 22

Name	Map Ref.	Page

Name	Map Ref.	Page

Name | Map Ref. | Page

Mambaí, Braz. C5 79
Mamberamo, stm., Indon. F10 38
Mambéré, stm., Cen. Afr. Rep. H4 56
Ma-Me-O Beach, Alta., Can. E21 102
Mamers, Fr. D7 14
Mamfe, Cam. G8 54
Mamiá, Lago, l., Braz. J11 84
Mamie, N.C., U.S. C11 112
Mamiña, Chile I7 82
Mammoth, Az., U.S. L6 120
Mammoth, W.V., U.S. I5 108
Mammoth Cave National Park, Ky., U.S. E10 114
Mammoth Lakes, Ca., U.S. G7 124
Mammoth Spring, Ar., U.S. F5 114
Mamonovo, Russia G2 22
Mamoré, stm., S.A. D9 82
Mamori, Lago, l., Braz. I12 84
Mamoriá, stm., Braz. B8 82
Mamou, Gui. F3 64
Mamou, La., U.S. L4 114
Mamoutzou, May. I16 67a
Mampikony, Madag. p22 67b
Mamry, Jezioro, l., Pol. A21 10
Mamuchi, China H6 32
Ma'mūn, Sud. K2 60
Mamuno, Bots. D5 66
Mamuru, stm., Braz. I14 84
Man, C. Iv. H6 64
Man, W.V., U.S. B5 112
Mana, Hi., U.S. o14 125a
Mana, stm., Fr. Gu. B8 76
Manabí, prov., Ec. H2 84
Manacacías, stm., Col. F6 84
Manacapuru, Braz. I12 84
Manacor, Spain F15 16
Manado, Indon. E7 38
Managua, Nic. E8 92
Managua, dept., Nic. E8 92
Managua, Lago de, l., Nic. E8 92
Manakara, Madag. s23 67b
Manāli, India D7 44
Manama see Al-Manāmah, Bahr. H11 48
Manambato, Madag. n23 67b
Manambolosy, Madag. p23 67b
Mánamo, Caño, mth., Ven. C11 84
Mananara, Madag. p23 67b
Mananjary, Madag. r23 67b
Manantenina, Madag. t22 67b
Manapiare, stm., Ven. E9 84
Manapire, stm., Ven. C9 84
Manaquiri, Lago, l., Braz. I12 84
Manaravolo, Madag. s21 67b
Manas, China C4 30
Manās, stm., Asia G14 44
Manas Hu, l., China B4 30
Manāslu, mtn., Nepal F11 44
Manasquan, N.J., U.S. G12 108
Manassa, Co., U.S. G11 120
Manassas, Va., U.S. I9 108
Manatí, Col. B5 84
Manatí, P.R. E11 94
Manaung, Mya. E2 40
Manaus, Braz. I12 84
Manawa, Wi., U.S. F7 110
Manawan Lake, l., Sask., Can. C11 104
Manbij, Syria C4 48
Mancelona, Mi., U.S. F10 110
Mancha Real, Spain H8 16
Manche, dept., Fr. C5 14
Manchester, Eng., U.K. H11 8
Manchester, Ct., U.S. F14 108
Manchester, Ga., U.S. G2 112
Manchester, Ia., U.S. H4 110
Manchester, Ky., U.S. B3 112
Manchester, Ma., U.S. E16 108
Manchester, Mi., U.S. H11 110
Manchester, N.H., U.S. E15 108
Manchester, Oh., U.S. I3 108
Manchester, Tn., U.S. G10 114
Manchester, Vt., U.S. D13 108
Manchón, Guat. C2 92
Manchuria, hist. reg., China B12 30
Máncora, Peru J2 84
Mancos, Co., U.S. G8 120
Mancos, stm., U.S. G8 120
Mandabe, Madag. r21 67b
Mandaguari, Braz. G3 79
Mandal, Nor. L10 6
Mandala, Puncak, mtn., Indon. F11 38
Mandalay, Mya. C4 40
Mandalgov', Mong. B8 30
Mandalī, Iraq E8 48
Mandan, N.D., U.S. E7 118
Mandara Mountains, mts., Afr. F9 54
Mandas, Italy J4 18
Mandeb, Bab el, strt. H3 47
Mandel, Afg. E16 48
Manderson, Wy., U.S. F18 122
Mandeville, Jam. E6 94
Mandeville, La., U.S. L6 114
Mandi, India E7 44
Mandiana, Gui. F5 64
Mandimba, Moz. D7 58
Mandioli, Pulau, i., Indon. F8 38
Mandioré, Lagoa, l., S.A. H13 82
Mandla, India A6 46
Mandoto, Madag. q22 67b
Mandouri, Togo F10 64
Mandra, Pak. D5 44
Mandritsara, Madag. o23 67b
Mandronarivo, Madag. r21 67b
Mandsaur, India H6 44
Manduria, Italy I12 18
Māndvi, India I3 44
Mandya, India F4 46
Manfalūt, Egypt D6 60
Manfredonia, Italy H10 18
Manfredonia, Golfo di, b., Italy H11 18
Manga, Braz. C7 79
Manga, Burkina F9 64
Mangabeiras, Chapada das, hills, Braz. F9 76
Mangalagiri, India D6 46
Mangalore, India F3 46
Mangaoka, Madag. n23 67b
Mangchang, China F8 30
Mange, China D10 44
Mange, S.L. G3 64
Mangham, La., U.S. J5 114
Manglares, Cabo, c., Col. G3 84
Mangochi, Mwi. D7 58
Mangoky, stm., Madag. r21 67b
Mangole, Pulau, i., Indon. F8 38
Mangoupa, Cen. Afr. Rep. O3 60
Mangrol, India J4 44
Mangrove Cay, i., Bah. B6 94
Mangueira, Lagoa, b., Braz. G12 80
Mangueirinha, Braz. C12 80
Mangulile, Hond. B8 92
Mangum, Ok., U.S. E7 116
Mangya, China D5 30
Manhattan, Ks., U.S. L11 118
Manhattan, Mt., U.S. E14 122
Manhuaçu, Braz. F7 79
Manhuaçu, stm., Braz. E8 79
Manhumirim, Braz. F8 79
Maniago, Italy C7 18
Maniamba, Moz. D7 58
Manic Deux, Réservoir, res., Que., Can. C5 106
Manicoré, Braz. A11 82
Manicoré, stm., Braz. B11 82
Manicouagan, stm., Que., Can. C5 106
Manicouagan, Réservoir, res., Que., Can. A5 106
Manic Trois, Réservoir, res., Que., Can. B5 106
Manignan, C. Iv. F6 64
Manigotagan, Man., Can. G18 104
Manigotagan, stm., Can. H19 104
Manila, Phil. n19 39b
Manila, Ar., U.S. G6 114
Manila, Ut., U.S. D7 120
Manila Bay, b., Phil. n19 39b
Manilla, Austl. H9 70
Manilla, Ia., U.S. J12 118
Manily, Russia E25 28
Maninpé, Mali D7 64
Manino, Russia H17 22
Manipur, state, India H15 44
Manipur, stm., Asia C2 40
Manisa, Tur. K11 20
Manissauá-Miçu, stm., Braz. A1 79
Manistee, Mi., U.S. F9 110
Manistee, stm., Mi., U.S. F9 110
Manistique, Mi., U.S. E9 110
Manistique, stm., Mi., U.S. D9 110
Manito, Il., U.S. B7 114
Manitoba, prov., Can. D17 104
Manitoba, Lake, l., Man., Can. H16 104
Manitou, Man., Can. I16 104
Manitou, stm., Ont., Can. I21 104
Manitou, stm., Que., Can. B8 106
Manitou, Lac, l., Que., Can. B10 106
Manitou, Lac, l., Que., Can. B8 106
Manitou Beach, Sask., Can. G9 104
Manitou Lake, l., Sask., Can. F5 104
Manitoulin Island, i., Ont., Can. E13 110
Manitou Springs, Co., U.S. F12 120
Manitowaning, Ont., Can. E14 110
Manitowish Waters, Wi., U.S. D6 110
Manitowoc, Wi., U.S. F8 110
Manitowoc, stm., Wi., U.S. F7 110
Maniwaki, Que., Can. A11 108
Manizales, Col. E5 84
Manja, Madag. r21 67b
Manjacaze, Moz. E11 66
Manjakandriana, Madag. q22 67b
Manjimup, Austl. F3 68
Mankato, Ks., U.S. L9 118
Mankato, Mn., U.S. F2 110
Mankayane, Swaz. F10 66
Mankota, Sask., Can. I7 104
Manlleu, Spain C14 16
Manly, Ia., U.S. G2 110
Manmād, India B3 46
Mannahill, Austl. I3 70
Mannar, Gulf of, b., Asia H5 46
Mannārgudi, India G5 46
Männedorf, Switz. D10 13
Mannford, Ok., U.S. C10 116
Mannheim, Ger. F8 10
Manni, China C12 44
Manning, Ia., U.S. J12 118
Manning, N.D., U.S. D5 118
Manning, S.C., U.S. F6 112
Mannington, W.V., U.S. H6 108
Mannum, Austl. J3 70
Mannville, Alta., Can. D23 102
Mano, stm., Afr. H4 64
Manoa, Bol. C9 82
Manoel Ribas, Braz. C13 80
Manokotak, Ak., U.S. G15 100
Manombo, Madag. s20 67b
Manono, Zaire C5 58
Manor, Sask., Can. I12 104
Manor, Tx., U.S. I9 116
Manosque, Fr. I12 14
Manouane, stm., Que., Can. B3 106
Manouane, Lac, l., Que., Can. B3 106
Manouanis, stm., Que., Can. A3 106
Manouanis, Lac, l., Que., Can. B3 106
Manp'o, N. Kor. B14 32
Manresa, Spain D13 16
Mānsa, India F6 44
Mansa, Zam. D5 58
Mansel Island, i., N.W. Ter., Can. D17 96
Mansfield, Austl. K7 70
Mansfield, Ar., U.S. G2 114
Mansfield, Ga., U.S. F3 112
Mansfield, Il., U.S. B8 114
Mansfield, La., U.S. J3 114
Mansfield, Ma., U.S. E15 108
Mansfield, Mo., U.S. E4 114
Mansfield, Oh., U.S. G4 108
Mansfield, Pa., U.S. F9 108
Mansfield, Tx., U.S. G9 116
Mansfield, Mount, mtn., Vt., U.S. C14 108
Mansión, C.R. G9 92
Mansle, Fr. G7 14
Manso, stm., Braz. F13 82
Manson, Ia., U.S. I13 118
Manson, stm., B.C., Can. B11 102
Manson Creek, B.C., Can. B10 102
Mansura see Al-Manṣūrah, Egypt B6 60
Mansura, La., U.S. K4 114
Manta, Ec. H2 84
Manta, Bahía de, b., Ec. H2 84
Mantagao, stm., Man., Can. G17 104
Mantaro, stm., Peru E4 82
Manteca, Ca., U.S. G4 124
Mantecal, Ven. D8 84
Manteno, Il., U.S. I8 110
Manteo, N.C., U.S. D11 112
Mantes-la-Jolie, Fr. D8 14
Manti, Ut., U.S. E5 120
Mantiqueira, Serra da, mts., Braz. G6 79
Manton, Mi., U.S. F10 110
Mantorville, Mn., U.S. F3 110
Mantos Blancos, Chile B3 80
Mantova, Italy D5 18
Mantua, Cuba C2 94
Mantua see Mantova, Italy D5 18
Mantua, Oh., U.S. F5 108
Manturovo, Russia C27 22
Mäntyharju, Fin. K20 6
Manu, Peru E6 82
Manú, stm., Peru E6 82
Manua Islands, is., Am. Sam. J23 126
Manuel, Mex. F10 90
Manuel Antonio, Parque Nacional, C.R. H10 92
Manuel Benavides, Mex. C8 90
Manuel Derqui, Arg. D9 80
Manuel Urbano, Braz. C7 82
Manuripe (Manuripi), stm., S.A. D8 82
Manuripi, stm., Bol. E8 82
Manus Island, i., Pap. N. Gui. k16 68a
Manvel, N.D., U.S. C10 118
Many, La., U.S. K3 114
Manyana, Bots. D5 66
Manyara, Lake, l., Tan. B7 58
Manyberries, Alta., Can. I4 104
Manyč, stm., Russia H6 26
Many Island Lake, l., Can. H4 104
Manzanares, Spain F8 16
Manzanillo, Cuba D6 94
Manzanillo, Mex. H7 90
Manzanillo, Punta, c., Pan. H15 92
Manzanillo Bay, b., N.A. E9 94
Manzano, N.M., U.S. J10 120
Manzanola, Co., U.S. M4 118
Manzano Peak, mtn., N.M., U.S. J10 120
Manzhouli, China B10 30
Manzini, Swaz. F10 66
Mao, Chad F4 56
Mao, Dom. Rep. E9 94
Maó, Spain F16 16
Maoke, Pegunungan, mts., Indon. F10 38
Maoming, China G9 30
Maouri, Dallol, val., Niger E11 64
Mapari, stm., Braz. I9 84
Mapastepec, Mex. J13 90
Mapia, Kepulauan, is., Indon. E9 38
Mapimí, Mex. E8 90
Mapimí, Bolsón de, des., Mex. D8 90
Maping, China D2 34
Mapinhane, Moz. D12 66
Mapire, Ven. D10 84
Mapiri, Bol. F7 82
Mapiri, stm., Bol. D8 82
Mapixari, Ilha, i., Braz. I10 84
Maple, stm., U.S. F9 118
Maple, stm., Ia., U.S. I12 118
Maple, stm., Mi., U.S. G11 110
Maple, stm., N.D., U.S. E10 118
Maple Creek, Sask., Can. I5 104
Maple Lake, Mn., U.S. E1 110
Maple Mount, Ky., U.S. E9 114
Maplesville, Al., U.S. J10 114
Mapleton, Ia., U.S. I12 118
Mapleton, Mn., U.S. G2 110
Mapleton, Or., U.S. F2 122
Mapleton, Ut., U.S. D5 120
Mapuera, stm., Braz. H14 84
Mapulanguene, Moz. E11 66
Maputo, Moz. E11 66
Maputo, stm., Afr. F11 66
Maqna, Sau. Ar. G3 48
Maquela do Zombo, Ang. C3 58
Maquereau, Pointe au, c., Que., Can. D9 106
Maquilaú, stm., Braz. G11 84
Maquinchao, Arg. E3 78
Maquoketa, Ia., U.S. H5 110
Maquoketa, stm., Ia., U.S. H5 110
Mar, Serra do, clf, Braz. C14 80
Mara, Peru F5 82
Mara, stm., Afr. B6 58
Maraã, Braz. H10 84
Marabá, Braz. E9 76
Maracá, Ilha de, i., Braz. F12 84
Maracaí, Braz. G3 79
Maracaibo, Ven. B7 84
Maracaibo, Lago de, l., Ven. C7 84
Maracaju, Braz. F1 79
Maracaju, Serra de, hills, S.A. F1 79
Maracanã, stm., Braz. C12 82
Maracás, Braz. B8 79
Maracay, Ven. B9 84
Marādah, Libya C4 56
Maradi, Niger E13 64
Maradi, Goulbin, stm., Afr. E13 64
Marāgheh, Iran C9 48
Maragogipe, Braz. F11 76
Maragogipe, Braz. B9 79
Marahuaca, Cerro, mtn., Ven. F10 84
Maraiche Lake, l., Sask., Can. D12 104
Marais des Cygnes, stm., U.S. D1 114
Marajó, Baía de, b., Braz. D9 76
Marajó, Ilha de, i., Braz. D9 76
Marakabei, Leso. G9 66
Maralal, Kenya A7 58
Maralaleng, Bots. E6 66
Marampa, S.L. G3 64
Maramureș, co., Rom. B8 20
Maran, Malay. M7 40
Marana, Az., U.S. L5 120
Marand, Iran B8 48
Marangani, Peru F6 82
Maranguape, Braz. D11 76
Maranhão, stm., Braz. C4 79
Maranoa, stm., Austl. E9 70
Marañón, stm., Peru D3 76
Marapanim, Braz. D9 76
Marapi, stm., Braz. G14 84
Maras, Peru E5 82
Marathon, Austl. C5 70
Marathon, Ont., Can. B9 110
Marathón, Grc. K7 20
Marathon, N.Y., U.S. E10 108
Marathon, Tx., U.S. I3 116
Marathon, Wi., U.S. F6 110
Maraú, Braz. C9 79
Marau, Braz. E12 80
Marauiá, stm., Braz. H10 84
Maravilha, Braz. D12 80
Maravillas, Mex. D7 90
Marawī, Sud. H6 60
Marayes, Arg. F4 80
Marbach, Switz. E8 13
Marbella, Spain I7 16
Marble, Mn., U.S. C2 110
Marble, N.C., U.S. D3 112
Marble Bar, Austl. D3 68
Marble Canyon, val., Az., U.S. H5 120
Marble Falls, Tx., U.S. I8 116
Marble Hall, S. Afr. E9 66
Marblehead, Oh., U.S. F4 108
Marble Hill, Mo., U.S. E7 114
Marble Rock, Ia., U.S. H3 110
Marburg, Ger. E8 10
Marcala, Hond. C6 92
Marcali, Hung. I17 10
Marcaria, Italy D5 18
Marceau, Lac, l., Que., Can. A7 106
Marcelin, Sask., Can. F8 104
Marceline, Mo., U.S. C4 114
Marcelino Ramos, Braz. D13 80
Marcellus, Mi., U.S. H10 110
March (Morava), stm., Eur. G16 10
Marcha, stm., Russia E15 28
Marche, prov., Italy F8 18
Marche, hist. reg., Fr. F8 14
Marche-en-Famenne, Bel. H7 12
Marchegg, Aus. G16 10
Marchena, Spain H6 16
Mar Chiquita, Laguna, b., Arg. I10 80
Mar Chiquita, Laguna, l., Arg. F7 80
Marcigny, Fr. F11 14
Marcola, Or., U.S. F3 122
Marcona, Peru F4 82
Marcos Juárez, Arg. G7 80
Marcos Paz, Arg. H9 80
Marcus, Ia., U.S. I12 118
Marcus Baker, Mount, mtn., Ak., U.S. F21 100
Marcy, Mount, mtn., N.Y., U.S. C13 108
Mardān, Pak. C5 44
Mardarivka, Ukr. B13 20
Mar del Plata, Arg. J10 80
Mardin, Tur. C6 48
Marea de Portillo, Cuba E6 94
Marechal Cândido Rondon, Braz. C11 80
Marechal Taumaturgo, Braz. C5 82
Mareeba, Austl. A6 70
Marengo, Il., U.S. H7 110
Marengo, In., U.S. D10 114
Marengo, Ia., U.S. I3 110
Marenisco, Mi., U.S. D6 110
Marfa, Tx., U.S. I2 116
Margaree, N.S., Can. F12 106
Margaree Harbour, N.S., Can. F12 106
Margaret Bay, B.C., Can. F7 102
Margaretville, N.Y., U.S. E12 108
Margarita, Isla, i., Col. C5 84
Margarita, Isla de, i., Ven. B10 84
Margarita Belén, Arg. D9 80
Margate, S. Afr. H10 66
Margate, Eng., U.K. J15 8
Margate, Fl., U.S. M6 112
Margate City, N.J., U.S. H12 108
Margecany, Slov. G21 10
Margherita Peak, mtn., Afr. A5 58
Marghī, Afg. C2 44
Margilan, Uzb. I12 26
Margos, Peru D3 82
Margot Lake, l., Ont., Can. F21 104
Margow, Dasht-e, des., Afg. F17 48
Marguerite Bay, b., Ant. B12 73
Marhanets', Ukr. H4 26
María Cleofas, Isla, i., Mex. G6 90
María Elena, Chile B4 80
Maria Gail, Aus. I13 10
María Ignacia (Vela), Arg. I9 80
Maria Island, i., Austl. N8 70
María la Baja, Col. C5 84
María Madre, Isla, i., Mex. G6 90
María Magdalena, Isla, i., Mex. G6 90
Mariana, Braz. F7 79
Mariana Islands, is., Oc. G18 126
Mariana Trench G18 126
Mariāni, India G16 44
Marian Lake, l., N.W. Ter., Can. D9 96
Marianna, Ar., U.S. H6 114
Marianna, Fl., U.S. I1 112
Mariano I. Loza, Arg. E9 80
Mariano Moreno, Arg. J3 80
Mariánské Lázně, Czech. F12 10
Marias, stm., Mt., U.S. B15 122
Marías, Islas, is., Mex. G6 90
Marias Pass, Mt., U.S. B12 122
María Teresa, Arg. H8 80
Mariato, Punta, c., Pan. D2 84
Mā'rib, Yemen G4 47
Maribor, Slo. C10 18
Marica (Évros) (Meriç), stm., Eur. H10 20
Marico, stm., Afr. E8 66
Maricopa, Az., U.S. K4 120
Maricopa, Ca., U.S. I6 124
Maricunga, Salar de, pl., Chile D4 80
Marié, stm., Braz. H9 84
Marie Byrd Land, reg., Ant. C10 73
Marie-Galante, i., Guad. G14 94
Mariehamn, Fin. K16 6
Mari El see Marij El, state, Russia F7 26
Marie Lake, l., Alta., Can. D4 104
Marienbad see Mariánské Lázně, Czech. F12 10
Marienburg see Malbork, Pol. A19 10
Mariental, Nmb. E3 66
Marienville, Pa., U.S. F7 108
Maries, stm., Mo., U.S. D4 114
Mariestad, Swe. L13 6
Marieta, stm., Ven. E9 84
Marietta, Ga., U.S. F2 112
Marietta, Mn., U.S. F11 118
Marietta, Oh., U.S. H5 108
Marietta, Ok., U.S. F9 116
Marieville, Que., Can. B13 108
Mariga, stm., Nig. F13 64
Marignane, Fr. I12 14
Marigot, Dom. G14 94
Marigot, Guad. E13 94
Mariinsk, Russia F9 28
Marijampole, Lith. G6 22
Marij El, state, Russia F7 26
Marikana, S. Afr. E8 66
Marília, Braz. G4 79
Marimari, stm., Braz. J13 84
Marimba, Ang. C3 58
Marín, Spain C3 16
Marina di Ravenna, Italy E7 18
Marina Fall, wtfl, Guy. E13 84
Marine City, Mi., U.S. H13 110
Marinette, Wi., U.S. E8 110
Maringá, Braz. G3 79
Maringouin, La., U.S. L5 114
Maringuè, Moz. A12 66
Marion, Al., U.S. J9 114
Marion, Ar., U.S. G6 114
Marion, Il., U.S. E8 114
Marion, In., U.S. B11 114
Marion, Ia., U.S. H4 110
Marion, Ks., U.S. M10 118
Marion, Ky., U.S. E8 114
Marion, La., U.S. J4 114
Marion, Mi., U.S. F10 110
Marion, Ms., U.S. J8 114
Marion, N.C., U.S. D4 112
Marion, N.D., U.S. E9 118
Marion, Oh., U.S. G3 108
Marion, S.C., U.S. E7 112
Marion, S.D., U.S. H10 118
Marion, Va., U.S. C5 112
Marion, Wi., U.S. F7 110
Marion, Lake, res., S.C., U.S. F6 112
Marion Junction, Al., U.S. J9 114
Marion Lake, res., Ks., U.S. M10 118
Marion Reef, rf., Austl. B10 70
Marionville, Mo., U.S. E3 114
Mariópolis, Braz. D12 80
Maripa, Ven. D10 84
Mariposa, Ca., U.S. G6 124
Mariquita, Col. E5 84
Mariscal Estigarribia, Para. B8 80
Marissa, Il., U.S. D7 114
Maritime Alps, mts., Eur. H14 14
Maritime Atlas see Atlas Tellien, mts., Alg. C11 62
Mariupol' (Ždanov), Ukr. H5 26
Mariusa, Caño, mth., Ven. C12 84
Marīvān, Iran D9 48
Märjamaa, Est. C7 22
Marjina Gorka, Bela. H11 22
Marjinsko, Russia C11 22
Marka, Som. H9 56
Markala, Mali E6 64
Markdale, Ont., Can. F15 110
Marked Tree, Ar., U.S. G6 114
Markesan, Wi., U.S. G7 110
Markham, Ont., Can. G16 110
Markham, Tx., U.S. K10 116
Markham, Mount, mtn., Ant. D8 73
Markham Bay, b., N.W. Ter., Can. D18 96
Markle, In., U.S. B11 114
Markleeville, Ca., U.S. F6 124
Markovo, Russia D23 22
Markovo, Russia E26 28
Marks, Russia G7 26
Marks, Ms., U.S. H6 114
Marksville, La., U.S. K4 114
Marktheidenfeld, Ger. F9 10
Marktoberdorf, Ger. H10 10
Marktredwitz, Ger. E12 10
Mark Twain Lake, res., Mo., U.S. C5 114
Markundi, Sud. L2 60
Marlboro, Alta., Can. D18 102
Marlboro, N.Y., U.S. F13 108
Marlborough, Austl. D8 70
Marlborough, Guy. D13 84
Marlborough, Eng., U.K. J12 8
Marlborough, Ma., U.S. E15 108
Marle, Fr. C10 14
Marlette, Mi., U.S. G12 110
Marlin, Tx., U.S. H10 116
Marlinton, W.V., U.S. I6 108
Marlow, Ok., U.S. E9 116
Marmaduke, Ar., U.S. F6 114
Marmande, Fr. H7 14
Marmara Denizi (Sea of Marmara), Tur. I12 20
Marmara Ereğlisi, Tur. I11 20
Marmaris, Tur. M12 20
Marmarth, N.D., U.S. E4 118
Marmaton, stm., U.S. E2 114
Marmelos, Braz. B11 82
Marmelos, Rio dos, stm., Braz. B11 82
Marmet, W.V., U.S. I5 108
Marmora, Ont., Can. F18 110
Mar Muerto, Laguna, b., Mex. I12 90
Marnay, Fr. E12 14
Marne, Mi., U.S. G10 110
Marne, dept., Fr. D11 14
Marne, stm., Fr. C10 14
Marne au Rhin, Canal de la, Fr. D13 14
Maroa, Il., U.S. B8 114
Maroa, Ven. F9 84
Maroala, Madag. o22 67b
Maroantsetra, Madag. o23 67b
Maroelaboom, Nmb. B4 66
Marolambo, Madag. r23 67b
Maromme, Fr. C8 14
Maromokotro, mtn., Madag. o23 67b
Marondera, Zimb. B10 66
Maroni, stm., S.A. C8 76
Maros (Mureș), stm., Eur. C4 20
Maroseranana, Madag. q23 67b
Maroua, Cam. F9 54
Marovato, Madag. o23 67b
Marovoay, Madag. p22 67b
Marquand, Mo., U.S. E6 114
Marquesas Islands see Marquises, Îles, is., Fr. Poly. I26 126
Marquesas Keys, is., Fl., U.S. O4 112
Marquette, Ks., U.S. M10 118
Marquette, Mi., U.S. D8 110
Marquise, Fr. B8 14
Marquises, Îles (Marquesas Islands), is., Fr. Poly. I26 126
Marrah, Jabal, mtn., Sud. K3 60
Marrakech, Mor. E6 62
Marrawah, Austl. M6 70
Marree, Austl. G3 70
Marrero, La., U.S. M6 114
Marromeu, Moz. B12 66
Mars, Pa., U.S. G6 108
Marsā al-Burayqah, Libya B4 56
Marsabit, Kenya H8 56
Marsala, Italy L7 18
Marsā Maṭrūḥ, Egypt B4 60
Marsden, Austl. I7 70
Marseille, Fr. I12 14
Marseille-en-Beauvaisis, Fr. C8 14
Marseilles, Il., U.S. I7 110
Marshall, Lib. G4 54
Marshall, Lib. H4 64
Marshall, Ar., U.S. G4 114
Marshall, Il., U.S. C9 114
Marshall, Mi., U.S. H11 110
Marshall, Mn., U.S. G12 118
Marshall, Mo., U.S. C3 114
Marshall, N.C., U.S. D4 112
Marshall, Tx., U.S. J2 114
Marshall, Va., U.S. I9 108
Marshallberg, N.C., U.S. E10 112
Marshall Islands, ctry., Oc. H20 126
Marshalltown, Ia., U.S. H3 110
Marshallville, Ga., U.S. G3 112
Marshfield, Mo., U.S. E4 114
Marshfield, Wi., U.S. F5 110
Marsh Harbour, Bah. A6 94
Mars Hill, N.C., U.S. D4 112
Marsh Island, i., La., U.S. M5 114
Marsh Lake, l., Yukon, Can. F27 100
Marsh Peak, mtn., Ut., U.S. D7 120
Marshville, N.C., U.S. E6 112
Marsing, Id., U.S. G9 122
Mart, Tx., U.S. H10 116
Martaban, Mya. F4 40
Martaban, Gulf of, b., Mya. F4 40
Martapura, Indon. F5 38
Marten Mountain, mtn., Alta., Can. B20 102
Marte R. Gómez, Presa, res., Mex. D10 90
Martha's Vineyard, i., Ma., U.S. F16 108
Martí, Cuba D6 94
Martigny, Switz. F7 13
Martigues, Fr. I12 14
Martil, Mor. J6 16
Martin, Slov. F18 10
Martin, Ky., U.S. B4 112
Martin, Mi., U.S. H10 110
Martin, N.D., U.S. D7 118
Martin, S.D., U.S. H6 118
Martin, Tn., U.S. F8 114
Martina Franca, Italy I12 18
Martindale, Tx., U.S. J9 116
Martinez, Ca., U.S. F3 124
Martinez, Ga., U.S. F4 112
Martínez de la Torre, Mex. G11 90
Martinho Campos, Braz. E6 79
Martinique, dep., N.A. G14 94
Martinique Passage, strt., N.A. G14 94
Martin Lake, res., Al., U.S. J11 114
Martinniemi, Fin. I19 6
Martinsberg, Aus. G15 10
Martinsburg, Pa., U.S. G8 108
Martinsburg, W.V., U.S. H9 108
Martins Ferry, Oh., U.S. G6 108
Martinsville, Il., U.S. C9 114
Martinsville, In., U.S. C10 114
Martinsville, Va., U.S. C7 112
Martin Vaz, Ilhas, is., Braz. G12 74
Martisovo, Russia E14 22
Martos, Spain H8 16
Martre, Lac la, l., N.W. Ter., Can. D9 96
Martti, Fin. H21 6
Maru, Nig. E13 64
Marugame, Japan M8 36
Marula, Zimb. C9 66
Marunga, Ang. A5 66
Marungu, mts., Zaire C5 58
Ma'rūt, Afg. E2 44
Marv Dasht, Iran G12 48
Marvejols, Fr. H10 14
Marvell, Ar., U.S. H6 114
Marvine, Mount, mtn., Ut., U.S. F5 120
Marwayne, Alta., Can. E4 104
Mary, Turk. J10 26
Maryborough, Austl. E10 70
Maryborough, Austl. K5 70
Marydale, S. Afr. G6 66
Maryfield, Sask., Can. I13 104
Mary Kathleen, Austl. C3 70
Maryland, state, U.S. D11 98
Maryneal, Tx., U.S. G6 116
Marys, stm., Nv., U.S. C10 124
Marystown, Newf., Can. E18 106
Marysvale, Ut., U.S. F4 120
Marysville, B.C., Can. H19 102
Marysville, N.B., Can. G7 106
Marysville, Ca., U.S. E4 124
Marysville, Ks., U.S. L11 118
Marysville, Mi., U.S. H13 110
Marysville, Oh., U.S. G3 108
Marysville, Pa., U.S. G10 108
Marysville, Wa., U.S. B3 122
Maryville, Mo., U.S. B2 114
Maryville, Tn., U.S. D3 112
Marzagão, Braz. D4 79
Marzo, Punta, c., Col. D4 84
Marzūq, Libya C3 56
Marzūq, Ṣaḥrā', des., Libya D3 56
Masachapa, Nic. F8 92
Masada see Meẓada, Ḥorvot, hist., Isr. F4 50
Masagua, Guat. C4 92
Masai Steppe, plat., Tan. B7 58
Masaka, Ug. B6 58
Masallı, Azer. B10 48
Masan, S. Kor. H16 32
Masasi, Tan. D7 58
Masatepe, Nic. F8 92
Masaya, Nic. F8 92
Masaya, dept., Nic. E8 92
Masbate, Phil. C7 38
Mascarene Islands, is., Afr. F11 58
Mascasín, Arg. F5 80
Mascot, Tn., U.S. C3 112
Mascota, Mex. G7 90
Mascoutah, Il., U.S. D7 114
Masefield, Sask., Can. I7 104
Maseru, Leso. G8 66
Mashaba Mountains, mts., Zimb. B10 66
Mashābih, i., Sau. Ar. I4 48
Mashar, Sud. M4 60
Mashhad, Iran C15 48
Mashīz, Iran G14 48
Māshkel, Hāmūn-i-, l., Pak. G17 48
Māshkel, Rūd-i- (Māshkīd), stm., Asia G17 48
Mashra'ur-Raqq, Sud. M5 60
Masi Manimba, Zaire B3 58
Maṣīrah, Khalīj, b., Oman E11 47
Masisea, Peru C4 82
Masjed-e Soleymān, Iran F10 48
Mask, Lough, l., Ire. H4 8
Maska, Nig. F13 64
Maskanah, Syria C5 48
Maskin, Oman C10 47
Maskwa, stm., Man., Can. H19 104
Masoala, Madag. o24 67b
Masoala, Cap, c., Madag. o24 67b
Masoala, Presqu'île de, pen., Madag. o24 67b
Masoarivo, Madag. q21 67b
Masomeloka, Madag. r23 67b
Mason, Mi., U.S. H11 110
Mason, Oh., U.S. H2 108
Mason, Tn., U.S. G7 114
Mason, Tx., U.S. I7 116
Mason, W.V., U.S. H4 108
Mason City, Il., U.S. B7 114
Mason City, Ia., U.S. G2 110
Mason City, Ne., U.S. J8 118
Masqaṭ (Muscat), Oman C11 47
Massa, Italy E5 18
Massachusetts, state, U.S. C12 98
Massachusetts Bay, b., Ma., U.S. E16 108
Massafra, Italy I12 18
Massa Marittima, Italy F5 18
Massangena, Moz. C11 66
Massarosa, Italy F5 18
Massena, Ia., U.S. J13 118
Massena, N.Y., U.S. C12 108
Massenya, Chad F4 56
Masset, B.C., Can. C2 102
Masset Inlet, b., B.C., Can. D2 102
Masseube, Fr. I7 14
Massey, Ont., Can. D13 110
Massillon, Oh., U.S. G5 108
Massina, reg., Mali E7 64
Massinga, Moz. D12 66
Massive, Mount, mtn., Co., U.S. E10 120
Mastābah, Sau. Ar. D1 47
Maştağa, Azer. I8 26
Masterson, Tx., U.S. D5 116
Masterton, N.Z. D5 72
Mastung, Pak. F2 44
Mastūrah, Sau. Ar. C1 47
Masuda, Japan M6 36
Masvingo, Zimb. C10 66
Matachewan, Ont., Can. C15 110
Matacuni, stm., Ven. F10 84
Mata de São João, Braz. B9 79
Matadi, Zaire C2 58
Matador, Tx., U.S. E6 116
Matagalpa, Nic. E9 92
Matagalpa, dept., Nic. E9 92
Matagami, Que., Can. G17 96
Matagorda, Tx., U.S. K11 116
Matagorda Bay, b., Tx., U.S. K10 116
Matagorda Island, i., Tx., U.S. K10 116
Matale, Sri L. I6 46
Matam, Sen. D3 64
Matama, Cerro, mtn., C.R. H11 92
Matamoras, Pa., U.S. F12 108
Matamoros, Mex. E11 90
Matamoros, Mex. E8 90
Matane, Que., Can. D6 106
Matanuska, stm., Ak., U.S. F20 100
Matanzas, Cuba C4 94
Matanzas, Mex. G9 90
Matapalo, Cabo, c., C.R. I11 92
Matape, stm., Mex. C4 90
Matapédia, Que., Can. E7 106
Matapédia, Lac, l., Que., Can. D6 106
Mataquito, stm., Chile H3 80
Matará, Peru B2 82
Matara, Sri L. J6 46
Mataram, Indon. G6 38
Matarani, Peru G5 82
Mataró, Spain D14 16
Matatiele, S. Afr. H9 66
Mataurá, stm., Braz. B11 82
Mateare, Nic. E8 92

Mate-Meza

Name — Map Ref. — Page

Matehuala, Mex. F9 90
Matera, Italy I11 18
Mátészalka, Hung. H22 10
Mateur, Tun. L4 18
Matewan, W.V., U.S. B4 112
Mather, Man., Can. I15 104
Mather, Pa., U.S. H6 108
Matheson, Ont., Can. B15 110
Matheson Island, Man., Can. G18 104
Mathews, Va., U.S. B10 112
Mathis, Tx., U.S. K9 116
Mathura, India G7 44
Matiacoali, Burkina E10 64
Matias Barbosa, Braz. F7 79
Matías Romero, Mex. I12 90
Matícora, stm., Ven. B7 84
Matignon, Fr. D4 14
Matiguás, Nic. E9 92
Matipó, Braz. F7 79
Matiyure, stm., Ven. D8 84
Matlamanyane, Bots. B7 66
M'atlevo, Russia G18 22
Matmata, Tun. D15 62
Mato, stm., Ven. D10 84
Mato, Cerro, mtn., Ven. D10 84
Matočkin Šar, proliv, strt., Russia C8 26
Mato Grosso, state, Braz. D13 82
Mato Grosso, Planalto do, plat., Braz. G7 76
Matonipi, stm., Que., Can. A4 106
Matopo Hills, hills, Zimb. C9 66
Matos, stm., Bol. F9 82
Matosinhos, Port. D3 16
Matou, Tai. L9 34
Matoury, Fr. Gu. C8 76
Matouying, China D6 32
Mato Verde, Braz. C7 79
Matozinhos, Braz. E6 79
Maṭraḥ, Oman C11 47
Matrei in Osttirol, Aus. H12 10
Matru, S.L. H3 64
Matsapha, Swaz. F10 66
Matsudo, Japan L14 36
Matsue, Japan L8 36
Matsumae, Japan F15 36
Matsumoto, Japan K12 36
Matsu Tao, i., Tai. I8 34
Matsuyama, Japan N7 36
Mattagami, stm., Ont., Can. F16 96
Mattagami, stm., Ont., Can. B14 110
Mattagami Heights, Ont., Can. B14 110
Mattawa, Ont., Can. D17 110
Mattawa, Wa., U.S. D6 122
Mattawamkeag, Me., U.S. B18 108
Mattawamkeag, stm., Me., U.S. B18 108
Matterhorn, mtn., Eur. G14 14
Matterhorn, mtn., Nv., U.S. C10 124
Mattersburg, Aus. H16 10
Matthews Ridge, Guy. D12 84
Matthew Town, Bah. D8 94
Maṭṭī, Sabkhat, l., Asia J12 48
Mattighofen, Aus. G13 10
Mattoon, Il., U.S. C8 114
Mattoon, Wi., U.S. E6 110
Mattydale, N.Y., U.S. D10 108
Matuba, Moz. E11 66
Matucana, Peru D3 82
Maturín, Ven. C11 84
Maturino, Russia B20 22
Matutina, Braz. E6 79
Maú (Ireng), stm., S.A. E13 84
Maúa, Moz. D7 58
Maubeuge, Fr. B10 14
Maud, Ok., U.S. D10 116
Maud, Tx., U.S. I2 114
Maude, Austl. J6 70
Maués, Braz. I14 84
Maués, stm., Braz. I14 84
Maui, i., Hi., U.S. q17 125a
Mauldin, S.C., U.S. E4 112
Maule, prov., Chile H2 80
Maule, stm., Chile H2 80
Maule, Laguna del, l., Chile I3 80
Mauléon, Fr. F6 14
Maumee, Oh., U.S. F3 108
Maumee, stm., U.S. F2 108
Maun, Bots. C6 66
Mauna Kea, vol., Hi., U.S. r18 125a
Maunaloa, Hi., U.S. p16 125a
Mauna Loa, vol., Hi., U.S. r18 125a
Maunath Bhanjan, India H10 44
Maunatlala, Bots. D8 66
Maungdaw, Mya. D2 40
Maunoir, Lac, l., N.W. Ter., Can. C32 100
Maupin, Or., U.S. E4 122
Mau Rānīpur, India H8 44
Maure-de-Bretagne, Fr. E5 14
Maurepas, Lake, l., La., U.S. L6 114
Mauri, stm., Bol. G7 82
Mauriac, Fr. G9 14
Mauritania (Mauritanie), ctry., Afr. D4 54
Mauritius, ctry., Afr. F11 58
Mauritius, i., Mrts. v18 67c
Mauron, Fr. D4 14
Maury Channel, strt., N.W. Ter., Can. A13 96
Mauston, Wi., U.S. G5 110
Mauterndorf, Aus. H13 10
Mauthausen, Aus. G14 10
Mauvezin, Fr. I7 14
Mavaca, stm., Ven. F10 84
Maverick, Az., U.S. K7 120
Mavinga, Ang. E4 58
Mawchi, Mya. E4 40
Maw-daung Pass, Asia I5 40
Mawdesley Lake, l., Man., Can. D14 104
Mawkhi, Mya. F5 40
Mawlaik, Mya. C3 40
Mawlamyine (Moulmein), Mya. F4 40
Maw Taung, mtn., Asia I5 40
Max, N.D., U.S. D6 118
Maxcanú, Mex. G15 90
Maxixe, Moz. D12 66
Maxton, N.C., U.S. E7 112
Maxville, Ont., Can. B12 108
Maxwell, Ca., U.S. E3 124
Maxwell, Ia., U.S. I2 110
Maxwell, Ne., U.S. J7 118
Maxwell, N.M., U.S. C2 116
Maxwell Bay, b., N.W. Ter., Can. B15 96
May, Tx., U.S. H8 116
May, stm., Alta., Can. B23 102
May, Cape, pen., N.J., U.S. I12 108
May, Mount, mtn., Alta., Can. C15 102
Mayaguana, i., Bah. C8 94
Mayaguana Passage, strt., Bah. C8 94
Mayagüez, P.R. E11 94
Mayaky, Ukr. C14 20
Mayales, Punta, c., Nic. F9 92
Maya Mountains, mts., N.A. I15 90
Mayapan, hist., Mex. G15 90
Mayarí, Cuba D7 94
Maybeury, W.V., U.S. B5 112
Maybole, Scot., U.K. F9 8
Mayenne, Fr. M13 8
Mayenne, dept., Fr. D6 14
Mayer, Az., U.S. J4 120
Mayersville, Ms., U.S. J5 114
Mayerthorpe, Alta., Can. D19 102
Mayfield, Ky., U.S. F8 114
Mayfield, Ut., U.S. E5 120
Mayflower, Ar., U.S. H4 114
May Inlet, b., N.W. Ter., Can. A12 96
May Jirgui, Niger E14 64
Maymont, Sask., Can. F7 104
Maymyo, Mya. C4 40
Maynard, Ia., U.S. H4 110
Maynardville, Tn., U.S. C3 112
Mayne, stm., Austl. D4 70
Mayo, Yukon, Can. E27 100
Mayo, Fl., U.S. I3 112
Mayo, co., Ire. H4 8
Mayo, stm., Col. G4 84
Mayo, stm., Mex. D5 90
Mayo, stm., Peru B3 82
Mayodan, N.C., U.S. C7 112
Mayo Lake, l., Yukon, Can. E27 100
Mayon Volcano, vol., Phil. o20 39b
Mayor Buratovich, Arg. J7 80
Mayor Pablo Lagerenza, Para. H11 82
Mayotte, dep., Afr. D9 58
May Pen, Jam. F6 94
Mayrhofen, Aus. H11 10
Mays Landing, N.J., U.S. H12 108
Maysville, Ky., U.S. I3 108
Maysville, Mo., U.S. C2 114
Maysville, N.C., U.S. E9 112
Maysville, Ok., U.S. E9 116
Mayumba, Gabon B2 58
Māyūram, India G5 46
Mayville, Mi., U.S. G12 110
Mayville, N.Y., U.S. E7 108
Mayville, N.D., U.S. D10 118
Mayville, Wi., U.S. G7 110
Maywood, Ne., U.S. K7 118
Maza, Arg. I7 80
Mazabuka, Zam. E5 58
Mazagan see El-Jadida, Mor. D6 62
Mazagão, Braz. D8 76
Mazamet, Fr. I9 14
Mazán, stm., Peru I6 84
Mazār, Jabal, mtn., Asia A6 50
Mazara del Vallo, Italy L7 18
Mazār-e Sharīf, Afg. B2 44
Mazaruni, stm., Guy. E13 84
Mazatenango, Guat. C3 92
Mazatlán, Mex. F6 90
Mazatzal Peak, mtn., Az., U.S. J5 120
Mažeikiai, Lith. E5 22
Mazenod, Sask., Can. I8 104
Mazeppa, Mn., U.S. F3 110
Mazhuang, China C3 34
Mazirbe, Lat. D5 22
Mazoe, stm., Afr. E6 58
Mazomanie, Wi., U.S. G6 110
Mazon, Il., U.S. I7 110
Mazsalaca, Lat. D8 22
Mazunga, Zimb. C9 66
Mazury, reg., Pol. B20 10
Mbabane, Swaz. F10 66
Mbacké, Sen. D2 64
Mbage, Cen. Afr. Rep. O3 60
Mbaïki, Cen. Afr. Rep. H4 56
Mbala, Zam. C6 58
Mbale, Ug. A6 58
Mbalmayo, Cam. H9 54
Mbamba Bay, Tan. D6 58
Mbandaka (Coquilhatville), Zaire A3 58
Mbanga, Cam. I14 64
M'banza Congo, Ang. C2 58
Mbanza-Ngungu, Zaire C2 58
Mbarara, Ug. B6 58
Mbari, stm., Cen. Afr. Rep. G5 56
Mbashe, stm., S. Afr. I9 66
M'bengué, C. Iv. F7 64
Mbeya, Tan. C6 58
Mbinda, Congo B2 58
Mbini, Eq. Gui. H8 54
Mbomou (Bomu), stm., Afr. H5 56
Mbonge, Cam. I14 64
Mboro, Sud. N5 60
Mbour, Sen. D1 64
Mbout, Maur. C3 64
Mbuji-Mayi (Bakwanga), Zaire C4 58
Mburucuyá, Arg. E9 80
McAdam, N.B., Can. G6 106
McAdoo, Pa., U.S. G11 108
McAlester, Ok., U.S. E11 116
McAllen, Tx., U.S. M8 116
McArthur, Oh., U.S. H4 108
McAuley, Man., Can. H13 104
McBain, Mi., U.S. F10 110
McBee, S.C., U.S. E6 112
McBeth Fjord, N.W. Ter., Can. C19 96
McBride, B.C., Can. D14 102
McCall, Id., U.S. F9 122
McCall Creek, Ms., U.S. K6 114
McCallum, Newf., Can. E17 106
McCamey, Tx., U.S. H4 116
McCammon, Id., U.S. H13 122
McCauley Island, i., B.C., Can. D4 102
McCaysville, Ga., U.S. E2 112
McClarty Lake, l., Man., Can. D14 104
McCleary, Wa., U.S. C2 122
McClellanville, S.C., U.S. F7 112
McClintock, Mount, mtn., Ant. D8 73
McCloud, Ca., U.S. C3 124
McClure, Il., U.S. E7 114
McClure, Pa., U.S. G9 108
McClusky, N.D., U.S. D7 118
McColl, S.C., U.S. E7 112
McComas, W.V., U.S. B5 112
McComb, Ms., U.S. K6 114
McComb, Oh., U.S. F3 108
McConaughy, Lake, res., Ne., U.S. J6 118
McConnell Range, mts., N.W. Ter., Can. E33 100
McConnellsburg, Pa., U.S. H9 108
McConnelsville, Oh., U.S. H5 108
McCook, Ne., U.S. K7 118
McCormick, S.C., U.S. F4 112
McCoy Lake, l., Ont., Can. F22 104
McCreary, Man., Can. H15 104
McCrory, Ar., U.S. G5 114
McCune, Ks., U.S. N12 118
McCurtain, Ok., U.S. D12 116
McCusker, stm., Sask., Can. C5 104
McDade, Tx., U.S. I9 116
McDavid, Fl., U.S. L9 114
McDermitt, Nv., U.S. C8 124
McDermott, Oh., U.S. I3 108
McDonald, Ks., U.S. L6 118
McDonough, Ga., U.S. F2 112
Mcensk, Russia H19 22
McEwen, Tn., U.S. F9 114
McFadden, Wy., U.S. C10 120
McFarland, Ca., U.S. I6 124
McFarland, Wi., U.S. G6 110
McGavock Lake, l., Man., Can. B13 104
McGehee, Ar., U.S. I5 114
McGill, Nv., U.S. E11 124
McGrath, Ak., U.S. E17 100
McGraw, N.Y., U.S. E10 108
McGregor, Ia., U.S. G4 110
McGregor, Tx., U.S. H9 116
McGregor, stm., B.C., Can. C13 102
McGregor Lake, l., Alta., Can. G22 102
McGregor Range, mts., Austl. F5 70
McHenry, Il., U.S. H7 110
McHenry, Ms., U.S. L7 114
Mchinji, Mwi. D6 58
McInnes Lake, l., Ont., Can. F21 104
McIntosh, Al., U.S. K8 114
McIntosh, Mn., U.S. D12 118
McIntosh, S.D., U.S. F6 118
McIntosh Lake, l., Sask., Can. C9 104
McIntyre Bay, b., B.C., Can. C3 102
McKeand, stm., N.W. Ter., Can. D19 96
McKee, Ky., U.S. B3 112
McKeesport, Pa., U.S. G7 108
McKenzie, Al., U.S. K10 114
McKenzie, Tn., U.S. F8 114
McKenzie Bridge, Or., U.S. F3 122
McKenzie Island, Ont., Can. G21 104
McKenzie Lake, l., Sask., Can. D12 104
McKinley, Mount, mtn., Ak., U.S. E19 100
McKinleyville, Ca., U.S. D1 124
McKinney, Tx., U.S. F10 116
McKnight Lake, l., Man., Can. B13 104
McLain, Ms., U.S. K8 114
McLaughlin, S.D., U.S. F7 118
McLaughlin, stm., Man., Can. E18 104
McLaurin, Ms., U.S. K7 114
McLean, Sask., Can. H10 104
McLean, Il., U.S. B7 114
McLean, Tx., U.S. D6 116
McLean Lake, l., Sask., Can. B5 104
McLeansboro, Il., U.S. D8 114
McLennan, Alta., Can. B18 102
McLeod, stm., Alta., Can. D19 102
McLeod Bay, b., N.W. Ter., Can. D10 96
McLeod Lake, B.C., Can. C11 102
M'Clintock Channel, strt., N.W. Ter., Can. B12 96
McLoughlin, Mount, mtn., Or., U.S. H3 122
McLoughlin Bay, b., N.W. Ter., Can. C13 96
McLouth, Ks., U.S. L12 118
McLure, B.C., Can. F14 102
M'Clure Strait, strt., N.W. Ter., Can. B9 96
McMahon, Sask., Can. H7 104
McMillan, Lake, res., N.M., U.S. G2 116
McMinnville, Or., U.S. E2 122
McMinnville, Tn., U.S. G11 114
McMurdo, sci., Ant. C8 73
McMurdo Sound, strt., Ant. C8 73
McNary, Az., U.S. J7 120
McNeil, Ar., U.S. I3 114
McNeil, Mount, mtn., B.C., Can. C4 102
McNeill, Ms., U.S. L7 114
McPhail, stm., Man., Can. F19 104
McPherson, Ks., U.S. M10 118
McPherson Range, mts., Austl. G10 70
McQueeney, Tx., U.S. J8 116
McRae, Ar., U.S. G5 114
McRae, Ga., U.S. G4 112
McRoberts, Ky., U.S. B4 112
McVeigh, Ky., U.S. B4 112
McVille, N.D., U.S. D9 118
McWilliams, Al., U.S. K9 114
M'Daourouch, Alg. M2 18
Meacham, Sask., Can. F9 104
Mead, Ne., U.S. J11 118
Mead, Lake, res., U.S. H2 120
Meade, Ks., U.S. N7 118
Meaden Peak, mtn., Co., U.S. D9 120
Meadow, Tx., U.S. F4 116
Meadow, Ut., U.S. F4 120
Meadow Lake, Sask., Can. D6 104
Meadow Lake, l., Sask., Can. D6 104
Meadow Lake Provincial Park, Sask., Can. D5 104
Meadowview, Va., U.S. C5 112
Meadville, Ms., U.S. K6 114
Meadville, Mo., U.S. C3 114
Meadville, Pa., U.S. F6 108
Meaford, Ont., Can. F15 110
Meaghers Grant, N.S., Can. H10 106
Méan, Bel. H7 12
Meana, Turk. C16 48
Meandarra, Austl. F8 70
Meander River, Alta., Can. E9 96
Meath, co., Ire. H7 8
Meath, hist. reg., Ire. H6 8
Meaux, Fr. D9 14
Mebane, N.C., U.S. C7 112
Mecaya, stm., Col. G5 84
Mecca see Makkah, Sau. Ar. D1 47
Mechanic Falls, Me., U.S. C16 108
Mechanicsburg, Oh., U.S. G3 108
Mechanicsville, Ia., U.S. I4 110
Mechanicsville, Va., U.S. B9 112
Mechanicville, N.Y., U.S. E13 108
Mechelen (Malines), Bel. F5 12
Mechita, Arg. H8 80
Mechra Safsaf, Mor. K9 16
Mechriyya, Alg. D10 62
Mechroha, Alg. M2 18
Mecklenburg, hist. reg., Ger. B12 10
Mecklenburger Bucht, b., Ger. A11 10
Mecklenburg-Vorpommern, state, Ger. B12 10
Meda, Port. E4 16
Medan, Indon. M5 40
Médanos, Arg. J7 80
Medanosa, Punta, c., Arg. F3 78
Medaryville, In., U.S. A10 114
Mede, Italy D3 18
Medeiros Neto, Braz. D8 79
Medellín, Col. D5 84
Médenine, Tun. D16 62
Mederdra, Maur. C2 64
Medford, Ok., U.S. C9 116
Medford, Or., U.S. H3 122
Medford, Wi., U.S. E5 110
Medgidia, Rom. E12 20
Mediapolis, Ia., U.S. I4 110
Mediaș, Rom. C8 20
Medical Lake, Wa., U.S. C8 122
Medicina, Italy E6 18
Medicine Bow, Wy., U.S. C10 120
Medicine Bow, stm., Wy., U.S. B10 120
Medicine Bow Mountains, mts., U.S. C10 120
Medicine Bow Peak, mtn., Wy., U.S. C10 120
Medicine Hat, Alta., Can. F10 96
Medicine Hat, Alta., Can. H4 104
Medicine Lake, Mt., U.S. C3 118
Medicine Lodge, Ks., U.S. N9 118
Medicine Lodge, stm., U.S. B8 116
Medina, Braz. D8 79
Medina see Al-Madīnah, Sau. Ar. B1 47
Medina, N.Y., U.S. D8 108
Medina, N.D., U.S. E8 118
Medina, Oh., U.S. F5 108
Medina, Tx., U.S. J7 116
Medina, stm., Tx., U.S. J8 116
Medina del Campo, Spain D7 16
Medininkai, Lith. G8 22
Medinīpur, India I12 44
Medio, Punta, c., Chile D3 80
Mediterranean Sea E9 52
Medjerda, Monts de la, mts., Afr. M3 18
Mednogorsk, Russia G9 26
Mednoje, Russia E18 22
Mednyj, ostrov, i., Russia G25 28
Médoc, reg., Fr. G6 14
Medora, In., U.S. D10 114
Medora, N.D., U.S. E4 118
Médouneu, Gabon A2 58
Medstead, Sask., Can. E6 104
Meductic, N.B., Can. F6 106
Medveđa, Yugo. G5 20
Medvedevskoje, Russia C18 22
Medvedica, stm., Russia G6 26
Medvežjegorsk, Russia E4 26
Medvežji ostrova, is., Russia C24 28
Medway, stm., N.S., Can. H9 106
Medyn', Russia G18 22
Meekatharra, Austl. E3 68
Meeker, Co., U.S. D9 120
Meeks Bay, Ca., U.S. E5 124
Meelpaeg Lake, res., Newf., Can. D17 106
Meer, Bel. F6 12
Meerane, Ger. E12 10
Meerut, India F7 44
Meeteetse, Wy., U.S. F17 122
Mega, Eth. H8 56
Mégantic, Lac, l., Que., Can. B16 108
Mégara, Grc. K7 20
Megargel, Tx., U.S. F8 116
Meghālaya, state, India H14 44
Meghna, stm., Bngl. H14 44
Mehadia, Rom. E6 20
Mehar, Pak. G2 44
Mehdia, Alg. C11 62
Mehedinți, co., Rom. E6 20
Meherrin, stm., U.S. C9 112
Mehrān, Iran E9 48
Meia Ponte, Rio da, stm., Braz. D4 79
Meigs, Ga., U.S. H2 112
Meiktila, Mya. D3 40
Meilie, China I6 34
Meiners Oaks, Ca., U.S. J6 124
Meiningen, Ger. E10 10
Meiringen, Switz. E9 13
Meissen, Ger. D13 10
Meixian, China K5 34
Meiyino, Sud. N8 60
Meizhai, China B10 40
Mejerda, Oued (Oued Medjerda), stm., Afr. M4 18
Mejez el Bab, Tun. M4 18
Mejicanos, El Sal. D5 92
Mejillones, Chile B3 80
Mejillones, Península, pen., Chile B3 80
Mejillones del Sur, Bahía de, b., Chile B3 80
Mékambo, Gabon A2 58
Mekele, Eth. K10 60
Meknès, Mor. D8 62
Mekong, stm., Asia H8 40
Mekoryuk, Ak., U.S. F11 100
Mékrou, stm., Afr. F7 54
Melado, stm., Chile H3 80
Melaka, Malay. M7 40
Melanesia, is., Oc. I19 126
Melbourne, Austl. K6 70
Melbourne, Ar., U.S. F5 114
Melbourne, Fl., U.S. K6 112
Melbourne, Ia., U.S. I2 110
Melbourne Island, i., N.W. Ter., Can. C12 96
Melby House, Scot., U.K. A12 8
Melcher, Ia., U.S. I2 110
Melchor Múzquiz, Mex. D9 90
Meldorf, Ger. A9 10
Meldrum Bay, Ont., Can. E12 110
Meldrum Creek, B.C., Can. E12 102
Melechovo, Russia E24 22
Melegnano, Italy D4 18
Melenki, Russia F24 22
Meleuz, Russia G9 26
Mélèzes, Rivière aux, stm., Que., Can. E18 96
Melfi, Chad F4 56
Melfi, Italy H10 18
Melfort, Sask., Can. F10 104
Melgaço, Port. C3 16
Melgar, Col. E5 84
Melghir, Chott, l., Alg. C14 62
Melhus, Nor. J12 6
Meli, stm., Afr. G4 64
Meliane, Oued, stm., Tun. M5 18
Melide, Switz. G10 13
Melilla, Sp. N. Afr. C9 62
Melincué, Arg. G8 80
Melipilla, Chile G3 80
Melita, Man., Can. I13 104
Melitopol', Ukr. F15 4
Mellègue, Oued, stm., Afr. M3 18
Mellen, Wi., U.S. D5 110
Mellette, S.D., U.S. F9 118
Mělník, Czech. E14 10
Mel'nytsya-Podil's'ka, Ukr. A10 20
Melo, Ur. G11 80
Melo, stm., Para. I12 82
Melong, Cam. I14 64
Melos see Mílos, i., Grc. M8 20
Melrose, Mn., U.S. F13 118
Melrose, N.M., U.S. E3 116
Melrose, Wi., U.S. F5 110
Melstone, Mt., U.S. D18 122
Melton Mowbray, Eng., U.K. I13 8
Melúa, Col. F6 84
Melun, Fr. D9 14
Melun, Mya. D2 40
Melvern, Ks., U.S. M12 118
Melville, Sask., Can. H12 104
Melville, La., U.S. L5 114
Melville, Détroit de see Viscount Melville Sound, strt., N.W. Ter., Can. B11 96
Melville, Lake, l., Newf., Can. F21 96
Melville Bugt, b., Grnld. B13 86
Melville Hills, hills, N.W. Ter., Can. B33 100
Melville Island, i., Austl. B6 68
Melville Island, i., N.W. Ter., Can. B8 86
Melville Peninsula, pen., N.W. Ter., Can. C16 96
Melville Sound, strt., N.W. Ter., Can. C11 96
Melvin, Il., U.S. J7 110
Melvin, Ky., U.S. B4 112
Melvin, Tx., U.S. H7 116
Melvin, Lough, l., Eur. G5 8
Melvin Lake, l., Man., Can. A14 104
Melyana, Alg. B12 62
Melzo, Italy D4 18
Memel, S. Afr. F9 66
Memel see Nemunas, stm., Eur. F6 22
Memmingen, Ger. H10 10
Memo, stm., Ven. C9 84
Mémót, Camb. I9 40
Mempawah, Indon. N10 40
Memphis, Fl., U.S. L4 112
Memphis, Mi., U.S. H13 110
Memphis, Mo., U.S. B4 114
Memphis, Tn., U.S. G6 114
Memphis, Tx., U.S. E6 116
Memphremagog, Lake, l., N.A. B14 108
Mena, Ar., U.S. H2 114
Menahga, Mn., U.S. E12 118
Ménaka, Mali D11 64
Menaldum, Neth. B8 12
Menan, Id., U.S. G14 122
Menard, Tx., U.S. I7 116
Menasha, Wi., U.S. F7 110
Menawashei, Sud. K3 60
Mendawai, stm., Indon. F5 38
Mende, Fr. H10 14
Mendenhall, Ms., U.S. K7 114
Méndez, Mex. E10 90
Mendi, Eth. M8 60
Mendi, Pap. N. Gui. G11 38
Mendocino, Ca., U.S. E2 124
Mendocino, Cape, c., Ca., U.S. D1 124
Mendon, Il., U.S. B5 114
Mendon, Mi., U.S. H10 110
Mendota, Ca., U.S. H5 124
Mendota, Il., U.S. I6 110
Mendoza, Arg. G4 80
Mendoza, Peru B3 82
Mendoza, prov., Arg. H4 80
Mendoza, stm., Arg. G4 80
Ménéac, Fr. D4 14
Mene de Mauroa, Ven. B7 84
Mene Grande, Ven. C7 84
Menemen, Tur. K11 20
Menen (Menin), Bel. G3 12
Menfi, Italy L7 18
Mengcheng, China E10 30
Menggala, Indon. F4 38
Menggu, China A7 40
Menghai, China C6 40
Mengla, China D6 40
Mengzhi, China B5 40
Mengzi, China C7 40
Menihek Lakes, l., Newf., Can. F19 96
Menindee, Austl. I5 70
Menindee Lake, l., Austl. I5 70
Menlo Park, Ca., U.S. G3 124
Menno, S.D., U.S. H10 118
Meno, Ok., U.S. C8 116
Menominee, Mi., U.S. E8 110
Menominee, stm., U.S. E8 110
Menomonee Falls, Wi., U.S. G7 110
Menomonie, Wi., U.S. F4 110
Menongue, Ang. D3 58
Menorca, i., Spain F16 16
Mens, Fr. H12 14
Mentasta Mountains, mts., Ak., U.S. E23 100
Mentawai, Kepulauan, is., Indon. F2 38
Mentawai, Selat, strt., Indon. F3 38
Menton, Fr. I14 14
Mentone, Tx., U.S. H3 116
Mentor, Oh., U.S. F5 108
Menzel Bourguiba, Tun. L4 18
Menzel Bou Zelfa, Tun. M5 18
Menzel Djemil, Tun. L4 18
Menzel Temime, Tun. M5 18
Menzies, Austl. E4 68
Menzies, Mount, mtn., Ant. C5 73
Meoqui, Mex. C7 90
Meota, Sask., Can. E6 104
Meppel, Neth. C9 12
Meppen, Ger. C7 10
Meqerghane, Sebkha, pl., Alg. G11 62
Mequon, Wi., U.S. G8 110
Mer, Fr. E8 14
Meramec, stm., Mo., U.S. D5 114
Merano (Meran), Italy C6 18
Merasheen, Newf., Can. E19 106
Merasheen Island, i., Newf., Can. E19 106
Merate, Italy D4 18
Merauke, Indon. G11 38
Mercaderes, Col. G4 84
Mercāra, India F3 46
Merced, Ca., U.S. G5 124
Merced, stm., Ca., U.S. G5 124
Mercedario, Cerro, mtn., Arg. F3 80
Mercedes, Arg. H9 80
Mercedes, Arg. E9 80
Mercedes, Arg. G6 80
Mercedes, Tx., U.S. M9 116
Mercedes, Ur. G9 80
Mercer, Mo., U.S. B3 114
Mercer, Pa., U.S. F6 108
Mercer, Wi., U.S. D5 110
Mercersburg, Pa., U.S. H9 108
Merchants Bay, b., N.W. Ter., Can. C20 96
Merchtem, Bel. G5 12
Mercoal, Alta., Can. D17 102
Mercury, Nv., U.S. H10 124
Mercy, Cape, c., N.W. Ter., Can. D20 96
Mercy Bay, b., N.W. Ter., Can. B9 96
Meredith, N.H., U.S. D15 108
Meredith, Lake, res., Tx., U.S. D5 116
Meredosia, Il., U.S. C6 114
Mereeg, Som. H10 56
Merenkurkku (Norra Kvarken), strt., Eur. J17 6
Merevari, stm., Ven. E10 84
Merewa, Eth. N9 60
Mergui (Myeik), Mya. H5 40
Mergui Archipelago, is., Mya. H5 40
Meriç (Marica) (Évros), stm., Eur. H10 20
Mérida, Mex. G15 90
Mérida, Spain G5 16
Mérida, Ven. C7 84
Mérida, state, Ven. C7 84
Mérida, Cordillera de, mts., Ven. C7 84
Meriden, Ct., U.S. F14 108
Meridian, Ga., U.S. H5 112
Meridian, Id., U.S. G9 122
Meridian, Ms., U.S. J8 114
Meridian, Tx., U.S. H9 116
Meridianville, Al., U.S. H10 114
Mérignac, Fr. H6 14
Merigold, Ms., U.S. I6 114
Merimbula, Austl. K8 70
Merín, Laguna (Lagoa Mirim), b., S.A. G12 80
Merino, Co., U.S. K4 118
Merinos, Ur. G10 80
Merkel, Tx., U.S. G6 116
Merkendorf, Ger. F10 10
Merkinė, Lith. G7 22
Merkulovičі, Bela. I13 22
Merlin, Ont., Can. H13 110
Merlin, Or., U.S. H2 122
Merlo, Arg. G6 80
Merna, Ne., U.S. J8 118
Mernye, Hung. I17 10
Meron, Hare, mtn., Isr. C4 50
Merredin, Austl. F3 68
Merrickville, Ont., Can. C11 108
Merrill, Ia., U.S. I11 118
Merrill, Mi., U.S. G11 110
Merrill, Or., U.S. H4 122
Merrill, Wi., U.S. E6 110
Merrillan, Wi., U.S. F5 110
Merrillville, In., U.S. A9 114
Merrimack, stm., U.S. D15 108
Merriman, Ne., U.S. I6 118
Merritt, B.C., Can. G14 102
Merritt Island, Fl., U.S. K6 112
Merriwa, Austl. I9 70
Mer Rouge, La., U.S. J5 114
Merryville, La., U.S. L3 114
Mersch, Lux. I9 12
Merseburg, Ger. D11 10
Mersey, stm., Austl. M7 70
Mersey, stm., N.S., Can. H9 106
Mersing, Malay. M7 40
Mērsrags, Lat. D6 22
Merthyr Tydfil, Wales, U.K. J10 8
Mértola, Port. H4 16
Mertzon, Tx., U.S. H6 116
Méru, Fr. C9 14
Meru, Kenya A7 58
Meru, Mount, mtn., Tan. B7 58
Mervin, Sask., Can. E6 104
Méry, Fr. D10 14
Merzig, Ger. F6 10
Mesa, Az., U.S. K5 120
Mesa, stm., Spain D10 16
Mesabi Range, hills, Mn., U.S. C3 110
Mesagne, Italy I12 18
Mesa Mountain, mtn., Co., U.S. G10 120
Mesa Verde National Park, Co., U.S. G8 120
Mescalero, N.M., U.S. K11 120
Meschede, Ger. D8 10
Meščovsk, Russia G18 22
Mesfinto, Eth. K9 60
Mesgouez, Lac, l., Que., Can. F17 96
Meshgīn Shahr, Iran B9 48
Mesick, Mi., U.S. F10 110
Mesilinka, stm., B.C., Can. A10 102
Mesilla, N.M., U.S. L10 120
Meskiana, Alg. C14 62
Meslay-du-Maine, Fr. E6 14
Mesocco, Switz. F11 13
Mesolóngion, Grc. K5 20
Mesopotamia, hist. reg., Asia D8 48
Mesquita, Braz. E7 79
Mesquite, Nv., U.S. H11 124
Mesquite, Tx., U.S. G10 116
Messalo, stm., Moz. D7 58
Messina, Italy K10 18
Messina, S. Afr. D10 66
Messina, Stretto di, strt., Italy K10 18
Messini, Grc. L6 20
Messiniakós Kólpos, b., Grc. M6 20
Messix Peak, mtn., Ut., U.S. C4 120
Messojacha, stm., Russia D13 26
Mestá, Grc. K9 20
Mesta (Néstos), stm., Eur. H7 20
Mestasa, Mor. C8 62
Mestghanem, Alg. C11 62
Mestre, Italy D7 18
Meszah Peak, mtn., B.C., Can. G29 100
Meta, dept., Col. F6 84
Meta, stm., S.A. D9 84
Meta Incognita Peninsula, pen., N.W. Ter., Can. D19 96
Metairie, La., U.S. M6 114
Metaline Falls, Wa., U.S. B8 122
Metamora, Il., U.S. J6 110
Metán, Arg. C6 80
Metapán, El Sal. C5 92
Meteghan, N.S., Can. H7 106
Metema, Eth. K9 60
Meteor Crater, crat., Az., U.S. I5 120
Methóni, Grc. M5 20
Methow, stm., Wa., U.S. B5 122
Metiskow, Alta., Can. F4 104
Metković, Cro. F12 18
Metlakatla, B.C., Can. C4 102
Metlakatla, Ak., U.S. I29 100
Metlaoui, Tun. C15 62
Metlatonoc, Mex. I10 90
Meto, Bayou, stm., Ar., U.S. H5 114
Metolius, stm., Or., U.S. F4 122
Metropolis, Il., U.S. E8 114
Metropolitan, Mi., U.S. D8 110
Metsematluku, Bots. E7 66
Metter, Ga., U.S. G4 112
Mettuppālaiyam, India G4 46
Mettūr, India G4 46
Metu, Eth. M8 60
Metulla, Isr. B5 50
Metz, Fr. C13 14
Meulan, Fr. C8 14
Meureudu, Indon. L4 40
Meurthe, stm., Fr. D13 14
Meurthe-et-Moselle, dept., Fr. D13 14
Meuse, dept., Fr. D12 14
Meuse (Maas), stm., Eur. E5 10
Meuselwitz, Ger. D12 10
Mexia, Tx., U.S. H10 116
Mexiana, Ilha, i., Braz. D9 76
Mexicali, Mex. A2 90
Mexican Hat, Ut., U.S. G7 120
Mexico, Me., U.S. C16 108
Mexico, Mo., U.S. C5 114
Mexico, N.Y., U.S. D10 108
México, state, Mex. H10 90
Mexico (México), ctry., N.A. F9 90
Mexico, Gulf of, b., N.A. C6 88
Mexico Beach, Fl., U.S. J1 112
Mexico City see Ciudad de México, Mex. H10 90
Meximieux, Fr. G12 14
Meycauayan, Phil. n19 39b
Meyers Chuck, Ak., U.S. I28 100
Meyersdale, Pa., U.S. H7 108
Meyísti, i., Grc. H13 4
Meymac, Fr. G9 14
Meymaneh, Afg. C1 44
Meymeh, stm., Asia E9 48
Meyrargues, Fr. I12 14
Meyronne, Sask., Can. I8 104
Meẕada, Ḥorvot (Masada), hist., Isr. F4 50

Name	Map Ref.	Page
Mezapa, Hond.	B7	92
Mezcala, Mex.	I10	90
Mezcalapa, stm., Mex.	I13	90
Meždurečensk, Russia	G9	28
Mèze, Fr.	I10	14
Mezen', Russia	D6	26
Mezen', stm., Russia	D6	26
Meziadin Lake, l., B.C., Can.	A5	102
Mézin, Fr.	H7	14
Mezinovskij, Russia	F23	22
Mezőberény, Hung.	I21	10
Mezőcsát, Hung.	H20	10
Mezőkovácsháza, Hung.	I20	10
Mezőkövesd, Hung.	H20	10
Mezőtúr, Hung.	H20	10
Mezquital, Mex.	F7	90
Mezquital, stm., Mex.	F7	90
Mglin, Russia	H15	22
M'goun, Irhil, mtn., Mor.	E7	62
Mhow, India	I6	44
Miahuatlán de Porfirio Díaz, Mex.	I11	90
Miajadas, Spain	F6	16
Miami, Man., Can.	I16	104
Miami, Az., U.S.	K6	120
Miami, Fl., U.S.	N6	112
Miami, Ok., U.S.	C12	116
Miami, Tx., U.S.	D6	116
Miami Beach, Fl., U.S.	N6	112
Miami Canal, Fl., U.S.	M6	112
Miamisburg, Oh., U.S.	H2	108
Miami Springs, Fl., U.S.	N6	112
Mīāndoāb, Iran	C9	48
Miandrivazo, Madag.	q21	67b
Mīāneh, Iran	C9	48
Miangas, Pulau, i., Indon.	D8	38
Mianhu, China	L5	34
Miānwāli, Pak.	D4	44
Mianyang, China	E7	30
Mianyang, China	E2	34
Miaoli, Tai.	K9	34
Miarinavaratra, Madag.	r22	67b
Miass, Russia	G10	26
Miastko, Pol.	A17	10
Micanopy, Fl., U.S.	J4	112
Micaúne, Moz.	B13	66
Michajlov, Russia	G22	22
Michajlovka, Russia	G6	26
Michanoviči, Bela.	H10	22
Michaud, Point, c., N.S., Can.	G13	106
Micheal Peak, mtn., B.C., Can.	D8	102
Michel, B.C., Can.	H20	102
Miches, Dom. Rep.	E10	94
Michigamme, stm., Mi., U.S.	D7	110
Michigan, N.D., U.S.	C9	118
Michigan, state, U.S.	C9	98
Michigan, Lake, l., U.S.	F8	110
Michigan Center, Mi., U.S.	H11	110
Michigan City, In., U.S.	A10	114
Michipicoten Island, i., Ont., Can.	C10	110
Michnevo, Russia	F20	22
Michoacán, state, Mex.	H9	90
Mico, stm., Nic.	E10	92
Mico, Montañas del, mts., Guat.	B6	92
Micronesia, is., Oc.	G19	126
Micronesia, Federated States of, ctry., Oc.	H19	126
Mičurinsk, Russia	I23	22
Midale, Sask., Can.	I11	104
Midar, Mor.	C9	62
Mid-Atlantic Ridge	F9	128
Middelburg, Neth.	E4	12
Middelburg, S. Afr.	H7	66
Middelburg, S. Afr.	E9	66
Middelfart, Den.	N11	6
Middelharnis, Neth.	E5	12
Middelpos, S. Afr.	H5	66
Middelwater, S. Afr.	D10	66
Middenmeer, Neth.	C7	12
Middle, stm., B.C., Can.	B9	102
Middle, stm., Ia., U.S.	A2	114
Middle America Trench	H10	86
Middle Andaman, i., India	H2	40
Middle-Bay, Que., Can.	A16	106
Middleboro, Ma., U.S.	F16	108
Middlebourne, W.V., U.S.	H6	108
Middlebro, Man., Can.	I19	104
Middle Brook, Newf., Can.	D19	106
Middleburg, N.Y., U.S.	E12	108
Middleburg, Pa., U.S.	G9	108
Middlebury, Vt., U.S.	C13	108
Middle Caicos, i., T./C. Is.	D9	94
Middle Channel, mth., N.W. Ter., Can.	B27	100
Middle Fabius, stm., Mo., U.S.	C4	114
Middlefield, Oh., U.S.	F5	108
Middle Loup, stm., Ne., U.S.	J8	118
Middle Musquodoboit, N.S., Can.	G10	106
Middle Point, Oh., U.S.	G2	108
Middleport, Oh., U.S.	H4	108
Middlesboro, Ky., U.S.	C3	112
Middlesbrough, Eng., U.K.	G12	8
Middlesex, Belize	I15	90
Middlesex, N.C., U.S.	D8	112
Middle Stewiacke, N.S., Can.	G10	106
Middleton, N.S., Can.	H8	106
Middleton, Mi., U.S.	G11	110
Middleton, Tn., U.S.	G8	114
Middleton, Wi., U.S.	G6	110
Middleton Island, i., Ak., U.S.	G21	100
Middletown, Ca., U.S.	F3	124
Middletown, Ct., U.S.	F14	108
Middletown, De., U.S.	H11	108
Middletown, Il., U.S.	B7	114
Middletown, In., U.S.	B11	114
Middletown, Ky., U.S.	D11	114
Middletown, Md., U.S.	H9	108
Middletown, N.Y., U.S.	F12	108
Middletown, Oh., U.S.	H2	108
Middletown, Pa., U.S.	G10	108
Middletown, R.I., U.S.	F15	108
Middletown, Va., U.S.	H8	108
Middleville, Mi., U.S.	H10	110
Midelt, Mor.	D8	62
Midgic, N.B., Can.	G9	106
Mid Glamorgan, co., Wales, U.K.	J10	8
Midi, Canal du, Fr.	I9	14
Midi de Bigorre, Pic du, mtn., Fr.	J7	14
Midland, Ont., Can.	F16	110
Midland, Ca., U.S.	K11	124
Midland, Mi., U.S.	G11	110
Midland, N.C., U.S.	D6	112
Midland, S.D., U.S.	G6	118
Midland, Tx., U.S.	H4	116
Midlothian, Tx., U.S.	G10	116
Midnapore, Alta., Can.	G20	102
Midongy Sud, Madag.	s22	67b
Miduzhen, China	B6	40
Midvale, Id., U.S.	F9	122
Midville, Ga., U.S.	G4	112
Midway, B.C., Can.	H16	102
Midway, Al., U.S.	J11	114
Midway, Ky., U.S.	I2	108
Midway, Tx., U.S.	H11	116
Midway, Ut., U.S.	D5	120
Midway Islands, dep., Oc.	F22	126
Midway Park, N.C., U.S.	E9	112
Midwest, Wy., U.S.	A10	120
Midwest City, Ok., U.S.	D9	116
Midyat, Tur.	C6	48
Midžor (Midžur), mtn., Eur.	F6	20
Miechów, Pol.	E20	10
Międzychód, Pol.	C15	10
Międzyrzec Podlaski, Pol.	C22	10
Międzyrzecz, Pol.	C15	10
Miélan, Fr.	I7	14
Mielec, Pol.	E21	10
Mier, Mex.	D10	90
Miercurea-Ciuc, Rom.	C9	20
Mieres, Spain	B6	16
Mier y Noriega, Mex.	F9	90
Miesbach, Ger.	H11	10
Mifflinburg, Pa., U.S.	G9	108
Migdal, Isr.	C5	50
Miguel Alemán, Presa, res., Mex.	H11	90
Miguel Auza, Mex.	E8	90
Miguel de la Borda, Pan.	H14	92
Miguel Hidalgo, Presa, res., Mex.	D5	90
Miguelópolis, Braz.	F4	79
Miguel Riglos, Arg.	I7	80
Mihara, Japan	M8	36
Mijdaḥah, Yemen	G6	47
Mikaševiči, Bela.	I10	22
Mikhrot Shelomo Hamelekh (Timna') (King Solomon's Mines), hist., Isr.	I3	50
Mikkeli, Fin.	K20	6
Mikkelin lääni, prov., Fin.	J20	6
Mikkwa, stm., Alta., Can.	E10	96
Mikołajki, Pol.	B21	10
Mikołów, Pol.	E18	10
Míkonos, Grc.	L9	20
Mikun', Russia	E8	26
Milaca, Mn., U.S.	E2	110
Milagro, Ec.	I3	84
Milan see Milano, Italy	D4	18
Milan, Ga., U.S.	G3	112
Milan, In., U.S.	C11	114
Milan, Mi., U.S.	H12	110
Milan, Mn., U.S.	F12	118
Milan, Mo., U.S.	B3	114
Milan, N.M., U.S.	I9	120
Milan, Tn., U.S.	G8	114
Milano (Milan), Italy	D4	18
Milano, Tx., U.S.	I10	116
Milanoa, Madag.	n23	67b
Milazzo, Italy	K10	18
Milbank, S.D., U.S.	F11	118
Milbanke Sound, strt., B.C., Can.	E6	102
Milburn, Ok., U.S.	E10	116
Milden, Sask., Can.	G7	104
Mildmay, Ont., Can.	F14	110
Mildred, Pa., U.S.	F10	108
Mildura, Austl.	J5	70
Mile, China	B7	40
Miles, Austl.	F9	70
Miles, Tx., U.S.	H6	116
Miles City, Mt., U.S.	D20	122
Mile Seven Hundred Thirty Three, Yukon, Can.	F29	100
Milestone, Sask., Can.	H10	104
Milevsko, Czech.	F14	10
Milford, Ct., U.S.	F13	108
Milford, De., U.S.	I11	108
Milford, Il., U.S.	J8	110
Milford, In., U.S.	A11	114
Milford, Ia., U.S.	H12	118
Milford, Me., U.S.	C18	108
Milford, Ma., U.S.	E15	108
Milford, Mi., U.S.	H12	110
Milford, N.H., U.S.	E15	108
Milford, N.J., U.S.	G11	108
Milford, Pa., U.S.	F12	108
Milford, Ut., U.S.	F3	120
Milford Center, Oh., U.S.	G3	108
Milford Haven, Wales, U.K.	J8	8
Milford Station, N.S., Can.	G10	106
Milḥ, Bahr al-, l., Iraq	E7	48
Milicz, Pol.	D17	10
Milk, stm., N.A.	B19	122
Mil'kovo, Russia	G23	28
Milk River, Alta., Can.	H22	102
Milk River Ridge Reservoir, res., Alta., Can.	H22	102
Millard, Ne., U.S.	J11	118
Millau, Fr.	H10	14
Millboro, Va., U.S.	B7	112
Millbrook, Ont., Can.	F17	110
Millbrook, N.Y., U.S.	F13	108
Mill City, Or., U.S.	F3	122
Millcreek, Pa., U.S.	E6	108
Millcreek, Ut., U.S.	D5	120
Mill Creek, W.V., U.S.	I7	108
Milledgeville, Ga., U.S.	F3	112
Milledgeville, Il., U.S.	I6	110
Mille Lacs, Lac des, l., Ont., Can.	B5	110
Mille Lacs Lake, l., Mn., U.S.	D2	110
Millen, Ga., U.S.	G5	112
Miller, Mo., U.S.	E3	114
Miller, S.D., U.S.	G9	118
Miller Mountain, mtn., Nv., U.S.	F7	124
Millerovo, Russia	H6	26
Miller Peak, mtn., Az., U.S.	M6	120
Millersburg, Ky., U.S.	I2	108
Millersburg, Mi., U.S.	E11	110
Millersburg, Oh., U.S.	G5	108
Millersburg, Pa., U.S.	G10	108
Millers Ferry, Al., U.S.	J9	114
Millersport, Oh., U.S.	H4	108
Millersville, Pa., U.S.	H10	108
Millerton, N.Y., U.S.	F13	108
Millertown, Newf., Can.	D17	106
Millertown Junction, Newf., Can.	C17	106
Millet, Alta., Can.	D21	102
Millett, Tx., U.S.	K7	116
Millevaches, Plateau de, plat., Fr.	G9	14
Mill Hall, Pa., U.S.	F9	108
Millicent, Austl.	K4	70
Milligan, Fl., U.S.	L10	114
Milligan, Ne., U.S.	K10	118
Millington, Mi., U.S.	G12	110
Millington, Tn., U.S.	G7	114
Millinocket, Me., U.S.	B18	108
Mill Island, i., N.W. Ter., Can.	D17	96
Millmerran, Austl.	F9	70
Millport, Al., U.S.	I8	114
Millry, Al., U.S.	K8	114
Mills, Wy., U.S.	B10	120
Mills Lake, l., N.W. Ter., Can.	D9	96
Millstatt, Aus.	I13	10
Millstream Chichester National Park, Austl.	D3	68
Milltown, In., U.S.	D10	114
Milltown, Mt., U.S.	D12	122
Milltown, Wi., U.S.	E3	110
Mill Valley, Ca., U.S.	G3	124
Millville, N.J., U.S.	H11	108
Millwood, Va., U.S.	H8	108
Millwood Lake, res., Ar., U.S.	I2	114
Milne Bay, b., Pap. N. Gui.	B10	68
Milnor, N.D., U.S.	E10	118
Milo, Alta., Can.	G22	102
Milo, Ia., U.S.	I2	110
Milo, Me., U.S.	B18	108
Mílos, Grc.	M8	20
Mílos, i., Grc.	M8	20
Miloslavskoje, Russia	H22	22
Milparinka, Austl.	G4	70
Milpitas, Ca., U.S.	G4	124
Milroy, In., U.S.	C11	114
Milroy, Pa., U.S.	G9	108
Miltenberg, Ger.	F9	10
Milton, Ont., Can.	G16	110
Milton, N.Z.	G2	72
Milton, De., U.S.	I11	108
Milton, Fl., U.S.	L9	114
Milton, Ia., U.S.	J3	110
Milton, N.D., U.S.	C9	118
Milton, Pa., U.S.	F10	108
Milton, Vt., U.S.	C13	108
Milton, W.V., U.S.	I4	108
Milton, Wi., U.S.	H7	110
Milton-Freewater, Or., U.S.	E7	122
Miltonvale, Ks., U.S.	L10	118
Milverton, Ont., Can.	G15	110
Milwaukee, Wi., U.S.	G8	110
Milwaukee, stm., Wi., U.S.	G7	110
Milwaukie, Or., U.S.	E3	122
Mim, Ghana	H8	64
Mimbres, stm., N.M., U.S.	L9	120
Mimoso, Braz.	C4	79
Mimoso, Braz.	G14	82
Mimoso do Sul, Braz.	F8	79
Mims, Fl., U.S.	K6	112
Min, stm., China	E7	30
Min, stm., China	I7	34
Mina, Nv., U.S.	F7	124
Mīnāb, Iran	H14	48
Mina El Limón, Nic.	E8	92
Minago, stm., Man., Can.	D16	104
Minahasa, pen., Indon.	E7	38
Minamata, Japan	O5	36
Minami-Daitō-jima, i., Japan	F13	30
Mina Pirquitas, Arg.	B5	80
Minas, Cuba	D6	94
Minas, Ur.	H11	80
Minas, Sierra de las, mts., Guat.	B5	92
Minas Basin, b., N.S., Can.	G9	106
Minas Channel, strt., N.S., Can.	G9	106
Minas de Barroterán, Mex.	D9	90
Minas de Corrales, Ur.	F11	80
Minas de Matahambre, Cuba	C3	94
Minas de Oro, Hond.	C7	92
Minas Gerais, state, Braz.	E6	79
Minas Novas, Braz.	D7	79
Minatare, Ne., U.S.	J4	118
Minatitlán, Mex.	I12	90
Minbu, Mya.	D3	40
Minco, Ok., U.S.	D9	116
Mindanao, i., Phil.	D8	38
Mindelo, C.V.	k16	64a
Mindemoya, Ont., Can.	E13	110
Minden, Ont., Can.	F17	110
Minden, Ger.	C8	10
Minden, La., U.S.	J3	114
Minden, Ne., U.S.	K9	118
Minden, Nv., U.S.	F6	124
Minden, W.V., U.S.	J5	108
Minden City, Mi., U.S.	G13	110
Mindenmines, Mo., U.S.	E2	114
Mindon, Mya.	E3	40
Mindoro, i., Phil.	C7	38
Mindoro Strait, strt., Phil.	C7	38
Mine Centre, Ont., Can.	B3	110
Mineiros, Braz.	D2	79
Mineola, Tx., U.S.	G11	116
Miner, stm., Yukon, Can.	C25	100
Mineral, Wa., U.S.	D3	122
Mineral de Cucharas, Mex.	F7	90
Mineral'nyje Vody, Russia	I6	26
Mineral Point, Wi., U.S.	H5	110
Mineral Springs, Ar., U.S.	I3	114
Mineral Wells, Tx., U.S.	G8	116
Minersville, Pa., U.S.	G10	108
Minersville, Ut., U.S.	F4	120
Minerva, Oh., U.S.	G5	108
Minervino Murge, Italy	H11	18
Mineville, N.Y., U.S.	C13	108
Minfeng, China	D3	30
Mingäçevir, Azer.	I7	26
Mingan, Que., Can.	B9	106
Mingan, stm., Que., Can.	B10	106
Mingan, Îles de, is., Que., Can.	B10	106
Mingan Archipelago National Park, Que., Can.	B10	106
Mingela, Austl.	B7	70
Minggang, China	C3	34
Mingo Junction, Oh., U.S.	G6	108
Minhang, China	D10	34
Minhla, Mya.	F3	40
Minho, hist. reg., Port.	D3	16
Minho (Miño), stm., Eur.	D3	16
Minhou, China	I8	34
Minicoy Island, i., India	H2	46
Minier, Il., U.S.	B7	114
Minīn, Syria	A6	50
Miniota, Man., Can.	H13	104
Ministikwan Lake, l., Sask., Can.	D5	104
Minitonas, Man., Can.	F13	104
Minjar, Russia	F9	26
Min'kovo, Russia	B26	22
Minlaton, Austl.	J2	70
Minle, China	D7	30
Minna, Nig.	G13	64
Minneapolis, Ks., U.S.	L10	118
Minneapolis, Mn., U.S.	F2	110
Minnedosa, Man., Can.	H15	104
Minnehaha, Wa., U.S.	E3	122
Minneola, Ks., U.S.	N7	118
Minneota, Mn., U.S.	G12	118
Minnesota, state, U.S.	B8	98
Minnesota, stm., Mn., U.S.	F2	110
Minnesota Lake, Mn., U.S.	G2	110
Minnewanka, Lake, l., Alta., Can.	F19	102
Minnewaukan, N.D., U.S.	C8	118
Minnitaki Lake, l., Ont., Can.	I22	104
Mino, Japan	L11	36
Miño (Minho), stm., Eur.	D3	16
Minocqua, Wi., U.S.	E6	110
Minong, Wi., U.S.	D4	110
Minonk, Il., U.S.	J6	110
Minot, N.D., U.S.	C6	118
Minsk, Bela.	H10	22
Mińsk Mazowiecki, Pol.	C21	10
Minster, Oh., U.S.	G2	108
Mintaka Pass, Asia	B6	44
Minto, Man., Can.	I14	104
Minto, N.B., Can.	F7	106
Minto, Yukon, Can.	E26	100
Minto, Ak., U.S.	D20	100
Minto, N.D., U.S.	C10	118
Minto, Lac, l., Que., Can.	E17	96
Minto, Mount, mtn., Ant.	C8	73
Minto Inlet, b., N.W. Ter., Can.	B9	96
Minton, Sask., Can.	I10	104
Minturn, Co., U.S.	E10	120
Minturno, Italy	H8	18
Minusinsk, Russia	G10	28
Minxian, China	E7	30
Minya see Al-Minyā, Egypt	C6	60
Minya Konka see Gongga Shan, mtn., China	F7	30
Mio, Mi., U.S.	F11	110
Miory, Bela.	F10	22
Mir, Bela.	H9	22
Mira, Port.	E3	16
Mira, stm., N.S., Can.	G13	106
Mira, stm., Col.	G3	84
Mira Bay, b., N.S., Can.	F14	106
Miracema do Tocantins, Braz.	E9	76
Mirador, Braz.	E10	76
Miradouro, Braz.	F7	79
Miraflores, Arg.	E6	80
Miraflores, Col.	E6	84
Miraflores, Col.	G6	84
Miraflores, Esclusas de, Pan.	I15	92
Mīrah, Wādī al-, val., Asia	B11	60
Miraj, India	D3	46
Miramar, Arg.	J10	80
Miramar, Arg.	F7	80
Miramar, C.R.	G10	92
Miramas, Fr.	I12	14
Miramichi Bay, b., N.B., Can.	E9	106
Miranda, Braz.	I13	82
Miranda, Col.	F4	84
Miranda, Ca., U.S.	D2	124
Miranda, state, Ven.	B9	84
Miranda, stm., Braz.	H13	82
Miranda de Ebro, Spain	C9	16
Miranda do Douro, Port.	D5	16
Mirande, Fr.	I7	14
Mirandela, Port.	D4	16
Mirando City, Tx., U.S.	L7	116
Mirandola, Italy	E6	18
Mirante do Paranapanema, Braz.	G3	79
Mirapuxi, stm., Braz.	B3	79
Mira Taglio, Italy	D7	18
Miravalles, Volcán, vol., C.R.	G9	92
Mirbāṭ, Oman	F9	47
Mirebeau-sur-Bèze, Fr.	E12	14
Mirecourt, Fr.	D13	14
Miri, Malay.	E5	38
Miriam Vale, Austl.	E9	70
Mirim, Lagoa (Laguna Merín), b., S.A.	G12	80
Miriñay, stm., Arg.	E10	80
Miritiparaná, stm., Col.	H7	84
Mīrjāveh, Iran	G16	48
Mirnyj, Russia	E14	28
Mirnyy, sci., Ant.	B6	73
Mirond Lake, l., Sask., Can.	C12	104
Mirow, Ger.	B12	10
Mīrpur, Pak.	D5	44
Mīrpur Khās, Pak.	H3	44
Mirria, Niger	E14	64
Mirror, Alta., Can.	E21	102
Mirzāpur, India	H10	44
Misāḥah, Bi'r, well, Egypt	F4	60
Misantla, Mex.	H11	90
Miscou Centre, N.B., Can.	E9	106
Miscou Island, i., N.B., Can.	E9	106
Miscou Point, c., N.B., Can.	D9	106
Misenheimer, N.C., U.S.	D6	112
Mishagua, stm., Peru	D5	82
Mishan, China	B13	30
Mishawaka, In., U.S.	A10	114
Mishbiḥ, Jabal, mtn., Egypt	J3	48
Mishicot, Wi., U.S.	F8	110
Misikan, China	C13	44
Misilmeri, Italy	K8	18
Misiones, prov., Arg.	D11	80
Misiones, dept., Para.	D10	80
Misión San Francisco de Laishí, Arg.	D9	80
Misión San Vicente, Mex.	B1	90
Miskī, Sud.	J3	60
Miskito Channel, strt., Nic.	C11	92
Miskitos, Cayos, is., Nic.	C12	92
Miskitos Reef, rf., Nic.	C12	92
Miskolc, Hung.	G20	10
Mislata, Spain	A10	62
Misool, Pulau, i., Indon.	F9	38
Misquamaebin Lake, l., Ont., Can.	E23	104
Misrātah, Libya	B4	56
Missinaibi, stm., Ont., Can.	F16	96
Missinaibi Lake, l., Ont., Can.	B12	110
Mission, S.D., U.S.	H7	118
Mission, Tx., U.S.	M8	116
Mission City, B.C., Can.	H12	102
Mississauga, Ont., Can.	G16	110
Mississinewa, stm., U.S.	B11	114
Mississippi, state, U.S.	E9	98
Mississippi, stm., U.S.	E8	98
Mississippi Delta, La., U.S.	M7	114
Mississippi Sound, strt., U.S.	L8	114
Mississippi State, Ms., U.S.	I8	114
Missoula, Mt., U.S.	D12	122
Missouri, state, U.S.	D8	98
Missouri, stm., U.S.	C7	98
Missouri Valley, Ia., U.S.	J12	118
Mistaken Point, c., Newf., Can.	F20	106
Mistanipisipou, stm., Que., Can.	A11	106
Mistassibi, stm., Que., Can.	G18	96
Mistassibi Nord-Est, stm., Que., Can.	B2	106
Mistassini, Que., Can.	F18	96
Mistassini, Lac, l., Que., Can.	F18	96
Mistatim, Sask., Can.	F11	104
Mistawasis Indian Reserve, Sask., Can.	E8	104
Mistelbach, Aus.	G16	10
Misterbianco, Italy	L10	18
Misterei, Sud.	K2	60
Misti, Volcán, vol., Peru	G6	82
Mistikokan, stm., Man., Can.	B23	104
Mistretta, Italy	L9	18
Mita, Punta, c., Mex.	G7	90
Mitchell, Austl.	F7	70
Mitchell, Ont., Can.	G14	110
Mitchell, In., U.S.	D10	114
Mitchell, Ne., U.S.	J4	118
Mitchell, Or., U.S.	F5	122
Mitchell, S.D., U.S.	H9	118
Mitchell, stm., Austl.	K7	70
Mitchell, Lake, res., Al., U.S.	J10	114
Mitchell, Mount, mtn., N.C., U.S.	D4	112
Mitchell Lake, l., B.C., Can.	E14	102
Mitchellville, Ia., U.S.	I2	110
Mitilíni, Grc.	J10	20
Mitis, Lac, l., Que., Can.	D6	106
Mitishto, stm., Man., Can.	D15	104
Mitla, hist., Mex.	I11	90
Mito, Japan	K15	36
Mitsamiouli, Com.	k15	67a
Mitsinjo, Madag.	p21	67b
Mitsio, Nosy, i., Madag.	n23	67b
Mitsiwa (Massawa), Erit.	J10	60
Mittellandkanal, Ger.	C9	10
Mittenwald, Ger.	H11	10
Mittersill, Aus.	H12	10
Mitú, Col.	G7	84
Mitumba, Monts, mts., Zaire	B5	58
Mitwaba, Zaire	C5	58
Mitzic, Gabon	A2	58
Miura, Japan	L14	36
Mixco Viejo, hist., Guat.	C4	92
Miyake-jima, i., Japan	M14	36
Miyako, Japan	H16	36
Miyakonojō, Japan	P6	36
Miyazaki, Japan	P6	36
Miyazu, Japan	L10	36
Miyun, China	C4	32
Mizan Teferi, Eth.	N8	60
Mizdah, Libya	B3	56
Mize, Ms., U.S.	K7	114
Mizen Head, c., Ire.	J4	8
Mizhhir'ya, Ukr.	A7	20
Mizoram, state, India	I15	44
Miẓpé Ramon, Isr.	G3	50
Mizque, Bol.	G9	82
Mizque, stm., Bol.	H9	82
Mjøsa, l., Nor.	K12	6
Mladá Boleslav, Czech.	E14	10
Mladenovac, Yugo.	E4	20
Mlanje Peak see Sapitwa, mtn., Mwi.	E7	58
Mława, Pol.	B20	10
Mmabatho, S. Afr.	E7	66
Mmadinare, Bots.	C8	66
Mo, Nor.	H14	6
Mo, stm., Afr.	G10	64
Moa, stm., Afr.	G4	54
Moa, stm., Braz.	B5	82
Moab, Ut., U.S.	F7	120
Moaco, stm., Braz.	C7	82
Moa Island, i., Austl.	B8	68
Moama, Austl.	K6	70
Moanda, Gabon	B2	58
Moar Lake, l., Can.	F19	104
Mobara, Japan	L15	36
Mobaye, Cen. Afr. Rep.	H5	56
Mobeetie, Tx., U.S.	D6	116
Moberly, Mo., U.S.	C4	114
Moberly, stm., B.C., Can.	A13	102
Moberly Lake, B.C., Can.	B13	102
Moberly Lake, l., B.C., Can.	B13	102
Mobile, Al., U.S.	L8	114
Mobile, Az., U.S.	K4	120
Mobile, stm., Al., U.S.	L8	114
Mobile Bay, b., Al., U.S.	L8	114
Mobridge, S.D., U.S.	F7	118
Moca, Dom. Rep.	E9	94
Mocal, stm., N.A.	C6	92
Moçambique, Moz.	E8	58
Mocanal, Spain	p23	17b
Mocha see Al-Makhā', Yemen	H3	47
Mocha, Isla, i., Chile	J2	80
Moche, stm., Peru	C2	82
Moche, hist., Peru	C2	82
Mochudi, Bots.	E8	66
Mocímboa da Praia, Moz.	D8	58
Mocksville, N.C., U.S.	D6	112
Moclips, Wa., U.S.	C1	122
Môco, Serra do, mtn., Ang.	D3	58
Mocoa, Col.	G4	84
Mococa, Braz.	F5	79
Mocoduene, Moz.	D12	66
Mocoretá, Arg.	F10	80
Mocorito, Mex.	E6	90
Moctezuma, Mex.	C5	90
Moctezuma, stm., Mex.	C5	90
Moctezuma, stm., Mex.	G10	90
Mocuba, Moz.	E7	58
Modane, Fr.	G13	14
Modderrivier, S. Afr.	G7	66
Modena, Italy	E5	18
Modesto, Ca., U.S.	G5	124
Modica, Italy	M9	18
Mödling, Aus.	G16	10
Moe, Austl.	L7	70
Moeda, Braz.	F6	79
Moema, Braz.	E6	79
Moengo, Sur.	B8	76
Moenkopi, Az., U.S.	H5	120
Moffit, N.D., U.S.	E7	118
Moga, India	E6	44
Mogadiscio see Muqdisho, Som.	H10	56
Mogadishu see Muqdisho, Som.	H10	56
Mogán, Spain	p25	17b
Mogapinyana, Bots.	D8	66
Mogaung, Mya.	B4	40
Mogil'ov, Bela.	H13	22
Mogincual, Moz.	E8	58
Mogliano Veneto, Italy	D7	18
Mogoča, Russia	G15	28
Mogogh, Sud.	M6	60
Mogok, Mya.	C4	40
Mogollon Rim, clf, Az., U.S.	J6	120
Mogotes, Col.	D6	84
Mogotón, mtn., N.A.	D8	92
Moguer, Spain	H5	16
Mogzon, Russia	G14	28
Mohács, Hung.	J18	10
Mohall, N.D., U.S.	C6	118
Mohammedia (Fedala), Mor.	D7	62
Mohave, Lake, res., U.S.	I11	124
Mohawk, Mi., U.S.	C7	110
Mohawk, stm., N.Y., U.S.	E12	108
Mohe, China	A11	30
Moho, stm., Belize	A6	92
Mohyliv-Podil's'kyy, Ukr.	H3	26
Moinești, Rom.	C10	20
Mointy, Kaz.	H12	26
Moiporá, Braz.	D3	79
Mõisaküla, Est.	C8	22
Moisés Ville, Arg.	F8	80
Moisie, Que., Can.	B7	106
Moisie, stm., Que., Can.	F19	96
Moisie, stm., Que., Can.	B7	106
Moisie, Baie de, b., Que., Can.	B8	106
Moissac, Fr.	H8	14
Moitaco, Ven.	C10	84
Mojana, Brazo, mth., Col.	C5	84
Mojave, Ca., U.S.	I7	124
Mojave Desert, des., Ca., U.S.	J8	124
Mojicuaçu, stm., Braz.	F5	79
Mojimirim, Braz.	G5	79
Mojjero, stm., Russia	D12	28
Mojo, Eth.	M10	60
Mokāma, India	H11	44
Mokelumne, stm., Ca., U.S.	F4	124
Moknine, Tun.	N5	18
Mokp'o, S. Kor.	I14	32
Mokrisset, Mor.	K6	16
Mokša, stm., Russia	G24	22
Mokwa, Nig.	G12	64
Mol, Bel.	F7	12
Mola di Bari, Italy	H12	18
Molalla, Or., U.S.	E3	122
Molanosa, Sask., Can.	D9	104
Moldau see Vltava, stm., Czech.	F14	10
Moldavia, hist. reg., Rom.	B11	20
Moldavia see Moldova, ctry., Eur.	F13	4
Molde, Nor.	J10	6
Moldova, ctry., Eur.	F13	4
Moldoveanu, Vârful, mtn., Rom.	D8	20
Môle, Cap du, c., Haiti	E8	94
Molega Lake, l., N.S., Can.	H9	106
Molepolole, Bots.	E7	66
Molėtai, Lith.	F8	22
Molfetta, Italy	H11	18
Molina, Chile	H3	80
Molina de Segura, Spain	G10	16
Moline, Il., U.S.	I5	110
Moline, Ks., U.S.	N11	118
Molino, Fl., U.S.	L9	114
Molinos, Arg.	C5	80
Molins de Rei, Spain	D14	16
Molise, prov., Italy	H9	18
Mollendo, Peru	G5	82
Mollepata, Peru	E5	82
Mölln, Ger.	B10	10
Mölndal, Swe.	M13	6
Moločnoje, Russia	B22	22
Molodečno, Bela.	G9	22
Mologa, stm., Russia	C19	22
Molokai, i., Hi., U.S.	p16	125a
Molong, Austl.	I8	70
Molopo, stm., Afr.	F5	66
Molotov see Perm', Russia	F9	26
Molou, Chad	K1	60
Molsheim, Fr.	D14	14
Molson Lake, l., Man., Can.	D18	104
Molteno, S. Afr.	H8	66
Moluccas see Maluku, is., Indon.	F8	38
Molucca Sea see Maluku, Laut, Indon.	F7	38
Molukkensee see Maluku, Laut, Indon.	F7	38
Moma, Moz.	E7	58
Moma, stm., Russia	D20	28
Momanga, Nmb.	B5	66
Mombachito, Cerro, mtn., Nic.	E9	92
Mombacho, Volcán, vol., Nic.	F9	92
Mombasa, Kenya	B7	58
Mombetsu, Japan	c18	36a
Momence, Il., U.S.	I8	110
Momotombo, Volcán, vol., Nic.	E8	92
Mompós, Col.	C5	84
Mona, Ut., U.S.	E5	120
Mona, Canal de la, strt., N.A.	E11	94
Mona, Isla de, i., P.R.	E11	94
Mona, Punta, c., C.R.	H12	92
Monaca, Pa., U.S.	G6	108
Monaco, ctry., Eur.	G9	4
Monadnock Mountain, mtn., N.H., U.S.	E14	108
Monagas, state, Ven.	C11	84
Monaghan, co., Ire.	G6	8
Monagrillo, Pan.	D2	84
Monahans, Tx., U.S.	H4	116
Monango, N.D., U.S.	E9	118
Monarch, S.C., U.S.	E5	112
Monarch Mountain, mtn., B.C., Can.	F9	102
Monarch Pass, Co., U.S.	F10	120
Monashee Mountains, mts., B.C., Can.	F16	102
Monashee Provincial Park, B.C., Can.	G16	102
Monastir see Bitola, Mac.	H5	20
Monastir, Tun.	N5	18
Monastyrščina, Russia	G14	22
Moncalieri, Italy	D2	18
Monção, Braz.	D9	76
Mončegorsk, Russia	D4	26
Mönchengladbach, Ger.	D6	10
Moncks Corner, S.C., U.S.	F6	112
Monclova, Mex.	D9	90
Moncontour, Fr.	D4	14
Moncoutant, Fr.	F6	14
Moncton, N.B., Can.	F9	106
Mondaí, Braz.	D12	80
Monday, stm., Para.	C11	80
Mondoro, Mali	D9	64
Mondoubleau, Fr.	E7	14
Mondovi, Wi., U.S.	F4	110
Mondragone, Italy	H8	18
Monero, N.M., U.S.	H10	120
Moneron, ostrov, i., Russia	a16	36a
Monessen, Pa., U.S.	G7	108
Monesterio, Spain	G5	16
Monett, Mo., U.S.	F3	114
Monette, Ar., U.S.	G6	114
Monfalcone, Italy	D8	18
Monflanquin, Fr.	H7	14
Monforte, Port.	F4	16
Monforte de Lemos, Spain	C4	16
Mongaguá, Braz.	H5	79
Mongalla, Sud.	G7	56
Mong Cai, Viet.	D9	40
Monger, Îles, is., Que., Can.	A15	106
Mongers Lake, l., Austl.	E3	68
Möng Hsat, Mya.	D5	40
Möng Mit, Mya.	C4	40
Mongo, Chad	F4	56
Mongo, stm., Afr.	G4	64
Mongol Altajn nuruu, mts., Asia	H16	26
Mongolia (Mongol Ard Uls), ctry., Asia	B8	30
Mongororo, Chad	K2	60
Möng Pai, Mya.	E4	40
Mongu, Zam.	E4	58
Möng Yawng, Mya.	D6	40
Monheim, Ger.	G10	10
Monico, Wi., U.S.	E6	110
Monida Pass, U.S.	F13	122
Monino, Russia	F21	22
Moniquirá, Col.	E6	84
Monistrol-sur-Loire, Fr.	G11	14
Monitor Range, mts., Nv., U.S.	F9	124
Monitor Valley, val., Nv., U.S.	F9	124
Monkey River, Belize	A6	92
Mońki, Pol.	B22	10
Monkira, Austl.	E4	70
Monmouth, Il., U.S.	J5	110
Monmouth, Or., U.S.	F2	122
Monmouth Mountain, mtn., B.C., Can.	F11	102
Mono, stm., Afr.	G7	54
Mono, Caño, stm., Col.	E8	84
Mono, Punta, c., Nic.	F11	92
Mono Lake, l., Ca., U.S.	F7	124
Monon, In., U.S.	B10	114
Monona, Ia., U.S.	G4	110
Monona, Wi., U.S.	G6	110
Monongahela, stm., U.S.	H7	108
Monopoli, Italy	I12	18
Monòver, Spain	G11	16
Monreale, Italy	K8	18
Monroe, Ga., U.S.	F3	112
Monroe, Ia., U.S.	I2	110
Monroe, La., U.S.	J4	114
Monroe, Mi., U.S.	I12	110
Monroe, Ne., U.S.	J10	118
Monroe, N.Y., U.S.	F12	108
Monroe, N.C., U.S.	E6	112
Monroe, Or., U.S.	F2	122
Monroe, Ut., U.S.	F4	120
Monroe, Va., U.S.	B7	112
Monroe, Wa., U.S.	C4	122
Monroe, Wi., U.S.	H6	110
Monroe City, In., U.S.	D9	114
Monroe City, Mo., U.S.	C5	114
Monroe Lake, res., In., U.S.	C10	114
Monroeville, Al., U.S.	K9	114
Monroeville, In., U.S.	B12	114
Monroeville, Oh., U.S.	F4	108
Monroeville, Pa., U.S.	G7	108
Monrovia, Lib.	H4	64
Mons (Bergen), Bel.	H4	12

Name	Map Ref.	Page
Monsefú, Peru	B2	82
Monselice, Italy	D6	18
Monson, Me., U.S.	B17	108
Montabaur, Ger.	E7	10
Montagnana, Italy	D6	18
Montagu, S. Afr.	I5	66
Montague, P.E.I., Can.	F11	106
Montague, Ca., U.S.	C3	124
Montague, Mi., U.S.	G9	110
Montague, Tx., U.S.	F9	116
Montague, Isla, i., Mex.	B2	90
Montague Island, i., Ak., U.S.	F21	100
Montagu Island, i., S. Geor.	A2	73
Montaigu, Fr.	F5	14
Montalcino, Italy	F6	18
Montalegre, Port.	D4	16
Montana, Bul.	F7	20
Montana, Switz.	F7	13
Montana, state, U.S.	B4	98
Montana Indian Reserve, Alta., Can.	E21	102
Montargis, Fr.	D9	14
Montauban, Fr.	H8	14
Montauk, N.Y., U.S.	F15	108
Montauk Point, c., N.Y., U.S.	F15	108
Montbard, Fr.	E11	14
Montbarrey, Fr.	E12	14
Montbéliard, Fr.	E13	14
Mont Belvieu, Tx., U.S.	J12	116
Mont Blanc, Tunnel du, Eur.	G6	13
Montbrison, Fr.	G11	14
Montbron, Fr.	G7	14
Montceau [-les-Mines], Fr.	F11	14
Montcevelles, Lac, l., Que., Can.	A13	106
Montchanin, Fr.	F11	14
Montclair, Ca., U.S.	J8	124
Montclair, N.J., U.S.	G12	108
Mont-de-Marsan, Fr.	I6	14
Montdidier, Fr.	C9	14
Monte, Laguna del, l., Arg.	I7	80
Monteagle, Tn., U.S.	G11	114
Monteagudo, Bol.	H10	82
Monte Albán, hist., Mex.	I11	90
Monte Alegre, Braz.	D8	76
Monte Alegre de Goiás, Braz.	B5	79
Monte Alegre de Minas, Braz.	E4	79
Monte Azul, Braz.	C7	79
Monte Azul Paulista, Braz.	F4	79
Montebello, Que., Can.	B12	108
Monte Bello Islands, is., Austl.	D3	68
Monte Buey, Arg.	G7	80
Montecarlo, Arg.	D11	80
Monte Caseros, Arg.	F10	80
Montecassino, Abbazia di, Italy	H8	18
Montecatini-Terme, Italy	F5	18
Montecillos, Cordillera de, mts., Hond.	C7	92
Montecito, Ca., U.S.	J6	124
Monte Comán, Arg.	H5	80
Monte Creek, B.C., Can.	G15	102
Monte Cristi, Dom. Rep.	E9	94
Montecristi, Ec.	H2	84
Monte Cristo, Bol.	F11	82
Monte Escobedo, Mex.	F8	90
Montego Bay, Jam.	E6	94
Monte Grande, Chile	F3	80
Montegut, La., U.S.	M6	114
Monteith, Mount, mtn., B.C., Can.	B12	102
Montelíbano, Col.	C5	84
Montélimar, Fr.	H11	14
Montelindo, stm., Para.	B9	80
Montellano, Spain	H6	16
Montello, Nv., U.S.	C11	124
Montello, Wi., U.S.	G6	110
Monte Maíz, Arg.	G7	80
Montemorelos, Mex.	E10	90
Montemor-o-Novo, Port.	G3	16
Montemor-o-Velho, Port.	E3	16
Montendre, Fr.	G6	14
Montenegro, Braz.	E13	80
Montenegro see Crna Gora, state, Yugo.	G2	20
Monte Pascoal, Parque Nacional de, Braz.	D9	79
Monte Patria, Chile	F3	80
Montepuez, Moz.	D7	58
Montepulciano, Italy	F6	18
Monte Quemado, Arg.	C7	80
Montereau-Faut-Yonne, Fr.	D9	14
Monterey, Ca., U.S.	H4	124
Monterey, Tn., U.S.	F11	114
Monterey, Va., U.S.	I7	108
Monterey Bay, b., Ca., U.S.	H4	124
Montería, Col.	C5	84
Montero, Bol.	G10	82
Monteros, Arg.	D6	80
Monterotondo, Italy	G7	18
Monterrey, Mex.	E9	90
Montesano, Italy	I10	18
Montesano, Wa., U.S.	D2	122
Monte Sant'Angelo, Italy	H10	18
Montesarchio, Italy	H9	18
Montes Claros, Braz.	D7	79
Montevallo, Al., U.S.	I10	114
Montevarchi, Italy	F6	18
Montevideo, Mn., U.S.	G12	118
Montevideo, Ur.	H10	80
Monte Vista, Co., U.S.	G10	120
Montezuma, Ga., U.S.	G2	112
Montezuma, In., U.S.	C9	114
Montezuma, Ia., U.S.	I3	110
Montezuma, Ks., U.S.	N7	118
Montfort, Fr.	D5	14
Montfort, Wi., U.S.	H5	110
Montgomery, Al., U.S.	J10	114
Montgomery, La., U.S.	K4	114
Montgomery, Mn., U.S.	F2	110
Montgomery, Pa., U.S.	F10	108
Montgomery, Tx., U.S.	I11	116
Montgomery, W.V., U.S.	I5	108
Montgomery City, Mo., U.S.	D5	114
Monthermé, Fr.	C11	14
Monthey, Switz.	F6	13
Monthois, Fr.	C11	14
Monticello, Ar., U.S.	I5	114
Monticello, Fl., U.S.	I3	112
Monticello, Ga., U.S.	F3	112
Monticello, Il., U.S.	B8	114
Monticello, In., U.S.	B10	114
Monticello, Ia., U.S.	H4	110
Monticello, Ky., U.S.	F12	114
Monticello, Mn., U.S.	E2	110
Monticello, Ms., U.S.	K6	114
Monticello, Mo., U.S.	B5	114
Monticello, N.Y., U.S.	F12	108
Monticello, Ut., U.S.	G7	120
Monticello, Wi., U.S.	H6	110
Montichiari, Italy	D5	18
Montignac, Fr.	G8	14
Montigny-le-Roi, Fr.	D12	14
Montigny-sur-Aube, Fr.	E11	14
Montijo, Pan.	D2	84
Montijo, Port.	G3	16
Montijo, Spain	G5	16
Montijo, Golfo de, b., Pan.	D2	84
Montilla, Spain	H7	16
Montividiu, Braz.	D3	79
Montivilliers, Fr.	C7	14
Mont-Joli, Que., Can.	D5	106
Mont-Laurier, Que., Can.	G17	96
Mont-Louis, Fr.	J9	14
Montluçon, Fr.	F9	14
Montluel, Fr.	G12	14
Montmagny, Que., Can.	F3	106
Montmédy, Fr.	C12	14
Montmirail, Fr.	D10	14
Montmorency see Beauport, Que., Can.	F2	106
Montmorency, stm., Que., Can.	E2	106
Montmorillon, Fr.	F7	14
Monto, Austl.	E9	70
Montoro, Spain	G7	16
Montour Falls, N.Y., U.S.	E10	108
Montoursville, Pa., U.S.	F10	108
Montpelier, Id., U.S.	H14	122
Montpelier, In., U.S.	G1	108
Montpelier, Ms., U.S.	I8	114
Montpelier, Oh., U.S.	F2	108
Montpelier, Vt., U.S.	C14	108
Montpellier, Fr.	I10	14
Montpon-Ménesterol, Fr.	G7	14
Montréal, Que., Can.	B13	108
Montreal, Wi., U.S.	D5	110
Montreal, stm., Sask., Can.	D9	104
Montreal Lake, Sask., Can.	D9	104
Montreal Lake, l., Sask., Can.	D9	104
Montreal Lake Indian Reserve, Sask., Can.	D9	104
Montreuil, Fr.	B8	14
Montreux, Switz.	F6	13
Montrevel [-en-Bresse], Fr.	F12	14
Montrose, Scot., U.K.	E11	8
Montrose, Co., U.S.	F9	120
Montrose, Ia., U.S.	J4	110
Montrose, Mi., U.S.	G12	110
Montrose, Pa., U.S.	F11	108
Montrose, S.D., U.S.	H10	118
Montross, Va., U.S.	I10	108
Monts, Pointe des, c., Que., Can.	C6	106
Mont-Sainte-Anne, Parc du, Que., Can.	E3	106
Mont-Saint-Michel see Le Mont-Saint-Michel, Fr.	D5	14
Montserrat, dep., N.A.	F13	94
Montvale, Va., U.S.	B7	112
Monument, Or., U.S.	F6	122
Monument Peak, mtn., Id., U.S.	H11	122
Monument Valley, val., U.S.	G6	120
Monywa, Mya.	C3	40
Monza, Italy	D4	18
Monzón, Peru	C3	82
Monzón, Spain	D12	16
Moodie Island, i., N.W. Ter., Can.	D19	96
Moody, Tx., U.S.	H9	116
Mooirivier, S. Afr.	G9	66
Mookane, Bots.	E7	66
Moolawatana, Austl.	G3	70
Moonie, stm., Austl.	F8	70
Moonta, Austl.	J2	70
Moora, Austl.	F3	68
Moorcroft, Wy., U.S.	G3	118
Moore, Id., U.S.	G12	122
Moore, Mt., U.S.	D16	122
Moore, Ok., U.S.	D9	116
Moore, Tx., U.S.	J7	116
Moore, Lake, l., Austl.	E3	68
Moorefield, W.V., U.S.	H8	108
Moore Haven, Fl., U.S.	M5	112
Mooreland, Ok., U.S.	C7	116
Mooresville, In., U.S.	C10	114
Mooresville, N.C., U.S.	D6	112
Moorhead, Mn., U.S.	E11	118
Moorhead, Ms., U.S.	I6	114
Mooringsport, La., U.S.	J3	114
Moornanyah Lake, l., Austl.	I5	70
Moorreesburg, S. Afr.	I4	66
Moosburg, Ger.	G11	10
Moosehead Lake, l., Me., U.S.	B17	108
Moose Heights, B.C., Can.	D12	102
Moose Island, i., Man., Can.	G17	104
Moose Jaw, Sask., Can.	H9	104
Moose Jaw, stm., Sask., Can.	H9	104
Moose Lake, Man., Can.	E14	104
Moose Lake, Mn., U.S.	D3	110
Moose Lake, l., Alta., Can.	C24	102
Moose Lake, l., Man., Can.	E15	104
Mooselookmeguntic Lake, l., Me., U.S.	C16	108
Moose Mountain, mtn., Sask., Can.	I12	104
Moose Mountain Creek, stm., Sask., Can.	H11	104
Moose Mountain Provincial Park, Sask., Can.	I12	104
Moose Pass, Ak., U.S.	F20	100
Moosomin, Sask., Can.	H13	104
Moosomin Indian Reserve, Sask., Can.	E6	104
Moosonee, Ont., Can.	F16	96
Mopane, S. Afr.	D9	66
Mopipi, Bots.	C7	66
Mopti, Mali	D7	64
Moquegua, Peru	G6	82
Moquegua, dept., Peru	G6	82
Mór, Hung.	H18	10
Mora, Spain	F8	16
Mora, Swe.	K14	6
Mora, Mn., U.S.	E2	110
Mora, N.M., U.S.	I11	120
Mora, stm., N.M., U.S.	H11	120
Morādābād, India	F8	44
Morada Nova de Minas, Braz.	E6	79
Moradel, Montaña de, mtn., Hond.	B8	92
Mora de Rubielos, Spain	E11	16
Morafenobe, Madag.	p21	67b
Mórahalom, Hung.	I19	10
Mor'akovskij Zaton, Russia	F14	26
Moraleda, Canal, strt., Chile	E2	78
Morales, Guat.	B6	92
Morales, Peru	B3	82
Morales, Laguna, b., Mex.	F11	90
Moran, Ks., U.S.	N12	118
Moran, Mi., U.S.	E11	110
Moran, Tx., U.S.	G7	116
Morant Bay, Jam.	F6	94
Morant Cays, is., Jam.	F7	94
Morant Point, c., Jam.	F6	94
Moratalla, Spain	G10	16
Moratuwa, Sri L.	I5	46
Morava, hist. reg., Czech.	F17	10
Morava (March), stm., Eur.	G16	10
Moravia, C.R.	H11	92
Moravia, Ia., U.S.	J3	110
Moravia, N.Y., U.S.	E10	108
Moravia see Morava, hist. reg., Czech.	F17	10
Morawhanna, Guy.	C13	84
Moraya, Bol.	I9	82
Moray Firth, est., Scot., U.K.	D10	8
Morazán, Guat.	C4	92
Morazán, Hond.	B7	92
Morbegno, Italy	C4	18
Morbi, India	I4	44
Morbihan, dept., Fr.	E4	14
Morcenx, Fr.	H6	14
Morden, Man., Can.	I16	104
Mordovija, state, Russia	G6	26
Mordovo, Russia	I23	22
Mordves, Russia	G21	22
Mordvinia see Mordovija, state, Russia	G6	26
Moreau, stm., S.D., U.S.	F6	118
Moreauville, La., U.S.	K5	114
Moree, Austl.	G8	70
Morée, Fr.	E8	14
Morehead, Ky., U.S.	I3	108
Morehead City, N.C., U.S.	E10	112
Morehouse, Mo., U.S.	F7	114
Moreland, Ga., U.S.	F2	112
Moreland, Ky., U.S.	E12	114
Morelia, Mex.	H9	90
Morell, P.E.I., Can.	F11	106
Morelos, Mex.	D6	90
Morelos, state, Mex.	H10	90
Moremi Wildlife Reserve, Bots.	B6	66
Morena, India	G8	44
Morena, Sierra, mts., Spain	G6	16
Morenci, Az., U.S.	K7	120
Morenci, Mi., U.S.	I11	110
Moreno, Bahía, b., Chile	B3	80
Møre og Romsdal, co., Nor.	J10	6
Moresby Island, i., B.C., Can.	E3	102
Mores Island, i., Bah.	A6	94
Moresnet, Bel.	G8	12
Moreton Island, i., Austl.	F10	70
Moreuil, Fr.	C9	14
Morez, Fr.	F13	14
Morgan, Ga., U.S.	H2	112
Morgan, Mn., U.S.	G13	118
Morgan, Tx., U.S.	G9	116
Morgan, Ut., U.S.	C5	120
Morgan City, Al., U.S.	H10	114
Morgan City, La., U.S.	M5	114
Morganfield, Ky., U.S.	E9	114
Morgan Hill, Ca., U.S.	G4	124
Morganito, Ven.	E9	84
Morganton, N.C., U.S.	D5	112
Morgantown, In., U.S.	C10	114
Morgantown, Ky., U.S.	E10	114
Morgantown, Ms., U.S.	K5	114
Morgantown, Ms., U.S.	K7	114
Morgantown, W.V., U.S.	H7	108
Morganza, La., U.S.	L5	114
Morgenzon, S. Afr.	F9	66
Morghāb (Murgab), stm., Asia	B16	48
Moriah, Mount, mtn., Nv., U.S.	E11	124
Moriarty, N.M., U.S.	J10	120
Moribaya, Gui.	G5	64
Morice, stm., B.C., Can.	C7	102
Morice Lake, l., B.C., Can.	C7	102
Morichal Largo, stm., Ven.	C11	84
Moriki, Nig.	E13	64
Moringen, Ger.	D9	10
Morino, Russia	D13	22
Morinville, Alta., Can.	D21	102
Morioka, Japan	H16	36
Morisset, Austl.	I9	70
Morkill, stm., B.C., Can.	D14	102
Morkiny Gory, Russia	D19	22
Morkoka, stm., Russia	D14	28
Morlaix, Fr.	D3	14
Morley, Mi., U.S.	G10	110
Mormal', Bela.	I12	22
Morney, Austl.	E4	70
Morning Sun, Ia., U.S.	I4	110
Mornington, Austl.	L6	70
Mornington, Isla, i., Chile	F1	78
Mornington Island, i., Austl.	A3	70
Moro, Or., U.S.	E5	122
Moro, stm., Afr.	H4	64
Morobe, Pap. N. Gui.	m16	68a
Morocco, In., U.S.	B9	114
Morocco (Al-Magreb), ctry., Afr.	B5	54
Morococala, Bol.	H8	82
Morococha, Peru	D3	82
Morogoro, Tan.	C7	58
Moro Gulf, b., Phil.	D7	38
Moroleón, Mex.	G9	90
Morombe, Madag.	r20	67b
Morón, Arg.	H9	80
Morón, Cuba	C5	94
Mörön, Mong.	B7	30
Morón, Ven.	B8	84
Morona, stm., Peru	I4	84
Morona-Santiago, prov., Ec.	I3	84
Morondava, Madag.	r21	67b
Morón de la Frontera, Spain	H6	16
Moroni, Com.	k15	67a
Moroni, Ut., U.S.	E5	120
Morotai, i., Indon.	E8	38
Morozovsk, Russia	H6	26
Morrill, Ne., U.S.	J4	118
Morrilton, Ar., U.S.	G4	114
Morrin, Alta., Can.	F22	102
Morrinhos, Braz.	D4	79
Morrinsville, N.Z.	B5	72
Morris, Man., Can.	I17	104
Morris, Il., U.S.	I7	110
Morris, Mn., U.S.	F12	118
Morris, Ok., U.S.	D11	116
Morris, stm., Man., Can.	I17	104
Morrisburg, Ont., Can.	C11	108
Morris Jesup, Kap, c., Grnld.	A16	86
Morrison, Arg.	G7	80
Morrison, Il., U.S.	I6	110
Morrisonville, Il., U.S.	C7	114
Morristown, Az., U.S.	K4	120
Morristown, In., U.S.	C11	114
Morristown, Mn., U.S.	F2	110
Morristown, S.D., U.S.	F6	118
Morristown, Tn., U.S.	C3	112
Morrisville, N.Y., U.S.	E11	108
Morrisville, Pa., U.S.	G12	108
Morrisville, Vt., U.S.	C14	108
Morrito, Nic.	F9	92
Morro, Ec.	I2	84
Morro, Punta, c., Mex.	H14	90
Morro Bay, Ca., U.S.	I5	124
Morro del Jable, Spain	o26	17b
Morro do Chapéu, Braz.	F10	76
Morropón, Peru	A1	82
Morrosquillo, Golfo de, b., Col.	C5	84
Morrow, La., U.S.	L4	114
Morrumbene, Moz.	D12	66
Moršansk, Russia	H24	22
Morse, Sask., Can.	H7	104
Morse, La., U.S.	L4	114
Morse, Tx., U.S.	C5	116
Morson, Ont., Can.	I20	104
Mortagne, Fr.	D7	14
Mortagne-sur-Sèvre, Fr.	E6	14
Mortain, Fr.	D6	14
Mortara, Italy	D3	18
Morteau, Fr.	E13	14
Morteros, Arg.	F7	80
Mortes, Rio das, stm., Braz.	B3	79
Mortesoro, Sud.	L8	60
Mortlach, Sask., Can.	H8	104
Mortlake, Austl.	L5	70
Morton, Il., U.S.	J6	110
Morton, Mn., U.S.	G13	118
Morton, Ms., U.S.	J7	114
Morton, Tx., U.S.	F4	116
Morton, Wa., U.S.	D3	122
Mortons Gap, Ky., U.S.	E9	114
Moruya, Austl.	J9	70
Morven, Austl.	F7	70
Morven, Ga., U.S.	I3	112
Morven, N.C., U.S.	E6	112
Morwell, Austl.	L7	70
Morženga, Russia	B23	22
Mosal'sk, Russia	G17	22
Moščnyj, ostrov, i., Russia	A10	22
Moscow see Moskva, Russia	F20	22
Moscow, Id., U.S.	D9	122
Mosel (Moselle), stm., Eur.	C13	14
Moselle, Ms., U.S.	K7	114
Moselle, dept., Fr.	D13	14
Moselle (Mosel), stm., Eur.	D13	14
Mosers River, N.S., Can.	H11	106
Moses Lake, Wa., U.S.	C6	122
Moses Point, Ak., U.S.	D13	100
Mosetse, Bots.	C8	66
Moshanpu, China	F1	34
Moshaweng, stm., S. Afr.	F6	66
Mosheim, Tn., U.S.	C4	112
Moshi, Tan.	B7	58
Mosina, Pol.	C16	10
Mosinee, Wi., U.S.	F6	110
Mosjøen, Nor.	I13	6
Moskva (Moscow), Russia	F20	22
Moskva, stm., Russia	F21	22
Moskvy, kanal imeni, Russia	E20	22
Mošok, Russia	F24	22
Mosolovo, Russia	G23	22
Mosomane, Bots.	E8	66
Mosonmagyaróvár, Hung.	H17	10
Mosopa, Bots.	E7	66
Mosquera, Col.	F3	84
Mosquero, N.M., U.S.	D3	116
Mosquito, Punta, c., Pan.	C4	84
Mosquito, Riacho, stm., Para.	B9	80
Mosquito Creek Lake, res., Oh., U.S.	F6	108
Mosquito Indian Reserve, Sask., Can.	F6	104
Mosquitos, Costa de, hist. reg., Nic.	D11	92
Mosquitos, Golfo de los, b., Pan.	H13	92
Moss, Nor.	L12	6
Mossaka, Congo	B3	58
Mossâmedes, Braz.	D3	79
Mossbank, Sask., Can.	I9	104
Mosselbaai, S. Afr.	J6	66
Mossendjo, Congo	B2	58
Mossleigh, Alta., Can.	G21	102
Mossoró, Braz.	E11	76
Moss Point, Ms., U.S.	L8	114
Moss Vale, Austl.	J9	70
Mossy, stm., Man., Can.	G15	104
Mossy, stm., Sask., Can.	D11	104
Most, Czech.	E13	10
Mosta, Russia	E25	22
Mostar, Bos.	F12	18
Mostardas, Braz.	F13	80
Mostok, Bela.	H13	22
Mostoos Hills, hills, Sask., Can.	C5	104
Mosty, Bela.	H7	22
Mostys'ka, Ukr.	F23	10
Mosul see Al-Mawṣil, Iraq	C7	48
Mota, Eth.	L9	60
Motagua, stm., N.A.	B6	92
Motala, Swe.	L14	6
Motatán, Ven.	C7	84
Motherwell, Scot., U.K.	F9	8
Motihāri, India	G11	44
Motloutse, Bots.	C8	66
Motozintla de Mendoza, Mex.	J13	90
Motril, Spain	I8	16
Motru, Rom.	E7	20
Mott, N.D., U.S.	E5	118
Mottola, Italy	I12	18
Motueka, N.Z.	D4	72
Motul [de Felipe Carrillo Puerto], Mex.	G15	90
Motupe, Peru	B2	82
Mouaskar, Alg.	C11	62
Mouchoir Passage, strt., N.A.	D9	94
Moudjéria, Maur.	C3	64
Moudon, Switz.	E6	13
Mouila, Gabon	B2	58
Mouit, Maur.	C3	64
Mouka, Cen. Afr. Rep.	N1	60
Moulamein, Austl.	J6	70
Moulay-Idriss, Mor.	C8	62
Moulins, Fr.	F10	14
Moulins-la-Marche, Fr.	D7	14
Moulmein see Mawlamyine, Mya.	F4	40
Moulmeingyun, Mya.	F3	40
Moulouya, Oued, stm., Mor.	C9	62
Moulton, Al., U.S.	H9	114
Moulton, Ia., U.S.	J3	110
Moulton, Tx., U.S.	J9	116
Moultrie, Ga., U.S.	H3	112
Moultrie, Lake, res., S.C., U.S.	F6	112
Mound Bayou, Ms., U.S.	I6	114
Mound City, Il., U.S.	E7	114
Mound City, Ks., U.S.	M13	118
Mound City, Mo., U.S.	B1	114
Mound City, S.D., U.S.	F7	118
Moundou, Chad	G4	56
Moundridge, Ks., U.S.	M10	118
Mounds, Il., U.S.	E7	114
Mounds, Ok., U.S.	D10	116
Moundsville, W.V., U.S.	H6	108
Moundville, Al., U.S.	J9	114
Mounlapamôk, Laos	G8	40
Mountain, Wi., U.S.	E7	110
Mountain, stm., N.W. Ter., Can.	D30	100
Mountainair, N.M., U.S.	J10	120
Mountainaire, Az., U.S.	I5	120
Mountain Brook, Al., U.S.	I10	114
Mountain City, Ga., U.S.	E3	112
Mountain City, Nv., U.S.	C10	124
Mountain City, Tn., U.S.	C5	112
Mountain Creek, Al., U.S.	J10	114
Mountain Grove, Mo., U.S.	E4	114
Mountain Home, Ar., U.S.	F4	114
Mountain Home, Id., U.S.	G10	122
Mountain Iron, Mn., U.S.	C3	110
Mountain Lake, Mn., U.S.	H13	118
Mountain Nile (Baḥr al-Jabal), stm., Sud.	M6	60
Mountain Park, Alta., Can.	E17	102
Mountain Pine, Ar., U.S.	H3	114
Mountain Point, Ak., U.S.	I29	100
Mountain View, Ar., U.S.	G4	114
Mountain View, Ca., U.S.	G3	124
Mountain View, Mo., U.S.	F5	114
Mountain View, Ok., U.S.	D8	116
Mountain View, Wy., U.S.	C6	120
Mountain View, Wy., U.S.	B10	120
Mountain Village, Ak., U.S.	E13	100
Mount Airy, Md., U.S.	H9	108
Mount Airy, N.C., U.S.	C6	112
Mount Alida, S. Afr.	G10	66
Mount Angel, Or., U.S.	E3	122
Mount Assiniboine Provincial Park, B.C., Can.	G19	102
Mount Ayr, Ia., U.S.	K13	118
Mount Barker, Austl.	F3	68
Mount Barker, Austl.	J3	70
Mount Brydges, Ont., Can.	H14	110
Mount Calm, Tx., U.S.	H10	116
Mount Carleton Provincial Park, N.B., Can.	E7	106
Mount Carmel, Newf., Can.	E20	106
Mount Carmel, Il., U.S.	D9	114
Mount Carmel, Pa., U.S.	G10	108
Mount Carroll, Il., U.S.	H6	110
Mount Clare, W.V., U.S.	H6	108
Mount Clemens, Mi., U.S.	H13	110
Mount Currie Indian Reserve, B.C., Can.	G12	102
Mount Desert Island, i., Me., U.S.	C18	108
Mount Dora, Fl., U.S.	K5	112
Mount Edgecumbe, Ak., U.S.	H27	100
Mount Enterprise, Tx., U.S.	K2	114
Mount Forest, Ont., Can.	G15	110
Mount Gambier, Austl.	K4	70
Mount Garnet, Austl.	A6	70
Mount Gay, W.V., U.S.	J4	108
Mount Gilead, N.C., U.S.	D6	112
Mount Gilead, Oh., U.S.	G4	108
Mount Hagen, Pap. N. Gui.	G11	38
Mount Holly, N.C., U.S.	D5	112
Mount Holly Springs, Pa., U.S.	G9	108
Mount Hope, Austl.	J1	70
Mount Hope, Ks., U.S.	N10	118
Mount Hope, W.V., U.S.	J5	108
Mount Horeb, Wi., U.S.	G6	110
Mount Ida, Ar., U.S.	H3	114
Mount Isa, Austl.	C3	70
Mount Jackson, Va., U.S.	I8	108
Mount Jewett, Pa., U.S.	F8	108
Mount Juliet, Tn., U.S.	F10	114
Mount Kisco, N.Y., U.S.	F13	108
Mount Lebanon, Pa., U.S.	G6	108
Mount Magnet, Austl.	E3	68
Mount Manara, Austl.	I5	70
Mount Morgan, Austl.	D9	70
Mount Morris, Il., U.S.	H6	110
Mount Morris, Mi., U.S.	G12	110
Mount Morris, N.Y., U.S.	E9	108
Mount Mulligan, Austl.	A6	70
Mount Olive, Il., U.S.	C7	114
Mount Olive, Ms., U.S.	K7	114
Mount Olive, N.C., U.S.	D8	112
Mount Olivet, Ky., U.S.	I2	108
Mount Orab, Oh., U.S.	H3	108
Mount Perry, Austl.	E9	70
Mount Pleasant, Ont., Can.	G15	110
Mount Pleasant, Ia., U.S.	J4	110
Mount Pleasant, Mi., U.S.	G11	110
Mount Pleasant, N.C., U.S.	D6	112
Mount Pleasant, Pa., U.S.	G7	108
Mount Pleasant, S.C., U.S.	G7	112
Mount Pleasant, Tn., U.S.	G9	114
Mount Pleasant, Tx., U.S.	F12	116
Mount Pleasant, Ut., U.S.	E5	120
Mount Pulaski, Il., U.S.	B7	114
Mount Rainier National Park, Wa., U.S.	D4	122
Mount Revelstoke National Park, B.C., Can.	F16	102
Mount Revelstoke Reservoir, res., B.C., Can.	F16	102
Mount Robson Provincial Park, B.C., Can.	E15	102
Mount Savage, Md., U.S.	H8	108
Mount Seymour Provincial Park, B.C., Can.	H12	102
Mount Shasta, Ca., U.S.	C3	124
Mount Sterling, Il., U.S.	C6	114
Mount Sterling, Ky., U.S.	A3	112
Mount Sterling, Oh., U.S.	H3	108
Mount Stewart, P.E.I., Can.	F11	106
Mount Stewart, S. Afr.	I7	66
Mount Surprise, Austl.	B6	70
Mount Uniacke, N.S., Can.	H10	106
Mount Union, Pa., U.S.	G9	108
Mount Vernon, Al., U.S.	K8	114
Mount Vernon, Ga., U.S.	G4	112
Mount Vernon, Il., U.S.	D8	114
Mount Vernon, In., U.S.	E9	114
Mount Vernon, Ia., U.S.	I4	110
Mount Vernon, Ky., U.S.	B2	112
Mount Vernon, Mo., U.S.	E3	114
Mount Vernon, Oh., U.S.	G4	108
Mount Vernon, Or., U.S.	F6	122
Mount Vernon, S.D., U.S.	H9	118
Mount Vernon, Tx., U.S.	F11	116
Mount Vernon, Wa., U.S.	B3	122
Mount Victory, Oh., U.S.	G3	108
Mount Wolf, Pa., U.S.	G10	108
Moura, Austl.	E8	70
Moura, Braz.	H12	84
Moura, Port.	G4	16
Mourdi, Dépression du, depr., Chad	E5	56
Mourdiah, Mali	D6	64
Mourne Mountains, mts., N. Ire., U.K.	G7	8
Moussoro, Chad	F4	56
Moutier, Switz.	D7	13
Moûtiers, Fr.	G13	14
Mouzon, Fr.	C12	14
Moville, Ire.	F6	8
Moville, Ia., U.S.	I11	118
Moweaqua, Il., U.S.	C7	114
Moya, Com.	I16	67a
Moya, Peru	E4	82
Moyahua, Mex.	G8	90
Moyamba, S.L.	G3	64
Moyen Atlas, mts., Mor.	D8	62
Moyeuvre-Grande, Fr.	C13	14
Moyie, B.C., Can.	H19	102
Moyie Springs, Id., U.S.	B9	122
Moyobamba, Peru	B3	82
Moyogalpa, Nic.	F9	92
Moyuta, Volcán, vol., Guat.	C4	92
Možajsk, Russia	F19	22
Mozambique (Moçambique), ctry., Afr.	E7	58
Mozambique Channel, strt., Afr.	E8	58
Mozarlândia, Braz.	C3	79
Mozdok, Russia	I6	26
Možga, Russia	F8	26
Mozyr', Bela.	G3	26
Mphoengs, Zimb.	C8	66
Mpika, Zam.	D6	58
Mpraeso, Ghana	H9	64
Mpwapwa, Tan.	C7	58
Mqanduli, S. Afr.	H9	66
Mrągowo, Pol.	B21	10
M'Ramani, Com.	I16	67a
Mrkopalj, Cro.	D9	18
M'Saken, Tun.	N5	18
M'Sila, Alg.	C13	62
Mšinskaja, Russia	B12	22
Msta, Russia	D17	22
Msta, stm., Russia	C14	22
Mstera, Russia	E24	22
Mstislavl', Bela.	G14	22
Mszczonów, Pol.	D20	10
Mtamvuna, stm., S. Afr.	H9	66
Mtwara, Tan.	D8	58
Mu, Cerro, mtn., S.A.	C6	84
Muanda, Zaire	C2	58
Muang Hôngsa, Laos	E6	40
Muang Huang, Laos	E7	40
Muang Khammouan, Laos	F8	40
Muang Khi, Laos	E6	40
Muang Không, Laos	G8	40
Muang Khôngxédôn, Laos	G8	40
Muang Long, Laos	D6	40
Muang Ngoy, Laos	D7	40
Muang Ou Nua, Laos	C6	40
Muang Ou Tai, Laos	C6	40
Muang Pak-Lay, Laos	E6	40
Muang Pakxan, Laos	E7	40
Muang Phiang, Laos	E6	40
Muang Phoun, Laos	E7	40
Muang Sing, Laos	D6	40
Muang Souy, Laos	E7	40
Muang Thadua, Laos	E6	40
Muang Vangviang, Laos	E7	40
Muang Vapi, Laos	G8	40
Muang Xaignabouri, Laos	E6	40
Muang Xay, Laos	D6	40
Muang Xépôn, Laos	F9	40
Muang Xon, Laos	D7	40
Muang You, Laos	E7	40
Muar (Bandar Maharani), Malay.	M7	40
Muarasiberut, Indon.	F2	38
Mucajaí, stm., Braz.	F12	84
Muchanovo, Russia	E21	22
Muchinga Mountains, mts., Zam.	D6	58
Muchtolovo, Russia	F26	22
Muckadilla, Austl.	F8	70
Mučkapskij, Russia	J25	22
Muconda, Ang.	D4	58
Mucuchíes, Ven.	C7	84
Mucugê, Braz.	B8	79
Mucuim, stm., Braz.	B9	82
Muçum, Braz.	E13	80
Mucupia, Moz.	B13	66
Mucupina, Monte, mtn., Hond.	B8	92
Mucur, Tur.	B3	48
Mucuri, Braz.	E9	79
Mucuri, stm., Braz.	E9	79
Mucusso, Ang.	B5	66
Mud, stm., Ky., U.S.	E10	114
Mud, stm., W.V., U.S.	I4	108
Mudan, stm., China	B12	30
Mudanjiang, China	C12	30
Muddy, stm., Nv., U.S.	H11	124
Mudgee, Austl.	I8	70
Mudjatik, stm., Sask., Can.	B7	104
Mudjuga, Russia	J26	6
Mudon, Mya.	F4	40
Mudu, China	D9	34
Muelle de los Bueyes, Nic.	E10	92
Muenster, Tx., U.S.	F9	116
Muerto, stm., Arg.	B7	80
Mufulira, Zam.	D5	58
Mu Gia, Deo, Asia	F8	40
Muğla, Tur.	L12	20
Mugron, Fr.	I6	14
Muḥammad, Ra's, c., Egypt	D8	60
Muḥammad Qawl, Sud.	G9	60
Mühlacker, Ger.	G8	10
Mühldorf, Ger.	G12	10
Mühlhausen, Ger.	D10	10
Mühlig-Hofmann Mountains, mts., Ant.	C3	73
Muhu, i., Est.	C6	22
Muhu väin, strt., Est.	C6	22
Muiron Islands, is., Austl.	D2	68
Muisne, Ec.	G2	84
Mujang-ni, S. Kor.	H14	32
Mujezerskij, Russia	J22	6
Mujnak, Uzb.	I9	26
Muju, S. Kor.	G15	32
Mukacheve, Ukr.	H2	26
Mukah, Malay.	E5	38
Mukdahan, Thai.	F8	40
Mukden see Shenyang, China	B11	32
Mukilteo, Wa., U.S.	C3	122
Mukry, Turk.	J11	26
Muktsar, India	E6	44
Mukutawa, stm., Man., Can.	E18	104
Mukwonago, Wi., U.S.	H7	110
Mula, Spain	G10	16
Mulanje, Mwi.	E7	58
Mulas, Punta de, c., Cuba	D7	94
Mulatos, Mex.	C5	90
Mulberry, Ar., U.S.	G2	114
Mulberry, Fl., U.S.	L5	112
Mulberry, In., U.S.	B10	114
Mulberry, stm., Ar., U.S.	G3	114
Mulberry Fork, stm., Al., U.S.	I9	114
Mulchatna, stm., Ak., U.S.	F17	100
Mulchén, Chile	I2	80
Mulde, stm., Ger.	D12	10
Muldoon, Tx., U.S.	J9	116
Muldraugh, Ky., U.S.	E11	114
Muldrow, Ok., U.S.	G2	114
Mule, Lac la, l., Que., Can.	A8	106
Mulegé, Mex.	D3	90
Mulegns, Switz.	E12	13
Muleshoe, Tx., U.S.	E4	116
Mulgowie, Austl.	F10	70
Mulgrave, N.S., Can.	G12	106
Mulhacén, mtn., Spain	H8	16
Mulhall, Ok., U.S.	C9	116
Mulhouse, Fr.	E14	14
Mull, Island of, i., Scot., U.K.	E7	8
Mullan, Id., U.S.	C10	122
Mullen, Ne., U.S.	I6	118
Mullengudgery, Austl.	H7	70
Mullens, W.V., U.S.	B5	112
Muller, Pegunungan, mts., Indon.	E5	38
Mullett Lake, l., Mi., U.S.	E11	110
Mullewa, Austl.	E3	68
Mullica, stm., N.J., U.S.	H12	108
Mulligan, stm., Austl.	D3	70
Mullin, Tx., U.S.	H8	116
Mullingar, Ire.	H6	8
Mullins, S.C., U.S.	E7	112
Mullinville, Ks., U.S.	N8	118
Mullumbimby, Austl.	G10	70
Multān, Pak.	E4	44
Mulvane, Ks., U.S.	N10	118
Mulyah Mountain, mtn., Austl.	H6	70
Mumbwa, Zam.	D5	58
Mumford, Tx., U.S.	I10	116
Mumu, Sud.	K2	60
Mumungwe, Bots.	C8	66
Mun, stm., Thai.	G8	40
Muna, Mex.	G15	90
Munā, Sau. Ar.	D1	47
Muna, stm., Russia	D15	28
Münchberg, Ger.	E11	10
München (Munich), Ger.	G11	10
München-Gladbach see Mönchengladbach, Ger.	D6	10
Münchenstein, Switz.	C8	13
Munchique, Cerro, mtn., Col.	F4	84
Munch'ŏn, N. Kor.	D15	32
Muncie, In., U.S.	B11	114
Muncy, Pa., U.S.	F10	108
Mundare, Alta., Can.	D22	102
Munday, Tx., U.S.	F7	116
Mundelein, Il., U.S.	H7	110
Münden, Ger.	D9	10
Mundo Novo, Braz.	A8	79
Mundubbera, Austl.	E9	70
Munene, Zimb.	C10	66
Munford, Tn., U.S.	G7	114
Munfordville, Ky., U.S.	E11	114
Mungallala, Austl.	F7	70

Name	Map Ref.	Page
Nesslau, Switz.	D11	13
Nesterov, Russia	G5	22
Néstos (Mesta), stm., Eur.	H8	20
Nestoyita, Ukr.	B13	20
Nesviž, Bela.	H9	22
Nes Ẓiyyona, Isr.	E3	50
Netanya, Isr.	D3	50
Netherdale, Austl.	C8	70
Netherlands (Nederland), ctry., Eur.	E9	4
Netherlands Antilles (Nederlandse Antillen), dep., N.A.	H10	94
Netrakona, Bngl.	H14	44
Nettilling Fiord, N.W. Ter., Can.	C19	96
Nettilling Lake, l., N.W. Ter., Can.	C18	96
Nettleton, Ms., U.S.	H8	114
Nettuno, Italy	H7	18
Neubrandenburg, Ger.	B13	10
Neuburg an der Donau, Ger.	G11	10
Neuchâtel, Switz.	E6	13
Neuchâtel, state, Switz.	D6	13
Neuchâtel, Lac de, l., Switz.	E6	13
Neudorf, Sask., Can.	H12	104
Neuenhagen, Ger.	C13	10
Neuf-Brisach, Fr.	D14	14
Neufchâteau, Bel.	I7	12
Neufchâteau, Fr.	D12	14
Neufchâtel-en-Bray, Fr.	C8	14
Neuhausen, Switz.	C10	13
Neu-Isenburg, Ger.	E8	10
Neumarkt [im Hausruckkreis], Aus.	G13	10
Neumarkt in der Oberpfalz, Ger.	F11	10
Neumarkt in Steiermark, Aus.	H14	10
Neumarkt-Sankt Veit, Ger.	G12	10
Neumünster, Ger.	A9	10
Neunburg vorm Wald, Ger.	F12	10
Neunkirchen/Saar, Ger.	F7	10
Neuquén, Arg.	J4	80
Neuquén, prov., Arg.	J4	80
Neuquén, stm., Arg.	J4	80
Neurara, Chile	C4	80
Neuruppin, Ger.	C12	10
Neuschwanstein, Schloss, Ger.	C14	13
Neuse, stm., N.C., U.S.	E10	112
Neusiedl am See, Aus.	H16	10
Neusiedler See, l., Eur.	H16	10
Neustadt [an der Aisch], Ger.	F10	10
Neustadt an der Waldnaab, Ger.	F12	10
Neustadt an der Weinstrasse, Ger.	F8	10
Neustadt bei Coburg, Ger.	E11	10
Neustadt in Holstein, Ger.	A10	10
Neustrelitz, Ger.	B13	10
Neutral Hills, hills, Alta., Can.	F4	104
Neu-Ulm, Ger.	G10	10
Neuville-sur-Saône, Fr.	G11	14
Neuwied, Ger.	E7	10
Neva, stm., Russia	B13	22
Nevada, Ia., U.S.	H2	110
Nevada, Mo., U.S.	E2	114
Nevada, Oh., U.S.	G3	108
Nevada, state, U.S.	D3	98
Nevada, Sierra, mts., Spain	H8	16
Nevada, Sierra, mts., Ca., U.S.	F6	124
Nevada City, Ca., U.S.	E4	124
Nevado, Cerro, mtn., Arg.	H4	80
Nevado, Cerro, mtn., Col.	C4	76
Nevado, Cerro, mtn., Col.	F5	84
Nevado de Colima, Parque Nacional del, Mex.	H8	90
Nevado de Toluca, Parque Nacional, Mex.	H9	90
Nevel', Russia	E12	22
Nevel'sk, Russia	H20	28
Never, Russia	G16	28
Nevers, Fr.	E10	14
Nevertire, Austl.	H7	70
Nevesinje, Bos.	F2	20
Nevinnomyssk, Russia	I6	26
Nevis, i., St. K./N.	F13	94
Nevis, Ben, mtn., Scot., U.K.	E9	8
Nevjansk, Russia	F10	26
Nevşehir, Tur.	B3	48
New, stm., Belize	H15	90
New, stm., Guy.	F14	84
New, stm., N.A.	L10	124
New, stm., U.S.	B6	112
New, stm., S.C., U.S.	G6	112
New, stm., Tn., U.S.	C2	112
New Albany, In., U.S.	D11	114
New Albany, Ms., U.S.	H7	114
New Albin, Ia., U.S.	G4	110
New Alfa, Sud.	J8	60
New Amsterdam, Guy.	D14	84
Newark, Ar., U.S.	G5	114
Newark, De., U.S.	H11	108
Newark, N.J., U.S.	G12	108
Newark, N.Y., U.S.	D9	108
Newark, Oh., U.S.	G4	108
Newark-on-Trent, Eng., U.K.	H13	8
Newark Valley, N.Y., U.S.	E10	108
New Athens, Il., U.S.	D7	114
New Augusta, Ms., U.S.	K7	114
Newaygo, Mi., U.S.	G10	110
New Baden, Il., U.S.	D7	114
New Baltimore, Mi., U.S.	H13	110
New Bedford, Ma., U.S.	F16	108
Newberg, Or., U.S.	E3	122
New Berlin, Il., U.S.	C7	114
New Berlin, N.Y., U.S.	E11	108
New Berlin, Wi., U.S.	H7	110
Newbern, Al., U.S.	J9	114
New Bern, N.C., U.S.	D9	112
Newbern, Tn., U.S.	F7	114
Newberry, Fl., U.S.	J4	112
Newberry, Mi., U.S.	D10	110
Newberry, S.C., U.S.	E5	112
New Bethlehem, Pa., U.S.	F7	108
New Bight, Bah.	B7	94
New Bloomfield, Pa., U.S.	G9	108
New Boston, Il., U.S.	I5	110
New Boston, Oh., U.S.	I4	108
New Boston, Tx., U.S.	I2	114
New Braunfels, Tx., U.S.	J8	116
New Bremen, Oh., U.S.	G2	108
New Britain, Ct., U.S.	F14	108
New Britain, i., Pap. N. Gui.	m17	68a
New Brockton, Al., U.S.	K11	114
Newbrook, Alta., Can.	C22	102
New Brunswick, N.J., U.S.	G12	108
New Brunswick, prov., Can.	G19	96
New Buffalo, Mi., U.S.	I9	110
Newburg, Mo., U.S.	E5	114
Newburgh, Ont., Can.	F19	110
Newburgh, In., U.S.	E9	114
Newburgh, N.Y., U.S.	F12	108
Newbury, Eng., U.K.	J12	8
Newburyport, Ma., U.S.	E16	108
New Caledonia, dep., Oc.	K20	126
New-Carlisle, Que., Can.	D8	106
New Carlisle, Oh., U.S.	H2	108
Newcastle, Austl.	I9	70
Newcastle, N.B., Can.	E8	106
Newcastle, Ont., Can.	G17	110
Newcastle, S. Afr.	F9	66
Newcastle, Ca., U.S.	F4	124
New Castle, Co., U.S.	E9	120
New Castle, De., U.S.	H11	108
New Castle, In., U.S.	C11	114
New Castle, Ky., U.S.	D11	114
Newcastle, Ne., U.S.	I11	118
Newcastle, Ok., U.S.	D9	116
New Castle, Pa., U.S.	F6	108
Newcastle, Tx., U.S.	F8	116
New Castle, Va., U.S.	B6	112
Newcastle, Wy., U.S.	H3	118
Newcastle Mine, Alta., Can.	F22	102
Newcastle-under-Lyme, Eng., U.K.	H11	8
Newcastle upon Tyne, Eng., U.K.	G12	8
Newcastle Waters, Austl.	C6	68
New City, N.Y., U.S.	F13	108
Newcomerstown, Oh., U.S.	G5	108
New Concord, Oh., U.S.	H5	108
New Cumberland, W.V., U.S.	G6	108
New Dayton, Alta., Can.	H22	102
Newdegate, Austl.	F3	68
New Delhi, India	F7	44
New Denver, B.C., Can.	H17	102
New Edinburg, Ar., U.S.	I4	114
New Effington, S.D., U.S.	F11	118
New Egypt, N.J., U.S.	G12	108
Newell, Ia., U.S.	I12	118
Newell, S.D., U.S.	G4	118
Newell, W.V., U.S.	G6	108
Newell, Lake, l., Alta., Can.	G23	102
New Ellenton, S.C., U.S.	F5	112
Newellton, La., U.S.	J5	114
New England, N.D., U.S.	E5	118
New England Range, mts., Austl.	H9	70
Newfane, N.Y., U.S.	D8	108
Newfane, Vt., U.S.	E14	108
New Florence, Mo., U.S.	D5	114
New Florence, Pa., U.S.	G7	108
Newfound Gap, U.S.	D3	112
Newfoundland, prov., Can.	F21	96
Newfoundland, i., Newf., Can.	D17	106
New Franklin, Mo., U.S.	C4	114
New Freedom, Pa., U.S.	H10	108
New Galloway, Scot., U.K.	F9	8
Newgate, B.C., Can.	H19	102
New Georgia, i., Sol.Is.	A11	68
New Germany, N.S., Can.	H9	106
New Glarus, Wi., U.S.	H6	110
New Glasgow, N.S., Can.	G11	106
New Guinea, i.	m15	68a
Newgulf, Tx., U.S.	J11	116
Newhalem, Wa., U.S.	B4	122
Newhalen, Ak., U.S.	G17	100
Newhall, Ca., U.S.	J7	124
New Hamburg, Ont., Can.	G15	110
New Hampshire, state, U.S.	C12	98
New Hampton, Ia., U.S.	G3	110
New Hanover, i., Pap. N. Gui.	k17	68a
New Harmony, In., U.S.	D9	114
New Hartford, Ct., U.S.	F14	108
New Hartford, Ia., U.S.	H3	110
Newhaven, Eng., U.K.	K14	8
New Haven, Ct., U.S.	F14	108
New Haven, Il., U.S.	E8	114
New Haven, In., U.S.	A11	114
New Haven, Ky., U.S.	E11	114
New Haven, Mo., U.S.	D5	114
New Haven, W.V., U.S.	I5	108
New Hazelton, B.C., Can.	B7	102
New Hebrides see Vanuatu, ctry., Oc.	J20	126
New Hebrides Trench	K21	126
Newhebron, Ms., U.S.	K7	114
New Holland, Oh., U.S.	H3	108
New Holland, Pa., U.S.	G10	108
New Holstein, Wi., U.S.	G7	110
New Hope, Al., U.S.	H10	114
New Iberia, La., U.S.	L5	114
New Ireland, i., Pap. N. Gui.	k17	68a
New Jersey, state, U.S.	C12	98
New Johnsonville, Tn., U.S.	F9	114
New Kensington, Pa., U.S.	G7	108
New Kent, Va., U.S.	B10	112
Newkirk, Ok., U.S.	C9	116
New Kowloon, H.K.	M3	34
Newland, N.C., U.S.	C5	112
Newlands, Austl.	C7	70
New Leipzig, N.D., U.S.	E6	118
New Lexington, Oh., U.S.	H4	108
New Lisbon, Wi., U.S.	G5	110
New Liskeard, Ont., Can.	C16	110
Newllano, La., U.S.	K3	114
New London, Ct., U.S.	F14	108
New London, Ia., U.S.	J4	110
New London, Mn., U.S.	F13	118
New London, Mo., U.S.	C5	114
New London, N.H., U.S.	D15	108
New London, Oh., U.S.	F4	108
New London, Tx., U.S.	J2	114
New London, Wi., U.S.	F7	110
New Madrid, Mo., U.S.	F7	114
Newman, Austl.	D3	68
Newman, Ca., U.S.	G4	124
Newman, Il., U.S.	C9	114
Newman Grove, Ne., U.S.	J10	118
Newmarket, Ont., Can.	F16	110
Newmarket, Ire.	I4	8
Newmarket, Eng., U.K.	I14	8
New Market, Al., U.S.	H10	114
New Market, Ia., U.S.	K13	118
Newmarket, N.H., U.S.	D16	108
New Market, Va., U.S.	I8	108
New Martinsville, W.V., U.S.	H6	108
New Meadows, Id., U.S.	F9	122
New Mexico, state, U.S.	E5	98
New Milford, Ct., U.S.	F13	108
New Milford, Pa., U.S.	F11	108
Newnan, Ga., U.S.	F2	112
New Norfolk, Austl.	N7	70
New Norway, Alta., Can.	E22	102
New Orleans, La., U.S.	M6	114
New Oxford, Pa., U.S.	H9	108
New Paltz, N.Y., U.S.	F12	108
New Paris, Oh., U.S.	H2	108
New Philadelphia, Oh., U.S.	G5	108
New Pine Creek, Or., U.S.	I5	122
New Plymouth, N.Z.	C5	72
New Plymouth, Id., U.S.	G9	122
Newport, Que., Can.	D9	106
Newport, Wales, U.K.	I9	8
Newport, Ar., U.S.	G5	114
Newport, In., U.S.	C9	114
Newport, Ky., U.S.	H2	108
Newport, Me., U.S.	C17	108
Newport, N.H., U.S.	D14	108
Newport, N.C., U.S.	E10	112
Newport, Or., U.S.	F1	122
Newport, Pa., U.S.	G9	108
Newport, R.I., U.S.	F15	108
Newport, Tn., U.S.	D3	112
Newport, Vt., U.S.	C14	108
Newport, Wa., U.S.	B8	122
Newport Beach, Ca., U.S.	K8	124
Newport News, Va., U.S.	C10	112
Newport [-on-Tay], Scot., U.K.	E11	8
New Port Richey, Fl., U.S.	K4	112
New Prague, Mn., U.S.	F2	110
New Providence, Tn., U.S.	F9	114
New Providence, i., Bah.	B6	94
New Richland, Mn., U.S.	G2	110
New-Richmond, Que., Can.	D8	106
New Richmond, Oh., U.S.	I2	108
New Richmond, Wi., U.S.	E3	110
New Road, N.S., Can.	H10	106
New Roads, La., U.S.	L5	114
New Rochelle, N.Y., U.S.	G13	108
New Rockford, N.D., U.S.	D8	118
New Ross, N.S., Can.	H9	106
New Ross, Ire.	I7	8
Newry, N. Ire., U.K.	G7	8
Newry, S.C., U.S.	E4	112
New Salem, N.D., U.S.	E6	118
New Schwabenland, reg., Ant.	C2	73
New Sharon, Ia., U.S.	I3	110
New Siberian Islands see Novosibirskoje ostrova, is., Russia	B20	28
New Smyrna Beach, Fl., U.S.	J6	112
New South Wales, state, Austl.	F9	68
New Stuyahok, Ak., U.S.	G16	100
New Tazewell, Tn., U.S.	C3	112
New Thunderchild Indian Reserve, Sask., Can.	E6	104
Newtok, Ak., U.S.	F12	100
Newton, Ga., U.S.	H2	112
Newton, Il., U.S.	D8	114
Newton, Ia., U.S.	I2	110
Newton, Ks., U.S.	M10	118
Newton, Ma., U.S.	E15	108
Newton, Ms., U.S.	J7	114
Newton, N.J., U.S.	F12	108
Newton, N.C., U.S.	D5	112
Newton, Tx., U.S.	L3	114
Newton Abbot, Eng., U.K.	K10	8
Newton Falls, N.Y., U.S.	C12	108
Newton Stewart, Scot., U.K.	G9	8
Newtown, Newf., Can.	C20	106
New Town, N.D., U.S.	D5	118
Newtownabbey, N. Ire., U.K.	G8	8
New Ulm, Mn., U.S.	G13	118
New Ulm, Tx., U.S.	J10	116
New Vienna, Oh., U.S.	H3	108
Newville, Pa., U.S.	G9	108
New Vineyard, Me., U.S.	C16	108
New Washington, Oh., U.S.	G4	108
New Waterford, N.S., Can.	F13	106
New Waverly, Tx., U.S.	I11	116
New Westminster, B.C., Can.	H12	102
New Whiteland, In., U.S.	C10	114
New Wilmington, Pa., U.S.	F6	108
New World Island, i., Newf., Can.	C19	106
New York, N.Y., U.S.	G12	108
New York, state, U.S.	C11	98
New York Mills, Mn., U.S.	E12	118
New York State Barge Canal, N.Y., U.S.	D8	108
New Zealand, ctry., Oc.	D4	72
Ney Lake, l., Can.	D22	104
Neyrīz, Iran	G13	48
Neyshābūr, Iran	C15	48
Nezahualcóyotl, Mex.	H10	90
Nezahualcóyotl, Presa, res., Mex.	I13	90
Neznanovo, Russia	G23	22
Nezperce, Id., U.S.	D9	122
Ngami, Lake, l., Bots.	C6	66
Ngamiland, dept., Bots.	B6	66
Ngamo, Zimb.	B8	66
Ngangla Ringco, l., China	E10	44
Nganglong Kangri, mts., China	D10	44
Ngaoundéré, Cam.	G9	54
Ngezi Recreational Park, Zimb.	B10	66
Ngoko, stm., Afr.	A3	58
Ngolo, Cen. Afr. Rep.	M2	60
Ngoring Hu, l., China	E6	30
Ngotwane, stm., Afr.	E8	66
Nguigmi, Niger	F9	54
Nguiroungou, Cen. Afr. Rep.	N2	60
Nguru, Nig.	F9	54
Nhamundá, Braz.	I14	84
Nhamundá, stm., Braz.	H14	84
Nhandeara, Braz.	F3	79
Nha Trang, Viet.	H10	40
Nhill, Austl.	K4	70
Niafounké, Mali	D7	64
Niagara, Wi., U.S.	E8	110
Niagara Falls, Ont., Can.	G16	110
Niagara Falls, N.Y., U.S.	D7	108
Niagara-on-the-Lake, Ont., Can.	G16	110
Niamey, Niger	E11	64
Niangara, Zaire	H6	56
Niangoloko, Burkina	F7	64
Niangua, stm., Mo., U.S.	E4	114
Niantic, Il., U.S.	C7	114
Niaro, Sud.	L6	60
Nias, Pulau, i., Indon.	N4	40
Nica, stm., Russia	F10	26
Nicaragua, ctry., N.A.	E9	92
Nicaragua, Lago de, l., Nic.	F9	92
Nicastro, Italy	K11	18
Nice, Fr.	I14	14
Niceville, Fl., U.S.	L10	114
Nichinan, Japan	P6	36
Nicholas Channel, strt., N.A.	C4	94
Nicholasville, Ky., U.S.	B2	112
Nicholls, Ga., U.S.	H4	112
Nicholl's Town, Bah.	B5	94
Nicholson, Ms., U.S.	L7	114
Nicholson, Pa., U.S.	F11	108
Nicholson, stm., Austl.	A2	70
Nickerie, dept., Sur.	E14	84
Nickerie, stm., Sur.	E14	84
Nickerson, Ks., U.S.	M9	118
Nicobar Islands, is., India	J2	40
Nicola, B.C., Can.	G14	102
Nicola, stm., B.C., Can.	G14	102
Nicola Lake, l., B.C., Can.	G14	102
Nicola Mameet Indian Reserve, B.C., Can.	G14	102
Nicolet, Que., Can.	A14	108
Nicolet, Lake, l., Mi., U.S.	D11	110
Nicollet, Mn., U.S.	F1	110
Nicosia (Levkosía), Cyp.	D2	48
Nicosia (Levkoşa), N. Cyp.	D2	48
Nicosia, Italy	L9	18
Nicotera, Italy	K10	18
Nicoya, C.R.	G9	92
Nicoya, Golfo de, b., C.R.	H10	92
Nicoya, Península de, pen., C.R.	H9	92
Nictheroy see Niterói, Braz.	H10	76
Nida, Lith.	F4	22
Nidzica, Pol.	B20	10
Niederbronn-les-Bains, Fr.	D14	14
Niederösterreich, state, Aus.	G15	10
Niedersachsen, state, Ger.	C8	10
Niedu, China	J3	34
Niekerkshoop, S. Afr.	G6	66
Niellé, C. Iv.	F7	64
Niemodlin, Pol.	E17	10
Niéna, Mali	F6	64
Nienburg, Ger.	C9	10
Niers, stm., Eur.	E9	12
Niesky, Ger.	D14	10
Nieszawa, Pol.	C18	10
Nieu Bethesda, S. Afr.	H7	66
Nieuw Amsterdam, Sur.	B7	76
Nieuwegein, Neth.	D7	12
Nieuweschans, Neth.	B11	12
Nieuwe Tonge, Neth.	E5	12
Nieuw Nickerie, Sur.	E14	84
Nieuwolda, Neth.	B10	12
Nieuwoudtville, S. Afr.	H4	66
Nieuwpoort (Nieuport), Bel.	F2	12
Nieuw-Schoonebeek, Neth.	C10	12
Nieva, stm., Peru	J4	84
Nièvre, dept., Fr.	E10	14
Niga, Mali	E7	64
Niğde, Tur.	C3	48
Nigei Island, i., B.C., Can.	G7	102
Niger, ctry., Afr.	E8	54
Niger, stm., Afr.	G8	54
Nigeria, ctry., Afr.	F8	54
Nigríta, Grc.	I7	20
Nihing (Nahang), stm., Asia	H17	48
Nihuil, Embalse del, res., Arg.	H4	80
Niigata, Japan	J14	36
Niihama, Japan	N8	36
Niihau, i., Hi., U.S.	p13	125a
Nii-jima, i., Japan	M14	36
Nijil, Jord.	G5	50
Nijkerk, Neth.	D8	12
Nijmegen, Neth.	E8	12
Nijvel (Nivelles), Bel.	G5	12
Nijverdal, Neth.	D9	12
Nikel', Russia	G22	6
Nikip Lake, l., Ont., Can.	F23	104
Nikki, Benin	G11	64
Nikkō, Japan	K14	36
Nikolajevo, Russia	C12	22
Nikolajevsk-na-Amure, Russia	G20	28
Nikol'sk, Russia	F7	26
Nikol'sk, Russia	G7	26
Nikolski, Ak., U.S.	J10	100
Nikol'skij, Russia	K24	6
Nikopol', Ukr.	H4	26
Nīkshahr, Iran	H16	48
Nikšić, Yugo.	G2	20
Nikulino, Russia	C27	22
Niland, Ca., U.S.	K10	124
Nile (Nahr an-Nīl), stm., Afr.	C7	56
Niles, Il., U.S.	H8	110
Niles, Mi., U.S.	I9	110
Niles, Oh., U.S.	F6	108
Nilkitkwa, stm., B.C., Can.	B8	102
Nīmach, India	H6	44
Nimba, Mont, mtn., Afr.	G5	54
Nimba Range, mts., Afr.	G5	54
Nîmes, Fr.	I11	14
Nimmitabel, Austl.	K8	70
Nimpkish Lake, l., B.C., Can.	G8	102
Nimule, Sud.	H7	56
Nindigully, Austl.	G8	70
Nindirí, Nic.	E8	92
Nine Degree Channel, strt., India	H2	46
Ninette, Man., Can.	I15	104
Ninety Mile Beach, Austl.	L7	70
Ninety Six, S.C., U.S.	E4	112
Ninga, Man., Can.	I15	104
Ningari, Mali	D8	64
Ningbo, China	F10	34
Ningcheng (Tianyi), China	B7	32
Ningdu, China	I4	34
Ninghai, China	F10	34
Ningi, Nig.	F14	64
Ningming, China	C9	40
Ningshan, China	E8	30
Ningsia see Yinchuan, China	D8	30
Ningwu, China	D9	30
Ningxia Huizu Zizhiqu (Ningsia Hui), prov., China	D8	30
Ningxiang, China	G1	34
Ninh Binh, Viet.	D8	40
Ninhue, Chile	I2	80
Ninilchik, Ak., U.S.	F19	100
Ninnescah, stm., Ks., U.S.	N10	118
Nioaque, Braz.	I14	82
Nioaque, stm., Braz.	I14	82
Niobrara, Ne., U.S.	I9	118
Niobrara, stm., U.S.	I9	118
Nioki, Zaire	B3	58
Niono, Mali	D6	64
Nioro du Sahel, Mali	D5	64
Niort, Fr.	F6	14
Niota, Tn., U.S.	D2	112
Nipan, Austl.	E9	70
Nipāni, India	D3	46
Nipawin, Sask., Can.	E10	104
Nipawin Provincial Park, Sask., Can.	D10	104
Nipe, Bahía de, b., Cuba	D7	94
Nipekamew, stm., Sask., Can.	D9	104
Nipekamew Lake, l., Sask., Can.	D10	104
Nipigon, Ont., Can.	A7	110
Nipigon, Lake, l., Ont., Can.	G15	96
Nipin, stm., Sask., Can.	C6	104
Nipisi Lake, l., Alta., Can.	B20	102
Nipissing, Lake, l., Ont., Can.	D16	110
Nipissis, Lac, l., Que., Can.	A7	106
Nipisso, Lac, l., Que., Can.	B8	106
Nipomo, Ca., U.S.	I5	124
Nippers Harbour, Newf., Can.	C18	106
Niquelândia, Braz.	C4	79
Niquero, Cuba	D6	94
Niquivil, Arg.	F4	80
Nirgua, Ven.	B8	84
Nirmal, India	C5	46
Niš, Yugo.	F5	20
Nisa (Neisse) (Nysa Łużycka), stm., Eur.	E15	10
Niṣāb, Sau. Ar.	G8	48
Niscemi, Italy	L9	18
Nishio, Japan	M12	36
Niska Lake, l., Sask., Can.	C6	104
Nisling, stm., Yukon, Can.	E25	100
Nisqually, stm., Wa., U.S.	D3	122
Nisswa, Mn., U.S.	D1	110
Nisutlin, stm., Yukon, Can.	F28	100
Niterói, Braz.	G7	79
Nithi River, B.C., Can.	C9	102
Nitinat Lake, l., B.C., Can.	I10	102
Nitra, Slov.	G18	10
Nitro, W.V., U.S.	I5	108
Niubu, China	D6	34
Niue, dep., Oc.	K23	126
Niut, Gunung, mtn., Indon.	N10	40
Niutuo, China	D4	32
Niuzhuang, China	C10	32
Nive, stm., Austl.	E7	70
Nivelles (Nijvel), Bel.	G5	12
Nivernais, hist. reg., Fr.	E10	14
Niverville, Man., Can.	I17	104
Nivskij, Russia	H23	6
Nixa, Mo., U.S.	E3	114
Nixon, Nv., U.S.	E6	124
Nixon, Tx., U.S.	J9	116
Nizāmābād, India	C5	46
Nizām Sāgar, res., India	C4	46
Nizhyn, Ukr.	G4	26
Nizip, Tur.	C4	48
Nízke Tatry, mts., Slov.	G19	10
Nižn'aja Pojma, Russia	F11	28
Nižn'aja Tunguska, stm., Russia	E10	28
Nižn'aja Tura, Russia	F9	26
Nižneudinsk, Russia	G11	28
Nižnevartovsk, Russia	E13	26
Nižnij Novgorod (Gor'kij), Russia	E27	22
Nižnij P'andž, Taj.	J11	26
Nižnij Tagil, Russia	F9	26
Nizwā, Oman	C10	47
Niẕẕana, Isr.	G2	50
Njazidja (Grande Comore), i., Com.	k15	67a
Njombe, Tan.	C6	58
Nkhata Bay, Mwi.	D6	58
Nkhotakota, Mwi.	D6	58
Nkongsamba, Cam.	H8	54
Nkurenkuru, Nmb.	A4	66
Nmai, stm., Mya.	B4	40
Noākhāli, Bngl.	I14	44
Noatak, Ak., U.S.	C13	100
Nobeoka, Japan	O6	36
Noble, Il., U.S.	D8	114
Noble, Ok., U.S.	D9	116
Noblesville, In., U.S.	B10	114
Noboribetsu, Japan	e16	36a
Nobres, Braz.	F13	82
Nobsa, Col.	E6	84
Nocatee, Fl., U.S.	L5	112
Nocera [Inferiore], Italy	I9	18
Noci, Italy	I12	18
Nockatunga, Austl.	F5	70
Nocona, Tx., U.S.	F9	116
Nocupétaro, Mex.	H9	90
Nodaway, stm., U.S.	B1	114
Noel, Mo., U.S.	F2	114
Noetinger, Arg.	G7	80
Nogales, Chile	G3	80
Nogales, Mex.	B4	90
Nogales, Az., U.S.	M6	120
Nogara, Eth.	K9	60
Nogaro, Fr.	I6	14
Nōgata, Japan	N5	36
Nogent-le-Rotrou, Fr.	D7	14
Noginsk, Russia	F21	22
Nogoa, stm., Austl.	D7	70
Nogoyá, Arg.	G9	80
Nógrád, co., Hung.	H19	10
Noirmoutier, Île de, i., Fr.	E4	14
Nokaneng, Bots.	B6	66
Nokomis, Sask., Can.	G9	104
Nokomis, Fl., U.S.	L4	112
Nokomis, Il., U.S.	C7	114
Nokomis Lake, l., Sask., Can.	B11	104
Nola, Italy	I9	18
Nolichucky, stm., U.S.	C3	112
Nolin, stm., Ky., U.S.	E10	114
Nolin Lake, res., Ky., U.S.	E10	114
Nolinsk, Russia	F7	26
Nombre de Dios, Mex.	F7	90
Nombre de Dios, Pan.	C3	84
Nombre de Dios, Cordillera, mts., Hond.	B8	92
Nome, Ak., U.S.	D12	100
Nomgon, Mong.	C8	30
Nominingue, Que., Can.	A11	108
Nonacho Lake, l., N.W. Ter., Can.	D11	96
Nondalton, Ak., U.S.	F17	100
Nondweni, S. Afr.	G10	66
Nong'an, China	C12	30
Nong Khai, Thai.	F7	40
Nongoma, S. Afr.	F10	66
Nono, Eth.	M9	60
Nonoai, Braz.	D12	80
Nonoava, Mex.	D6	90
Nonogasta, Arg.	E5	80
Nonsan, S. Kor.	G15	32
Nonthaburi, Thai.	H6	40
Nontron, Fr.	G7	14
Nooksack, stm., Wa., U.S.	B3	122
Noonan, N.D., U.S.	C4	118
Noord-Brabant, prov., Neth.	E6	12
Noord-Holland, prov., Neth.	C6	12
Noordoewer, Nmb.	G3	66
Noordoostpolder, reg., Neth.	C8	12
Noordwijk aan Zee, Neth.	D5	12
Noordzeekanaal, Neth.	D5	12
Noorvik, Ak., U.S.	C14	100
Nootka Island, i., B.C., Can.	H8	102
Nootka Sound, strt., B.C., Can.	H8	102
Nóqui, Ang.	C2	58
Norah, i., Erit.	E9	56
Noralee, B.C., Can.	D8	102
Nora Springs, Ia., U.S.	G2	110
Norberto de la Riestra, Arg.	H9	80
Norborne, Mo., U.S.	C3	114
Norcatur, Ks., U.S.	L7	118
Norcia, Italy	G8	18
Norcross, Ga., U.S.	F2	112
Nord, dept., Fr.	B10	14
Nord, Grand lac du, l., Que., Can.	B6	106
Nord, Petit lac du, l., Que., Can.	B6	106
Nordaustlandet, i., Sval.	B3	24
Nordegg, Alta., Can.	E18	102
Nordegg, stm., Alta., Can.	E19	102
Norden, Ger.	B7	10
Nordenham, Ger.	B8	10
Nordenšel'da, archipelag, is., Russia	B11	28
Nordenskiold, stm., Yukon, Can.	F26	100
Norderstedt, Ger.	B10	10
Nordhausen, Ger.	D10	10
Nordheim, Tx., U.S.	K9	116
Nordhorn, Ger.	C7	10
Nordkapp, c., Nor.	F19	6
Nordland, co., Nor.	H14	6
Nördlingen, Ger.	G10	10
Nordostrundingen, c., Grnld.	A18	86
Nord-Ostsee-Kanal, Ger.	A9	10
Nordreisa, Nor.	G17	6
Nordrhein-Westfalen, state, Ger.	D7	10
Nord-Trøndelag, co., Nor.	I12	6
Nore, Nor.	K11	6
Norfolk, Ne., U.S.	I10	118
Norfolk, Va., U.S.	C10	112
Norfolk, co., Eng., U.K.	I15	8
Norfolk Island, dep., Oc.	K20	126
Norfork Lake, res., U.S.	F4	114
Noril'sk, Russia	D9	28
Norlina, N.C., U.S.	C8	112
Normal, Al., U.S.	H10	114
Normal, Il., U.S.	J7	110
Norman, Ar., U.S.	H3	114
Norman, Ok., U.S.	D9	116
Norman, stm., Austl.	B4	70
Norman, Lake, res., N.C., U.S.	D6	112
Normandie, hist. reg., Fr.	D6	14
Normandie, Collines de, hills, Fr.	D6	14
Normandy see Normandie, hist. reg., Fr.	D6	14
Normangee, Tx., U.S.	H10	116
Norman Park, Ga., U.S.	H3	112
Normanton, Austl.	A4	70
Norman Wells, N.W. Ter., Can.	D31	100
Norogachi, Mex.	D6	90
Norphlet, Ar., U.S.	I4	114
Norquay, Sask., Can.	G12	104
Norra Kvarken (Merenkurkku), strt., Eur.	J17	6
Norrbottens Län, co., Swe.	H16	6
Norridgewock, Me., U.S.	C17	108
Norris, Tn., U.S.	C2	112
Norris Arm, Newf., Can.	C18	106
Norris City, Il., U.S.	E8	114
Norris Lake, res., Tn., U.S.	C3	112
Norris Point, Newf., Can.	C16	106
Norristown, Pa., U.S.	G11	108
Norrköping, Swe.	L15	6
Norrtälje, Swe.	L16	6
Norseman, Austl.	F4	68
Norsk, Russia	G17	28
Norte, Canal do, strt., Braz.	C8	76
Norte, Serra do, plat., Braz.	D12	82
Norte de Santander, state, Col.	J8	94
Norte de Santander, dept., Col.	C6	84
Nortelândia, Braz.	F13	82
North, S.C., U.S.	F5	112
North, stm., Newf., Can.	E20	96
North, stm., Al., U.S.	I9	114
North, stm., Ia., U.S.	I2	110
North, Cape, c., N.S., Can.	E13	106
North Adams, Ma., U.S.	E13	108
North Adams, Mi., U.S.	I11	110
North Albany, Or., U.S.	F2	122
Northam, Austl.	F3	68
North America	E9	86
Northampton, Austl.	E2	68
Northampton, Eng., U.K.	I13	8
Northampton, Ma., U.S.	E14	108
Northampton, Pa., U.S.	G11	108
Northamptonshire, co., Eng., U.K.	I13	8
North Andaman, i., India	H2	40
North Anna, stm., Va., U.S.	B9	112
North Anson, Me., U.S.	C17	108
North Asheboro, N.C., U.S.	D7	112
North Atlanta, Ga., U.S.	F2	112
North Augusta, S.C., U.S.	F5	112
North Aulatsivik Island, i., Newf., Can.	E20	96
North Baltimore, Oh., U.S.	F3	108
North Battleford, Sask., Can.	F6	104
North Bay, Ont., Can.	D16	110
North Bend, B.C., Can.	H13	102
North Bend, Ne., U.S.	J11	118
North Bend, Or., U.S.	G1	122
North Bennington, Vt., U.S.	E13	108
North Berwick, Scot., U.K.	E11	8
North Berwick, Me., U.S.	D16	108
North Bourke, Austl.	H6	70
North Branch, Mi., U.S.	G12	110
North Branch, Mn., U.S.	E3	110
North Caicos, i., T./C. Is.	D9	94
North Canadian, stm., Ok., U.S.	D10	116
North Canton, Ga., U.S.	E2	112
North Canton, Oh., U.S.	G5	108
North Cape, c., P.E.I., Can.	E9	106
North Cape, c., N.Z.	A4	72
North Cape see Nordkapp, c., Nor.	F19	6
North Caribou Lake, l., Ont., Can.	F14	96
North Carolina, state, U.S.	D11	98
North Cascades National Park, Wa., U.S.	B4	122
North Channel, strt., Ont., Can.	D12	110
North Channel, strt., U.K.	F8	8
North Charleston, S.C., U.S.	G7	112
North Chicago, Il., U.S.	H8	110
North College Hill, Oh., U.S.	H2	108
North Collins, N.Y., U.S.	E8	108
North Conway, N.H., U.S.	C15	108
North Creek, N.Y., U.S.	D13	108
North Crossett, Ar., U.S.	I5	114
North Dakota, state, U.S.	B6	98
North East, Md., U.S.	H11	108
North East, Pa., U.S.	E7	108
North-East, dept., Bots.	C8	66
North East Point, c., Bah.	D8	94
North East Point, c., Bah.	C8	94
Northeast Providence Channel, strt., Bah.	B6	94
Northeim, Ger.	D10	10
North English, Ia., U.S.	I3	110
Northern Arm, Newf., Can.	C18	106
Northern Cape, prov., S. Afr.	G5	66
Northern Dvina see Severnaja Dvina, stm., Russia	E6	26
Northern Indian Lake, l., Man., Can.	E13	96
Northern Ireland, ter., U.K.	G7	8
Northern Mariana Islands, dep., Oc.	G19	126
Northern Territory, ter., Austl.	C6	68
Northern Transvaal, prov., S. Afr.	D9	66
North Fabius, stm., U.S.	B4	114
Northfield, Ma., U.S.	E14	108
Northfield, Mn., U.S.	F2	110
Northfield, Vt., U.S.	C14	108
North Flinders Range, mts., Austl.	H3	70
North Fond du Lac, Wi., U.S.	G7	110
North Foreland, c., Eng., U.K.	J15	8
North Fork, Ca., U.S.	G6	124
North Fork, stm., U.S.	F4	114
North Fort Myers, Fl., U.S.	M5	112
North Freedom, Wi., U.S.	G6	110
North Frisian Islands, is., Eur.	A8	10
Northglenn, Co., U.S.	E12	120
North Gulfport, Ms., U.S.	L7	114
North Henderson, N.C., U.S.	C8	112
North Henik Lake, l., N.W. Ter., Can.	D13	96
North Hero, Vt., U.S.	C13	108
North Highlands, Ca., U.S.	F4	124
North Island, i., N.Z.	B4	72
North Judson, In., U.S.	A10	114
North Kenai, Ak., U.S.	F19	100
North Kingsville, Oh., U.S.	F6	108
North Knife Lake, l., Man., Can.	E13	96
North La Junta, Co., U.S.	N4	118
North Lakhimpur, India	G16	44
North Las Vegas, Nv., U.S.	H10	124
North La Veta Pass, Co., U.S.	G11	120
North Liberty, In., U.S.	A10	114
North Little Rock, Ar., U.S.	H4	114
North Logan, Ut., U.S.	C5	120
North Loon Mountain, mtn., Id., U.S.	E10	122
North Loup, Ne., U.S.	J9	118
North Loup, stm., Ne., U.S.	J9	118
North Macmillan, stm., Yukon, Can.	E28	100
North Magnetic Pole	B9	86
North Mamm Peak, mtn., Co., U.S.	E9	120
North Manchester, In., U.S.	A11	114

Name / Map Ref. / Page

Painted Desert, des., Az., U.S. I5 120
Painted Rock Reservoir, res., Az., U.S. K4 120
Paint Lake, l., Man., Can. C17 104
Paint Rock, Tx., U.S. H7 116
Paint Rock, stm., Al., U.S. H10 114
Paintsville, Ky., U.S. B4 112
Paisley, Scot., U.K. F9 8
Paisley, Or., U.S. H5 122
Paita, Peru A1 82
Paita, Bahía de, b., Peru A1 82
Paizhou, China E2 34
Pajala, Swe. H18 6
Pajan, Ec. H2 84
Pájara, Spain o26 17b
Pajjer, gora, mtn., Russia D10 26
Pakaraima Mountains, mts., S.A. E12 84
Pak Ban, Laos D7 40
Pakch'ŏn, N. Kor. D13 32
Pakeng, Sud. N6 60
Pakhoi see Beihai, China G8 30
Pakistan (Pākistān), ctry., Asia C9 42
Pakokku, Mya. D3 40
Pakouabo, C. Iv. H7 64
Pakowki Lake, l., Alta., Can. I4 104
Pākpattan, Pak. E5 44
Pak Phanang, Thai. J6 40
Pak Phraek, Thai. J6 40
Pakrac, Cro. D12 18
Pakruojis, Lith. F6 22
Paks, Hung. I18 10
P'akupur, stm., Russia E7 28
Pakwash Lake, l., Ont., Can. H21 104
Pakxé, Laos G8 40
Pala, Chad G3 56
Palacca Point, c., Bah. D8 94
Palacios, Tx., U.S. K10 116
Palacios, stm., Bol. G10 82
Palagonia, Italy L9 18
Palagruža, Otoci, is., Cro. G11 18
Pālakodu, India D6 46
Palamós, Spain D15 16
Palana, Russia F23 28
Palanga, Lith. F4 22
Palangkaraya, Indon. F5 38
Palani, India G4 46
Pālanpur, India H5 44
Palapye, Bots. D8 66
Palatka, Russia E22 28
Palatka, Fl., U.S. J5 112
Palau (Belau), dep., Oc. E9 38
Palauk, Mya. H5 40
Palawan, i., Phil. D6 38
Pālayankottai, India H4 46
Palca, Bol. G8 82
Palca, Peru D4 82
Palcamayo, Peru D4 82
Pal'co, Russia H17 22
Paldiski, Est. B7 22
Palech, Russia E24 22
Palembang, Indon. F3 38
Palena, Italy H9 18
Palencia, Spain C7 16
Palenque, Mex. I14 90
Palenque, hist., Mex. I13 90
Palenque, Punta, c., Dom. Rep. E9 94
Palermo, Col. F5 84
Palermo, Italy K8 18
Palermo, Ur. G11 80
Palestina, Braz. F4 79
Palestine, Ar., U.S. H6 114
Palestine, Il., U.S. C9 114
Palestine, Tx., U.S. H11 116
Palestine, hist. reg., Asia D4 50
Palestine, Lake, res., Tx., U.S. G11 116
Palestrina, Italy H7 18
Paletwa, Mya. D2 40
Pālghāt, India G4 46
Pāli, India H5 44
Palín, Guat. C4 92
Palisade, Co., U.S. E8 120
Palisade, Ne., U.S. K6 118
Palisades, Id., U.S. G14 122
Palisades Reservoir, res., U.S. G14 122
Paliseul, Bel. I7 12
Pālitāna, India B1 46
Palivere, Est. C6 22
Palizada, Mex. H13 90
Palk Bay, b., Asia H5 46
Palk Strait, strt., Asia H5 46
Palla Bianca (Weisskugel), mtn., Eur. E14 13
Pallasca, Peru C2 82
Palling, B.C., Can. C9 102
Palliser, Cape, c., N.Z. D5 72
Palma, Braz. F7 79
Palma, Moz. D8 58
P'al'ma, Russia J24 6
Palma, stm., Braz. B5 79
Palma del Río, Spain H6 16
Palma [de Mallorca], Spain F14 16
Palma di Montechiaro, Italy L8 18
Palmar, stm., Ven. B6 84
Palmar Camp, Belize I15 90
Palmar de los Sepúlveda, Mex. E6 90
Palmar de Varela, Col. B5 84
Palmares, Braz. E11 76
Palmares, C.R. G10 92
Palmares, C.R. H11 92
Palmares do Sul, Braz. F13 80
Palmarito, Ven. D7 84
Palmar Sur, C.R. I11 92
Palmas, Braz. F9 76
Palmas, Braz. D12 80
Palmas Bellas, Pan. C2 84
Palmas de Monte Alto, Braz. C7 79
Palma Soriano, Cuba D6 94
Palm Bay, Fl., U.S. K6 112
Palm Beach, Fl., U.S. M6 112
Palmdale, Ca., U.S. J7 124
Palm Desert, Ca., U.S. K9 124
Palmeira, Braz. C13 80
Palmeira, C.V. k17 64a
Palmeira das Missões, Braz. D12 80
Palmeira d'Oeste, Braz. F3 79
Palmeiras, Braz. B8 79
Palmeiras, stm., Braz. C3 79
Palmelo, Braz. D4 79
Palmer, Ak., U.S. F20 100
Palmer, Ma., U.S. E14 108
Palmer, Ms., U.S. K7 114
Palmer, Ne., U.S. J9 118
Palmer, Tn., U.S. G11 114
Palmer, Tx., U.S. G10 116
Palmer, sci., Ant. B12 73
Palmer Lake, Co., U.S. F12 120
Palmer Land, reg., Ant. C12 73
Palmerston, Ont., Can. G15 110
Palmerston, N.Z. F3 72
Palmerston, Cape, c., Austl. C8 70
Palmerston North, N.Z. D5 72
Palmerton, Pa., U.S. G11 108
Palmetto, Fl., U.S. L4 112
Palmetto, Ga., U.S. F2 112
Palmetto, La., U.S. L5 114
Palmi, Italy K10 18
Palminópolis, Braz. D3 79
Palmira, Arg. G4 80
Palmira, Col. F4 84
Palmira, Cuba C4 94
Palmira, Ec. I3 84
Palmitas, Ur. G10 80
Palmitos, Braz. D12 80
Palm Springs, Ca., U.S. K9 124
Palmyra see Tudmur, Syria D5 48
Palmyra, Il., U.S. C7 114
Palmyra, Mo., U.S. C5 114
Palmyra, N.Y., U.S. D9 108
Palmyra, Pa., U.S. G10 108
Palmyra, Va., U.S. B8 112
Palmyra, hist., Syria D5 48
Palmyra Atoll, atoll, Oc. H23 126
Palo Alto, Ca., U.S. G3 124
Palo Flechado Pass, N.M., U.S. H11 120
Paloich, Sud. L7 60
Palomar Mountain, mtn., Ca., U.S. K9 124
Palomas Viejo, Mex. B6 90
Palo Negro, Ven. B9 84
Palo Pinto, Tx., U.S. G8 116
Palopo, Indon. F7 38
Palora, stm., Ec. H3 84
Palos see Palos de la Frontera, Spain H5 16
Palos, Cabo de, c., Spain H11 16
Palo Santo, Arg. C9 80
Palos de la Frontera, Spain H5 16
Palouse, Wa., U.S. D8 122
Palouse, stm., U.S. D7 122
Palo Verde, Ca., U.S. K11 124
Palo Verde, Parque Nacional, C.R. G9 92
Palpa, Peru F4 82
Palpalá, Arg. C6 80
Palu, Indon. F6 38
Palwal, India F7 44
Pama, Burkina F10 64
Pāmban Island, i., India H5 46
Pambeguwa, Nig. F14 64
Pamekasan, Indon. j16 39a
Pamiers, Fr. I8 14
Pamir, mts., Asia B5 44
Pamlico, stm., N.C., U.S. D10 112
Pamlico Sound, strt., N.C., U.S. D11 112
Pampa, Tx., U.S. D6 116
Pampã, stm., Braz. D8 79
Pampa, reg., Arg. I6 80
Pampa Almirón, Arg. D9 80
Pampacolca, Peru F5 82
Pampa del Chañar, Arg. F4 80
Pampa del Indio, Arg. D9 80
Pampa del Infierno, Arg. D8 80
Pampa de los Guanacos, Arg. D8 80
Pampa Grande, Bol. H9 82
Pampas, Peru E4 82
Pampas, stm., Peru E5 82
Pamplico, S.C., U.S. F7 112
Pamplona, Col. D6 84
Pamplona, Spain C10 16
Pampoenpoort, S. Afr. H6 66
Pamunkey, stm., Va., U.S. B9 112
Pana, Il., U.S. C7 114
Panabá, Mex. G15 90
Panaca, Nv., U.S. G11 124
Panacea, Fl., U.S. I2 112
Panaji (Panjim), India E2 46
Panamá, Braz. E4 79
Panamá, Pan. C3 84
Panama, Il., U.S. C7 114
Panama, Ok., U.S. G2 114
Panamá, prov., Pan. I15 92
Panama (Panamá), ctry., N.A. G8 88
Panamá, Bahía de, b., Pan. C3 84
Panamá, Canal de, Pan. H15 92
Panamá, Golfo de, b., Pan. C3 84
Panamá, Istmo de, Pan. C2 84
Panama City, Fl., U.S. L11 114
Panamá Vieja, hist., Pan. H15 92
Panambi, Braz. E12 80
Panamint Range, mts., Ca., U.S. H8 124
Panao, Peru C3 82
Pančevo, Yugo. E4 20
Pandamatenga, Bots. B7 66
Pan de Azúcar, Ur. H11 80
Pandėlys, Lith. E8 22
Pandharpur, India D3 46
Pāndhurna, India B5 46
Pando, dept., Bol. D8 82
P'andž (Panj), stm., Asia A4 44
Panevėžys, Lith. F7 22
Panfang, China H4 34
Panfilov, Kaz. I14 26
Pangala, Congo B2 58
Pangalanes, Canal des, Madag. q23 67b
Pangani, Tan. C7 58
Pangburn, Ar., U.S. G5 114
Pangfou see Bengbu, China E10 30
Pangi, Zaire B5 58
Pangkalanbuun, Indon. F5 38
Pangkalpinang, Indon. F4 38
Pangman, Sask., Can. I10 104
Pangnirtung, N.W. Ter., Can. C19 96
Pangong Tso, l., Asia D8 44
Panguitch, Ut., U.S. G4 120
Panhandle, Tx., U.S. D5 116
Panino, Russia E17 22
Pānīpat, India F7 44
Panj (P'andž), stm., Asia B4 44
Panjāb, Afg. C2 44
Panjgūr, Pak. H18 48
Panjim see Panaji, India E2 46
Pankshin, Nig. G14 64
Panlong (Lo), stm., Asia C8 40
P'anmunjŏm, N. Kor. F14 32
Panna, India H9 44
Pannawonica, Austl. D3 68
Panola, Al., U.S. K10 114
Panora, Ia., U.S. J13 118
Panorama, Braz. F3 79
Pansik, Rápido, wtfl, N.A. C9 92
Pantelleria, Isola di, i., Italy M7 18
Pantha, Mya. C3 40
Pánuco, Mex. F10 90
Pánuco, stm., Mex. G10 90
Panuke Lake, l., N.S., Can. H9 106
Panxian, China B8 40
Panxidu, China H3 32
Panyam, Nig. G14 64
Panyang, Sud. L5 60
Panyu, China M2 34
Panzós, Guat. B5 92
Pao, stm., Ven. C8 84
Pao, stm., Ven. C10 84
Paola, Italy J11 18
Paola, Ks., U.S. M13 118
Paoli, In., U.S. D10 114
Paonia, Co., U.S. F9 120
Paotow see Baotou, China C8 30
P'aozero, ozero, l., Russia H22 6
Paozi, China A10 32
Pápa, Hung. H17 10
Papagaio, stm., Braz. I11 84
Papagayo, Golfo de, b., C.R. G9 92
Papaikou, Hi., U.S. r18 125a
Papantla [de Olarte], Mex. G11 90
Papenburg, Ger. B7 10
Papilė, Lith. E5 22
Papillion, Ne., U.S. J11 118
Papineau-Labelle, Réserve, Que., Can. B11 108
Paposo, Chile C3 80
Papua, Gulf of, b., Pap. N. Gui. m15 68a
Papua New Guinea, ctry., Oc. m15 68a
Papudo, Chile G3 80
Papun, Mya. E4 40
Papunáua, stm., Col. G7 84
Papurí, stm., S.A. G7 84
Paquera, C.R. H10 92
Pará, state, Braz. B13 82
Pará, stm., Braz. D9 76
Pará, stm., Braz. E6 79
Paraburdoo, Austl. D3 68
Paracari, stm., Braz. A13 82
Paracas, Bahía de, b., Peru E3 82
Paracas, Península de, pen., Peru E3 82
Paracatu, Braz. D5 79
Paracatu, stm., Braz. D6 79
Paracatu, stm., Braz. D6 79
Paracel Islands see Xisha Qundao, is., China B5 38
Parachilna, Austl. H3 70
Paracho de Verduzco, Mex. H8 90
Parachute, Co., U.S. E8 120
Paraćin, Yugo. F5 20
Parád, Hung. H20 10
Parada, Punta, c., Peru F4 82
Paradas, Spain H6 16
Paradise, Guy. D14 84
Paradise, Ca., U.S. E4 124
Paradise, Mt., U.S. C11 122
Paradise, Nv., U.S. H10 124
Paradise, Tx., U.S. F9 116
Paradise Hill, Sask., Can. E5 104
Paradise Valley, Az., U.S. K5 120
Paradise Valley, Nv., U.S. C8 124
Parado, stm., Braz. D14 82
Paragonah, Ut., U.S. G4 120
Paragould, Ar., U.S. F6 114
Paraguá, stm., Bol. E11 82
Paragua, stm., Ven. D11 84
Paraguaçu, stm., Braz. B9 79
Paraguaçu Paulista, Braz. G3 79
Paraguaipoa, Ven. B7 84
Paraguaná, Península de, pen., Ven. B8 84
Paraguarí, Para. C10 80
Paraguarí, dept., Para. D10 80
Paraguay, ctry., S.A. G9 74
Paraguay (Paraguai), stm., S.A. G9 74
Paraíba do Sul, stm., Braz. F7 79
Paraíso, Braz. E2 79
Paraíso, C.R. H11 92
Paraíso, Mex. H13 90
Paraiso, Pan. C3 84
Paraíso do Norte, Braz. G2 79
Paraisópolis, Braz. G6 79
Paraitinga, stm., Braz. G6 79
Parakou, Benin G11 64
Paramakkudi, India H5 46
Paramaribo, Sur. B7 76
Paramirim, Braz. B7 79
Paramirim, stm., Braz. B7 79
Paramonga, Peru D3 82
Paramušir, ostrov, i., Russia G23 28
Paran, Nahal (Wādī al-Jirāfī), val. H3 50
Paraná, Arg. F8 80
Paranã, Braz. B5 79
Paraná, state, Braz. C13 80
Paranã, stm., Braz. B5 79
Paraná, stm., S.A. G9 80
Paranaguá, Braz. C14 80
Paranaguá, Baía de, b., Braz. C14 80
Paranaíba, Braz. E3 79
Paranaíba, stm., Braz. E3 79
Paranaíta, stm., Braz. C13 82
Paranam, Sur. B7 76
Paranapanema, stm., Braz. G3 79
Paranapiacaba, Serra do, mts., Braz. C14 80
Paranavaí, Braz. G2 79
Parângu Mare, Vârful, mtn., Rom. D7 20
Paranhos, Braz. G1 79
Paranoá, Lago do, l., Braz. C5 79
Paraopeba, Braz. E6 79
Parapara, Ven. C9 84
Parapetí, stm., Bol. H10 82
Paras, Peru E4 82
Paratinga, Braz. B7 79
Parauari, stm., Braz. J13 84
Paraúna, Braz. D3 79
Paray-le-Monial, Fr. F11 14
Pārbati, stm., India H7 44
Pārbatipur, Bngl. H13 44
Parbhani, India C4 46
Parchment, Mi., U.S. H10 110
Parczew, Pol. D22 10
Pardeeville, Wi., U.S. G6 110
Pardes Hanna-Karkur, Isr. D3 50
Pardo, stm., Braz. C6 79
Pardo, stm., Braz. F4 79
Pardo, stm., Braz. G4 79
Pardo, stm., Braz. C9 79
Pardo, stm., Braz. F2 79
Pardo, stm., Braz. E12 80
Pardubice, Czech. E15 10
Parecis, Braz. F13 82
Parecis, stm., Braz. E13 82
Parecis, Chapada dos, mts., Braz. F12 82
Paredón, Mex. E9 90
Paren', stm., Russia E24 28
Parent, Que., Can. G18 96
Parepare, Indon. F6 38
Parera, Arg. H6 80
Parfino, Russia D14 22
Paria, stm., U.S. H5 120
Paria, Gulf of, b. B11 84
Paria, Península de, pen., Ven. B11 84
Pariaguán, Ven. C10 84
Pariaman, Indon. O6 40
Pariamanu, stm., Peru E6 82
Pariči, Bela. I12 22
Paricutín, vol., Mex. H8 90
Parida, Isla, i., Pan. I12 92
Parika, Guy. D13 84
Parima, stm., Braz. F11 84
Parima, Sierra, mts., S.A. F10 84
Pariñas, Punta, c., Peru J2 84
Parintins, Braz. I14 84
Pariquera-Açu, Braz. C15 80
Paris, Ont., Can. G15 110
Paris, Fr. D9 14
Paris, Ar., U.S. G3 114
Paris, Id., U.S. H14 122
Paris, Il., U.S. C9 114
Paris, Ky., U.S. I2 108
Paris, Me., U.S. C16 108
Paris, Mo., U.S. C4 114
Paris, Tn., U.S. F8 114
Paris, Tx., U.S. F11 116
Parismina, C.R. G11 92
Parismina, stm., C.R. G11 92
Parita, Bahía de, b., Pan. I14 92
Parit Buntar, Malay. L6 40
Park, stm., N.D., U.S. C10 118
Parkano, Fin. J18 6
Park City, Ks., U.S. N10 118
Park City, Mt., U.S. E17 122
Park City, Ut., U.S. D5 120
Parkdale, P.E.I., Can. F10 106
Parkdale, Or., U.S. E4 122
Parker, Az., U.S. J2 120
Parker, Co., U.S. L3 118
Parker, Fl., U.S. L11 114
Parker, S.D., U.S. H10 118
Parker, Cape, c., N.W. Ter., Can. A17 96
Parker City, In., U.S. B11 114
Parker Dam, Ca., U.S. J11 124
Parkersburg, Il., U.S. D8 114
Parkersburg, Ia., U.S. H3 110
Parkersburg, W.V., U.S. H5 108
Parkers Prairie, Mn., U.S. E12 118
Parkes, Austl. I8 70
Park Falls, Wi., U.S. E5 110
Park Forest, Il., U.S. I8 110
Parkhill, Ont., Can. G14 110
Parkin, Ar., U.S. G6 114
Parkland, Wa., U.S. C3 122
Park Range, mts., Co., U.S. D10 120
Park Rapids, Mn., U.S. E12 118
Park River, N.D., U.S. C10 118
Parkrose, Or., U.S. E3 122
Parksley, Va., U.S. B11 112
Parkston, S.D., U.S. H10 118
Parksville, B.C., Can. H10 102
Parkville, Md., U.S. H10 108
Parkville, Mo., U.S. C2 114
Parkwater, Wa., U.S. C8 122
Parla, Spain E8 16
Parlākimidi, India C8 46
Parle, Lac qui, l., Mn., U.S. F11 118
Parli, India C4 46
Parma, Italy E5 18
Parma, Id., U.S. G9 122
Parma, Mo., U.S. F7 114
Parma, Oh., U.S. F5 108
Parnaguá, Braz. F10 76
Parnaíba, Braz. D10 76
Parnaíba, stm., Braz. D10 76
Parnassós, mtn., Grc. K6 20
Pärnu, Est. C7 22
Pärnu-Jaagupi, Est. C7 22
Paro, Bhu. G13 44
Paromaj, Russia G20 28
Paroo, stm., Austl. H5 70
Páros, i., Grc. L9 20
Parowan, Ut., U.S. G4 120
Parpaillon, mts., Fr. H13 14
Parpan, Switz. E12 13
Parral, Chile I3 80
Parral see Hidalgo del Parral, Mex. D7 90
Parral, stm., Mex. D7 90
Parramatta, Austl. I9 70
Parras de la Fuente, Mex. E8 90
Parrish, Al., U.S. I9 114
Parrish, Fl., U.S. L4 112
Parrita, C.R. H10 92
Parrita, stm., C.R. H10 92
Parrsboro, N.S., Can. G9 106
Parry, Cape, c., N.W. Ter., Can. B8 96
Parry, Mount, mtn., B.C., Can. E6 102
Parry Bay, b., N.W. Ter., Can. C16 96
Parry Channel, strt., N.W. Ter., Can. B9 86
Parry Peninsula, pen., N.W. Ter., Can. B32 100
Parry Sound, Ont., Can. E15 110
Parsberg, Ger. F11 10
Parseier Spitze, mtn., Aus. D13 13
Parshall, N.D., U.S. D5 118
Parsnip, stm., B.C., Can. C12 102
Parsons, Ks., U.S. N12 118
Parsons, Tn., U.S. G8 114
Parsons, W.V., U.S. H7 108
Parson's Pond, Newf., Can. B16 106
Parsons Pond, l., Newf., Can. B16 106
Pärsti, Est. C8 22
Partanna, Italy L7 18
Parthenay, Fr. F6 14
Partinico, Italy K8 18
Partizansk, Russia I18 28
Partridge Crop Lake, l., Man., Can. C17 104
Partridge Point, c., Newf., Can. B17 106
Paru, stm., Braz. D8 76
Parú, stm., Ven. E10 84
Paru de Oeste, stm., Braz. D7 76
Paruro, Peru E6 82
Pārvatīpuram, India C7 46
Paryang, China E10 44
Pasaco, Guat. D4 92
Pasadena, Newf., Can. C16 106
Pasadena, Ca., U.S. J7 124
Pasadena, Tx., U.S. J11 116
Pasado, Cabo, c., Ec. H2 84
Pasaje, Ec. I3 84
Pasaje, stm., Arg. C6 80
Pa Sak, stm., Thai. G6 40
Pasawng, Mya. E4 40
Pascagoula, Ms., U.S. L8 114
Pascagoula, stm., Ms., U.S. L8 114
Pașcani, Rom. B10 20
Pasco, Wa., U.S. D6 122
Pasco, dept., Peru D4 82
Pascoag, R.I., U.S. F15 108
Pascua, Isla de (Easter Island), i., Chile G4 74
Pas-de-Calais, dept., Fr. B9 14
Pasewalk, Ger. B14 10
Pasig, Phil. n19 39b
P'asina, stm., Russia C9 28
Pasinler, Tur. B6 48
P'asino, ozero, l., Russia D9 28
P'asinskij zaliv, b., Russia C14 26
Pasir Puteh, Malay. L7 40
Pasley Bay, b., N.W. Ter., Can. B13 96
Pasmore, stm., Austl. H3 70
Pasni, Pak. I17 48
Paso del Cerro, Ur. F11 80
Paso de los Libres, Arg. E10 80
Paso de los Toros, Ur. G10 80
Paso de Patria, Para. D9 80
Paso Hondo, Mex. J13 90
Pasorapa, Bol. H9 82
Paso Robles, Ca., U.S. I5 124
Pasqua Indian Reserve, Sask., Can. H10 104
Pasquel, Punta, c., Mex. E4 90
Pasquia Hills, hills, Sask., Can. E12 104
Pasquotank, stm., N.C., U.S. C10 112
Pasrūr, Pak. D6 44
Passadumkeag, Me., U.S. B18 108
Passage Point, c., N.W. Ter., Can. B9 96
Passaic, N.J., U.S. G12 108
Passamaquoddy Bay, b., N.A. G7 106
Passau, Ger. G13 10
Passero, Capo, c., Italy M10 18
Pass Island, Newf., Can. E17 106
Pašškij Perevoz, Russia A15 22
Passo Fundo, Braz. E12 80
Passos, Braz. F5 79
Pastaza, prov., Ec. H4 84
Pastaza, stm., S.A. J4 84
Pastecho, stm., Alta., Can. B20 102
Pasteur, Lac, l., Que., Can. B7 106
Pasto, Col. G4 84
Pastora Peak, mtn., Az., U.S. H7 120
Pasuruan, Indon. j16 39a
Pasvalys, Lith. E7 22
Pásztó, Hung. H19 10
Patacamaya, Bol. G8 82
Patagonia, Az., U.S. M6 120
Patagonia, reg., Arg. F3 78
Pātan, India I5 44
Patargān, Daqq-e, sw., Asia E16 48
Pătârlagele, Rom. D10 20
Pataz, Peru B3 82
Patchewollock, Austl. J5 70
Patchogue, N.Y., U.S. G13 108
Patea, N.Z. C5 72
Pategi, Nig. G12 64
Pate Island, i., Kenya B8 58
Patensie, S. Afr. I7 66
Paterna, Spain F11 16
Paternion, Aus. I13 10
Paternò, Italy L9 18
Pateros, Wa., U.S. B6 122
Paterson, S. Afr. I7 66
Paterson, N.J., U.S. G12 108
Pathānkot, India D6 44
Pathein (Bassein), Mya. F3 40
Pathfinder Reservoir, res., Wy., U.S. B10 120
Pathiong, Sud. N6 60
Patía, Col. F4 84
Patía, stm., Col. F3 84
Patiāla, India E7 44
P'atigorsk, Russia I6 26
Pativilca, Peru D3 82
Pativilca, stm., Peru D3 82
Pātkai Range, mts., Asia G16 44
Patna, India H11 44
Pato Branco, Braz. D12 80
Patoka, Il., U.S. D7 114
Patoka, stm., In., U.S. D9 114
Patos, Braz. E11 76
Patos, Lagoa dos, b., Braz. F13 80
Patos, Río de los, stm., Arg. F4 80
Patos, Rio dos, stm., Braz. E13 82
Patos de Minas, Braz. E5 79
P'atovskij, Russia G19 22
Patquía, Arg. F5 80
Pátrai, Grc. K5 20
Patraïkós Kólpos, b., Grc. K5 20
Patras see Pátrai, Grc. K5 20
Patrocínio, Braz. E5 79
Patrocínio Paulista, Braz. F5 79
Pattada, Italy I4 18
Pattani, Thai. K6 40
Patten, Me., U.S. B18 108
Patterson, Ca., U.S. G4 124
Patterson, Ga., U.S. H4 112
Patterson, La., U.S. M5 114
Patterson, Mount, mtn., Yukon, Can. D27 100
Patti, Italy K9 18
Pattison, Ms., U.S. K6 114
Patton, Pa., U.S. G8 108
Pattonsburg, Mo., U.S. B2 114
Pattullo, Mount, mtn., B.C., Can. H30 100
Patuca, stm., Hond. B10 92
Patuca, Punta, c., Hond. B10 92
Patul, Cerro, mtn., Ec. I3 84
Patulul, Guat. C3 92
Patuxent, stm., Md., U.S. I10 108
Pátzcuaro, Mex. H9 90
Patzicía, Guat. C4 92
Patzún, Guat. C3 92
Pau, Fr. I6 14
Pau Brasil, Braz. C9 79
Paucarbamba, Peru E4 82
Paucarpata, Peru G6 82
Paucartambo, Peru E6 82
Pauini, Braz. B8 82
Pauini, stm., Braz. B8 82
Pauini, stm., Braz. H11 84
Pauk, Mya. D3 40
Paul, Id., U.S. H12 122
Paul, Lac à, l., Que., Can. C3 106
Paulaya, stm., Hond. B9 92
Paulding, Ms., U.S. J7 114
Paulding, Oh., U.S. F2 108
Paulhan, Fr. I10 14
Paulicéia, Braz. F3 79
Paulina Peak, mtn., Or., U.S. G4 122
Pauline, Mount, mtn., Can. D15 102
Paulistana, Braz. E10 76
Paulistas, Braz. E7 79
Paullina, Ia., U.S. I12 118
Paull Lake, l., Sask., Can. B10 104
Paulo Afonso, Braz. E11 76
Paulo de Faria, Braz. F4 79
Pauloff Harbor (Pavlof Harbor), Ak., U.S. I13 100
Paulpietersburg, S. Afr. F10 66
Pauls Valley, Ok., U.S. E9 116
Paungbyin, Mya. B3 40
Paungde, Mya. E3 40
Pausa, Peru F5 82
Paute, Ec. I3 84
Paute, stm., Ec. I3 84
Pauto, stm., Col. E7 84
Pāveh, Iran D9 48
Pavelec, Russia H22 22
Pavia, Italy D4 18
Pavilion, B.C., Can. G13 102
Pavillion, Wy., U.S. A8 120
Pavilly, Fr. C7 14
Pāvilosta, Lat. E4 22
Pavlikeni, Bul. F9 20
Pavlodar, Kaz. G7 28
Pavlovo, Russia F26 22
Pavlovsk, Russia B13 22
Pavlovskij Posad, Russia F21 22
Pavo, Ga., U.S. H2 112
Pavón, Col. F6 84
Paw Creek, N.C., U.S. D6 112
Pawhuska, Ok., U.S. C10 116
Pawnee, Il., U.S. C7 114
Pawnee, Ok., U.S. C10 116
Pawnee, stm., Ks., U.S. M8 118
Pawnee City, Ne., U.S. K11 118
Pawnee Rock, Ks., U.S. M9 118
Paw Paw, Il., U.S. I7 110
Paw Paw, Mi., U.S. H10 110
Paw Paw, W.V., U.S. H8 108
Paw Paw Lake, Mi., U.S. H9 110
Pawtucket, R.I., U.S. F15 108
Paxton, Il., U.S. J7 110
Paxton, Ne., U.S. J6 118
Paya, Hond. B9 92
Payakumbuh, Indon. O6 40
Payas, Cerro, mtn., Hond. B9 92
Payerne, Switz. E6 13
Payette, Id., U.S. F9 122
Payette, stm., Id., U.S. G9 122
Payne, Oh., U.S. F2 108
Payne, Lac, l., Que., Can. E18 96
Payne Bay, b., Can. D19 96
Paynesville, Mn., U.S. F13 118
Paynton, Sask., Can. E6 104
Paysandú, Ur. G9 80
Payson, Az., U.S. J5 120
Payson, Il., U.S. C5 114
Payson, Ut., U.S. D5 120
Payún, Cerro, mtn., Arg. I4 80
Paz, stm., N.A. D4 92
Pazardžik, Bul. G8 20
Pazarköy, Tur. J11 20
Paz de Ariporo, Col. E7 84
Paz de Río, Col. E6 84
P'ažijeva Sel'ga, Russia K24 6
Pazin, Cro. D8 18
Pazña, Bol. H8 82
Pea, stm., U.S. K10 114
Peabody, Ks., U.S. M10 118
Peabody, Ma., U.S. E16 108
Peace, stm., Can. E10 96
Peace, stm., Fl., U.S. L5 112
Peace Canyon Dam, B.C., Can. B13 102
Peace River, Alta., Can. A17 102
Peach Creek, W.V., U.S. J5 108
Peachland, B.C., Can. H15 102
Peach Orchard, Ga., U.S. F4 112
Peach Springs, Az., U.S. I3 120
Peacock Hills, hills, N.W. Ter., Can. C11 96
Peak Hill, Austl. E3 68
Peak Hill, Austl. I8 70
Peale, Mount, mtn., Ut., U.S. F7 120
Pearce, Az., U.S. M7 120
Pearisburg, Va., U.S. B6 112
Pearl, Il., U.S. C6 114
Pearl, Ms., U.S. J6 114
Pearl, stm., U.S. L7 114
Pearland, Tx., U.S. J11 116
Pearl Harbor, b., Hi., U.S. p16 125a
Pearl Peak, mtn., Nv., U.S. D10 124
Pearl River, La., U.S. L7 114
Pearl River, N.Y., U.S. F12 108
Pearsall, Tx., U.S. K7 116
Pearse Island, i., B.C., Can. C4 102
Pearsoll Peak, mtn., Or., U.S. H2 122
Pearson, Ga., U.S. H4 112
Pearson Lake, l., Man., Can. B17 104
Pearston, S. Afr. I7 66
Peary Land, reg., Grnld. A16 86
Pebane, Moz. E7 58
Pebas, Peru I7 84
Peć, Yugo. G4 20
Pecan Bayou, stm., Tx., U.S. H7 116
Pecan Gap, Tx., U.S. F11 116
Peçanha, Braz. E7 79
Peças, Ilha das, i., Braz. C14 80
Pecatonica, Il., U.S. H6 110
Pecatonica, stm., U.S. H6 110
Pečenga, Russia D4 26
Pechenizhyn, Ukr. A8 20
Pechora see Pečora, stm., Russia D8 26
Pecica, Rom. C5 20
Peck, Mi., U.S. G13 110
Pečora, Russia D9 26
Pečora, stm., Russia D8 26
Pečorskaja guba, b., Russia D8 26
Pečorskoje more, Russia D8 26
Pečory, Russia D10 22
Pecos, N.M., U.S. I11 120
Pecos, Tx., U.S. H3 116
Pecos, stm., U.S. J5 116
Pécs, Hung. I18 10
Pedasí, Pan. D2 84
Peddāpuram, India D7 46
Pedder, Lake, res., Austl. N7 70
Pedernales, Arg. H9 80
Pedernales, Dom. Rep. E9 94
Pedernales, Ven. C11 84
Pedernales, stm., Tx., U.S. I7 116
Pedernales, Salar de, pl., Chile D4 80
Pedra Azul, Braz. D8 79
Pedra Grande, Recifes da, rf., Braz. D9 79
Pedra Lume, C.V. k17 64a
Pedras, Braz. I14 84
Pedras Negras, Braz. E10 82
Pedraza, Col. B5 84
Pedregal, Pan. C1 84
Pedregal, Ven. B7 84
Pedregulho, Braz. F5 79
Pedreiras, Braz. D10 76
Pedriceña, Mex. E8 90
Pedro Afonso, Braz. E9 76
Pedro Cays, is., Jam. F6 94
Pedrógão Grande, Port. F3 16
Pedro Gomes, Braz. E1 79
Pedro II, Braz. D10 76
Pedro II, Ilha, i., S.A. G9 84
Pedro Juan Caballero, Para. B11 80
Pedro Leopoldo, Braz. E6 79
Pedro Luro, Arg. J7 80
Pedro Muñoz, Spain F9 16
Pedro Osório, Braz. F12 80
Pedro R. Fernández, Arg. E9 80
Peebinga, Austl. J4 70
Peebles, Oh., U.S. I3 108
Pee Dee, stm., U.S. D6 112
Peekskill, N.Y., U.S. F13 108
Peel, I. of Man G9 8
Peel, stm., Can. C27 100
Peel Channel, mth., N.W. Ter., Can. C27 100
Pe Ell, Wa., U.S. D2 122
Peel Point, c., N.W. Ter., Can. B10 96
Peel Sound, strt., N.W. Ter., Can. B13 96
Peene, stm., Ger. B13 10
Peepeekisis Indian Reserve, Sask., Can. H11 104
Peerless, Mt., U.S. B20 122
Peers, Alta., Can. D18 102
Peesane, Sask., Can. F11 104
Peetz, Co., U.S. K4 118
Pegasus Bay, b., N.Z. E4 72
Pegnitz, Ger. F11 10
Pegnitz, stm., Ger. F11 10
Pego, Spain G11 16
Pegu see Bago, Mya. F4 40
Peguis Indian Reserve, Man., Can. G17 104
Pegu Yoma, mts., Mya. E3 40
Pehčevo, Mac. H6 20
Pehuajó, Arg. H8 80
Peigan Indian Reserve, Alta., Can. H21 102
Peikang, Tai. L9 34
Peine, Ger. C10 10
Peipus, Lake see Čudskoje ozero, l., Eur. C10 22
Peissenberg, Ger. H11 10
Peixe, Braz. B4 79
Peixe, Rio do, stm., Braz. C3 79
Peixe, Rio do, stm., Braz. G3 79
Peixian, China E10 30
Peiziyan, China H3 32
Pekalongan, Indon. j14 39a
Pekanbaru, Indon. N6 40
Pekin, Il., U.S. J6 110
Pekin, In., U.S. D10 114
Peking see Beijing, China D4 32
Peklino, Russia H16 22
Pelabuhan Kelang, Malay. M6 40
Pelagie, Isole, is., Italy N7 18

Name	Map Ref.	Page
Pistolet Bay, b., Newf., Can.	A18	106
Pisz, Pol.	B21	10
Pit, stm., Ca., U.S.	D3	124
Pital, Col.	F5	84
Pitalito, Col.	G4	84
Pitanga, Braz.	C13	80
Pitangueiras, Braz.	F4	79
Pitangui, Braz.	E6	79
Pitcairn, dep., Oc.	K27	126
Piteå, Swe.	I17	6
Pitelino, Russia	G24	22
Pitești, Rom.	E8	20
Pithapuram, India	D7	46
Pithiviers, Fr.	D9	14
Pitigliano, Italy	G6	18
Pitiquito, Mex.	B3	90
Pitk'aranta, Russia	K22	6
Pitt Island, i., B.C., Can.	D5	102
Pitt Lake, l., B.C., Can.	H12	102
Pittsboro, Ms., U.S.	I7	114
Pittsboro, N.C., U.S.	D7	112
Pittsburg, Ks., U.S.	N13	118
Pittsburg, Tx., U.S.	G12	116
Pittsburgh, Pa., U.S.	G7	108
Pittsfield, Il., U.S.	C6	114
Pittsfield, Me., U.S.	C17	108
Pittsfield, Ma., U.S.	E13	108
Pittsfield, N.H., U.S.	D15	108
Pittsford, Mi., U.S.	I11	110
Pittston, Pa., U.S.	F11	108
Pittsview, Al., U.S.	J11	114
Pittsworth, Austl.	F9	70
Pituil, Arg.	E5	80
Pitumarca, Peru	E6	82
Pium, Braz.	F9	76
Piura, Peru	A1	82
Piura, dept., Peru	A1	82
Piura, stm., Peru	A1	82
Pivan', Russia	G19	28
Pivdennyy Buh, stm., Ukr.	H4	26
Pivijay, Col.	B5	84
Pixley, Ca., U.S.	I6	124
Pizzo, Italy	K11	18
Placentia, Newf., Can.	E20	106
Placentia Bay, b., Newf., Can.	E19	106
Placerville, Ca., U.S.	F5	124
Placetas, Cuba	C5	94
Plácido de Castro, Braz.	D8	82
Plácido Rosas, Ur.	G12	80
Plain City, Oh., U.S.	G3	108
Plain City, Ut., U.S.	C4	120
Plain Dealing, La., U.S.	J3	114
Plainfield, Ct., U.S.	F15	108
Plainfield, In., U.S.	C10	114
Plainfield, N.J., U.S.	G12	108
Plainfield, Wi., U.S.	F6	110
Plains, Ga., U.S.	G2	112
Plains, Ks., U.S.	N7	118
Plains, Mt., U.S.	C11	122
Plains, Tx., U.S.	F4	116
Plainview, Mn., U.S.	F3	110
Plainview, Ne., U.S.	I10	118
Plainview, Tx., U.S.	E5	116
Plainville, In., U.S.	D9	114
Plainville, Ks., U.S.	L8	118
Plainwell, Mi., U.S.	H10	110
Plaisance, Baie de, b., Que., Can.	E12	106
Plaistow, N.H., U.S.	E15	108
Plakhtiyivka, Ukr.	C13	20
Plamondon, Alta., Can.	C22	102
Planada, Ca., U.S.	G5	124
Planalto, Braz.	C8	79
Planalto, Braz.	D12	80
Planeta Rica, Col.	C5	84
Plankinton, S.D., U.S.	H9	118
Plano, Il., U.S.	I7	110
Plano, Tx., U.S.	F10	116
Plantagenet, Ont., Can.	B11	108
Plantation, Fl., U.S.	M6	112
Plant City, Fl., U.S.	K4	112
Plantersville, Al., U.S.	J10	114
Plantersville, Ms., U.S.	H8	114
Plantsite, Az., U.S.	K7	120
Plaquemine, La., U.S.	L5	114
Plasencia, Spain	E5	16
Plast, Russia	G10	26
Plaster Rock, N.B., Can.	F6	106
Plata, Isla de la, i., Ec.	H2	84
Plata, Río de la, est., S.A.	H10	80
Plato, Col.	C5	84
Platonovka, Russia	I24	22
Platta, Switz.	E10	13
Platte, S.D., U.S.	H9	118
Platte, stm., Mn., U.S.	D1	110
Platte, stm., Ne., U.S.	J11	118
Platte, stm., Wi., U.S.	H5	110
Platte Center, Ne., U.S.	J10	118
Platte City, Mo., U.S.	C2	114
Platteville, Co., U.S.	D12	120
Platteville, Wi., U.S.	H5	110
Plattsburg, Mo., U.S.	C2	114
Plattsburgh, N.Y., U.S.	C13	108
Plattsmouth, Ne., U.S.	J12	118
Platveld, Nmb.	B3	66
Plau, Ger.	B12	10
Plauen, Ger.	E12	10
Plav, Yugo.	G3	20
Pļaviņas, Lat.	E8	22
Plavsk, Russia	H20	22
Playa Azul, Mex.	I8	90
Playa Bonita, C.R.	H10	92
Playa del Carmen, Mex.	G16	90
Playa Noriega, Laguna, l., Mex.	C4	90
Playas Lake, l., N.M., U.S.	M8	120
Playa Vicente, Mex.	I12	90
Play Cu, Viet.	H10	40
Playgreen Lake, l., Man., Can.	D16	104
Plaza, N.D., U.S.	C6	118
Plaza de Caisán, Pan.	I12	92
Plaza Huincul, Arg.	J4	80
Pleasant, Lake, res., Az., U.S.	K4	120
Pleasant, Mount, hill, N.B., Can.	G7	106
Pleasant Bay, N.S., Can.	F13	106
Pleasantdale, Sask., Can.	F10	104
Pleasant Gap, Pa., U.S.	G9	108
Pleasant Garden, N.C., U.S.	D7	112
Pleasant Grove, Ut., U.S.	D5	120
Pleasant Hill, Il., U.S.	C6	114
Pleasant Hill, La., U.S.	K3	114
Pleasant Hill, Mo., U.S.	D2	114
Pleasanton, Ks., U.S.	M13	118
Pleasanton, Tx., U.S.	K8	116
Pleasant Plains, Il., U.S.	C7	114
Pleasantville, Ia., U.S.	I2	110
Pleasantville, N.J., U.S.	H12	108
Pleasantville, Pa., U.S.	F7	108
Plechanovo, Russia	G20	22
Pléneuf, Fr.	D4	14
Plenty, Sask., Can.	G6	104
Plenty, Bay of, b., N.Z.	B6	72
Plentywood, Mt., U.S.	C3	118
Pleščenicy, Bela.	G10	22
Pleseck, Russia	E6	26
Plessisville, Que., Can.	A15	108
Pleszew, Pol.	D17	10
Plétipi, Lac, l., Que., Can.	F18	96
Pleven, Bul.	F8	20
Plevna, Mt., U.S.	E3	118
Pljevlja, Yugo.	F3	20
Płock, Pol.	C19	10
Plöckenpass, Eur.	I12	10
Ploërmel, Fr.	E4	14
Ploești see Ploiești, Rom.	E10	20
Ploiești, Rom.	E10	20
Plomárion, Grc.	K10	20
Plön, Ger.	A10	10
Plonge, Lac la, l., Sask., Can.	C7	104
Płońsk, Pol.	C20	10
Pl'os, Russia	D24	22
Ploskoje, Russia	I21	22
Plottier, Arg.	J4	80
Plouay, Fr.	E3	14
Ploudalmézeau, Fr.	D2	14
Plouguenast, Fr.	D4	14
Plouha, Fr.	D4	14
Plovdiv, Bul.	G8	20
Plover, stm., Wi., U.S.	F6	110
Plumas, Man., Can.	H15	104
Plumerville, Ar., U.S.	G4	114
Plummer, Id., U.S.	C9	122
Plumtree, Zimb.	C8	66
Plungė, Lith.	F4	22
Pl'ussa, Russia	C12	22
Pl'ussa, stm., Russia	C11	22
Plutarco Elías Calles, Presa, res., Mex.	C5	90
Plymouth, Monts.	F13	94
Plymouth, Eng., U.K.	K9	8
Plymouth, Ca., U.S.	F5	124
Plymouth, Il., U.S.	B6	114
Plymouth, In., U.S.	A10	114
Plymouth, Ma., U.S.	F16	108
Plymouth, Ne., U.S.	K11	118
Plymouth, N.H., U.S.	D15	108
Plymouth, N.C., U.S.	D10	112
Plymouth, Oh., U.S.	F4	108
Plymouth, Pa., U.S.	F11	108
Plymouth, Wi., U.S.	G8	110
Plzeň, Czech.	F13	10
Pô, Burkina	F9	64
Po, stm., Italy	E7	18
Poana, stm., Braz.	G14	84
Poás, Volcán, vol., C.R.	G10	92
Pobé, Benin	H11	64
Pobeda, gora, mtn., Russia	D21	28
Pobeda Ice Island, i., Ant.	B6	73
Pobedino, Russia	H20	28
Pobedy, pik, mtn., Asia	I14	26
Pocahontas, Ar., U.S.	F6	114
Pocahontas, Il., U.S.	D7	114
Pocahontas, Ia., U.S.	I13	118
Pocatalico, stm., W.V., U.S.	I5	108
Pocatello, Id., U.S.	H13	122
Počep, Russia	I16	22
Pöchlarn, Aus.	G15	10
Pochvistnevo, Russia	G8	26
Počinok, Russia	G15	22
Pocitos, Salar, pl., Arg.	C5	80
Pocoata, Bol.	H8	82
Poções, Braz.	C8	79
Pocola, Ok., U.S.	G2	114
Pocomoke, stm., U.S.	J11	108
Pocomoke City, Md., U.S.	I11	108
Pocona, Bol.	G9	82
Poconé, Braz.	G13	82
Pocono Mountains, hills, Pa., U.S.	F11	108
Pocono Summit, Pa., U.S.	F11	108
Poços de Caldas, Braz.	F5	79
Pocrane, Braz.	E8	79
Pocrí, Pan.	I14	92
Podberezje, Russia	E13	22
Podborovje, Russia	B18	22
Poddorje, Russia	D14	22
Poděbrady, Czech.	E15	10
Podgorica, Yugo.	G3	20
Podkamennaja Tunguska, stm., Russia	E11	28
Podol'sk, Russia	F20	22
Podor, Maur.	C2	64
Podoz'orskij, Russia	D23	22
Podporožje, Russia	E4	26
Podravska Slatina, Cro.	D1	20
Podsvilje, Bela.	F10	22
Podujevo, Yugo.	G5	20
Podu Turcului, Rom.	C11	20
Pofadder, S. Afr.	G4	66
Pogan, China	G5	34
Pogar, Russia	I16	22
Poggibonsi, Italy	F6	18
Pogoanele, Rom.	E11	20
Pogoreloje Gorodišče, Russia	E17	22
Pogost, Bela.	H12	22
Pograničnyj, Russia	I18	28
P'ohang, S. Kor.	G17	32
Pohénégamook, Que., Can.	E4	106
Pohjois-Karjalan lääni, prov., Fin.	J21	6
Poinsett, Cape, c., Ant.	B6	73
Point, Tx., U.S.	G11	116
Point Arena, Ca., U.S.	F2	124
Point Au Fer Island, i., La., U.S.	M5	114
Point Comfort, Tx., U.S.	K10	116
Pointe-à-la-Frégate, Que., Can.	C9	106
Pointe-à-la-Garde, Que., Can.	D7	106
Pointe a la Hache, La., U.S.	M7	114
Pointe-à-Maurier, Que., Can.	B14	106
Pointe-à-Pitre, Guad.	F14	94
Point Edward, Ont., Can.	G13	110
Pointe-Noire, Congo	B2	58
Point Fortin, Trin.	I14	94
Point Hope, Ak., U.S.	B11	100
Point Imperial, mtn., Az., U.S.	H5	120
Point Lake, l., N.W. Ter., Can.	C10	96
Point Leamington, Newf., Can.	C18	106
Point Marion, Pa., U.S.	H7	108
Point Pelee National Park, Ont., Can.	I13	110
Point Pleasant, N.J., U.S.	G12	108
Point Pleasant, W.V., U.S.	I4	108
Point Sapin, N.B., Can.	F9	106
Poisson Blanc, Réservoir du, res., Que., Can.	A11	108
Poissy, Fr.	D9	14
Poitiers, Fr.	F7	14
Poix, Fr.	C8	14
Pojarkovo, Russia	H17	28
Pojo, Bol.	G9	82
Pojoaque Valley, N.M., U.S.	I10	120
Pojuca, Braz.	B9	79
Pojuca, stm., Braz.	B9	79
Pokharā, Nepal	F10	44
Pokrov, Russia	F22	22
Pokrovsk, Russia	E17	28
Pokrovskoje, Russia	I19	22
Pola, Russia	D14	22
Polacca, Az., U.S.	I6	120
Pola de Lena, Spain	B6	16
Polān, Iran	I16	48
Polanco, Ur.	G11	80
Poland (Polska), ctry., Eur.	E11	4
Polanów, Pol.	A16	10
Pol'arnyj, Russia	D4	26
Polatlı, Tur.	B2	48
Polcura, Chile	I3	80
Pol-e Khomrī, Afg.	C3	44
Polesje, reg., Eur.	G3	26
Polessk [Labiau], Russia	G4	22
Polevskoj, Russia	F10	26
Polgár, Hung.	H21	10
Pŏlgyo, S. Kor.	I15	32
Police, Pol.	B14	10
Poligny, Fr.	F12	14
Pólis, Cyp.	D2	48
Polistena, Italy	K11	18
Políyiros, Grc.	I7	20
Polk, Ne., U.S.	J10	118
Polk, Pa., U.S.	F7	108
Polkton, N.C., U.S.	D6	112
Polla, Italy	I10	18
Pollāchi, India	G4	46
Pöllau, Aus.	H15	10
Pollock, La., U.S.	K4	114
Pollock, S.D., U.S.	F7	118
Pol'noje-Jaltunovo, Russia	H24	22
Polo, Il., U.S.	I6	110
Polo, Mo., U.S.	C2	114
Polochic, stm., Guat.	B5	92
Polock, Bela.	F11	22
Polonio, Cabo, c., Ur.	H12	80
Polonnaruwa, Sri L.	I6	46
Polotn'anyj, Russia	G19	22
Polson, Mt., U.S.	C11	122
Poltava, Ukr.	H4	26
Poltimore, Que., Can.	B11	108
Põltsamaa, Est.	C8	22
Poluj, stm., Russia	D11	26
Polunočnoje, Russia	E10	26
Polynesia, is., Oc.	I24	126
Polysajevo, Russia	G15	26
Pomabamba, Peru	C3	82
Pomacanchi, Peru	F6	82
Pomata, Peru	G7	82
Pombal, Port.	F3	16
Pomene, Moz.	D12	66
Pomerania, hist. reg., Pol.	A16	10
Pomeranian Bay, b., Eur.	A14	10
Pomerene, Az., U.S.	M6	120
Pomerode, Braz.	D14	80
Pomeroon, stm., Guy.	D13	84
Pomeroy, Ia., U.S.	I13	118
Pomeroy, Oh., U.S.	H4	108
Pomeroy, Wa., U.S.	D8	122
Pomme de Terre, stm., Mn., U.S.	F11	118
Pomme de Terre, stm., Mo., U.S.	E3	114
Pomona, Ca., U.S.	J8	124
Pomona, Ks., U.S.	M12	118
Pomona Park, Fl., U.S.	J5	112
Pompano Beach, Fl., U.S.	M6	112
Pompei, hist., Italy	I9	18
Pompéia, Braz.	G3	79
Pompéu, Braz.	E6	79
Pompton Lakes, N.J., U.S.	F12	108
Pomquet, N.S., Can.	G12	106
Ponask Lake, l., Ont., Can.	D22	104
Ponass Lakes, l., Sask., Can.	F11	104
Ponca, Ne., U.S.	I11	118
Ponca City, Ok., U.S.	C9	116
Ponce, P.R.	E11	94
Ponce de Leon, Fl., U.S.	L11	114
Ponchatoula, La., U.S.	L6	114
Pond, stm., Ky., U.S.	E9	114
Pondcreek, Ok., U.S.	C9	116
Pondicherry, India	G5	46
Pondicherry, ter., India	G5	46
Pond Inlet, N.W. Ter., Can.	B17	96
Pond Inlet, b., N.W. Ter., Can.	B17	96
Pondoland, hist. reg., S. Afr.	H9	66
Pondosa, Ca., U.S.	C4	124
Ponferrada, Spain	C5	16
Ponhook Lake, l., N.S., Can.	H9	106
Ponnūru Nidubrolu, India	D6	46
Ponoj, stm., Russia	D5	26
Ponoka, Alta., Can.	E21	102
Ponorogo, Indon.	j15	39a
Pons, Fr.	G6	14
Ponta do Sol, Port.	m20	17a
Ponta Grossa, Braz.	C13	80
Pontalina, Braz.	D4	79
Ponta Porã, Braz.	G1	79
Pontarlier, Fr.	F13	14
Pontassieve, Italy	F6	18
Pont-Audemer, Fr.	C7	14
Pont-Aven, Fr.	E3	14
Pont Canavese, Italy	D2	18
Pontchartrain, Lake, l., La., U.S.	L6	114
Pont-d'Ain, Fr.	F12	14
Pont-de-Vaux, Fr.	F11	14
Ponte Alta do Bom Jesus, Braz.	B5	79
Ponte Branca, Braz.	D2	79
Pontedera, Italy	F5	18
Ponteix, Sask., Can.	I7	104
Ponte Nova, Braz.	F7	79
Ponte Serrada, Braz.	D13	80
Pontevedra, Spain	C3	16
Ponte Vedra Beach, Fl., U.S.	I5	112
Pontiac, Il., U.S.	J7	110
Pontiac, Mi., U.S.	H12	110
Pontianak, Indon.	F4	38
Pontivy, Fr.	D4	14
Pont-l'Abbé, Fr.	E2	14
Pont-l'Évêque, Fr.	C7	14
Pontoise, Fr.	C9	14
Pontorson, Fr.	D5	14
Pontotoc, Ms., U.S.	H8	114
Pontotoc, Tx., U.S.	I8	116
Pontremoli, Italy	E4	18
Pontresina, Switz.	F12	13
Ponts, Spain	D13	16
Pont-sur-Yonne, Fr.	D10	14
Pontypridd, Wales, U.K.	J10	8
Pony, Mt., U.S.	E14	122
Ponyri, Russia	I19	22
Ponziane, Isole, is., Italy	I7	18
Poole, Eng., U.K.	K12	8
Pooler, Ga., U.S.	G5	112
Pooley Island, i., B.C., Can.	E6	102
Pool's Cove, Newf., Can.	E18	106
Poolville, Tx., U.S.	G9	116
Poona see Pune, India	C2	46
Poopo, Bol.	H8	82
Poopó, Lago, l., Bol.	H8	82
Poor Man Indian Reserve, Sask., Can.	G10	104
Popa, Isla, i., Pan.	H12	92
Popayán, Col.	F4	84
Pope, Ms., U.S.	H7	114
Poperinge, Bel.	G2	12
Popham Bay, b., N.W. Ter., Can.	D19	96
Popigaj, stm., Russia	C14	28
Popiltah Lake, l., Austl.	I4	70
Poplar, Mt., U.S.	C2	118
Poplar, Wi., U.S.	D4	110
Poplar, stm., Can.	F18	104
Poplar, stm., Mn., U.S.	D11	118
Poplar Bluff, Mo., U.S.	F6	114
Poplar Hill, Ont., Can.	F20	104
Poplar Point, Man., Can.	H17	104
Poplarville, Ms., U.S.	L7	114
Poplevinskij, Russia	H22	22
Popocatépetl, Volcán, vol., Mex.	H10	90
Popokabaka, Zaire	C3	58
Popoli, Italy	G8	18
Popondetta, Pap. N. Gui.	m16	68a
Popovo, Bul.	F10	20
Poppel, Bel.	F7	12
Poppi, Italy	F6	18
Popple, stm., Wi., U.S.	E7	110
Poprad, Slov.	F20	10
Poprad, stm., Eur.	F20	10
Pŏptong, N. Kor.	E15	32
Poptún, Guat.	A5	92
Poquoson, Va., U.S.	B10	112
Porangatu, Braz.	B4	79
Porbandar, India	J3	44
Porce, stm., Col.	D5	84
Porcher Island, i., B.C., Can.	D4	102
Porchov, Russia	D12	22
Porciúncula, Braz.	F7	79
Porco, Bol.	H9	82
Porcos, Rio dos, stm., Braz.	B6	79
Porcuna, Spain	H7	16
Porcupine, stm., N.A.	C23	100
Porcupine Hills, hills, Can.	F13	104
Pordenone, Italy	D7	18
Porecatu, Braz.	G3	79
Porečje, Bela.	H7	22
Porečje Rybnoje, Russia	D22	22
Pori, Fin.	K17	6
Porlamar, Ven.	B11	84
Poroma, Bol.	H9	82
Poronajsk, Russia	H20	28
Poroshkove, Ukr.	G22	10
Porosozero, Russia	J23	6
Porozovo, Bela.	I7	22
Porpoise Bay, b., Ant.	B7	73
Porrentruy, Switz.	D7	13
Portachuelo, Bol.	G10	82
Port Adelaide, Austl.	J3	70
Portadown, N. Ire., U.K.	G7	8
Portage, Mi., U.S.	H10	110
Portage, Ut., U.S.	C4	120
Portage, Wi., U.S.	G6	110
Portage, stm., Oh., U.S.	F3	108
Portage Bay, b., Man., Can.	G16	104
Portage-la-Prairie, Man., Can.	I16	104
Portageville, Mo., U.S.	F7	114
Portal, Ga., U.S.	G5	112
Portal, N.D., U.S.	C5	118
Port Alberni, B.C., Can.	H10	102
Portal del Infierno, wtfl, Hond.	C9	92
Portales, N.M., U.S.	E3	116
Port Alfred (Kowie), S. Afr.	I8	66
Port Alice, B.C., Can.	G7	102
Port Allegany, Pa., U.S.	F8	108
Port Allen, La., U.S.	L5	114
Port Angeles, Wa., U.S.	B2	122
Port Anson, Newf., Can.	C18	106
Port Antonio, Jam.	E6	94
Port Aransas, Tx., U.S.	L9	116
Port Arthur, Austl.	N7	70
Port Arthur see Thunder Bay, Ont., Can.	B6	110
Port Arthur see Lüshun, China	E9	32
Port Arthur, Tx., U.S.	M3	114
Port Augusta, Austl.	I2	70
Port au Port, Newf., Can.	D15	106
Port au Port Bay, b., Newf., Can.	D15	106
Port au Port Peninsula, pen., Newf., Can.	D14	106
Port-au-Prince, Haiti	E8	94
Port-au-Prince, Baie de, b., Haiti	E8	94
Port Austin, Mi., U.S.	F13	110
Port-aux-Basques see Channel-Port-aux-Basques, Newf., Can.	E14	106
Port Barre, La., U.S.	L5	114
Port-Bergé, Madag.	o22	67b
Port Blair, India	I2	40
Port Blandford, Newf., Can.	D19	106
Port Borden, P.E.I., Can.	F10	106
Port-Bouët, C. Iv.	I8	64
Port Broughton, Austl.	I2	70
Port Byron, Il., U.S.	I5	110
Port Canning, India	I13	44
Port-Cartier, Que., Can.	B7	106
Port-Cartier Sept-Îles, Réserve, Que., Can.	B6	106
Port Chalmers, N.Z.	F3	72
Port Charlotte, Fl., U.S.	M4	112
Port Chester, N.Y., U.S.	F13	108
Port Clements, B.C., Can.	D2	102
Port Clinton, Oh., U.S.	F4	108
Port Clyde, Me., U.S.	D17	108
Port Colborne, Ont., Can.	H16	110
Port Coquitlam, B.C., Can.	H12	102
Port Credit, Ont., Can.	G16	110
Port-Daniel, Réserve, Que., Can.	D9	106
Port-de-Paix, Haiti	E8	94
Port Dickson, Malay.	M6	40
Port Dover, Ont., Can.	H15	110
Porte Crayon, Mount, mtn., W.V., U.S.	I7	108
Port Edward, B.C., Can.	C4	102
Port Edward, S. Afr.	H10	66
Port Edwards, Wi., U.S.	F6	110
Portegolpe, C.R.	G9	92
Porteirinha, Braz.	C7	79
Portel, Braz.	D8	76
Port Elgin, N.B., Can.	F9	106
Port Elgin, Ont., Can.	F14	110
Port Elizabeth, S. Afr.	I7	66
Port-en-Bessin, Fr.	C6	14
Porter, Ok., U.S.	D11	116
Porter, Tx., U.S.	I11	116
Porter Lake, l., Sask., Can.	B7	104
Porterville, Ca., U.S.	H6	124
Porterville, Ms., U.S.	J8	114
Port Essington, B.C., Can.	C5	102
Portete, Bahía, b., Col.	A6	84
Port Fairy, Austl.	L5	70
Port Gamble, Wa., U.S.	C3	122
Port Gentil, Gabon	B1	58
Port Germein, Austl.	I3	70
Port Gibson, Ms., U.S.	K6	114
Port Graham, Ak., U.S.	G19	100
Port Greville, N.S., Can.	G9	106
Port Harcourt, Nig.	I13	64
Port Hardy, B.C., Can.	G7	102
Port Hawkesbury, N.S., Can.	G12	106
Port Hedland, Austl.	D3	68
Port Henry, N.Y., U.S.	C13	108
Port Hill, P.E.I., Can.	F10	106
Port Hood, N.S., Can.	F12	106
Port Hope, Ont., Can.	G17	110
Port Hope, Mi., U.S.	G13	110
Port Howe, Bah.	B7	94
Port Huron, Mi., U.S.	H13	110
Port-İliç, Azer.	B10	48
Portimão, Port.	H3	16
Port Isabel, Tx., U.S.	M9	116
Port Jervis, N.Y., U.S.	F12	108
Port Kembla, Austl.	J9	70
Portland, Austl.	I9	70
Portland, Austl.	L4	70
Portland, Ar., U.S.	I5	114
Portland, In., U.S.	B12	114
Portland, Me., U.S.	D16	108
Portland, Mi., U.S.	H11	110
Portland, N.D., U.S.	D10	118
Portland, Or., U.S.	E3	122
Portland, Tn., U.S.	F10	114
Portland, Tx., U.S.	L9	116
Portland, Bill of, c., Eng., U.K.	K11	8
Portland, Cape, c., Austl.	M7	70
Portland Bay, b., Austl.	L4	70
Portland Bight, Jam.	F6	94
Portland Canal, b., N.A.	B4	102
Portland Creek Pond, l., Newf., Can.	B16	106
Portland Inlet, b., B.C., Can.	C4	102
Portland Point, c., Jam.	F6	94
Port Laoise, Ire.	H6	8
Port Lavaca, Tx., U.S.	K10	116
Port Leyden, N.Y., U.S.	D11	108
Port Lincoln, Austl.	J1	70
Port Lions, Ak., U.S.	H18	100
Port Loko, S.L.	G3	64
Port-Louis, Fr.	E3	14
Port Louis, Mrts.	v18	67c
Port Macquarie, Austl.	H10	70
Port Maitland, N.S., Can.	I7	106
Port Maria, Jam.	E6	94
Port McNeill, B.C., Can.	G7	102
Port McNicoll, Ont., Can.	F16	110
Port Mellon, B.C., Can.	H11	102
Port-Menier, Que., Can.	C9	106
Port Moody, B.C., Can.	H12	102
Port Moresby, Pap. N. Gui.	m16	68a
Port Morien, N.S., Can.	F14	106
Port Mouton, N.S., Can.	I9	106
Port Neches, Tx., U.S.	M3	114
Port Nelson, Man., Can.	A22	104
Portneuf, stm., Que., Can.	D4	106
Portneuf, stm., Id., U.S.	H13	122
Portneuf, Lac, l., Que., Can.	C3	106
Portneuf-sur-Mer, Que., Can.	D4	106
Port Neville, B.C., Can.	G8	102
Port Nolloth, S. Afr.	G3	66
Port Norris, N.J., U.S.	H11	108
Porto, Port.	D3	16
Porto Acre, Braz.	C8	82
Porto Alegre, Braz.	F13	80
Porto Amboim, Ang.	D2	58
Porto Belo, Braz.	D14	80
Portobelo, Pan.	C3	84
Port O'Connor, Tx., U.S.	K10	116
Porto de Moz, Braz.	D8	76
Porto de Pedras, Braz.	E11	76
Porto Empedocle, Italy	L8	18
Porto Esperança, Braz.	H13	82
Porto Esperidião, Braz.	F12	82
Porto Farina, Tun.	L5	18
Porto Feliz, Braz.	G5	79
Porto Ferreira, Braz.	F5	79
Port of Spain, Trin.	I14	94
Portogruaro, Italy	D7	18
Porto Inglês, C.V.	m17	64a
Portola, Ca., U.S.	E5	124
Porto Lucena, Braz.	D11	80
Pörtom (Pirttikylä), Fin.	J17	6
Porto Mendes, Braz.	C11	80
Porto Murtinho, Braz.	I13	82
Porto Nacional, Braz.	F9	76
Porto-Novo, Benin	H11	64
Port Orange, Fl., U.S.	J6	112
Port Orchard, Wa., U.S.	C3	122
Porto Recanati, Italy	F8	18
Port Orford, Or., U.S.	H1	122
Porto San Giorgio, Italy	F8	18
Porto Santo, i., Port.	I21	17a
Porto São José, Braz.	G2	79
Porto Seguro, Braz.	D9	79
Porto-Séguro, Togo	H10	64
Porto Torres, Italy	I3	18
Porto União, Braz.	D13	80
Porto Válter, Braz.	C5	82
Porto-Vecchio, Fr.	m24	15a
Porto Velho, Braz.	C10	82
Portoviejo, Ec.	H2	84
Port Perry, Ont., Can.	F17	110
Port Phillip Bay, b., Austl.	L6	70
Port Pirie, Austl.	I3	70
Port Rexton, Newf., Can.	D20	106
Port Richey, Fl., U.S.	K4	112
Port Rowan, Ont., Can.	H15	110
Port Royal, Pa., U.S.	G9	108
Port Royal, S.C., U.S.	G6	112
Port Royal National Historic Park, N.S., Can.	H8	106
Port Said see Būr Saʿīd, Egypt	B7	60
Port Saint Joe, Fl., U.S.	J1	112
Port Saint Johns, S. Afr.	H9	66
Port Saint Lucie, Fl., U.S.	L6	112
Port-Saint-Servan, Que., Can.	A15	106
Port Sanilac, Mi., U.S.	G13	110
Port Saunders, Newf., Can.	B16	106
Portsea, Austl.	L6	70
Port Shepstone, S. Afr.	H10	66
Portsmouth, Eng., U.K.	K12	8
Portsmouth, N.H., U.S.	D16	108
Portsmouth, Oh., U.S.	I4	108
Portsmouth, Va., U.S.	C10	112
Portsoy, Scot., U.K.	D11	8
Port Stanley, Ont., Can.	H14	110
Port Sudan see Būr Sūdān, Sud.	H9	60
Port Sulphur, La., U.S.	M7	114
Port Talbot, Wales, U.K.	J10	8
Port Taufiq see Būr Tawfīq, Egypt	G2	48
Porttipahdan tekojärvi, res., Fin.	G20	6
Port Townsend, Wa., U.S.	B3	122
Portugal, ctry., Eur.	H6	4
Portugal, Cachoeira, wtfl, Braz.	C9	82
Portugal Cove South, Newf., Can.	F20	106
Portugalete, Spain	B8	16
Portuguesa, state, Ven.	C8	84
Portuguesa, stm., Ven.	C9	84
Portuguese Guinea see Guinea-Bissau, ctry., Afr.	F3	54
Port Union, Newf., Can.	D20	106
Port-Vendres, Fr.	J10	14
Portville, N.Y., U.S.	E8	108
Port Wakefield, Austl.	J3	70
Port Wakefield, Ak., U.S.	G18	100
Port Washington, Wi., U.S.	G8	110
Port Wentworth, Ga., U.S.	G5	112
Port Wing, Wi., U.S.	D4	110
Porum, Ok., U.S.	D11	116
Porvenir, Chile	G2	78
Porvenir, Mex.	B7	90
Porzuna, Spain	F7	16
Posada, Italy	I4	18
Posadas, Arg.	D11	80
Posadas, Spain	H6	16
Poschiavo, Switz.	F13	13
Pošechon'e, Russia	C22	22
Posen see Poznań, Pol.	C16	10
Posen, Mi., U.S.	E12	110
Positano, Italy	I9	18
Posjet, Russia	I18	28
Posse, Braz.	C5	79
Possession Islands, is., Ant.	C8	73
Pössneck, Ger.	E11	10
Possum Kingdom Lake, res., Tx., U.S.	G8	116
Post, Tx., U.S.	F5	116
Postavy, Bela.	F9	22
Poste-de-la-Baleine, Que., Can.	E17	96
Postelle, Tn., U.S.	D2	112
Poste Ramartina, Madag.	q21	67b
Post Falls, Id., U.S.	C9	122
Postojna, Slo.	D9	18
P'ostraja Dresva, Russia	E23	28
Postrevalle, Bol.	H10	82
Postville, Ia., U.S.	G4	110
Pótam, Mex.	D4	90
Potaro, stm., Guy.	E13	84
Potaro Landing, Guy.	E13	84
Poté, Braz.	D8	79
Poteau, Ok., U.S.	G2	114
Poteau, stm., U.S.	G2	114
Poteet, Tx., U.S.	J8	116
Potenza, Italy	I10	18
Potes, Spain	B7	16
Potgietersrus, S. Afr.	E9	66
Poth, Tx., U.S.	J8	116
Potholes Reservoir, res., Wa., U.S.	C6	122
Poti, Geor.	I6	26
Poti, stm., Braz.	E10	76
Potiraguá, Braz.	C9	79
Potirendaba, Braz.	F4	79
Potiskum, Nig.	F9	54
Potlatch, Id., U.S.	D9	122
Potomac, Il., U.S.	B9	114
Potomac, stm., U.S.	I10	108
Potomac Heights, Md., U.S.	I9	108
Potosí, Bol.	H9	82
Potosi, Mo., U.S.	E6	114
Potosí, dept., Bol.	I8	82
Potrerillos, Chile	D4	80
Potrerillos, Hond.	B7	92
Potrerillos Arriba, Pan.	I12	92
Potrero, C.R.	G9	92
Potrero Grande, C.R.	H11	92
Potro, Cerro del, mtn., S.A.	E4	80
Potsdam, Ger.	C13	10
Potsdam, N.Y., U.S.	C12	108
Potter, Ne., U.S.	J4	118
Potterville, Mi., U.S.	H11	110
Potts Camp, Ms., U.S.	H7	114
Pottstown, Pa., U.S.	G11	108
Pottsville, Pa., U.S.	G10	108
Potwin, Ks., U.S.	N10	118
P'otzu, Tai.	L9	34
Pouancé, Fr.	E5	14
Pouce-Coupe, B.C., Can.	B14	102
Pouce Coupé, stm., Can.	A15	102
Pouch Cove, Newf., Can.	E21	106
Poughkeepsie, N.Y., U.S.	F13	108
Poulan, Ga., U.S.	H3	112
Poulin-de-Courval, Lac, l., Que., Can.	D3	106
Poulsbo, Wa., U.S.	C3	122
Poultney, Vt., U.S.	D13	108
Poŭn, S. Kor.	G15	32
Pound, Va., U.S.	B4	112
Poundmaker Indian Reserve, Sask., Can.	F5	104
Pouso Alegre, Braz.	G6	79
Pouso Redondo, Braz.	D14	80
Poŭthĭsăt, Camb.	H7	40
Považská Bystrica, Slov.	F18	10
Povenec, Russia	J24	6
Póvoa de Varzim, Port.	D3	16
Povorino, Russia	G6	26
Povungnituk, Que., Can.	D17	96
Povungnituk, Rivière de, stm., Que., Can.	D18	96
Powassan, Ont., Can.	D16	110
Poway, Ca., U.S.	L8	124
Powder, stm., U.S.	B5	98
Powder, stm., Or., U.S.	F8	122
Powderly, Ky., U.S.	E9	114
Powderly, Tx., U.S.	F11	116
Powell, Wy., U.S.	F17	122
Powell, stm., U.S.	C3	112
Powell, Lake, res., U.S.	G6	120
Powell, Mount, mtn., Co., U.S.	E10	120
Powellhurst, Or., U.S.	E3	122
Powell Lake, l., B.C., Can.	G10	102
Powell River, B.C., Can.	H10	102
Powellton, W.V., U.S.	I5	108
Powers, Mi., U.S.	E8	110
Powers, Or., U.S.	H1	122
Powers Lake, N.D., U.S.	C5	118
Powhatan, La., U.S.	K3	114
Powhatan, Va., U.S.	B9	112
Powhatan Point, Oh., U.S.	H6	108
Powys, co., Wales, U.K.	I10	8
Poxoréo, Braz.	C1	79
Poyang Hu, l., China	F5	34
Poyen, Ar., U.S.	H4	114
Poygan, Lake, l., Wi., U.S.	F7	110
Poynette, Wi., U.S.	G6	110
Požarevac, Yugo.	E5	20
Poza Rica, Mex.	G11	90
Poznań, Pol.	C16	10
Pozo Almonte, Chile	I7	82
Pozoblanco, Spain	G7	16
Pozo Colorado, Para.	B9	80
Pozo del Molle, Arg.	G7	80
Pozo del Tigre, Arg.	C8	80
Pozo Hondo, Arg.	D6	80
Pozo Negro, Spain	o27	17b
Pozuelo de Alarcón, Spain	E8	16
Pozuelos, Ven.	B10	84
Pozuelos, Laguna, l., Arg.	B6	80
Pozuzo, Peru	D4	82
Pozuzo, stm., Peru	C4	82
Pozzallo, Italy	M9	18
Pozzuoli, Italy	I9	18
Prachin Buri, Thai.	G6	40
Prachuap Khiri Khan, Thai.	I5	40
Pradera, Col.	F4	84
Prades, Fr.	J9	14
Prado, Braz.	D9	79
Prados, Braz.	F6	79
Prague see Praha, Czech.	E14	10
Prague, Ne., U.S.	J11	118
Prague, Ok., U.S.	D10	116
Praha (Prague), Czech.	E14	10
Prahova, co., Rom.	D10	20
Praia, C.V.	m17	64a
Praia Grande, Braz.	E14	80
Prainha Nova, Braz.	B11	82
Prairie, stm., Mn., U.S.	C2	110
Prairie, stm., Wi., U.S.	E6	110
Prairie City, Il., U.S.	J5	110
Prairie City, Ia., U.S.	I2	110
Prairie City, Or., U.S.	F7	122
Prairie du Chien, Wi., U.S.	G4	110
Prairie du Sac, Wi., U.S.	G6	110
Prairie Grove, Ar., U.S.	G2	114
Prairie River, Sask., Can.	F11	104
Prairies, Lake of the, res., Can.	G13	104
Prairie View, Tx., U.S.	I11	116
Prairie Village, Ks., U.S.	M13	118
Prampram, Ghana	I10	64
Pran Buri, Thai.	H5	40
Praslin, Lac, l., Que., Can.	B4	106
Praslin Island, i., Sey.	B11	58
Prata, Braz.	E4	79
Prata, Rio da, stm., Braz.	D5	79
Prata, Rio da, stm., Braz.	E4	79
Pratāpgarh, India	H6	44
Pratápolis, Braz.	F5	79
Pratas Island see Tungsha Tao, i., Tai.	G10	30
Pratinha, Braz.	E5	79
Prato, Italy	F6	18
Pratt, Ks., U.S.	N9	118
Prattsburg, N.Y., U.S.	E9	108
Prattville, Al., U.S.	J10	114

Name	Map Ref.	Page

Name — Map Ref. — Page

Salto Grande, Braz. G4 79
Salton City, Ca., U.S. K10 124
Salton Sea, l., Ca., U.S. K10 124
Saltville, Va., U.S. C5 112
Saluda, S.C., U.S. E5 112
Saluda, Va., U.S. B10 112
Saluda, stm., S.C., U.S. E5 112
Sālūr, India C7 46
Saluzzo, Italy E2 18
Salvador, Braz. B9 79
Salvador, El see El Salvador, ctry., N.A. D6 92
Salvador, Lake, l., La., U.S. M6 114
Salvador Mazza, Arg. B7 80
Salvage, Newf., Can. D20 106
Salvaterra de Magos, Port. F3 16
Salvatierra, Mex. G9 90
Salwā, Dawhat, b., Asia I11 48
Salwā Baḥrī, Egypt E7 60
Salween (Nu) (Thanlwin), stm., Asia D5 40
Salyan, Azer. J7 26
Salyān, Nepal F10 44
Salyer, Ca., U.S. D2 124
Salyersville, Ky., U.S. B3 112
Salzach, stm., Eur. G12 10
Salzburg, Aus. H13 10
Salzburg, state, Aus. H13 10
Salzgitter, Ger. C10 10
Salzkammergut, reg., Aus. H13 10
Salzwedel, Ger. C11 10
Samā, Jord. D6 50
Sama, stm., Peru G6 82
Samacá, Col. E6 84
Sama [de Langreo], Spain B6 16
Samaipata, Bol. H10 82
Samalá, stm., Guat. C3 92
Sāmalkot, India D7 46
Samālūt, Egypt C6 60
Samambaia, stm., Braz. G2 79
Samaná, Dom. Rep. E10 94
Samaná, Bahía de, b., Dom. Rep. E10 94
Samaná, Cabo, c., Dom. Rep. E10 94
Samana Cay, i., Bah. C8 94
Samandağı, Tur. C3 48
Samaniego, Col. G4 84
Samar, Isr. I4 50
Samara (Kujbyšev), Russia G8 26
Samara, stm., Russia G8 26
Samarai, Pap. N. Gui. n17 68a
Samaria, Id., U.S. H13 122
Samariapo, Ven. E9 84
Samarinda, Indon. F6 38
Samarkand, Uzb. J11 26
Sāmarrā', Iraq D7 48
Samastīpur, India H11 44
Samaúna, Braz. B11 82
Şamaxı, Azer. A10 48
Sambalpur, India J10 44
Sambas, Indon. N10 40
Sambava, Madag. o24 67b
Sambawizi, Zimb. B8 66
Sambhal, India F8 44
Sāmbhar, India G6 44
Sambir, Ukr. F23 10
Sâmbor, Camb. H8 40
Samborombón, stm., Arg. H10 80
Samborombón, Bahía, b., Arg. I10 80
Samborondón, Ec. H3 84
Sambre, stm., Eur. B11 14
Sambú, stm., Pan. C3 84
Sambusu, Nmb. A4 66
Samch'ŏk, S. Kor. F17 32
Samch'ŏnp'o, S. Kor. I16 32
Samedan, Switz. E12 13
Samho, N. Kor. D15 32
Samiria, stm., Peru J5 84
Samnaungruppe, mts., Eur. D13 13
Samnye, S. Kor. H15 32
Samoa Islands, is., Oc. J22 126
Samo Alto, Chile F3 80
Samoded, Russia E6 26
Sámos, Grc. L11 20
Sámos, i., Grc. L10 20
Samoset, Fl., U.S. L4 112
Samosir, Pulau, i., Indon. M5 40
Samothrace see Samothráki, i., Grc. I9 20
Samothráki (Samothrace), i., Grc. I9 20
S'amozero, Russia K23 6
Sampacho, Arg. G6 80
Sampit, Indon. F5 38
Sampués, Col. C5 84
Sampur, Russia I24 22
Sam Rayburn Reservoir, res., Tx., U.S. K2 114
Samre, Eth. K10 60
Samreboi, Ghana I8 64
Samson, Al., U.S. K10 114
Samson Indian Reserve, Alta., Can. E21 102
Samsun, Tur. G15 4
Samtown, La., U.S. K4 114
Samuhú, Arg. D8 80
Samui, Ko, i., Thai. J6 40
Samut Prakan, Thai. H6 40
Samut Sakhon, Thai. H6 40
Samut Songkhram, Thai. H6 40
S'amža, Russia A24 22
San, Mali E7 64
San (Xan), stm., Asia H9 40
San, stm., Eur. E22 10
Saña, Peru B2 82
Şan'ā', Yemen G4 47
Sanaba, stm., Afr. D4 64
Sanaga, stm., Cam. J14 64
San Agustín, Arg. J9 80
San Agustín, Arg. F6 80
San Agustín, Col. G4 84
San Agustín de Valle Fértil, Arg. F5 80
San Alejo, El Sal. D7 92
Sanalona, Presa, res., Mex. E6 90
San Ambrosio, Isla, i., Chile B1 78
Sanana, Pulau, i., Indon. F8 38
Sanandaj, Iran D9 48
Sanandita, Bol. I10 82
San Andreas, Ca., U.S. F5 124
San Andrés, Col. H4 94
San Andrés, Mex. D2 90
San Andrés, Pan. I12 92
San Andrés, Isla de, i., Col. H4 94
San Andrés de Giles, Arg. H9 80
San Andres Mountains, mts., N.M., U.S. L10 120
San Andrés Sajcabajá, Guat. B4 92
San Andrés Tuxtla, Mex. H12 90
San Andrés y Providencia, ter., Col. H4 94
Sananduva, Braz. D13 80
San Angelo, Tx., U.S. H6 116
San Anselmo, Ca., U.S. G3 124
San Antero, Col. C5 84
San Antonio, Arg. C6 80
San Antonio, Arg. E6 80
San Antonio, Belize A5 92
San Antonio, Chile D3 80
San Antonio, Chile G3 80
San Antonio, Col. F5 84
San Antonio, C.R. G9 92
San Antonio, Peru B3 82
San Antonio, N.M., U.S. I10 120
San Antonio, Tx., U.S. J8 116
San Antonio, Ur. F10 80
San Antonio, stm., Mex. B2 90
San Antonio, stm., Tx., U.S. K9 116
San Antonio, Cabo, c., Arg. I10 80
San Antonio, Cabo de, c., Cuba D2 94
San Antonio, Mount, mtn., Ca., U.S. J8 124
San Antonio, Punta, c., Mex. C2 90
San Antonio, Punta, c., Mex. D4 90
San Antonio, Río, stm., U.S. H10 120
San Antonio Bay, b., Tx., U.S. K10 116
San Antonio de Areco, Arg. H9 80
San Antonio de los Baños, Cuba C3 94
San Antonio de los Cobres, Arg. C5 80
San Antonio del Táchira, Ven. D6 84
San Antonio de Tamanaco, Ven. C9 84
San Antonio El Bravo, Mex. B7 90
San Antonio Mountain, mtn., N.M., U.S. H10 120
San Antonio Suchitepéquez, Guat. C3 92
Sanatorium, Ms., U.S. K7 114
San Augustine, Tx., U.S. K2 114
San Augustin Pass, N.M., U.S. L10 120
San Bartolomé, Spain n27 17b
San Benedetto del Tronto, Italy G8 18
San Benedicto, Isla, i., Mex. H4 90
San Benito, Bol. G9 82
San Benito, Guat. I15 90
San Benito, Peru B2 82
San Benito, Tx., U.S. M9 116
San Benito, stm., Ca., U.S. H4 124
San Bernardino, Switz. F11 13
San Bernardino, Ca., U.S. J8 124
San Bernardino Mountains, mts., Ca., U.S. J9 124
San Bernardo, Arg. D8 80
San Bernardo, Chile G3 80
San Bernardo, Mex. E7 90
San Bernardo, Isla, i., Nic. F9 92
San Bernardo, Islas de, is., Col. C4 84
San Bernardo del Viento, Col. C5 84
San Blas, Mex. G7 90
San Blas, Mex. D5 90
San Blas, Cape, c., Fl., U.S. J1 112
San Blas, Golfo de, b., Pan. C3 84
San Blas, Serranía De, mts., Pan. C3 84
San Blas de los Sauces, Arg. E5 80
San Borja, Bol. F8 82
Sanborn, Ia., U.S. H12 118
Sanborn, Mn., U.S. G12 118
Sanborn, N.D., U.S. E9 118
San Bruno, Ca., U.S. G3 124
San Buenaventura, Bol. F8 82
San Buenaventura, Mex. D9 90
Sancang, China C9 34
San Carlos, Arg. D11 80
San Carlos, Arg. G4 80
San Carlos, Arg. C6 80
San Carlos, Chile I3 80
San Carlos, Mex. C9 90
San Carlos, Mex. E10 90
San Carlos, Nic. F10 92
San Carlos, Pan. C3 84
San Carlos, Para. B10 80
San Carlos, Phil. C7 38
San Carlos, Phil. n19 39b
San Carlos, Az., U.S. K6 120
San Carlos, Ca., U.S. G3 124
San Carlos, Ur. H11 80
San Carlos, Ven. C8 84
San Carlos, stm., C.R. G10 92
San Carlos, stm., Ven. C8 84
San Carlos, Riacho, stm., Para. B9 80
San Carlos Centro, Arg. F8 80
San Carlos de Bariloche, Arg. E2 78
San Carlos de Bolívar, Arg. I8 80
San Carlos de Guaroa, Col. F6 84
San Carlos del Zulia, Ven. C7 84
San Carlos de Río Negro, Ven. G9 84
San Cataldo, Italy L8 18
San Cayetano, Arg. J9 80
Sancerre, Fr. E9 14
Sánchez, Dom. Rep. E10 94
Sanch'ŏng, S. Kor. H15 32
San Ciro de Acosta, Mex. G10 90
San Clemente, Spain F9 16
San Clemente, Ca., U.S. K8 124
San Clemente, Cerro, mtn., Chile F2 78
San Clemente Island, i., Ca., U.S. L7 124
San Cosme, Arg. D9 80
San Cristóbal, Arg. F8 80
San Cristóbal, Dom. Rep. E9 94
San Cristóbal, Ven. D6 84
San Cristóbal, Bahía, b., Mex. D2 90
San Cristóbal, Isla, i., Ec. j14 84a
San Cristóbal, Volcán, vol., Nic. E7 92
San Cristóbal de la Laguna, Spain o24 17b
San Cristóbal de las Casas, Mex. I13 90
San Cristóbal Totonicapán, Guat. C3 92
San Cristóbal Verapaz, Guat. B4 92
Sancti Spíritus, Cuba D5 94
Sancy, Puy de, mtn., Fr. G9 14
Sand, stm., Alta., Can. D3 104
San Damián, Peru E3 82
Sandaré, Mali D4 64
Sand Coulee, Mt., U.S. C14 122
Sanders, Az., U.S. I7 120
Sanderson, Tx., U.S. I4 116
Sandersville, Ga., U.S. G4 112
Sandersville, Ms., U.S. K7 114
Sandfly Lake, l., Sask., Can. C8 104
Sand Fork, W.V., U.S. I6 108
Sandgate, Austl. F10 70
Sand Hill, stm., Mn., U.S. D11 118
Sand Hills, hills, Ne., U.S. J6 118
Sandia, Peru F7 82
Sandia Crest, mtn., N.M., U.S. I10 120
San Diego, Ca., U.S. L8 124
San Diego, Tx., U.S. L8 116
San Diego, stm., Ca., U.S. L9 124
San Diego, Cabo, c., Arg. G3 78
San Diego Aqueduct, Ca., U.S. K8 124
San Diego de la Unión, Mex. G9 90
San Dionisio, Nic. E9 92
Sand Lake, l., Ont., Can. H20 104
Sandoa, Zaire C4 58
Sandomierz, Pol. E21 10
Sandoná, Col. G4 84
San Donà di Piave, Italy D7 18
Sandoval, Il., U.S. D7 114
Sandovalina, Braz. G3 79
Sandovo, Russia C19 22
Sandoway, Mya. E3 40
Sandpoint, Id., U.S. B9 122
Sandringham, Eng., U.K. I13 8
Sandspit, B.C., Can. D3 102
Sand Springs, Ok., U.S. C10 116
Sand Springs, Tx., U.S. G5 116
Sandston, Va., U.S. B9 112
Sandstone, Austl. E3 68
Sandstone, Mn., U.S. D3 110
Sandu Ao, b., China I8 34
Sandusky, Mi., U.S. G13 110
Sandusky, Oh., U.S. F4 108
Sandusky, stm., Oh., U.S. F3 108
Sandvika, Nor. L12 6
Sandviken, Swe. K15 6
Sandwich, Il., U.S. I7 110
Sandwich, Ma., U.S. F16 108
Sandwich Bay, b., Newf., Can. F21 96
Sandwick, B.C., Can. H10 102
Sandwīp Island, i., Bngl. I14 44
Sandy, Or., U.S. E3 122
Sandy, Ut., U.S. D5 120
Sandy, stm., Me., U.S. C17 108
Sandy Bay, b., Nic. C11 92
Sandy Bay Indian Reserve, Man., Can. H16 104
Sandy Cape, c., Austl. E10 70
Sandy Hook, Ky., U.S. A3 112
Sandy Hook, Ms., U.S. K7 114
Sandy Hook, spit, N.J., U.S. G12 108
Sandykači, Turk. J10 26
Sandy Lake, l., Newf., Can. C17 106
Sandy Lake, l., Ont., Can. E22 104
Sandy Point Town, St. K./N. F13 94
Sandy Springs, Ga., U.S. F2 112
San Elizario, Tx., U.S. M10 120
San Enrique, Arg. H8 80
San Estanislao, Para. C10 80
San Esteban, Hond. B9 92
San Esteban, Isla, i., Mex. C3 90
San Felipe, Chile G3 80
San Felipe, Col. G9 84
San Felipe, Mex. B2 90
San Felipe, Mex. G9 90
San Felipe, Phil. n19 39b
San Felipe, Ven. B8 84
San Felipe, Castillo de, hist., Guat. B5 92
San Felipe, Cayos de, is., Cuba D3 94
San Felipe de Vichayal, Peru A1 82
San Felipe Nuevo Mercurio, Mex. E8 90
San Felipe Pueblo, N.M., U.S. I10 120
San Félix, stm., Pan. I13 92
San Félix, Isla, i., Chile G6 74
San Fernando, Chile H3 80
San Fernando, Mex. E10 90
San Fernando, Phil. m19 39b
San Fernando, Phil. n19 39b
San Fernando, Spain I5 16
San Fernando, Trin. I14 94
San Fernando, Ca., U.S. J7 124
San Fernando, Ven. D9 84
San Fernando de Atabapo, Ven. E9 84
San Fernando del Valle de Catamarca, Arg. E6 80
Sanford, Co., U.S. G11 120
Sanford, Fl., U.S. K5 112
Sanford, Me., U.S. D16 108
Sanford, Mi., U.S. G11 110
Sanford, N.C., U.S. D7 112
Sanford, Tx., U.S. D5 116
Sanford, Mount, mtn., Ak., U.S. E22 100
San Francisco, Arg. F7 80
San Francisco, Col. G4 84
San Francisco, C.R. H9 92
San Francisco, El Sal. D6 92
San Francisco, Pan. I14 92
San Francisco, Ca., U.S. G3 124
San Francisco, stm., Arg. B6 80
San Francisco, stm., U.S. K8 120
San Francisco, Paso de, S.A. D4 80
San Francisco Bay, b., Ca., U.S. G3 124
San Francisco de Borja, Mex. D6 90
San Francisco de la Paz, Hond. C8 92
San Francisco del Chañar, Arg. E7 80
San Francisco del Monte de Oro, Arg. G5 80
San Francisco del Oro, Mex. D7 90
San Francisco del Rincón, Mex. G9 90
San Francisco de Macorís, Dom. Rep. E9 94
San Francisco de Mostazal, Chile G3 80
San Francisco Libre, Nic. E8 92
San Franco, Cerro, mtn., Hond. B7 92
San Gabriel, Ec. G4 84
San Gabriel, stm., Tx., U.S. I9 116
San Gabriel Chilac, Mex. H11 90
San Gabriel Mountains, mts., Ca., U.S. J7 124
Sangamner, India C3 46
Sangamon, stm., Il., U.S. B6 114
Sanga Puitã, Braz. G1 79
Sangay, vol., Ec. H3 84
Sangayán, Isla, i., Peru E3 82
Sangchungshih, Tai. J10 34
Sang-e Māsheh, Afg. D2 44
Sanger, Ca., U.S. H6 124
Sanger, Tx., U.S. F9 116
Sāngera, Mol. B12 20
Sangerhausen, Ger. D11 10
San Germán, Cuba D6 94
San Germán, P.R. E11 94
Sangerville, Me., U.S. B17 108
Sanggan, stm., China C9 30
Sangha, stm., Afr. A3 58
Sangihe, Kepulauan, is., Indon. E8 38
Sangihe, Pulau, i., Indon. E8 38
San Gil, Col. D6 84
San Gimignano, Italy F6 18
San Giovanni in Fiore, Italy J11 18
San Giovanni in Persiceto, Italy E6 18
San Giovanni Rotondo, Italy H10 18
San Giovanni Valdarno, Italy F6 18
Sangju, S. Kor. G16 32
Sāngli, India D3 46
Sangolquí, Ec. H3 84
San Gorgonio Mountain, mtn., Ca., U.S. J9 124
San Gottardo, Passo del, Switz. E10 13
Sangre de Cristo Mountains, mts., U.S. G11 120
San Gregorio, Arg. H7 80
San Gregorio, Ur. G11 80
Sangre Grande, Trin. I14 94
Sangrūr, India E6 44
Sanguandian, China D7 34
Sangudo, Alta., Can. D20 102
Sangue, Rio do, stm., Braz. D12 82
Sanhecun, China A17 32
San Hipólito, Punta, c., Mex. D3 90
Sanibel Island, i., Fl., U.S. M4 112
San Ignacio, Arg. D11 80
San Ignacio, C.R. H10 92
San Ignacio, Hond. C7 92
San Ignacio, Mex. D3 90
San Ignacio, Mex. F9 90
San Ignacio, Para. D10 80
San Ignacio, Isla, i., Mex. E5 90
San Ignacio, Laguna, l., Mex. D3 90
San Ignacio de Moxo, Bol. F9 82
San Ignacio de Velasco, Bol. G11 82
San Ildefonso, Cerro, mtn., Hond. B6 92
San Isidro, Arg. H9 80
San Isidro, Arg. E6 80
San Isidro, C.R. H11 92
San Isidro, Nic. E8 92
San Isidro, Tx., U.S. M8 116
San Jacinto, Col. C5 84
San Jacinto, Ca., U.S. K9 124
San Jacinto, West Fork, stm., Tx., U.S. I11 116
San Javier, Arg. D11 80
San Javier, Arg. F9 80
San Javier, Bol. F9 82
San Javier, Bol. G10 82
San Javier, Ur. G9 80
San Javier, stm., Arg. E9 80
San Javier de Loncomilla, Chile H3 80
Sanjāwi, Pak. E3 44
San Jerónimo, Guat. B4 92
San Jerónimo Norte, Arg. F8 80
Sanjō, Japan J13 36
San Joaquín, Bol. E9 82
San Joaquín, Para. C10 80
San Joaquín, stm., Bol. E10 82
San Joaquin, stm., Ca., U.S. G4 124
San Joaquin Valley, val., Ca., U.S. H5 124
San Jon, N.M., U.S. D3 116
San Jorge, Arg. F8 80
San Jorge, El Sal. D6 92
San Jorge, Nic. F9 92
San Jorge, stm., Col. C5 84
San Jorge, Bahía, b., Mex. B3 90
San Jorge, Golfo, b., Arg. F3 78
San José, Arg. D11 80
San José, C.R. H10 92
San José, Para. C10 80
San Jose, Phil. n19 39b
San Jose, Ca., U.S. G4 124
San Jose, Il., U.S. B7 114
San Jose, N.M., U.S. I11 120
San José, prov., C.R. H11 92
San Jose, stm., B.C., Can. F13 102
San José, Isla, i., Mex. E4 90
San José, Isla, i., Pan. C3 84
San Jose, Rio, stm., N.M., U.S. J9 120
San José Batuc, Mex. C5 90
San José Buena Vista, Guat. D4 92
San José de Bácum, Mex. D4 90
San José de Chiquitos, Bol. G11 82
San José de Copán, Hond. C6 92
San José de Feliciano, Arg. F9 80
San José de Guanipa, Ven. C10 84
San José de Guaribe, Ven. C10 84
San José de Jáchal, Arg. F4 80
San José de la Esquina, Arg. G8 80
San José de las Lajas, Cuba C3 94
San José de las Raíces, Mex. E9 90
San José del Cabo, Mex. F5 90
San José del Guaviare, Col. F6 84
San José de los Molinos, Peru E4 82
San José de Mayo, Ur. H10 80
San José de Ocuné, Col. E7 84
San José de Sisa, Peru B3 82
San José de Tiznados, Ven. C9 84
San Jose Island, i., Tx., U.S. K10 116
San Juan, Arg. F4 80
San Juan, Guat. B6 92
San Juan, Peru F4 82
San Juan, P.R. E11 94
San Juan, prov., Arg. F4 80
San Juan, stm., Arg. G5 80
San Juan, stm., Col. E4 84
San Juan, stm., Mex. E10 90
San Juan, stm., N.A. G10 92
San Juan, stm., Peru E4 82
San Juan, stm., S.A. G3 84
San Juan, stm., U.S. G6 120
San Juan, stm., Ven. B11 84
San Juan, Pico, mtn., Cuba D4 94
San Juan Bautista, Para. D10 80
San Juan Bautista, Ca., U.S. H4 124
San Juan Cotzal, Guat. B3 92
San Juan de Abajo, Mex. G7 90
San Juan de Colón, Ven. C6 84
San Juan de Guadalupe, Mex. E8 90
San Juan [de la Maguana], Dom. Rep. E9 94
San Juan del Cesar, Col. B6 84
San Juan del Norte, Nic. G11 92
San Juan del Oro, stm., Bol. I9 82
San Juan de los Cayos, Ven. B8 84
San Juan de los Morros, Ven. C9 84
San Juan del Río, Mex. E7 90
San Juan del Río, Mex. G9 90
San Juan del Sur, Nic. F9 92
San Juan de Micay, stm., Col. F4 84
San Juan de Payara, Ven. D9 84
San Juan Evangelista, Mex. I12 90
San Juanico, Mex. D3 90
San Juanillo, C.R. G9 92
San Juan Islands, is., Wa., U.S. B3 122
San Juanito, Isla, i., Mex. G6 90
San Juan Mountains, mts., Co., U.S. G9 120
San Juan Nepomuceno, Col. C5 84
San Juan Nepomuceno, Para. D11 80
San Juan Sacatepéquez, Guat. C4 92
San Juan Teotihuacán, Mex. H10 90
San Justo, Arg. F8 80
Sankarani, stm., Afr. F5 64
Sankosh, stm., Asia G14 44
Sankt Aegyd am Neuwalde, Aus. H15 10
Sankt Anton [am Arlberg], Aus. H10 10
Sankt Gallen, Aus. H14 10
Sankt Gallen, Switz. D11 13
Sankt Gallen, state, Switz. D11 13
Sankt Gilgen, Aus. H13 10
Sankt Goar, Ger. E7 10
Sankt Goarshausen, Ger. E7 10
Sankt Ingbert, Ger. F7 10
Sankt Johann im Pongau, Aus. H13 10
Sankt Johann in Tirol, Aus. H12 10
Sankt Moritz, Switz. E12 13
Sankt Niklaus, Switz. F8 13
Sankt Paul [im Lavanttal], Aus. I14 10
Sankt Peter, Ger. A8 10
Sankt-Peterburg (Saint Petersburg), Russia B13 22
Sankt Pölten, Aus. G15 10
Sankt Valentin, Aus. G14 10
Sankt Veit an der Glan, Aus. I14 10
Sankt Vith (Saint-Vith), Bel. H9 12
Sankt Wendel, Ger. F7 10
San Lázaro, Para. B10 80
San Lázaro, Cabo, c., Mex. E3 90
San Leandro, Ca., U.S. G3 124
Sanlicheng, China D3 34
Şanlıurfa, Tur. C5 48
San Lope, Col. D7 84
San Lorenzo, Arg. E9 80
San Lorenzo, Arg. G8 80
San Lorenzo, Bol. I9 82
San Lorenzo, Ec. G3 84
San Lorenzo, Hond. D7 92
San Lorenzo, Mex. E8 90
San Lorenzo, Nic. E9 92
San Lorenzo, Ven. C7 84
San Lorenzo, stm., Mex. E6 90
San Lorenzo, Bahía de, b., Hond. D7 92
San Lorenzo, Cabo, c., Ec. H2 84
San Lorenzo, Isla, i., Mex. C3 90
San Lorenzo, Isla, i., Peru E3 82
San Lorenzo de El Escorial, Spain E7 16
Sanlúcar de Barrameda, Spain I5 16
Sanlúcar la Mayor, Spain H5 16
San Lucas, Bol. I9 82
San Lucas, Ec. I3 84
San Lucas, Mex. F5 90
San Lucas, Cabo, c., Mex. F5 90
San Luis, Arg. G5 80
San Luis, Cuba D7 94
San Luis, Guat. A5 92
San Luis, Az., U.S. L5 120
San Luis, Co., U.S. G11 120
San Luis, Ven. B8 84
San Luis, prov., Arg. H5 80
San Luis, Laguna, l., Bol. E9 82
San Luis, Sierra de, mts., Arg. G6 80
San Luis de la Paz, Mex. G9 90
San Luis del Cordero, Mex. E7 90
San Luis del Palmar, Arg. D9 80
San Luis Gonzaga, Mex. E4 90
San Luis Gonzaga, Bahía, b., Mex. C2 90
San Luis Jilotepeque, Guat. C5 92
San Luis Obispo, Ca., U.S. I5 124
San Luis Peak, mtn., Co., U.S. G10 120
San Luis Potosí, Mex. F9 90
San Luis Potosí, state, Mex. F9 90
San Luis Reservoir, res., Ca., U.S. G4 124
San Luis Río Colorado, Mex. A2 90
San Luis Valley, val., Co., U.S. G10 120
Sanluri, Italy J3 18
San Manuel, Arg. I9 80
San Manuel, Az., U.S. L6 120
San Marcial, stm., Mex. C4 90
San Marcos, Chile F3 80
San Marcos, Col. C5 84
San Marcos, C.R. H10 92
San Marcos, El Sal. D5 92
San Marcos, Guat. C3 92
San Marcos, Hond. C6 92
San Marcos, Hond. B6 92
San Marcos, Mex. I10 90
San Marcos, Tx., U.S. J9 116
San Marcos, dept., Guat. B3 92
San Marcos, stm., Tx., U.S. J9 116
San Marcos, Isla, i., Mex. D3 90
San Marcos de Colón, Hond. D8 92
San Marino, S. Mar. F7 18
San Marino, ctry., Eur. G10 4
San Martín, Arg. E6 80
San Martín, Arg. G4 80
San Martín, Col. F6 84
San Martín, dept., Peru B3 82
San Martín, stm., Bol. D8 82
San Martín, stm., Bol. E10 82
San Martín, Lago (Lago O'Higgins), l., S.A. F2 78
San Martín de los Andes, Arg. E2 78
San Martín Texmelucan, Mex. H10 90
San Mateo, Ca., U.S. G3 124
San Mateo, Fl., U.S. J5 112
San Mateo, N.M., U.S. I9 120
San Mateo, Ven. C10 84
San Mateo Ixtatán, Guat. B3 92
San Matías, Bol. G12 82
San Matías, Golfo, b., Arg. E4 78
Sanmenxia, China E9 30
San Miguel, Arg. E10 80
San Miguel, Bol. G11 82
San Miguel, Ec. H3 84
San Miguel, El Sal. D6 92
San Miguel, Mex. C9 90
San Miguel, Pan. C3 84
San Miguel, Peru E5 82
San Miguel, Spain o24 17b
San Miguel, Ca., U.S. I5 124
San Miguel, stm., Bol. F10 82
San Miguel (Cuilco), stm., N.A. B2 92
San Miguel, stm., S.A. H11 82
San Miguel, stm., Co., U.S. F8 120
San Miguel, Cerro, hill, Bol. H11 82
San Miguel, Golfo de, b., Pan. C3 84
San Miguel, Volcán de, vol., El Sal. D6 92
San Miguel de Allende, Mex. G9 90
San Miguel de Cruces, Mex. E7 90
San Miguel del Monte, Arg. H9 80
San Miguel de Pallaques, Peru B2 82
San Miguel de Salcedo, Ec. H3 84
San Miguel de Tucumán, Arg. D6 80
San Miguel el Alto, Mex. G8 90
San Miguelito, Nic. F10 92
San Miguel Ixtahuacán, Guat. B3 92
San Miniato, Italy F5 18
Sannār, Sud. K7 60
Sannicandro Garganico, Italy H10 18
San Nicolás, Hond. B6 92
San Nicolás, Peru F4 82
San Nicolás, Spain p25 17b
San Nicolás, stm., Mex. H7 90
San Nicolás de los Arroyos, Arg. G8 80
San Nicolás de los Garza, Mex. E9 90
San Nicolas Island, i., Ca., U.S. K6 124
Sânnicolau Mare, Rom. C4 20
Sannikova, proliv, strt., Russia C20 28
Sanniquellie, Lib. H5 64
Sano, Japan K14 36
Sañogasta, Arg. E5 80
Sanok, Pol. F22 10
San Onofre, Col. C5 84
San Pablo, Col. G4 84
San Pablo, Phil. n19 39b
San Pablo, stm., Bol. F10 82
San Pablo, stm., Pan. I13 92
San Pablo Bay, b., Ca., U.S. F3 124
San Pedro, Arg. G9 80
San Pedro, Arg. C6 80
San Pedro, Arg. D6 80
San Pedro, Chile A4 80
San Pedro, Chile G3 80
San Pédro, C. Iv. I6 64
San Pedro, Col. C5 84
San Pedro, C.R. H10 92
San Pedro, Para. C10 80
San Pedro, Tx., U.S. L9 116
San Pedro, Ven. C7 84
San Pedro, dept., Para. C10 80
San Pedro, stm., Mex. B5 90
San Pedro, stm., N.A. I14 90
San Pedro, stm., N.A. L6 120
San Pedro, Punta, c., Chile C3 80
San Pedro, Volcán, vol., Chile A4 80
San Pedro Ayampuc, Guat. C4 92
San Pedro Carchá, Guat. B4 92
San Pedro Channel, strt., Ca., U.S. K7 124
San Pedro de Atacama, Chile B4 80
San Pedro de Buena Vista, Bol. H9 82
San Pedro de Curahuara, Bol. G7 82
San Pedro de la Cueva, Mex. C5 90
San Pedro de las Colonias, Mex. E8 90
San Pedro del Gallo, Mex. E7 90
San Pedro de Lloc, Peru B2 82
San Pedro del Norte, Nic. D10 92
San Pedro del Paraná, Para. D10 80
San Pedro de Macorís, Dom. Rep. E10 94
San Pedro Peaks, mts., N.M., U.S. H10 120
San Pedro Pinula, Guat. C5 92
San Pedro Pochutla, Mex. J11 90
San Pedro Sacatepéquez, Guat. C3 92
San Pedro Sula, Hond. B6 92
San Pedro Tabasco, Mex. I14 90
San Pelayo, Col. C5 84
San Pitch, stm., Ut., U.S. E5 120
Sanpoil, stm., Wa., U.S. B7 122
San Quintín, Cabo, c., Mex. B1 90
San Rafael, Arg. H4 80
San Rafael, Chile H3 80
San Rafael, Mex. E9 90
San Rafael, Ca., U.S. G3 124
San Rafael, N.M., U.S. I9 120
San Rafael, Ven. B7 84
San Rafael, stm., Bol. H12 82
San Rafael, stm., Ut., U.S. F6 120
San Rafael del Norte, Nic. D8 92
San Rafael del Sur, Nic. F8 92
San Rafael Desert, des., Ut., U.S. F6 120
San Rafael Oriente, El Sal. D6 92
San Rafael Swell, plat., Ut., U.S. F6 120
San Rafael Tasajera, El Sal. D6 92
San Ramón, Arg. D6 80
San Ramón, Bol. E8 82
San Ramón, C.R. G10 92
San Ramón, Hond. C10 92
San Ramón, Peru D4 82
San Ramón, Ur. H11 80
San Ramón de la Nueva Orán, Arg. B6 80
Sanrao, China L5 34
San Remo, Italy F2 18
San Román, stm., Guat. A4 92
San Román, Cabo, c., Ven. A7 84
San Roque, Arg. E9 80
San Roque, Arg. F4 80
San Roque, Spain I6 16
San Roque, Punta, c., Mex. D2 90
San Rosendo, Chile I2 80
San Saba, Tx., U.S. H8 116
San Saba, stm., Tx., U.S. I7 116
San Salvador, Arg. E10 80
San Salvador, Arg. F9 80
San Salvador, El Sal. D5 92
San Salvador (Watling Island), i., Bah. B7 94
San Salvador, Volcán de, vol., El Sal. D5 92
San Salvador de Jujuy, Arg. C6 80
Sansanné-Mango, Togo F10 64
San Sebastián, El Sal. D6 92
San Sebastián, Guat. C3 92
San Sebastián, Hond. C6 92
San Sebastián de la Gomera, Spain o23 17b
San Sebastián de Yalí, Nic. D8 92
Sansepolcro, Italy F7 18
San Severo, Italy H10 18
Sanshui, China L1 34
San Simon, Az., U.S. L7 120
San Simón, stm., Bol. E10 82
San Simon, stm., Az., U.S. L7 120
Sanso, Mali F6 64
San Solano, Arg. F6 80
Sans-Souci, hist., Haiti E8 94
Santa, Peru C2 82
Santa, stm., Peru C2 82
Santa, Isla del, i., Peru C2 82
Santa Adélia, Braz. F4 79
Santa Albertina, Braz. F3 79
Santa Ana, Arg. D11 80
Santa Ana, Bol. H12 82
Santa Ana, Col. C5 84
Santa Ana, Ec. H2 84
Santa Ana, El Sal. D5 92
Santa Ana, Mex. E9 90
Santa Ana, Mex. B4 90
Santa Ana, Ca., U.S. K8 124
Santa Ana, Ven. C10 84
Santa Ana, Volcán de, vol., El Sal. D5 92
Santa Ana del Alto Beni, Bol. F8 82
Santa Anna, Tx., U.S. H7 116

Name	Map Ref.	Page
Santa Bárbara, Chile	I2	80
Santa Barbara, Col.	E5	84
Santa Bárbara, Hond.	C6	92
Santa Bárbara, Mex.	D7	90
Santa Barbara, Ca., U.S.	J6	124
Santa Bárbara, Ven.	F9	84
Santa Bárbara, Ven.	D7	84
Santa Bárbara, dept., Hond.	B6	92
Santa Bárbara, stm., Bol.	G11	82
Santa Barbara Channel, strt., Ca., U.S.	J5	124
Santa Bárbara do Sul, Braz.	E12	80
Santa Catalina, Arg.	A5	80
Santa Catalina, Gulf of, b., Ca., U.S.	L7	124
Santa Catalina, Isla, i., Mex.	E4	90
Santa Catalina Island, i., Ca., U.S.	K7	124
Santa Catalina o Calovébora, Pan.	I13	92
Santa Catarina, Mex.	E9	90
Santa Catarina, state, Braz.	D13	80
Santa Catarina, Ilha de, i., Braz.	D14	80
Santa Cecília, Braz.	D13	80
Santa Clara, Col.	I8	84
Santa Clara, Cuba	C5	94
Santa Clara, Mex.	C6	90
Santa Clara, Ca., U.S.	G4	124
Santa Clara, Ut., U.S.	G3	120
Santa Clara, stm., Ut., U.S.	G3	120
Santa Clara de Olimar, Ur.	G11	80
Santa Clotilde, Peru	I6	84
Santa Coloma de Farners, Spain	D14	16
Santa Comba Dão, Port.	E3	16
Santa Cruz, Braz.	E8	79
Santa Cruz, Chile	H3	80
Santa Cruz, C.R.	G9	92
Santa Cruz, Peru	B2	82
Santa Cruz, Phil.	n19	39b
Santa Cruz, Phil.	o20	39b
Santa Cruz, Port.	m21	17a
Santa Cruz, Ca., U.S.	H3	124
Santa Cruz, Ven.	C7	84
Santa Cruz, dept., Bol.	G11	82
Santa Cruz, stm., Arg.	G2	78
Santa Cruz, stm., N.A.	L5	120
Santa Cruz, Isla, i., Ec.	j13	84a
Santa Cruz, Sierra de, mts., Guat.	B5	92
Santa Cruz Cabrália, Braz.	D9	79
Santa Cruz de Goiás, Braz.	D4	79
Santa Cruz de la Palma, Spain	o23	17b
Santa Cruz de la Sierra, Bol.	G10	82
Santa Cruz del Quiché, Guat.	B3	92
Santa Cruz del Sur, Cuba	D5	94
Santa Cruz de Tenerife, Spain	o24	17b
Santa Cruz de Tenerife, prov., Spain	o23	17b
Santa Cruz do Rio Pardo, Braz.	G4	79
Santa Cruz do Sul, Braz.	E12	80
Santa Cruz Island, i., Ca., U.S.	J6	124
Santa Cruz Islands, is., Sol.Is.	J20	126
Santa Elena, Arg.	F9	80
Santa Elena, Ec.	I2	84
Santa Elena, El Sal.	D6	92
Santa Elena, Mex.	D8	90
Santa Elena, stm., Bol.	G8	82
Santa Elena, Bahía de, b., Ec.	I2	84
Santa Elena, Cabo, c., C.R.	G9	92
Santa Elena, Golfo de, b., C.R.	G9	92
Santa Elena, Punta, c., Ec.	I2	84
Santa Elena de Uairén, Ven.	E12	84
Santa Eugenia, Spain	C2	16
Santa Eulalia, Guat.	B3	92
Santa Eulària del Riu, Spain	G13	16
Santa Fe, Arg.	F8	80
Santa Fé, Braz.	C3	79
Santa Fé, Braz.	G3	79
Santa Fe, Hond.	B8	92
Santa Fé, Pan.	I13	92
Santa Fe, Spain	H8	16
Santa Fe, N.M., U.S.	I11	120
Santa Fe, prov., Arg.	F8	80
Santa Fe, stm., N.M., U.S.	I10	120
Santa Fe Baldy, mtn., N.M., U.S.	I11	120
Santa Fe de Bogotá, Col.	E5	84
Santa Fé do Sul, Braz.	F3	79
Santa Filomena, Braz.	E9	76
Santa Helena de Goiás, Braz.	D3	79
Santai, China	E8	30
Santa Inês, Braz.	B9	79
Santa Inés, Bahía, b., Mex.	D4	90
Santa Inés, Isla, i., Chile	G2	78
Santa Isabel, Arg.	I5	80
Santa Isabel, Arg.	G8	80
Santa Isabel, Ec.	I3	84
Santa Isabel, i., Sol.Is.	I19	126
Santa Isabel, stm., Guat.	B5	92
Santa Isabel de Sihuas, Peru	G5	82
Santa Juliana, Braz.	E5	79
Santa Lucía, Arg.	E9	80
Santa Lucía, Arg.	F4	80
Santa Lucía, Cuba	D6	94
Santa Lucía, Ur.	H10	80
Santa Lucía, Ven.	C8	84
Santa Lucía Cotzumalguapa, Guat.	C3	92
Santa Lucia Range, mts., Ca., U.S.	H4	124
Santa Luzia, i., C.V.	E2	54
Santa Magdalena, Arg.	H7	80
Santa Margarita, Ca., U.S.	I5	124
Santa Margarita, Isla, i., Mex.	E4	90
Santa Margherita Ligure, Italy	E4	18
Santa María, Arg.	D5	80
Santa Maria, Braz.	E12	80
Santa Maria, C.V.	k17	64a
Santa María, C.R.	H11	92
Santa María, Pan.	I14	92
Santa Maria, Switz.	F11	13
Santa Maria, Switz.	E13	13
Santa Maria, Ca., U.S.	J5	124
Santa Maria, stm., Braz.	F11	80
Santa Maria, stm., Braz.	A11	80
Santa María, stm., Mex.	B6	90
Santa María, stm., Mex.	G10	90
Santa María, stm., Pan.	I14	92
Santa María, Bahía, b., Mex.	E5	90
Santa María, Cabo, c., Ur.	H11	80
Santa Maria, Cabo de, c., Ang.	D2	58
Santa Maria, Cape, c., Bah.	C7	94
Santa María, Isla, i., Chile	I2	80
Santa María, Isla, i., Ec.	j13	84a
Santa María, Laguna, l., Mex.	B6	90
Santa María, Volcán, vol., Guat.	C3	92
Santa Maria Asunción Tlaxiaco, Mex.	I11	90
Santa Maria Capua Vetere, Italy	H9	18
Santa María Colotepec, Mex.	J11	90
Santa Maria da Vitória, Braz.	B6	79
Santa María de Huazamota, Mex.	F7	90
Santa María de Ipire, Ven.	C10	84
Santa Maria de Itabira, Braz.	E7	79
Santa María del Oro, Mex.	E7	90
Santa María del Río, Mex.	G9	90
Santa Mariá de Mohovano, Mex.	D8	90
Santa Maria di Leuca, Capo, c., Italy	J13	18
Santa Maria do Suaçuí, Braz.	E7	79
Santa Maria Madalena, Braz.	F7	79
Santa-Maria-Siché, Fr.	m23	15a
Santa Marinella, Italy	G6	18
Santa Marta, Col.	B5	84
Santa Marta, Guat.	D3	92
Santa Marta, Cerro, mtn., Mex.	H12	90
Santa Marta, Ciénaga Grande, b., Col.	B5	84
Santa Marta Grande, Cabo de, c., Braz.	E14	80
Santa Monica, Ca., U.S.	J7	124
Santa Monica Bay, b., Ca., U.S.	K7	124
Santana, Braz.	B6	79
Santana, Port.	m21	17a
Santana, stm., Braz.	E3	79
Santana, Coxilha de, hills, S.A.	F11	80
Santana da Boa Vista, Braz.	F12	80
Santana do Livramento, Braz.	F11	80
Santander, Col.	F4	84
Santander, Spain	B8	16
Santander, dept., Col.	D6	84
Santander Jiménez, Mex.	E10	90
Santanilla, Islas, is., Hond.	F3	94
Sant Antoni de Portmany, Spain	G13	16
Santa Paula, Ca., U.S.	J6	124
Santaquin, Ut., U.S.	E5	120
Santarém, Braz.	D8	76
Santarém, Port.	F3	16
Santaren Channel, strt., Bah.	C5	94
Santa Rita, Col.	G6	84
Santa Rita, Hond.	B7	92
Santa Rita, Mex.	C4	90
Santa Rita, Ven.	B7	84
Santa Rita de Catuna, Arg.	F5	80
Santa Rita do Araguaia, Braz.	D2	79
Santa Rita do Weil, Braz.	I8	84
Santa Rosa, Arg.	I6	80
Santa Rosa, Arg.	B6	80
Santa Rosa, Bol.	F8	82
Santa Rosa, Bol.	D8	82
Santa Rosa, Bol.	G10	82
Santa Rosa, Braz.	B6	78
Santa Rosa, Braz.	C5	79
Santa Rosa, Braz.	D11	80
Santa Rosa, Col.	F8	84
Santa Rosa, C.R.	G9	92
Santa Rosa, Ec.	I3	84
Santa Rosa, Para.	D10	80
Santa Rosa, Para.	I11	82
Santa Rosa, Ca., U.S.	F3	124
Santa Rosa, N.M., U.S.	E2	116
Santa Rosa, Tx., U.S.	M9	116
Santa Rosa, Ven.	C8	84
Santa Rosa, dept., Guat.	C4	92
Santa Rosa, Parque Nacional, C.R.	G9	92
Santa Rosa Beach, Fl., U.S.	L10	114
Santa Rosa de Aguán, Hond.	B9	92
Santa Rosa de Amanadona, Ven.	G9	84
Santa Rosa de Cabal, Col.	E5	84
Santa Rosa [de Copán], Hond.	C6	92
Santa Rosa del Conlara, Arg.	G6	80
Santa Rosa de Leales, Arg.	D6	80
Santa Rosa de Lima, El Sal.	D7	92
Santa Rosa del Palmar, Bol.	G10	82
Santa Rosa de Osos, Col.	D5	84
Santa Rosa de Río Primero, Arg.	F7	80
Santa Rosa de Sucumbíos, Ec.	G4	84
Santa Rosa de Viterbo, Col.	E6	84
Santa Rosa Island, i., Ca., U.S.	K5	124
Santa Rosa Island, i., Fl., U.S.	L10	114
Santa Rosalía, Mex.	D3	90
Santa Rosalía, Ven.	C8	84
Santa Rosa Range, mts., Nv., U.S.	C8	124
Šantarskije ostrova, is., Russia	F19	28
Santa Sylvina, Arg.	D8	80
Santa Teresa, Braz.	E8	79
Santa Teresa, Mex.	E11	90
Santa Teresa, stm., Braz.	B4	79
Santa Teresa, Embalse de, res., Spain	E6	16
Santa Tereza de Goiás, Braz.	B4	79
Santa Vitória, Braz.	E3	79
Santa Vitória do Palmar, Braz.	G12	80
Santa Ynez, stm., Ca., U.S.	J5	124
Sant Carles de la Ràpita, Spain	E12	16
Santee, Ca., U.S.	L9	124
Santee, stm., S.C., U.S.	F7	112
Sant Feliu de Guíxols, Spain	D15	16
Santhià, Italy	D3	18
Santiago, Bol.	H12	82
Santiago, Braz.	E11	80
Santiago, Chile	G3	80
Santiago, Mex.	F5	90
Santiago, Pan.	C2	84
Santiago, Para.	D10	80
Santiago, Peru	F4	82
Santiago, i., C.V.	G4	52
Santiago, i., C.V.	m17	64a
Santiago, stm., Mex.	E7	90
Santiago, stm., S.A.	I4	84
Santiago, Cerro, mtn., Pan.	I13	92
Santiago, Isla, i., Ec.	j13	84a
Santiago, Serranía de, mts., Bol.	H12	82
Santiago Atitlán, Guat.	C3	92
Santiago Choapan, Mex.	I12	90
Santiago de Cao, Peru	B2	82
Santiago de Chocorvos, Peru	E4	82
Santiago de Chuco, Peru	C2	82
Santiago de Compostela, Spain	C3	16
Santiago de Cuba, Cuba	D7	94
Santiago de Huari, Bol.	H8	82
Santiago de Huata, Bol.	G7	82
Santiago del Estero, Arg.	D6	80
Santiago del Estero, prov., Arg.	E7	80
Santiago [de los Caballeros], Dom. Rep.	E9	94
Santiago de Machaca, Bol.	G7	82
Santiago de Méndez, Ec.	I3	84
Santiago Ixcuintla, Mex.	G7	90
Santiago Jamiltepec, Mex.	I11	90
Santiago Larre, Arg.	H9	80
Santiago Papasquiaro, Mex.	E7	90
Santiaguillo, Laguna, l., Mex.	E7	90
Santiam Pass, Or., U.S.	F4	122
San Timoteo, Ven.	C7	84
Säntis, mtn., Switz.	D11	13
Sant Jordi, Golf de, b., Spain	E13	16
Santo, Tx., U.S.	G8	116
Santo Amaro, Braz.	B9	79
Santo Anastácio, Braz.	F3	79
Santo André, Braz.	G5	79
Santo Ângelo, Braz.	E11	80
Santo Antão, i., C.V.	k16	64a
Santo António, S. Tom./P.	A1	58
Santo Antônio, stm., Braz.	E6	79
Santo Antônio da Patrulha, Braz.	E13	80
Santo Antônio de Jesus, Braz.	B9	79
Santo Antônio de Pádua, Braz.	F7	79
Santo Antônio do Amparo, Braz.	F6	79
Santo Antônio do Içá, Braz.	I9	84
Santo Antônio do Leverger, Braz.	F13	82
Santo Antônio do Rio Verde, Braz.	D5	79
Santo Antônio do Sudoeste, Braz.	D12	80
Santo Augusto, Braz.	D12	80
Santo Corazón, Bol.	G12	82
Santo Domingo, Dom. Rep.	E10	94
Santo Domingo, Mex.	E3	90
Santo Domingo, Nic.	E9	92
Santo Domingo, stm., Mex.	A3	92
Santo Domingo de los Colorados, Ec.	H3	84
Santo Domingo Pueblo, N.M., U.S.	I10	120
Santo Domingo Tehuantepec, Mex.	I12	90
Santo Domingo Zanatepec, Mex.	I12	90
Santo Estêvão, Braz.	B9	79
San Tomé, Ven.	C10	84
Santoña, Spain	B8	16
Santo Onofre, stm., Braz.	B7	79
Santorini see Thíra, i., Grc.	M9	20
Santos, Braz.	G5	79
Santos Dumont, Braz.	F7	79
Santos Tomás del Norte, Nic.	D8	92
Santo Tomás, Col.	B5	84
Santo Tomás, Mex.	B1	90
Santo Tomás, Nic.	E9	92
Santo Tomás, Peru	B3	82
Santo Tomás, Peru	F5	82
Santo Tomás, stm., Peru	F5	82
Santo Tomás, Punta, c., Mex.	B1	90
Santo Tomé, Arg.	E10	80
Santo Tomé, Arg.	F8	80
Santuario de Quillacas, Bol.	H8	82
Santunying, China	C6	32
San Ubaldo, Nic.	F9	92
San Vicente, Arg.	E6	80
San Vicente, El Sal.	D6	92
San Vicente, Volcán de, vol., El Sal.	D6	92
San Vicente de Cañete, Peru	E3	82
San Vicente de Chucurí, Col.	D6	84
San Vicente del Caguán, Col.	F5	84
San Vicente de Tagua-Tagua, Chile	H3	80
San Vincenzo, Italy	F5	18
San Vito, C.R.	I12	92
San Vito, Italy	J4	18
San Vito dei Normanni, Italy	I12	18
San Ygnacio, Tx., U.S.	L7	116
Sanyuan, China	E8	30
Sanza Pombo, Ang.	C3	58
Sanzha, China	B2	32
São Benedito, stm., Braz.	C13	82
São Bento, Braz.	D10	76
São Bento do Sul, Braz.	D14	80
São Borja, Braz.	E10	80
São Caetano do Sul, Braz.	G5	79
São Carlos, Braz.	G5	79
São Cristóvão, Braz.	F11	76
São Domingos, Braz.	B5	79
São Domingos, Braz.	D12	80
São Domingos, Gui.-B.	E1	64
São Domingos, stm., Braz.	B5	79
São Domingos, stm., Braz.	E3	79
São Domingos, stm., Braz.	E2	79
São Domingos, stm., Braz.	E9	82
São Felipe, Braz.	C8	79
São Filipe, C.V.	m16	64a
São Francisco, Braz.	C6	79
São Francisco, stm., Braz.	E11	76
São Francisco, stm., Braz.	C8	79
São Francisco, stm., Braz.	B7	79
São Francisco, Baía de, b., Braz.	D14	80
São Francisco, Ilha de, i., Braz.	D14	80
São Francisco de Assis, Braz.	E11	80
São Francisco de Goiás, Braz.	C4	79
São Francisco de Paula, Braz.	E13	80
São Francisco do Sul, Braz.	D14	80
São Gabriel, Braz.	F11	80
São Gabriel da Palha, Braz.	E8	79
São Gabriel de Goiás, Braz.	C5	79
São Gonçalo do Abaeté, Braz.	E6	79
São Gonçalo do Sapucaí, Braz.	F6	79
São Gonçalo dos Campos, Braz.	B9	79
Sao Hill, Tan.	C7	58
São Jerônimo, Braz.	E13	80
São Jerônimo, Serra de, plat., Braz.	D1	79
São Jerônimo da Serra, Braz.	G3	79
São João, stm., Braz.	B3	79
São João da Barra, Braz.	F8	79
São João da Boa Vista, Braz.	F5	79
São João D'Aliança, Braz.	C5	79
São João da Madeira, Port.	E3	16
São João da Ponte, Braz.	C6	79
São João del-Rei, Braz.	F6	79
São João do Araguaia, Braz.	E9	76
São João do Paraíso, Braz.	C7	79
São João Evangelista, Braz.	E7	79
São Joaquim, Braz.	E14	80
São Joaquim, Parque Nacional de, Braz.	E14	80
São Joaquim da Barra, Braz.	F5	79
São José, Braz.	D14	80
São José, stm., Braz.	E8	79
São José de Anauá, Braz.	G12	84
São José do Cedro, Braz.	D12	80
São José do Norte, Braz.	G12	80
São José do Rio Preto, Braz.	F4	79
São José dos Campos, Braz.	G6	79
São José dos Pinhais, Braz.	C14	80
São Leopoldo, Braz.	E13	80
São Lourenço, Braz.	G6	79
São Lourenço, Pantanal de, sw., Braz.	G13	82
São Lourenço do Oeste, Braz.	D12	80
São Lourenço do Sul, Braz.	F13	80
São Luís, Braz.	D10	76
São Luís de Montes Belos, Braz.	D3	79
São Luís Gonzaga, Braz.	E11	80
São Manuel, Braz.	G4	79
São Manuel, stm., Braz.	C13	82
São Marcos, stm., Braz.	D5	79
São Mateus, Braz.	E9	79
São Mateus, Braço Norte, stm., Braz.	E8	79
São Mateus do Sul, Braz.	C13	80
São Miguel, i., Port.	m21	62a
São Miguel, stm., Braz.	D8	79
São Miguel do Araguaia, Braz.	B3	79
São Miguel d'Oeste, Braz.	D12	80
Saona, Isla, i., Dom. Rep.	E10	94
Saône, stm., Fr.	F11	14
Saône-et-Loire, dept., Fr.	F11	14
São Nicolau, i., C.V.	k16	64a
São Paulo, Braz.	G5	79
São Paulo, state, Braz.	G4	79
São Paulo de Olivença, Braz.	I8	84
São Pedro, Braz.	E3	79
São Pedro, stm., Braz.	D8	79
São Pedro do Sul, Braz.	E11	80
São Pedro do Sul, Port.	E3	16
São Raimundo Nonato, Braz.	E10	76
São Romão, Braz.	D6	79
São Roque, Braz.	G5	79
São Roque, Cabo de, c., Braz.	E11	76
São Sebastião, Braz.	G6	79
São Sebastião, Ilha de, i., Braz.	G6	79
São Sebastião, Ponta, c., Moz.	D12	66
São Sebastião do Maranhão, Braz.	E7	79
São Sebastião do Paraíso, Braz.	F5	79
São Sebastião do Rio Claro, Braz.	C3	79
São Sepé, Braz.	F12	80
São Simão, Braz.	E3	79
São Simão, Braz.	F5	79
São Tiago, Braz.	F6	79
São Timóteo, Braz.	B7	79
São Tomé, S. Tom./P.	A1	58
São Tomé, i., S. Tom./P.	A1	58
São Tomé, stm., Braz.	C13	82
São Tomé, Cabo de, c., Braz.	F8	79
Sao Tome and Principe (São Tomé e Principe), ctry., Afr.	A1	58
Saoura, Oued, val., Alg.	F10	62
São Vicente, Braz.	G5	79
São Vicente, i., C.V.	k16	64a
São Vicente, Cabo de (Cape Saint Vincent), c., Port.	H2	16
São Vicente de Minas, Braz.	F6	79
Sapé, Braz.	E11	76
Sapele, Nig.	I12	64
Sapello, stm., N.M., U.S.	I11	120
Sapelo Island, i., Ga., U.S.	H5	112
Şaphane, Tur.	J13	20
Šapitwa, mtn., Mwi.	E7	58
Šapki, Russia	B14	22
Sa Pobla, Spain	F15	16
Sapodilla Cays, i., Belize	A6	92
Saponé, Burkina	E9	64
Saposoa, Peru	B3	82
Sapožok, Russia	H23	22
Sapporo, Japan	d16	36a
Sapri, Italy	I10	18
Saptakośī, stm., Nepal	G12	44
Sapulpa, Ok., U.S.	D10	116
Sāqiat al-'Abd, Sud.	G6	60
Saqqez, Iran	C9	48
Saquena, Peru	A5	82
Saquisilí, Ec.	H3	84
Sarāb, Iran	C9	48
Saraburi, Thai.	G6	40
Saracura, stm., Braz.	B8	79
Saragosa, Tx., U.S.	H3	116
Saragossa see Zaragoza, Spain	D11	16
Saraguro, Ec.	I3	84
Sarai, Russia	H24	22
Sarajevo, Bos.	F2	20
Sarakhs, Iran	C16	48
Saraland, Al., U.S.	L8	114
Saran', Kaz.	H12	26
Saranac, Mi., U.S.	H10	110
Saranac, stm., N.Y., U.S.	C13	108
Saranac Lake, N.Y., U.S.	C12	108
Sarandi, Braz.	D12	80
Sarandí del Yi, Ur.	G11	80
Sarandí Grande, Ur.	G10	80
Saransk, Russia	G7	26
Sarapiquí, stm., C.R.	G11	92
Sarapul, Russia	F8	26
Sarare, Ven.	C8	84
Sara Sara, Nevado, mtn., Peru	F5	82
Sarasota, Fl., U.S.	L4	112
Sarata, Ukr.	C13	20
Saratoga, Ca., U.S.	G3	124
Saratoga, Tx., U.S.	I12	116
Saratoga, Wy., U.S.	C10	120
Saratoga Springs, N.Y., U.S.	D13	108
Saratov, Russia	G7	26
Saratovskoje vodochranilišče, res., Russia	G7	26
Saraurcu, mtn., Ec.	H4	84
Saravan, Laos	G9	40
Sarawak, hist. reg., Malay.	E5	38
Saraya, Gui.	F4	64
Sarayköy, Tur.	L12	20
Sarbāz, Iran	H16	48
Sárbogárd, Hung.	I18	10
Sarcee Indian Reserve, Alta., Can.	G20	102
Sarcoxie, Mo., U.S.	E2	114
Sārda (Mahākālī), stm., Asia	F9	44
Sardārshahr, India	F6	44
Sardegna, prov., Italy	I4	18
Sardegna (Sardinia), i., Italy	I4	18
Sardinal, C.R.	G9	92
Sardinata, Col.	C6	84
Sardinia see Sardegna, i., Italy	I4	18
Sardis, Al., U.S.	J10	114
Sardis, Ga., U.S.	G5	112
Sardis, Ms., U.S.	H7	114
Sardis, Tn., U.S.	G8	114
Sardis Lake, res., Ms., U.S.	H7	114
Sar-e Pol, Afg.	B1	44
Sarepta, La., U.S.	J3	114
Sargans, Switz.	D11	13
Sargasso Sea	B8	74
Sargent, Ga., U.S.	F2	112
Sargent, Ne., U.S.	J8	118
Sargodha, Pak.	D5	44
Sarh, Chad	G4	56
Sārī, Iran	C12	48
Saric, Mex.	B4	90
Şarif, Yemen	F7	47
Sarıkamış, Tur.	A7	48
Sarina, Austl.	C8	70
Sariñena, Spain	D11	16
Sarīr, Libya	D2	60
Sarita, Tx., U.S.	B9	116
Şariwŏn, N. Kor.	E13	32
Šarja, Russia	F7	26
Sark, i., Guernsey	L11	8
Sarkad, Hung.	I21	10
Şarkışla, Tur.	B4	48
Šarkovščina, Bela.	F10	22
Şarköy, Tur.	I11	20
Šarlauk, Turk.	B13	48
Sarles, N.D., U.S.	C9	118
Sármellék, Hung.	I17	10
Sarmiento de Gamboa, Cerro, mtn., Chile	G2	78
Särna, Swe.	K13	6
Sarnen, Switz.	E9	13
Sarnia, Ont., Can.	H13	110
Sarno, Italy	I9	18
Saron, S. Afr.	I4	66
Saronikós Kólpos, b., Grc.	L7	20
Saronno, Italy	D4	18
Sárospatak, Hung.	G21	10
Sarpsborg, Nor.	L12	6
Sarralbe, Fr.	C14	14
Sarrebourg, Fr.	D14	14
Sarreguemines, Fr.	C14	14
Sarre-Union, Fr.	D14	14
Sarro, Mali	E7	64
Sarstoon (Sarstún), stm., N.A.	B5	92
Sarstún (Sarstoon), stm., N.A.	B5	92
Sartang, stm., Russia	D18	28
Sartell, Mn., U.S.	E1	110
Sartène, Fr.	H3	18
Sarthe, dept., Fr.	D7	14
Sartilly, Fr.	D5	14
Saruhanlı, Tur.	K11	20
Sarūr, Oman	C11	47
Sárvár, Hung.	H16	10
Sarvestān, Iran	G12	48
Saryg-Sep, Russia	G17	26
Sarykol'skij chrebet, mts., Asia	A6	44
Saryozek, Kaz.	I13	26
Sarysu, stm., Kaz.	H11	26
Sary-Taš, Kyrg.	J12	26
Sarzana, Italy	E4	18
Sasaginnigak Lake, l., Man., Can.	G19	104
Sasakwa, Ok., U.S.	E10	116
Sāsarām, India	H11	44
Sásd, Hung.	I18	10
Sasebo, Japan	N4	36
Saskatchewan, prov., Can.	F11	96
Saskatchewan, stm., Can.	E13	104
Saskatoon, Sask., Can.	F8	104
Saslaya, Cerro, mtn., Nic.	H2	94
Sasolburg, S. Afr.	F8	66
Sasovo, Russia	G24	22
Saspamco, Tx., U.S.	J8	116
Sassafras, Ky., U.S.	B3	112
Sassafras Mountain, mtn., U.S.	D4	112
Sassandra, C. Iv.	I6	64
Sassandra, stm., C. Iv.	I6	64
Sassari, Italy	I3	18
Sassoferrato, Italy	F7	18
Sasso Marconi, Italy	E6	18
S'as'stroj, Russia	A15	22
Sassuolo, Italy	E5	18
Sastown, Lib.	I5	64
Sastre, Arg.	F8	80
Sasyk, ozero, l., Ukr.	D13	20
Satah Mountain, mtn., B.C., Can.	E10	102
Šatalovo, Russia	G15	22
Sata-misaki, c., Japan	Q5	36
Satanta, Ks., U.S.	N7	118
Sātāra, India	D2	46
Satara, S. Afr.	E10	66
Satélite, Mex.	B6	90
Satellite Beach, Fl., U.S.	K6	112
Satipo, Peru	D4	82
Satīt (Tekeze), stm., Afr.	J9	60
Satka, Russia	F9	26
Satna, India	H9	44
Sátoraljaújhely, Hung.	G21	10
Sātpura Range, mts., India	J7	44
Satsuma, Al., U.S.	L8	114
Satsunan-shotō, is., Japan	r4	37b
Sattahip, Thai.	H6	40
Satthwa, Mya.	F3	40
Satu Mare, Rom.	B6	20
Satu Mare, co., Rom.	B6	20
Şatun, Thai.	K6	40
Šatura, Russia	F22	22
Şaturnino M. Laspiur, Arg.	F7	80
Šaturtorf, Russia	F22	22
Sauce, Arg.	F9	80
Sauce, Peru	B3	82
Sauce, Ur.	H10	80
Sauce Corto, Arroyo, stm., Arg.	I8	80
Saucier, Ms., U.S.	L7	114
Saucillo, Mex.	C7	90
Sauda, Nor.	L10	6
Saudi Arabia (Al-'Arabīyah as-Su'ūdīyah), ctry., Asia	D4	42
Sauer (Sûre), stm., Eur.	I10	12
Saueruiná, stm., Braz.	E12	82
Sauê-Uiná, stm., Braz.	E12	82
Saugatuck, Mi., U.S.	H9	110
Saugerties, N.Y., U.S.	E13	108
Saugstad, Mount, mtn., B.C., Can.	E8	102
Saujil, Arg.	E5	80
Sauk, stm., Mn., U.S.	E1	110
Sauk Centre, Mn., U.S.	F13	118
Sauk City, Wi., U.S.	G6	110
Sauk Rapids, Mn., U.S.	E1	110
Saukville, Wi., U.S.	G8	110
Saül, Fr. Gu.	C8	76
Saulgau, Ger.	G9	10
Saulieu, Fr.	E11	14
Saulkrasti, Lat.	D7	22
Sault-au-Mouton, Que., Can.	D4	106
Sault aux Cochons, Rivière du, stm., Que., Can.	D4	106
Saulteaux, stm., Alta., Can.	C20	102
Saulteaux Indian Reserve, Sask., Can.	E6	104
Sault Sainte Marie, Ont., Can.	D11	110
Sault Sainte Marie, Mi., U.S.	D11	110
Saumarez Reef, rf., Austl.	C10	70
Saumons, Riviere aux, stm., Que., Can.	C11	106
Saumur, Fr.	E6	14
Saunders Island, i., S. Geor.	A2	73
Saunders Island, i., S. Geor.	J12	74
Sauquoit, N.Y., U.S.	D11	108
Saurimo, Ang.	C4	58
Sausalito, Ca., U.S.	G3	124
Sauveterre-de-Béarn, Fr.	I6	14
Sauvo, Fin.	K18	6
Sava, Italy	I12	18
Sava, stm., Eur.	F11	4
Savage, Md., U.S.	H10	108
Savage, Mt., U.S.	D3	118
Savai'i, i., W. Sam.	J22	126
Savalou, Benin	H10	64
Savane, stm., Que., Can.	A2	106
Savanna, Il., U.S.	H5	110
Savanna, Ok., U.S.	E11	116
Savannah, Ga., U.S.	G5	112
Savannah, Mo., U.S.	C2	114
Savannah, Tn., U.S.	G8	114
Savannah, stm., U.S.	G5	112
Savannakhét, Laos	F8	40
Savanna-la-Mar, Jam.	E5	94
Savé, Benin	G11	64
Save (Sabi), stm., Afr.	C12	66
Sāveh, Iran	D11	48
Savelli, Italy	J11	18
Saverdun, Fr.	I8	14
Saverne, Fr.	D14	14
Savigliano, Italy	E2	18
Savino, Russia	E24	22
Şavinskij, Russia	J27	6
Šavnik, Yugo.	G3	20
Savognin, Switz.	E12	13
Savoie, dept., Fr.	G13	14
Savona, B.C., Can.	G14	102
Savona, Italy	E3	18
Savoonga, Ak., U.S.	E9	100
Savoy, Tx., U.S.	F10	116
Savran', Ukr.	A14	20
Savu Sea see Sawu, Laut, Indon.	G7	38
Sawahlunto, Indon.	O6	40
Sawāi Mādhopur, India	H7	44
Sawākin, Sud.	H9	60
Sawankhalok, Thai.	F5	40
Sawatch Range, mts., Co., U.S.	E10	120
Sawdā', Jabal, mtn., Sau. Ar.	E3	47
Sawdā', Jabal as-, hills, Libya	C4	56
Sawdā', Qurnat as-, mtn., Leb.	D4	48
Sawdirī, Sud.	J5	60
Sawhāj, Egypt	D6	60
Sawknah, Libya	C4	56
Şawqirah, Ghubbat, b., Oman	E10	47
Sawu, Laut (Savu Sea), Indon.	G7	38
Sawu, Pulau, i., Indon.	H7	38
Sawyer, Mi., U.S.	I9	110
Sawyer, N.D., U.S.	C6	118
Sawyers Hill, hill, Newf., Can.	E20	106
Saxby, stm., Austl.	B4	70
Saxis, Va., U.S.	B11	112
Saxon, Switz.	F7	13
Saxon, Wi., U.S.	D5	110
Saxony see Sachsen, state, Ger.	C9	10
Saxton, Pa., U.S.	G8	108
Say, Niger	E11	64
Sayán, Peru	D3	82
Sayan Mountains (Sajany), mts., Asia	G11	28
Sayaxché, Guat.	I14	90
Saybrook, Il., U.S.	B8	114
Şaydā (Sidon), Leb.	A4	50
Sayḩūt, Yemen	G7	47
Sayil, hist., Mex.	G15	90
Saylorville Lake, res., Ia., U.S.	I2	110
Saylūn, Khirbat (Shiloh), hist., Isr. Occ.	D4	50
Sayre, Ok., U.S.	D7	116
Sayre, Pa., U.S.	F10	108
Sayreville, N.J., U.S.	G12	108
Sayula, Mex.	H8	90
Sayward, B.C., Can.	G9	102
Saywūn, Yemen	G6	47
Şazonovo, Russia	B18	22
Šazud, Taj.	B5	44
Sba, Alg.	F10	62
Sbeïtla, Tun.	N4	18
Sbiba, Tun.	N4	18
Scafell Pikes, mtn., Eng., U.K.	G10	8
Scalea, Italy	J10	18
Scammon, Ks., U.S.	N13	118
Scandia, Ks., U.S.	L10	118
Scanlon, Mn., U.S.	D3	110
Scapa, Alta., Can.	F23	102
Scapa Flow, b., Scot., U.K.	C10	8
Scapegoat Mountain, mtn., Mt., U.S.	C13	122
Ščapino, Russia	F23	28
Scappoose, Or., U.S.	E3	122
Scarborough, Ont., Can.	G16	110
Scarborough, Trin.	I14	94
Scarborough, Eng., U.K.	G13	8
Scatarie Island, i., N.S., Can.	G14	106
Şcawfell Island, i., Austl.	C8	70
Ščelkovo, Russia	F21	22
Şceptre, Sask., Can.	H5	104
Ščerbinka, Russia	F20	22
Schaerbeek (Schaarbeek), Bel.	G5	12
Schaffhausen, Switz.	C10	13
Schaffhausen, state, Switz.	C10	13
Schaller, Ia., U.S.	I12	118
Schärding, Aus.	G13	10
Schefferville, Que., Can.	F19	96
Scheibbs, Aus.	G15	10
Scheinfeld, Ger.	F10	10
Schelde (Escaut), stm., Eur.	D4	10
Schenectady, N.Y., U.S.	E13	108
Schertz, Tx., U.S.	J8	116
Schesslitz, Ger.	F11	10
Scheveningen, Neth.	D5	12
Schiedam, Neth.	E5	12
Schiermonnikoog, Neth.	B9	12
Schiermonnikoog, i., Neth.	B9	12
Schiltigheim, Fr.	D14	14
Schio, Italy	D6	18
Schipbeek, stm., Eur.	D9	12
Schkeuditz, Ger.	D12	10
Schladming, Aus.	H13	10
Schlater, Ms., U.S.	I6	114
Schleswig, Ger.	A9	10
Schleswig, Ia., U.S.	I12	118
Schleswig-Holstein, state, Ger.	A9	10
Schleusingen, Ger.	E10	10
Schlieren, Switz.	D9	13
Schlitz, Ger.	E9	10
Schlüchtern, Ger.	E9	10
Schmalkalden, Ger.	E10	10
Schmidmühlen, Ger.	F11	10
Schmölln, Ger.	E12	10
Schneverdingen, Ger.	B9	10

Name Map Ref. Page

Schodn'a, Russia F20 22
Schofield, Wi., U.S. F6 110
Schoharie, N.Y., U.S. E12 108
Schönebeck, Ger. C11 10
Schongau, Ger. H10 10
Schoolcraft, Mi., U.S. H10 110
Schopfheim, Ger. H7 10
Schorndorf, Ger. G9 10
Schouten Island, i., Austl. N8 70
Schouwen, i., Neth. E4 12
Schramberg, Ger. G8 10
Schreiber, Ont., Can. B8 110
Schriever, La., U.S. M6 114
Schroffenstein, mtn., Nmb. F4 66
Schulenburg, Tx., U.S. J10 116
Schultz Lake, l., N.W. Ter., Can. D13 96
Schumacher, Ont., Can. B14 110
Schüpfheim, Switz. E9 13
Schuyler, Ne., U.S. J10 118
Schuyler, Va., U.S. B8 112
Schuylkill, stm., Pa., U.S. G11 108
Schuylkill Haven, Pa., U.S. G10 108
Schwabach, Ger. F11 10
Schwaben, hist. reg., Ger. G10 10
Schwäbische Alb, mts., Ger. G9 10
Schwäbisch Gmünd, Ger. G9 10
Schwäbisch Hall, Ger. F9 10
Schwabmünchen, Ger. G10 10
Schwanden, Switz. D11 13
Schwandorf, Ger. F12 10
Schwaner, Pegunungan, mts., Indon. F5 38
Schwarza, Ger. E11 10
Schwarzach im Pongau, Aus. H13 10
Schwarzenburg, Switz. E7 13
Schwarzwald (Black Forest), mts., Ger. G8 10
Schwaz, Aus. H11 10
Schwedt, Ger. B14 10
Schweinfurt, Ger. E10 10
Schweizer Nationalpark, Switz. E13 13
Schwerin, Ger. B11 10
Schwyz, Switz. D10 13
Schwyz, state, Switz. D10 13
Sciacca, Italy L8 18
Scicli, Italy M9 18
Scilla, Italy K10 18
Scilly, Isles of, is., Eng., U.K. L7 8
Scio, Oh., U.S. G5 108
Scio, Or., U.S. F3 122
Scioto, stm., Oh., U.S. I3 108
Scipio, Ut., U.S. E4 120
Ścobey, Mt., U.S. B20 122
Ščokino, Russia G20 22
Scone, Austl. I9 70
Scooba, Ms., U.S. J8 114
Scordia, Italy L9 18
Scotia, Ne., U.S. J9 118
Scotia, N.Y., U.S. E13 108
Scotia Sea, S.A. A1 73
Scotland, Ont., Can. G15 110
Scotland, S.D., U.S. H10 118
Scotland, Tx., U.S. F8 116
Scotland, ter., U.K. D9 8
Scotland Neck, N.C., U.S. C9 112
Scotlandville, La., U.S. L5 114
Scotsburn, N.S., Can. G11 106
Scott, Sask., Can. F6 104
Scott, Ms., U.S. I5 114
Scott, stm., Ca., U.S. C3 124
Scott, Cape, c., B.C., Can. G6 102
Scott, Mount, mtn., Or., U.S. H3 122
Scott Base, sci., Ant. C8 73
Scottburgh, S. Afr. H10 66
Scott City, Ks., U.S. M7 118
Scott City, Mo., U.S. E7 114
Scottdale, Pa., U.S. G7 108
Scott Islands, is., B.C., Can. G6 102
Scott Mountain, mtn., Id., U.S. F10 122
Scott Reef, rf., Austl. B4 68
Scottsbluff, Ne., U.S. J4 118
Scottsboro, Al., U.S. H10 114
Scottsburg, In., U.S. D11 114
Scottsdale, Austl. M7 70
Scottsdale, Az., U.S. K5 120
Scotts Hill, Tn., U.S. G8 114
Scottsville, Ky., U.S. F10 114
Scottville, Mi., U.S. G9 110
Scout Lake, Sask., Can. I8 104
Scranton, Ia., U.S. I13 118
Scranton, N.D., U.S. E4 118
Scranton, Pa., U.S. F11 108
Screven, Ga., U.S. H4 112
Scribner, Ne., U.S. J11 118
Ščučin, Bela. H7 22
Ščučinsk, Kaz. G12 26
Scuol (Schuls), Switz. E13 13
Scurry, Tx., U.S. G10 116
Scutari, Lake, l., Eur. G3 20
Seabird Island Indian Reserve, B.C., Can. H13 102
Seaboard, N.C., U.S. C9 112
Seadrift, Tx., U.S. K10 116
Seaford, De., U.S. I11 108
Seaforth, Ont., Can. G14 110
Seager Wheeler Lake, l., Sask., Can. D11 104
Seagraves, Tx., U.S. G4 116
Seahorse Point, c., N.W. Ter., Can. D16 96
Sea Islands, is., U.S. I5 112
Sea Isle City, N.J., U.S. H12 108
Seal, stm., Man., Can. E13 96
Sea Lake, Austl. J5 70
Seal Cays, is., T./C. Is. D9 94
Seal Cove, N.B., Can. H7 106
Seal Cove, Newf., Can. C17 106
Seale, Al., U.S. J11 114
Sealevel, N.C., U.S. E10 112
Seal Island, i., N.S., Can. I7 106
Seal Lake, l., Newf., Can. F20 96
Sealy, Tx., U.S. J10 116
Seara, Braz. D12 80
Searchlight, Nv., U.S. I11 124
Searcy, Ar., U.S. G5 114
Searsport, Me., U.S. C18 108
Seaside, Ca., U.S. H4 124
Seaside, Or., U.S. E2 122
Seaside Park, N.J., U.S. H12 108
Seattle, Wa., U.S. C3 122
Seattle, Mount, mtn., N.A. F25 100
Sébaco, Nic. E8 92
Sebago Lake, l., Me., U.S. D16 108
Sebakwe Recreational Area, Zimb. B10 66
Šebalino, Russia G15 26
Sebastian, Tx., U.S. M9 116
Sebastián Vizcaíno, Bahía, b., Mex. C2 90
Sebastopol, Ca., U.S. F3 124
Sebastopol, Ms., U.S. J7 114
Sebderat, Erit. J9 60
Sebeka, Mn., U.S. E12 118
Seberi, Braz. D12 80
Sebeş, Rom. D7 20
Sebes Körös (Crişul Repede), stm., Eur. B5 20
Sebewaing, Mi., U.S. G12 110
Sebež, Russia E11 22
Şebinkarahisar, Tur. A5 48

Sebiş, Rom. C6 20
Sebnitz, Ger. E14 10
Sebree, Ky., U.S. E9 114
Sebring, Fl., U.S. L5 112
Secas, Islas, is., Pan. J12 92
Sechelt, B.C., Can. H11 102
Sechura, Peru A1 82
Sechura, Bahía de, b., Peru A1 82
Sechura, Desierto de, des., Peru A1 82
Seclantás, Arg. C5 80
Seco, stm., Arg. B7 80
Sečovce, Slov. G21 10
Section, Al., U.S. H11 114
Sécure, stm., Bol. F9 82
Security, Co., U.S. M3 118
Seda, China E7 30
Seda, Lat. D8 22
Seda, Lith. E5 22
Sedalia, Alta., Can. G4 104
Sedalia, Mo., U.S. D3 114
Sedan, Fr. C11 14
Sedan, Ks., U.S. N11 118
Sedano, Spain C8 16
Sedel'nikovo, Russia F13 26
Sederot, Isr. E3 50
Sedgefield, N.C., U.S. D6 112
Sedgewick, Alta., Can. E23 102
Sedgwick, Co., U.S. K5 118
Sedgwick, Ks., U.S. N10 118
Sedgwick, Mount, mtn., N.M., U.S. I8 120
Sedini, Italy I3 18
Sedlčany, Czech. F14 10
Sedom (Sodom), hist., Isr. F4 50
Sedona, Az., U.S. J5 120
Sedot Yam, Isr. D3 50
Sedova, pik, mtn., Russia C8 26
Sedrata, Alg. M2 18
Sedro Woolley, Wa., U.S. B3 122
Šeduva, Lith. F6 22
Seeberg, Switz. D8 13
Seeber Lake, l., Ont., Can. E21 104
Seefeld in Tirol, Aus. H11 10
Seehausen, Ger. C11 10
Seeheim, Nmb. F3 66
Seeis, Nmb. D3 66
Seekaskootch Indian Reserve, Sask., Can. E5 104
Seeley Lake, Mt., U.S. C12 122
Seelow, Ger. C14 10
Seelyville, In., U.S. C9 114
Seengen, Switz. D9 13
Sées, Fr. D7 14
Seesen, Ger. D10 10
Sefadu, S.L. G4 64
Sefar, hist., Alg. H15 62
Sefare, Bots. D8 66
Sefīd Ābeh, Iran F16 48
Sefrou, Mor. D8 62
Segamat, Malay. M7 40
Şegarcea, Rom. E7 20
Šegbana, Benin F11 64
Segbwema, S.L. G4 64
Segeža, Russia E4 26
Segni, Italy H8 18
Segorbe, Spain F11 16
Ségou, Mali E6 64
Segovia, Col. D5 84
Segovia, Spain E7 16
Segozero, ozero, l., Russia J23 6
Segre, stm., Eur. D12 16
Séguédine, Niger D9 54
Séguéla, C. Iv. H6 64
Séguéla, Mali D6 64
Seguí, Arg. F8 80
Seguin, Tx., U.S. J9 116
Segundo, Co., U.S. N3 118
Segundo, stm., Arg. F7 80
Segura, Port. F5 16
Segura, stm., Spain G11 16
Sehithwa, Bots. C6 66
Seia, Port. E4 16
Seibert, Co., U.S. L5 118
Seiling, Ok., U.S. C8 116
Seilo, Sud. K2 60
Sein, Île de, i., Fr. D2 14
Seinäjoki, Fin. J18 6
Seine, stm., Man., Can. I18 104
Seine, stm., Ont., Can. B3 110
Seine, stm., Fr. C7 14
Seine, Baie de la, b., Fr. C6 14
Seine-et-Marne, dept., Fr. D10 14
Seine-Maritime, dept., Fr. C8 14
Seival, Port. G2 16
Sejm, stm., Eur. G4 26
Sejmčan, Russia E22 28
Seke, Eth. M10 60
Šeki, Azer. I7 26
Šeki, Japan L11 36
Seki, Tur. M13 20
Sekoma, Bots. E6 66
Sekondi-Takoradi, Ghana I9 64
Šekota, Eth. K10 60
Šeksna, Russia B21 22
Šelagskij, mys, c., Russia C26 28
Selah, Wa., U.S. D5 122
Selaru, Pulau, i., Indon. G9 38
Selatan, Tanjung, c., Indon. F5 38
Selawik, Ak., U.S. C14 100
Selayar, Pulau, i., Indon. G7 38
Selb, Ger. E12 10
Selbu, Nor. J12 6
Selby, S.D., U.S. F7 118
Selbyville, De., U.S. I11 108
Sel'co, Russia H17 22
Selden, Ks., U.S. L7 118
Seldovia, Ak., U.S. G19 100
Selebi Phikwe, Bots. D8 66
Selenga (Selenge), stm., Asia G19 26
Selenge (Selenga), stm., Asia B7 30
Selenn'ach, stm., Russia D20 28
Sélestat, Fr. D14 14
Selezn'ovo, Russia A11 22
Selfridge, N.D., U.S. E7 118
Šelibaby, Maur. D3 64
Šelichova, zaliv, b., Russia F23 28
Seliger, ozero, l., Russia D16 22
Seligman, Az., U.S. I4 120
Seligman, Mo., U.S. F3 114
Selinsgrove, Pa., U.S. G10 108
Selišče, Russia E16 22
Seližarovo, Russia E16 22
Selje, Nor. J9 6
Seljord, Nor. L11 6
Selkirk, Man., Can. H18 104
Selkirk, Scot., U.K. F11 8
Selkirk Mountains, mts., N.A. F16 102
Seller Lake, l., Man., Can. C20 104
Sellers, S.C., U.S. E7 112
Sellersburg, In., U.S. D11 114
Sells, Az., U.S. M5 120
Selm, Ger. D7 10
Selma, Al., U.S. J9 114
Selma, Ca., U.S. H6 124
Selma, N.C., U.S. D8 112
Selmer, Tn., U.S. G8 114
Selmont, Al., U.S. J9 114
Selous, Mount, mtn., Yukon, Can. E28 100
Seltz, Fr. D15 14
Selva, Arg. E7 80
Selvas, for., Braz. E6 76
Selwyn, Austl. C4 70

Selwyn, Mount, mtn., B.C., Can. B11 102
Selwyn Lake, l., Can. E12 96
Selwyn Mountains, mts., Can. D28 100
Selwyn Range, mts., Austl. C4 70
Seman, stm., Alb. I3 20
Semans, Sask., Can. G10 104
Semarang, Indon. j15 39a
Semenivka, Ukr. I15 22
Semeru, Gunung, mtn., Indon. k16 39a
Semeževo, Bela. I10 22
Semibratovo, Russia D22 22
Seminary, Ms., U.S. K7 114
Seminoe Reservoir, res., Wy., U.S. B10 120
Seminole, Ok., U.S. D10 116
Seminole, Tx., U.S. G4 116
Seminole, Lake, res., U.S. I2 112
Semipalatinsk, Kaz. G8 28
Semmens Lake, l., Man., Can. C20 104
Semnān, Iran D12 48
Semois, stm., Eur. I7 12
Semonaicha, Kaz. G14 26
Sem'onov, Russia F6 26
Semple Lake, l., Man., Can. C19 104
Semporna, Malay. E6 38
Semuliki, stm., Afr. A5 58
Semur-en-Auxois, Fr. E11 14
Sena, Bol. D8 82
Sena, Moz. E7 58
Senador Canedo, Braz. D4 79
Senador Firmino, Braz. F7 79
Senador Pompeu, Braz. E11 76
Senahú, Guat. B5 92
Sena Madureira, Braz. C7 82
Senanga, Zam. E4 58
Senate, Sask., Can. I5 104
Senath, Mo., U.S. F6 114
Senatobia, Ms., U.S. H7 114
Sendafa, Eth. M10 60
Sendai, Japan I15 36
Sêndo, China E15 44
Seneca, Il., U.S. I7 110
Seneca, Ks., U.S. L11 118
Seneca, Mo., U.S. F2 114
Seneca, Or., U.S. F7 122
Seneca, S.C., U.S. E4 112
Seneca Falls, N.Y., U.S. E10 108
Seneca Lake, l., N.Y., U.S. E10 108
Senegal (Sénégal), ctry., Afr. F4 54
Sénégal, stm., Afr. E4 54
Senekal, S. Afr. G8 66
Senftenberg, Ger. D14 10
Sengés, Braz. H4 79
Senhor do Bonfim, Braz. F10 76
Senica, Slov. G17 10
Senigallia, Italy F8 18
Senise, Italy I11 18
Senj, Cro. E9 18
Senja, i., Nor. G15 6
Šenkursk, Russia E6 26
Senlac, Sask., Can. F5 104
Senlis, Fr. C9 14
Senmonorom, Camb. H9 40
Sennori, Italy I3 18
Senoia, Ga., U.S. F2 112
Senqu see Orange, stm., Afr. G4 66
Sens, Fr. D10 14
Sensuntepeque, El Sal. D6 92
Senta, Yugo. D4 20
Sentinel, Ok., U.S. D7 116
Sentinel Peak, mtn., B.C., Can. C13 102
Seo de Urgel, Spain C13 16
Seoni, India I8 44
Seoul see Sŏul, S. Kor. F14 32
Sepatini, stm., Braz. B9 82
Sepetiba, Baía de, b., Braz. G7 79
Sepik, stm., Pap. N. Gui. k15 68a
Sępólno Krajeńskie, Pol. B17 10
Sepopa, Bots. B6 66
Sepoti, stm., Braz. B11 82
Sepotuba, stm., Braz. F13 82
Sept-Îles (Seven Islands), Que., Can. B7 106
Sepulga, stm., Al., U.S. K10 114
Sequatchie, stm., Tn., U.S. D1 112
Sequeros, Spain E5 16
Sequim, Wa., U.S. B2 122
Sequoia National Park, Ca., U.S. H7 124
Šerabad, Uzb. B2 44
Serachs, Turk. C16 48
Serafimovič, Russia H6 26
Seraidi, Alg. M2 18
Seraing, Bel. G7 12
Seram (Ceram), i., Indon. F8 38
Seram, Laut (Ceram Sea), Indon. F8 38
Serang, Indon. j13 39a
Serbia see Srbija, state, Yugo. F4 20
Serdobsk, Russia G6 26
Serebr'anyje Prudy, Russia G21 22
Sered', Slov. G17 10
Seredejskij, Russia G18 22
Seredina-Buda, Ukr. I17 22
Seredžius, Lith. F6 22
Seremban, Malay. M6 40
Serengeti Plain, pl., Tan. B6 58
Serenje, Zam. D6 58
Šereševo, Bela. I7 22
Seret (Siret), stm., Eur. A9 20
Sergeant Bluff, Ia., U.S. I11 118
Sergeja Kirova, ostrova, is., Russia B15 26
Sergejevka, Russia I18 28
Sergijev Posad, Russia E21 22
Seria, Bru. E5 38
Serian, Malay. N11 40
Sérifos, i., Grc. L8 20
Sérigny, stm., Que., Can. E19 96
Serkhe, Cerro, mtn., Bol. G7 82
Šerlovaja Gora, Russia G15 28
Sermata, Pulau, i., Indon. G8 38
Serodino, Arg. G8 80
Serov, Russia F10 26
Serowe, Bots. D8 66
Serpa, Port. H4 16
Serpent, Rivière au, stm., Que., Can. C2 106
Serpents Mouth, strt. C12 84
Serpuchov, Russia G20 22
Serra, Braz. F8 79
Serra do Navio, Braz. C8 76
Serra do Salitre, Braz. E5 79
Sérrai, Grc. H7 20
Serrana, Braz. F5 79
Serrânia, Braz. F5 79
Serranópolis, Braz. E2 79
Serra Talhada, Braz. E11 76
Serrezuela, Arg. F6 80
Serrinha, Braz. F11 76
Serro, Braz. E7 79
Sersale, Italy J11 18
Sertânia, Braz. E11 76
Seruini, stm., Braz. C8 82
Serule, Bots. C8 66
Sêrxü, China E6 30
Sesfontein, Nmb. B1 66
Sesheke, Zam. E4 58
Seskar, ostrov, i., Russia A11 22

Sessa Aurunca, Italy H8 18
Sestao, Spain B8 16
Sestri Levante, Italy E4 18
Šestroreck, Russia A12 22
Šešupe, stm., Eur. G5 22
Setana, Japan e14 36a
Sète, Fr. I10 14
Sete Barras, Braz. C15 80
Sete de Setembro, stm., Braz. B2 79
Sete Lagoas, Braz. E6 79
Sete Quedas, Parque Nacional de, Braz. C11 80
Seth Ward, Tx., U.S. E5 116
Set Net, Punta, c., Nic. E11 92
Seto, Japan L12 36
Seto-naikai, Japan M7 36
Seton Lake, l., B.C., Can. G12 102
Seton Portage, B.C., Can. G12 102
Settat, Mor. D7 62
Setté Cama, Gabon B1 58
Sette-Daban, chrebet, mts., Russia E19 28
Settee Lake, l., Man., Can. A18 104
Setting Lake, l., Man., Can. C16 104
Setúbal, Port. G3 16
Setúbal, Baía de, b., Port. G3 16
Seui, Italy J4 18
Seul, Lac, l., Ont., Can. H22 104
Seurre, Fr. E12 14
Sevan, Arm. A8 48
Sevan, ozero, l., Arm. I7 26
Sévaré, Mali D7 64
Sevastopol', Ukr. I4 26
Seven Islands see Sept-Îles, Que., Can. B7 106
Seven Persons, Alta., Can. I4 104
Seven Sisters Peaks, mts., B.C., Can. C6 102
Seventy Mile House, B.C., Can. F13 102
Severn, stm., Ont., Can. E15 96
Severn, stm., U.K. J11 8
Severnaja Dvina, stm., Russia E6 26
Severnaja Osetija, state, Russia I6 26
Severnaja Sos'va, stm., Russia E4 28
Severnaja Zeml'a, is., Russia B17 26
Severna Park, Md., U.S. H10 108
Severn Lake, l., Ont., Can. E24 104
Severnyje uvaly, hills, Russia B27 22
Severodvinsk, Russia E5 26
Severo-Dvinskij kanal, Russia B21 22
Severomorsk, Russia D4 26
Severo-Sibirskaja nizmennost', pl., Russia C18 26
Severoural'sk, Russia E9 26
Severo-Zadonsk, Russia G21 22
Severy, Ks., U.S. N11 118
Sevier, stm., Ut., U.S. E4 120
Sevier Desert, des., Ut., U.S. E4 120
Sevier Lake, l., Ut., U.S. F3 120
Sevierville, Tn., U.S. D3 112
Sevilla, Col. E5 84
Sevilla (Seville), Spain H6 16
Sevilla, Isla, i., Pan. I12 92
Seville see Sevilla, Spain H6 16
Seville, Fl., U.S. J5 112
Seville, Oh., U.S. F5 108
Şevketiye, Tur. I11 20
Sevsk, Russia I17 22
Sewanee, Tn., U.S. G11 114
Seward, Ak., U.S. F20 100
Seward, Ne., U.S. K10 118
Seward, Pa., U.S. G7 108
Seward Glacier, N.A. F24 100
Seward Peninsula, pen., Ak., U.S. D13 100
Sewell, Chile H3 80
Sexsmith, Alta., Can. B16 102
Sextín, stm., Mex. E7 90
Seybaplaya, Mex. H14 90
Seychelles, ctry., Afr. B11 58
Seydisfjördur, Ice. B6 6a
Seylac, Som. F9 56
Seymour, Austl. K6 70
Seymour, S. Afr. I8 66
Seymour, Ct., U.S. F13 108
Seymour, In., U.S. D11 114
Seymour, Ia., U.S. J2 110
Seymour, Mo., U.S. E4 114
Seymour, Tx., U.S. F7 116
Seymour, Wi., U.S. F7 110
Seymour, stm., B.C., Can. F8 102
Seymour Inlet, b., B.C., Can. F7 102
Seymourville, La., U.S. L5 114
Seyssel, Fr. G12 14
Sezela, S. Afr. H10 66
Sfântu Gheorghe, Rom. D9 20
Sfântu Gheorghe, Ostrovul, i., Rom. D13 20
Sfax, Tun. C16 62
Sfizef, Alg. C10 62
's-Gravenbrakel see Braine-le-Comte, Bel. G5 12
's-Gravenhage (The Hague), Neth. D5 12
Shaanxi (Shensi), prov., China D8 30
Shabeelle (Shebele), stm., Afr. H9 56
Shabwah, Yemen G5 47
Shache (Yarkand), China A7 44
Shackan Indian Reserve, B.C., Can. G13 102
Shackleton Ice Shelf, Ant. B6 73
Shādegān, Iran F10 48
Shady Cove, Or., U.S. H3 122
Shady Grove, Fl., U.S. I3 112
Shadyside, Oh., U.S. H6 108
Shafer Butte, mtn., Id., U.S. G9 122
Shafter, Ca., U.S. I6 124
Shagamu, Nig. H11 64
Shageluk, Ak., U.S. E15 100
Shag Rocks, S. Geor. G8 78
Shāhābād, India E7 44
Shāhābād, India D4 46
Shah Alam, Malay. M6 40
Shahdād, Namakzār-e, pl., Iran F15 48
Shahdol, India I9 44
Shahe, China I6 32
Shāhjahānpur, India G8 44
Shāh Jūy, Afg. D2 44
Shāhpur, Pak. F3 44
Shāhpura, India H6 44
Shahrak, Afg. C1 44
Shahr-e Bābak, Iran F13 48
Shahr-e Kord, Iran E11 48
Shā'īb al-Banāt, Jabal, mtn., Egypt H2 48
Shaikou, China H6 34
Shakawe, Bots. B5 66
Shaker Heights, Oh., U.S. F5 108
Shaki, Nig. G11 64
Shākir, Jazīrat, i., Egypt H2 48
Shakopee, Mn., U.S. F2 110
Shaktoolik, Ak., U.S. D14 100
Shala, Lake, l., Eth. N10 60
Shalalth, B.C., Can. G12 102

Shalatayn, Bi'r, well, Egypt J3 48
Shaler Mountains, mts., N.W. Ter., Can. B10 96
Shaleshanto, Bots. B6 66
Shallotte, N.C., U.S. F8 112
Shallowater, Tx., U.S. F5 116
Shām, Bādiyat ash- (Syrian Desert), des., Asia E6 48
Shām, Jabal ash-, mtn., Oman C10 47
Shamattawa, Man., Can. C22 104
Shambe, Sud. N6 60
Shambu, Eth. M9 60
Shamīl, Iran H14 48
Shāmli, India F7 44
Shamokin, Pa., U.S. G10 108
Shamrock, Fl., U.S. J3 112
Shamrock, Tx., U.S. D6 116
Shamva, Zimb. E6 58
Shanany, ozero, l., Ukr. D13 20
Shanbiao, China H1 32
Shandī, Sud. I7 60
Shandong (Shantung), prov., China D10 30
Shandong Bandao (Shantung Peninsula), pen., China F8 32
Shangani, Zimb. B9 66
Shangani, stm., Zimb. B9 66
Shangcheng, China D4 34
Shangfu, China G3 34
Shanggu, China C6 32
Shanghai, China D10 34
Shanghai Shi, China E11 30
Shangjiaodao, China F8 34
Shangping, China K3 34
Shangqing, China G6 34
Shangqiu (Zhuji), China A4 34
Shangrao, China G6 34
Shangshui, China B3 34
Shangxian, China E8 30
Shangxingzhen, China D8 34
Shangyuan, China B8 32
Shangzhi, China B12 30
Shangzhuang, China C7 32
Shankou, China G3 34
Shannon, S. Afr. G8 66
Shannon, Ga., U.S. E1 112
Shannon, Il., U.S. H6 110
Shannon, Ms., U.S. H8 114
Shannon, stm., Ire. I4 8
Shannontown, S.C., U.S. F6 112
Shanpo, China E3 34
Shansi see Shanxi, prov., China D9 30
Shāntipur, India I13 44
Shantou (Swatow), China L5 34
Shanxi (Shansi), prov., China D9 30
Shanxian, China I4 32
Shanxu, China C9 40
Shanyin, China D9 30
Shaodian, China B3 34
Shaoguan, China K2 34
Shaowu, China H6 34
Shaoxing, China E9 34
Shaoyang, China F9 30
Shaqqā, Syria C7 50
Shaqrā', Sau. Ar. I8 48
Shaqrā', Yemen H4 47
Sharafkhāneh, Iran B8 48
Sharbatāt, Ra's ash-, c., Oman F10 47
Sharbot Lake, Ont., Can. F19 110
Share, Nig. G12 64
Shark Bay, b., Austl. E2 68
Sharktooth Mountain, mtn., B.C., Can. E7 96
Sharktooth Mountain, mtn., B.C., Can. G31 100
Sharm ash-Shaykh, Egypt D8 60
Sharon, N.D., U.S. D10 118
Sharon, Pa., U.S. F6 108
Sharon, Tn., U.S. F8 114
Sharon, Wi., U.S. H7 110
Sharon Springs, Ks., U.S. M6 118
Sharpe, Lake, res., S.D., U.S. G8 118
Sharpe Lake, l., Man., Can. D21 104
Sharqī, Al-Jabal ash- (Anti-Lebanon), mts., Asia A6 50
Sharqīyah, Aş-Şahrā' ash- (Arabian Desert), des., Egypt D7 60
Shasha, Eth. N8 60
Shashe, stm., Afr. C9 66
Shashemene, Eth. N10 60
Shashi, China E9 30
Shasta, Ca., U.S. D3 124
Shasta, stm., Ca., U.S. C3 124
Shasta, Mount, vol., Ca., U.S. C3 124
Shasta Lake, res., Ca., U.S. D3 124
Shatawī, Sud. J7 60
Shattuck, Ok., U.S. C7 116
Shatuji, China H3 32
Shaunavon, Sask., Can. I6 104
Shaw, Ms., U.S. I6 114
Shawano, Wi., U.S. F7 110
Shawinigan, Que., Can. G18 96
Shawnee, Ks., U.S. L13 118
Shawnee, Oh., U.S. H4 108
Shawnee, Ok., U.S. D10 116
Shawneetown, Il., U.S. E8 114
Shawo, China G3 34
Shawville, Que., Can. B10 108
Shaybārā, i., Sau. Ar. I4 48
Shay Gap, Austl. D4 68
Shaykh, Jabal ash- (Mount Hermon), mtn., Asia B5 50
Shaykh 'Uthmān, Yemen H4 47
Shayuan, China H9 34
Shebele (Shabeelle), stm., Afr. G9 56
Shebelē Wenz, stm., Afr. H3 42
Sheberghān, Afg. B1 44
Sheboygan, Wi., U.S. G8 110
Sheboygan, stm., Wi., U.S. G8 110
Sheboygan Falls, Wi., U.S. G8 110
Shechem see Nābulus, Isr. Occ. D4 50
Shediac, N.B., Can. F9 106
Shedin Peak, mtn., B.C., Can. B7 102
Sheenjek, stm., Ak., U.S. C23 100
Sheep, stm., Alta., Can. G20 102
Sheep Creek, stm., Alta., Can. D15 102
Sheep Mountain, mtn., Wy., U.S. G15 122
Sheet Harbour, N.S., Can. H11 106
Shefar'am, Isr. C4 50
Sheffield, N.Z. E4 72
Sheffield, Eng., U.K. H12 8
Sheffield, Al., U.S. H9 114
Sheffield, Il., U.S. I6 110
Sheffield, Ia., U.S. H2 110
Sheffield, Pa., U.S. F7 108
Sheffield, Tx., U.S. I5 116
Sheffield Lake, l., Newf., Can. C17 106
Shegaon, India B4 46
Sheho, Sask., Can. G11 104
Sheikh Hasan, Eth. K8 60
Shekatika, Que., Can. A15 106
Shekhūpura, Pak. E5 44

Shelagyote Peak, mtn., B.C., Can. B7 102
Shelbina, Mo., U.S. C4 114
Shelburn, In., U.S. C9 114
Shelburne, N.S., Can. I8 106
Shelburne, Ont., Can. F15 110
Shelburne Falls, Ma., U.S. E14 108
Shelby, Ia., U.S. J12 118
Shelby, Mi., U.S. G9 110
Shelby, Ms., U.S. I6 114
Shelby, Mt., U.S. B14 122
Shelby, Ne., U.S. J10 118
Shelby, N.C., U.S. D5 112
Shelby, Oh., U.S. G4 108
Shelbyville, Il., U.S. C8 114
Shelbyville, In., U.S. C11 114
Shelbyville, Ky., U.S. D11 114
Shelbyville, Mo., U.S. C4 114
Shelbyville, Tn., U.S. G10 114
Shelbyville, Lake, res., Il., U.S. C8 114
Sheldon, Ia., U.S. H12 118
Sheldon, Mo., U.S. E2 114
Shelikof Strait, strt., Ak., U.S. H17 100
Shell, stm., Man., Can. G13 104
Shellbrook, Sask., Can. E8 104
Shell Brook, stm., Sask., Can. E8 104
Shelley, B.C., Can. C12 102
Shelley, Id., U.S. G13 122
Shellharbour, Austl. J9 70
Shell Lake, Sask., Can. E7 104
Shell Lake, Wi., U.S. E4 110
Shellman, Ga., U.S. H2 112
Shellmouth Dam, Man., Can. H13 104
Shell Rock, Ia., U.S. H3 110
Shell Rock, stm., U.S. G2 110
Shellsburg, Ia., U.S. H4 110
Shelton, Ct., U.S. F13 108
Shelton, Ne., U.S. K9 118
Shelton, Wa., U.S. C2 122
Shemogue, N.B., Can. F9 106
Shemya Station, Ak., U.S. j2 101a
Shenandoah, Ia., U.S. K12 118
Shenandoah, Pa., U.S. G10 108
Shenandoah, Va., U.S. I8 108
Shenandoah, stm., U.S. H9 108
Shenandoah National Park, Va., U.S. I8 108
Shendam, Nig. G14 64
Shengang, China H5 34
Shengtian, China H2 34
Shengze, China E9 34
Shenqiu, China B4 34
Shensi see Shaanxi, prov., China D8 30
Shenyang (Mukden), China B11 32
Shenzhen, China M3 34
Sheopur, India H7 44
Shepard, Alta., Can. G21 102
Shepetivka, Ukr. G3 26
Shepherd, Mi., U.S. G11 110
Shepherd, Tx., U.S. L1 114
Shepherdstown, W.V., U.S. H9 108
Shepherdsville, Ky., U.S. E11 114
Sheppard Peak, mtn., B.C., Can. H28 100
Shepparton, Austl. K6 70
Sheqi, China B1 34
Sherab, Sud. L3 60
Sherada, Eth. N9 60
Sherard, Cape, c., N.W. Ter., Can. B16 96
Sherbro Island, i., S.L. H3 64
Sherbrooke, N.S., Can. G12 106
Sherbrooke, Que., Can. B15 108
Sherbrooke Lake, l., N.S., Can. H9 106
Sherburn, Mn., U.S. H13 118
Sherburne, N.Y., U.S. E11 108
Sheridan, Ar., U.S. H4 114
Sheridan, In., U.S. B10 114
Sheridan, Mt., U.S. E13 122
Sheridan, Or., U.S. E2 122
Sheridan, Tx., U.S. J10 116
Sheridan, Wy., U.S. F19 122
Sherman, Ms., U.S. H8 114
Sherman, N.Y., U.S. E7 108
Sherman, Tx., U.S. F10 116
Sherman Mills, Me., U.S. B18 108
Sherman Station, Me., U.S. B18 108
Sherpur, Bngl. H14 44
Sherrard, Il., U.S. I5 110
Sherridon, Man., Can. C13 104
Sherrill, N.Y., U.S. D11 108
Shertallai, India H4 46
's-Hertogenbosch, Neth. E7 12
Sherwood, P.E.I., Can. F10 106
Sherwood, Ar., U.S. H4 114
Sherwood, N.D., U.S. C6 118
Sherwood, Oh., U.S. F2 108
Sherwood, Tn., U.S. G11 114
Sherwood Park, Alta., Can. D21 102
Sherwood Shores, Tx., U.S. I8 116
Sheshea, stm., Peru C5 82
Shetland, prov., Scot., U.K. A12 8
Shetland Islands, is., Scot., U.K. A12 8
Shevchenkove, Ukr. D13 20
Shewa Gimira, Eth. N8 60
Shexian, China F7 34
Sheyenne, N.D., U.S. D8 118
Sheyenne, stm., N.D., U.S. E10 118
Sheykhābād, Afg. C3 44
Shḥim, Leb. A4 50
Shiba, China F5 34
Shibām, Yemen G6 47
Shibarni, Sud. J3 60
Shibata, Japan J14 36
Shibetsu, Japan c17 36a
Shibīn al-Kawm, Egypt B6 60
Shicheng, China I5 34
Shickley, Ne., U.S. K10 118
Shickshinny, Pa., U.S. F10 108
Shidao, China G10 32
Shidler, Ok., U.S. C10 116
Shields, stm., Mt., U.S. E15 122
Shifodian, China C4 34
Shigaib, Sud. J2 60
Shigezhuang, China E4 32
Shihan, Wādī, val., Asia E8 47
Shihe, China D9 32
Shijiazhuang, China E2 32
Shijing, China K7 34
Shikārpur, Pak. G3 44
Shikohābād, India G8 44
Shikoku, i., Japan N8 36
Shiliguri, India G13 44
Shillelagh, Ire. I7 8
Shillington, Pa., U.S. G11 108
Shillong, India H14 44
Shilo, Canadian Forces Base, mil., Man., Can. I15 104
Shiloh, Oh., U.S. H2 108
Shiloh see Saylūn, Khirbat, hist., Isr. Occ. D4 50
Shilong, China L2 34
Shimabara, Japan O5 36
Shimada, Japan M13 36
Shimbiris, mtn., Som. F10 56
Shimen, China D6 32
Shimian, China F7 30
Shimiaozi, China C11 32
Shimizu, Japan L13 36
Shimla, India E7 44

Name	Map Ref.	Page
Taiobeiras, Braz.	C7	79
T'aipei, Tai.	J10	34
T'aipeihsien, Tai.	J10	34
Taiping, China	M2	34
Taiping, Malay.	L6	40
Taishun, China	H8	34
Taitao, Península de, pen., Chile	F1	78
Taitouying, China	C7	32
T'aitung, Tai.	M10	34
Taiwan (T'aiwan), ctry., Asia	G11	30
Taiwan Strait, strt., Asia	K8	34
Taixian, China	C9	34
Taixing, China	C9	34
Ṭaiyiba, Isr.	D4	50
Taiyuan, China	D9	30
Taizhou, China	C8	34
Ta'izz, Yemen	H4	47
Tajerouine, Tun.	N3	18
Tajga, Russia	F9	28
Tajgonos, mys, c., Russia	E24	28
Tajikistan, ctry., Asia	J12	26
Tajimi, Japan	L12	36
Tajique, N.M., U.S.	J10	120
Tajitos, Mex.	B3	90
Tajmura, stm., Russia	E17	26
Tajmyr, ozero, l., Russia	C18	26
Tajmyr, poluostrov, pen., Russia	B18	26
Tajšet, Russia	F11	28
Tajumulco, Volcán, vol., Guat.	B3	92
Tak, Thai.	F5	40
Takāb, Iran	C9	48
Takachu, Bots.	D5	66
Takahashi, Japan	M8	36
Takahe, Mount, mtn., Ant.	C11	73
Takaka, N.Z.	D4	72
Takakkaw Falls, wtfl, B.C., Can.	F18	102
Takamatsu, Japan	M9	36
Takaoka, Japan	K12	36
Takapuna, N.Z.	B5	72
Takasaki, Japan	K14	36
Takatsuki, Japan	M10	36
Takayama, Japan	K12	36
Takefu, Japan	L11	36
Takenake, China	C9	44
Takengon, Indon.	L4	40
Take-shima, i., Japan	q5	37b
Take-shima (Tok-to), is., Asia	J6	36
Tākestān, Iran	C10	48
Takêv, Camb.	I8	40
Takhli, Thai.	G6	40
Takijuk Lake, l., N.W. Ter., Can.	C10	96
Takikawa, Japan	d16	36a
Takla Lake, l., B.C., Can.	B9	102
Takla Landing, B.C., Can.	B9	102
Taklimakan Shamo, des., China	D3	30
Takrouna, Tun.	M5	18
Taku, stm., N.A.	G28	100
Takua Pa, Thai.	J5	40
Taku Glacier, Ak., U.S.	G27	100
Takum, Nig.	H14	64
Takutu (Tacutu), stm., S.A.	F13	84
Takysie Lake, B.C., Can.	D9	102
Tala, Mex.	G8	90
Tala, Ur.	H11	80
Talagang, Pak.	D5	44
Talagante, Chile	G3	80
Talamanca, Cordillera de, mts., C.R.	H11	92
Talara, Peru	J2	84
Talas, Kyrg.	I12	26
Talasea, Pap. N. Gui.	m17	68a
Talata Mafara, Nig.	E13	64
Talaud, Kepulauan, is., Indon.	E8	38
Talavera de la Reina, Spain	F7	16
Talawdī, Sud.	L6	60
Talbot Lake, l., Man., Can.	D15	104
Talbotton, Ga., U.S.	G2	112
Talbragar, stm., Austl.	I8	70
Talca, Chile	H3	80
Talcahuano, Chile	I2	80
Talchichitle, Isla, i., Mex.	E5	90
Talco, Tx., U.S.	F11	116
Taldom, Russia	E20	22
Taldy-Kurgan, Kaz.	H13	26
Talent, Or., U.S.	H3	122
Tālesh, Iran	C10	48
Talgar, Kaz.	I13	26
Taliabu, Pulau, i., Indon.	F7	38
Talica, Russia	F10	26
Talickij Čamlyk, Russia	I23	22
Talihina, Ok., U.S.	E11	116
Taliouine, Mor.	E7	62
Tali Post, Sud.	O6	60
Talish Mountains (Kūhhā-ye Tavālesh, mts., Asia	B10	48
Tal'ka, Bela.	H11	22
Talkeetna, Ak., U.S.	E19	100
Talladega, Al., U.S.	I10	114
Tall 'Afar, Iraq	C7	48
Tallah, Egypt	C6	60
Tallahassee, Fl., U.S.	I2	112
Tallahatchie, stm., Ms., U.S.	I6	114
Tallangatta, Austl.	K7	70
Tallapoosa, Ga., U.S.	F1	112
Tallapoosa, stm., U.S.	J10	114
Tallassee, Al., U.S.	J11	114
Tallinn, Est.	B7	22
Tall Kalakh, Syria	D4	48
Tallmadge, Oh., U.S.	F5	108
Tallula, Il., U.S.	C7	114
Tallulah, La., U.S.	J5	114
Talmage, Ca., U.S.	E2	124
Talmage, Ne., U.S.	K11	118
Tal'menka, Russia	G14	26
Talmont, Fr.	F5	14
Talo, mtn., Eth.	L9	60
Taloga, Ok., U.S.	C8	116
Talpa, Tx., U.S.	H7	116
Talsi, Lat.	D5	22
Taltal, Chile	C3	80
Taltapin Lake, l., B.C., Can.	C9	102
Taltson, stm., N.W. Ter., Can.	D10	96
Talwood, Austl.	G8	70
Tama, Arg.	F5	80
Tama, Ia., U.S.	I3	110
Tamacuarí, Pico, mtn., S.A.	G10	84
Tamadjert, Alg.	H14	62
Tamalameque, Col.	C6	84
Tamale, Ghana	G9	64
Tamana, Japan	O5	36
Tamaná, Cerro, mtn., Col.	E4	84
Tamanaco, stm., Ven.	C10	84
Tamaniquá, Braz.	I10	84
Tamano, Japan	M8	36
Tamanquaré, Ilha, i., Braz.	H10	84
Tamapatz, Mex.	G10	90
Tamaqua, Pa., U.S.	G11	108
Tamar, stm., Austl.	M7	70
Támara, Col.	E6	84
Tamarac, stm., Mn., U.S.	C10	118
Tamaroa, Il., U.S.	D7	114
Tamarugal, Pampa del, pl., Chile	I7	82
Tamási, Hung.	I18	10
Tamaské, Niger	D12	64
Tamaulipas, state, Mex.	F10	90
Tamaya, stm., Peru	C4	82
Tamazula, Mex.	E6	90
Tamazula de Gordiano, Mex.	H8	90
Tamazulapan del Progreso, Mex.	I11	90
Tamazunchale, Mex.	G10	90
Tambacounda, Sen.	E3	64
Tamba Dabatou, Gui.	F4	64
Tāmbaram, India	F6	46
Tambelan, Kepulauan, is., Indon.	N9	40
Tamberías, Arg.	F4	80
Tambo, Austl.	E7	70
Tambo, Peru	E4	82
Tambo, stm., Austl.	K7	70
Tambo, stm., Peru	G6	82
Tambo, stm., Peru	D5	82
Tamboara, Braz.	G2	79
Tambo Grande, Peru	A1	82
Tambohorano, Madag.	p20	67b
Tambopata, stm., S.A.	E7	82
Tambor, C.R.	H9	92
Tamboritha, Mount, mtn., Austl.	K7	70
Tamboryacu, stm., Peru	H5	84
Tambov, Russia	I24	22
Tambura, Sud.	O4	60
Tamchaket, Maur.	C4	64
Tame, Col.	D7	84
Tameapa, Mex.	E6	90
Tameghza, Tun.	C14	62
Tamel Aike, Arg.	F2	78
Tamelelt, Mor.	E7	62
Tamenghest, Alg.	I13	62
Tamenghest, Oued, val., Alg.	I11	62
Tamiahua, Mex.	G11	90
Tamiahua, Laguna de, b., Mex.	G11	90
Tamiami Canal, Fl., U.S.	N5	112
Tamil Nādu, state, India	G5	46
Tamiš (Timiş), stm., Eur.	D4	20
Tamitatoala, stm., Braz.	B2	79
Tam Ky, Viet.	G10	40
Tamms, Il., U.S.	E7	114
Tamnum, Yemen	G7	47
Tampa, Fl., U.S.	L4	112
Tampa Bay, b., Fl., U.S.	L4	112
Tampaón, stm., Mex.	G10	90
Tampere, Fin.	K18	6
Tampico, Mex.	F11	90
Tampico, Il., U.S.	I6	110
Tampin, Malay.	M7	40
Tam Quan, Viet.	G10	40
Tamri, Mor.	E6	62
Tamsagbulag, Mong.	B10	30
Tamsalu, Est.	B9	22
Tamshiyacu, Peru	J6	84
Tamsweg, Aus.	H13	10
Tamworth, Austl.	H9	70
Tamyang, S. Kor.	H14	32
Tana, Chile	H7	82
Tana (Teno), stm., Eur.	F20	6
Tana, Lake, l., Eth.	K9	60
Tanabe, Japan	N10	36
Tanabi, Braz.	F4	79
Tanacross, Ak., U.S.	E23	100
Tanahbala, Pulau, i., Indon.	O5	40
Tanahmasa, Pulau, i., Indon.	O5	40
Tanami Desert, des., Austl.	C5	68
Tan An, Viet.	I9	40
Tanana, Ak., U.S.	D18	100
Tanana, stm., Ak., U.S.	D19	100
Tananarive see Antananarivo, Madag.	q22	67b
Tancheng, China	I6	32
Tanchoj, Russia	G13	28
Tanch'ŏn, N. Kor.	C16	32
Tancítaro, Pico de, mtn., Mex.	H8	90
Tānda, India	G10	44
Tandaltī, Sud.	K6	60
Tandil, Arg.	I9	80
Tandou Lake, l., Austl.	I5	70
Tanega-shima, i., Japan	q6	37b
Tan Emellel, Alg.	G15	62
Taneytown, Md., U.S.	H9	108
Tanezrouft, des., Afr.	D6	54
Tanga, Tan.	C7	58
Tangail, Bngl.	H13	44
Tangainony, Madag.	s22	67b
Tangalla, Sri L.	I6	46
Tanganyika, Lake, l., Afr.	C5	58
Tangarana, stm., Peru	I5	84
Tangcun, China	J2	34
Tanger (Tangier), Mor.	C8	62
Tangermünde, Ger.	C11	10
Tanggou, China	B7	34
Tanggu, China	D5	32
Tanggula Shan, mts., China	D13	44
Tangier, N.S., Can.	H11	106
Tangier see Tanger, Mor.	C8	62
Tangier, Va., U.S.	B11	112
Tangipahoa, stm., U.S.	K6	114
Tangjiagou, China	E6	34
Tangjin, S. Kor.	G14	32
Tangra Yumco, l., China	E12	44
Tangsanying, China	B5	32
Tangshan, China	D6	32
Tanguiéta, Benin	F10	64
Tangxian, China	E2	32
Tanimbar, Kepulauan, is., Indon.	G9	38
Taninges, Fr.	F13	14
Tanjiafang, China	G6	32
Tanjiang, China	K5	34
Tanjungbalai, Indon.	M5	40
Tanjungpandan, Indon.	F4	38
Tanjungpinang, Indon.	N8	40
Tanjungselor, Indon.	E6	38
Tānk, Pak.	D4	44
Tan Kena, Alg.	G15	62
Tännäs, Swe.	J13	6
Tanner, Al., U.S.	H10	114
Tanner, Mount, mtn., B.C., Can.	H16	102
Tannu-Ola, chrebet, mts., Asia	G10	28
Tannūrah, Ra's, c., Sau. Ar.	H11	48
Tano, stm., Afr.	I8	64
Tânout, Niger	D14	64
Tanquinho, Braz.	A9	79
Tanshui, Tai.	J10	34
Tánsin, Isla de, i., Hond.	B11	92
Tánsin, Laguna de, b., Hond.	B11	92
Ṭanṭā, Egypt	B6	60
Tan-Tan, Mor.	F5	62
Tantoyuca, Mex.	G10	90
Tanuku, India	D6	46
Tanyang, S. Kor.	G16	32
Tanzania, ctry., Afr.	C6	58
Tao, stm., China	E7	30
Taochong, China	D7	34
Tao'er, stm., China	B11	30
Taolakepa, China	D11	44
Taoling, China	E7	34
Taormina, Italy	L10	18
Taos, Mo., U.S.	D4	114
Taos, N.M., U.S.	H11	120
Taos Pueblo, N.M., U.S.	H11	120
Taoudenni, Mali	I8	62
Taounate, Mor.	C8	62
Taoura, Alg.	M3	18
Taourirt, Mor.	C9	62
Taoussa, Mali	C9	64
Taoyuan, China	J6	34
Tapa, Est.	B8	22
Tapacari, Bol.	G8	82
Tapachula, Mex.	J13	90
Tapah, Malay.	L6	40
Tapaje, stm., Col.	F3	84
Tapajós, stm., Braz.	D7	76
Tapalqué, Arg.	I8	80
Tapanahony, stm., Sur.	C7	76
Tapauá, Braz.	A10	82
Tapauá, stm., Braz.	A9	82
Tapejara, Braz.	E12	80
Tapera, Braz.	E12	80
Taperas, Bol.	G11	82
Taperoá, Braz.	B9	79
Tapes, Braz.	F13	80
Tapeta, Lib.	H5	64
Taphan Hin, Thai.	F6	40
Tāpi, stm., India	B2	46
Tapiche, stm., Peru	A5	82
Taping (Daying), stm., Asia	B4	40
Tapiraí, Braz.	E5	79
Tāplejungg, Nepal	G12	44
Tapoa, stm., Afr.	E11	64
Tapolca, Hung.	I17	10
Tappahannock, Va., U.S.	B10	112
Tappen, N.D., U.S.	E8	118
Tappi-zaki, c., Japan	F15	36
Tappo, Ghana	F8	64
Tapurucuara, Braz.	H10	84
Taqātu' Hayyā, Sud.	H9	60
Taquara, Braz.	E13	80
Taquaras, Ponta das, c., Braz.	D14	80
Taquari, Braz.	D2	79
Taquari, Braz.	E13	80
Taquari, stm., Braz.	E13	80
Taquari, stm., Braz.	H13	82
Taquari, Pantanal do, sw., Braz.	H13	82
Taquaritinga, Braz.	F4	79
Taquaruçu, stm., Braz.	F2	79
Tar, stm., N.C., U.S.	D9	112
Tara, Austl.	F9	70
Tara, Russia	F6	28
Taraba, stm., Nig.	G9	54
Tarabine, Oued ti-n-, val., Afr.	J14	62
Tarabuco, Bol.	H9	82
Ṭarābulus (Tripoli), Leb.	D3	48
Ṭarābulus (Tripoli), Libya	B3	56
Ṭarābulus (Tripolitania), hist. reg., Libya	B3	56
Taraclia, Mol.	D12	20
Tarago, Austl.	J8	70
Taraira (Traíra), stm., S.A.	H8	84
Tarakan, Indon.	E6	38
Taranaki, Mount see Egmont, Mount, mtn., N.Z.	C4	72
Tarancón, Spain	E8	16
Taranto, Italy	I12	18
Taranto, Golfo di, b., Italy	I12	18
Tarapacá, Col.	I8	84
Tarapoto, Peru	B3	82
Taraquá, Braz.	G8	84
Tarare, Fr.	G11	14
Tarariras, Ur.	H10	80
Tarāsa Dwīp, i., India	J2	40
Tarascon, Fr.	J8	14
Tarascon, Fr.	I11	14
Tarat, Alg.	G15	62
Tarata, Bol.	G8	82
Tarata, Peru	G6	82
Tarauacá, Braz.	C6	82
Tarauacá, stm., Braz.	B6	82
Tarawa, atoll, Kir.	H21	126
Tarawera, N.Z.	C6	72
Tarazona, Spain	D10	16
Tarazona de la Mancha, Spain	F10	16
Tarbagataj, chrebet, mts., Asia	H8	28
Tarbes, Fr.	I7	14
Tarboro, N.C., U.S.	D9	112
Tarbū, Libya	C4	56
Tarcento, Italy	C8	18
Tarcoola, Austl.	F6	68
Tardajos, Spain	C8	16
Tardoki-Jani, gora, mtn., Russia	H19	28
Taree, Austl.	H10	70
Tärendö, Swe.	H18	6
Tarentum, Pa., U.S.	G7	108
Ṭarfā', Ra's aṭ-, c., Sau. Ar.	F3	47
Ṭarfā', Wādī aṭ-, val., Egypt	G1	48
Tarfaya, Mor.	G4	62
Targhee Pass, U.S.	F14	122
Tărgovište, Bul.	F10	20
Târgovişte, Rom.	E9	20
Târgu Bujor, Rom.	D11	20
Târgu Cărbuneşti, Rom.	E7	20
Targuist, Mor.	C8	62
Târgu Jiu, Rom.	D7	20
Târgu Mureş, Rom.	C8	20
Târgu-Neamţ, Rom.	B10	20
Târgu Ocna, Rom.	C10	20
Târguşor, Rom.	E12	20
Tarhjijt, Mor.	F6	62
Tarhūnah, Libya	B3	56
Tari, Pap. N. Gui.	G11	38
Táriba, Ven.	D6	84
Tarifa, Spain	I6	16
Tarifa, Punta de, c., Spain	I6	16
Tarija, Bol.	I9	82
Tarija, dept., Bol.	I9	82
Tarīm, Yemen	F6	47
Tarim, stm., China	C3	30
Tarim Pendi, China	A9	44
Taritatu, stm., Indon.	F10	38
Tarka, Niger	D13	64
Tarkastad, S. Afr.	I8	66
Tarkio, Mo., U.S.	B1	114
Tarkio, stm., U.S.	K12	118
Tarkwa, Ghana	I9	64
Tarlac, Phil.	n19	39b
Tarm, Den.	N11	6
Tarma, Peru	D4	82
Tarn, dept., Fr.	I9	14
Tärnaby, Swe.	I14	6
Târnăveni, Rom.	C8	20
Tarn-et-Garonne, dept., Fr.	H8	14
Tarnobrzeg, Pol.	E21	10
Tarnów, Pol.	E21	10
Tarnowskie Góry, Pol.	E18	10
Taroom, Austl.	E8	70
Taroudant, Mor.	E6	62
Tarpon Springs, Fl., U.S.	K4	112
Tarqui, Peru	H5	84
Tarra, stm., Ven.	C6	84
Tarrafal, C.V.	k16	64a
Tarrafal, C.V.	m17	64a
Tarragona, Spain	D13	16
Tarraleah, Austl.	N7	70
Tarrant City, Al., U.S.	I10	114
Tàrrega, Spain	D13	16
Tarsus, Tur.	C3	48
Tartagal, Arg.	B7	80
Tartagal, Arg.	E9	80
Tartu, Est.	C9	22
Ṭarṭūs, Syria	D3	48
Tarumirim, Braz.	E8	79
Tarusa, Russia	G20	22
Tarutung, Indon.	M5	40
Tarutyne, Ukr.	C13	20
Tarvisio, Italy	C8	18
Tarvo, stm., S.A.	F11	82
Tarzan, Tx., U.S.	G5	116
Tašauz, Turk.	I9	26
Tasejeva, stm., Russia	F16	26
Tasejevo, Russia	F16	26
Taseko, stm., B.C., Can.	F11	102
Taseko Lakes, l., B.C., Can.	F11	102
Taseko Mountain, mtn., B.C., Can.	F11	102
Tashi Gang Dzong, Bhu.	G14	44
Ṭashk, Daryācheh-ye, l., Iran	G12	48
Tashkent see Taškent, Uzb.	I11	26
Tasikmalaya, Indon.	j14	39a
Taškent, Uzb.	I11	26
Taškepri, Turk.	J10	26
Tasman Bay, b., N.Z.	D4	72
Tasmania, state, Austl.	H9	68
Tasmania, i., Austl.	N7	70
Tasman Peninsula, pen., Austl.	N7	70
Tasman Sea, Oc.	L19	126
Tăşnad, Rom.	B6	20
Tassara, Niger	C12	64
Tassialouc, Lac, l., Que., Can.	E18	96
Taštagol, Russia	G9	28
Tastiota, Mex.	C4	90
Tata, Hung.	H18	10
T'at'a, vulkan, vol., Russia	c21	36a
Tatabánya, Hung.	H18	10
Tataouine, Tun.	D16	62
Tatarbunary, Ukr.	D13	20
Tatarija, state, Russia	F8	26
Tatarka, Bela.	H11	22
Tatarlar, Tur.	H10	20
Tatarsk, Russia	F7	28
Tatarskij proliv, strt., Russia	H20	28
Tatarstan see Tatarija, state, Russia	F8	26
Tatar Strait see Tatarskij proliv, strt., Russia	H20	28
Tate, Ga., U.S.	E2	112
Tate, stm., Austl.	A6	70
Tathlina Lake, l., N.W. Ter., Can.	D9	96
Tatitlek, Ak., U.S.	F21	100
Tatla Lake, B.C., Can.	F10	102
Tatla Lake, l., B.C., Can.	F10	102
Tatlayoko Lake, B.C., Can.	F10	102
Tatlayoko Lake, l., B.C., Can.	F10	102
Tatlow, Mount, mtn., B.C., Can.	F11	102
Tatnam, Cape, c., Man., Can.	E14	96
Tatrang, China	A11	44
Tatta, Pak.	H2	44
Tatuk Lake, l., B.C., Can.	D10	102
Tatum, N.M., U.S.	F3	116
Tatum, Tx., U.S.	J2	114
Tatvan, Tur.	B7	48
Taubaté, Braz.	G6	79
Tauberbischofsheim, Ger.	F9	10
Taučik, Kaz.	I8	26
Tauini, stm., Braz.	G13	84
Taulabé, Hond.	C7	92
Taumarunui, N.Z.	C5	72
Taum Sauk Mountain, mtn., Mo., U.S.	E6	114
Taunay, Braz.	I13	82
Taung, S. Afr.	F7	66
Taungdwingyi, Mya.	D3	40
Taunggyi, Mya.	D4	40
Taungup, Mya.	E3	40
Taunton, Eng., U.K.	J10	8
Taunton, Ma., U.S.	F15	108
Taupo, N.Z.	C6	72
Taupo, Lake, l., N.Z.	C5	72
Tauragė, Lith.	F5	22
Tauranga, N.Z.	B6	72
Taurianova, Italy	K11	18
Tauripampa, Peru	E3	82
Taurisma, Peru	F5	82
Tauroa Point, c., N.Z.	A4	72
Taurus Mountains see Toros Dağları, mts., Tur.	H14	4
Tauste, Spain	D10	16
Tavaí, Para.	D11	80
Tavanasa, Switz.	E11	13
Tavares, Fl., U.S.	K5	112
Tavda, Russia	F11	26
Tavda, stm., Russia	F10	26
Tavernes de Valldigna, Spain	F11	16
Tavernier, Fl., U.S.	N6	112
Tavira, Port.	H4	16
Tavistock, Ont., Can.	G15	110
Tavolžan, Kaz.	G13	26
Tavor, Har (Mount Tabor), mtn., Isr.	C4	50
Tavoy see Dawei, Mya.	G5	40
Tavşanlı, Tur.	J13	20
Tawakoni, Lake, res., Tx., U.S.	G10	116
Tawas City, Mi., U.S.	F12	110
Ṭawīlah, Juzur, is., Egypt	H2	48
Ṭawkar, Sud.	H9	60
Taxco de Alarcón, Mex.	H10	90
Taxisco, Guat.	C4	92
Taxkorgan, China	D2	30
Tay, stm., Yukon, Can.	E28	100
Tay, stm., Scot., U.K.	E10	8
Tayabamba, Peru	C3	82
Taylor, B.C., Can.	A14	102
Taylor, Az., U.S.	J6	120
Taylor, Ar., U.S.	I3	114
Taylor, Ne., U.S.	J8	118
Taylor, Tx., U.S.	I9	116
Taylor, Mount, mtn., N.M., U.S.	I9	120
Taylors, S.C., U.S.	E4	112
Taylorsville, In., U.S.	C11	114
Taylorsville, Ky., U.S.	D11	114
Taylorsville, Ms., U.S.	K7	114
Taylorsville, N.C., U.S.	D5	112
Taylorville, Il., U.S.	C7	114
Taymā', Sau. Ar.	H5	48
Taymouth, N.B., Can.	F7	106
Taymyr Peninsula see Tajmyr, poluostrov, pen., Russia	B12	28
Tay Ninh, Viet.	I9	40
Tayoltita, Mex.	E7	90
Tayside, prov., Scot., U.K.	E10	8
Taytay, Phil.	C6	38
Tayyārah, Sud.	K6	60
Taz, stm., Russia	D8	28
Taza, Mor.	C8	62
Tazenakht, Mor.	E7	62
Tazewell, Tn., U.S.	C3	112
Tazewell, Va., U.S.	B5	112
Tazin, stm., Can.	D10	96
Tazin Lake, l., Sask., Can.	E11	96
Tazovskaja guba, b., Russia	D7	28
Tazovskij poluostrov, pen., Russia	D13	26
Tazrouk, Alg.	I14	62
Tazumal, hist., El Sal.	D5	92
Tazungdām, Mya.	F17	44
Tbessa, Alg.	C15	62
Tbilisi, Geor.	I6	26
Tchamba, Togo	G10	64
Tchaourou, Benin	G11	64
Tchefuncta, stm., La., U.S.	L6	114
Tchentlo Lake, l., B.C., Can.	B9	102
Tchériba, Burkina	E8	64
Tchesinkut Lake, l., B.C., Can.	C9	102
Tchetti, Benin	H10	64
Tchibanga, Gabon	B2	58
Tchien, Lib.	G5	54
Tchin-Tabáradene, Niger	D12	64
Tchula, Ms., U.S.	I6	114
Tczew, Pol.	A18	10
Teá, stm., Braz.	H10	84
Teaca, Rom.	C8	20
Teacapan, Mex.	F7	90
Teague, Tx., U.S.	H10	116
Te Anau, Lake, l., N.Z.	F1	72
Teano, Italy	H9	18
Teapa, Mex.	I13	90
Te Awamutu, N.Z.	C5	72
Teba, Spain	I7	16
Tebicuary, stm., Para.	D10	80
Tebicuary-Mí, stm., Para.	D10	80
Tebingtinggi, Indon.	M5	40
Tebingtinggi, Pulau, i., Indon.	N7	40
Tébourba, Tun.	M4	18
Téboursouk, Tun.	M4	18
Tecalitlán, Mex.	H8	90
Tecamachalco, Mex.	H11	90
Tecate, Mex.	A1	90
Teche, Bayou, stm., La., U.S.	L5	114
Techirghiol, Rom.	E12	20
Techlé, W. Sah.	J3	62
Tecklenburg, Ger.	C7	10
Tecomán, Mex.	H8	90
Tecopa, Ca., U.S.	I9	124
Tecpan de Galeana, Mex.	I9	90
Tecpán Guatemala, Guat.	C3	92
Tecuala, Mex.	F7	90
Tecuamburro, Volcán, vol., Guat.	C4	92
Tecuci, Rom.	D11	20
Tecumseh, Mi., U.S.	H12	110
Tecumseh, Ne., U.S.	K11	118
Tecumseh, Ok., U.S.	D10	116
Tedžen, Turk.	J10	26
Tedžen (Harīrūd), stm., Asia	C16	48
Teec Nos Pos, Az., U.S.	H7	120
Teeli, Russia	G16	26
Tees, stm., Eng., U.K.	G12	8
Teesside see Middlesbrough, Eng., U.K.	G12	8
Teeswater, Ont., Can.	F14	110
Tefé, Braz.	I10	84
Tefé, stm., Braz.	D5	76
Tefé, Lago, l., Braz.	I10	84
Tegal, Indon.	j14	39a
Tegelen, Neth.	F9	12
Tegernsee, Ger.	H11	10
Tegina, Nig.	F13	64
Tegucigalpa, Hond.	C7	92
Teguise, Spain	n27	17b
Tehachapi, Ca., U.S.	I7	124
Tehachapi Pass, Ca., U.S.	I7	124
Tehamiyam, Sud.	H9	60
Tehek Lake, l., N.W. Ter., Can.	D13	96
Téhini, C. Iv.	G8	64
Tehrān, Iran	D11	48
Tehrathum, Nepal	G12	44
Tehuacán, Mex.	H11	90
Tehuantepec, Golfo de, b., Mex.	J12	90
Tehuantepec, Istmo de, Mex.	I12	90
Teide, Pico de, mtn., Spain	o24	17b
Teixeira Pinto, Gui.-B.	E3	64
Teixeira Soares, Braz.	C13	80
Tejamén, Mex.	E7	90
Tejkovo, Russia	E23	22
Tejo see Tagus, stm., Eur.	F3	16
Tejupan, Punta, c., Mex.	H8	90
Tejupilco de Hidalgo, Mex.	H9	90
Tekamah, Ne., U.S.	J11	118
Tekapo, Lake, l., N.Z.	E3	72
Tekax, Mex.	G15	90
Tekeli, Kaz.	I13	26
Tekeze, stm., Afr.	F8	56
Tekirdağ, Tur.	I11	20
Tekoa, Wa., U.S.	C8	122
Tekonsha, Mi., U.S.	H11	110
Te Kuiti, N.Z.	C5	72
Tela, Hond.	B7	92
Tela, Bahía de, b., Hond.	B7	92
Télagh, Alg.	C10	62
Tel Aviv-Yafo, Isr.	D3	50
Telde, Spain	o25	17b
Telechany, Bela.	I8	22
Telefomin, Pap. N. Gui.	G11	38
Telegraph Cove, B.C., Can.	G8	102
Telegraph Creek, B.C., Can.	H29	100
Telemark, co., Nor.	L11	6
Telembí, stm., Col.	G4	84
Telén, Arg.	I6	80
Teleneşti, Mol.	B12	20
Teleorman, co., Rom.	F8	20
Telertheba, Djebel, mtn., Alg.	H14	62
Telescope Peak, mtn., Ca., U.S.	H8	124
Telfs, Aus.	H11	10
Telica, stm., Hond.	C8	92
Telica, Volcán, vol., Nic.	E8	92
Telkwa, B.C., Can.	C7	102
Telkwa, stm., B.C., Can.	C7	102
Tell City, In., U.S.	E10	114
Teller, Ak., U.S.	D11	100
Tellicherry, India	G3	46
Tellico, stm., U.S.	D2	112
Tellico Plains, Tn., U.S.	D2	112
Tello, Col.	F5	84
Telluride, Co., U.S.	G9	120
Tel Megiddo (Armageddon), hist., Isr.	C4	50
Tel Mond, Isr.	D3	50
Telok Anson, Malay.	L6	40
Teloloapan, Mex.	H10	90
Telpaneca, Nic.	D8	92
Telšiai, Lith.	F5	22
Telti, Italy	I4	18
Teltow, Ger.	C13	10
Tema, Ghana	I10	64
Temagami, Lake, l., Ont., Can.	C15	110
Temax, Mex.	G15	90
Tembenči, stm., Russia	D11	28
Temblador, Ven.	C11	84
Tembleque, Spain	F8	16
Temecula, Ca., U.S.	K8	124
Temera, Mor.	D7	62
Temirtau, Kaz.	G12	26
Témiscamie, Lac, l., Que., Can.	A1	106
Témiscouata, Lac, l., Que., Can.	E5	106
Temora, Austl.	J7	70
Temosachic, Mex.	C6	90
Tempe, Az., U.S.	K5	120
Temperance, Mi., U.S.	I12	110
Tempio Pausania, Italy	I4	18
Tempisque, stm., C.R.	G9	92
Temple, Ok., U.S.	E8	116
Temple, Tx., U.S.	H9	116
Templeton, stm., Austl.	C3	70
Templin, Ger.	B13	10
Tempoal, stm., Mex.	G10	90
Tempoal de Sánchez, Mex.	G10	90
Tempy, Russia	E20	22
Temr'uk, Russia	H5	26
Temuco, Chile	J2	80
Tena, Ec.	H4	84
Tenabo, Mex.	G14	90
Tenaha, Tx., U.S.	K2	114
Tenakee Springs, Ak., U.S.	H27	100
Tenāli, India	D6	46
Tenasserim, Mya.	H5	40
Tendaho, Eth.	F9	56
Tende, Col de, Eur.	H14	14
Ten Degree Channel, strt., India	J2	40
Tenente Marques, stm., Braz.	D11	82
Tenente Portela, Braz.	D12	80
Ténéré, des., Niger	E9	54
Tenerife, i., Spain	o24	17b
Ténès, Alg.	B11	62
Teng'aopu, China	B10	32
Tengchong, China	B5	40
Tenggara, Nusa (Lesser Sunda Islands), is., Indon.	G7	38
Tengiz, ozero, l., Kaz.	G11	26
Tengtian, China	H4	34
Tengtiao (Na), stm., Asia	C7	40
Tengxian, China	H5	32
Teniente Rodolfo Marsh, sci., Ant.	B1	73
Tenino, Wa., U.S.	D3	122
Tenkāsi, India	H4	46
Tenke, Zaire	D5	58
Tenkiller Ferry Lake, res., Ok., U.S.	D11	116
Tenkodogo, Burkina	F9	64
Ten Mile Lake, l., Newf., Can.	A17	106
Tennant Creek, Austl.	C6	68
Tennessee, state, U.S.	D9	98
Tennessee, stm., U.S.	D9	98
Tennille, Ga., U.S.	G4	112
Teno, Chile	H3	80
Teno (Tana), stm., Eur.	F20	6
Tenosique, Mex.	I14	90
Tenryū, Japan	M12	36
Tensas, stm., La., U.S.	K5	114
Tensed, Id., U.S.	C9	122
Ten Sleep, Wy., U.S.	F18	122
Tenterfield, Austl.	G10	70
Ten Thousand Islands, is., Fl., U.S.	N5	112
Teocaltiche, Mex.	G8	90
Teodelina, Arg.	H8	80
Teófilo Otoni, Braz.	D8	79
Teo Lakes, l., Sask., Can.	G5	104
Teotihuacán, hist., Mex.	H10	90
Tepalcatepec, Mex.	H8	90
Tepeaca, Mex.	H11	90
Tepehuanes, Mex.	E7	90
Tepehuanes, stm., Mex.	E7	90
Tepeji de Ocampo, Mex.	H10	90
Tepelenë, Alb.	I4	20
Tepi, Eth.	N8	60
Tepic, Mex.	G7	90
Teplice, Czech.	E13	10
Teplovo, Russia	F25	22
Tepoca, Bahía, b., Mex.	B3	90
Tepoca, Punta, c., Mex.	C3	90
Tepopa, Cabo, c., Mex.	C3	90
Téra, Niger	D10	64
Tera, stm., Spain	D6	16
Teramo, Italy	G8	18
Terang, Austl.	L5	70
Terborg, Neth.	E9	12
Terbuny, Russia	I21	22
Terceira, i., Port.	k21	62a
Tercero, stm., Arg.	G7	80
Terechovka, Bela.	I14	22
Tereida, Sud.	L6	60
Terek, stm., Russia	I7	26
Terence Bay, N.S., Can.	H10	106
Terenino, Russia	G16	22
Terenos, Braz.	F1	79
Teresina, Braz.	E10	76
Teresópolis, Braz.	G7	79
Terespol, Pol.	C23	10
Teresva, Ukr.	A7	20
Terhorne, Neth.	B8	12
Teribe, stm., N.A.	H12	92
Terlingua, Tx., U.S.	J3	116
Termas de Río Hondo, Arg.	D6	80
Termez, Uzb.	J11	26
Termini Imerese, Italy	L8	18
Términos, Laguna de, b., Mex.	H14	90
Termoli, Italy	G10	18
Ternate, Indon.	E8	38
Ternberg, Aus.	H14	10
Ternej, Russia	H19	28
Terneuzen, Neth.	F4	12
Terni, Italy	G7	18
Ternivka, Ukr.	A13	20
Ternopil', Ukr.	H3	26
Teror, Spain	o25	17b
Terpenija, mys, c., Russia	H20	28
Terpenija, zaliv, b., Russia	H20	28
Terra Alta, W.V., U.S.	H7	108
Terra Bella, Ca., U.S.	I6	124
Terrace, B.C., Can.	C6	102
Terrace Bay, Ont., Can.	B8	110
Terracina, Italy	H8	18
Terral, Ok., U.S.	F9	116
Terralba, Italy	J3	18
Terra Nova Lake, l., Newf., Can.	D19	106
Terra Nova National Park, Newf., Can.	D20	106
Terra Rica, Braz.	G2	79
Terra Roxa, Braz.	C12	80
Terra Santa, Braz.	I14	84
Terrassa, Spain	D14	16
Terrebonne Bay, b., La., U.S.	M6	114
Terre Haute, In., U.S.	C9	114
Terrell, Tx., U.S.	G10	116
Terrell Hills, Tx., U.S.	J8	116
Terrenceville, Newf., Can.	E19	106
Terror Point, c., B.C., Can.	D5	102
Terry, Ms., U.S.	J6	114
Terry, Mt., U.S.	E2	118
Terry Peak, mtn., S.D., U.S.	G4	118
Terschelling, i., Neth.	B7	12
Teruel, Col.	F5	84
Teruel, Spain	E10	16
Terzaghi Dam, B.C., Can.	G12	102
Teša, Russia	F25	22
Tesalia, Col.	F5	84
Tešanj, Bos.	E2	20
Tes-Chem (Tesijn), stm., Asia	A5	30
Tescott, Ks., U.S.	L10	118
Teseney, Erit.	J9	60
Tesijn (Tes-Chem), stm., Asia	B6	30
Teslić, Bos.	E1	20
Teslin, Yukon, Can.	F28	100
Teslin, stm., Can.	F27	100
Teslin Lake, l., Can.	F28	100
Tesouras, stm., Braz.	C3	79
Tesouro, Braz.	D2	79
Tessala, Monts du, mts., Alg.	J11	16
Tessalit, Mali	A10	64
Tessaoua, Niger	E13	64
Tessenderlo, Bel.	F7	12
Tessy-sur-Vire, Fr.	D5	14
Testour, Tun.	M4	18
Tesuque, N.M., U.S.	I11	120

U

Name	Map Ref.	Page
Ujungkulon National Park, Indon.	j12	39a
Ujungpandang, Indon.	G6	38
Ukiah, Ca., U.S.	E2	124
Ukiah, Or., U.S.	E7	122
Ukmergė, Lith.	F7	22
Ukraine, ctry., Eur.	F14	4
Ulaanbaatar, Mong.	B8	30
Ulaangom, Mong.	B5	30
Ulan, Austl.	I8	70
Ulan Bator see Ulaanbaatar, Mong.	B8	30
Ulang, stm., Nic.	C11	92
Ulan-Ude, Russia	G13	28
Ulazów, Pol.	E23	10
Ulchin, S. Kor.	G17	32
Ulcinj, Yugo.	H3	20
Ulco, S. Afr.	G7	66
Ulcumayo, Peru	D4	82
Uldz, stm., Asia	H14	28
Ulen, Mn., U.S.	D11	118
Ulhäsnagar, India	C2	46
Uliastaj, Mong.	B6	30
Uljanovka, Russia	B13	22
Uljanovsk, Russia	G7	26
Ulla, Bela.	F12	22
Ulladulla, Austl.	J9	70
Ullapool, Scot., U.K.	D8	8
Ullin, Il., U.S.	E7	114
Ulm, Ger.	G10	10
Ulm, Mt., U.S.	C14	122
Ulmarra, Austl.	G10	70
Ulongué, Moz.	D6	58
Ulricehamn, Swe.	B9	12
Ulrum, Neth.	B9	12
Ulsan, S. Kor.	H17	32
Ulster, hist. reg., Eur.	G6	8
Ultraoriental, Cordillera (Serra do Divisor), mts., S.A.	C5	82
Ulu, Russia	E17	28
Ulúa, stm., Hond.	B6	92
Ulubey, Tur.	K13	20
Ulukışla, Tur.	C3	48
Ulungur, stm., China	B4	30
Ulungur Hu, l., China	B4	30
Uluru National Park, Austl.	E6	68
Ulverstone, Austl.	M7	70
Ul'yanovka, Ukr.	A14	20
Ulysses, Ks., U.S.	N6	118
Ulysses, Ne., U.S.	J10	118
Ulzë, Alb.	H3	20
Uman, Mex.	G15	90
Uman', Ukr.	H4	26
Umarkot, Pak.	H3	44
Umari, stm., Braz.	B9	82
Umatilla, Fl., U.S.	K5	112
Umatilla, Or., U.S.	E6	122
Umatilla, stm., Or., U.S.	E6	122
Umbertide, Italy	F7	18
Umboi Island, i., Pap. N. Gui.	m16	68a
Umbrail, Pass, Eur.	E13	13
Umbria, prov., Italy	G7	18
Umbuzero, ozero, l., Russia	H24	6
Umeå, Swe.	J17	6
Umfreville Lake, l., Ont., Can.	H20	104
Umfuli, stm., Zimb.	A9	66
Umhlanga Rocks, S. Afr.	G10	66
Umkomaas, S. Afr.	H10	66
Umm al-Birak, Sau. Ar.	C1	47
Umm al-Qaywayn, U.A.E.	B9	47
Umm al-Qittayn, Jord.	D7	50
Umm Badr, Sud.	J4	60
Umm Dabbī, Sud.	J6	60
Umm Dhibbān, Sud.	J5	60
Umm Digulgulaya, Sud.	L3	60
Umm Durmān (Omdurman), Sud.	J7	60
Umm el Fahm, Isr.	C4	50
Umm Jamālah, Sud.	J4	60
Umm Kaddādah, Sud.	K4	60
Umm Kuwaykah, Sud.	K7	60
Umm Lajj, Sau. Ar.	I4	48
Umm Mirdi, Sud.	H7	60
Umm Qaṣr, Iraq	F9	48
Umm Quṣayr, Jord.	E5	50
Umm Ruwābah, Sud.	K6	60
Umm Sayyālah, Sud.	J6	60
Umm Shalīl, Sud.	L2	60
Umm Shuṭūr, Sud.	N7	60
Umm Walad, Syria	C6	50
Um'ot, Russia	G25	22
Um'ot, Russia	I25	22
Umpqua, stm., Or., U.S.	G2	122
Umred, India	B5	46
Umreth, India	I5	44
Ümsŏng, S. Kor.	G15	32
Umtata, S. Afr.	H9	66
Umtentweni, S. Afr.	H10	66
Umuahia, Nig.	I13	64
Umuarama, Braz.	G2	79
Umzinto, S. Afr.	H10	66
Una, Braz.	C9	79
Unadilla, Ga., U.S.	G3	112
Unadilla, N.Y., U.S.	E11	108
Unadilla, stm., N.Y., U.S.	E11	108
Unaí, Braz.	D5	79
Unalakleet, Ak., U.S.	E14	100
Unalaska, Ak., U.S.	J11	100
Unare, stm., Ven.	C10	84
'Unayzah, Sau. Ar.	H7	48
'Unayzah, Jabal, mtn., Asia	E5	48
'Unayzah, Jabal, mtn., Jord.	G5	50
Uncía, Bol.	H8	82
Uncompahgre, stm., Co., U.S.	F9	120
Uncompahgre Peak, mtn., Co., U.S.	F8	120
Uncompahgre Plateau, plat., Co., U.S.	F8	120
Underwood, N.D., U.S.	D6	118
Undva nina, c., Est.	C7	22
Uneča, Russia	I15	22
Uneiuxi, stm., Braz.	H10	84
Ungarie, Austl.	I7	70
Ungava, Péninsule d', pen., Que., Can.	E18	96
Ungava Bay, b., Can.	E19	96
Unggi, N. Kor.	A18	32
União, Braz.	D10	76
União da Vitória, Braz.	D13	80
União dos Palmares, Braz.	E11	76
Unicoi, Tn., U.S.	C4	112
Unimak Island, i., Ak., U.S.	I12	100
Unimak Pass, strt., Ak., U.S.	I12	100
Unini, stm., Braz.	H12	84
Unión, Arg.	H6	80
Union, Or., U.S.	E9	122
Unión, Para.	C10	80
Union, Ia., U.S.	H2	110
Union, La., U.S.	L6	114
Union, Ms., U.S.	J7	114
Union, Mo., U.S.	D5	114
Union, N.J., U.S.	G12	108
Union, Or., U.S.	E8	122
Union, S.C., U.S.	E5	112
Union, Wa., U.S.	C2	122
Union, W.V., U.S.	B6	112
Union Bay, B.C., Can.	H10	102
Union City, Ga., U.S.	F2	112
Union City, In., U.S.	B11	114
Union City, Mi., U.S.	H10	110
Union City, Oh., U.S.	G2	108
Union City, Pa., U.S.	F7	108
Union City, Tn., U.S.	F7	114
Unión de Reyes, Cuba	C4	94
Unión de Tula, Mex.	H7	90
Union Gap, Wa., U.S.	D5	122
Union Grove, Wi., U.S.	H1	110
Union Park, Fl., U.S.	K5	112
Union Point, Ga., U.S.	F3	112
Union Springs, Al., U.S.	J11	114
Union Springs, N.Y., U.S.	E10	108
Uniontown, Al., U.S.	J9	114
Uniontown, Ky., U.S.	E9	114
Uniontown, Pa., U.S.	H7	108
Unionville, Mi., U.S.	G12	110
Unionville, Mo., U.S.	B3	114
Unipouheos Indian Reserve, Alta., Can.	E4	104
United, Pa., U.S.	G7	108
United Arab Emirates (Al-Imārāt al-'Arabīyah al-Muttaḥidah), ctry., Asia	E5	42
United Arab Republic see Egypt, ctry., Afr.	C7	56
United Kingdom, ctry., Eur.	E7	4
United States, ctry., N.A.	F5	104
Unity, Sask., Can.	F5	104
Universal City, Tx., U.S.	J8	116
University, Ms., U.S.	H7	114
University City, Mo., U.S.	D6	114
University Park, N.M., U.S.	L10	120
University Park, Tx., U.S.	G10	116
Unjha, India	I5	44
Uno, Canal Numero, Arg.	I10	80
Unp'a, N. Kor.	E13	32
Unquillo, Arg.	F6	80
Unža, stm., Russia	D26	22
Unža, stm., Russia	C27	22
Uozu, Japan	K12	36
Upano, stm., Ec.	I3	84
Upata, Ven.	C11	84
Upemba, Lac, l., Zaire	C5	58
Upham, N.D., U.S.	C7	118
Upía, stm., Col.	E6	84
Upington, S. Afr.	D8	26
Upire, stm., Ven.	B8	84
Upleta, India	I4	44
Upolu, i., W. Sam.	J22	126
Upolu Point, c., Hi., U.S.	q18	125a
Upper Arlington, Oh., U.S.	G3	108
Upper Arrow Lake, l., B.C., Can.	G17	102
Upper Blackville, N.B., Can.	F8	106
Upper Darby, Pa., U.S.	H11	108
Upper Demerara-Berbice, prov., Guy.	D13	84
Upper Fraser, B.C., Can.	C13	102
Upper Goose Lake, l., Ont., Can.	G22	104
Upper Hat Creek, B.C., Can.	G13	102
Upper Humber, stm., Newf., Can.	C16	106
Upper Iowa, stm., U.S.	G4	110
Upper Island Cove, Newf., Can.	E20	106
Upper Klamath Lake, l., Or., U.S.	H4	122
Upper Lake, Ca., U.S.	E3	124
Upper Liard, Yukon, Can.	F30	100
Upper Manitou Lake, l., Ont., Can.	I22	104
Upper Musquodoboit, N.S., Can.	G11	106
Upper Red Lake, l., Mn., U.S.	C13	118
Upper Sandusky, Oh., U.S.	G3	108
Upper Sheila, N.B., Can.	E9	106
Upper Takutu-Upper Essequibo, prov., Guy.	F13	84
Upper Windigo Lake, l., Ont., Can.	F23	104
Uppsala see Uppsala, Swe.		
Uppsala, Swe.	L15	6
Upton, Ky., U.S.	E11	114
Upton, Wy., U.S.	G3	118
Uquía, Cerro, mtn., Ven.	E11	84
Urabá, Golfo de, b., Col.	C4	84
Uracoa, Ven.	C11	84
Uraj, Russia	E10	26
Ural, stm., Russia	H8	26
Uralla, Austl.	H9	70
Ural Mountains see Ural'skije gory, mts., Russia	E9	26
Ural'sk, Kaz.	G8	26
Ural'skije gory (Ural Mountains), mts., Russia	E9	26
Urana, Austl.	J7	70
Urandangi, Austl.	C3	70
Urandi, Braz.	C7	79
Urangan, Austl.	E10	70
Urania, La., U.S.	K4	114
Uranium City, Sask., Can.	E11	96
Urariá, Paraná, mth., Braz.	I14	84
Uraricaá, stm., Braz.	F11	84
Uraricoera, Braz.	F12	84
Uraricoera, stm., Braz.	F12	84
Ura-T'ube, Taj.	J11	26
Uravan, Co., U.S.	F8	120
Urawa, Japan	L14	36
Urbana, Ar., U.S.	I4	114
Urbana, Il., U.S.	B8	114
Urbana, Mo., U.S.	E3	114
Urbana, Oh., U.S.	G3	108
Urbandale, Ia., U.S.	A3	114
Urbania, Italy	F7	18
Urbino, Italy	F7	18
Urcos, Peru	E6	82
Urdinarrain, Arg.	G9	80
Uré, Col.	C4	84
Urečje, Bela.	H10	22
Ureña, Ven.	D6	84
Ures, Mex.	C4	90
Urgenč, Uzb.	I10	26
Urgüp, Tur.	B3	48
Uri, state, Switz.	E10	13
Uriah, Al., U.S.	K9	114
Uriah, Mount, mtn., N.Z.	E3	72
Uribante, stm., Ven.	D7	84
Uribe, Col.	F5	84
Uribia, Col.	B6	84
Urich, Mo., U.S.	D2	114
Urique, Mex.	D6	90
Urique, stm., Mex.	D6	90
Urituyacu, stm., Peru	J5	84
Uriu, Tur.	K10	20
Urmia see Orūmīyeh, Iran	C8	48
Uroš:vac, Braz.	G5	20
Urrao, Col.	D4	84
Ursa, Il., U.S.	B5	114
Uršel'skij, Russia	F23	22
Urtigueira, Braz.	C13	80
Uru, stm., Braz.	C4	79
Uruaçu, Braz.	C4	79
Uruana, Braz.	C4	79
Uruapan del Progreso, Mex.	H8	90
Urubamba, Peru	E5	82
Urubamba, stm., Peru	D5	82
Urubaxi, stm., Braz.	H10	84
Urubu, stm., Braz.	I13	84
Urucará, Braz.	I14	84
Urucu, stm., Braz.	J10	84
Uruçuca, Braz.	C9	79
Urucuia, stm., Braz.	D6	79
Urucurituba, Braz.	I14	84
Uruguaiana, Braz.	E10	80
Uruguay (Uruguai), ctry., S.A.	C5	78
Uruguay (Uruguai), stm., S.A.	G9	80
Ürümçi see Ürümqi, China	C4	30
Ürümqi, China	C4	30
Urundel, Arg.	B6	80
Urup, ostrov, i., Russia	H22	28
Urupá, stm., Braz.	D10	82
Urupadi, stm., Braz.	J14	84
Urupês, Braz.	F4	79
Ur'upinsk, Russia	G6	26
Urussanga, Braz.	E14	80
Urutaí, Braz.	D4	79
Urutaú, Arg.	C7	80
Urzum, Russia	F8	26
Usa, Japan	N6	36
Usa, stm., Russia	D9	26
Uşak, Tur.	F11	22
Uşak, Tur.	K13	20
Ušaki, Russia	B13	22
Usakos, Nmb.	D2	66
Usedom, i., Eur.	A14	10
'Usfān, Sau. Ar.	D1	47
Ushant see Ouessant, Île d', i., Fr.	D1	14
'Ushayrah, Sau. Ar.	D2	47
Ushuaia, Arg.	G3	78
Usingen, Ger.	E8	10
Usk, B.C., Can.	C6	102
Usk, Wa., U.S.	B8	122
Uslar, Ger.	D9	10
Usman', Russia	I22	22
Usolje-Sibirskoje, Russia	G12	28
Usoro, Nig.	I13	64
Uspallata, Arg.	G4	80
Uspanapa, stm., Mex.	I12	90
Ussuri (Wusuli), stm., Asia	B13	30
Ustaritz, Fr.	I5	14
Ust'-Barguzin, Russia	G13	28
Ust'-Chorna, Ukr.	A7	20
Ust'-Cil'ma, Russia	D8	26
Ust'-Dolysy, Russia	E12	22
Uster, Switz.	D10	13
Ust'-Ilimskoje vodochraniliŝče, res., Russia	F18	28
Ústí nad Labem, Czech.	E14	10
Ústí nad Orlicí, Czech.	F16	10
Ust'-íšim, Russia	F12	26
Ustje, Russia	D22	22
Ustka, Pol.	A16	10
Ust'-Kamčatsk, Russia	F24	28
Ust'-Kamenogorsk, Kaz.	H8	28
Ust'-Katav, Russia	G9	26
Ust'-Koksa, Russia	G15	26
Ust'-Kut, Russia	F13	28
Ust'-Luga, Russia	B11	22
Ust'-Nera, Russia	E20	28
Ust'-Omčug, Russia	E21	28
Ust'-Ordynskij, Russia	G12	28
Ust'uckoje, Russia	C18	22
Ust'urt, plato, plat., Asia	I9	26
Ust'-Usa, Russia	D9	26
Ust'užna, Russia	C19	22
Usu, China	C3	30
Usulután, El Sal.	D6	92
Usumacinta, stm., N.A.	I14	90
Ušumun, Russia	G17	28
Utah, state, U.S.	D4	98
Utah Lake, l., Ut., U.S.	D5	120
Utapi, Nmb.	A2	66
Utashinai, Japan	d17	36a
Ute, Ia., U.S.	I12	118
Utembo, stm., Ang.	E4	58
Utena, Lith.	F8	22
Utete, Tan.	C7	58
Uthai Thani, Thai.	E6	40
Utiariti, Braz.	E12	82
Utica, Ks., U.S.	M7	118
Utica, Mi., U.S.	H12	110
Utica, Ms., U.S.	J6	114
Utica, Ne., U.S.	K10	118
Utica, N.Y., U.S.	D11	108
Utica, Oh., U.S.	G4	108
Utiel, Spain	F10	16
Utikoomak Lake Indian Reserve, Alta., Can.	B19	102
Utikuma Lake, l., Alta., Can.	B19	102
Utila, Hond.	A8	92
Utila, Isla de, i., Hond.	A8	92
Utinga, stm., Braz.	L5	18
Utopia, Tun.	L5	18
Uto, Japan	O5	36
Utopia, Tx., U.S.	J7	116
Utorgoš, Russia	C13	22
Utrecht, Neth.	D7	12
Utrecht, S. Afr.	F10	66
Utrecht, prov., Neth.	D7	12
Utrera, Spain	H6	16
Utsunomiya, Japan	K14	36
Uttaradit, Thai.	F6	40
Uttar Pradesh, state, India	G9	44
Utuado, P.R.	E11	94
Uusikaupunki (Nystad), Fin.	K17	6
Uuskaarlepyy (Nykarleby), Fin.	K19	6
Uvá, Braz.	C3	79
Uvá, stm., Col.	F8	84
Uvalda, Ga., U.S.	F3	112
Uvalde, Tx., U.S.	J7	116
Uvarovka, Russia	I13	22
Uvarovo, Russia	J25	22
Uvat, Russia	F11	26
Uvinza, Tan.	C6	58
Uvira, Zaire	B5	58
Uvs nuur, l., Asia	A5	30
Uwajima, Japan	N7	36
Uwayl, Sud.	M4	60
'Uwaynāt, Jabal al-, mtn., Afr.	D5	56
Uxbridge, Ont., Can.	F16	110
Uxmal, hist., Mex.	G15	90
Uyuni, Bol.	I8	82
Uyuni, Salar de, pl., Bol.	I8	82
Uźava, Lat.	D4	22
Uzbekistan, ctry., Asia	I10	26
Uzboj, stm., Turk.	B13	48
Uzda, Bela.	H10	22
Uzdin, Yugo.	D4	20
Užice, Yugo.	F3	20
Uzlovaja, Russia	H21	22
Uzunköprü, Tur.	H10	20
Užur, Russia	F9	28
Užventis, Lith.	F5	22

V

Name	Map Ref.	Page
Vääksy, Fin.	K19	6
Vaala, Fin.	I20	6
Vaalserberg, mtn., Neth.	G9	12
Vaalwater, S. Afr.	E9	66
Vaasa (Vasa), Fin.	K18	6
Vabalninkas, Lith.	F7	22
Vabkent, Uzb.	A18	48
Vác, Hung.	H19	10
Vaca, Bol.	H10	82
Vača, Russia	F25	22
Vacacaí, stm., Braz.	F11	80
Vacaria, Braz.	E13	80
Vacaria, stm., Braz.	D7	79
Vacaria, stm., Braz.	F1	79
Vacaville, Ca., U.S.	F4	124
Vaccarès, Étang de, b., Fr.	I11	14
Vach, stm., Russia	E8	26
Vache, Île à, i., Haiti	C8	94
Vachš, stm., Taj.	J11	26
Vacoas, Mrts.	v18	67c
Vadino, Russia	F16	22
Vadodara, India	I5	44
Vado Ligure, Italy	E3	18
Vaduz, Liech.	E16	14
Vaga, stm., Russia	E6	26
Vagaj, Russia	F11	26
Vågåmo, Nor.	K11	6
Vágar, i., Faer. Is.	D8	6b
Váh, stm., Slov.	G17	10
Vaiden, Ms., U.S.	I7	114
Vaihingen, Ger.	B9	22
Vail, Co., U.S.	E10	120
Vail, Ia., U.S.	I12	118
Vailly-sur-Aisne, Fr.	C10	14
Vainode, Lat.	E4	22
Vajgač, ostrov, i., Russia	C9	26
Valais (Wallis), state, Switz.	F7	13
Valašské Meziříčí, Czech.	F17	10
Valatie, N.Y., U.S.	E13	108
Vâlcea, co., Rom.	E8	20
Valcheta, Arg.	E3	78
Valdagno, Italy	D6	18
Valdai Hills see Valdajskaja vozvyšennost', hills, Russia	D15	22
Valdaj, Russia	D16	22
Valdajskaja vozvyšennost', hills, Russia	D16	22
Valdelândia, Braz.	C3	79
Valdemārpils, Lat.	D5	22
Valdepeñas, Spain	G8	16
Valders, Wi., U.S.	F8	110
Valdés, Península, pen., Arg.	E4	78
Val-des-Bois, Que., Can.	B11	108
Valdese, N.C., U.S.	D5	112
Valdéz, Ec.	G3	84
Valdez, Ak., U.S.	F21	100
Val-d'Isère, Fr.	G13	14
Valdivia, Chile	D2	78
Valdivia, Col.	D5	84
Valdobbiadene, Italy	D7	18
Val-d'Oise, dept., Fr.	C9	14
Valdosta, Ga., U.S.	I3	112
Vale, Or., U.S.	G8	122
Valemount, B.C., Can.	E15	102
Valença, Braz.	C9	79
Valença, Port.	C3	16
Valençay, Fr.	E8	14
Valence, Fr.	H11	14
Valencia, Hond.	C9	92
València, Spain	F11	16
Valencia, Ven.	B8	84
Valencia, prov., Spain	F11	16
València, Golf de, b., Spain	F12	16
Valencia, Lago de, l., Ven.	B9	84
Valencia de Alcántara, Spain	F4	16
Valenciennes, Fr.	B10	14
Valentine, Ne., U.S.	I7	118
Valentine, Tx., U.S.	I2	116
Valenza, Italy	D3	18
Valera, Ven.	C7	84
Valga, Est.	D9	22
Valiente, Península, pen., Pan.	C2	84
Valiente, Punta, c., Pan.	H13	92
Valier, Il., U.S.	D7	114
Valier, Mt., U.S.	B13	122
Valjevo, Yugo.	E3	20
Valka, Lat.	D9	22
Valkininkas, Lith.	G7	22
Valladolid, Ec.	J3	84
Valladolid, Mex.	G15	90
Valladolid, Spain	D7	16
Valldal, Nor.	J10	6
Valle, Lat.	E7	22
Valle, Spain	B7	16
Valle, dept., Hond.	D7	92
Vallecitos, N.M., U.S.	H10	120
Valle d'Aosta, prov., Italy	D2	18
Valle de Guanape, Ven.	C10	84
Valle de la Pascua, Ven.	C9	84
Valle del Cauca, dept., Col.	F4	84
Valle de Olivos, Mex.	D6	90
Valle de Santiago, Mex.	G9	90
Valle de Zaragoza, Mex.	D7	90
Valledupar, Col.	B6	84
Valle Edén, Ur.	F10	80
Vallegrande, Bol.	H9	82
Valle Hermoso, Arg.	F6	80
Vallehermoso, Spain	E11	90
Vallejo, Ca., U.S.	F3	124
Vallenar, Chile	E3	80
Valles Caldera, crat., N.M., U.S.	I10	120
Valletta, Malta	N9	18
Valley, Al., U.S.	J11	114
Valley, Ne., U.S.	J11	118
Valley, stm., Man., Can.	G14	104
Valley Bend, W.V., U.S.	I7	108
Valley Center, Ks., U.S.	N10	118
Valley City, N.D., U.S.	E10	118
Valley Falls, Ks., U.S.	L12	118
Valley Farms, Az., U.S.	L5	120
Valleyfield, Newf., Can.	C20	106
Valley Head, Al., U.S.	H11	114
Valley Head, W.V., U.S.	I6	108
Valley Mills, Tx., U.S.	H9	116
Valley of the Kings, hist., Egypt	E7	60
Valley Springs, S.D., U.S.	H11	118
Valley Station, Ky., U.S.	D11	114
Valleyview, Alta., Can.	B17	102
Valley View, Tx., U.S.	F9	116
Valliant, Ok., U.S.	E11	116
Vallimanca, Arroyo, stm., Arg.	H8	80
Vallorbe, Switz.	E6	13
Valls, Spain	D13	16
Val-Marie, Sask., Can.	I7	104
Valmaseda, Spain	B8	16
Valmeyer, Il., U.S.	D5	114
Valmiera, Lat.	D8	22
Valognes, Fr.	C5	14
Valonga, Port.	D3	16
Vālpārai, India	G4	46
Valparaíso, Chile	G3	80
Valparaíso, Braz.	F3	79
Valparaiso, In., U.S.	A9	114
Valparaíso, Mex.	F7	90
Valparaíso, prov., Chile	G3	80
Valréas, Fr.	H11	14
Vals, Tanjung, c., Indon.	G10	38
Valsbaai, S. Afr.	J4	66
Valsetz, Or., U.S.	F2	122
Valtimo, Fin.	J21	6
Valujki, Russia	G5	26
Valverde del Camino, Spain	H5	16
Van, Tur.	B7	48
Van, Tx., U.S.	G11	116
Van Alstyne, Tx., U.S.	F10	116
Vananda, B.C., Can.	H10	102
Van Buren, Ar., U.S.	G2	114
Van Buren, Mo., U.S.	F5	114
Vanč, Taj.	J12	26
Vanceboro, Me., U.S.	B19	108
Vanceburg, Ky., U.S.	I3	108
Vancleave, Ms., U.S.	L8	114
Vancouver, B.C., Can.	H11	102
Vancouver, Wa., U.S.	E3	122
Vancouver, Cape, c., Austl.	G3	68
Vancouver, Cape, c., Ak., U.S.	F12	100
Vancouver, Mount, mtn., N.A.	F25	100
Vancouver Island, i., B.C., Can.	H9	102
Vancouver Island Ranges, mts., B.C., Can.	H9	102
Vandalia, Il., U.S.	D7	114
Vandalia, Mo., U.S.	C5	114
Vandalia, Oh., U.S.	H2	108
Vandekerckhove Lake, l., Man., Can.	A13	104
Vanderbijlpark, S. Afr.	F8	66
Vanderbilt, Mi., U.S.	E11	110
Vanderbilt, Tx., U.S.	K10	116
Vandergrift, Pa., U.S.	G7	108
Vanderhoof, B.C., Can.	C10	102
Vanderlin Island, i., Austl.	C7	68
Vandervoort, Ar., U.S.	H2	114
Van Diemen Gulf, b., Austl.	B6	68
Vändra, Est.	C8	22
Vanegas, Mex.	F9	90
Vänern, l., Swe.	L13	6
Vänersborg, Swe.	L13	6
Vangaindrano, Madag.	s22	67b
Van Gölü, l., Tur.	B7	48
Vangsnes, Nor.	K10	6
Vanguard, Sask., Can.	I7	104
Van Horn, Tx., U.S.	H2	116
Van Horne, Ia., U.S.	H3	110
Vanier, Ont., Can.	B11	108
Vanimo, Pap. N. Gui.	F11	38
Vanino, Russia	H20	28
Vāniyambādi, India	F5	46
Vankleek Hill, Ont., Can.	B12	108
Van Lear, Ky., U.S.	B3	112
Vanndale, Ar., U.S.	G6	114
Vannes, Fr.	E4	14
Van Ninh, Viet.	H10	40
Van Rees, Pegunungan, mts., Indon.	F10	38
Vanrhynsdorp, S. Afr.	H4	66
Vansant, Va., U.S.	B4	112
Vansittart Island, i., N.W. Ter., Can.	C16	96
Vanskoje, Russia	C19	22
Vanstadensrus, S. Afr.	G8	66
Vanua Levu, i., Fiji	J21	126
Vanuatu, ctry., Oc.	J20	126
Van Vleck, Tx., U.S.	J11	116
Van Wert, Oh., U.S.	G2	108
Vanzylsrus, S. Afr.	F6	66
Vapnjarka, Ukr.	A12	20
Var, dept., Fr.	I13	14
Var, stm., Fr.	I13	14
Varaklāni, Lat.	E9	22
Varallo, Italy	D3	18
Vārānasi (Benares), India	H10	44
Varangerfjorden, Nor.	G22	6
Varangerhalvøya, pen., Nor.	F21	6
Varaždin, Cro.	C11	18
Varazze, Italy	E3	18
Varberg, Swe.	M13	6
Vardak, prov., Afg.	C3	44
Vardar (Axiós), stm., Eur.	H6	20
Varde, Nor.	F22	6
Varegovo, Russia	D22	22
Varel, Ger.	B8	10
Varela, Arg.	H5	80
Vārena, Lith.	G7	22
Vareš, Bos.	E2	20
Varese, Italy	D3	18
Vârfurile, Rom.	C6	20
Varginha, Braz.	D4	79
Varkaus, Fin.	J20	6
Värmlands Län, co., Swe.	L13	6
Varna, Bul.	F11	20
Värnamo, Swe.	M14	6
Varnsdorf, Czech.	E14	10
Varnville, S.C., U.S.	G5	112
Várpalota, Hung.	H18	10
Vârșca, Est.	D10	22
Vârtopu, Rom.	E7	20
Várzea, Rio da, stm., Braz.	D12	80
Várzea da Palma, Braz.	E7	79
Várzea Grande, Braz.	F13	82
Varzelo, Braz.	C14	80
Vas, co., Hung.	H16	10
Vasalemma, Est.	B7	22
Vashkivtsi, Ukr.	A11	20
Vashkivtsi, Ukr.	A9	20
Vasilečiči, Bela.	I12	22
Vasilika, Grc.	o23	17b
Vasiljevski Moch, Russia	D18	22
Vasiljevskoje, Russia	E24	22
Vaskelovo, Russia	A13	22
Vasloi, co., Rom.	C11	20
Vass, N.C., U.S.	D7	112
Vassar, Mi., U.S.	G12	110
Vasto, Italy	G9	18
Vas'ugan, stm., Russia	F13	26
Vas'uganje, sw., Russia	F7	28
Vatan, Fr.	E8	14
Vatican City (Città del Vaticano), ctry., Eur.	H7	18
V'atka, stm., Russia	F8	26
Vatnajökull, Ice.	B5	6a
Vatneyri, Ice.	B2	6a
Vatomandry, Madag.	q23	67b
Vatra Dornei, Rom.	B9	20
V'atskij Baskunčak, Russia	H7	18
Vatican, Taj.		
Vatican City, Braz.		
Vättern, l., Swe.	L14	6
Vaucluse, dept., Fr.	I12	14
Vaucouleurs, Fr.	D12	14
Vaud, state, Switz.	E6	13
Vaughan, N.M., U.S.	J11	120
Vaupés, col., Fr.	C5	14
Vaupés [Uaupés], stm., S.A.	G7	84
Vauréal, Chute, wtfl, Que., Can.	C11	106
Vauvert, Fr.	I11	14
Vauxhall, Alta., Can.	G22	102
Vavatenina, Madag.	p23	67b
Vavoua, C. Iv.	H6	64
Väyksy, Fin.		
Växjö, Swe.	M14	6
Vazante, Braz.	E5	79
Vazante Grande, stm., Braz.	H13	82
Važgort, Russia	F22	22
V'az'emskij, Russia	H18	28
V'az'ma, Russia	F17	22
V'azniki, Russia	E25	22
Veazie, Me., U.S.	C18	108
Veblen, S.D., U.S.	F10	118
Vecht, stm., Eur.	C9	12
Vechta, Ger.	C8	10
Vecsés, Hung.	H19	10
Vedea, Rom.	E8	20
Vedersburg, In., U.S.	B9	114
Veedersburg, In., U.S.	B9	114
Veendam, Neth.	B10	12
Veenendaal, Neth.	D8	12
Vega, Tx., U.S.	D4	116
Veghel, Neth.	E8	12
Vegreville, Alta., Can.	D22	102
Veguita, N.M., U.S.	J10	120
Veinticinco de Mayo, Arg.	H4	80
Veinticinco de Mayo, Arg.	H10	80
Veintiocho de Mayo, Ec.	I3	84
Veintisiete de Abril, C.R.	G9	92
Veisiejai, Lith.	G6	22
Vejer de la Frontera, Spain	I6	16
Vejle, Den.	N11	6
Velardeña, Mex.	E8	90
Velas, Cabo c., C.R.	G9	92
Velázquez, Ur.	H11	80
Velddrif, S. Afr.	I4	66
Velden, Ger.	G12	19
Veldhoven, Neth.	F7	12
Velet'ma, Russia	F25	22
Vélez, Col.	D6	84
Velez de la Gomera, Peñón de, i., Sp. N. Afr.	J7	16
Vélez-Málaga, Spain	I7	16
Vel'gija, Russia	C16	22
Velhas, Rio das, stm., Braz.	D6	79
Velika Morava, stm., Yugo.	E5	20
Velika Plana, Yugo.	E5	20
Velikije Luki, Russia	E13	22
Velikij Ust'ug, Russia	E7	26
Velikodvorskij, Russia	F23	22
Veliko Gradište, Yugo.	E5	20
Velikoje, Russia	D22	22
Veliko Tărnovo, Bul.	F9	20
Vélingara, Sen.	F4	54
Veliž, Russia	F14	22
Velletri, Italy	H7	18
Vellore, India	F5	46
Velma, Ok., U.S.	E9	116
Velp, Neth.	D8	12
Velsen, Neth.	E6	26
Velten, Ger.	C13	10
Velva, N.D., U.S.	C7	118
Velyka Koshnytsya, Ukr.	A12	20
Velyka Mykhaylivka, Ukr.	B13	20
Velyki Luchky, Ukr.	A6	20
Velykoploske, Ukr.	B13	20
Velykyy Bereznyy, Ukr.	G22	10
Velykyy Bychkiv, Ukr.	B8	20
Venado, Col.	E5	84
Venado, Isla del, i., Nic.	F11	92
Venado Tuerto, Arg.	G8	80
Venâncio Aires, Braz.	E12	80
Vence, Fr.	I14	14
Venceslau Braz, Braz.	G4	79
Venda, hist. reg., S. Afr.	D10	66
Venda Nova, Port.	D4	16
Vendas Novas, Port.	G3	16
Vendée, dept., Fr.	F5	14
Vendeuvre-sur-Barse, Fr.	D11	14
Vendôme, Fr.	E8	14
Vendychany, Ukr.	A11	20
Venecia, C.R.	G10	92
Veneto, prov., Italy	G18	14
Venev, Russia	G21	22
Venezia (Venice), Italy	D7	18
Venezia, ctry., S.A.	B5	76
Venezuela, Golfo de, b., S.A.	B7	84
Vengerovo, Russia	F13	26
Veniaminof, Mount, mtn., Ak., U.S.	H15	100
Venice see Venezia, Italy	D7	18
Venice, Fl., U.S.	L4	112
Venice, La., U.S.	M7	114
Venice, Gulf of, b., Eur.	D8	18
Vénissieux, Fr.	G11	14
Venlo, Neth.	F9	12
Vennesa, Italy	I10	18
Vent, Aus.	I11	13
Ventanas, Ec.	H3	84
Ventersburg, S. Afr.	F8	66
Ventersdorp, S. Afr.	F8	66
Venterstad, S. Afr.	H7	66
Ventimiglia, Italy	F2	18
Ventspils, Lat.	D4	22
Ventuari, stm., Ven.	E9	84
Ventura, Ca., U.S.	J6	124
Venus, Fl., U.S.	L5	112
Venustiano Carranza, Mex.	I13	90
Venustiano Carranza, Mex.	H8	90
Venustiano Carranza, Bahía, b., Mex.	H16	90
Venustiano Carranza, Presa, res., Mex.	D9	90
Vera, Arg.	E8	80
Vera, Spain	H12	90
Veracruz [Llave], Mex.	H11	90
Veraguas, prov., Pan.	I13	92
Veranópolis, Braz.	E13	80
Vērāval, India	J4	44
Verbania, Italy	D3	18
Verbilki, Russia	E20	22
Vercelli, Italy	D3	18
Vercel [-Villedieu-le-Camp], Fr.	E13	14
Verchn'aja Inta, Russia	D10	26
Verchn'aja Salda, Russia	F10	26
Verchn'aja Tura, Russia	F9	26
Verchn'aja Troica, Russia	D20	22
Verchnedneprovskij, Russia	G16	22
Verchnetulomskoje vodochranilišče, res., Russia	G22	6
Verchnevil'ujsk, Russia	E16	28
Verchnij Ufaley, Russia	F10	26
Verchnij Ufaley, Russia	D18	28
Verchojanskij chrebet, mts., Russia	D17	28
Verchojansk, Russia	D17	28
Verchotur'je, Russia	F10	26
Verchovje, Russia	I20	22
Vercors, reg., Fr.	H12	14
Verda, Ky., U.S.	C3	112
Verde, stm., Braz.	C4	79
Verde, stm., Braz.	G4	79
Verde, stm., Braz.	E4	79
Verde, stm., S.A.	F11	82
Verde, stm., Az., U.S.	K5	120
Verde, Arroyo, stm., Bol.	E8	82
Verde, Cape, c., Bah.	C7	94
Verde Grande, stm., Braz.	C7	79
Verde Pequeno, stm., Braz.	C7	79
Verdigre, Ne., U.S.	I9	118
Verdigris, stm., U.S.	C11	116

Name — Map Ref. — Page

Verdinho, stm., Braz. D3 79
Verdon, Ne., U.S. K12 118
Verdun, Que., Can. B13 108
Verdun, Fr. I8 14
Verdun-sur-le-Doubs, Fr. F12 14
Verdun-sur-Meuse, Fr. C12 14
Vereeniging, S. Afr. F8 66
Veregin, Sask., Can. G12 104
Vereja, Russia F19 22
Veremejki, Bela. H14 22
Vereščagino, Russia F8 26
Vergara, Ur. G12 80
Vergennes, Vt., U.S. C13 108
Verín, Spain D4 16
Veriora, Est. C10 22
Veríssimo, Braz. E4 79
Verkhovyna, Ukr. A8 20
Verkhoyansk see Verchojansk, Russia D18 28
Vermejo, stm., N.M., U.S. H12 120
Vermelho, stm., Braz. C3 79
Vermette Lake, l., Sask., Can. C5 104
Vermilion, Alta., Can. D24 102
Vermilion, Oh., U.S. F4 108
Vermilion, stm., Alta., Can. E3 104
Vermilion, stm., Il., U.S. I7 110
Vermilion, stm., La., U.S. M4 114
Vermilion, stm., Mn., U.S. B3 110
Vermilion Bay, Ont., Can. I21 104
Vermilion Bay, b., La., U.S. M4 114
Vermilion Lake, l., Ont., Can. H22 104
Vermilion Lake, l., Mn., U.S. C3 110
Vermilion Pass, Can. F18 102
Vermillion, S.D., U.S. I11 118
Vermillion, stm., S.D., U.S. H11 118
Vermont, Il., U.S. B6 114
Vermont, state, U.S. C12 98
Vernal, Ut., U.S. D7 120
Vernayaz, Switz. F7 13
Verndale, Mn., U.S. E12 118
Verner, Ont., Can. D15 110
Verneuil, Fr. D7 14
Vernon, B.C., Can. G15 102
Vernon, Fr. C8 14
Vernon, Al., U.S. I8 114
Vernon, Ct., U.S. F14 108
Vernon, Fl., U.S. L11 114
Vernon, In., U.S. D11 114
Vernon, Tx., U.S. E7 116
Vernon, Ut., U.S. D4 120
Vernonia, Or., U.S. E2 122
Vernon River, P.E.I., Can. F11 106
Verny, Fr. C13 14
Vero Beach, Fl., U.S. L6 112
Véroia, Grc. I6 20
Verona, Ont., Can. F19 110
Verona, Italy D6 18
Verona, Ms., U.S. H8 114
Verona, Wi., U.S. H6 110
Verónica, Arg. H10 80
Verrettes, Haiti E8 94
Versailles, Fr. D9 14
Versailles, Il., U.S. C6 114
Versailles, In., U.S. C11 114
Versailles, Ky., U.S. D12 114
Versailles, Mo., U.S. D4 114
Versailles, Oh., U.S. G2 108
Veršino-Darasunskij, Russia G15 28
Vert, Cap, c., Sen. D1 64
Verte, Île, i., Que., Can. D4 106
Vertientes, Cuba D5 94
Vertou, Fr. E5 14
Verviers, Bel. G8 12
Vervins, Fr. C10 14
Vescovato, Fr. G4 18
Vesjegonsk, Russia C20 22
Vesoul, Fr. E13 14
Vespasiano, Braz. E7 79
Vesta, C.R. H11 92
Vest-Agder, co., Nor. L10 6
Vestavia Hills, Al., U.S. I10 114
Vesterålen, is., Nor. G14 6
Vestfjorden, Nor. H14 6
Vestfold, co., Nor. L12 6
Vestmannaeyjar, Ice. C3 6a
Vesuvio, vol., Italy I9 18
Vesuvius see Vesuvio, vol., Italy I9 18
Veszprém, Hung. H17 10
Veszprém, co., Hung. H17 10
Vésztő, Hung. I21 10
Vetluga, Russia F7 26
Vetralla, Italy G7 18
Vetrino, Bela. F11 22
Vetrişoaia, Rom. C12 20
Vetschau, Ger. D14 10
Veurne (Furnes), Bel. F2 12
Vevay, In., U.S. D11 114
Vevey, Switz. F6 13
Vézelise, Fr. D13 14
Viacha, Bol. G7 82
Viadana, Italy E5 18
Viadutos, Braz. D12 80
Viale, Arg. F8 80
Viamão, Braz. F13 80
Viamonte, Arg. G7 80
Vian, Ok., U.S. D12 116
Viana, Braz. D9 76
Viana do Alentejo, Port. G3 16
Viana do Castelo, Port. D3 16
Viangchan (Vientiane), Laos F7 40
Viangphoukha, Laos D6 40
Viareggio, Italy F5 18
Vibank, Sask., Can. H11 104
Viborg, Den. M11 6
Viborg, S.D., U.S. H10 118
Vibo Valentia, Italy K11 18
Vibraye, Fr. D7 14
Viburnum, Mo., U.S. E5 114
Vic (Vich), Spain D14 16
Vícam, Mex. D4 90
Vicco, Ky., U.S. B3 112
Vic-en-Bigorre, Fr. I7 14
Vicente Guerrero, Mex. F8 90
Vicente López, Arg. H9 80
Vicente Noble, Dom. Rep. E9 94
Vicenza, Italy D6 18
Viceroy, Sask., Can. I9 104
Vichada, dept., Col. E8 84
Vichada, stm., Col. E8 84
Vichadero, Ur. F11 80
Vichigasta, Arg. E5 80
Vichuquén, Chile H2 80
Vichy, Fr. F10 14
Vici, Ok., U.S. C7 116
Vicksburg, Mi., U.S. H10 110
Vicksburg, Ms., U.S. J6 114
Vico, Fr. I23 15a
Viçosa, Braz. F7 79
Victor, Id., U.S. G14 122
Victor, Ia., U.S. I3 110
Victor, Mt., U.S. D11 122
Victor, Lac, l., Que., Can. B12 106
Victor Harbor, Austl. J3 70
Victoria, Arg. G8 80
Victoria, Cam. I14 64
Victoria, B.C., Can. I11 102
Victoria, P.E.I., Can. F10 106
Victoria, Chile J2 80
Victoria, Gren. H14 94
Victoria (Xianggang), H.K. M3 34
Victoria, Malay. D6 38
Victoria, Sey. B11 58
Victoria, Ks., U.S. M8 118
Victoria, Tx., U.S. K9 116
Victoria, Va., U.S. C8 112
Victoria, state, Austl. G9 68
Victoria, stm., Austl. C6 68
Victoria, stm., Newf., Can. D17 106
Victoria, Lake, l., Afr. B6 58
Victoria, Lake, l., Austl. I4 70
Victoria, Mount, mtn., Mya. D2 40
Victoria, Mount, mtn., Pap. N. Gui. A9 68
Victoria Beach, Man., Can. H18 104
Victoria Falls, Zimb. A7 66
Victoria Falls, wtfl, Afr. A7 66
Victoria Harbour, Ont., Can. F16 110
Victoria Island, i., N.W. Ter., Can. B10 96
Victoria Lake, res., Newf., Can. D16 106
Victoria Land, reg., Ant. C8 73
Victoria Nile, stm., Ug. H7 56
Victoria Peak, mtn., Belize I15 90
Victoria Peak, mtn., B.C., Can. G8 102
Victoria River Downs, Austl. C6 68
Victoria Strait, strt., N.W. Ter., Can. C12 96
Victoriaville, Que., Can. A15 108
Victoria West, S. Afr. H6 66
Victorica, Arg. I6 80
Victorino, Ven. F9 84
Victorino de la Plaza, Arg. I7 80
Victorville, Ca., U.S. J8 124
Vičuga, Russia D24 22
Vicuña, Chile F3 80
Vicuña Mackenna, Arg. G6 80
Vidalia, Ga., U.S. G4 112
Vidalia, La., U.S. K5 114
Vidal Ramos, Braz. D14 80
Vidauban, Fr. I13 14
Videira, Braz. D13 80
Vidigueira, Port. G4 16
Vidin, Bul. F6 20
Vidisha, India I7 44
Vidlica, Russia K23 6
Vidor, Tx., U.S. L2 114
Vidzeme, hist. reg., Lat. D8 22
Vidzy, Bela. F9 22
Viechtach, Ger. F12 10
Viedma, Arg. E4 78
Viedma, Lago, l., Arg. F2 78
Viejo, Cerro, mtn., Peru J3 84
Viekšniai, Lith. E5 22
Viella, Spain C12 16
Vienna see Wien, Aus. G16 10
Vienna, Ga., U.S. G3 112
Vienna, Il., U.S. E8 114
Vienna, Md., U.S. I11 108
Vienna, Mo., U.S. D5 114
Vienna, S.D., U.S. G10 118
Vienna, W.V., U.S. H5 108
Vienne, Fr. G11 14
Vienne, dept., Fr. F7 14
Vienne, stm., Fr. E7 14
Vientiane see Viangchan, Laos F7 40
Vieques, P.R. E12 94
Vieques, Isla de, i., P.R. E12 94
Vierfontein, S. Afr. F8 66
Vierwaldstättersee, l., Switz. D9 13
Vierzon, Fr. E9 14
Viesca, Mex. E8 90
Viesīte, Lat. E8 22
Vieste, Italy H11 18
Vietnam, ctry., Asia B4 38
Viet Tri, Viet. D8 40
Vieux-Fort, Que., Can. A16 106
Vieux Fort, St. Luc. H14 94
Vievis, Lith. G7 22
Vieytes, Arg. H10 80
Vigan, Phil. m19 39b
Vigeland, Nor. L10 6
Vigevano, Italy D3 18
Vigneulles-lès-Hattonchâtel, Fr. D12 14
Vignola, Italy E6 18
Vigo, Spain C3 16
Vihowa, Pak. E4 44
Viitasaari, Fin. J19 6
Vijāpur, India I5 44
Vijayawāda, India D6 46
Vijosë (Aóös), stm., Eur. I4 20
Viking, Alta., Can. D23 102
Vikna, i., Nor. C10 4
Vikno, Ukr. A9 20
Vikramasingapuram, India H4 46
Vila da Ribeira Brava, C.V. m16 64a
Vila de Manica, Moz. B11 66
Vila do Bispo, Port. H3 16
Vila Fontes, Moz. A12 66
Vilafranca del Penedès, Spain D13 16
Vila Gomes da Costa, Moz. E11 66
Viļaka, Lat. D10 22
Vilama, Laguna de, l., Arg. B5 80
Vila Machado, Moz. B12 66
Vilanculos, Moz. E12 66
Viļāni, Lat. E9 22
Vila Nova de Foz Côa, Port. D4 16
Vila Nova de Gaia, Port. D3 16
Vilanova i la Geltrú, Spain D13 16
Vila Novo de Ourém, Port. F3 16
Vila Paiva de Andrada, Moz. B12 66
Vila Real, Port. D4 16
Vila Real de Santo António, Port. H4 16
Vilar Formoso, Port. E5 16
Vila Velha, Braz. F8 79
Vila Velha de Ródão, Port. F4 16
Vila Verde, Port. D3 16
Vil'che, Ukr. F22 10
Vilejka, Bela. G9 22
Vilelas, Arg. D7 80
Vilhelmina, Swe. I15 6
Vilhena, Braz. E11 82
Viljandi, Est. C8 22
Viljoenskroon, S. Afr. F8 66
Vilkaviškis, Lith. G6 22
Vil'kickogo, ostrov, i., Russia C13 26
Vil'kickogo, proliv, strt., Russia B18 26
Vilkija, Lith. F6 22
Villa Abecia, Bol. I9 82
Villa Aberastain, Arg. F4 80
Villa Alemana, Chile G3 80
Villa Ana, Arg. E9 80
Villa Ángela, Arg. D8 80
Villa Atamisqui, Arg. E7 80
Villa Atuel, Arg. H5 80
Villa Bella, Bol. D9 82
Villa Berthet, Arg. D8 80
Villa Bruzual, Ven. C8 84
Villa Cañás, Arg. H8 80
Villacañas, Spain F8 16
Villa Carlos Paz, Arg. F6 80
Villacarrillo, Spain G8 16
Villa Castelli, Arg. E4 80
Villach, Aus. I13 10
Villacidro, Italy J3 18
Villa Comaltitlan, Mex. B2 92
Villa Concepción del Tío, Arg. F7 80
Villa Constitución, Arg. G8 80
Villada, Spain C7 16
Villa de Arista, Mex. F9 90
Villa de Arriaga, Mex. G9 90
Villa de Cos, Mex. F8 90
Villa de Cura, Ven. B9 84
Villa del Carmen, Arg. G6 80
Villa del Rosario, Arg. F7 80
Villa del Rosario, Arg. F10 80
Villa de María, Arg. E7 80
Villa de Nova Sintra, C.V. m16 64a
Villa de San Antonio, Hond. C7 92
Villa de San Francisco, Hond. C8 92
Villa de Soto, Arg. F6 80
Villadiego, Spain C7 16
Villa Dolores, Arg. F6 80
Villa Elisa, Arg. G9 80
Villa Flores, Mex. I13 90
Villa Florida, Para. D10 80
Villafranca de los Barros, Spain G5 16
Villafranca di Verona, Italy D5 18
Village, Ok., U.S. D9 116
Villa General Roca, Arg. G5 80
Villagrán, Mex. E10 90
Villa Grove, Il., U.S. C8 114
Villaguay, Arg. F9 80
Villa Guerrero, Mex. H10 90
Villa Guillermina, Arg. E9 80
Villa Hayes, Para. C10 80
Villahermosa, Mex. I13 90
Villa Hernandarias, Arg. F9 80
Villa Hidalgo, Mex. G8 90
Villa Huidobro, Arg. H6 80
Villaines-la-Juhel, Fr. D6 14
Villa Insurgentes, Mex. E4 90
Villa Iris, Arg. J7 80
Villa Juárez, Mex. D5 90
Villa Krause, Arg. F4 80
Villa Larca, Arg. G6 80
Villaldama, Mex. D9 90
Villalonga, Arg. D4 78
Villa Mainero, Mex. E10 90
Villa María, Arg. G7 80
Villa María Grande, Arg. F9 80
Villa Martín, Bol. I8 82
Villa Matoque, Arg. C7 80
Villa Mazán, Arg. E5 80
Villa Media Agua, Arg. F4 80
Villa Mercedes, Arg. F4 80
Villamontes, Bol. I10 82
Villa Nueva, Arg. G7 80
Villa Nueva, Arg. G4 80
Villanueva, Col. B6 84
Villa Nueva, Guat. C4 92
Villanueva, Hond. B6 92
Villanueva, Mex. F8 90
Villanueva, Nic. E8 92
Villanueva, N.M., U.S. I11 120
Villanueva de Córdoba, Spain G7 16
Villanueva de la Serena, Spain G6 16
Villanueva del Río y Minas, Spain H6 16
Villa Ocampo, Arg. E9 80
Villa Ojo de Agua, Arg. E7 80
Villa Oliva, Para. D10 80
Villa Oropeza, Bol. H9 82
Villapinzón, Col. E6 84
Villa Quinteros, Arg. D6 80
Villa Ramírez, Arg. G8 80
Villarcayo, Spain C8 16
Villa Regina, Arg. J5 80
Villa Reynolds, Arg. G6 80
Villa Rica, Ga., U.S. F2 112
Villa Rivero, Bol. G9 82
Villarrica, Chile D2 78
Villarrica, Col. F5 84
Villarrica, Para. C10 80
Villarrobledo, Spain F9 16
Villas, N.J., U.S. H12 108
Villa Sandino, Nic. E10 92
Villa San José, Arg. G9 80
Villa San Martín, Arg. E6 80
Villa Santa, Montaña, mtn., Hond. C8 92
Villa Santo Domingo, Mex. F9 90
Villasayas, Spain D9 16
Villa Serrano, Bol. H9 82
Villasimius, Italy J4 18
Villasor, Italy J3 18
Villa Tunari, Bol. G9 82
Villa Unión, Arg. E4 80
Villa Unión, Arg. E7 80
Villa Unión, Mex. C9 90
Villa Unión, Mex. F6 90
Villa Valeria, Arg. H6 80
Villavicencio, Col. E6 84
Villaviciosa, Spain B6 16
Villa Viscarra, Bol. G9 82
Villazón, Bol. J9 82
Villé, Fr. D14 14
Villedieu, Fr. D5 14
Villefort, Fr. H10 14
Villefranche, Fr. G11 14
Villena, Spain G11 16
Villeneuve-d'Aveyron, Fr. H9 14
Villeneuve-Saint-Georges, Fr. D9 14
Villeneuve-sur-Lot, Fr. H7 14
Ville Platte, La., U.S. L4 114
Villers-Bocage, Fr. C9 14
Villers-Bocage, Fr. C6 14
Villersexel, Fr. E13 14
Villerupt, Fr. C12 14
Ville-Saint-Georges see Saint-Georges, Que., Can. A16 108
Villeta, Col. E5 84
Villeurbanne, Fr. G11 14
Villiers, S. Afr. F9 66
Villingen-Schwenningen, Ger. G8 10
Villisca, Ia., U.S. K13 118
Vilna, Alta., Can. C23 102
Vilnius, Lith. G8 22
Vilshofen, Ger. G13 10
Vil'uj, stm., Russia E16 28
Vil'ujsk, Russia E16 28
Vil'ujskoje vodochranilišče, res., Russia E20 26
Vimianzo, Spain B2 16
Vimoutiers, Fr. D7 14
Vimperk, Czech. F13 10
Vina, Ca., U.S. E3 124
Vina, stm., Cam. G9 54
Viñac, Peru E4 82
Viña del Mar, Chile G3 80
Vinalhaven, Me., U.S. C18 108
Vinaròs, Spain E12 16
Vincennes, In., U.S. D9 114
Vincennes Bay, b., Ant. B6 73
Vincent, Al., U.S. I10 114
Vinces, Ec. H3 84
Vinchina, Arg. E4 80
Vinchos, Peru E4 82
Vindhya Range, mts., India I7 44
Vinegar Hill, mtn., Or., U.S. F7 122
Vine Grove, Ky., U.S. E11 114
Vineland, N.J., U.S. H11 108
Vinemont, Al., U.S. H10 114
Vineyard Haven, Ma., U.S. F16 108
Ving Ngün, Mya. C5 40
Vinh, Viet. E8 40
Vinh Long, Viet. I8 40
Vinita, Ok., U.S. C11 116
Vinkovci, Cro. D2 20
Vinnytsya, Ukr. H3 26
Vinson Massif, mtn., Ant. C12 73
Vinton, Ia., U.S. H3 110
Vinton, La., U.S. L3 114
Vinton, Va., U.S. B7 112
Viny, Russia C15 22
Viola, Il., U.S. I5 110
Viola, Wi., U.S. G5 110
Violín, Isla, i., C.R. I11 92
Vipiteno, Italy C6 18
Vipos, Arg. D6 80
Virac, Phil. C7 38
Virac, Phil. m19 39b
Viradouro, Braz. F4 79
Virago Sound, strt., B.C., Can. C2 102
Viramgām, India I5 44
Viranşehir, Tur. C5 48
Virbalis, Lith. G5 22
Virden, Man., Can. I14 104
Virden, Il., U.S. C7 114
Virden, N.M., U.S. L7 120
Vire, Fr. D6 14
Virelles, Bel. H5 12
Virgem da Lapa, Braz. D7 79
Virgil, Ks., U.S. N11 118
Virgilina, Va., U.S. C8 112
Virgin, stm., U.S. H2 120
Virgin Gorda, i., Br. Vir. Is. E12 94
Virginia, S. Afr. G8 66
Virginia, Il., U.S. C6 114
Virginia, Mn., U.S. C3 110
Virginia, state, U.S. D11 98
Virginia Beach, Va., U.S. C11 112
Virginia City, Mt., U.S. E14 122
Virginia City, Nv., U.S. E6 124
Virginia Falls, wtfl, N.W. Ter., Can. F32 100
Virginiatown, Ont., Can. B16 110
Virgin Islands, dep., N.A. E12 94
Virginópolis, Braz. E7 79
Virgolândia, Braz. E7 79
Virôchey, Camb. H9 40
Virojoki, Fin. K20 6
Viroqua, Wi., U.S. G5 110
Virovitica, Cro. D12 18
Virrat, Fin. J18 6
Virtaniemi, Fin. G21 6
Virtsu, Est. C6 22
Virú, Peru C2 82
Virudunagar, India H4 46
Virungu, Zaire C5 58
Viru-Nigula, Est. B9 22
Vis, Cro. F11 18
Vis (Fish), stm., Nmb. E3 66
Vis, Otok, i., Cro. F11 18
Visalia, Ca., U.S. H6 124
Visayan Sea, Phil. C7 38
Visby, Swe. M16 6
Viscount, Sask., Can. G9 104
Viscount Melville Sound, strt., N.W. Ter., Can. B11 96
Visé (Wezet), Bel. G8 12
Višegrad, Bos. F3 20
Viseu, Port. E4 16
Vishākhapatnam, India D7 46
Vislinskij zaliv, b., Eur. A19 10
Visnagar, India I5 44
Viso, Monte, mtn., Italy E2 18
Visoko, Bos. F2 20
Visokoi Island, i., S. Geor. A2 73
Visp, Switz. F8 13
Visselhövede, Ger. C9 10
Vista, Ca., U.S. K8 124
Vista Alegre, Arg. J4 80
Vista Flores, Arg. G4 80
Vistula see Wisła, stm., Pol. A18 10
Vita, Man., Can. I18 104
Vita, stm., Col. E8 84
Vitarte, Peru E3 82
Vitebsk, Bela. F13 22
Viterbo, Italy G7 18
Vitichi, Bol. I9 82
Viti Levu, i., Fiji J21 126
Vitim, stm., Russia F14 28
Vitor, Peru G6 82
Vitor, stm., Peru G6 82
Vitória, Braz. F8 79
Vitoria (Gasteiz), Spain C9 16
Vitória da Conquista, Braz. C8 79
Vitré, Fr. D5 14
Vitry-le-François, Fr. D11 14
Vittangi, Swe. H17 6
Vitteaux, Fr. E11 14
Vittel, Fr. D12 14
Vittoria, Italy M9 18
Vittorio Veneto, Italy D7 18
Viver, Spain F11 16
Vivi, stm., Russia D11 26
Vivian, La., U.S. J3 114
Vivoratá, Arg. I10 80
Vivorillo, Cayos, is., Hond. B11 92
Vizcaíno, Desierto de, des., Mex. D3 90
Vize, Tur. H11 20
Vize, ostrov, i., Russia B13 26
Vizianagaram, India C7 46
Vizzini, Italy L9 18
Vlaardingen, Neth. E5 12
Vladikavkaz, Russia I6 26
Vladimir, Russia E23 22
Vladimirskij Tupik, Russia F16 22
Vladivostok, Russia I18 28
Vlasenica, Bos. E2 20
Vlasotince, Yugo. G6 20
Vlieland, i., Neth. B7 12
Vlissingen (Flushing), Neth. F4 12
Vlonë see Vlorë, Alb. I3 20
Vlorë, Alb. I3 20
Vlorës, Gji i, b., Alb. I3 20
Vltava, stm., Czech. F14 10
Vnukovo, Russia F20 22
Vochtoga, Russia B23 22
Voca, Tx., U.S. I7 116
Vodlozero, ozero, l., Russia J25 6
Vodňany, Czech. F14 10
Vogelsberg, mts., Ger. E9 10
Voghera, Italy E4 18
Vohenstrauss, Ger. F12 10
Vohibinany, Madag. q23 67b
Vohilava, Madag. r23 67b
Vohimarina, Madag. n24 67b
Vohipeno, Madag. s22 67b
Võhma, Est. C8 22
Void, Fr. D12 14
Voinjama, Lib. G5 64
Voiron, Fr. G12 14
Voitsberg, Aus. H15 10
Voj-Vož, Russia E8 26
Volary, Czech. G13 10
Volcán, Arg. B6 80
Volcán, Pan. C1 84
Volcano, Hi., U.S. r18 125a
Volcán Poás, Parque Nacional, C.R. G10 92
Volchov, Russia B15 22
Volchov, stm., Russia B15 22
Volga, Russia D21 22
Volga, Ia., U.S. H4 110
Volga, S.D., U.S. G11 118
Volga, stm., Russia H7 26
Volgino, Russia C16 22
Volgo-Baltijskij kanal, Russia L26 6
Volgodonsk, Russia H6 26
Volgograd (Stalingrad), Russia H6 26
Volgogradskoje vodochranilišče, res., Russia H7 26
Volintiri, Mol. C13 20
Volkach, Ger. F10 10
Völkermarkt, Aus. I14 10
Völklingen, Ger. F6 10
Volkovysk, Bela. H7 22
Volksrust, S. Afr. F9 66
Volockaja, Russia A25 22
Volodarsk, Russia E26 22
Volodarskoje, Kaz. G11 26
Vologda, Russia B22 22
Vologda, stm., Russia B22 22
Volokolamsk, Russia E18 22
Vólos, Grc. J6 20
Volosovo, Russia B12 22
Volot, Russia D13 22
Volovets', Ukr. A7 20
Volovo, Russia H21 22
Voložin, Bela. G9 22
Vol'sk, Russia G7 26
Volta, stm., Ghana I10 64
Volta, Lake, res., Ghana H9 64
Volta Blanche (White Volta), stm., Afr. F6 54
Volta Noire (Black Volta), stm., Afr. F6 54
Volta Redonda, Braz. G6 79
Volta Rouge, stm., Afr. F9 64
Volterra, Italy F5 18
Voltri, Italy E3 18
Volyně, Czech. F13 10
Volžsk, Russia F7 26
Volžskij, Russia H6 26
Vonda, Sask., Can. F8 104
Vondrozo, Madag. s22 67b
Vopnafjörður, Ice. B6 6a
Vorarlberg, state, Aus. H9 10
Vorau, Aus. H15 10
Vorden, Neth. D9 12
Vorder-Grauspitz, mtn., Eur. D12 13
Vorderrhein, stm., Switz. E10 13
Vordingborg, Den. N12 6
Vóreion Aiyaíon, prov., Grc. K9 20
Vorga, Russia H15 22
Vórioi Sporádhes, is., Grc. J7 20
Vorkuta, Russia D10 26
Vormsi, i., Est. B6 22
Vorob'jovo, Russia B23 22
Vorokhta, Ukr. A8 20
Voroncov, Mol. B13 20
Voronež, Russia G5 26
Voronovo, Bela. G8 22
Voropajevo, Bela. F10 22
Voroshilovsk see Stavropol', Russia H6 26
Vorošilovgrad see Luhans'k, Ukr. H5 26
Vorpommern, hist. reg., Ger. B13 10
Vorsma, Russia F26 22
Võrtsjärv, l., Est. C9 22
Võru, Est. D10 22
Vosges, dept., Fr. D13 14
Vosges, mts., Fr. D14 14
Voskresensk, Russia F21 22
Voskresenskoje, Russia B20 22
Voskresenskoje, Russia D20 22
Voss, Nor. K10 6
Vostočno-Sibirskoje more (East Siberian Sea), Russia C23 28
Vostočnyj Sajan, mts., Russia G11 28
Vostok, sci., Ant. C6 73
Votkinsk, Russia F8 26
Votuporanga, Braz. F4 79
Voulou, Cen. Afr. Rep. M2 60
Vouziers, Fr. C11 14
Voves, Fr. D8 14
Voyageurs National Park, Mn., U.S. B3 110
Vože, ozero, l., Russia K26 6
Vožega, Russia A23 22
Voznesens'k, Ukr. H4 26
Voznesenskoje, Russia G25 22
Vraca, Bul. F7 20
Vrådal, Nor. L11 6
Vrancea, co., Rom. D10 20
Vrangel'a, ostrov, i., Russia C28 28
Vranje, Yugo. G5 20
Vrbas, Yugo. D3 20
Vrede, S. Afr. F9 66
Vredenburg, S. Afr. I3 66
Vredenburgh, Al., U.S. K9 114
Vredendal, S. Afr. H4 66
Vreed en Hoop, Guy. D13 84
Vrindāvan, India G7 44
Vrondádhes, Grc. K10 20
Vršac, Yugo. D5 20
Vryburg, S. Afr. F7 66
Vryheid, S. Afr. F10 66
Vsetín, Czech. F17 10
Vsevidof, Mount, mtn., Ak., U.S. J10 100
Vtoryje Levyje Lamki, Russia H24 22
Vukovar, Cro. D3 20
Vulcan, Alta., Can. G21 102
Vulcan, Rom. D7 20
Vulcan, Mi., U.S. E8 110
Vulcăneşti, Mol. D12 20
Vung Tau, Viet. I9 40
Vuohijärvi, Fin. K20 6
Vuokenniska, Fin. K21 6
Vuotso, Fin. G20 6
Vuyyūru, India D6 46
Vyborg, Russia A11 22
Vyborgskij zaliv, b., Russia A11 22
Vyčegda, stm., Russia E7 26
Vygoniči, Russia H17 22
Vygozero, ozero, l., Russia J24 6
Vyksa, Russia F25 22
Vyľkove, Ukr. D13 20
Vynohradiv, Ukr. A7 20
Vypolzovo, Russia D16 22
Vyrica, Russia B13 22
Vyša, Russia H25 22
Vyšgorodok, Russia D11 22
Vyškov, Czech. F17 10
Vyškov, Russia I14 22
Vyšnij Voloček, Russia D17 22
Vysock, Russia A11 22
Vysoké Tatry, mts., Eur. F20 10
Vysokiniči, Russia G19 22
Vysokogornyj, Russia G19 28
Vysokoje, Bela. I6 22
Vysokoje, Russia E17 22
Vysokovsk, Russia E19 22
Vyšší Brod, Czech. G14 10
Vytegra, Russia E5 26
Vyzhnytsya, Ukr. A9 20

W

Wa, Ghana F8 64
Waal, stm., Neth. E7 12
Waao, China B8 40
Wabag, Pap. N. Gui. G11 38
Wabamun, Alta., Can. D20 102
Wabamun Indian Reserve, Alta., Can. D20 102
Wabamun Lake, l., Alta., Can. D20 102
Wabana, Newf., Can. E21 106
Wabasca, Alta., Can. A21 102
Wabasca, stm., Alta., Can. E9 96
Wabasca Indian Reserve, Alta., Can. B21 102
Wabash, In., U.S. B11 114
Wabash, stm., U.S. E9 114
Wabasha, Mn., U.S. F3 110
Wabasso, Fl., U.S. L6 112
Wabasso, Mn., U.S. G12 118
Wabeno, Wi., U.S. E7 110
Wabigoon Lake, l., Ont., Can. I22 104
Wabowden, Man., Can. D16 104
Wąbrzeźno, Pol. B18 10
W.A.C. Bennett Dam, B.C., Can. A12 102
Waccamaw, stm., U.S. F8 112
Wachapreague, Va., U.S. B11 112
Wacissa, Fl., U.S. I3 112
Waco, Tx., U.S. H9 116
Waconda Lake, res., Ks., U.S. L9 118
Waconia, Mn., U.S. F2 110
Wacouno, stm., Que., Can. A8 106
Wad Al-Haddād, Sud. K7 60
Wad Bandah, Sud. K4 60
Wad Ban Naqa, Sud. I7 60
Waddenzee, Neth. B7 12
Waddington, N.Y., U.S. C11 108
Waddington, Mount, mtn., B.C., Can. F9 102
Wade, Mount, mtn., Ant. D9 73
Wadena, Sask., Can. G11 104
Wadena, Mn., U.S. E12 118
Wädenswil, Switz. D10 13
Wadesboro, N.C., U.S. E6 112
Wad Hāmid, Sud. I7 60
Wadham Islands, is., Newf., Can. C20 106
Wadhams, B.C., Can. F7 102
Wādī as-Sīr, Jord. E5 50
Wādī Halfā', Sud. G6 60
Wadley, Al., U.S. I11 114
Wadley, Ga., U.S. G4 112
Wad Madanī, Sud. J7 60
Wadowice, Pol. F19 10
Wadsworth, Nv., U.S. E6 124
Wadsworth, Oh., U.S. F5 108
Waegwan, S. Kor. H16 32
Waelder, Tx., U.S. J9 116
Wafang, China B6 32
Wafrah, Kuw. G10 48
Wageningen, Neth. E8 12
Wageningen, Sur. E14 84
Wager Bay, b., N.W. Ter., Can. C15 96
Wagga Wagga, Austl. J7 70
Wagin, Austl. F3 68
Waging am See, Ger. H12 10
Wagner, S.D., U.S. H9 118
Wagoner, Ok., U.S. D11 116
Wagon Mound, N.M., U.S. C2 116
Wągrowiec, Pol. C17 10
Waha, Libya C4 56
Wāh Cantonment, Pak. D5 44
Wahiawa, Hi., U.S. p15 125a
Wahoo, Ne., U.S. J11 118
Wahpeton, N.D., U.S. E11 118
Wahran (Oran), Alg. C10 62
Waialua, Hi., U.S. p15 125a
Waianae, Hi., U.S. p15 125a
Waiau, N.Z. E4 72
Waiblingen, Ger. G9 10
Waidhofen an der Thaya, Aus. G15 10
Waidhofen an der Ybbs, Aus. H14 10
Waigeo, Pulau, i., Indon. F9 38
Waihi, N.Z. B5 72
Waikato, stm., N.Z. C5 72
Waikerie, Austl. J3 70
Wailuku, Hi., U.S. q17 125a
Waimate, N.Z. F3 72
Waimea, Hi., U.S. p15 125a
Wainganga, stm., India C6 46
Waingapu, Indon. G7 38
Waini, stm., Guy. D13 84
Wainwright, Alta., Can. E24 102
Wainwright, Ak., U.S. A14 100
Waipara, N.Z. E4 72
Waipukurau, N.Z. C6 72
Wairoa, N.Z. C6 72
Waitara, N.Z. C5 72
Waite Park, Mn., U.S. E1 110
Waitsburg, Wa., U.S. D7 122
Waiuku, N.Z. B5 72
Wajima, Japan J11 36
Waka, Eth. N9 60
Waka, Tx., U.S. C5 116
Wakarusa, In., U.S. A10 114
Wakarusa, stm., Ks., U.S. M12 118
Wakaw, Sask., Can. F9 104
Wakaw Lake, l., Sask., Can. F9 104
Wakayama, Japan M10 36
WaKeeney, Ks., U.S. L8 118
Wakefield, Ks., U.S. L10 118
Wakefield, Ne., U.S. I11 118
Wakefield, R.I., U.S. F15 108
Wakefield, Va., U.S. C10 112
Wake Forest, N.C., U.S. D8 112
Wake Island, dep., Oc. G20 126
Wakema, Mya. F3 40
Wakeman, stm., B.C., Can. F8 102
Wake Village, Tx., U.S. I2 114
Wakita, Ok., U.S. C9 116
Wakkanai, Japan b16 36a
Wakonda, S.D., U.S. H10 118
Waku Kundo, Ang. D3 58
Walachia, hist. reg., Rom. E8 20
Wałbrzych (Waldenburg), Pol. E16 10
Walcha, Austl. H9 70
Walcheren, i., Neth. F4 12
Walcott, B.C., Can. C8 102
Walcott, Ia., U.S. I5 110
Walcott, N.D., U.S. E11 118
Wałcz, Pol. B16 10
Wald, Switz. D10 13
Waldbillig, Lux. I9 12
Waldeck, Ger. D9 10
Walden, Co., U.S. D10 120
Walden, N.Y., U.S. F12 108
Walden Ridge, mtn., Tn., U.S. G11 114
Waldheim, Sask., Can. F8 104
Waldkirchen, Ger. G13 10
Waldmünchen, Ger. F12 10
Waldo, B.C., Can. H19 102
Waldo, Ar., U.S. I3 114
Waldoboro, Me., U.S. C17 108
Waldorf, Md., U.S. I10 108
Waldport, Or., U.S. F1 122
Waldron, Sask., Can. H12 104
Waldron, Ar., U.S. H2 114
Waldron, In., U.S. C11 114
Waldron, Mi., U.S. I11 110
Waldshut, Ger. H8 10
Waldviertel, reg., Aus. G15 10
Walenstadt, Switz. D11 13
Wales, Ak., U.S. D10 100
Wales, ter., U.K. I10 8
Wales Island, i., B.C., Can. C4 102
Wales Island, i., N.W. Ter., Can. C15 96
Walgett, Austl. H8 70

Name	Map Ref.	Page
Walgreen Coast, Ant.	C11	73
Walhachin, B.C., Can.	G14	102
Walhalla, N.D., U.S.	C10	118
Walhalla, S.C., U.S.	E3	112
Walker, Ia., U.S.	H4	110
Walker, Mn., U.S.	C1	110
Walker, stm., Nv., U.S.	E7	124
Walker, Lac, l., Que., Can.	B6	106
Walker Lake, l., Man., Can.	D18	104
Walker Lake, l., Nv., U.S.	F7	124
Walkersville, Md., U.S.	H9	108
Walkerton, Ont., Can.	F14	110
Walkerton, In., U.S.	A10	114
Walkertown, N.C., U.S.	C6	112
Walkerville, Mt., U.S.	D13	122
Wall, S.D., U.S.	H5	118
Wallace, Id., U.S.	C10	122
Wallace, Ne., U.S.	K6	118
Wallace, N.C., U.S.	E9	112
Wallaceburg, Ont., Can.	H13	110
Wallangarra, Austl.	G9	70
Wallaroo, Austl.	I2	70
Walla Walla, Wa., U.S.	D7	122
Waller, Tx., U.S.	I11	116
Wallingford, Ct., U.S.	F14	108
Wallingford, Vt., U.S.	D14	108
Wallis, Tx., U.S.	J10	116
Wallis and Futuna, dep., Oc.	J22	126
Wallisellen, Switz.	D10	13
Wall Lake, Ia., U.S.	I12	118
Wallowa, Or., U.S.	E8	122
Wallowa, stm., Or., U.S.	E8	122
Wallowa Mountains, mts., Or., U.S.	E8	122
Walls, Ms., U.S.	H6	114
Wallula, Lake, res., U.S.	D7	122
Walnut, Il., U.S.	I6	110
Walnut, Ia., U.S.	A1	114
Walnut, Ks., U.S.	N12	118
Walnut, Ms., U.S.	H8	114
Walnut, N.C., U.S.	D4	112
Walnut, stm., Ks., U.S.	N10	118
Walnut Cove, N.C., U.S.	C6	112
Walnut Grove, Mn., U.S.	G12	118
Walnut Grove, Ms., U.S.	J7	114
Walnut Ridge, Ar., U.S.	F6	114
Walnut Springs, Tx., U.S.	G9	116
Walpeup, Austl.	J5	70
Walpole, N.H., U.S.	D14	108
Walsenburg, Co., U.S.	G12	120
Walsh, Alta., Can.	I4	104
Walsh, Co., U.S.	N5	118
Walsrode, Ger.	C9	10
Walterboro, S.C., U.S.	G6	112
Walter F. George Lake, res., U.S.	H1	112
Walters, Ok., U.S.	E8	116
Waltershausen, Ger.	E10	10
Waltersville, Ms., U.S.	J6	114
Walthall, Ms., U.S.	I7	114
Waltham, Ma., U.S.	E15	108
Walthill, Ne., U.S.	I11	118
Walton, N.S., Can.	G9	106
Walton, In., U.S.	B10	114
Walton, Ky., U.S.	I2	108
Walton, N.Y., U.S.	E11	108
Walvis Bay, Nmb.	D2	66
Walworth, Wi., U.S.	H7	110
Wamba, Nig.	G14	64
Wamba, stm., Afr.	C3	58
Wamego, Ks., U.S.	L11	118
Wampsville, N.Y., U.S.	D11	108
Wampú, Hond.	B9	92
Wampú, stm., Hond.	B9	92
Wampum, Pa., U.S.	G6	108
Wamsutter, Wy., U.S.	I18	122
Wanaaring, Austl.	G6	70
Wanaka, N.Z.	F2	72
Wanamingo, Mn., U.S.	F3	110
Wan'an, China	I3	34
Wanbi, Austl.	J4	70
Wanblee, S.D., U.S.	H6	118
Wanchese, N.C., U.S.	D11	112
Wandering, stm., Alta., Can.	B22	102
Wando, S. Kor.	I14	32
Wandoan, Austl.	F8	70
Wanette, Ok., U.S.	E9	116
Wanfoxia, China	C6	30
Wanganui, N.Z.	C5	72
Wangaratta, Austl.	K7	70
Wangary, Austl.	J1	70
Wangdu Phodrang, Bhu.	G13	44
Wanghu, China	D1	32
Wanghuzhuang, China	E5	32
Wangjiang, China	E5	34
Wangpan Yang, b., China	E11	30
Wangsi, China	E4	32
Wangtuan, China	F10	32
Wangzhong, China	H4	32
Wangzhuangbu, China	D1	32
Wanham, Alta., Can.	B16	102
Wani, India	B5	46
Wanigela, Pap. N. Gui.	A9	68
Wanipigow, stm., Can.	G19	104
Wānkāner, India	I4	44
Wanli, China	D9	34
Wanneroo, Austl.	F3	68
Wanxian, China	E8	30
Wanzai, China	G3	34
Wanzleben, Ger.	C11	10
Wapakoneta, Oh., U.S.	G2	108
Wapanucka, Ok., U.S.	E10	116
Wapato, Wa., U.S.	D5	122
Wapawekka Hills, hills, Sask., Can.	D10	104
Wapawekka Lake, l., Sask., Can.	D10	104
Wapella, Sask., Can.	H12	104
Wapello, Ia., U.S.	I4	110
Wapesi Lake, l., Ont., Can.	H22	104
Wapisu Lake, l., Man., Can.	C15	104
Wapiti, stm., Can.	B15	102
Wappingers Falls, N.Y., U.S.	F13	108
Wapsipinicon, stm., U.S.	I5	110
Wapus Lake, l., Sask., Can.	B12	104
Waqqāş, Jord.	C5	50
War, W.V., U.S.	B5	112
Warangal, India	C5	46
Waratah, Austl.	M6	70
Warbreccan, Austl.	E5	70
Warburg, Ger.	D9	10
Warburton, Austl.	K6	70
Warburton Bay, b., N.W. Ter., Can.	D10	96
Warburton Creek, stm., Austl.	E7	68
Ward, stm., Austl.	E7	70
Ward Cove, Ak., U.S.	B3	102
Warden, Wa., U.S.	D6	122
Wardha, India	B5	46
Wardha, stm., India	C5	46
Wardlow, Alta., Can.	G23	102
Wardner, B.C., Can.	H19	102
Ware, Ma., U.S.	E14	108
Ware, stm., Ma., U.S.	E14	108
Waregem, Bel.	G3	12
Wareham, Eng., U.K.	K11	8
Wareham, Ma., U.S.	F16	108
Waremme (Borgworm), Bel.	G7	12
Waren, Ger.	B12	10
Warendorf, Ger.	D7	10
Ware Shoals, S.C., U.S.	E4	112
Wargla, Alg.	E13	62
Warialda, Austl.	G9	70
Warin Chamrap, Thai.	G8	40
Warkworth, Ont., Can.	F18	110
Warman, Sask., Can.	F8	104
Warmbad, Nmb.	G4	66
Warmbad, S. Afr.	E9	66
Warminster, Eng., U.K.	J11	8
Warminster, Pa., U.S.	G11	108
Warm Springs, Ga., U.S.	G2	112
Warm Springs, Mt., U.S.	D13	122
Warm Springs, Or., U.S.	F4	122
Warm Springs, Va., U.S.	A7	112
Warm Springs, stm., Or., U.S.	E4	122
Warner, Alta., Can.	H22	102
Warner, N.H., U.S.	D15	108
Warner, Ok., U.S.	D11	116
Warner Lakes, l., Or., U.S.	H6	122
Warner Mountains, mts., U.S.	C5	124
Warner Peak, mtn., Or., U.S.	H6	122
Warner Robins, Ga., U.S.	G3	112
Warnes, Arg.	H8	80
Warnes, Bol.	G10	82
Warpath, stm., Man., Can.	F16	104
Warracknabeal, Austl.	K5	70
Warr Acres, Ok., U.S.	D9	116
Warragul, Austl.	L6	70
Warrego, stm., Austl.	G6	70
Warrego Range, mts., Austl.	E7	70
Warren, Austl.	H7	70
Warren, Ar., U.S.	I4	114
Warren, Il., U.S.	H6	110
Warren, Mi., U.S.	H12	110
Warren, Mn., U.S.	C11	118
Warren, Oh., U.S.	F6	108
Warren, Pa., U.S.	F7	108
Warren Point, c., N.W. Ter., Can.	B28	100
Warrens, Wi., U.S.	F5	110
Warrensburg, Mo., U.S.	D3	114
Warrensburg, N.Y., U.S.	D13	108
Warrenton, S. Afr.	G7	66
Warrenton, Ga., U.S.	F4	112
Warrenton, Mo., U.S.	D5	114
Warrenton, N.C., U.S.	C8	112
Warrenton, Or., U.S.	D2	122
Warrenton, Va., U.S.	I9	108
Warri, Nig.	I12	64
Warrington, Fl., U.S.	L9	114
Warrior, Al., U.S.	I10	114
Warrnambool, Austl.	L5	70
Warroad, Mn., U.S.	C12	118
Warsaw see Warszawa, Pol.	C21	10
Warsaw, Il., U.S.	J4	110
Warsaw, In., U.S.	A11	114
Warsaw, Ky., U.S.	D12	114
Warsaw, Mo., U.S.	D3	114
Warsaw, N.Y., U.S.	E8	108
Warsaw, N.C., U.S.	E8	112
Warsaw, Oh., U.S.	G4	108
Warsaw, Va., U.S.	B10	112
Warspite, Alta., Can.	C22	102
Warszawa (Warsaw), Pol.	C21	10
Warta, stm., Pol.	C15	10
Wartburg, Tn., U.S.	C2	112
Wartburg, hist., Ger.	E10	10
Wartrace, Tn., U.S.	G10	114
Warud, India	B5	46
Warunta, Laguna de, l., Hond.	B10	92
Warwick, Austl.	G10	70
Warwick, Que., Can.	B15	108
Warwick, Eng., U.K.	I12	8
Warwick, R.I., U.S.	F15	108
Warwick Channel, strt., Austl.	B7	68
Warwickshire, co., Eng., U.K.	I12	8
Wasaga Beach, Ont., Can.	F15	110
Wasagu, Nig.	F12	64
Wasatch Plateau, plat., Ut., U.S.	E5	120
Wasatch Range, mts., Ut., U.S.	D5	120
Wascana Creek, stm., Sask., Can.	H10	104
Wasco, Ca., U.S.	I6	124
Wasco, Or., U.S.	E5	122
Waseca, Mn., U.S.	F2	110
Wasekamio Lake, l., Sask., Can.	B6	104
Washademoak Lake, l., N.B., Can.	G8	106
Washburn, Il., U.S.	J6	110
Washburn, N.D., U.S.	D6	118
Washburn, Wi., U.S.	D5	110
Washburn Lake, l., N.W. Ter., Can.	B11	96
Washicoutai, Que., Can.	B13	106
Washington, D.C., U.S.	I9	108
Washington, Ga., U.S.	F4	112
Washington, Il., U.S.	J6	110
Washington, In., U.S.	D9	114
Washington, Ia., U.S.	I4	110
Washington, Ks., U.S.	L10	118
Washington, Ky., U.S.	I3	108
Washington, La., U.S.	L4	114
Washington, Mo., U.S.	D5	114
Washington, N.C., U.S.	D9	112
Washington, Pa., U.S.	G6	108
Washington, Tx., U.S.	I10	116
Washington, Ut., U.S.	G3	120
Washington, Va., U.S.	I8	108
Washington, state, U.S.	B2	98
Washington, Mount, mtn., N.H., U.S.	C15	108
Washington Court House, Oh., U.S.	H3	108
Washington Island, Wi., U.S.	E9	110
Washington Island, i., Wi., U.S.	E9	110
Washington Terrace, Ut., U.S.	C5	120
Washita, stm., U.S.	E10	116
Washow Bay, b., Man., Can.	G18	104
Washtucna, Wa., U.S.	D7	122
Wasilków, Pol.	B23	10
Wasilla, Ak., U.S.	F20	100
Waskada, Man., Can.	I14	104
Waskaganish, Que., Can.	F17	96
Waskahigan, stm., Alta., Can.	C17	102
Waskaiowaka Lake, l., Man., Can.	B18	104
Waskatenau, Alta., Can.	C22	102
Waskesiu Lake, l., Sask., Can.	E8	104
Waskom, Tx., U.S.	J2	114
Waspam, Nic.	C11	92
Waspuk, stm., Nic.	C10	92
Wassen, Switz.	E10	13
Wassenaar, Neth.	D5	12
Wasseralfingen, Ger.	G10	10
Wasserbillig, Lux.	I10	12
Wasserburg am Inn, Ger.	G12	10
Wass Lake, l., Man., Can.	E19	104
Wassou, Gui.	F3	64
Wassy, Fr.	D11	14
Watampone, Indon.	F7	38
Watapi Lake, l., Sask., Can.	C5	104
Waterberg, Nmb.	C3	66
Waterberg Plateau Park, Nmb.	C3	66
Waterbury, Ct., U.S.	F13	108
Waterbury, Vt., U.S.	C14	108
Waterdown, Ont., Can.	G16	110
Wateree, stm., S.C., U.S.	F6	112
Wateree Lake, res., S.C., U.S.	E6	112
Waterford, Ont., Can.	H15	110
Waterford, Ire.	I6	8
Waterford, Ca., U.S.	G5	124
Waterford, Pa., U.S.	F7	108
Waterford, Wi., U.S.	H7	110
Waterford, co., Ire.	I6	8
Waterhen, stm., Sask., Can.	D6	104
Waterhen Lake, l., Man., Can.	F15	104
Waterhen Lake, l., Sask., Can.	D6	104
Waterloo, Bel.	G5	12
Waterloo, Ont., Can.	G15	110
Waterloo, Que., Can.	B14	108
Waterloo, Al., U.S.	H8	114
Waterloo, Il., U.S.	D6	114
Waterloo, Ia., U.S.	H3	110
Waterloo, N.Y., U.S.	E10	108
Waterloo, Wi., U.S.	G7	110
Waterman, Il., U.S.	I7	110
Waterproof, La., U.S.	K5	114
Watersmeet, Mi., U.S.	D6	110
Waterton, stm., N.A.	H21	102
Waterton-Glacier International Peace Park, N.A.	B12	122
Waterton Lakes National Park, Alta., Can.	H21	102
Watertown, N.Y., U.S.	D11	108
Watertown, S.D., U.S.	G10	118
Watertown, Wi., U.S.	G7	110
Water Valley, Ms., U.S.	H7	114
Waterville, N.S., Can.	G9	106
Waterville, Ks., U.S.	L11	118
Waterville, Me., U.S.	C17	108
Waterville, Mn., U.S.	F2	110
Waterville, Oh., U.S.	F3	108
Waterville, Wa., U.S.	C5	122
Watervliet, N.Y., U.S.	E13	108
Watford, Ont., Can.	H14	110
Watford City, N.D., U.S.	D4	118
Wathaman, stm., Sask., Can.	A11	104
Wathaman Lake, l., Sask., Can.	B11	104
Wathena, Ks., U.S.	L13	118
Watino, Alta., Can.	B17	102
Watkins Glen, N.Y., U.S.	E10	108
Watkinsville, Ga., U.S.	F3	112
Watling Island see San Salvador, i., Bah.	B7	94
Watonga, Ok., U.S.	D8	116
Watonwan, stm., Mn., U.S.	G13	118
Watrous, Sask., Can.	G9	104
Watrous, N.M., U.S.	I12	120
Watseka, Il., U.S.	J8	110
Watson, Sask., Can.	F10	104
Watson Lake, Yukon, Can.	F30	100
Watsontown, Pa., U.S.	F10	108
Watsonville, Ca., U.S.	H4	124
Wattens, Aus.	H11	10
Wattenwil, Switz.	E8	13
Watts Bar Lake, res., Tn., U.S.	D2	112
Watts Mills, S.C., U.S.	E4	112
Wattwil, Switz.	D11	13
Watubela, Kepulauan, is., Indon.	F9	38
Watzmann, mtn., Ger.	H12	10
Waubay, S.D., U.S.	F10	118
Wauchope, Austl.	H10	70
Wauchula, Fl., U.S.	L5	112
Wauconda, Wa., U.S.	B6	122
Waugh, Man., Can.	I19	104
Waugh Mountain, mtn., Id., U.S.	E11	122
Waukaringa, Austl.	I3	70
Waukegan, Il., U.S.	H8	110
Waukesha, Wi., U.S.	G7	110
Waukomis, Ok., U.S.	C9	116
Waukon, Ia., U.S.	G4	110
Waunakee, Wi., U.S.	G6	110
Wauneta, Ne., U.S.	K6	118
Waupaca, Wi., U.S.	F6	110
Waupun, Wi., U.S.	G7	110
Waurika, Ok., U.S.	E9	116
Wausa, Ne., U.S.	I10	118
Wausau, Wi., U.S.	F6	110
Wausaukee, Wi., U.S.	E8	110
Wauseon, Oh., U.S.	F2	108
Wautoma, Wi., U.S.	F6	110
Wauwatosa, Wi., U.S.	G7	110
Wauzeka, Wi., U.S.	G5	110
Wave Hill, Austl.	C6	68
Waveland, Ms., U.S.	L7	114
Waverly, Al., U.S.	J11	114
Waverly, Il., U.S.	C7	114
Waverly, Ia., U.S.	H3	110
Waverly, Ks., U.S.	M12	118
Waverly, Mn., U.S.	E2	110
Waverly, Mo., U.S.	C3	114
Waverly, Ne., U.S.	K11	118
Waverly, N.Y., U.S.	E10	108
Waverly, Oh., U.S.	H4	108
Waverly, Tn., U.S.	F9	114
Waverly, Va., U.S.	B9	112
Waverly Hall, Ga., U.S.	G2	112
Wavre (Waver), Bel.	G6	12
Wāw, Sud.	N4	60
Wawa, Ont., Can.	C11	110
Wawa, Sud.	G6	60
Wawa, stm., Nic.	C11	92
Wāw al-Kabīr, Libya	C4	56
Wawanesa, Man., Can.	I15	104
Wawota, Sask., Can.	I12	104
Waxahachie, Tx., U.S.	G10	116
Waxhaw, N.C., U.S.	E6	112
Wayabula, Indon.	E8	38
Waycross, Ga., U.S.	H4	112
Wayland, Ia., U.S.	I4	110
Wayland, Ky., U.S.	B4	112
Wayland, Mi., U.S.	H10	110
Wayland, N.Y., U.S.	E9	108
Waylyn, S.C., U.S.	G7	112
Wayne, Alta., Can.	F22	102
Wayne, Mi., U.S.	H12	110
Wayne, Ne., U.S.	I10	118
Wayne, N.J., U.S.	G12	108
Wayne, Ok., U.S.	E9	116
Wayne, W.V., U.S.	I4	108
Wayne City, Il., U.S.	D8	114
Waynesboro, Ga., U.S.	F4	112
Waynesboro, Ms., U.S.	K8	114
Waynesboro, Pa., U.S.	H9	108
Waynesboro, Tn., U.S.	G9	114
Waynesboro, Va., U.S.	A8	112
Waynesburg, Oh., U.S.	G5	108
Waynesburg, Pa., U.S.	H6	108
Waynesville, Il., U.S.	B8	114
Waynesville, Mo., U.S.	E4	114
Waynesville, N.C., U.S.	D4	112
Waynoka, Ok., U.S.	C8	116
Wāzah Khwāh, Afg.	D3	44
Wāzin, Libya	E16	62
Wazīrābād, Pak.	D6	44
We, Pulau, i., Indon.	L3	40
Weagamow Lake, l., Ont., Can.	F23	104
Weatherford, Ok., U.S.	D8	116
Weatherford, Tx., U.S.	G9	116
Weatherly, Pa., U.S.	G11	108
Weaubleau, Mo., U.S.	E3	114
Weaver, Al., U.S.	I11	114
Weaver Lake, l., Man., Can.	F18	104
Weaverville, Ca., U.S.	D3	124
Weaverville, N.C., U.S.	D4	112
Webb, Sask., Can.	H6	104
Webb, Ms., U.S.	I6	114
Webb City, Mo., U.S.	E2	114
Webber Lake, l., Man., Can.	D20	104
Webbwood, Ont., Can.	D14	110
Weber, stm., Ut., U.S.	D5	120
Weber, Mount, mtn., B.C., Can.	B6	102
Weber City, Va., U.S.	C4	112
Weberi Bekera, Eth.	M10	60
Webster, Alta., Can.	B16	102
Webster, Fl., U.S.	K4	112
Webster, Ma., U.S.	E15	108
Webster, S.D., U.S.	F10	118
Webster, Wi., U.S.	E3	110
Webster City, Ia., U.S.	H2	110
Webster Springs, W.V., U.S.	I6	108
Weda, Indon.	E8	38
Weddell Sea, Ant.	B1	73
Wedderburn, Austl.	K5	70
Wedge Mountain, mtn., B.C., Can.	G12	102
Wedgeport, N.S., Can.	I8	106
Wedowee, Al., U.S.	I11	114
Wedweil, Sud.	M4	60
Wedza, Zimb.	B10	66
Weed, Ca., U.S.	C3	124
Weedsport, N.Y., U.S.	D10	108
Weedville, Pa., U.S.	F8	108
Weems, Va., U.S.	B10	112
Weenen, S. Afr.	G10	66
Weeping Water, Ne., U.S.	K11	118
Weert, Neth.	F8	12
Weesp, Neth.	D7	12
Wee Waa, Austl.	H8	70
Węgrów, Pol.	C22	10
Wei, stm., China	E8	30
Weiden in der Oberpfalz, Ger.	F12	10
Weifang, China	G7	32
Weihai, China	F10	32
Weilburg, Ger.	E8	10
Weilheim, Ger.	H11	10
Weimar, Ger.	E11	10
Weimar, Tx., U.S.	J10	116
Weinan, China	E8	30
Weiner, Ar., U.S.	G6	114
Weinfelden, Switz.	C11	13
Weinheim, Ger.	F8	10
Weipa, Austl.	B8	68
Weippe, Id., U.S.	D10	122
Weir, Ks., U.S.	N13	118
Weir, Ms., U.S.	I7	114
Weir, stm., Austl.	F9	70
Weir, stm., Man., Can.	B21	104
Weir River, Man., Can.	B20	104
Weirsdale, Fl., U.S.	K5	112
Weirton, W.V., U.S.	G6	108
Weisburd, Arg.	D7	80
Weiser, Id., U.S.	F9	122
Weiser, stm., Id., U.S.	F9	122
Weishan (Xiazhen), China	I5	32
Weishancheng, China	C2	34
Weisner Mountain, mtn., Al., U.S.	H11	114
Weissenburg, Switz.	E7	13
Weissenburg in Bayern, Ger.	F10	10
Weissenfels, Ger.	D11	10
Weisshorn, mtn., Switz.	F8	13
Weisskugel (Palla Bianca), mtn., Eur.	E14	13
Weiss Lake, res., U.S.	E1	112
Weitou, China	K7	34
Weitra, Aus.	G14	10
Weiz, Aus.	H15	10
Weizhen, China	F2	32
Weizhou Wan, b., Asia	K7	34
Wejherowo, Pol.	A18	10
Wekusko Lake, l., Man., Can.	D15	104
Welaka, Fl., U.S.	J5	112
Welch, Ok., U.S.	C11	116
Welch, Tx., U.S.	G4	116
Welch, W.V., U.S.	B5	112
Welcome, Mn., U.S.	H13	118
Welcome, S.C., U.S.	E4	112
Weldon, Sask., Can.	E9	104
Weldon, Il., U.S.	B8	114
Weldon, N.C., U.S.	C9	112
Weldon, stm., U.S.	B3	114
Weldona, Co., U.S.	K4	118
Weleetka, Ok., U.S.	D10	116
Welkite, Eth.	M9	60
Welkom, S. Afr.	F8	66
Welland, Ont., Can.	H16	110
Welland, stm., Ont., Can.	G16	110
Wellborn, Fl., U.S.	I4	112
Wellborn, Tx., U.S.	I10	116
Wellesley Islands, is., Austl.	A3	70
Wellesley Lake, l., Yukon, Can.	E25	100
Wellfleet, Ma., U.S.	F16	108
Wellington, Austl.	I8	70
Wellington, Ont., Can.	G18	110
Wellington, N.Z.	D5	72
Wellington, S. Afr.	I4	66
Wellington, Eng., U.K.	I11	8
Wellington, Co., U.S.	D11	120
Wellington, Ks., U.S.	N10	118
Wellington, Mo., U.S.	C3	114
Wellington, Oh., U.S.	F4	108
Wellington, Tx., U.S.	E6	116
Wellington, Ut., U.S.	E6	120
Wellington, Isla, i., Chile	F2	78
Wellington Bay, b., N.W. Ter., Can.	C11	96
Wellington Channel, strt., N.W. Ter., Can.	A14	96
Wellington Station, P.E.I., Can.	F9	106
Wellman, Ia., U.S.	I4	110
Wellman, Tx., U.S.	F4	116
Wells, B.C., Can.	D13	102
Wells, Mi., U.S.	E8	110
Wells, Mn., U.S.	G2	110
Wells, Nv., U.S.	C11	124
Wells, N.Y., U.S.	D12	108
Wells, Tx., U.S.	K2	114
Wellsboro, Pa., U.S.	F9	108
Wellsburg, Ia., U.S.	H3	110
Wellsburg, W.V., U.S.	G6	108
Wellsford, N.Z.	B5	72
Wells Gray Provincial Park, B.C., Can.	E15	102
Wells Lake, l., Man., Can.	A13	104
Wells-next-the-Sea, Eng., U.K.	I14	8
Wellston, Oh., U.S.	H4	108
Wellston, Ok., U.S.	D9	116
Wellsville, Ks., U.S.	M12	118
Wellsville, Mo., U.S.	C5	114
Wellsville, N.Y., U.S.	E9	108
Wellsville, Oh., U.S.	G6	108
Wellsville, Ut., U.S.	C5	120
Wellton, Az., U.S.	L2	120
Wels, Aus.	G14	10
Welsford, N.B., Can.	G7	106
Welsh, La., U.S.	L4	114
Welwitschia, Nmb.	C2	66
Wembley, Alta., Can.	B15	102
Wenatchee, Wa., U.S.	C5	122
Wenatchee, stm., Wa., U.S.	C5	122
Wenatchee Mountains, mts., Wa., U.S.	C5	122
Wenchow see Wenzhou, China	G9	34
Wendell, Id., U.S.	H11	122
Wendell, N.C., U.S.	D8	112
Wenden, Az., U.S.	K3	120
Wendeng, China	F10	32
Wendo, Eth.	N10	60
Wendover, Ut., U.S.	D2	120
Wengyang, China	G9	34
Wengyuan, China	K3	34
Wenling, China	G10	34
Wenlock, stm., Austl.	B8	68
Wenona, Il., U.S.	I6	110
Wenshan, China	C8	40
Wentworth, Austl.	J4	70
Wentworth, N.C., U.S.	C7	112
Wentworth, S.D., U.S.	H11	118
Wenzhou, China	G9	34
Werda, Bots.	E6	66
Werdau, Ger.	E12	10
Werder, Ger.	C12	10
Were Ilu, Eth.	L10	60
Wernigerode, Ger.	D10	10
Werra, stm., Ger.	E10	10
Werribee, Austl.	K6	70
Werris Creek, Austl.	H9	70
Wertheim, Ger.	F9	10
Wertingen, Ger.	G10	10
Wesel, Ger.	D6	10
Weser, stm., Ger.	B8	10
Weskan, Ks., U.S.	M6	118
Weslaco, Tx., U.S.	M9	116
Wesley, Ia., U.S.	G2	110
Wesleyville, Newf., Can.	C20	106
Wesleyville, Pa., U.S.	E6	108
Wessel, Cape, c., Austl.	B7	68
Wessel Islands, is., Austl.	B7	68
Wessington, S.D., U.S.	G9	118
Wessington Springs, S.D., U.S.	G9	118
Wesson, Ms., U.S.	K6	114
West, Ms., U.S.	I7	114
West, Tx., U.S.	H9	116
West, stm., Vt., U.S.	D14	108
West Alexandria, Oh., U.S.	H2	108
West Allis, Wi., U.S.	G7	110
Westbank, B.C., Can.	H15	102
West Bank, hist. reg., Isr. Occ.	E4	50
West Bay, N.S., Can.	G12	106
Westbay, Fl., U.S.	L11	114
West Bay, b., Tx., U.S.	J12	116
West Bend, Ia., U.S.	I13	118
West Bend, Wi., U.S.	G7	110
West Bengal, state, India	I12	44
West Blocton, Al., U.S.	I9	114
Westbourne, Man., Can.	H16	104
West Branch, Ia., U.S.	I4	110
West Branch, Mi., U.S.	F11	110
Westbridge, B.C., Can.	H16	102
Westbrook, Me., U.S.	D16	108
Westbrook, Mn., U.S.	G12	118
Westbrook, Tx., U.S.	G5	116
West Burlington, Ia., U.S.	J4	110
West Butte, mtn., Mt., U.S.	B14	122
Westby, Mt., U.S.	C3	118
Westby, Wi., U.S.	G5	110
West Caicos, i., T./C. Is.	D8	94
West Carlisle, Tx., U.S.	F5	116
West Channel, mth., N.W. Ter., Can.	B27	100
West Chester, Pa., U.S.	H11	108
Westchester Station, N.S., Can.	G10	106
Westcliffe, Co., U.S.	F11	120
West Columbia, S.C., U.S.	F5	112
West Columbia, Tx., U.S.	J11	116
West Concord, Mn., U.S.	F3	110
West Des Moines, Ia., U.S.	I2	110
West Elk Mountains, mts., Co., U.S.	F9	120
West Elk Peak, mtn., Co., U.S.	F9	120
West End, Bah.	A5	94
West End, Ar., U.S.	H4	114
West End, N.C., U.S.	D7	112
Westerlo, Bel.	F6	12
Westerly, R.I., U.S.	F15	108
Western, Ne., U.S.	K10	118
Western, stm., Austl.	D5	70
Western Australia, state, Austl.	E4	68
Western Cape, prov., S. Afr.	I5	66
Western Channel, strt., Asia	I16	32
Western Desert see Gharbīyah, Aş-Şaḥrā' al-, des., Egypt	D4	60
Western Ghāts, mts., India	D2	46
Western Isles, prov., Scot., U.K.	D6	8
Westernport, Md., U.S.	H7	108
Western Sahara, dep., Afr.	D4	54
Western Samoa, ctry., Oc.	J22	126
Western Shore, N.S., Can.	H9	106
Westerschelde, est., Neth.	F4	12
Westerstede, Ger.	B7	10
Westerville, Oh., U.S.	G4	108
West Falkland, i., Falk. Is.	G4	78
West Fargo, N.D., U.S.	E11	118
Westfield, Il., U.S.	C8	114
Westfield, In., U.S.	B10	114
Westfield, Ma., U.S.	E14	108
Westfield, N.J., U.S.	G12	108
Westfield, N.Y., U.S.	E7	108
Westfield, Pa., U.S.	F9	108
Westfield, Wi., U.S.	G6	110
West Fiord, N.W. Ter., Can.	A14	96
West Fork, Ar., U.S.	G2	114
West Frankfort, Il., U.S.	E8	114
Westgate, Austl.	F7	70
West Glacier, Mt., U.S.	B12	122
West Glamorgan, co., Wales, U.K.	J10	8
West Hamlin, W.V., U.S.	I4	108
West Hartford, Ct., U.S.	F14	108
Westhaven, Ca., U.S.	C1	124
West Haven, Ct., U.S.	F14	108
West Helena, Ar., U.S.	H6	114
Westhoff, Tx., U.S.	J9	116
Westhope, N.D., U.S.	C6	118
West Ice Shelf, Ant.	B5	73
West Indies, is.	E9	94
West Jefferson, N.C., U.S.	C5	112
West Jefferson, Oh., U.S.	H3	108
West Jordan, Ut., U.S.	D5	120
West Kettle, stm., B.C., Can.	H15	102
West Kingston, R.I., U.S.	F15	108
West Lafayette, In., U.S.	B10	114
West Lafayette, Oh., U.S.	G5	108
Westlake, La., U.S.	L3	114
West Laramie, Wy., U.S.	C11	120
West Lebanon, In., U.S.	B9	114
West Liberty, Ia., U.S.	I4	110
West Liberty, Ky., U.S.	B3	112
West Liberty, Oh., U.S.	G3	108
Westlock, Alta., Can.	C21	102
West Lorne, Ont., Can.	H14	110
Westmeath, co., Ire.	H6	8
West Melbourne, Fl., U.S.	K6	112
West Memphis, Ar., U.S.	G6	114
West Mifflin, Pa., U.S.	G7	108
Westminster, Co., U.S.	E11	120
Westminster, Md., U.S.	H10	108
Westminster, S.C., U.S.	E3	112
West Monroe, La., U.S.	J4	114
Westmont, Pa., U.S.	G8	108
Westmoreland, Ks., U.S.	L11	118
Westmoreland, Tn., U.S.	F10	114
Westmorland, Ca., U.S.	K10	124
West Nicholson, Zimb.	C9	66
West Nishnabotna, stm., Ia., U.S.	K12	118
Weston, Co., U.S.	G12	120
Weston, Id., U.S.	H14	122
Weston, Mo., U.S.	C2	114
Weston, Ne., U.S.	J11	118
Weston, Oh., U.S.	F3	108
Weston, Or., U.S.	E7	122
Weston, W.V., U.S.	H6	108
Weston-super-Mare, Eng., U.K.	J11	8
West Orange, Tx., U.S.	L3	114
Westover, Tn., U.S.	G8	114
Westover, W.V., U.S.	H7	108
West Palm Beach, Fl., U.S.	M6	112
West Paris, Me., U.S.	C16	108
West Pensacola, Fl., U.S.	L9	114
Westphalia, Ks., U.S.	M12	118
West Plains, Mo., U.S.	F5	114
West Point, Ca., U.S.	F5	124
West Point, Ga., U.S.	G1	112
West Point, Ia., U.S.	J4	110
West Point, Ky., U.S.	E11	114
West Point, Ms., U.S.	I8	114
West Point, Ne., U.S.	J11	118
West Point, N.Y., U.S.	F13	108
West Point, Va., U.S.	B10	112
West Point, c., Austl.	J2	70
West Point, c., P.E.I., Can.	F9	106
West Point Lake, res., U.S.	F1	112
Westport, Newf., Can.	C17	106
Westport, N.S., Can.	H7	106
Westport, Ont., Can.	F19	110
Westport, N.Z.	D3	72
Westport, Ct., U.S.	F13	108
Westport, In., U.S.	C11	114
Westport, Or., U.S.	D2	122
Westport, Wa., U.S.	D1	122
West Portsmouth, Oh., U.S.	I3	108
West Prairie, stm., Alta., Can.	B18	102
West Quoddy Head, c., Me., U.S.	C20	108
West Richland, Wa., U.S.	D6	122
West Road, stm., B.C., Can.	D11	102
West Rutland, Vt., U.S.	D13	108
West Sacramento, Ca., U.S.	F4	124
West Saint Marys, stm., N.S., Can.	G11	106
West Saint Modeste, Newf., Can.	A17	106
West Salem, Il., U.S.	D8	114
West Salem, Oh., U.S.	G4	108
West Salem, Wi., U.S.	G4	110
West Shoal Lake, l., Man., Can.	H17	104
West Siberian Plain see Zapadno-Sibirskaja ravnina, pl., Russia	E13	26
West Slope, Or., U.S.	E3	122
West Spanish Peak, mtn., Co., U.S.	G12	120
West Sussex, co., Eng., U.K.	K13	8
West Terre Haute, In., U.S.	C9	114
West Union, Ia., U.S.	H4	110
West Union, Oh., U.S.	I3	108
West Union, W.V., U.S.	H6	108
West Unity, Oh., U.S.	F2	108
West Valley, Mt., U.S.	D12	122
West Valley City, Ut., U.S.	D5	120
West Vancouver, B.C., Can.	H11	102
Westville, N.S., Can.	G11	106
Westville, In., U.S.	A10	114
Westville, Ok., U.S.	G2	114
West Virginia, state, U.S.	D10	98
West-Vlaanderen, prov., Bel.	F2	12
West Warwick, R.I., U.S.	F15	108
West Webster, N.Y., U.S.	D9	108
Westwego, La., U.S.	M6	114
Westwold, B.C., Can.	G15	102
Westwood, Ca., U.S.	D4	124
Westwood Lakes, Fl., U.S.	N6	112
West Wyalong, Austl.	I7	70
West Yellowstone, Mt., U.S.	F14	122
Wetar, Pulau, i., Indon.	G8	38
Wetaskiwin, Alta., Can.	E21	102
Wete, Tan.	C7	58
Wethersfield, Ct., U.S.	F14	108
Wetiko Hills, hills, Can.	D22	104
Wetmore, Ks., U.S.	L12	118
Wet Mountains, mts., Co., U.S.	F11	120
Wetteren, Bel.	F4	12
Wetumka, Ok., U.S.	D10	116
Wetumpka, Al., U.S.	J10	114
Wetzikon, Switz.	D10	13
Wetzlar, Ger.	E8	10
Wewahitchka, Fl., U.S.	I1	112
Wewak, Pap. N. Gui.	k15	68a
Wewoka, Ok., U.S.	D10	116
Wexford, Ire.	I7	8
Wexford, co., Ire.	I7	8
Weyakwin Lake, l., Sask., Can.	D8	104
Weyauwega, Wi., U.S.	F7	110
Weyburn, Sask., Can.	I11	104
Weymouth, N.S., Can.	H7	106
Weymouth, Eng., U.K.	K11	8
Weymouth, Ma., U.S.	E16	108
Whakatane, N.Z.	B6	72
Whangarei, N.Z.	A5	72
Wharton, Tx., U.S.	J10	116
Wharton, W.V., U.S.	J5	108
Wharton Lake, l., N.W. Ter., Can.	D13	96
Whataroa, N.Z.	E3	72
What Cheer, Ia., U.S.	I3	110
Whatley, Al., U.S.	K9	114
Whatshan Lake, l., B.C., Can.	G16	102
Wheatland, Ca., U.S.	E4	124
Wheatland, Ia., U.S.	I5	110
Wheatland, Wy., U.S.	B12	120
Wheatley, Ont., Can.	H13	110
Wheatley, Ar., U.S.	H5	114
Wheaton, Il., U.S.	A8	114
Wheaton, Md., U.S.	H9	108
Wheaton, Mn., U.S.	F11	118
Wheat Ridge, Co., U.S.	E11	120
Wheeler, Ms., U.S.	H8	114
Wheeler, Tx., U.S.	D6	116
Wheeler, stm., Que., Can.	E19	96
Wheeler, stm., Sask., Can.	A9	104
Wheeler Lake, res., Al., U.S.	H9	114
Wheeler Peak, mtn., Ca., U.S.	F6	124
Wheeler Peak, mtn., Nv., U.S.	F11	124
Wheeler Peak, mtn., N.M., U.S.	H11	120
Wheeling, W.V., U.S.	G6	108
Wheelwright, Arg.	G8	80
Wheelwright, Ky., U.S.	B4	112